CASTLES
Made of
SAND

Also by André Gerolymatos

RED ACROPOLIS, BLACK TERROR

THE BALKAN WARS

GUERRILLA WARFARE AND ESPIONAGE IN GREECE, 1940–1944

ESPIONAGE AND TREASON

CASTLES

Made of

SAND

A CENTURY OF ANGLO-AMERICAN ESPIONAGE
AND INTERVENTION IN THE MIDDLE EAST

André Gerolymatos

THOMAS DUNNE BOOKS ☙ NEW YORK
ST. MARTIN'S PRESS

THOMAS DUNNE BOOKS.
An imprint of St. Martin's Press.

CASTLES MADE OF SAND. Copyright © 2010 by André Gerolymatos. All rights reserved. Printed in the United States of America. For information, address St. Martin's Press, 175 Fifth Avenue, New York, N.Y. 10010.

www.thomasdunnebooks.com
www.stmartins.com

Book design by Susan Yang

ISBN 978-0-312-35569-2

First Edition: December 2010

10 9 8 7 6 5 4 3 2 1

TO BEVERLEY,

the beautiful sunsets are never ending.

CONTENTS

ACKNOWLEDGMENTS

This project has been a unique journey that has afforded me the opportunity to gain insight into the complex and, at times, tragic history of Anglo-American intelligence operations and their impact on the Muslim world from the Middle East to South Asia.

If this book falls short of achieving its objectives, and for any errors, the fault is mine; however, it is my pleasant duty to thank all those who have given of their time and energy in order for me to complete this study. As always, I am grateful to my agent, Bill Hanna, whose support and guidance over the years has made it possible for me to undertake and complete several books. I also would like to acknowledge Thomas Dunne of St. Martin's Press for having faith in this project and Rob Kirkpatrick for his insightful editorial suggestions and valuable comments.

I am thankful to Graham Fuller, a former vice chairman of the National Intelligence Council of the CIA, for useful comments on parts of the manuscript. Furthermore, I am indebted to Professors Amikam Nachmani and Shlomo Shpiro at Bar Ilan University for their valuable help with research in Israel. The support of the Social Sciences and Humanities Research Council of Canada provided me with a generous grant that made the research possible.

The book would not have been realized without a group of students from Simon Fraser University who ably assisted me in the research phase. Vanessa Rockel and Julian Brooks worked with me from the beginning and later were joined by Adrian O'Sullivan, Kelly Hammond, Simon Pratt, Lucia Petersen, and Inbal Negbi. I am appreciative of the staff of the Hellenic Studies Program, Maria Hamilton and Trina Mateus, for their help with a variety of administrative tasks.

Finally, to my wife, Beverley, editor, lifelong companion, and best friend for her patience, encouragement, and faith in me, I owe the greatest debt.

PREFACE

Anglo-American intelligence operations hold a unique place in the history of Middle East and Muslim politics. Directly and indirectly, first British and later American intelligence officers served as catalysts to events that forever changed the region. During the colonial period, from the nineteenth century to the end of the Second World War, the men (and a few women) of the covert services were a critical part of the control mechanism that enabled the British Empire to rule the Middle East and South Asia with minimal military forces. The method of control adopted by the British, and followed by the Americans, was to try to exploit Islam as an ally in maintaining their hegemony over the region.

The rapid decolonization of the Middle East after the Second World War coincided with an Arab nationalism that swept aside the corrupt monarchies of the Middle East (later the new secular rulers indulged in the same corruption). The rapid change challenged how London and Washington perceived the future development of the Middle East and how they coped with the aggressive Soviets, who were ready to establish their own hegemony over the region. However, the wartime allies, notwithstanding the special Anglo-American relationship, did not share a common approach in dealing with the postcolonial Middle East. In 1956, the British, along with the French and Israelis attempted to use raw military power to impose their will on Egypt's Gamal Abdel Nasser and regain control of the Suez Canal, but the effort ended in dismal failure when the United States condemned the operation.

Although the Americans were opposed to colonialism and while President Dwight Eisenhower fumed over the Suez Crisis debacle, the CIA was trying to implement Operation Straggle to overthrow the government of Syria. Consequently, it was not that Washington was opposed to interference in the Middle East, but rather to the British mechanisms of intervention. The American preference was for the use of covert operations with a penchant for coups led by a favorite regional puppet. But the frequent exposure of failed CIA coups made a mockery of secrecy, revealing naked American intervention. A climate of pending conspiracy anticipating American machinations prevailed in the capitals of most of the Middle East countries, particularly those that followed either a policy of neutrality or maintained warm relations with the Soviet Union.

Nonalignment and failure to cater to American strategic and economic interests guaranteed U.S. intervention through the CIA.

In Syria, the American efforts (sometimes in concert with the British) at
regime change ultimately solidified the dictatorship of Hafiz al-Asad and expanded Soviet influence in Damascus as well as in Cairo. Not remarkably, the
same cycle of coups and countercoups followed American policy in Iraq and
led to the dictatorship of Saddam Hussein.

After the Second World War, and until September 11, 2001, the role of British
and American intelligence services in the Middle East remained relatively obscure. In the public imagination, spies working for the CIA and MI6 were primarily identified with operations against the Soviet Union in Europe, to a
lesser extent in South America, and only rarely with events in the Middle East
or South Asia.

Interest in the Middle East was generally limited to oil supplies and the price
of gasoline, punctuated by the highjacking of airplanes by the PLO, the Palestine
Liberation Organization, and a terrorist outrage in Israel. There were exceptions,
when the Middle East came to the forefront of events, such as during the 1980s,
when Muslim extremists in Lebanon kidnapped American diplomats and CIA
officers. The 444-day drama of the American hostages in Tehran and the cata-
strophic failure of the CIA and U.S. Special Forces to effect a rescue captured
public interest, but it dissipated after the hostages were released. The Middle East
dominated the headlines for a short period with the onset of the first Persian Gulf
War, but interest waned again after the successful end of the conflict.

Fundamentally, the Middle East, and certainly South Asia, pose the greatest challenge to Western security and a major problem for Anglo-American
secret services. Berlin and the Eastern bloc may have served as the backdrop to
the Cold War, but Cairo, Jerusalem, Beirut, Damascus, and the Northwest
Frontier command the attention of the CIA, MI6, and the successor organizations of the KGB.

The tragedy of 9/11 and the rhetoric of weapons of mass destruction that
escalated into the War on Terror that preceded the second Persian Gulf War in
March 2003 will forever filter perceptions of the Middle East. Over the course
of both conflicts, Saddam Hussein became a household demon and the central
figure in the War on Terror. Indeed, the new enemy in Iraq quickly superseded
the short-term American victory in Afghanistan.

The demonized Hussein was only one of a series of Middle East strongmen
and dictators who were, depending on the occasion, first courted, then vilified
by the British and the Americans. In fact, the first steps down the path to 9/11
were set in motion when in the 1950s the Americans began to flirt with militant

Islamic organizations to checkmate Arab nationalism. In this context the Saddam Hussein type of bogeyman mirrored U.S. attitudes toward Abdel Nasser in the 1950s. Remarkably, both men initially had been covert allies of the United States and to a considerable degree owed their achieving power to the machinations of the CIA.

But, ultimately, Hussein and Nasser were just two in a parade of characters spewed out by the upheavals of the post-Ottoman Muslim world. Indeed, the eclipse of the Ottoman Empire and the termination of the Caliphate led to the destabilization of the spiritual center of the Sunni Muslim community. Ironically, both the American intelligence services and the followers of political Islam, with divergent interests, have been trying to find a suitable replacement. What follows is a modest attempt to tell the story of the efforts of the Anglo-American intelligence community to find a credible substitute for the Caliphate in order to contain nationalist and other unwelcome leadership stirring in the Muslim world.

The focus of this book is the history of British and American intelligence establishments and the Muslim organizations they tried to exploit. Although it has not been possible to examine all the countries of the Muslim world in detail because of the lack of sources, some such as Egypt, Arabia, Israel, Syria, Iran, and the region of South Asia offer excellent historical case studies to understand the relationship between the Anglo-American intelligence communities and Islam. This study is an account of the historical events that were, to a considerable extent, catalysts to 9/11 and its aftermaths in Iraq and Afghanistan.

A NOTE ON SOURCES

Writing intelligence history on the basis of archival records can be a baffling exercise in frustration. Of course, it comes as no surprise that the U.S. government should want to conceal documents that might connect Western intelligence agencies with Islamic fundamentalist groups in the aftermath of the events of September 11, 2001. However, the scale of the reclassification of intelligence-related documents has been described as excessive.[1]

A case in point would be the experience of two of my researchers who in the spring of 2006 looked for files regarding alleged OSS and early CIA contacts with radical Islamic organizations. When informed of their project, a CIA archivist just laughed, saying that the files were classified and inaccessible. In fact, a digital archive of CIA files is available through the CIA's CREST computer database, but many of these declassified files are heavily sanitized.

For example, my search for a CIA officer who reportedly met regularly with Muslim Brotherhood founder Hassan al-Banna turned up only a few trivialities, such as an invitation to the agent's retirement party. A State Department archivist was not much more encouraging, suggesting that the best avenue would be to go through department files in relevant geographical areas, on the chance that one might find a document that was missed by the censors. While this strategy did reveal some interesting anecdotes and circumstantial evidence, it did not yield documentation that would provide concrete proof of connections between intelligence operatives and Islamic militants.

President Bill Clinton's Executive Order 12958 of 1995 required the release of all classified U.S. government historical records after twenty-five years. However, thanks to the work of former National Security Agency officer Matthew M. Aid, it became publicly known in 2006 that various American government agencies had been involved in several large-scale document reclassification projects. Because of resistance to EO 12958 by the CIA and other American intelligence agencies, only 1,400 documents were actually reclassified between 1999 and 2000. Under the administration of George W. Bush the reclassification program was endorsed and expanded. It was further intensified after the events of 9/11, which led to a revision of EO 12958. Since 2001, some 9,500 documents have been reclassified, often in a somewhat wholesale fashion. Many of these documents concern intelligence dating back to the Second World War.[2]

If the Americans cut swaths with a sword, British censors tend to operate with scalpels. There are plenty of declassified files in the British archives that concern topics of potential interest to intelligence historians. The release of such files during the 1990s can be credited to the Waldergrave Initiative, launched in 1992 to release more documents to the public. Prominent intelligence historian Richard Aldrich calls the initiative a "qualified success" in terms of the quantity of material released.[3] Aldrich points to major breakthroughs, such as the release of records concerning British intelligence operations to investigate military science in Warsaw Pact countries during the Cold War, but other areas remain less accessible. As my researchers discovered, it is often not that a file has been withheld, but that it has been "weeded" of its key documents that might yield vital evidence. According to Aldrich, weeding can be of varying quality, involving weeders who know little of the material they are working on nor the subject area in general.[4]

One weeder with plenty of experience is J. R. Green of the Prime Minister's Office. Mr. Green's treatment of the Records of the Prime Minister's Office (PREM) has touched a number of files relevant to this study. Some documents have been removed from files, while others have been removed and destroyed. For instance PREM 11/515—regarding Iran in the months prior to the 1953 Anglo-American coup—has had some twenty-nine documents removed. By the British National Archives' own admission, many of the recently released records of the security service have been heavily weeded. Most of these files contain only photocopies; some pages have words blacked out.

Notwithstanding the obstructions and the efforts of the likes of Mr. Green, the CIA, and the Bush minions, sufficient documents have survived that, combined with diaries, autobiographies, biographies, and histories of the region, have enabled this historian to piece together the history of Anglo-American intelligence in the Middle East. There are other sources; however, I would rather keep such information from the weeders in the U.S. and U.K. archives. Despite these drawbacks, I am grateful to the staff of the National Archives in Maryland and Kew for their help in wading through thousands of documents. Like many researchers, I wish that John Taylor, a pioneer in archival research and one who guided me in the initial stage of this work, had lived to see the publication of this book.

CASTLES
Made of
SAND

PROLOGUE:
STORIES FROM THE BAZAAR

The storyteller sits on a tattered rug spread across the grime and dust of the ground near the edge of the bazaar.[1] He will mesmerize his audience with stories of war, intrigue, and guile from a bygone golden age. In the modest bazaars of small towns and out-of-the-way neighborhoods in large cities, he is the connection between past and present, and a sojourn into escapism for the humble folk who can spare a coin or two. The priests and mullahs may have the souls of the faithful, but this street historian captures and holds their imagination—if only for a brief time.

A man such as our storyteller lacks the practical skills to secure employment in the cities or villages and drifts from place to place scratching out a living on the fringes of society. In the Balkans, men such as these are usually Gypsies leading a tumbleweed existence from town to town, effortlessly crossing in and out of state borders.

In the Middle East, storytellers do not belong to the nomadic tribes that have drifted across the deserts for millennia. Besides, such men would be too old and too weary to take part in punishing raids for booty or revenge. Our storyteller is equally unsuitable to the dozens of secret societies and paramilitary organizations challenging local authorities for control of the street. No, our conjurer of tales is a loner. His stories are distilled from a variety of conspiracy theories legitimized over time and by sheer repetition, as well as from historical accounts filtered through myth and legend. Yet, despite the inaccuracies and convoluted interpretations of the past, for a brief moment in time, the storyteller reigns supreme in the marketplace.

After a small crowd gathers, the storyteller is ready to begin his performance. He shifts the weight of his body and, crossing his legs, settles in a comfortable position. His theme is the Crusades, but more importantly the story that he cobbles together from parts of history, myth, and conspiracy theory will stress that the success of Western armies was a shabby victory won by subterfuge, clandestine tricks, and unspeakably brutal force. For an instant, he glances at the eager faces of the young and the expectant faces of the old who have distilled into a small crowd around him. He takes a deep gulp of the cool evening air and in a soft melodic voice begins his tale with the hindsight of nostalgia.

In the late 1950s, I came across such a storyteller in a small bazaar on the outskirts of Athens. He transfixed his audience with tragic and grisly tales spun out of the Crusades. He was a Gypsy, and the bazaar at that time was as common in Greece as it is today in some parts of the Middle East. It struck me that he drew on the Crusades for the theme of his stories and assumed that, by elaborating on the cruelty of Western Christians against the Muslims, this theme would find resonance with an Eastern Orthodox audience. He was not far off, at least with respect to the Fourth Crusade.

In the convoluted cauldron of Balkan myth and legend, the sack of Constantinople by the Fourth Crusade in 1204 remains a bitter and painful legacy. Accordingly, the sympathy of the Eastern Orthodox, insofar as the Fourth Crusade is concerned, lies with the Muslims; the Franks (the general name for the Crusaders) are depicted as the scourge of civilization.

My storyteller also touched on another important theme that appealed to his audience—the notion of waging war against a superior force by subterfuge, cunning, espionage, and intrigue. Generally the role of spy and saboteur is frowned upon by most cultures and considered beneath the martial dignity of a warrior, although in times of defeat and occupation by a foreign opponent it was, and still is, acceptable in most societies to resort to clandestine warfare.[2] In the Middle East, such stories (along with others) of deception, espionage, and subterfuge are transmitted via the unofficial culture that exists (and continues to do so) beyond the watchful eye of the authorities.

As was the case in the bazaar in Athens, which operated without official sanction, the marketplace in the Middle East is a venue for the transmission of unedited ideas and information carried by word of mouth that provide the building blocks of legend and mythology. The "Arab Street," the masses that make up the urban poor, feed on the retelling of a variety of stories, including that of the Crusades, along with ample doses of conspiracy theories. At the end of the twentieth century, the notion of the Crusades as a grand conspiracy of the West received new impetus when in 1990 President George H. W. Bush proclaimed "a new world order."

Although Bush's remarks referred to the post–Cold War era in the Middle East, writes the controversial Daniel Pipes, "the phrase was widely understood as signaling a plan for 'the United States, master of the new world' to establish hegemony over the entire globe."[3] Hence perceptions in the Middle East point to the "new world order" as further evidence of a policy of "crushing Islam and its people" and "a Jewish plan for a Greater Israel and a Christian 'spirit of the Crusades.'"[4]

Yet this conspiracy theory is a by-product of the legacy of the Crusades that has continued to resonate in the region since the end of the thirteenth century. As noted by Carole Hillenbrand, Akbar Ahmed, a prominent Islamic scholar, remarks:

> The memory of the Crusades lingers in the Middle East and colours Muslim perceptions of Europe. It is the memory of an aggressive, backward and religiously fanatic Europe. This historical memory would be reinforced in the nineteenth and twentieth centuries as imperial Europeans once again arrived to subjugate and colonize territories in the Middle East. Unfortunately this legacy of bitterness is overlooked by most Europeans when thinking of the Crusades.[5]

Another scholar, Amin Maalouf, echoes with similar sentiments:

> It is often surprising to discover the extent to which the attitude of the Arabs (and of Muslims in general) towards the West is still influenced, even today, by events that supposedly ended some seven centuries ago.

> Today, on the eve of the third millennium, the political and religious leaders of the Arab world constantly refer to Saladin, to the fall of Jerusalem and its recapture. In the popular mind, and in some official discourse too, Israel is regarded as a new Crusader state. . . . In his days of glory, President Nasser was regularly compared to Saladin, who, like him, had united Syria and Egypt—and even Yemen! The Arabs perceived the Suez expedition of 1956 as a Crusade by the French and the English, similar to that of 1191.[6]

More recently, Osama bin Laden has frequently used the term "Crusaders" and "Crusade" in his characterization of the West and its role in the Middle East. But it was President George W. Bush who inadvertently linked the Crusades with the clandestine war on the extremists and fanatics in the Muslim world. In a speech on the future course of American action eight days after 9/11, he cast the war against terror (what essentially would be a series of intelligence and covert operations) as "a crusade" against terrorism, thus inadvertently invoking the specter of a religious, as well as secular, conflict against Islam.

Perhaps this is not such an outlandish concept. In the Middle East, the Crusades inexplicably continue to cast a long shadow. These "holy" wars between

East and West have filtered the perceptions of the West to generations of Muslims. In the present, these notions are further reinforced by the exigencies of the war on terror waged by covert means around the world and primarily aimed against Muslims, as well as by the ground conflicts in Iraq and Afghanistan.

Like the Crusades, this conflict is waged essentially outside the rules of war. Notorious though the concept of crusading may be, however, it has always been subject, by and large, to a set of self-imposed regulations observed by warring states in the West. Their genesis originated in the medieval code of chivalry, but they only applied to fellow Christians. The twentieth-century Geneva Convention, on the other hand, was designed for conventional warfare and did not make provisions for covert operations or espionage.[7] So, in this context, both the Crusades and the murky world of covert operations are conflicts waged without recourse to any universal rules.

In the twentieth and twenty-first centuries, both the Anglo-American and the Axis intelligence organizations (followed later by the Soviets) became the point of contact between the West and the nationalists, militant Muslim groups, and any other radicals in the Middle East. Necessity in the First and Second World Wars created the momentum for a secret relationship between the intelligence services of Great Britain (and later the United States) with the emerging secular radicals in the various Arab nationalist movements and conservative religious organizations, such as the Muslim Brotherhood. The Anglo-American secret services desperately needed agents to use, first against the Ottomans and later against the Axis, and finally as a means to contain the rising Arab nationalism that British operatives such as T. E. Lawrence had helped to instigate in 1916. In most cases the relationship was, at best, qualified by expediency and mutual suspicion.

Throughout the course of this unusual association, the Middle Eastern perceptions of the British and Americans, as well as of other representatives of the Western powers, were—and still are—to a degree defined by the Crusades. Hence the Crusades are, at least for most Muslims, part of the negative cultural construct that has typified the Western presence in the region.

The Crusaders not only brought war and destruction to the Middle East; they also attempted to graft European medieval feudalism onto an entrenched culture and religion that anchored the societies of the freshly conquered territories to a different reality. For instance, the most important nobles assumed regal titles and carved out their realms as islands of Christendom within a sea of Islamic civilization.

Despite the eventual triumph of Islam in the Holy Land, the Crusades engendered a cycle of defeat for many Muslims. They also serve as stock themes for the blend of mythology, history, and romanticism with which storytellers entertain the Arab Street in the bazaar. To radical Muslim and Arab national-ists, the struggle against the European hegemony (and later the United States), as well as against those Muslims perceived to be working with the West, had to be waged underground through urban warfare, assassination, propaganda, es-pionage, and subversion.

One such instance is the 1979 incident that took place in the Great Mosque of Mecca.[8] In the early morning of November 20, just before the beginning of the Islamic New Year, approximately two hundred well-armed men, as well as women and children, seized the al-Masjid al-Haram Mosque in Mecca. Most of them were students at the Islamic University of Medina, and some were locals, as well as Muslims from other countries. They were led by Juhaiman al-Utaibi and Abdullah ah-Qahtani. Utaibi came from a prominent Arab family, and he, along with the other militants, were members of the puritanical Wahhabi sect, which is also the official state version of Islam in Saudi Arabia.

A number of the militants were also members of the Egyptian Muslim Brotherhood, a radical organization calling for a return to pure Islam and the overthrow of secular governments throughout the Islamic world.[9] The presence of Brotherhood adherents in Saudi Arabia was an example of regional blowback. King Faysal had invited the MB to Arabia in the 1960s as part of a scheme to undermine Nasser of Egypt. Nasser had ruthlessly suppressed the Brotherhood because of its opposition to his rule, as well as its religious militancy.[10] Many MB members accepted Faysal's asylum and became active in several of the new reli-gious universities established by the Saudi royal family and had come into con-tact with Juhaiman al-Utaibi and Abdullah al-Qahtani.

The capture of the Great Mosque was not only a religious act but was also meant to stir up an Islamic uprising against the Saudi royal family. After he took over the mosque, Utaibi announced that he and his followers were condemning the House of Saud for its moral laxity, corruption, and the destruction of Saudi culture by imitating the West. According to him, the Saudi monarchy had lost its legitimacy and thus had to be removed. He also proclaimed that Abdullah al-Qahtani was the true "Mahdi"[11] and asked the imam leading the morning prayers to proclaim him as such.[12]

The seizure of one of the most sacred mosques in Islam stunned Muslims throughout the world and had considerable repercussions for the United States and its allies. A flurry of rumors, conspiracy theories, and outright fantasies carried the crisis in Mecca to every corner of the Muslim world. In Islamabad, Pakistan, a Pakistani newspaper proclaimed that an American operation was in the process of landing a task force in Arabia in order to take control of the Persian Gulf. A short while later the same newspaper revealed that Israeli paratroopers were to be dropped on Mecca or Medina, perhaps both. The theocratic regime in Tehran immediately accused the United States and Israel.

> It is not far far-fetched to assume that this act has been perpetrated by the criminal American imperialism so that it can infiltrate the solid ranks of Muslims by such intrigues. It would not be far-fetched to assume that, as it has often indicated, Zionism intends to make the House of God Vulnerable.[13]

On November 21, the day after the Grand Mosque was seized, Pakistani students and militants from Pakistan's militant Islamic organizations stormed the American embassy in Islamabad and burned down the building as Pakistani police and security forces slowly came to the rescue of the Americans. The howling mobs were driven by the conviction that the United States had seized the Grand Mosque and they had to exact vengeance.[14] Although a major Kuwaiti newspaper, al-Siyassa, published large extracts of the musings of the rebels in the Grand Mosque on November 29, many Muslims continued to assume that the capture of the mosque was the work of a variety of hostile foreigners. Mobs of young militant Muslims and students attacked American institutions in Turkey, India, and Bangladesh and stormed the American embassy in Tripoli, Libya.

The Saudi government sealed off Mecca and severed all communications within the kingdom and between the kingdom and the outside world, in order to rule out the possibility of a coup supported by a foreign power. At the same time, any military action to retake the mosque had to wait because of the real possibility that the building would be damaged, thus earning for the Saudi royal family the enmity of the Muslim world. The question on whether to use force was submitted to the Ulema (the religious establishment), which, after some deliberation, sanctioned government use of force to remove the militants from the mosque.[15]

Once they got the green light, the Saudis deployed the National Guard, but their assault failed with the loss of twenty-one soldiers killed. What followed remains ensnared in purposeful obscurity. According to some accounts, the recapture of the mosque was accomplished by Pakistani troops in conjunction with French paratroopers. Others have proposed that there were some foreign troops but do not name them, while some make no reference to the presence of non-Muslims.[16]

Robert Fisk provides another explanation. He argues that the Saudis deployed ten thousand troops to retake the building, but many of the militants escaped into the labyrinth of caves and tunnels beneath the mosque. In the process the troops flooded the tunnels with water and inserted electric cables in order to electrocute the rebels.[17] In actual fact this did not take place. The retaking of the Grand Mosque was accomplished by Saudi troops under the direction of a French antiterrorist unit.

Officers from a French special unit, Groupe d'Intervention de la Gendermerie Nationale (GIGN) were brought to Mecca two weeks later and trained a select number of Saudi military. Under French supervision, from afar, the Saudis hunted down the militants by flooding the basement of the mosque and its tunnels with a chemical, dichlorobenzylidene-malononitrile (CB), which is essentially an irritant that blocks respiration and inhibits aggressiveness and nonlethal as long as the subject of the attack is removed in less than five minutes.[18] The operation was successful and a large number of the insurgents were captured. A short while later, sixty-three of the militants were publicly beheaded on January 9, 1980.

The event, regardless of the significance it had for the Saudi royal family—as well as for its major ally the United States and the Muslim world in general—was quickly overtaken by the Soviet invasion of Afghanistan and the aftershocks of the Ayatollah Khomeini's revolution in Iran. For most of the outside world, the incident at the Great Mosque was just that: yet another episode in a series of confrontations between radicals and state authority in the tumultuous Middle East. However, the rebels who challenged the legitimacy of the Saudi dynasty also signaled the rise of militant Sunni Islam in its various manifestation throughout the Muslim world.

But in 1979–1980 it was Khomeini's brand of Shiite Islam that was of major concern to the West and to the conservative regimes of the Middle East. Indeed, the United States was beginning to tap into the militant stream of Wahhabism in order to secure Islamic mujahidin (freedom fighters) for the covert war against the Soviet Union in Afghanistan. The Saudis, as well as other Middle East governments, anxious to get rid of potential troublemakers and to be of assistance to the Americans, killed two birds with one stone and facilitated the transportation of these new covert warriors to the Islamic jihad (holy war) in Afghanistan, including the infamous Osama bin Laden.[19]

In that unfortunate country, under the tutelage of experts from the Central Intelligence Agency working through Pakistan's Inter-Services Intelligence (ISI) agency, the mujahidin learned the tradecraft of espionage, sabotage, commando operations, psychological warfare, and counterintelligence, which they later successfully employed against the West.[20] In cases where the U.S. Congress had placed restrictions on some practices, the CIA outsourced them to the British. Gus Avrakotos, a veteran CIA officer who took part in organizing the jihad against the Soviets, commented:

> The Brits were eventually to buy things that we couldn't because it infringed on murder, assassination, and indiscriminate bombings. They could issue guns with silencers. We couldn't do that because a silencer immediately implied assassination—and heaven forbid car bombs! No way I could even suggest it, but I could say to the Brits, "Fadlallah in Beirut was really effective last week. They had a car bomb that killed three hundred people." I gave MI6 stuff in good faith. What they did with it was always their business.[21]

Although Afghanistan was the culmination of covert operations by the United States, the relationship between the Muslim militants, as well as nationalists, and the intelligence organizations of the West emerged from the First World War. Part of the British intelligence community remained focused on the Northwest Frontier, while other elements focused on Egypt.

ONE

Assassination

"What's all this nonsense about isolating Nasser?
I want him destroyed, can't you understand?"
—*Anthony Eden to Anthony Nutting*[1]

At 7:31 P.M. on a pleasantly cool evening with a light breeze from the sea, Gamal Abdel Nasser stood on the podium and began to speak—slowly and quietly at first. Then he grew excited, waving his right hand in sweeping gestures, and soon the crowd responded. Torrents of applause washed over him each time he recalled the past, to highlight Egypt's struggle for independence. Close to 250,000 spectators had jammed into the Midan el Tahir (Place of Liberation) in Alexandria on Tuesday, October 26, 1954, to hear Nasser proclaim the end of British rule in Egypt. Earlier, on October 19, Nasser had signed the formal Evacuation Agreement with Britain's representatives, but Tuesday was reserved for jubilation with the people of Egypt.[2]

As Nasser progressed through his speech, in the eighth row in front of the podium, a round-faced man with a clump of black hair hanging down over his forehead stood up. His hand shook slightly as he aimed a .36 caliber Italian revolver at Nasser and began shooting. The first bullet went wild. The second hit an electric light globe near Nasser's head. The man fired six more times, but remarkably he missed the Egyptian strongman.[3] Nasser heard the deadly explosions streaming past him, blinked, and brushed pieces of the shattered light globe from his shoulders. Despite the near-death experience, he remained calm and, looking at the crowd, shouted over and over: "This is Gamel Abdel Nasser speaking to you. My blood is your blood. My life is yours. You are all Gamel Abdel Nassers. If I had been killed, it would have made no difference, for you would carry on the struggle. You are all Gamel Abdel Nassers."[4]

Initial reports on Mahmud Abd al-Latif could not agree if the would-be assassin was a tinsmith, a carpenter, or a plumber. Eventually the authorities determined that he was a thirty-two-year-old tinsmith from Cairo and had been a Muslim Brother for sixteen years. After torture, he confessed that he had not acted alone but was part of a greater conspiracy organized by the Muslim Brotherhood to kill Nasser and eventually other members of the Revolutionary

Command Council. According to Latif, the MB contacted him in early October, and he had chosen to act on October 19, the day that Nasser signed the new Anglo-Egyptian treaty, which was condemned by the Brotherhood as an act of treason because it afforded the British the opportunity to reoccupy the Suez Canal in case of war. But he could not find the appropriate opportunity to execute the plan until October 26.[5] Although the treaty infuriated the Muslim Brothers, the failure of the Free Officers, who had seized power in 1952, to transform Egypt into an Islamic state was the primary motive for the plot to kill Nasser and overthrow the government.

The Muslim Brothers were not the only ones who despised Nasser enough to kill him. Anthony Eden, Britain's last imperial prime minister, had developed an almost pathological hatred for Egypt's new hero. In a fit of fury, Eden had ordered MI6, the British intelligence service, to kill Nasser at all costs.[6] Nasser, however, was convinced that the British were in collusion with the MB and said so in a victory speech on December 21, 1965, in which he accused the Brotherhood of holding conspiratorial meetings at the British embassy in Cairo.[7]

There may have been a grain of truth in this accusation, because MI6 had never quite developed sufficient expertise to deal with assassination and often outsourced such activity. During the course of the Second World War, for example, MI6 employed third parties to eliminate problematical Axis agents, but special operations and killing were practiced with considerable skill by its wartime equivalent, the Special Operations Executive (SOE). After the war, MI6 absorbed some sections of the SOE that included individuals who had experience in assassination into its Special Operations Branch, but elimination of unwanted elements was still farmed out to third parties. Although the British government had abandoned assassination as part of clandestine warfare by 1950, it continued to receive credence within certain ranks of MI6.[8]

Overall, the British attempts to kill Nasser, with one possible exception, bordered on the ludicrous. One plan involved flooding the ventilation system in one of Nasser's headquarters with nerve gas, but Eden rescinded it in favor of a joint French-Israeli operation that failed to bear fruit.[9] Another effort relied on using a group of renegade Egyptian officers, but that too collapsed when the weapons to be used proved defective. MI6 also contemplated using a dart tipped with poison and fired from a cigarette pack, but that also was scrapped because it would have been impossible to avoid a direct link between the British and Nasser's death.[10]

In 1956, a German mercenary was hired to murder the Egyptian leader. When he arrived in Cairo, however, the Egyptian authorities received an anonymous warning about him, and he surreptitiously left the country.[11] Other comic-book-style endeavors included giving Nasser a box of spiked chocolates and finding someone willing to lace his food with strychnine.[12]

Remarkably, after almost seventy years of dominion over Egyptian affairs, by the early 1950s the British presence in that country was rapidly fading. MI6 controlled a handful of agents in place, but few in senior positions in the Egyptian military and political establishment. Operating out of the well-respected Arab News Agency (ANA), however, Britain's intelligence service did manage to establish links with radical student and religious groups, as well as with cashiered officers. Other contacts included ties to the ousted royalist groups and exiled politicians.

Unfortunately, in 1956, what was left of MI6's intelligence network collapsed. In August of that year, the Egyptian security service raided the British-controlled ANA and arrested thirty of its staff, as well as expelling two members of the British embassy. The ANA not only served as a cover for MI6 in Cairo but also for intelligence operations throughout Egypt and the Middle East. Some of its agents were Britons working in Egypt as businessmen, journalists, or teachers, while the Egyptian agents were royalists and opponents of the Nasser regime.[13]

According to the Egyptian secret police, the Mukhabarat, those arrested constituted an espionage ring that, in addition to conducting intelligence work, was also planning the overthrow of the government. Of the thirty arrested, two Britons were eventually acquitted, while James Swinburn, the business manager of the ANA, was convicted in May 1957. Some of the Egyptians were executed, and others faced long prison sentences.[14] Other Britons, such as the representative of the Prudential Assurance Company, John Stanley, along with Alexander Reynolds, George Sweet, and George Rose, had already left for Britain and were tried in absentia.[15]

Swinburn, the accused ringleader of the plot, was subjected to intensive interrogation and confessed to collecting information on military deployments, confidential political meetings, Alexandria's defenses, and coordinating missions to communist countries. The Mukhabarat also claimed that documents found in Swinburn's house included reports on the disposition of Egyptian military units, information on new Soviet-built tank transports, antitank weapons, and considerable details on a new radar station on the outskirts of Cairo. Other agents working under journalistic cover provided by the ANA reported on communist activities in the Middle East.[16] The head of the ANA, Tom Little, who was a correspondent for *The Economist* and *The Times,* was the senior MI6 officer in Cairo, but the Egyptians left him free and fed him considerable disinformation, so that he could pass it on to MI6.[17]

J. G. Gove, head of the visa section of the British embassy, and J. B. Flux, commercial first secretary, had supervised the clandestine network and were expelled by the Egyptian government.[18] Mohamed Heikal, Nasser's confidant and longtime friend, writes that the two British diplomats had also been in contact with "student elements of a religious inclination" with the purpose of instigating Islamic fundamentalist riots and thus provoking foreign military intervention to protect the Europeans.[19] There is little doubt that the student elements were members of the Muslim Brotherhood or had links to the remnants of the organization.

Although the British lost a major intelligence network in Cairo and the Middle East, they persisted in trying to destabilize Egypt's government by a coup or by the assassination of Nasser. In 1953, MI6 recruited Mahmud Khalil, after he was appointed head of the intelligence directorate of the Egyptian air force. Khalil was first approached in August by Hussein Khayri, former deputy head of Egypt's military intelligence prior to the overthrow of the monarchy in 1952. Khalil remained cautious and noncommittal.

A few weeks later, the two men met at the Riviera Hotel in Beirut, and on this occasion Khayri introduced the Egyptian officer to John Farmer of MI6. During the course of this meeting, Khalil agreed to form a secret organization of Egyptian officers, with the aim of implementing a coup against the Nasser regime. Khalil, however, set one nonnegotiable condition—that he be in charge and the go-between for the British and the conspirators. Farmer accepted and handed over to Khalil an envelope containing £1,000. However, Khalil insisted that he would require at least £100,000 to maintain his organization, so Farmer agreed that sometime in the future this sum would be made available.[20]

Meanwhile, MI6 continued to hatch a variety of means to terminate Nasser, including Operation Unfasten, an unorthodox plan to be executed by Khalil's secret organization in Cairo. This particular plot was a cross between a comic-book fantasy and a James Bond movie. In actual fact, Operation Unfasten revolved around Nasser's beard. The Egyptian strongman had a heavy beard, which forced him to shave several times a day. The MI6 plan called for giving Nasser a Remington electric shaver filled with plastic explosive that would detonate the moment he switched the shaver on.[21]

In the meantime, MI6 wove an elaborate scheme to protect Khalil as a source. In order to justify Khalil's frequent journeys (secret meetings with representatives from MI6) to foreign countries, the British passed to him valuable intelligence about Israel, as well as providing substantial funds to maintain the secret organization of Egyptian army officers. Although bilateral relations between Britain and Israel were good, as they were between

Mossad (Israel's intelligence service) and MI6, the British had few qualms about divulging material detrimental to the Israelis to Khalil, in order to make their agent look good. Later, Yaacov Caroz, deputy chief of Mossad, wrote: "Harming Israel's security by handing over secret information about her did not apparently trouble the conscience of the British."[22] However, in the murky world of espionage, to paraphrase an oft-quoted maxim, "there is no such thing as a friendly intelligence agency, only rival agencies of friendly countries."

The plan to kill Nasser was shelved temporarily, although MI6 continued to shop around for a coup. From late August to early September 1957, Julian Amery and Neil "Billy" McLean, accompanied by two MI6 officers, held several secret meetings in the south of France with exiled Egyptian royalists and members of other groups hostile to Nasser. Amery and McLean were both participants in the so-called Suez Group, a collection of backbenchers, ex-ministers, former members of Britain's intelligence community, and young and newly elected MPs opposed to any proposed changes in the Anglo-Egyptian relationship affecting the Suez Canal.[23]

Julian Amery was the son-in-law of Harold Macmillan and secretary of the Suez Group. Both McLean and Amery had been officers in the SOE during the Second World War and took part in several special operations in the post-war period. In the late 1940s, Amery had been involved with the joint MI6-CIA operation to overthrow the communist government of Albania. Amery and McLean were not the only ex-intelligence officers either; others from Britain's wartime clandestine agencies, such as Fitzroy Maclean and Lord Hankey, the father of the British modern intelligence community, were members of this imperial caucus, and they cast a long shadow over MI6.[24]

In 1958, together with John Bruce Lockhart, another former MI6 officer, Amery had helped to organize covert operations in Cyprus against the local insurgents. In particular, Amery had blackmailed Archbishop Makarios, the Greek Cypriot prelate and political leader, about his homosexuality, and had forced Makarios to make concessions to the British. In effect, the Suez Group was both a customer of MI6's intelligence product and an instigator of covert operations.

After their meetings in France, Amery and McLean traveled to Geneva to meet with representatives of the Muslim Brotherhood, although they informed MI6 that they kept this part of their trip secret from other members of the Suez Group. Their efforts resulted in the establishment in Cairo of a "shadow government" ready to seize power at the first opportunity.[25] It is not certain what took place at this encounter in Geneva between Britain's lingering imperialists and Egypt's fundamentalist Muslims, but it was not the first time that these unlikely allies had collaborated against a common enemy.

On October 29, 1956, after the Israelis, based on a prearranged secret agreement, had attacked Egypt, the British and the French seized the Suez Canal. The military attempt failed, in large measure thanks to U.S. opposition, and finally brought the curtain down on imperial Anglo-French ambitions in Egypt and the Middle East. The invasion had placed a hold on any of the covert plans, but, after the debacle, MI6 reactivated the assassination plot.

In October 1957, an MI6 courier delivered the lethal razor to Khalil, along with £166,000.[26] The Saudis may have provided part or all of the money—not the first time that Arab petrodollars would be used to finance a coup.[27] The razor failed to explode. Then, on December 23 at a massive rally in Port Said celebrating the first anniversary of the Anglo-French withdrawal from the Suez Canal, Nasser unmasked the so-called Restoration Plot and claimed Khalil was a double agent who had been working for Egypt's security service. Nasser donated the £166,000 that Khalil received to Egyptians whose property had been damaged by the British naval bombardment of Alexandria during the Suez Crisis.[28] Nasser's revelation effectively gutted what was left of Britain's intelligence capability in Egypt.

The outcome of these events demonstrated that there was little coordination between the covert activities of MI6 and the grand strategy of the British government with respect to Egypt. Insofar as the British military and Foreign Office were concerned, clandestine intervention in Egypt was reserved as a last resort. Accordingly, such last-minute attempts, hastily organized, forced MI6 to work with unreliable individuals and often double agents.

British covert efforts in Egypt failed, to a great extent, because Eden and his close partners in the cabinet preferred to bypass not only the normal process within the governmental apparatus but also the chain of command in the intelligence community. The Suez Group, with its direct links to MI6 and powerful influence over Eden and succeeding prime ministers, blurred the lines between the government and the intelligence community. For that matter, MI6 was implementing its own policy, albeit loosely based on Eden's irrational loathing of Nasser and his directive to have the Egyptian leader eliminated.

As a result, covert operations, as well as the fate of agents, were at the mercy of several masters. The use of back channels in MI6 and the propensity to employ gifted amateurs, a long tradition in the history of British special operations, fragmented any serious efforts and compromised the handful of clandestine networks in Egypt. Since MI6 did not officially exist, ultimate responsibility for failure reverted to the government, while the organization was free to continue to launch maverick operations. Scott Lucas and Alistair Morey rightly point out that "MI6 could still withhold or, worse, fabricate intelligence and neglect to pass details of operations to its Foreign Office overseers."[29]

Furthermore, the intelligence fiascos in Cairo enabled the Egyptian security service to round up most of the opposition to Nasser, thus diminishing any future opportunity to recruit Egyptian agents. Finally, the destruction of the secular opposition left the field almost exclusively to Muslim extremists. Although the Brotherhood received a serious blow in 1954 following the assassination attempt against Nasser, it survived as an organization and also took root in several countries in the Middle East. At the same time, it inspired or spawned new extremist Muslim organizations, one of which, Egyptian Islamic Jihad, succeeded in assassinating Anwar al-Sadat, Nasser's successor.[30] Two decades later, Egyptian Islamic Jihad merged with al-Qaeda into the Qaeda al-Jihad.[31]

In the future, the Anglo-American intelligence community would face the impossible task of penetrating the Muslim opposition to the nationalist governments in the region. Even when the American or British intelligence agencies managed to establish links with the Muslim opposition to the Arab secular leadership, they only did so under conditions that suited the fundamentalists and were not able to access the rank and file. For most of the twentieth century, the Muslim Brotherhood, perhaps the most significant political-religious and clandestine network, remained beyond the reach of the U.S. and British intelligence establishment.

Although the Brotherhood was shunned by more radical organizations like Egyptian Islamic Jihad and al-Qaeda, it was one step in the evolution of what is now described as "political Islam."[32] The label of "political Islam," which lacks the intensity of other descriptions such as "fundamentalist Islam," "militant Islam," or "radical Islam," is closer to defining the religious-political movement that has gripped the Muslim world. Political Islam is not, however, a phenomenon of the twentieth or twenty-first centuries, but stems in part from reaction to the European colonization of the region, as well as to the endemic corruption that has plagued the Middle East from the nineteenth century.

Colonialism, writes Adeed Dawisha, was subsumed by imperialism and became the much needed "other" for Arab nationalism. This was particularly the case at the height of Arab nationalism between 1954 and 1967, personified by the regime of Nasser. The ideological construct of anti-imperialism was based on the notion that Dawisha describes as follows: "The 'imperialist forces' were outsiders, alien to the area, had committed many injustices against the Arab people, and therefore were 'deserving' of the abuse heaped upon them."[33] When the Nasser bubble burst, following the humiliating defeat in the 1967 war with Israel, it not only underscored the failure of Arab nationalism but, along with it, secularism. For the Arabs, as well as the other Muslims of the Middle East, secular leadership and secular states became synonymous with failure and systemic corruption.

For the practitioners of political Islam, defining the historic injustices perpetrated by the West remained integral in promoting jihad against the West. One familiar theme is the Crusades. In dredging the past to explain the present, the Crusades and U.S. support of Israel (and more recently the invasion and occupation of Iraq) bracket the rhetoric that dominates the discourse of political Islam.

TWO

The Mahdi

"One is what one has the nerve to pretend to be."
—*Alan Furst*[1]

D eath to the Christians!" With this cry, thousands of native Egyptians, accompanied by Bedouin, flooded into the European quarter of Alexandria on June 11, 1882.[2] The crescendo of thousands of voices, together with an army of feet pounding the streets, generated a deep roar that shattered the comfortable silence that embraces most Mediterranean cities and towns after noonday. This tidal wave of desperate humanity, roused to a murderous passion, poured into the narrow roads and alleys, crashing into the luckless Europeans found on the streets. In the initial moment of frenzy, the angry swarm greeted the foreigners with a barrage of clubs, mercilessly beating them down and trampling their victims underfoot. These clubs or *naboots*, which inflicted the most harm, were long thick pieces of wood used by the native watchmen.[3]

The instigator of the riot remained a mystery, but several developments quickly pointed to Tawfik, the Khedive of Egypt. Cartfuls of clubs had been distributed to the poor on instructions from the prefect of police, who was sympathetic to the Khedive.[4] Further evidence that the Egyptian ruler was behind the rampage that engulfed Alexandria was the presence of large numbers of armed Bedouin (also loyal to the Khedive) who had slipped into the city by the side streets and who later began to use their long rifles to shoot down Europeans.[5] Traditionally the Bedouin had little interest in constitutional reform and remained loyal to the head of state.[6] The signal for the onset of the massacre was a funeral procession accompanied by locals wearing green turbans that took place between 10:00 A.M. and noon. The dozens of warnings given to the Europeans by their Egyptian servants and tradesmen is further evidence that the pogrom unleashed in Alexandria was not spontaneous but carefully planned.

From early afternoon until sundown, mobs armed with a variety of makeshift weapons, along with some rifles and swords, attacked any foreigners on sight. Outside the Austrian post office, the frenzied horde beat to death a five-year-old boy.[7] Shortly afterward they caught a man staggering along the rue des Soeurs dripping with blood, but the sight only excited the mob, and they dispatched him with clubs. The rioters killed anyone they could get their hands on and then proceeded to strip the victims of all their belongings. That was not enough to satiate their thirst for violence; after the plunder they focused their fury on the corpses, leaving them horribly mutilated and then tossing them into the harbor.[8]

Throughout that afternoon the mob's fury gained further momentum, and more Europeans succumbed to stabbings, beatings, and gunshots. The blood-thirsty crowd poured into nearby shops, cafés, and any other establishment that was foreign-owned, to feed their anger and to fill their pockets. Members of the city's law enforcement detachments for the most part stood idly by and occasion-ally even joined the mob in beating to a pulp some hapless man, woman, or child who had the misfortune to seek asylum with the police. In the evening, Egyptian troops arrived, and the mob suddenly melted away. No arrests were made. How-ever, the violent episode was merely the first act in a course of events that trans-ferred Egyptian sovereignty from the court at Constantinople to London.

Ominously, in the harbor, Britain's Mediterranean fleet trained its guns on the city but did not fire a single shot in anger. In London, the government of William Gladstone sought a political solution in concert with the other Euro-pean powers but found no takers. The French, who had initially insisted on a show of force, now backed away from any involvement, except to offer the Brit-ish moral support. After a month of uneasy quiet a second riot exploded in the streets of Alexandria on July 11, leaving a longer trail of death and destruction. This time, the British fleet opened fire and began to demolish the harbor, but in the ensuing riot the looters satiated their appetite for hatred of the Europeans by consigning the city to flames. The next day, a British force of 250 sailors, along with 160 marines, established order among the burning rubble of Alexandria's European quarter. The troops came across the macabre spectacle of streets lit-tered with mutilated corpses and of women dousing rags and mattresses with petroleum and using them to burn the remaining houses. A portent of Britain's dependency on Egypt (in addition to the Suez Canal) was the shutting down of the Egyptian post offices, which left the Eastern Telegraph Company little choice but to withdraw its staff and instruments. Communication with India stopped, and the London Stock Exchange tumbled; millions of pounds sterling evaporated.

The mobs and the violence were products of deep-seated exasperation fu-eled by hatred for the foreigners and encouraged, behind the scenes, by Tawfik. Egypt's wretched ruler, desperate to regain absolute power, believed that the full fury of the Great Powers would descend on the Nationalists who had dimin-ished his power. He had tried to take advantage of a political crisis instigated by the British and French but had only succeeded in alienating the most influential sectors of Egyptian society, as well as the masses of peasants, who had to bear the brunt of the economic woes plaguing the country. Surrounded by a coterie of reactionary, landowning Turks and courtiers, Tawfik had lost touch with the realities of Egyptian society, concentrating almost exclusively on trying to out-maneuver the Nationalists and the Egyptian army. The Khedive's efforts, unfortunately, had only ushered in a series of plots and counterschemes, eventually drowning Egypt's body politic in a sea of conspiracies. Prior to the events in June and July, Tawfik's ineptitude had surrendered the political momentum for change and progress to the army, members of the Islamic establishment, and the small professional class.

The countdown to the June–July riots began in the winter of 1882, when the Chamber of Notables, whose majority was held by these groups, had proposed to give itself the right to vote on the disposition of half of Egypt's annual budget of £9 million, conceding that the other half was pledged to pay down the foreign debt. The chamber also proposed to increase military expenditures to promote native officers, as well as raising the army to eighteen thousand as decreed by the Ottoman Sultan. Unfortunately, the British and French controllers refused to relinquish their hold on Egypt's finances and rejected both recommendations.[9] Meanwhile, European bondholders, whose fortunes rested on financing the Egyptian debt, were becoming increasingly nervous at Egypt's endemic instability. The government, via the caprice of military coup, also shook the confidence of the French and British governments in Egypt's capability to pay down the enormous debts or service the interest on them.

In the late nineteenth century, financial insolvency had paved the way to gradual colonization of North Africa and the Middle East. As the rulers of the semiautonomous provinces of the Ottoman Empire foolishly fell victim to the siren call of the European moneylenders, they did not realize that with each loan they parceled out their sovereignty. Egypt's financial crisis was not unique amongst the territories of the Ottoman Sultan but part of a pattern that ushered in, in stages, European colonization of the Middle East. The Ottoman Viceroy of Tunisia, for example, had preceded the Egyptian Khedive in compiling huge debts and then declaring bankruptcy in 1869. A similar international debt commission was established, with representatives from France, Great Britain, and Italy.

However, at the Congress of Berlin in 1878, the Great Powers, not just for the sake of bond issues, but to preserve the balance of power in Europe, sacrificed the independence of Tunisia. Tunisia was the consolation prize to France for Britain's acquisition of Cyprus.[10] In April 1881, the French government took advantage of raids mounted by Tunisian tribesmen and compelled the Ottoman

Viceroy to accept a French protectorate. The Treaty of Bardo provided legal fi-
nesse to otherwise blatant annexation, but it also provoked uprisings in the
south and center of the country, which were contained by the deployment of
French troops. However, the rebels were joined by thousands of tribesmen, and
by June the initial French success had degenerated into a protracted conflict.[11]
Regardless, the French convinced themselves that rebellion in Tunisia was part
of a larger Muslim uprising that would expand into a pan-Islamic movement,
spilling over into Egypt and Algeria and undermining France's position in
North Africa.[12]

The British, on the other hand, had little concern over the situation in
Egypt and even less sympathy for the French predicament in Algeria and Tunisia. Furthermore, the liberal Gladstone was opposed to foreign interventions,
and felt that, if something had to be done about the internal Egyptian crisis, it
was a matter for the European Concert. Nonetheless, the Gladstone government was equally determined to maintain good relations with France and
agreed to issue a Joint Note on January 8, 1882, which assured the Khedive of
Anglo-French "support against the difficulties of various kinds which might
interfere with the course of public affairs in Egypt." The note went on to state:
"the assurance publicly given of their formal intentions in this respect will tend
to avert the dangers . . . to which the Government of the Khedive might be exposed, and which would certainly find England and France united to oppose
them."[13]

The Anglo-French guarantee to defend the Khedive against all enemies
from within or without, reinforced by the presence of the British warships in
Alexandria, set the irrevocable course that led to the riots of June and July and
ultimately stifled Egypt's sovereignty. Tawfik immediately embraced the protection of the foreign powers and, at the onset of the mob violence he himself
had inspired, sought refuge under the British guns in Alexandria. By so doing,
Tawfik forfeited his legitimacy to rule the Egyptians almost at the same time
that Islamic fundamentalism was emerging as the alternative to secular authority in the Sudan and Tunis.

Ironically, the French had urged intervention in order to check the perceived spread of a pan-Islamic movement, only to instigate it through the British
bombardment of Alexandria. The leader of the Nationalists, Ahmed Arabi's,
first reaction to the presence of the British warships was to communicate to
Gladstone that "use will be made of the religious zeal of the Mohammedans, to
preach a holy war in Syria, in Arabia and in India. . . . I repeat again and again,
that the first blow struck at Egypt by England or her allies will cause blood to
flow throughout the breadth of Asia and of Africa." In his letter to the British

prime minister, he also threatened to confiscate all European property, cancel the Dual Control, disown the debt, destroy the canal, and cut the telegraph connecting Britain to India.[14] There was little room for compromise, and events quickly catapulted into a violent confrontation. The British government, with Gladstone at its head, became convinced that Arabi and his followers had imposed a military dictatorship and organized the riots.

When the British guns leveled Alexandria's forts, Arabi and his followers took power and prepared for war. A reluctant Gladstone ordered direct military intervention, and 18,500 British troops landed on Egyptian soil. After several weeks of skirmishes, both armies finally clashed on September 13, 1883, at Tel-el-Kebir, north of the canal. After a hard-fought battle, British forces, commanded by Sir Garnet Wolseley, defeated Arabi's Egyptian army of fifteen thousand. Egypt was restored to the incompetent Tawfik. The British then decided to rule the country through the compliant Khedive, buttressed by a small army of British soldiers and a handful of civil servants. The foreigners soon returned to a rebuilt Alexandria and also spilled over to Cairo, quickly taking over Egypt's economy and trade.

The pan-Islam feared by the French did bubble to the surface—not in Egypt, Algeria, or Tunisia, but in the Sudan[15] under the banner of Muhammad Ahmad ibn Abd Allah, who, taking advantage of the discontent of the Sudanese against the Egyptian administration, proclaimed himself the Mahdi, "the Expected One," the redeemer of Islam.[16] His purpose was to revive the Islamic faith and practice of the Prophet through the restoration of the Koran and the establishment of an Islamic republic.[17] The Mahdi preached adherence to the teachings of Mohammed based on a return to the virtue of strict devotion, prayer, and simplicity as laid down in the Koran. He also condemned the use of tobacco and alcohol, and he advocated the segregation of women from male society.[18] He attracted a large following that expanded into hundreds of thousands. Although his theology was similar in extremism and austerity to that of the Wahhabi sect in Saudi Arabia, the Mahdi was trained in the Sufi school. However, he preached a fundamentalist and virulent strain of Islam that in time appealed to many Muslims beyond the Sudan.

To accomplish these ends, the Mahdi declared a jihad against the Egyptian administration; his followers gladly sought battle to achieve martyrdom. The Mahdi's armies of what British soldiers called "fuzzy-wuzzies"—half-naked Hadendoa warriors, armed with spears and swords and drunk with religious fervor—easily smashed the ill-led and ill-prepared forces sent by Cairo, and by 1883 had overrun most of the scattered Egyptian garrisons in the Sudan. Thousands of Egyptians were stranded and faced a cruel fate at the hands of the

Mahdi and his followers. A large number had sought refuge in Khartoum, one of the last garrisons still under Egyptian control.[19] In 1864, the British government asked General Charles Gordon to lead a relief force of native troops to rescue the stranded Egyptians.[20] General Gordon succeeded in evacuating about 2,500 women and children from Khartoum before the Mahdi's army laid siege to the city.

The British government, however, was less motivated by humanitarian sentiments than by the fact that the Mahdi's rebellion had engulfed the eastern Sudan and threatened the ports that guarded the southern exit of the Suez Canal, linking the Sudan with Jeddah and Mecca. The major concern was that, if the Mahdi succeeded in spreading his rebellion to the Arabian provinces of the Ottoman Empire, it could threaten the route to India. Furthermore, if he succeeded in capturing Khartoum, the Mahdi would control the Nile Valley from the Sudan to the Mediterranean. In London and Cairo the consensus among British officials was that, to contain the Mahdi uprising in the Sudan, they had to remain in Egypt.

Gladstone continued to preach that Britain would pull out of Egypt, but it was a hollow promise. What concerned his government was that there were insufficient resources to secure Egypt and restore control over the Sudan. When the Mahdi's armies succeeded in spreading the revolt in the eastern Sudan, the British government decided to consolidate its forces in Egypt, essentially abandoning Gordon and Khartoum. There was one serious attempt to relieve the siege and rescue Gordon, but it failed. On January 26, 1885, Khartoum fell, and General Gordon was hacked to pieces and beheaded. For the next ten years, the British forgot about Gordon and Khartoum and left the Sudan to the Mahdi and his successors.

"Egypt was the graveyard of Gladstonian diplomacy," writes Paul Kennedy.[21] In vain Gladstone kept assuring the British public that it was only a matter of time before all British officials and soldiers would leave the country, but the problem of the security of the Suez Canal persisted, skewing the great liberal's plans, quickly souring relations with the French, and holding every prospect of raising the specter of the Eastern Question. Egypt was still a province of the Ottoman Empire, whose ruler held power through the beneficence of the Sultan in Constantinople.

Albeit longstanding, the goodwill of the Sultan was ceremonial, but legally Egypt remained an appendage of the Ottoman domain, and any radical aggrandizement of the Sultan's territories would certainly invoke the interests of the other European powers. The 1884 Berlin Conference had established a modicum of broad understanding over the formal European exploitation of

Africa, and any dramatic change in Egypt and the Sudan could easily unravel the agreements.[22]

The security of the Suez Canal effectively left little recourse for the British, except to stay and consolidate their hold over Egypt, as well as over the immediate region. The process was made easier when the collapse of Italy's Ethiopian colonial ambitions facilitated Britain's expansion of Egypt to include the Sudan. On March 1, 1896, the Italian army suffered a disastrous defeat at Adowa in Abyssinia, losing over half of its soldiers to the well-organized forces of Menelik II, the emperor of Ethiopia.[23] The defeat encouraged Khalifa Abdullahi, the Mahdi's successor, to lay siege to the Italian fort at Kassala in the northeastern Sudan.[24] The Italians appealed for help in order to rescue their garrison and in the process triggered a chain of events that transformed the Sudan into another British colony.

The government of Lord Salisbury decided it was preferable to conquer the Sudan on the pretext of saving the Italians, rather than allow the French to move into the region.[25] In a single stroke, Salisbury satisfied imperial security and revenge for the death of General Gordon at Khartoum. After a grueling three-year campaign (1896–1899), Horatio Herbert Kitchener conquered the Sudan and captured Khartoum, ostensibly in the name of the Khedive, but in actual fact to secure the Suez Canal for Great Britain. According to A. J. P. Taylor:

> The British expedition to the Sudan completed the revolution in Mediterranean politics. Previously the British had intended to oppose Russia at the [Bosporus] Straits and therefore sought to keep France neutral. The collapse of Italy gave the final blow to this policy. The Italian fleet was useless: the Italians would need help instead of giving it. . . . Since the British could not pass the Straits, they decided to stay in Egypt permanently and to defend the Suez Canal by the armed forces stationed there.[26]

Although the Mahdi's Islamic state survived for only twenty years after his death, his rebellion and subsequent success attracted a great deal of attention throughout the Muslim world. During this brief interlude in the otherwise insatiable European expansion in the Middle East, the Mahdi's spectacular victories had clearly demonstrated that Islam could defeat the West. The lesson he taught was that a purified Islam, unified under the leadership of a Caliph (significantly his successor was designated as Caliph), could be a potent force.[27]

However, the legacy of the Mahdi left an equally strong impression on the Europeans, particularly the British and the Germans, who convinced themselves that manipulation of Islam's power by controlling the Caliph offered a considerable edge in the race for their looming imperial confrontation. Yet neither the British and the Germans, nor any of the other European powers, appreciated that the lure of a purified Islamic state, headed by the secular-theocratic Caliph, had already become an idée fixe for a small, but steadily growing, army of Muslim intellectuals, theologians, and students. These continued to morph into a variety of Muslim organizations and militant underground forces, culminating in the radical and terrorist groups that have played a disproportionate role in shaping the discourse of political Islam in the late twentieth- and early twenty-first centuries.

From the First World War until the 1970s, the Western intelligence services sought to harness the energy of political Islam for their own purposes. In 1914, imperial Germany, quickly followed by Great Britain, tried to exploit the spiritual influence of the Caliphate, to achieve specific strategic military objectives in the Middle East. The Germans convinced the Ottoman Sultan to declare a jihad that fell on deaf ears, while the British tried to set up the Sharif of Mecca, the steward of the holy cities of Mecca and Medina, as an Arab Caliph, in contrast to the Turkish Sultan, only to discover that it barely caused a ripple of interest in the Muslim world. Both empires misjudged and misunderstood the significance of the Caliphate and the degree to which political Islam could serve the interests of the West.

THREE

The Eclipse of Imperial Islam

"I think that this pan-Islamic movement is one of our greatest
dangers in the future, and is indeed far more of a
menace than the 'Yellow Peril.'"
—*Sir Arthur Nicolson, Permanent Undersecretary, Foreign Office*[1]

On March 3, 1924, at 5:30 A.M. a small convoy of three cars followed by a
truck snaked its way through the wet streets of Constantinople. Occasionally the cars got stuck in the muddy streets, and the gendarmes who escorted the party of eight had to get out and place stones under the tires to get
the vehicles moving. The convoy bounced along the Bosporus, over the Galata
Bridge, past the Bayezid Mosque, then through the Edirne Gate, circumventing
the ancient walls to Yedikule, and finally to the Catala train station. At 11:00
A.M. the last Caliph, Abdulmecit II, stepped out of the car followed by two of his
wives, his son and his daughter, and accompanied by his chief chamberlain, his
personal physician, and his private secretary.[2] The station manager offered Abdulmecit every courtesy and accommodated the party in his home located next
to the station. The police formed a cordon to keep away the faithful and the curious, as well as to ensure that Abdulmecit accepted the decision of the new Turkish parliament: to leave the country.[3]

At midnight and at a leisurely pace, the Orient Express puffed into the
station and in a short while was ready for the new passengers. Just before Abdulmecit boarded the special coach assigned to him, the governor of Istanbul
handed over to him an envelope containing £2,000 and temporary entry visas
issued by the Swiss consulate. And so, with little fanfare, the Ottoman Caliph,
supreme spiritual and political leader of the Sunni Muslim world, resigned his
office and stepped into oblivion.[4] The half millennium of the Ottoman imperium
drew to a hurried and shabby end on the platform of the Calata train station, a few
steps from the Orient Express, and the continuum with the successors of Mohammed was severed forever.[5] In his memoirs, Ismet Inönü, one of the founders of
the Turkish Republic and, along with Ataturk, an advocate of the abolition of the
Caliphate, recalled:

We encountered the greatest resistance when we abolished the caliphate. Abolishing the sultanate had been easier, as the survival of the caliphate had satisfied the partisans of the sultanate. But the two-headed system could not go on forever. It nourished the expectation that the sovereign would return under the guise of caliph . . . and gave hope to the [Ottoman dynasty]. This is why the abolition of the caliphate . . . had deeper effects and was to become the main source of conflict.[6]

Elsewhere reaction appeared to be muted; few people took notice and fewer still seemed to care when Abdulmecit issued a statement announcing his resignation after his train crossed the Turkish-Bulgarian border. However, it was impossible to gauge the sentiments of ordinary Muslims in the Middle East and beyond. Certainly in 1924 the European powers had swallowed major tracts of the Muslim regions, leaving only a handful of countries, including the new republic of Turkey, independent of foreign rule. It is unlikely that the European masters of these Islamic communities made any effort to measure the reaction of their new Muslim subjects to the momentous event at the Calata train station. Gilles Kepel has noted, "one of the greatest traumas to affect Islam in the early twentieth century was Ataturk's abolition of the Caliphate in 1924. The caliphate was already a spent political force at the time, but it represented the ideal of spiritual unity within the Muslim world."[7]

On the eve of the First World War, with a few exceptions, a large part of the Middle East had been within the tired grip of the Ottoman Empire. The Ottomans, a disparate assortment of Turks and Muslim converts, had gravitated from Central Asia as mercenaries and in time evolved into a formidable army that swept away the remnants of the Byzantine Empire. In 1453 the Ottomans conquered the great city of Constantinople and by the next century spread out from the Balkans and Asia Minor to envelop most of the Middle East. The Ottoman armies proved unbeatable, and by the sixteenth century they had conquered most of North Africa, all of southeastern Europe, and parts of Hungary, and had twice brought their armies to the gates of Vienna.

As Caliph, the Ottoman ruler represented the secular and the religious unity of Islam that reached beyond the confines of the empire to Muslims beyond its frontiers.[8] By the eighteenth century, Ottoman supremacy had eclipsed, and the empire began a long and almost irreversible decline until its final demise at the end of the First World War.[9] However, the Great Powers, particularly Britain, could not allow the total collapse of the Ottomans and the ensuing political vacuum in the Middle East, and they therefore undertook to prop up the Ottoman state. British fears were based on the real possibility that if the Ottoman Empire vanished, large parts of its territories would fall to Russia and expose the land route to India.

British policy, as well as that of France, Austria-Hungary, and Prussia, toward the "Sick Man" of Europe (the description of the Ottoman regime in the nineteenth century) was to maintain the integrity of the empire, in order to keep the Russian battle fleet and Russian influence locked up in the Black Sea. As long as the Ottoman Empire remained more or less intact, the Sultan, with the backing of the Royal Navy, could maintain sovereignty over the Straits (the Dardanelles and Bosporus) and thus deny the Russian Black Sea fleet access to the Mediterranean. However, in periods of weakness, it suited the Russians for the Sultan to keep the Straits closed to all warships and prevent Russia's rivals from entering the Black Sea. Of course, this did not deter Britain, France, Italy, and Russia from colonizing large tracts of Ottoman territories and finalizing partition of the former empire after the First World War.

In 1914, the Ottomans chose to link their fortunes with Imperial Germany in a desperate bid to reacquire lost territories and past glories. Initially, the Ottomans had tried to ally themselves with Britain, France, and even Russia, but each one had turned them down. The decision to join Germany placed the Ottoman Empire on the side of the defeated Central Powers and instigated a feeding frenzy amongst the Entente allies for the Sultan's lands in the Middle East. Events, once again, brought the Middle East full circle, and Western powers, in the period after the First World War, controlled most of the Islamic world. Muslim fundamentalists argue this is still the case in the twenty-first century.

During the war, the allies—particularly the British—needed the Arabs to fight against the Ottomans, but they also saw in the Arabs the key to countering the influence of the Sultan as Caliph of all Muslims and his ability to declare a jihad. The notion of holy war instigating a massive uprising of Britain's Muslim subjects dominated the thinking of British officials in Whitehall and Cairo as much as in Berlin. Politicians and bureaucrats on both sides were convinced that an appeal to Islam held a strategic advantage. Ultimately, neither the Sultan's role as Caliph nor declaration of a jihad had any significant impact on the war.

The Islamic factor, however, skewed British policy toward the Middle East both during and after the First World War, as bureaucrats, politicians, and intelligence officers in London and Cairo misunderstood religion and nationalism in the Middle East, assuming that they could control the former and manufacture the latter. In the decades after 1918, the British and later the Americans alternately attempted to manipulate religion and nationalism in order to secure their interests in the region, by seeking a strongman as the focal point of either Arab nationalism or as the centerpiece of Islamic unity.

The termination of the Caliphate left a significant void in the Muslim community which engendered several disparate movements that sought to reconstruct Islamic unity. However, for many a manifestation of a new Caliph held the strongest appeal.[10] One of the fundamental goals of the Muslim Brotherhood, established four years after the resignation of the Ottoman Caliph, was the political unity of Islam through the reconstitution of a new Caliphate.[11] Subsequently, the quest for the leadership of the international or regional Islamic community has oscillated between the claims of Islamic militants and ambitious Muslim secular leaders. Meanwhile, British and American intelligence officers assumed that a single master could direct a "monolithic" Islam, and that—through him—they could guide events in the Middle East. This assumption was held dear by the British, and later by some Muslim experts in the Anglo-American intelligence services; it was based on the notion that some kind of entity such as the Caliphate was the centrifugal force that held the loyalty of the Muslims and also transcended national boundaries. This tenuous political and theological construct emerged in the late nineteenth and early twentieth centuries in response to the perceived imminent demise of the Ottoman Empire.

The wholesale defeat of the Sultan's armies by the Russians in 1878 and the loss of more territory were further evidence of the decline and inevitable collapse of the Ottoman Empire. Under the terms of the 1878 Treaty of Berlin, which ended the Russo-Turkish War, the Ottoman Empire lost 8 percent of its territory and almost 20 percent of its population, of which a substantial number were Christians. A unique by-product of this consequence, especially after further losses of non-Muslim populations in the aftermath of the Balkan Wars (1912–1913), was that the Muslims now constituted most of the empire's subjects.[12] The multiethnic and denominational diversity that had characterized Ottomanism for almost half a millennium receded, and the empire's universality now rested exclusively on Islam.

The new demographic, however, created an opportunity to counter the demands for self-determination by the empire's minorities, most of which after 1878 were Muslim, by invoking Islamic unity. The Ottoman Sultan, Abdulhamid II, was convinced that to rescue the empire from the accelerating slide into oblivion, it was necessary to bring it back to its Islamic roots. He believed that efforts at modernization, which emulated Western political, economic, and social structures, were doomed to fail and to further erode the Sultan's power and ability to guide the Ottoman state. Consequently, for Abdulhamid, the secular Ottoman identity proclaimed by the modernizers no longer had any resonance for most of the empire's people. Caroline Finkel, in a recent history of the Ottoman Empire, writes that Islam offered a new ideology that enabled Abdulhamid to take "the latent notion of the Ottoman Sultan as caliph and [refashion] it to command the allegiance, not just of his own people but of all Muslims, asserting more insistently than any Ottoman sultan before him the potency of his identity as caliph, and the appropriateness of Islam as a focus of loyalty for the state."[13]

However, the perception of pending imperial doom and the appeal of Islam as a political force created new ambitions for the empire's Arab potentates, as well as for its European rivals. Although the attempt to establish an independent Arabia and to cast the Emir of Mecca as a new Sultan-Caliph is part of the Lawrence of Arabia legend, the British took the first tentative attempts toward this goal in the late nineteenth century. After the debacle of the Russo-Turkish War, Hussein Pasha, the Emir of Mecca, began to flirt with the British over the disposition of the Caliphate. Emir Hussein, while openly exhibiting absolute loyalty to the Sultan, initiated a subtle but cautious communication with the British in order to prove his bona fide pro-British credentials, while indirectly hinting that the transfer of the Caliphate from Istanbul to Mecca would benefit Great Britain.[14] As an Arab, a member of the Qurayshi tribe and of the Hashemite clan, as well as the Awn family, Hussein had direct access to the succession of the Caliphate.[15] The Ottoman claim was based on the Hanafi school of Islamic jurisprudence, which was more flexible than the orthodox view and which held that the Caliph had to be a member of the Qurayshi tribe.[16] The British responded cautiously but favorably and maintained contact with the Emir through their consul in Arabia.[17]

Initially, Abdulhamid II assumed that Egypt's rulers would emerge as rivals, would challenge the Ottomans for control of the Arab provinces, and would take over the Caliphate, thus ending the Ottoman monopoly over Islamic unity. Even after the deposition of the Khedive Ismail and the reduction of the Egyptian army to eighteen thousand men, rumors persisted that his successor, Tawfik, was conspiring in the Hejaz (the region of Mecca and Medina). It did not help Abdulhamid's paranoia that the exiled Ismail was sponsoring newspapers openly calling for the transfer of the Caliphate to Cairo.[18]

At about this time, reports of Emir Hussein's secret negotiations reached the Sultan, further fueling his suspicions that the British were promoting an independent Arab Caliphate. However, the assassination of the Emir by an obscure Afghan in 1880 brought to an end, for the time being, the prospect of a future Arab Caliph.[19] The respite over the machinations of the Caliphate as a counterweight to the Ottoman Sultan for the "hearts and minds" of Muslims remained in abeyance for twenty-four years, but resumed with a greater urgency after the opening salvos of the First World War.

One of the primary architects of Britain's Middle East policy in the First World War was Field Marshal Lord Kitchener, consul general and British agent in Cairo—in actual fact British proconsul in Egypt and as such the power behind the Khedive's throne. During his tenure in Cairo, Kitchener became convinced that if a hostile power controlled the Ottoman Caliphate it could challenge Britain's hold over the millions of Muslim subjects of the British Empire. Muslims accounted for 70 million of India's population and a significant percentage of the Indian army; many continued to regard the Ottoman Sultan-Caliph as the supreme Islamic authority.[20] In contrast, the population of the Ottoman Empire in 1897 was 39 million, which also included non-Muslim minorities.[21]

Furthermore, in the early twentieth century, the Ottoman Empire was the last Muslim state that retained its full sovereignty and autonomy, making it a focal point for all Sunni Muslims. Accordingly, Kitchener reasoned, a call to arms from the only independent Muslim ruler would inflame the Muslim communities in the British Empire. Certainly Kitchener was witness to the powerful emotions stirred by appeals to Islam and jihad. In the Sudan he had seen firsthand how religious zealotry and fanaticism animated Islamic warriors armed with spears and swords to fling themselves against an army equipped with machine guns and artillery. Islamic militancy had also fueled mass uprisings in Egypt, and religious fervor had been the cause of the Great Indian Mutiny in 1857–1859.

Accordingly, the disintegration of the Ottoman Empire would undermine British interests in the Near and Middle East and the Eastern Mediterranean. However, the ensuing vacuum would create a scramble for its provinces, with Russia as one of the main contenders. In this context, Kitchener was less concerned about Germany than about Russia, concludes David Fromkin, and even after the outbreak of the First World War, the field marshal continued to harbor suspicions that the Ottoman Sultan-Caliph would become a creature of the Russian Czar.[22] Germany was primarily a European problem, but after the First World War, Russia would remain Britain's primary challenger in Asia. To Kitchener, the entente that ended the Great Game and brought Britain and Russia into an alliance with France was simply a temporary convenience whose usefulness would terminate after the defeat of Germany.

FOUR

Jihad for All Occasions

"As a nation we dearly love the bogy of a fanatical army of
millions of desert Arabs yelling 'Allah!' and putting infidels to the
sword and I imagine the idea must have started about the
eleventh century during the First Crusade."
—*Colonel C. S. Jarvis (Libyan Desert, 1917)*[1]

On November 13, 1914, in the hall of the Popkapi Palace, where the relics of the Prophet Mohammed were kept, a solemn ceremony was performed to invoke the power of Islam's glorious past. In the presence of Sultan-Caliph Mehmet V Reshat, and of clerical, military, and political dignitaries, the Sheikul-islam invoked a series of fatwas allowing for the declaration of jihad, thus making it the binding duty of every Muslim to take part in a holy war against the Entente.[2] Unlike previous fatwas calling for jihad, this time it was not only addressed to the subjects of the Ottoman Empire, but also to Muslims under British, French, Russian, Serbian, and Montenegrin rule.[3]

The legitimacy of the proclamation of holy war was doubtful, since the Ottoman Empire was taking part in a war allied with Christian powers fighting against other Christian powers.[4] Nevertheless this resort to jihad was the culmination of German propaganda in the fervent assumption that the Ottoman Sultan-Caliph could provoke mass uprisings of Muslims in the British, French, and Russian empires. Yet, that fateful day in November evolved as a combination of theater and wishful thinking.

After several speeches, an attempt was made to link the events of 1914 with the roots of Islam and Mohammed. The call to holy war was followed by a procession on horseback, led by a band, through the streets of Istanbul, accompanied by two women representing the Prophet's wife, Aishah, and her attendant.[5] The procession stopped at the German embassy and was greeted by representatives from the Committee of Union and Progress (CUP), the ruling party, and a Turkish-speaking member of the German legation.

The theater continued as a Moroccan in French uniform gave a brief speech in Arabic praising the Germans for his liberation and condemning the treatment of Muslim soldiers in the French army. The crowd cheered the name of the German emperor as an ally of Islam. They then proceeded to the Austro-Hungarian embassy and, more or less, followed the same course. Afterward, some of the crowd became a mob and looted several Christian shops and houses.[6]

Gottfried Hagen has summarized the reactions of contemporary observers to the event as "curiosity, confusion, and some amusement. . . . An American report quotes rumors that the two women who represented Aishah and her attendant in their normal life sold roasted chickpeas on the bridge over the Golden Horn, as more respectable women had refused to participate."[7] The Moroccan Muslim patriot's motives turned out to be suspect. He had been taken prisoner on the Western Front and most likely had been coached on how to address the crowd. One German eyewitness, observing the scene from a balcony of the embassy, described the speech of the Moroccan soldier by stating: "I don't think that much of what he said was understood down there. People will hardly have understood his gibberish."[8]

Regardless of the issue of validity, on November 23, 1914, the Sultan, in his capacity as Caliph, formally issued the declaration of holy war throughout the Muslim world. Most scholars agree that the proclamation of jihad was the culmination of Germany's Ottoman policy rooted in the kaiser's Damascus promise to all Muslims of his eternal friendship.[9] Although the majority of members from the CUP (the real power in the Ottoman Empire) subscribed to a secular rather than religious outlook, they understood that harnessing Islam offered a means of sowing discontent among the Muslim subjects of the Entente.

The prospect of a mass uprising of Muslims after the Sultan-Caliph called the faithful to jihad had fixated the Germans and British, who expended considerable nervous energy and gold on stimulating or preventing a future holy war. Prior to the war, the Germans had established a pan-Islamic propaganda office in Berlin that focused on the Islamic issues in the Ottoman Empire, as well as in the territories of the Entente that included large numbers of Muslims.[10] For their part, the British concentrated their efforts on the Sharif of Mecca as a possible antidote to counter the Ottoman Sultan's proclamation of holy war.

In fact, German and British intelligence strategy in the Middle East was centered on the notion of jihad as the magic bullet with which to manipulate the 300 million Muslims around the globe to take up arms. Shiite Muslims were the exception; they did not belong to the Sunni branch of Islam with the Sultan-Caliph as its head. The Germans published millions of printed leaflets and had them distributed as far away as India, but the printed message was lost on millions of Muslims, who, for the most part, were illiterate.

Despite so much effort and determination to rouse the Muslims to war and to generate a pan-Islamic movement, the Sultan-Caliph's appeal to jihad failed. One factor was that while Abdulhamid was considered by a majority of Muslims, especially those outside the Ottoman Empire, as the legitimate Sultan and Caliph, the CUP had in fact toppled him.[11] Another consideration was that, by the end of the nineteenth century, the position of Caliph as a monopoly of the Ottoman Sultan faced legal and secular challenges.

Some authoritative Islamic scholars argued at the time that the Caliphate should be re-formed and restored to an Arab chieftain.[12] Ibn Saud, the Emir of the Nejd in Central Arabia and head of the puritanical Wahhabi sect, outright rejected the idea that the Sultan's role as Caliph gave him secular authority over the Muslim community. The British successfully countered the possible impact of the Sultan's jihad by securing legal opinions from Islamic legal experts and Muslim clerics in Egypt and India who asserted that it was the obligation of Muslims to obey the British authorities.[13]

Rudolph Peters, on the other hand, concludes that the main reason for the failure of the jihad "was that Pan-Islamism lacked any form of political mass organization. Despite the exaggerated notions with regard to its force and impact prevalent in Europe, it was no more than an idea espoused by some intellectuals as a reaction against the rapid spread of Western domination during the last quarter of the nineteenth century."[14]

Despite the collapse of the jihad, the fear of a pan-Islamic movement inflamed by religious fervor in an all-out holy war continued to haunt and intrigue the British—and later American—strategists. In early 1917, a few hundred Senussi tribesmen raided the Libyan Desert from Tripolitania,[15] although they were quickly defeated and scattered by a small number of British territorial forces. According to C. S. Jarvis, a British officer in the Western Desert, the raid reinforced the paranoia of an imminent jihad. Consequently, the British stationed thirty thousand troops on the western frontier, when they were badly needed elsewhere, in the conviction that the Senussi represented the vanguard of a much larger force. In all, about one thousand Senussi tribesmen tied up thirty thousand British troops desperately needed on other fronts. Jarvis went on to complain:

> It is very difficult to decide now who actually was to blame for this state of affairs—probably the Intelligence Department in the first place, as they imbued the soldiers with the idea that if the Senussi penetrated to the Nile Valley the whole of Egypt would rise in a holy war against us, which, to say the least, was a gross and absurd exaggeration. . . . For months our troops remained facing a perfectly empty desert, devoid

absolutely of water, in which the enemy could not move if he so desired, and they continued to do so until at last the authorities decided very regretfully that the Senussi was a myth.[16]

Two years later, Jarvis reported that the same paranoia seized British intelligence in Cairo, and they predicted another mass uprising of Arabs. Jarvis reminiscences that at the time:

> Telegrams were showering in on me to the effect that hordes of Arabs, estimated at 40,000, were marching on Cairo and Alexandria from the Libyan Desert. . . . After a two days' patrol that covered the greater part of the north-west portion of the Western Desert, I failed utterly to find anything in the nature of an organization and wired back to that effect. I was not believed, for the Powers that Be in Cairo had faithfully predicted that a rising of Arabs would be the natural sequence of events; and as a nation we have definitely a marked Arab complex.[17]

In the decades after the First World War, the fixation with a mass Arab uprising continued to color Whitehall's policies toward the Middle East. In 1946, R. H. S. Crossman, a Labour member of Parliament, remarked: "The danger of an Arab Holy War is now being used more and more intensively than ever by officials in the Colonial Service and in the various Middle East Embassies as an argument against the acceptance of the Anglo-American Report."[18] Although Crossman was a leading Zionist, his frustration with British diplomats and civil servants reflected an ingrained attitude that had less to do with the pro-Arab sentiments of some British officials than with an almost irrational fear of pan-Islam's leading to a jihad.[19]

In 1919, Indian Muslims organized to pressure the British government to preserve both the boundaries of the Ottoman Empire, as well as the spiritual and temporal authority of the Sultan-Caliph. For many of these officials, the Khilafat Movement that sprang up in India just after the end of the First World War served as further evidence of the latent power of pan-Islam. Yet, as the scholar Gail Minault demonstrates, the Khilafat movement was an attempt by Indian Muslim leaders to unite their community politically by means of religious and cultural symbols that could appeal to the entire community—in effect, a pan-Indian Islam.[20]

Although these Indian Muslim radicals were not unsympathetic to the fate of the Ottoman Caliph, British intelligence in India, as well as in Cairo and

London, did not understand the difference. Minault also adds that the leader- ship of the movement provided one set of arguments in English publications, whereas their message to Muslim Indians in Urdu and other local dialects was nuanced to reflect local ambitions.[21] Whether British intelligence officials in India ever considered the political propaganda aimed at the Indian Muslims remains an open question. As was the case in the Middle East, British colonial civil servants and intelligence officers focused their energies—and based their knowledge of Islamic factors—on regional elites.

Regardless of evidence to the contrary, neither the Ottoman Sultan nor the Sharif of Mecca succeeded in mobilizing a holy war or a mass uprising in 1914 or at any time during the First World War. Even in the period after the First World War, local rebellions in the Middle East, such as those by the Druze (an Islamic minority) and the Palestinians, as well as Rashid Ali's revolt in Iraq during the Second World War, failed to elicit sympathetic revolts in other Arab regions. Nevertheless, the same era served as a gestation period for far more intense and militant movements, such as the Muslim Brotherhood in Egypt, which aimed at resurrecting Islam as the binding force to unite all Muslims.

Although Muslim militancy had bubbled to the surface as early as the late nineteenth century, with the Mahdi in the Sudan, the end of the Ottoman Em- pire and the abolition of the Caliphate created a vacuum that a variety of move- ments and individuals have tried to fill. Yet Islamic militancy and pan-Islam have manifested themselves variously in different parts of the Middle East. For example, writes Gilles Kepel: "Present-day Pakistani Islam is the heir to a series of movements created in reaction to the British empire's dethronement of the last Muslim sovereign in 1897."[22]

Pakistan is but one example, followed by Saudi Arabia and Egypt, as well as Iran, which are home to strong currents of some form of pan-Islamic move- ment. In other regions of the Muslim world, such as Turkey, Islamic identity is quickly superseding secular nationalism. But even secular Turkey was anchored in the legacy of Mustapha Kemal Ataturk, who filled the role of a Sultan and Caliph stripped of Islamic trappings. The erosion of secularism after the 1980s has offered fertile ground for Turkish Muslims to try and reorganize Turkish society along Islamic principles.

The current term for militant pan-Islam is "political Islam," a concept that embraces the spiritual and cultural elements of Islam, as well as the notion of Islam as a political force mobilized for the purpose of creating a pan-Islamic state. Beyond certain shared tenets of Islam, it is perhaps the one common de- nominator found among both Sunni and Shiite Muslim militant ideologues.[23] The British and later the American intelligence organizations not only failed to notice this development, but attempted to harness Islam as a means to counter Arab and Iranian nationalism. Throughout most of the twentieth century, beginning after the First World War, Arab nationalism haunted the British and the Americans, who sought security for their interests in the Middle East by supporting Islamic militancy as a counterweight to nationalism and later communism.

Yet what the Anglo-American intelligence communities (as well as British colonial officials) failed to understand was that behind the veneer of Arab nationalism was the rise of pan-Islam. Equally significant is the fact that the manifestation of pan-Islam is a form of regional Muslim identity that is less centered on the concept of a universal Caliphate. However, the fog of militant Islam has clouded every other consideration. Ironically, Muslim militants, as well as British and American intelligence agencies, for opposite purposes and at various periods, have sought to find a variation of a new Caliphate that could unify the Islamic community to checkmate the Marxist and—regardless of the contradiction—the nationalist Middle East bogeyman. For the British, the search for a new Caliph originated in Arabia, which, in time, contributed to a ripple effect that inspired a new generation of Muslim militants.

FIVE

A New Caliph

"There is a dry wind blowing through the East, and the parched grasses
wait the spark. And the wind is blowing towards the Indian border."
—*John Buchan*[1]

Rifle fire tore through the stillness of the morning almost immediately after the faithful had finished prayers in the early dawn (June 10, 1916). The
bullets crashed through the wooden shutters and drilled into the polished floor
of the Hamidiya building that housed the offices of the Ottoman government
representatives in Mecca. Bullets continued to rip through the windows and
walls, igniting small explosions of wood slivers and raising tiny clouds of dust.
Bimbashi Mehmed Zia Bey, the acting governor and commander of the Turkish forces in Mecca, had instinctively dropped to the floor after the first shots
and remained low to escape the bullets whizzing just above his head.[2] He tried
to reach the nearby Turkish barracks but to no avail—the rebels had cut the
telephone lines, isolating the few Turkish troops within the city. Next he
phoned Sharif Hussein, the only man with authority over the Bedouin, whom
he suspected were behind the attack.[3]

Zia Bey assumed that, as had been the practice for centuries, local Arabs
were attempting to extort money from the Ottoman government by attacking
the nearby Turkish garrison. His discussion with Hussein was brief and dis-
concerting. Upon reaching the Emir, Zia Bey asked what all this (the firing)
meant, saying: "The Bedouins have revolted against the government; find a
way out." Sharif Hussein replied with cold sarcasm: "Of course we shall" and
hung up immediately.[4] Zia Bey tried to hold his position, but with few troops,
almost no ammunition, a lack of water, and no relief in sight, he capitulated.[5]

In the holiest city of Islam on that day, June 10, 1916, Sharif Hussein completed his break with the Ottoman Empire and threw in his lot with the British.[6] Yet the Great Arab Revolt was less of an explosion of Arab nationalism
than a fizzle of local politics, backed by Bedouin opportunism. For the British,
particularly the British intelligence community in Cairo, it came as a relief that
a major custodian of Islam, Sharif Hussein of Mecca, could now serve as a
counterbalance to the Sultan-Caliph of the Ottoman Empire—a factor that had

focused Britain's imperial legates in Egypt on reshaping the dynamics of Islamic authority and harnessing the power of Islam to serve British interests. British intelligence officers, as well as officials in Cairo and London, believed that Hussein's revolt would garner support in the Arab and Muslim worlds, as well as induce at least 100,000 Arab troops to abandon their posts with the Ottoman army and join the Sharif. Hussein was convinced—or at least tried to convince—the British that the number of Arab deserters would be as high as 250,000: almost all the combat troops of the Ottoman army.[7]

Hussein's rebellion was perceived both in Cairo and London as the culmination of Britain's intelligence efforts in Arabia. In fact, the sleight-of-hand of vague promises practiced by Lord Kitchener and his lieutenants in convincing Hussein to break from the Ottomans had little to do with the Sharif's decision.[8] David Fromkin, as well as other scholars, has observed that Hussein opted to take his chances in declaring independence for Arabia, because he became convinced that the Turks were planning to depose him as Sharif of Mecca.[9] Yet the illusion persisted, and not for the first time in the Middle East, Western policies toward the region were held hostage by ephemeral notions and self-delusion.

Unfortunately, in the same week that Sharif Hussein raised the standard of revolt against the Ottoman Empire, Lord Kitchener, the prime architect of an Arab Caliphate, was lost at sea. On June 5, 1916, Kitchener had sailed on the armored cruiser HMS *Hampshire* for the Russian port of Archangel. Despite warnings from naval intelligence that a German submarine had laid mines along the proposed path of the cruiser, British naval headquarters failed to take notice. At the same time, the weather got progressively worse, but Kitchener would not be deterred—he was in a hurry to get on with his visit to Russia. The *Hampshire* had set sail at 4:45 P.M.; almost three hours later the ship struck a mine. According to the sole survivor, he last saw Kitchener standing calmly on the ship's quarterdeck, and fifteen minutes later the *Hampshire* slipped under the stormy waves.[10]

Although Kitchener did not live to see the fruits of his labors with respect to the Arab uprising, he, more than anyone else, had set in motion the series of events that ultimately helped shape the future of the Middle East. In the late nineteenth century, Kitchener had dreaded the idea of the Ottoman Sultan-Caliph proclaiming, in a future war, a jihad against the British, at the behest of a rival power such as Russia or Germany. He believed that only the establishment of an Arab Caliphate could forestall such an eventuality.[11] To that end, he turned to Arabia in order to create a new Middle East strategic construct as a means of securing British interests in the region and guaranteeing the loyalty of Britain's Muslim subjects. Kitchener was convinced that he could achieve this by harnessing the power of Islam to counter the spiritual monopoly of the Ottoman Sultan over the Muslim world.

Events in the early twentieth century soon fortified Kitchener's fears. The Ottoman Empire continued to decline, as new military defeats in North Africa and the Balkans in 1912–1913 resulted in further territorial losses, along with the death of almost one and a half million Muslims and the influx of 400,000 refugees flooding over its shrinking borders.[12] Conspiracies and coups further compounded the empire's difficulties and added to the general political, economic, and cultural malaise. Opposition to the Sultan's absolute authority increased in tandem with every fresh defeat, together with the deterioration of the empire's finances.

In 1889, resistance to Sultan Abdulhamid coalesced in the creation of the Committee of Union and Progress, a disparate collection of underground forces and groups advocating a variety of agendas, but united in their opposition to the Sultan. The CUP did not, however, represent a popular movement or even attempt to mobilize a mass following, but remained an elitist assortment of competing political and military groups.[13] To some degree, the political upheaval in the Ottoman Empire, in which decaying traditional monarchical rule was replaced by secular military-political elites, would be mirrored in other parts of the Middle East later in the twentieth century. Although some of these groups achieved a limited degree of popularity, for example the Free Officers led by Gamal Nasser in Egypt—and certainly Nasser himself—they did not seize power at the head of a mass following.

Kitchener's other fear, that the Ottoman Empire would become a vassal of one of Britain's rivals, was also quickly realized, as German influence supplanted British preeminence in the Sultan's court. After the losses suffered by the Ottomans as a result of the Berlin Treaty, Abdulhamid had turned to Germany, the one Great Power with no traditional interests in the Near East, to buttress his increasingly vulnerable empire. Although Otto von Bismarck opposed German involvement in the Near East, he agreed to offer limited assistance to the Sultan. Beginning in 1880, German civilian advisors arrived with the promise that soon military experts would follow.[14] In March 1890, Kaiser Wilhelm II removed Bismarck from the position of imperial chancellor and assumed direct control over foreign policy; consequently, German interest in the Ottoman Empire expanded dramatically. The kaiser saw great financial and strategic opportunities in the Sultan's lands and intended that Germany should take over Britain's traditional role in propping up the Ottoman Empire.[15]

German companies acquired lucrative contracts to build Ottoman railways

and other major construction works, which contributed to the expansion of
Germany's heavy industry. One such project was the Baghdad Railway, which
was intended to expand the Ottoman Empire's reach to the Persian Gulf and
Egypt, as well as strengthen the Sultan's hold over Arabia and the holy cities of
Mecca and Medina. At the same time, the construction of the railway would
also carry German influence and goods to the Middle East.[16]

In October 1898, Wilhelm undertook a grand tour of the Middle East, beginning with Istanbul, followed by a stop in Jerusalem, and culminating in a
visit to Damascus. On November 8, carried away by the tumultuous reception
he had witnessed during his tour, the kaiser challenged Britain's hegemony
over the Middle East by appealing to the Muslims within and beyond the borders of the Ottoman Empire. At a banquet in his honor he proclaimed: "His
Majesty the Sultan and the 300 million Muslims scattered across the globe who
revere him as their Caliph, can rest assured that the German Emperor is, and
will at all times remain, their friend."[17]

Thanks to German propaganda experts, along with generous gifts to Ara-
bic and Turkish newspapers, the speech spread across the Muslim world as far
as British India and Central Asia—at least for those who could read.[18] For the
British, the kaiser's remarks underscored the increasing German influence in
Istanbul and held the very real prospect that, in the event of war, the Ottoman
Empire would side with the Central Powers. In that eventuality, the Sultan, as
Caliph, would proclaim a jihad, not only provoking Britain's Muslims, but also
closing their access to the annual pilgrimage to Mecca.

Kitchener surmised that the best means of counteracting the impact of a
jihad proclaimed by the Ottoman Sultan-Caliph was to co-opt Muslim religious leaders in Arabia and the Sharif of Mecca in particular. From his perspective, the Arab territories adjacent to the Suez Canal were an integral part
of Britain's security in the Eastern Mediterranean and belonged to Egypt, not
to the Ottoman Empire.[19] The key to these regions and concurrently the means to
preempt potential rivals for control of Islam was the Caliphate, and the road
to that institution lay through Mecca. Hussein's power and influence stemmed
from his inheritance and position. In the context of Islamic tradition and custom, his position was unique. George Antonius, a Christian Arab nationalist,
has described Hussein and his status in the following terms:

> He was a descendant of the Prophet and the custodian of the holy
> places; and this dual claim to reverence placed him in a category of his
> own in which he had no rival, and on an eminence from which, on an
> issue involving the safety of the holy cities, he might challenge the

authority of the Caliph himself. He was lord of Mecca, the metropolis and focus of Islam, to whose voice no devout Moslim—least of all an Arab Moslim—could remain deaf. To him and to him alone, would it fall to endorse the Sultan's clamor that the Holy Places of Mecca and Medina were in danger. So that, on an issue like the call to *jihad*, his acquiescence was an important, if not the determining, factor; and would be eagerly canvassed by the Turks for the same reason as it was feared by the Entente.[20]

Fortunately for Kitchener's plans, the Sharif of Mecca, Hussein, had a history of warm relations with the British.[21] In late 1912 or early 1913, Kitchener had met with Abdullah, Hussein's second son, when he had visited Cairo as a guest of the Khedive. Abdullah was shopping for British support in the event that the Ottomans attempted to remove his father.[22] However, Britain was not at war with the Ottoman Empire, and Kitchener could do little except sympathize.[23] Adding to Hussein's alarm, as well as that of the Bedouin chieftains, in the face of Ottoman intentions in the Hejaz was the construction of a railway connecting Damascus with Medina, with plans to eventually reach Mecca.[24]

For centuries the Bedouin had enjoyed monopoly over the camel trade to Mecca and as guardians of the annual pilgrimage route. The railway now threatened this lucrative sideline, in which the Sultan paid the Bedouin an annual fee essentially not to attack and rob the pilgrims. The railway also ended the relative isolation of the Hejaz, enabling the central government in Istanbul to supply the four divisions of Ottoman troops in western Arabia, as well as to intervene in the politics of the Hejaz. The railway would end the desert isolation that had served to buffer the Sharif of Mecca from the intrigues of the Sultan's court and which had given him a significant degree of local autonomy.

Shortly after the outbreak of the First World War, Kitchener was recalled to London to assume the post of secretary of state for war, but, despite his new responsibilities, he maintained his interest and influence over events in the Middle East. A few months later, Gilbert Layton, the official representative of the Sudan government in Cairo (and, after the outbreak of war, head of all British, as well as Egyptian, civil and military intelligence), convinced Kitchener to resume communication with Hussein and to encourage the Sharif of Mecca to break with the Ottomans. After the exchange of correspondence between Sir Henry McMahon, the British high commissioner in Egypt, and Hussein, Britain's officials in Cairo were committed to inciting a rebellion within the frontiers of the Ottoman Empire: a rebellion that would require use of irregular forces and foster the creation of a separate intelligence establishment in Cairo.

To Britain's imperial paladins responsible for Egypt, the imminent collapse of the Ottoman Empire offered the opportunity, proposed by Ronald Storrs, then oriental secretary of the British Agency (assistant to the senior British official in Egypt), to establish a "North African or Near-Eastern viceroyalty including Egypt and the Sudan and across the way from Aden to Alexandretta [that] would compare in interest and complexity, if not in actual size, with India itself."[25] Consequently, such imperial desiderata became intertwined with the prosecution of the intelligence war against the Ottomans in Arabia, whose practitioners pursued quasi-independent foreign policy objectives as part of the covert struggle against the Ottoman Empire in Arabia.

Underlying these considerations, however, was the issue of promises intimated to Hussein. The Sharif was convinced that a future Arabian kingdom, whose territories remained undefined, was to be his reward; the British were convinced that the Keeper of the Holy Places would replace the Ottoman Sultan as Caliph. However, during the exigencies of war, these arrangements afforded the British government in London considerable flexibility in making territorial promises to current and potential clients in the region, while at the same time bargaining with allies such as France over the future division of the Ottoman spoils in the Near and Middle East.

The purveyors of the contradictory promises and the conjurers of the Great Arab Revolt, such as T. E. Lawrence, not only acted as the intermediaries between London and the Arabs, but afterward established the myths and illusions that shaped the perceptions of the war in the Middle East. The men and women who filled the ranks of the intelligence community that sprouted in Cairo, both British and later American, were interconnected through social networks, as well as with their links to the clandestine world of espionage and special operations. The social and personal ties facilitated the ad hoc approach of the loose constellation of military intelligence officers, civil servants, scholars, Arabists, journalists, archaeologists, and not a few eccentrics, who eventually coalesced into the Arab Bureau. The cast of characters who emerged from the shadows in the Arabian covert war bypassed the official chain of command (both military and civil service) and guided events in the Middle East theater of operations in directions that still reverberate with consequences.

SIX

Middle East Delusions:
The Great Arab Revolt

"The whole thing was a castle in the air which would never materialize."
—*Sir Edward Grey to Austin Chamberlain*[1]

The bone-weary soldiers carelessly clustered around mud huts as the 100 degree heat beat down on them relentlessly. Hunger gnawed at the men; malaria and dysentery, as well as a host of other debilitating diseases, afflicted them. Hopelessness sapped the will of the strong and destroyed the weak. Death hunted freely in the makeshift hospitals and primitive barracks.[2] The survivors suffered constant torment from dense mists of flies that infiltrated every crevice and coated every morsel of food. Quickly all objects of nutrition vanished, and the men turned to anything remotely akin to sustenance; soon even the vile residue of unthinkable matter disappeared into empty stomachs. Men watched each other suspiciously, in case anyone held back on a moldy meal or horded a cache of bleached bones.

These unfortunates represented what was left of the British garrison of Kut, a village snuggled in a loop of the Tigris River, 350 kilometers upstream from Basra and approximately 170 kilometers from Baghdad. The soldiers of the 6th (Poona) Division of the Indian army suffered terribly from the calamities of defeat in this obscure and barren land: starvation, bad water, and disease carried by clouds of mosquitoes and flies. They had arrived in Mesopotamia (modern-day Iraq) in 1914 to preempt an attack on the oilfields of Persia, after the Ottoman Empire entered the war on the side of Germany. It was not the first time a Western army had been trapped in an Iraqi quagmire as a result of poor intelligence on the region and its inhabitants.

In the early stages of the British invasion, fighting the Turks was relatively easy, but as they advanced toward Baghdad, marshes, deserts, bad roads, and the meandering course of the Tigris, as well as constant skirmishing, had reduced the 6th Division from its original complement of 31,000 troops to only thirteen thousand officers and men by the time the division reached Kut on December 3, 1915.[3] There, in this nondescript village, they dug in, and after 146 days of siege, the commanding officer, Major General Charles Vere Ferrers Townshend, was compelled to surrender, although, before accepting the odium of defeat and capitulation, Townshend attempted to buy a reprieve for his doomed army. The British government concurred, and Aubrey Herbert and T. E. Lawrence, soon to become members of the Arab Bureau, attempted to negotiate with the Turks. They offered £2 million to free the garrison, but the Turkish commander rejected the offer.

On April 29, 1916, the 6th Indian Division passed into captivity. The attitude of the victorious Turks was varied: they were courteous with the British officers, even hospitable toward Townshend himself, merciless with the local population accused of aiding the enemy, and indifferent to the ordinary Indian troops. The Turks executed large numbers of local Arabs, even those merely suspected of collaboration with the British. The fortunate ones were hanged Turkish-style; the less fortunate were garroted.[4] The officers were separated from the men and transported in relative comfort to Baghdad. Townshend, wined and dined by Turkish generals, finally ended up in a luxurious villa on the island of Malki in the Sea of Marmara, where he sat out the war and forgot all about his men.

For the ordinary soldiers of the 6th Indian Division hell on earth began from the moment of surrender. Despite their desperate physical state, they had to march until dusk and were then fed hard biscuits tossed to the ground from the backs of camels. In addition to some meager nutrients, the biscuits contained straw and dirt, but the starving soldiers fell on them; some gnawed at the edges, while others used their boots to break them into smaller pieces. The few with patience soaked them for hours in water and noticed how dramatically the biscuits swelled in size. The next day, the men began to die, frothing at the mouth, while their bowels and stomachs disintegrated into a greenish slime. Almost all who ate the biscuits dehydrated and died moaning in agony.[5] This was the first stage of the Dante's Inferno that welcomed the soldiers of the 6th Indian Division. After endless marches, constant abuse, whippings, and almost no provisions, the survivors ended their days working on railway gangs in Anatolia. Only a few survived the ordeal, and handfuls of men returned home after the war, broken in body and spirit.[6]

This was the second humiliation heaped upon the British by the Ottomans. The defeat at Gallipoli had clearly demonstrated that the Ottomans still had resilience, and it was evident from the disaster at Kut that the empire's strength was formidable.[7] However, as long as the Western Front consumed armies on an industrial scale, the British could ill afford to divert significant forces to the Middle East. The alternative was to subvert the Ottoman Empire from within, as advocated by Kitchener's associates in Cairo and undertaken by the newly created Arab Bureau. The key to this strategy was the Arab provinces of the Ottoman Empire and the conviction that, with the appropriate leader who possessed the requisite secular and religious credentials, Arab nationalism would undermine Turkish control over the Middle East. Effectively, the defeats at Gallipoli and Kut added further momentum to the secret negotiations with Sharif Hussein that led to the rebellion in the Hejaz in the summer of 1916.

For the first time in the modern period, the intelligence service of a state undertook to wage clandestine and irregular warfare as an adjunct to military operations. However, a fundamental flaw with the strategy of the British intelligence establishment in Cairo was that it failed to understand the limited appeal of Arab nationalism. The Great Arab Revolt did achieve some relatively minor objectives: a small army of mostly paid Bedouin conducted successful raids against the Turkish railway lines in Arabia and other acts of sabotage. Sharif Hussein evaded the Sultan's declaration of jihad, but the declaration did not have the resonance in the Muslim world that the British and Germans had wrongly assumed it would have.[8] There was no mass uprising against the Ottoman Empire, and Britain's Muslim subjects remained relatively quiet.[9]

Despite the failure of the Sultan's call to jihad, most Arabs remained loyal to the Ottoman Empire, while raids against the Turkish railway in the Hejaz, if anything, soured the attitude of Muslims toward Hussein's rebellion, since the disruptions severely limited the annual pilgrimage to Mecca. Furthermore, to add insult to injury, the Hejaz railway was constructed with funds raised from Muslims throughout the world; every mile of rail blown up represented the loss of thousands of lira in contributions made up by both rich and poor Muslims.[10]

On the other hand, the British alliance with Sharif Hussein did guarantee access to Mecca for Britain's Muslims, and the refusal of Hussein to sanction the Sultan's call to jihad may have contributed to the collapse of an Islamic holy war against the British and the Entente. However, this was less a success for British intelligence than astute political manipulation on the part of the British, as well as Hussein.

T. E. Lawrence, whose exploits captured the popular imagination in Britain and America, compounded the problem by contributing to the illusion of the Great Arab Revolt. Part of it stemmed from his own account of the insurgency in Arabia, but that came later. The initial publicity that cemented the legend was spun by Lowell Thomas, an obscure American professor, who cast Lawrence as a romantic desert warrior, determined to give the Arabs a state.[11] However, history has been less kind to Lawrence, as historians over the decades have stripped each layer of the legend, exposing a complex yet politically astute charlatan. Perhaps H. V. F. Winstone offers the most fitting summary of Lawrence and the desert war in Arabia:

> . . . the story of "Lawrence of Arabia"; a story of stupefying naïveté that has fascinated generations of writers, historians, scholars, poets, and ordinary men and women. It is a myth to which men of academic distinction have devoted their working lives, scrambling endlessly through letters and diaries in search of the "truth" of this and that venture, writing volume after volume of appraisal and re-appraisal, countering every attempt to put the matter into some kind of perspective with charges of calumny, deliberate distortion, bullying, muckraking, and general vilification. . . . Even the Germans, whose concern for documentary evidence is usually such as to reduce the most adventurous tale to an indigestible recital of factual detail, have fallen victim to the unaccountable charisma that attaches to this diminutive, talkative soldier who looked like a girl in his pristine Arab dress and of whom few Arabs had ever heard until the publishing industry and the film-makers penetrated even their awareness, so that suddenly old men of the towns and villages of Syria and the Hejaz remembered.[12]

Although Lawrence was an extreme example, many of the men and one woman (Gertrude Bell) who formed the close-knit British intelligence community in the Middle East rarely had the opportunity to meet ordinary Arabs. For the archaeologists, geographers, historians, and other scholars, Arabia was a matter of topography, imperial politics, and academic curiosity. T. E. Lawrence, as was the case with most of his colleagues, was intimately familiar with the deserts and ruins of a bygone age but remarkably out of touch with the inhabitants. To the British, ordinary Arabs represented household help, camel drivers, waiters, farmers, shoeshine boys, and beggars, as well as the wandering Bedouin, but this constituency had no voice: political aspirations only reflected the opinions and convictions of their leaders.

In this respect, British intelligence analysis of the political sentiments of the mass of Muslims in the Middle East (and elsewhere) was filtered through Arabs in positions of authority. Compounding these difficulties was the fragmentation of Britain's intelligence efforts. In the Middle East, at least southwest of Mesopotamia, British individuals who gravitated to clandestine work coalesced in the Arab Bureau. Although not a centralized agency as originally proposed by Sir Mark Sykes, Kitchener's Middle East expert, the new organization was attached to the Cairo Intelligence Department.[13] Sykes had planned that the new agency would be a means of simplifying the competing layers of Britain's policymakers in London and throughout the empire.[14]

The Arab Bureau joined the other policy stakeholders in the Foreign Office, the War Office, the India Office, the government of India, the Colonial Office, the Admiralty, and the War Cabinet in attempting to guide British policy on the Middle East. At the same time, the Arab Bureau had to conduct a guerrilla war with Hussein's ragtag army of Bedouin and Arab deserters from the Turkish army, as well as coordinate intelligence operations in the Middle East. Hussein followed the British lead strictly out of self-interest, while relying on promises for his own state intimated through his exchange in the McMahon correspondence. Yet, at the beginning of February 1916, before the outbreak of the Great Arab Revolt and the establishment of the Arab Bureau, the Sykes-Picot Agreement divided the Ottoman provinces of the Middle East, including Arabia, among the Entente allies.[15] However, this arrangement was no less self-serving than the Sharif's deception that he represented anything more than himself—let alone the Arabs.

Whitehall recast Hussein's ambition for an Arab empire as a confederation of Arab states, each headed by an independent ruler, with the most viable and productive parts reserved for direct British and French administration. The officers of the Arab Bureau continued to maintain the illusion of a future Arab state with Hussein as head, while the wily Sharif pretended that he led a pan-Arab movement into rebellion against the Ottoman Empire. The Arab Bureau would have preferred indirect British and French rule through an obliging Arab prince, with Hussein as their primary candidate. Even Lawrence was skeptical about the viability of a truly independent Arab country, although he did not quite lose the duality of purpose that guided his sentiments toward the Arabs and a future Arabia. In a long report on Prince Feisal's, the son of Sharif, operations on October 30, 1916, which he published in the *Arab Bulletin*, Lawrence claimed:

> The Arab leaders have quite a number of intelligent levelheaded men among them, who if they do not do things as we would do them, are successful in their generation. Of course they lack experience—except of Turkish officialdom, which is a blind leader—and theory; for the study of practical economics has not been encouraged. However, I no longer question their capacity to form a government in the Hejaz, which is better, so far as the interests of their subjects are concerned, than the Turkish system which they have replaced.[16]

However, in a handwritten note attached to the report, he reached the opposite conclusion:

> They [the Arab leaders] are weak in material resources and always will be, for their world is agricultural and pastoral and can never be very rich or very strong. If it were otherwise we would have to weigh more deeply the advisability of creating in the Middle East a new power with such exuberant national sentiment. As it is, their military weakness which for the moment incommodes us should henceforward ensure us advantages immeasurably greater than the money, arms and ammunition we are now called upon to spare.[17]

Overall, the agreement was condemned as a postwar division of spoils that would result from the partition of the Ottoman Empire and a fraud with respect to the promises made to the Arabs. George Antonius, a well-known Arab nationalist (but a Christian) declares: "The Sykes-Picot Agreement is a shocking document. It is not only the product of greed at its worst, that is to say, of greed allied to suspicion and so leading to stupidity: it also stands out as a startling piece of double-dealing."[18] Other scholars have argued that the McMahon letters and accompanying promises to Hussein were not double-dealing but essentially proposed to create an Arab state, albeit one under British tutelage, to be ruled by the Sharif.[19] Certainly the members of the Arab Bureau, although pro-Arab, regretted the Sykes-Picot Agreement, but not its objective of a future Arab state attached as a client to the British Empire.[20]

In a recent study of the Arab Bureau, Bruce Westrate's view is that the policy of the Arab Bureau's Arab enthusiasts "was a more modern, and somehow more insidious, stratagem incorporating mechanisms of artifice and manipulation that would bestow the necessary flexibility to confront the rising tide of Arab nationalism and extend Britain's stay both in India and Egypt."[21] Toward this end, the Arab Bureau was to aid in the construction of an Arab nationalism that would be divided against itself and create a confederation of mutually hostile political and religious entities. Under this policy of divide-and-rule, control of Arabia and the accompanying new protectorates and subsequent territorial mandates in the Middle East, as well as leadership of the Muslim world, would pass to creatures of the British, including a new Caliph. Undoubtedly, the Sharif of Mecca and Keeper of the Holy Places fit the requirements of an able puppet. However, the failure of Hussein to ignite a bona fide Arab uprising or instigate mass desertions of Arabs serving in the Ottoman armies ultimately exposed the myth of a pan-Arab movement originating from Mecca.

Equally problematic is whether the Arab Bureau grossly overestimated the nationalist sentiments of the Arabs and indulged in the temptation of believing reports of secret societies in Syria or entertained the notion of a general rebellion against the Ottomans, which suited the interests of British officials in Cairo. The bureau's assessment of the potential of Arab nationalism and the prospects for engineering a revolt was based on reports from a young Arab officer in the Ottoman army. Lieutenant Muhammad Sharif al-Faruqi was a member of a secret society, al-Ahd, based in Damascus that included Arab officers in the Ottoman army, as well as Arab businessmen and political figures in Syria.[22] In the fall of 1915, Faruqi was posted to Gallipoli, where he crossed the lines and deserted to the British. He claimed to possess important information for British intelligence in Cairo and was transferred to Egypt.

Unfortunately Faruqi spoke little English; although several officers in Cairo's intelligence department were fluent in Arabic, some of what he said may have been lost in translation. However, he was able to convince particularly those who wished to be convinced that al-Ahd and al-Fatat (another secret society) were united in backing Hussein, and that the British should accept immediately the Sharif's demands for the creation of an independent Arab state.[23] In return, the societies would lead a rebellion against the Ottomans. He also emphasized that the Turks were offering the Arabs similar inducements to remain loyal to the Ottoman Empire, and that the societies were hard-pressed and had to respond to the Turkish offer. Faruqi told his interrogators that al-Ahd had the allegiance of 90 percent of the Arab officers in the Ottoman army, and that the society collected over 100,000 Turkish lira in membership dues. He also added that, after the union of the two societies, for which he claimed credit, they included a large number of civilian participants who had joined al-Ahd.[24]

Despite the fact that Faruqi was a junior officer and a deserter making bold claims about the intentions of secret Arab societies, the British accepted his information without reservation. Gilbert Clayton, the director of British military and political intelligence in Cairo, was convinced that al-Ahd and al-Fatat were legitimate, with extensive networks throughout the Arab provinces of the Ottoman Empire, and that because of their influence the Turks and Germans would not dare to destroy them.[25] As a result of Faruqi's information, the discussions with Hussein were concluded with McMahon, and the Sharif was assured of British support for an independent Arabia.[26]

Remarkably, just about everything Faruqi claimed to represent and the information he imparted was sheer fabrication. The members of al-Ahd represented not 90 percent, but less than 0.5 percent of the Arab officers in the

Ottoman army. According to Eliezer Tauber, "the entire society numbered at the outbreak of the war only about 50 activists, of whom 40 were officers; *al-Fatat* too numbered only about 40 activists at the beginning of the war."[27] At first, the goal of these societies, as well as those of similar organizations that had sprouted in Syria, Lebanon, and Mesopotamia, was to secure greater autonomy, while promoting the political and cultural standing of Arabs within the Ottoman Empire, rather than to achieve independence or sovereignty.

Equally significant was that part of the stated aims of the societies was their identification with Islam.[28] For some, Arab nationalism was local and specific to a particular region such as Syria or Iraq; for others, pan-Arabism was inexplicably linked to the Islamic religion and heritage. Even those who aspired to an Arab empire did so within an Islamic context. Faruqi omitted such references, while maintaining the fabrication of a pan-Arab movement committed to the Sharif. The appeal of a secular Arab nationalism was confined to Arab Christians, but they represented only a small minority.[29] However, the young Arab officer continued to impose his delusions and went so far as to write to Hussein, pretending to have influence with the British, while simultaneously telling them he represented Hussein.

Was Faruqi responsible for convincing the British to support Hussein, thus triggering the Arab Revolt? If so, it would have been a major failure of British intelligence. It is unlikely that those responsible for British intelligence in the Middle East accepted Faruqi's claims at their face value; it is much more likely that they used him to pursue an agenda driven by Cairo policy, first formulated by Kitchener, and then continued by Storrs, Clayton, and Sykes, the latter having become a recent convert to Arab independence. These men subscribed to the notion that Britain would not only act as a midwife to a new Arab state, but would use that state to expand the British Empire to encompass the Arab provinces of the Ottoman Empire.

Effectively, the intelligence service in Egypt, along with their patrons in London, implemented a separate foreign policy with respect to the Arab Middle East. On a tactical level, sowing sedition among Arab troops became necessary, as they had proven their worth fighting the British, as well as the other Entente forces, at Gallipoli. The Gallipoli front included most of the Arab divisions in the Ottoman army. Defeat at Gallipoli removed any hesitation in Whitehall with respect to using subversion and instigating rebellion to tie down Turkish units in Arab provinces of the Ottoman Empire. On the other hand, the fact that the Arabs fought well should have been an indication that Hussein's claim of mass desertions among Arab soldiers and officers was a hollow one.

In early 1916, the Arab Bureau became the hub of those ambitions and the driving force behind Hussein's Arab Revolt. The fact that the Sharif only represented himself and led an army of Bedouin, whose loyalty was bought with British gold, did not hinder the plans of the Arab Bureau for an Arabia under British tutelage. It suited their interests for Hussein not to lead a substantial Arab force or to head a pan-Arab mass-based movement. Under these conditions, it was far easier to control the Sharif's ambitions and divide the loyalties of the other Arab leaders in Arabia. However, the difficulty of a compartmentalized foreign policy was that it exposed regional interests to the dynamics of grand strategy for the postwar period, which was guided from London.

The Sykes-Picot Agreement complicated the relationship between Hussein and the British. Although the agreement was secret, T. E. Lawrence informed Feisal, Hussein's son, about it.[30] It mattered little that Lawrence betrayed the secret Anglo-French arrangement, because after the Russian Revolution in October 1917, the Bolsheviks published all secret treaties between Russia and the Entente, including the Sykes-Picot Agreement, in November 1917.[31] Regardless of the subsequent debate on what the agreement meant to achieve and to what degree the British betrayed or did not betray the Arab Revolt, the reaction in the Arab and Muslim world was negative and Sykes-Picot continues to be regarded as a fraud.[32] This was the second disillusionment: on November 2, 1917, the British government had issued the Balfour Declaration, committing Britain to the creation of a Jewish homeland in Palestine. Significantly, the McMahon–Hussein correspondence made no specific reference to Palestine, leaving advocates for both sides—then and later—to interpret the territorial stipulations in such a way as to support their respective points of view.

News of the Balfour Declaration caused considerable unrest and protest among the Arabs and throughout the Muslim world.[33] Together with the Sykes-Picot Agreement, it provided the building blocks for future Muslim accusations of British perfidy and betrayal by the West. Concurrently, the policy of the Arab Bureau in fostering the notion of an Arab state, regardless of its configuration and the realpolitik exercised by the political leadership in London, eventually engendered a duality in the Middle East that oscillated between the pursuit of Arab nationalism and the quest for the reestablishment of a state organized along Muslim principles and practices.

Both Arab nationalism and the rise of militant Islam gained considerable momentum after the First World War, but a contributing factor was the Arab reaction to the British and French division of the Ottoman Middle East, compounded by the consequences of the Balfour Declaration.[34] Certainly the British intelligence community in the region cultivated both nationalist and Muslim strains. The Arab Bureau lobbied for Hussein and Arab nationalism, which they assumed was secular, while promoting the Sharif as an Arab Caliph. Yet, with the exception of Christian Arabs and a small number of intellectuals, Arab nationalism was rooted in Islam. In attempting to play off one against the other, the British unknowingly succeeded in fortifying the Islamic identity of most Arabs. Secular Arab nationalism, except for a few decades after the Second World War, dissipated in a sea of corruption, poverty, and defeat. Ultimately, fanning the flames of Arab nationalism and Islam left a difficult legacy for the Middle East and complicated the role of Anglo-American intelligence in the region.

SEVEN

Spies, Adventurers, and Religious Warriors

"Generations of Pashas and Beys from Surrey and Kent had
devoted their lives to the Arab cause,
and had become emotionally identified with it."
—*Arthur Koestler*[1]

Captain William Shakespear was drawn to the desert and relished the loneliness that accompanied travelers daring to challenge its treacherous wilderness. He often slept and dined apart from his guides and servants, preferring solitude to campfire chitchat. He was born in the Punjab of a well-known British-Indian military family. Before the outbreak of war, Shakespear was serving as an Indian army officer and had originally been posted as political agent for the government of India with the Emir of Kuwait. Like Lawrence he was fluent in Arabic, as well as an avid traveler who made several long expeditions into the Arabian Desert along Kuwait's western frontier. In 1909, he met Abdul Aziz ibn Saud, when the latter came to visit the Emir of Kuwait, and formed a positive impression of the Emir of Nejd.[2]

One year later Shakespear had a formal meeting with Ibn Saud, who informed the Indian officer of his wish to establish an alliance with the British against the Turks. According to Shakespear's reports, Ibn Saud was the natural leader of an Arab uprising against the Ottomans, but Whitehall was opposed to the idea and considered it interference by the government of India.[3] In the spring of 1914, Shakespear paid a visit to Ibn Saud in Riyadh, where the Arab chieftain reaffirmed his desire for an alliance with Britain. Shakespear and the Wahhabi Emir became friends.

He would not be the last Englishman to fall under the desert chief's spell: a little later Harry St. John Philby, a noted geographer, senior British civil servant, and intelligence officer, would establish a close relationship with Ibn Saud. Meanwhile, after a series of meetings with him, Shakespear continued on foot and camelback for a journey of 1,800 miles eastward across the great Arabian Desert to the Hejaz and eventually reported to Lord Kitchener in Cairo.

Once again Shakespear tried to promote Ibn Saud as the future leader of the Arabs, but Kitchener and his associates remained committed to Hussein.[4]

When the Ottoman Empire opted to cast its future with the Germans, Whitehall became very interested in Arab chieftains and how to get them to join Britain or remain neutral. Shakespear was appointed political officer on special duty and was directed to secure Ibn Saud's allegiance to Britain; however, in the complex world of imperial British administration he would be acting in the interest of the government of India. He was instructed to stay with Ibn Saud and if necessary take up residence in Riyadh, the Emir's capital.[5] Ibn Saud had little love for the Turks, since the Ottoman Empire had traditionally supported his archenemy and rival for control of central Arabia, Ibn Rashid.

Before joining Ibn Saud in Arabia, Shakespear had behaved like a man haunted by a premonition. After so many dangerous adventures and missions, he was suddenly aware of his mortality. On December 11, 1914, he asked one of his colleagues to write to his mother in the event of his death; a few days later he wrote his last will and testament. Shakespear left Kuwait on December 12 and nineteen days later (December 31) joined Ibn Saud at his camp near Majmaa on the plain of Arma.[6] Ibn Saud was moving northward to make war on his pro-Turkish enemy, Ibn Rashid, Emir of Hail. Over campfires and along the trek, Shakespear and Ibn Saud managed to draft the outline of a treaty with Britain to the satisfaction of both, which Shakespear forwarded to Sir Percy Cox, the chief political agent in the Persian Gulf, on behalf of the government of India in Mesopotamia.[7]

On January 22, 1915, they camped near Zilfi, the largest town in the Sudair region, where Ibn Saud tried to convince Shakespear to leave, as it was not necessary for the British officer to take part in the upcoming battle. Shakespear refused. In the morning, Shakespear had a quick meal and decided to watch the battle from the dunes next to the sole field artillery gun, manned by a young Arab, supporting Ibn Saud's army. For a few moments, the two armies paused, and then with the cry of "Allahu Akbar" (God Is Great) they charged across the flat empty plain near the oasis of Jarab. Ibn Saud's forces, despite being outnumbered, fought well, and some of Ibn Rashid's units began to lose their cohesion.[8]

Shakespear, no longer a bystander, was directing the field gun, which was having a devastating affect on Ibn Rashid's soldiers, when it jammed. Ibn Saud's infantry lost heart and fell back, and—to make matters worse—the Ajman tribe, which made up a significant part of the cavalry, deserted to Ibn Rashid. Shakespear could easily see that Ibn Saud's army was falling victim to panic, so he tried to repair the gun, but by this time he was alone on the dune. Ibn Rashid's cavalry advanced to his position, sweeping over the British officer and the use-less gun. Several bullets struck Shakespear in the face and head, but he was still alive when one of Ibn Rashid's attendants slashed at the fallen officer with his sword and finished him off.[9]

Had Shakespear lived, he would have overshadowed the reputation of T. E. Lawrence, at least with respect to audacity and daring. He had ventured into the deserts of Arabia and traveled widely in Anatolia and Persia. He had earned the trust and respect of Ibn Saud and his followers; however, both his exploits and the policies of the government of India are examples of the fragmentation of Britain's intelligence efforts in the region. Shakespear's actions demonstrated just how the role of the secret services complicated postwar policies. He was working for the India Office and the government of India, while Lawrence and the Arab Bureau represented the interests of British officials in Cairo and like-minded officials in London, as well as their own policies.

Meanwhile, the recently established Secret Intelligence Service (SIS as well as MI6) was responsible for espionage in the rest of the world, but not in the Middle East.[10] One consideration was that jurisdiction for intelligence operations in the Middle East was divided in 1906 among the India Office, the War Office, and the Directorate of Military Intelligence in London, with the former assuming responsibility for all regions in southern Arabia from Aqaba to Basra (excluding Asir, Hejaz, and Yemen), while the latter took charge of the rest of Arabia, including the Ottoman provinces of Syria and Mesopotamia.[11] In 1916, the Arab Bureau's zone of operations in the Middle East was transferred to those areas of Arabia that fell under the control of military intelligence in Cairo.

After the death of Captain Shakespear, London and Cairo almost forgot about Ibn Saud and central Arabia, until the launching of the Great Arab Revolt made both the region and Ibn Saud interesting to British intelligence. At the very least it was necessary to secure Ibn Saud's benevolent neutrality toward Hussein—despite the fact that the Emir of Najd despised the Sharif of Mecca—and if possible to convince the Wahhabi leader to wage war against the pro-Turkish Ibn Rashid of Hail. In the years following Shakespear's demise, Ibn Saud had extended his power over the tribes of central Arabia and was in a strong position to cause considerable grief to the army of Hussein.

The man chosen for the mission was Harry St. John Philby.[12] In 1915, Philby joined Sir Percy Cox, the political officer in charge of the territory occupied by the British army in Mesopotamia.[13] Cox chose Philby because he was a gifted linguist and fluent in Urdu, Punjabi, Baluchi, Farsi, and a variety of Arabic dialects. Cox charged Philby with the tasks of establishing a political agency in Riyadh and wooing Ibn Saud to wage war against the pro-Turkish

Arab tribes, without attacking Hussein's forces in the Hejaz. In October 1917, Philby set out for central Arabia, accompanied by two other British officers, and by the end of November had reached Ibn Saud's capital. Philby undertook the journey by crossing central Arabia from east to west, which had only been accomplished once by an Englishman, and, in recognition of this feat, the Royal Geographical Society awarded him the Founder's Medal.[14]

After meeting and getting to know Ibn Saud, Philby became convinced that both British and Saudi interests would be best served by uniting the Arabian Peninsula under one government from the Red Sea to the Persian Gulf. Naturally this meant that the Saudis would assume the role of the Hashemites as Islamic Keepers of the Holy Places, while protecting shipping lanes on the Suez–Aden–Bombay route of the British Empire. Even though Ibn Saud was a legitimate Arab leader who was bringing Arabia under his control by war, fear, and faith, the British authorities in London and Cairo remained committed to Hussein. The Emir of Nejd was accomplishing what the Arab Bureau had planned for the Sharif of Mecca, while Hussein spent considerable effort on acquiring titles without the power to sustain his authority.

In 1917, Hussein had proclaimed himself King of the Arabs, but had had to modify the title to King of the Hejaz, further rankling Ibn Saud, who could not wait until he came to terms with the Sharif. In May 1919, Ibn Saud's fierce Wahhabi warriors, along with the forces of Khalid ibn Mansur ibn Luway, launched a lightning night raid on the British-trained army of Hussein's son Abdullah camped in the oasis of Kurma. Hussein's troops were taken by surprise and close to five thousand were slaughtered. Abdullah managed to escape only by running away in his nightshirt. After this disaster, which destroyed the Sharif's army, both sides agreed to a truce. Although Philby was in England on leave, he used Ibn Saud's victory to drive home the point with the British government that Ibn Saud was the only outstanding leader in Arabia.

Remarkably, the response from Whitehall was to proclaim Feisal king of Syria (and, after he was toppled by the French, the British gave him the newly constructed state of Iraq). They also awarded Transjordan (present-day Jordan) to Abdullah. In 1924, after Mustapha Kemal had abolished the Ottoman Empire and the Caliphate, the Sharif of Mecca declared himself Caliph—to the consternation of most Arabs and Muslims. Then, adding insult to injury, Hussein decided to ban all Wahhabi Muslims from taking part in the pilgrimage to Mecca.

This ill-conceived gesture only provoked Ibn Saud to launch another attack against the Hejaz, and within a short span of time he captured the holy cities of Mecca and Medina, and finally Jeddah. Ibn Saud assumed control of the holy places, as well as responsibility for the Hajj, giving him a powerful influence over Sunni Muslims. These events had little impact on Whitehall. T. E. Lawrence pronounced Ibn Saud's accomplishments in unifying Arabia as "a figment, built on sand."[15] Yet the British did not entirely abandon Ibn Saud: the Emir continued to receive a monthly stipend and military aid.

In 1929, after failing to prevent some Wahhabi tribesmen from carrying out raids and massacres, Ibn Saud attacked them. With the support of four British warplanes, and two hundred radio-equipped armored cars and troop carriers, he annihilated the entire force of Wahhabi cavalry, which was armed with old rifles, lances, and scimitars. Regardless of his overwhelming fire-power, it took Ibn Saud ten months to put down the rebels. In so doing, he effectively brought to an end the chronic tribal warfare that had plagued the region for millennia, establishing the Islamic-based nation-state of Saudi Arabia. However, the new Arabian state had few resources and even fewer links with the outside world, and it was vulnerable to British power.[16]

Philby missed out on most of these events in Arabia while on leave in England, and, after his return, the British closed down the mission in Riyadh. Shortly after, the war came to an end, but the peace did not grant the Arabs a single state. Even those new states that did not fall under the mandate system acquired only limited independence.[17] Philby was outraged and made his views known to anyone who would listen. After languishing without a posting, he was placed as advisor to the Iraqi minister of the interior in October 1920. Philby's appointment came in the aftermath of a major uprising in Mesopotamia, which was becoming known as Iraq.[18]

In this uprising, tribesmen, Shiite clergy, notables, and young intellectuals rose in rebellion, partly in response to British rule and partly from local grievances, such as high prices and taxes. The Turks, as well as the Bolsheviks, also had a hand in the revolt and had sent agents to encourage opposition to the British. It is not certain if the uprising was a national revolt or simply a coalition of disparate groups whose only common agenda was opposition to the British. Eliezer Tauber concludes, "to the local people the meaning of the national struggle was: a struggle for liberation from foreign rule, the achievement of independence, and the establishment of a local government."[19] In April 1920, at the Conference of San Remo, the League of Nations agreed to the British mandate over Iraq. This agreement left little doubt that the British would not leave Iraq and contributed to the causes of the uprising. Many intellectuals in Baghdad and other major cities in Iraq denounced the decision of the allies and called for the inhabitants of Iraq to fight against foreign rule.[20]

It was symptomatic of British attitudes toward the Middle East—and Arabs in particular—to ignore the interests of the local inhabitants. Despite promises of independence and U.S. President Woodrow Wilson's proclamation of self-determination, the British continued to rule most of the Middle East, convinced that they knew what was best for the Arabs. Captain Arnold Wilson and Gertrude Bell administered Iraq and, regardless of their differences, both believed they understood the sentiments and wishes of the locals. Wilson advocated direct rule, while Bell preferred a protectorate.[21]

However, both agreed that self-determination was not an option. Bell wrote: "the people of Mesopotamia, having witnessed the successful termination of the war, had taken it for granted that the country would remain under British control and were as a whole content to accept the decision of arms."[22] She went on to say that the notion of self-determination proposed at the Paris Peace Conference "opened up other possibilities which were regarded almost universally with anxiety, but gave opportunity for political intrigue to the less stable and more fanatical elements."[23] The British political leaders at Versailles were less concerned about what and how the new country was constituted, however, than with the problem of petroleum, which seemed to be abundant in Mesopotamia.[24]

As a result the British government decided to recast Mesopotamia as Iraq by lumping together the Ottoman provinces of Mosul, Basra, and Baghdad, regardless of the religious differences of the people inhabiting the region. The conflicting religious and national identities of the new citizens of Iraq remained with the country for the rest of the twentieth century and spilled into the twenty-first. At present, the West—particularly the United States—has yet to come to terms with the dynamics of Iraqi society and continues to apply the Western concept of nationalism to it. It does so despite the unique mix of Arabs, Kurds, and a small minority of Assyrians that underlies the delicate and often volatile relationships of the Shiite majority with the smaller Sunni and Christian minorities.

Bell wrote a lengthy report on the situation in Mesopotamia—her magnum opus in fact—which contributed to how the borders of the new country were finally delineated and which led to Sunni domination over the country, until the American intervention in 2003.[25] She held the conviction that Iraq had to be led by the Sunni minority, because the majority Shiites were "unworldly and apolitical," while the Sunnis were "educated, powerful, financially astute."[26] Like Shakespear and Wilson, Bell represented that unique combination of spy, explorer, bureaucrat, and adventurer which left its lasting imprint on the Middle East in one form or another. The Iraqi rebellion, however, terminated Wilson's tenure as chief civil administrator and, although he was sent home and given a knighthood, he could not accept the outcome and left the

British civil service.[27] Bell, on the other hand, remained and continued to play a critical role in the development of the new state. Percy Cox kept her employed in Iraq, since he shared her views about the final disposition of the new country and its relationship with Britain.

Philby also owed his new job in Iraq to Percy Cox, who had employed him in Mesopotamia during the early years of the First World War. When Cox arrived in early October 1921 and was given responsibility for Iraq, he moved quickly to establish a temporary all-Iraqi government, but one buttressed by British advisors. Although he supported the concept of Iraqi self-rule, Cox equally believed that the Arabs could govern themselves only up to a point, and beyond that he would remain the final and supreme authority.[28] The role of the British advisors was to guide the Iraqi ministers to make the correct decisions and, under these terms of reference, the first government of Iraq was established on October 25, 1920.

Philby accepted this arrangement, but his patience with the British system came to an end when Winston Churchill as colonial secretary, T. E. Lawrence, and Gertrude Bell engineered the election of Feisal as king of Iraq. Philby made his views known to anyone willing to listen, and in 1921 he was forced to leave after Feisal assumed the crown.[29] As compensation, he was sent to Transjordan as chief British representative.[30] After three years there, he had had enough, and so had the British high commissioner in Jerusalem, but Philby succeeded in tendering his resignation before he was relieved of his duties.[31] Whether this was a sudden act born of frustration or had been building up over the years, Philby decided to abandon the Indian civil service and transfer his allegiance to Ibn Saud. Although the change in loyalties did not come about that easily and quickly, the culmination of disappointments may explain Philby's motives for his ultimate metamorphosis from British civil servant and intelligence officer into advisor to King Abdul Aziz ibn Saud and convert to Islam.[32] Although most historians agree that Philby's conversion to Islam was cynical and self-serving, nonetheless his determination to curry favor with the Arab leader was such that he underwent a painful circumcision to meet all the requirements of being a Muslim.[33]

Philby was a courageous combination of explorer, adventurer, social misfit, and spy—and also an avid bird watcher.[34] Unlike T. E. Lawrence, Philby, regardless of his own selfish motives, was genuinely captivated by the austere Ibn Saud and saw him as a "great and outstanding figure."[35] Eventually he not only became the monarch's chief advocate, but also in the process betrayed his own country. In the years to come, his more famous son, Harold Adrian Russell "Kim" Philby, also deceived friends and colleagues, but Kim's "religion" was Marxism and the Soviet Union. In his memoirs, Kim Philby addresses the theories of certain writers:

> who have attributed the unusual course of my life to the influence of my father. It is possible that his eccentricities enabled me, in early youth, to resist some of the more outrageous prejudices of the English public-school system of forty years ago. But very little research would show that, [at] all decisive turning points in my life, he was thousands of miles out of reach. If he had lived a little longer to learn the truth, he would have been thunderstruck, but by no means disapproving.[36]

Few people who knew Kim Philby can ever be convinced of his comments regarding his life. Yuri Modin, the KGB officer responsible for the so-called Cambridge spies (the British moles recruited by Soviet intelligence in the 1930s), wrote in the endorsement section of Kim Philby's book:

> [Philby] never revealed his true self. Neither the British, nor the women he lived with, nor ourselves ever managed to pierce the armour of mystery that clad him. His great achievement in espionage was his life's work, and it fully occupied him until the day he died. But in the end I suspect that Philby made a mockery of everyone, including ourselves.[37]

Perhaps John le Carré's comments ring closer to the common traits shared by father and son:

> Philby has no home, no women, no faith. Behind the inbred upper-class arrogance, the taste for adventure, lies the self-hate of a vain misfit for whom nothing will ever be worthy of his loyalty. In the last instance, Philby is driven by the incurable drug of deceit itself.[38]

When the Saudi court interpreter, who knew the older Philby, read Kim's memoirs, he remarked that Kim was "a true replica of his father."[39] Like his son, the senior Philby remained a complex and unscrupulous individual throughout most of his life, never hesitating to use anyone to further his own ends. During the period between leaving the civil service and working for Ibn Saud, St. John Philby tried his hand at making money, but with little success. He set up a trading company in Riyadh, but he achieved less success with commerce than with exploring the deserts of Arabia. He became involved with a wealthy businessman, Remy Fisher, in order to secure lucrative contracts for himself. When Fisher showed an interest in Philby's wife, Dora, rather than being offended, Philby urged Dora to encourage Fisher's advances. The reason was to placate Fisher, so the Philby family could vacation on his estate in France.[40]

In May 1932, Francis B. Loomis, representing Standard Oil of California (SOCAL),[41] approached Philby through the American consul-general in London with a proposal for talks aimed at securing rights for oil concessions. Philby had been encouraging Ibn Saud to consider the possibility that under the soil of Arabia ran rivers of oil that could augment the Saudi kingdom's income. The prospect of petroleum deposits offered a new and desperately needed source of revenue for the Arabian monarch. The finances of the Kingdom were in dire straits: expenditure by Ibn Saud and his court exceeded revenue, and by the early 1930s they were defaulting on payments to their creditors.

On May 31, 1935, SOCAL discovered oil in Bahrain, which convinced the company that it was worthwhile to explore for petroleum deposits in Arabia. Representatives from SOCAL resumed contact with Philby and sought his help in convincing Ibn Saud to grant them rights to explore, as well as concessions in the event oil was discovered. Philby luxuriated in his new role as advisor to the king and simultaneously as middleman for SOCAL. Although he was hired as a paid consultant by SOCAL, he also, behind the back of the American company, approached the Iraq Petroleum Company (whose major shareholder was the Anglo-Persian Oil Company), in an effort to drive the price higher and secure further commissions for himself.

After much hard bargaining, the Saudis agreed, and SOCAL secured its first oil contract with Arabia. Philby acquired a lucrative monthly consulting fee of £1,000, as well as signing bonuses and other financial advantages.[42] The agreement was signed on May 29, 1933, and eventually SOCAL and its successors obtained exclusive access to one of the world's largest petroleum deposits.[43] The representatives from the Iraq Petroleum Company had given up much earlier and did not pursue further negotiations. Their interests were not so much in acquiring new sources of oil but essentially in preempting any future competitors.[44] This proved to be a strategic blunder, which deprived the British of another source of petroleum and billions of dollars in profits, as well as leaving them dependent on Persian oil wells, with all the consequences this held for Great Britain in the future.

One critical factor in how the Americans won the Saudi oil concessions was Philby's role on their behalf; another was British shortsightedness in failing to appreciate the potential of Saudi oil: perhaps Britain's greatest intelligence failure of all time. Philby's intentions were a combination of greed, ego, and—to some degree—revenge against Britain's Middle East policies. However, the renegade British spy and civil servant was also strapped for cash to pay his son's fees at Cambridge University, so that Kim Philby could complete his education. In effect, St. John Philby and his son underwrote the decline of British intelligence until the early 1960s and helped seal a Faustian bargain between America and Saudi Arabia.

SOCAL and its successors discovered vast reserves of petroleum, which generated considerable wealth for American oil companies and enriched the Saudi royal family beyond their wildest dreams. In 1950, the lopsided arrangement, which favored American petroleum companies to the detriment of the Saudis, was modified so that the spoils were divided on a 50–50 basis, which dramatically increased the Kingdom's revenue.[45] Great wealth infected common sense, and the House of Saud then followed the siren's song of greed that left it hostage to the foreign—and especially American—addiction to fossil fuel. In order to sustain their expanding appetite for almost limitless opulence, future kings and the extended royal family of approximately one thousand members surrendered Saudi society to the Wahhabi clerics, who kept their version of extreme Islam simmering.

By the end of the Second World War, St. John Philby had become increasingly disgusted by the corruption, poor administration, and avarice and indulgence of the Saudi royal family, and he said so publicly. This proved too much for Ibn Saud's successor, and he banished Philby. Ironically, the ex-Saudi advisor chose London as his place of banishment.[46] In April 1955, Harry St. John Bridger Philby returned home from Arabia, leaving behind him a legacy of oil, money, and corruption that served as the handmaidens to fanatical Islam.

EIGHT

Absolute Faith: The Muslim Brotherhood and the Politics of Intelligence

"My word will be stronger if they kill me."
—*Sayyid Qutb*[1]

On dank mornings at the end of August, the wind carries the flavors and scents of the desert to Cairo. Overnight, the sand sucks up the cool moisture and releases the wetness a few hours before dawn. The smells of Cairo at that hour are a confluence of the sterile odors of desert dampness with hints of the delta that combine manure and pungent whiffs of stagnant irrigation water. Later in the day, Cairo becomes engulfed by the signature aroma prevalent in most cities of the Middle East: a mélange of exhaust fumes, cheap incense, manure, and animal sweat.[2] To all outward appearances, August 29, 1966, seemed like a typical early morning in Egypt's capital. Yet a few hours later, the Egyptian government set in motion a chain of events that would mark that day as a new threshold for the Middle East. Later that morning, the execution of an Islamic theologian and ideologue of jihad provided Muslim militants with a fresh and influential martyr.

The prisoner in the special cell block of Tura prison, however, seemed almost impervious to his fate: wearing the traditional red burlap pajamas of a condemned man, he waited with resignation. Two policemen came by, just after the break of dawn, and, taking one arm each, practically carried Sayyid Qutb to a waiting automobile in the prison courtyard. It was part of a small convoy of police and military vehicles that sped quickly to the place for executions. Upon arrival, Qutb was taken to a makeshift hanging post, and a rope was placed around his neck. The executioner waited patiently under a black flag for the signal to initiate the final ordeal for the condemned man. As the guards and the other men sentenced to death waited for the killing to commence, a car screeched to a halt outside, and a senior Egyptian officer burst into the death chamber.

Anwar Sadat, a former member of the Muslim Brotherhood and a close associate of Nasser, entered the place of execution and offered Qutb a simple proposition: appeal the sentence, and Nasser would grant him mercy. Nasser had realized, especially as the streets of Cairo were beginning to bulge with demonstrators, that Qutb would be more dangerous dead. Qutb refused.[3] The hangman then proceeded to pull the rope, slowly lifting Qutb above the ground. Qutb gasped and thrashed violently; in a matter of minutes he had collapsed.

In a feeble attempt to put the genie back in the bottle, the Egyptian government refused to release the body to the family, in order to prevent the gravesite from becoming a shrine, but it was too late.[4] Even as the Muslim Brotherhood appeared at the point of disintegration, Qutb's execution and martyrdom represented a line in the sand in the evolution of political Islam, and his writings became essential scriptures for the disciples of modern jihad.[5] In a moment of supreme irony, Qutb's death helped relaunch the Brotherhood during the first decade of Nasser's Egypt (1954–1965), concurrently with the peak of secular Arab nationalism.[6]

To a great extent Qutb's life and death is a metaphor for the spiritual and ideological journey that has transported many men and women in the Middle East from a commitment to secular political ideals to the absolutism of political Islam. Initially, Qutb was a mild-mannered young schoolteacher who achieved a reputation in literary criticism. His political experience in the post–Second World War nationalism that was sweeping over Egypt and his contacts with the West convinced him to seek salvation in Islam. Sayyid Qutb became the spiritual guide of the Muslim Brotherhood and preached an interpretation of Islam that bridged the beliefs of the puritanical Wahhabis and those outside Arabia, which ultimately provided an intellectual and theological framework for Osama bin Laden and his followers in al-Qaeda.[7] Qutb despised the West, especially the United States, and was equally ill-disposed toward Nasser's Arab nationalism.

The Islamic martyr was born in 1906, in Mush, a small village in Upper Egypt. In 1921, he was sent to live with an uncle in Cairo to complete his studies and graduated from Dar al-'Ulum, a teacher-training institute. After graduation, he was sent to the provinces as a teacher, eventually returning to Cairo as an inspector of schools for the Egyptian Ministry of Education. In the 1930s and 1940s, he gained some distinction as a literary critic, writer, and journalist.[8] Like most Egyptians of his generation, he dabbled in politics and resented the British domination of Egypt. At this time, Qutb was not a religious activist but confined his interests to literary criticism, poetry, and—after

1945—Egyptian nationalism. He devoted himself to the cause of Egyptian nationalism with such fervor that he irritated King Farouk, who proposed to have him arrested. However, thanks to his political contacts, the Ministry of Education spirited him away to the United States in 1948 for further training.[9]

Qutb's experience in America was in effect his road to Damascus, transforming the young Egyptian man of letters into a committed Islamic ideologue. Almost immediately, his newfound resolve was tested on the ocean liner, as a drunken American woman attempted to seduce him. Qutb did not succumb, nor was he later won over by the charms of the American way of life. He was repelled by its prejudice against Arabs and shocked by the freedom that American men allowed their women. He described the churches as "entertainment centers and sexual playgrounds."

After two and a half years of exposure to Western civilization, Qutb realized that he despised everything about it. So, on his return to Egypt in 1951, he resigned from the Ministry of Education and joined the militant Muslim Brotherhood.[10] In 1954, Nasser's police arrested him and many other members of the MB. Qutb spent ten years in prison and, despite the harsh conditions, he was able to continue writing and publishing. He was released in 1964, but was arrested again in 1965 after members of the Brotherhood had attempted to assassinate Nasser.

Qutb became the most influential advocate of the contemporary concept of jihad. For many militants in the Middle East, his new interpretation of holy war legitimizes violent Muslim resistance to governments that claim to be Muslim, but whose implementation of Islamic precepts is flawed. Qutb is especially popular in Saudi Arabia, but his extensive publications have also been translated into most Muslim languages. In the 1960s and 1970s, when many Afghan religious scholars came under the influence of the Muslim Brotherhood, Qutb's ideas attracted particular interest in the faculty of religious law in Kabul, and the scholar Burhanuddin Rabbani translated his writings into the Afghan language, Dari.

Although Qutb is studied everywhere from Malaysia to Morocco, there are many versions of militant Islam, and his writings have been interpreted in a variety of ways. Some Muslim radicals have even written polemics against Qutb's version of Islam. Still, Qutb is regarded as the father of contemporary militant Islam, and the inspiration and influence for many radical Muslims, including Osama bin Laden.[11] Years later, Qutb's brother, Muhammad, was teaching at King Abdul-al-Aziz University, where he indoctrinated many young Arabs, including bin Laden. Another Muslim Brother, Abdullah Azzam, also an instructor at the Saudi university and a follower of Qutb, spent considerable time with the future terrorist in Peshawar, Pakistan, during the war in Afghanistan.[12]

Until the appearance of al-Qaeda in the 1990s, Qutb and the Muslim Brotherhood carried the banner of radical and—to Western, as well as established Muslim regimes—fanatical Islam. The Brotherhood had burrowed deep into Egyptian society, and its tentacles had spread throughout the Arab Muslim world. Although on the surface it appeared that Arab nationalism had captivated Egypt and other Arab states in the post–Second World War period, it was the Muslim Brotherhood that had captured the soul of Egypt's poor and young intellectuals.

Equally significantly, the Muslim Brothers had acquired powerful allies: in the late 1940s, the Central Intelligence Agency supported these Egyptian radicals to counterbalance the unsettling rise of Egyptian nationalism.[13] The Dulles brothers—Allen as director of the CIA (1953–1961) and John Foster as secretary of state (1953–1959)—came to regard Nasser as a pro-Soviet communist and believed that Islam was the magic bullet with which to kill Arab nationalism, thereby depriving Moscow of potential allies in the Middle East.[14] Accordingly, they encouraged Saudi Arabia and Jordan to aid and finance the MB's struggle against Nasser. The irony was that, only a few years earlier, the CIA had covertly supported Nasser.[15]

However, the Americans were not the first to seek Islamic militants as allies in containing nationalist and secular movements in Egypt. The British had implemented the same recipe during the First World War by trying to exploit Islam against the Ottoman Empire. In the late 1920s, they had donated £500 Egyptian, through the Suez Canal Company, to Hassan al-Banna and had helped establish the MB.[16] Ten years later, the Muslim Brothers began advocating nationalization of the canal.[17] Despite the apparent contradiction, the British had few reservations over tolerating and even supporting an organization that was antithetical to their presence in Egypt. This cynical approach was motivated, in part, because, like the British, the MB was also opposed to Egyptian nationalists, left-wing organizations, independent labor institutions, and communist entities in general.

The raison d'être of the Muslim Brotherhood was—and continues to be—cleansing Islam of all foreign elements and restoring it to its pristine essence as practiced at the time of the Prophet Mohammed. To accomplish this resurrection of the true faith, the Brotherhood and its later offshoots worked with grim determination and fanaticism toward the establishment of a theocratic Islamic republic. To this end, the Muslim Brothers have consigned themselves to do battle throughout the Middle East and beyond.

The foundation of the organization in the 1920s came at a time when the Muslim world was in disarray. Ataturk (Mustapha Kemal) had dismantled the Ottoman Empire in 1924 and had supplanted it with a secular Turkish republic. The Muslim territories, with the exception of Turkey, were parceled out by the victorious European powers and recast as "mandates," in order to avoid using the label "colonies." The end of the Ottoman Empire also spelled the end of the Caliphate and the fragmentation of Islam. Gilles Kepel asserts:

> The Muslim Brothers formed their society in Egypt in order to reclaim Islam's political dimension, which had formerly resided in the person of the now-fallen caliph. Confronted by the Egyptian nationalists of the time—who demanded independence, the departure of the British, and a democratic constitution—the Brothers responded with a slogan that is still current in the Islamist movement: "The Koran is our constitution."[18]

Ever since 1924, in one form or another, various Muslim organizations and individuals have been trying to re-create the Islamic unity that they perceive as having been represented by the Ottoman Caliph. The search for an all-embracing Islamic entity, through either the leadership of a single religious-political entity or that of an individual, remains at the crux of the Muslim restlessness that has marked the twentieth and early twenty-first centuries. The strange characters spewed forth by the chaos of the post-Ottoman Middle East came at the forefront of competing ideologies and movements offering pan-Arabism or pan-Islam, but with the purpose of uniting the disparate Muslim world. Secular Arab leaders advocated either local or regional nationalism; however, although Muslim activists welcomed the notion of unifying the Arabs, they saw this only as a first step to the establishment of an Islamic state to replace the central role of the Caliphate.[19]

Al-Banna and the Brotherhood attempted to fill that void by preaching Islam as the salvation of the Arabs, and later on of all Muslims beyond the frontiers of Egypt. Until 1936, the MB concentrated on acquiring members, creating branches in Egypt, and delivering social welfare. But after 1936, the Muslim Brothers expanded their activities beyond the borders of Egypt. The outbreak of the Arab rebellion against the British mandate in Palestine offered al-Banna a unique opportunity to engage the society in a cause that was quickly capturing the hearts and minds of Arabs and Muslims throughout the world.[20] He threw the weight of the Muslim Brothers into organizing a recruiting campaign for volunteers to fight in Palestine, as well as to raise money.

The Palestinian crisis of 1936 was neither the first nor the last, but one in a series of violent rebellions that ultimately became a major stimulant to radical movements within the Muslim world in the twentieth and the beginning of the twenty-first century.[21] Arab resistance to the British provided inspiration for the rise of Arab nationalism in Egypt. It also helped to instigate pan-Arabism, which many believed would come under Egyptian leadership, thus paving the way for Nasser's revolution of 1952. The Palestinian struggle beckoned secular Arab nationalists, because it underscored the fight by Arabs in Palestine for self-determination and statehood. At the same time, the position of Jerusalem in Islam acted as a magnet for the religious militants, who could not accept the loss of the third sacred city so critical in the Islamic faith.

At the center of the Palestinian conundrum stood Hajj Amin al-Husseini, the Mufti of Jerusalem, who owed his position to the British, and who was also their most bitter enemy before and after his appointment.[22] Al-Husseini has stalked the history of Palestine since the beginning of the British mandate until the present; he has cast a long shadow over the roots of political Islam. Remarkably, in 1921 he was not the first choice for Mufti; in fact, he received the lowest number of votes from the Muslim electors appointed by the British administration of Palestine to elect the Mufti.[23] However, al-Husseini and his supporters organized a campaign to promote his candidacy and with considerable venom negated the others. Letters of support from Palestinian notables (including leaders of the Christian communities), as well as petitions with hundreds of signatures, inundated the British authorities. Although these made some impact on the mandate administration, other factors conspired to confer the position of Mufti on al-Husseini.

One recent theory advocated by David Dalin and John Rothmann is that a key player in the appointment of al-Husseini was Ernest Richmond, the assistant political secretary of the British High Commission in Jerusalem. Richmond was the high commissioner's advisor on Arab affairs, but equally significantly, according to Dalin and Rothmann, "it was rumored that Richmond and al-Husseini were involved in a passionate homosexual relationship. As a result of their relationship, Richmond enthusiastically used his political influence to persuade Sir Herbert Samuel to appoint al-Husseini as mufti."[24] Equally interesting is the claim of these authors that "Richmond, who had previously been employed as a minor British government official in Cairo, had been brought to Jerusalem from Egypt by his longtime lover and mentor, Sir Ronald Storrs, the British mandatory governor of Palestine."[25]

There is little evidence for these outrageous assertions. Dalin and Rothmann base their theory on one single reference in a study by Elie Kedourie, in which he states that Richmond and Storrs had shared a house in Jerusalem—as they had also shared a flat earlier in Cairo.[26] Beyond that, Kedourie offers no further insight into the relationship between Richmond and Storrs, and he certainly provides no comment on any possible homosexual ménage-à-trois embracing al-Husseini, Richmond, and Storrs. However, Kedourie does stipulate that Richmond's intervention with Samuel was decisive and that it practically ensured al-Husseini's appointment.[27]

Perhaps Dalin and Rothmann's claim of a homosexual connection is in response to the widespread incredulity that someone as ill-qualified as al-Husseini should have been elected. He had neither the education nor the experience of the other contenders who could have been appointed by Samuel to the post of Mufti. Equally remarkable is the fact that Samuel was Jewish and a Zionist, while al-Husseini clearly demonstrated anti-British and anti-Jewish biases. It begs the question why someone with Samuel's convictions would have even considered such a poor choice, insofar as British and Zionist interests were concerned. Kedourie speculates that the choice of al-Husseini was a product of timing and the decisive intervention by Richmond. On the other hand, Philip Mattar argues that the Husseini family had monopolized the position of Mufti since the seventeenth century, thus affording al-Husseini religious legitimacy.[28]

Another possibility is that the British disingenuously appointed al-Husseini precisely because of his shortcomings. His lack of credentials, combined with the Husseini family history, made him a perfect candidate for manipulation.[29] The history of British imperial policy is replete with the concept of ruling through compliant indigenous leaders. To contain al-Husseini, the British confirmed him simply as Mufti, not Grand Mufti, and did not give him an official letter of appointment.[30] Furthermore, Samuel appointed al-Husseini president of the Supreme Muslim Council, which controlled the religious schools, orphanages, Islamic courts, mosques, and the funds of the awqaf (charitable foundations). This gave al-Husseini considerable power over Muslim affairs in Palestine.

One additional factor that may substantiate the theory that the British believed they could manipulate al-Husseini is that, according to Rashid Khalidi, the office of Mufti was refashioned to accommodate the interests of the mandate authority. First, the British changed his title to Grand Mufti of Palestine (as opposed to Mufti of Jerusalem); although important, the new office was limited in terms of geography and influence. The Mufti of Jerusalem, prior to the appointment of al-Husseini, had no authority over the other muftis in Palestine.[31] Under the terms of this new arrangement, with the title and powers of the reconstituted office, the Grand Mufti of Palestine, combined with the position of president of the Supreme Muslim Council, afforded the officeholder considerable jurisdiction and power over the lives of the Palestinians. Consequently, if the British could manipulate the Mufti, they could exercise through him a greater degree of control over the Muslims throughout Palestine.

Regardless of all these theories, al-Husseini proved to be a disastrous choice for the British and caused them endless difficulties. He instigated numerous riots and revolts; eventually he collaborated with the Nazis, spending most of the Second World War in Berlin, where he had the ear and protection of the German führer himself. By the end of the war, he had come full circle, and he was once again employed by the British. In the interim, al-Husseini had become yet another catalyst for political Islam and, perhaps more than anyone, was responsible for making the cause of the Palestinians the ethos of both Arab nationalists and Muslim militants.

The 1936 Arab Revolt in Palestine, led by al-Husseini, was more than an uprising both with respect to its duration (1936–1939) and its impact on pan-Arabism and Egypt.[32] Furthermore, the desire of the Palestinians to free themselves from British rule spilled outside the confines of Palestine and manifested itself as a cause espoused by Arab nationalists and Muslim militants, as well as ordinary people in the Middle East.[33] Indeed, the Palestinian struggle eventually became submerged in the rhetoric of pan-Arabists and militant Muslims, but also in that of radical and revolutionary organizations in the West.[34]

The Palestinian revolt was the first opportunity for the Muslim Brotherhood to blood many of its members. The three-year crisis and the eventual defeat of the Palestinians radicalized an entire generation of Arabs and engendered the notion of Egypt as the champion of the rights of all Arabs, eventually inspiring the establishment of the Arab League in Cairo on March 22, 1945. Consequently, the work of the Muslim Brothers in Palestine elevated the organization from the fringes of society to a rapprochement with mainstream Egyptian political elites.[35]

For the Mufti, the 1936 revolt was the beginning of a lifelong journey of running and hiding, all the while waging a relentless war against the British. By October of 1936, al-Husseini and the other Arab leaders were becoming conciliatory and came close to reaching an agreement with the British to end the rebellion. However, when the Peel Commission, set up to examine what led to the outbreak of violence, recommended the partition of Palestine, al-Husseini condemned it and on July 8, 1937, vowed to continue fighting the British and the Zionists.[36]

NINE

The British-Jewish Military Alliance

"Rags, wretchedness, poverty and dirt, those signs and symbols
that indicate the presence of Muslim rule
more surely than the crescent-flag itself."
—*Mark Twain*[1]

For millennia a strange and exotic assortment of characters has left its mark on the blood-drenched land of Palestine. Some were prophets, holy men, soothsayers, vagabonds, charlatans, evangelists, missionaries, zealots, pilgrims; but most were soldiers committed to wresting from history their version of the Holy Land. For others, Palestine was, and continues to remain, a land of religious imagination. During the nineteenth century, thousands of books, travel guides, histories, memoirs, and novels published in North America and Europe offered a Western-tainted version of Palestine as the land of the Bible. The notion of Palestine as the Christian Holy Land and Palestine as the home of the Jews shaped Western perceptions of the region.[2] Concurrently, millions of Muslims conceived of Palestine, particularly after 1948, as inextricably linked to their faith but lost to Islam. Regardless of religious affiliation or national identity, these unique individuals contributed to the legend that shaped the legacy of the region.

In 1938, one such character was a military pilgrim by the name of Orde Charles Wingate. Occasionally a perplexed passerby walking across the rolling fields and orchards of the Galilee would notice a bearded and pith-helmet-wearing British officer, with mismatched socks and twin revolvers slung over his hips, leading a ragged band of Jewish fighters and a handful of British soldiers.[3] According to one observer, Moshe Shertok, "He looked like a man devoured by a kind of inner fire, addicted to a single idea that had captured his imagination."[4] Basil Liddell Hart, Britain's distinguished military historian, described Wingate as a kind of Lawrence of the Jews.[5] He became such an ardent Zionist that he earned the term "Ha Yadid," or "The Friend."[6]

Yet Wingate's background should have predisposed him to be pro-Arab, as was the case with certain elements of the British army. In stark contrast to Wingate's staunch Zionist convictions, his cousin Sir Reginald, for example, was a former high commissioner who believed that the Jews had dragged the Ottoman Empire into war against the British.[7] Wingate was born in India, the son of a colonial officer, and had followed in the footsteps of his ancestors by pursuing a military career. As a young man he attended a prestigious school and early on he developed an interest in Arab affairs. In 1936 he arrived in Palestine as an intelligence officer and became obsessed with Zionism.[8]

The notoriously eccentric Wingate and his men comprised the Special Night Squads (SNS), effectively one of the first Special Forces units. The 1936 Arab uprising had expanded rapidly into full-blown rebellion and the British desperately needed reinforcements. Wingate organized his elite force of counterinsurgency troops to scatter, terrorize, and often kill the Arab guerrillas in nighttime ambushes. The SNS included four platoons comprising about two hundred soldiers, of which 150 were Jews, and operated in the Galilee. Ostensibly the task of the SNS was to guard the oil pipeline from Iraq, but its primary task was to counter terrorism with terrorism.[9]

Ultimately, Wingate's tactics laid the guidelines for the Israeli army and the basic framework for the organization and deployment of Israel's Special Forces. According to a publication issued by the Israeli Ministry of Defense, "The teaching of Orde Wingate, his character and leadership were a cornerstone for many of the Haganah's commanders, and his influence can be seen in the Israeli Defence Force's combat doctrine.[10]

British security cooperation with the Jewish fighters was not limited only to training, equipment, and logistical support but also included intelligence and espionage work. The Haganah also provided Arabic-speaking Jews who proved to be of considerable assistance to the British since the mandate authority lacked officers and men proficient in the language.[11] Committed pro-Zionists like Wingate were an exception. British-Jewish collaboration in Palestine was based on self-interest in response to the 1936 Arab rebellion, which dashed the prospect of any compromise between the Jews, Arabs, and the British over coexistence in Palestine.

Although, with some exceptions, the 1920s were comparatively peaceful, the British could not find a mechanism to balance Arab fears over Jewish immigration and increasingly extensive land purchases.[12] Both the issue of land and immigration were exacerbated in the 1930s by the anti-Semitic policies of Poland and by the mass persecution of Jews by Nazi Germany, which dramatically increased the number of Jewish refugees pressing on the shores of Palestine.

The 1936 rebellion was a multifaceted affair not necessarily driven by nationalism or religion exclusively, but it had a critical impact on the future of the

Arab Palestinians. The British had from the beginning of the mandate encouraged religion and supported traditional institutions as a means to counter nationalism. In this respect they created the precedent for the Americans, who followed the same policy in the twentieth and twenty-first centuries and also tried to use Islam to counter Egypt's Nasser and in 1979 armed and trained the mujahidin to counter the pro-Soviet secular regime in Afghanistan.

In Palestine the mandate officials tried to channel the leadership of the Palestinians away from nationalism by refashioning institutions such as the office of the Mufti and by the establishment of the Supreme Muslim Council. The British appointed Hajj Amin al-Husseini as Mufti in the belief that he would not oppose the mandate, and that this position, along with the Supreme Muslim Council, would undermine the emergence of a national and secular political leadership.[13] But the 1936 rebellion both politicized and internationalized the Palestinian issue and restructured the leadership of the Palestinian Arabs.

The 1936 rebellion trigger occurred on the evening of April 15, 1936, when a group of armed Arabs set up a roadblock near the village of Tulkarm to ambush passing Jewish and British convoys as well as extort donations from Arab drivers. On this occasion, they shot three Jewish drivers, one died immediately, another five days later, but the third survived.[14] Quickly the cyclone of vengeance and retribution sucked in Jews, Arabs, and the Arab Christians. The members of a radical Zionist organization, the Hairgun Hatzvai Haleumi Be Yisrael (National Military Organization, or IZL), killed two Arabs in a house near the city of Petah Tikva. A few days later, on April 19, mobs of Arab peasants vented their anger by rampaging through Jaffa, taking the lives of nine Jews and injuring another sixty. Muslim notables who spread rumors that the Jews had murdered an Arab woman and several Syrian workers incited the mob. From April 19–21 national strike committees sprouted in almost every Arab town from Gaza to Nablus. During the summer armed groups formed in the countryside, particularly in the rural regions of central and northern Palestine. Violence spread rapidly and labor strikes paralyzed several cities.[15]

The British were ill-prepared to deal with the rebellion since it lacked a particular center of geographic and leadership gravity. Effectively, the rebellion was driven by local and regional forces and not guided from the top. An attempt was made by the Mufti and by the existing political parties to seize control of events, but Arab leadership remained fragmented.[16] From the beginning of the mandate, Arab society was riddled with factions and local rivalries among the various notables—a condition that the British readily exploited, but it did them little good in the 1936 rebellion since the uprising was grass-roots-based.[17]

Because of cutbacks, after 1930 the mandate authority had at its disposal two infantry battalions and an RAF armored car squadron. Initially, the British response was restrained in the mistaken notion that the violence would quickly blow over. But in the first few weeks of the uprising the British forces were overwhelmed and an additional twenty thousand troops were brought from Egypt and Britain. Despite the reinforcements, by June 1936 the rural areas of Palestine came under the power of armed guerrilla bands and the British only maintained control over the cities.[18]

In September of 1937, after the intervention of the Arab leaders of Saudi Arabia, Iraq, Yemen, and Transjordan, the violence came to an end.[19] Peace was short-lived because the recommendations of the Peel Royal Commission, although tolerable to the Jews, were not acceptable to the Arabs. The Royal Commission recommended the end of the mandate and the partition of Palestine into a Jewish state and an Arab area. The Arab zone was to include 70 percent of the mandate territory, but would be merged with Transjordan; only 20 percent was allocated for a Jewish state; and 10 percent, the areas from Jaffa to Jerusalem, would be remain under a redefined British mandate.[20] The Jewish leadership responded with qualified support but the Arabs officially denounced the commission's proposals and demanded the establishment of an Arab state to include all of Palestine.

Unwittingly, the recommendations of the Peel Commission mobilized Arab opinion not only in Palestine but throughout the Arab world. The rebellion resumed with renewed ferocity. Despite the extensive and harsh British reprisals, the Arab infrastructure and capability for guerrilla warfare had remained intact. The British had failed to destroy or disarm the armed guerrilla bands during the previous year. In this case Arab lack of unity worked to the advantage of the insurgents. When the British eliminated a particular band of fighters another group quickly took its place. The absence of a central command and infrastructure did not afford the British the opportunity to strike at the core of the rebellion.

The Arabs, on the other hand, had the advantage of attacking stationary targets and targets of opportunity—police stations, the railway system, roads, telephone and telegraph lines, the pipeline of the Iraq Petroleum Company, and British convoys trying to supply isolated posts. The Arabs deployed snipers positioned in strategic locations who were able to shoot at patrols, vehicles, and civilian passersby.[21] Assassination of moderate Arabs as well as against individuals members of the mandate authority discouraged collaboration and kept the British confined in the cities and towns. For example, on September 26 Arab gunmen assassinated Lewis Y. Andrews, the acting district commissioner of the Galilee. During 1937, Arab rebels launched a total of 438 attacks, 109 against British military and police forces, 143 against Jewish settlements, and the remainder aimed at other Arabs. Ninety-seven people were killed and 149 wounded.[22]

Faced with an expanding and diffused insurgency, the British increased cooperation with the Palestinian Jews. As a result, the British received considerable intelligence on Arab activities from the far better informed Haganah intelligence service, Sherut Yediot (SHAI, or Information Service), in exchange for concessions to the Haganah's own attempts to expand militarily.[23] The British also created special military units to protect Jewish civilians and to mount joint operations against the Arab rioters. One of these, the special Jewish police force, called the Notrim, or Guards, also included an elite and mobile Settlement Police force, the Nodedot. Almost every member of the Notrim was part of the Haganah and thus the Nodedot had in addition to its official British chain of command an "illegal" Haganah commander.[24] The Haganah used the British training to evolve the Nodedot into the first unit that established a long tradition of the use of unconventional Special Forces, which have played a crucial and significant role in Israeli military history.[25] The other joint operations military unit was the Special Night Squads, formed in 1938 by Orde Wingate.

The Special Night Squads carried out their nighttime ambushes against Arab fighters from 1938 to 1939. Beginning in 1938, without authorization from his superiors, Wingate led small patrols at night of Haganah soldiers from the besieged kibbutz of Hanita in an effort to incite the Jewish fighters to go "beyond the fence" and switch their defensive mentality to an offensive one.[26] These patrols comprised the unofficial first actions of what would later become the single most effective counterinsurgency unit that the British forces ever employed against the Arab rebels in Palestine.

In spring of 1938, the British high command in Palestine approved Wingate's seventeen-page proposal for the recognition of the Special Night Squads as a joint Anglo-Jewish military unit deployed "to persuade the gangs that in their predatory raids there is every chance of running into a government gang which is determined to destroy them not by an exchange of shots in the distance but by bodily assault with bayonet and bomb."[27] Quartered in three north Jewish settlements,[28] the Anglo-Jewish squads succeeded in ambushing the majority of Arab attacks on the Haifa oil pipeline, and managed to end the siege on Kibbutz Hanita.[29]

On July 10, 1938, the Night Squads expanded its operations and advanced on Dabburiya, a small town on the slopes of Mount Tavor, approximately eight kilometers southeast of Nazareth, in response to rebel attacks against Nazareth.

Wingate's force included thirty-two British soldiers and fifty-five Jewish fighters, about half of the SNS. On July 11, he initially had moved on the town of Ein Mahil, but upon finding it free from insurgents proceeded to nearby Dabburiya. On the outskirts of Dabburiya, Wingate's men lost the element of surprise after engaging two Arab sentries and spent the next several hours exchanging fire with the rebels until the Arab guerrillas melted into the nearby hills.

Unfortunately, in the confusion—multiple squads pursuing fleeing guerrillas—one of the SNS units fired upon Wingate and several of his men, whose silhouetted figures were indistinguishable at night from those of the enemy. Wingate was hit five times in his extremities by ricocheting bullets, while a Jewish member of the unit was shot several times in the stomach and died shortly after. One of the British officers in the SNS recalled, "Though Wingate's face was white as a sheet and very taut, he was sitting there, in the hay, covered in blood and giving orders in English and in Hebrew quite calmly. . . . He was quite an extraordinary man." Zvi Brenner, a Jewish squad leader, recalled how Wingate refused to leave until all of his men were confirmed to be safe, despite his injuries: "He looked very pale and frightened and sorry for himself. He hated pain and the first thing he said to me was: 'I hope I'm not going to die because of you. I refused to leave until I made sure you were all right. Now take me to a hospital quickly.'"[30]

Further successful operations followed, with the Night Squads killing large numbers of Arab guerrillas while suffering almost no losses of their own. The most spectacular of these was possibly Wingate's fast response to the ongoing October 2 massacre of nineteen Jews (eleven of whom were children) in Tiberia. Rushing to the scene, the Night Squads managed to kill between forty and fifty of the Arab fighters with no losses. Furthermore, in a mop-up operation two days later at the port town of Dabburiya, Wingate radioed the local RAF squadron for tactical air support—unusual and innovative thinking for 1938. Emboldened by his success, Wingate intensified his training program at Ein Herod and began a school for Jewish officers there as well, though only one cohort would ever graduate, in early October 1938.[31] At the same time, however, he became more outwardly eccentric, growing a beard and donning an old pith helmet. On another occasion, he showed up to a wardroom party on a ship in Haifa in a filthy field uniform and carrying a bag of grenades over one shoulder.[32] For British officials in Palestine, the unprecedented and brutal battlefield successes of the largely Jewish-staffed SNS and its fervently Zionist commanding officer held uneasy portents for the future.

In the spring of 1939, the Arab rebellion was winding down and the mandate authorities decided to disband the SNS and to transfer Wingate out of

Palestine. The end of the crisis evaporated British interest in arming Zionists. A cascade of recriminations along with convenient hindsight followed on the heels of the British victory of the 1936 Arab rebellion. A conference of British officials voiced their opposition to "dressing Jews up as British soldiers . . . [and] to have a proportion of Jews in SNS detachments." Others held the ambush tactics of the SNS in distaste. Hugh Foot, who would later become Lord Caradon and Britain's last governor of Cyprus, complained that the SNS "forfeited our general reputation for fair fighting."[33]

On May 11, 1939, Wingate was reassigned, and though he offered to resign his commission and remain in Palestine illegally to assist the Zionist cause, on May 26 he departed Palestine, never to return. Cooperation between the British security forces and the Jewish community in Palestine came to an abrupt end but the exigencies of the Second World War forced the renewal of the relationship. Wingate was transferred to Britain and at the outbreak of the war commanded an antiaircraft gun but shortly after he secured a posting to the Sudan.

In East Africa he distinguished himself using similar Special Forces tactics he had developed in Palestine culminating in the establishment of the Gideon Force—a guerrilla group of approximately 1,700 composed of British, Sudanese, and Ethiopian soldiers in which he invited a number of veterans of the Haganah SNS to join him. During the East Africa campaign, Wingate's small force fought ferociously and at the end took the surrender of twenty thousand Italians. But victory did not result in promotion or recognition for his efforts. He was again sent home to Britain, and in February 1941 he arrived in Burma. Once again he organized mobile commando forces to strike behind enemy lines and achieved some success. Tragically, on March 24, 1944, Wingate flew to assess the situation of his commando forces in Burma, but on the return flight the American B-25 Mitchell crashed into the jungle-covered hills near Bishnupur in northwest India killing him and nine others.[34] He died at the age of forty-one.

For the Jews, the outbreak of the war in Europe offered an opportunity to aid their fellow Jews by joining the fight against the Nazis, while for the British the rapid victories of the Nazis left them vulnerable and they sought help from all quarters. However, the 1939 British Report, which had severely limited Jewish immigration to Palestine, strained relations between the Yishuv and the mandate authorities. Certainly, the British were anxious to avoid equipping and training a "Jewish army" that would eventually challenge the mandate and stir Arab dissent, despite the willingness of Palestinian Jews to fight against the Axis. David Ben-Gurion's (Zionist leader) famous declaration, "We must fight

Germany as though there were no White Paper, and fight the White Paper as though there were no war,"[35] encapsulated the Zionist policy. The British, on the other hand, officially rejected the notion of cooperating with the Jews, and instead established a clandestine relationship under the auspices of the British intelligence services.

In June 1940, the French surrendered and their colonies in Syria and Lebanon came under the control of the Vichy regime. In the same month Italy's Benito Mussolini threw in his lot with Adolf Hitler, and overnight Palestine came under threat of an Italian invasion. Underscoring the new crisis for both the British and Jews in Palestine, Italian planes bombed Haifa and Tel Aviv.[36] In September 1940, the British called for recruits of any nationality from Palestine—nearly ninety thousand men and over fifty thousand women (out of a total of 650,000 Jews living in the Yishuv) volunteered to join in various capacities.[37] Although cooperation with the British meant providing labor for constructing bases and roads throughout Palestine and industrial trade with the British army, approval for military participation or acceptance of Jewish volunteers into the British army was refused.[38] The official consensus in Whitehall was that the Jews should not be given a combat role in the war.

However, cooperation in clandestine activities between British intelligence and the Jewish Agency, which represented Jewish interests in Palestine, had begun as early as July 1940. Propaganda operations in Syria were conducted with Jewish assistance and a Free French radio transmitter was placed in the Haifa home of David Cohen, a high-ranking SHAI[39] agent. At the same time, a network of agents run by Yishuv intelligence officer Tuvya Arazi in Syria and Lebanon was distributing propaganda leaflets. These propaganda operations were carried out under the direction of Brigadier Iltyd Clayton, head of army intelligence at British headquarters in Cairo.[40]

The Special Operations Executive also initiated a secret relationship with Jewish organizations. The chief of SOE in Cairo, Sir John Pollock, worked clandestinely with the Jewish Agency to establish special units that included Jewish fighters from the Haganah who could operate undercover in Arab populations.[41] The plan was to send this "Arab Platoon" into Syria and Lebanon to collect intelligence and conduct sabotage, should the Germans occupy Syria after the surrender of the French army in June.[42] This collaboration was the first significant initiative between British intelligence and the Yishuv.

The majority of the members of the Arab Platoon (Arabic-speaking Jews) had come from Arab countries and were able to effectively blend in with native Arab populations. They received their training at the SOE school on Mount Carmel, near Haifa, and platoon members were taught Arab customs such as singing and dancing, games such as backgammon, and other similar cultural practices, alongside their military training. Even so, their training did not always keep them from being unmasked. On one occasion two of the undercover Arabs were arrested by the Vichy French security service in Damascus. Major Nick Hammond, the SOE liaison with the Arab Platoon, which involved sending two Palmach (the strike-force of the Hagana) agents disguised as British deserters, later extracted them in an elaborate scheme. C. M. Woodhouse also worked with Reuven Zaslany, a SHAI officer and the Jewish Agency but, like Hammond, was posted to the SOE mission with the Greek resistance.[43] Ultimately, as the Italians or the Germans did not invade Syria, the twelve Arab Platoon fighters in Damascus were left in place with little to do.[44]

In May 1941, when the Allies had finalized their plans to invade the Vichy-controlled Levant, SOE headquarters in Cairo employed Jewish agents from Palestine in a plan to infiltrate north into Lebanon and sabotage the oil refineries in Tripoli. On May 18, 1941, a group of twenty-three Haganah fighters embarked on the cutter *Sea Lion* in Haifa, under the command of Major Anthony Palmer, a well-connected young cavalry officer. Palmer, a twenty-six-year-old Royal Dragoon Guards officer, had left this elite unit for service with the SOE in occupied countries.[45]

An hour later the team ceased radio contact after reporting they had entered Lebanese waters. No trace was found of the boat and its crew for some time. Eventually the SOE received reports that members of a captured German radio post mentioned that an Italian submarine had intercepted a boat of Jews and British soldiers. Another report referred to a French officer who buried seven bodies washed ashore on a beach in Lebanon at the end of May 1941. Another witness reported that a Vichy judge in Tripoli had told him of a group of Palestinian prisoners transferred to Aleppo on May 22, 1939, and summarily executed—their boat having been destroyed by the explosives it had been carrying.[46]

On May 15, 1941, the Haganah created an elite military force, the Palmach (Plugot Sadeh or Storm Companies), to "carry out actions against the enemy . . . with or without the help of [British] forces." This decision was influenced by the SOE-Haganah reconnaissance patrols in Syria as well as by the Tripoli operation.[47] Nine companies of thirty volunteers each were organized and scattered throughout various kibbutzim (where they also worked part-time in the fields) in Palestine under the control of the Haganah.[48] The Palmach had two official objectives: to protect the Yishuv from Arabs and to defend Palestine in the event of a German invasion. In the latter case, the Palmach would use guerrilla tactics to disrupt German communication lines and sabotage enemy airfields.

The companies even boasted of a "German Platoon" composed of German and Austrian Jews who were familiar with all Wehrmacht arms and weapon systems.

Recruitment to the Palmach was conducted in secret, and Yitzhak Sadeh, the commander of the Palmach and the former commander of FOSH, and his company commanders personally screened each potential fighter carefully. By 1943 the Palmach consisted of more than one thousand fighters and included a naval commando unit, Palyam (Sea Companies), which trained its soldiers in amphibious landing, naval sabotage, and deep-sea operations, and an air force, Palavir (Air Companies), whose pilots flew gliders and small transport planes. Ultimately, the Palmach proved to be a training ground for Israel's ruling elite and Palmach veterans dominated the upper echelons of Israeli political and military leadership.[49]

The Palmach went into action for the Allies prior to the Anglo-American invasion of Syria and Lebanon. One hundred of the Palmach's Shachar Company, composed of Jews disguised as Arabs and influenced by the Arab Platoon of the Haganah, infiltrated into Vichy territory, where they assisted Free French agents in various clandestine operations and collected intelligence for the British.[50] Then, on the eve of the July 8 British invasion of Syria and Lebanon, the SOE sent two companies of the Palmach, commanded by Moshe Dayan and Yigal Allon, into Vichy territory to cut telephone lines, open routes for Australian army reconnaissance units, and seize and hold several bridges. Dayan lost his eye in this operation after his field glasses were struck by a French bullet and disintegrated into his face.[51] When a colonel from the Australian army's 7th Division offered to recommend the Palmach fighters for decorations for their bravery and skill in seizing a bridge spanning the Litani River in Lebanon, Allon declined and asked that he instead be permitted to keep any captured weapons. The colonel agreed, and out of gratitude even offered up an additional cache of arms seized from the French.[52]

Though Dayan was unfit for combat following the loss of his eye, Reuven Zaslany had another plan for his injured friend. As Dayan commented:

> British intelligence asked Zaslany for a proposal for the creation of an underground network that would gather military intelligence and relay it somehow to the British [in the event of a German invasion of Palestine]. I took it upon myself to organise this network . . . in August 1941 I submitted a detailed proposal . . . the British approved the plan and in September 1941 a course was held for 20 wireless operators . . . the network's official name was P.S. (for Palestine Scheme), but it was

known was "Moshe Dayan's network" . . . I suggested that if the Germans took Palestine, we would increase our intelligence gathering activities, and add to the group of wireless operators units of "Fake-Arabs" or "Fake-Germans" that we would train. As I saw it, the best way to gather information would be to enlist the help of Jews who could look, speak and behave like Arabs or Germans. . . . The idea of setting up a German unit and an Arab unit was later actually carried out in the Palmach.[53]

Zaslany was in charge of implementing the plan. He received the necessary operational details from the British officer in charge of the operation on January 12, 1942, and developed the training program for Dayan's men.[54] On March 8, 1942, the Haganah approved Zaslany's request to include Palmach companies in the scheme and by April the first training course for sharpshooting and explosives had begun at Kibbutz Mishmar Ha'Emek, with courses in reconnaissance. The first of the trainees graduated on May 30, 1942.[55]

The local mandate authorities were kept in the dark over the activities at the kibbutz, as it contravened British policy of maintaining neutrality among the Palestinian communities in order to avoid inciting political violence. Thus when the Palestine police discovered Palmach soldiers bearing arms and carrying out military exercises at the kibbutz, Captain Aubrey Eban,[56] a young South African working for army intelligence in Cairo, was dispatched to ensure that the SOE's operation and the Palmach units were left undisturbed. He was later appointed liaison between the SOE and Haganah HQ. He recalls this appointment:

> I was supposed to obtain my posting from the commander of the Special Operations Section in Cairo, Colonel Dumwill, known both for his courage and for his enormous capacity for alcohol. I therefore requested an appointment at ten in the morning, in order to be sure of finding him sober. Despite a large bottle of whiskey on the table, everything went well. I left his office with the impressive title of liaison officer between Special Operations and the Jewish Agency for Palestine.[57]

During the duration of the Mishmar Ha'Emek camp's operation, six hundred Palmach fighters were trained in groups of one hundred using the same sets of false papers in succession.[58] However, when the Axis forces faced defeat in North Africa, the cooperation between the Palmach and the SOE ended on a poor note. After the training camp at Mishmar Ha'Emek was closed, the British refused to return to the Haganah the arms that the Jewish militia had contributed and in retaliation a Palmach platoon broke into the SOE training school on Mount Carmel and stole 277 rifles and twenty-two machine guns from its arsenal.[59] That was end of SOE-Jewish cooperation for the duration of the Second World War, but not the end of the relationship between clandestine Jewish organizations with British intelligence.

Apart from the SOE, MI9, the "escape and evasion" unit of British intelligence, entered into a secret arrangement to employ the Jews of Palestine for covert operations. The officer in charge of the MI9 unit for southern Europe at the British armed forces headquarters in Cairo was Anthony Simmonds. Simmonds had served with Wingate in Palestine and Ethiopia, as well as with the SOE in Palestine.[60]

Early in 1943, Zaslany and Ze'ev Shind, a senior commander of Ha'Mossad le'Aliya Bet,[61] the illegal immigration department of the Jewish Agency's Istanbul branch, signed an agreement with Simmonds to use Jews for work behind enemy lines. The plan called for Jewish agents from Palestine to parachute into Nazi-occupied Europe and arrange the evacuation of Jews from Romania into Turkey as well as use their network to assist British soldiers who had escaped captivity. According to Shaul Avigur, of the thirty-two parachutists trained for this mission, twenty-six carried out operations, and twenty-one of them did so with MI9.[62]

The MI9 operation had some success, but also carried a heavy price. Reuven Dafni parachuted into Yugoslavia on March 13, 1944, and managed to organize the rescue of 124 British and American airmen. Unfortunately, by the end of the mission thirteen out of the original twenty-six agents were captured and seven of those were executed.

In addition to collaboration between the SOE and MI9, MI6 established a separate relationship with the Jewish clandestine organizations. In 1943, the Inter-Services Liaison Department (ISLD), the Secret Intelligence Service's code name in the Middle East, desperately needed radio operators for Romania and to maintain contact with Tito's partisans. The ISLD approached the Jewish Agency, and Zaslany of the SHAI in Haifa selected fourteen volunteers, who, once deployed, would be handled exclusively by the British. The first volunteer, Reuven Dafni, was ready to parachute into Yugoslavia in March 1943. However, the mission was delayed until May because the Jewish recruits refused to enlist in the British army contrary to the agreement between the ISLD and Zaslany. The problem was resolved and the operation continued until the summer of 1944.[63]

British contacts with clandestine Jewish organizations, although secret, were between directorates of Britain's intelligence community and organizations controlled by the Jewish Agency—the legitimate body representing Palestinian Jews. The British needed agents with fluency in a variety of languages, knowledge of European cities, and familiarity with the terrain in North Africa and the Middle East. The Jewish Agency and other Jewish organizations collaborated with the British and the Allies both to fight the common enemy and to exploit British as well as American military and intelligence expertise for the creation of an Israeli state.

However, the clandestine relationships with Jewish Palestinians extended beyond the quasi-legal departments of the Jewish Agency to much more radical groups committed to the use of terror and whose tactics would inflict considerable damage to the British in the postwar period.

TEN

Kill the Mufti:
Politics and Blowback

*"The Mufti's removal is unlikely to have ill effects, since it is strength,
not weakness, which is admired in the Arab world."*
—*British Chiefs of Staff, 1940*[1]

On September 26, 1937, when the Arab extremists killed Lewis Y. Andrews, district commissioner of Galilee, the British seized the opportunity to go after the Mufti and the other Arab leaders of the uprising. Over two hundred leading members of the Arab community were arrested, and the British stripped al-Husseini of his chairmanship of the Waqf (Islamic charity) Committee in Jerusalem. Fearing arrest, the Mufti slipped out of Jerusalem on the evening of October 14 and shortly after reached Lebanon. From exile, al-Husseini continued to direct the revolt, but after the collapse of the rebellion in Palestine, he made his way to Baghdad in late October 1939.

In Iraq, the Mufti helped instigate and became an integral part of the 1941 Iraqi revolt against the British. Al-Husseini attempted to orchestrate a common front of Arab leaders from Palestine, Iraq, Transjordan, and Syria. He also facilitated negotiations with the Germans to secure arms and political support from the Axis.[2] The British authorities in London believed that if Iraq reached a secret agreement with the Axis, this outcome would represent a major setback in the Middle East. Furthermore, a pro-Axis government in Baghdad would threaten Britain's supply of petroleum, as well as the overland and air routes to India.[3] In the spring of 1941, the tide of war was turning against the British, with defeats in mainland Greece, Crete, and North Africa. As such, the Iraqi revolt could not have come at a worse time for the British. Al-Husseini compounded matters by issuing a fatwa urging Arabs and Muslims to lend their support to free Iraq from the British.[4]

As early as October 1940, the British government had begun to consider several options for dealing with al-Husseini, including kidnapping. Leo Amery of the India Office speculated as follows: "Would it be possible for a few bold lads to kidnap the Mufti in Baghdad, run him south by car out to a waiting airplane, and then to Cyprus? Nashashibis[5] in Palestine, Jews, and indeed all the Middle East would laugh, and a real big danger would be averted."[6] However, the secretary of state for the colonies responded with less enthusiasm, pointing out:

> an attempt to kidnap the Mufti would not be practical politics. . . . No doubt the Nashashibis and the Palestine Jews would be pleased, but I am sure that the feelings aroused in Iraq, Egypt, and Saudi Arabia would be very different. I understand that in Baghdad the Mufti is now something of a popular hero, and any direct action against him at our instigation would be widely resented. Moreover, the Mufti has influential friends in Egypt, and we should have difficulty in explaining the position to the Egyptian Government and for that matter to Ibn Saud.[7]

He went on to caution:

> there can be no certainty that the kidnapping could be successfully carried out. I understand that the Mufti has his own private bodyguard. There would probably be resistance and one or two casualties. Perhaps the Mufti himself would be killed. Perhaps the kidnappers would be caught and imprisoned, and the whole story would come out in the Iraqi law courts. I fear that the outcome would be a severe blow to British prestige throughout the Middle East.[8]

The Chiefs of Staff, on the other hand, proposed to have al-Husseini eliminated. In a report to the War Cabinet, the chiefs stated: "There is ample evidence that [al-Husseini] is in enemy pay. The Mufti's removal is unlikely to have ill effects, since it is strength, not weakness, which is admired in the Arab world."[9] The Eastern Department of the Foreign Office was opposed to assassination and concerned over the possible repercussions, whether the event succeeded or failed since, they feared, it would undoubtedly alienate Arab public opinion. Churchill bypassed these objections by stating that the department concerned "could take action required to implement the various recommendations, which [the report of the Chiefs of Staff] contained."[10]

Effectively, Churchill's ambiguous ruling set into motion an attempt to eliminate the Mufti and thus crossed a critical threshold in clandestine operations by authorizing the use of assassination in wartime.[11] In July 1940, the British had established the Special Operations Executive with a mandate for subversion, sabotage, and propaganda. Implicit in this mandate was the use of assassination as an alternative means of achieving military and political objectives. Consequently, the policy framework was established, and the Mufti was to be the first target in what would eventually become a process, albeit clandestine, that would characterize British and American intelligence operations in the post–Second World War period.

However, there was still reluctance to link British policy with the odium of officially sanctioned murder. The response of the Foreign Office to the proposed killing of the Mufti was to caution that British personnel should not be involved in the assassination since "even if the murder was successfully carried out, it would probably not turn out to our advantage, whereas if the attempt were unsuccessful . . . the results might be disastrous . . . it would alienate Arab opinion throughout the Middle East."[12]

Ultimately, the consensus was to leave it to the Chiefs of Staff to decide on how and when to deal with the Mufti. The plan adopted by the Chiefs of Staff after April 1941 was to employ hitherto incarcerated members of the outlawed Irgun, disguised as Arabs, to undertake his assassination.[13] Consequently, General Archibald Wavell, C-in-C Middle East, ordered the release from a Palestine prison of David Raziel, head of the Irgun, along with several of his companions.[14]

On the evening of May 17, 1941, a Dakota aircraft landed at RAF Habbaniya, the British airbase in Iraq. Four armed men deplaned and proceeded to the makeshift headquarters of the British army. Ostensibly, their mission was to destroy Iraqi supplies of aviation fuel in Baghdad. However, before the commandos were to proceed with blowing up the storage tanks, the British commanding general instructed them to make contact with the officer in charge of an Indian unit and ascertain from him the number and strength of Iraqi units facing his army.

Raziel and a British major accompanied two of the Irgun men (Yaakov Meridor and a companion) to the outskirts of the city and sent them off on a small boat for a reconnaissance mission. Not long after they located the major in command of the Indian unit. Raziel, the British major, and the third member of the Irgun team returned to their car, but just as Raziel asked for a cigarette a bomb from a German airplane scored a direct hit on the automobile. The driver lost both legs, while the British officer and Raziel were killed instantly; only one man survived unscathed.[15]

The fact that the operation failed did not deter the British from adopting assassination as a means of achieving strategic or tactical objectives in the future. For example, in the course of the desert campaign in 1941–1942, the British made several efforts to assassinate Field Marshal Erwin Rommel, commander of the Afrika Korps. Middle East headquarters decided that if Rommel, a charismatic general whose continued victories against the British were proving embarrassing, were killed, it would destroy the morale of the Afrika Korps, as well as making it easier for the Eighth Army to defeat the Germans.[16]

The attempts, all of which failed, were implemented by Britain's embryonic Special Forces and took place behind enemy lines. On each occasion, the casualties were high, but the notion of assassination had taken root in British strategic thinking. In fact, the British had dabbled for some time in the use of Special Forces deployed behind enemy lines; to some degree the variety of commando-type units that emerged in North Africa during the Second World War drew inspiration from T. E. Lawrence and his use of Bedouin in raids and sabotage against the Ottoman forces in the Arabian Peninsula during the First World War.

In Europe, the first target for assassination was a senior Nazi officer in occupied Europe who posed a serious threat to the future course of European resistance. On May 27, 1942, two Free Czech agents, trained by the SOE, parachuted into German-occupied Czechoslovakia and killed one of Hitler's favorite SS officers, Reinhard Heydrich, by throwing a bomb at his automobile. Operation Daylight achieved its objectives by removing a vicious yet very competent Nazi leader who might have influenced Hitler in a way that would have prolonged the war.[17] However, the reprisals against the Czechs were extensive and cruel.[18]

As demonstrated in subsequent situations in Europe and the Middle East, the SS reprisals only served to radicalize the local population and contribute to the expansion of resistance activities. Not so remarkably, the assassination of Heydrich by the British SOE caused the Germans to overreact, taking revenge against the local population and thus swelling the ranks of the Czech resistance. Yet, in Palestine, the British would make the very same mistake as the Germans, by trying to suppress the Jewish resistance movement through the use of intimidation and other dubious counterinsurgency tactics. Although often harsh and violent, the actions of the British Palestinian authorities hardly compared with those of the Nazis; they did, however, succeed in alienating the Jews and leaving them little choice but to join radical and extreme paramilitary organizations.

Meanwhile, during the first years of the Second World War, the British, out of desperation, not only resorted to assassination but also organized an extensive program of cooperation with underground groups in occupied Europe. This involved training individuals in clandestine warfare, supplying them with weapons and explosives, and providing them with expertise in intelligence tradecraft and propaganda methods. Equally significant was the decision to permit the SOE to form covert alliances with organizations that were antithetical to prewar British interests and values.

Toward this end, the SOE and MI6, as well as an alphabet soup of Allied intelligence, propaganda, and security organizations, collaborated with communist resistance forces in occupied Europe and Asia; with republicans in countries that had royalist governments-in-exile in London; and with anarchists, Trotskyites, labor leaders, and Christian conservatives. In some cases, the SOE had contact with extreme-right-wing organizations and even groups that had also collaborated with the Axis. It was only a matter of time before the list extended to Jewish groups, such as the Irgun, which the British had outlawed and labeled as terrorist, and, not surprisingly under the circumstances, even to Muslim extremists.

By the beginning of the Second World War, the Arabs and the Jews had taken sides with respect to the belligerents. The Arabs for the most part supported the Axis and looked to the Nazis to help eliminate the Jews in Palestine.[19] The Jewish community, on the other hand, opted to support the British, despite the White Paper issued by London in May 1939 severely limiting the number of Jews who could immigrate to Palestine. Even so, the Jewish Agency, the de facto government of the Jewish community in Palestine, made every effort to assist the British. As early as 1940, Section D (forerunner of the SOE) began to recruit Jews to take part in covert operations in occupied Eastern Europe. Equally important for the British was the fact that the Jewish Agency could provide them with information on German activities in Palestine, as well as enabling them to exploit Jewish-Arab contacts in Syria.[20]

In 1940, it seemed probable, despite Nazi anti-Semitic policies, that Jewish communities in Eastern Europe could provide assistance to British clandestine operations. In June 1941, the Palmach, a Jewish commando force established with the connivance of the British, provided forty reconnaissance experts and sappers to the Allied campaign against the Vichy French forces in Lebanon and Syria.[21] During the period of 1943–1945, the Palmach and Haganah provided approximately twenty-five Palestinian Jews with facility in European languages to work as agents for MI6 Cairo who, after training in sabotage and radio communications, were parachuted into Nazi-occupied Europe.[22] After the war, some of the survivors of these missions joined the Mossad. The arrangement between the British intelligence services and the Jewish Agency was that information collected by the Palestinian agents was to be shared.[23]

Later, however, the SOE became less enthusiastic about employing Jewish agents in the Middle East. SOE headquarters in Cairo feared political problems with the Arabs and was reticent about supporting Zionist ambitions in the postwar period. The British Secret Intelligence Service and the SOE took exception to publications by the Jewish Agency advertising their collaboration with the British, and also feared that the Jews were trying to penetrate Britain's intelligence and security organizations in Palestine.[24] Their suspicions were not unfounded.

Over 26,000 Palestinian Jewish men and women joined the British armed forces and received some degree of military training, which became useful in the postwar struggle to create a state of Israel. In contrast, twelve thousand Arabs served with the British in the Second World War.[25] It is not known how many Jews or Arabs were employed by Britain's clandestine services. As early as 1942, the SIS (MI6) in the Middle East estimated that the Haganah had thirty thousand armed fighters out of a total of about fifty thousand to seventy thousand men and women in its ranks. A year later, Field Marshal Harold Alexander, C-in-C Middle East, warned that there was a probability that the Jewish community in Israel would rebel after the end of the war.[26]

This was certainly the case with one Jewish paramilitary group, known as the Stern Gang—and later as the Freedom Fighters of Israel (FFI)—which even from the beginning of the Second World War was violently opposed to the British. Breakaway members of the Irgun who were disenchanted with the truce between the British and the Jewish community established the organization in 1939–1941, and they were committed to a life-and-death struggle toward the establishment of an Israeli state that would include all the Jews from Europe and Russia. Abraham Stern, the head of the organization, was convinced that British interests in the Middle East were diametrically opposed to the establishment of a Jewish state. Furthermore, Stern and his followers shared the view that, although Arabs were the ultimate adversaries, the British were the immediate enemy.[27] The Stern Gang was not as numerous as the Irgun, but it was structured to wage a clandestine urban war through the use of assassination, sabotage, and fear: in effect a terrorist organization.

Stern believed that, since it was the British who were preventing the Jews from escaping Europe, Britain had to be defeated if the persecuted Jews of Europe were to find refuge in Palestine. To this end, the Stern Gang even went so far as to attempt an alliance with Nazi Germany. Late in 1940, Stern tried to establish contact with Otto von Hentig, the German emissary in Syria, to find common ground in the struggle against the British, but he was contemptuously rebuffed.[28] This did not deter Stern; later he sent a representative to meet a Nazi official in Beirut. The Jewish extremists offered the Germans military, political, and intelligence assistance, but the Nazis were not interested. Other attempts were foiled by the British security services, who arrested representatives of the Stern Gang before they could meet with Nazi officials in neutral countries, often thanks to tips from the Haganah.[29]

Unlike the mainstream Jewish organizations that had secure funding from supporters around the globe, the Stern Gang had to initiate a campaign of bank robberies to finance their operations. These actions resulted in the killing of British soldiers and, by mistake, Jewish policemen. At the same time, the shootings and acts of sabotage also killed innocent bystanders and earned the Stern Gang little support from the Jewish community in Palestine. Such unsavory tactics made it easy for the British security services, as well as the Palestine police, to find informers and eliminate many Stern Gang members. On February 12, 1942, the British cornered Abraham Stern at his safe house and shot him dead.[30] By this time only two of the Stern Gang's founding members remained, and they decided to end all violent activity while they rebuilt the organization from the ranks of inactive and reserve followers. Two years later, the Stern Gang reemerged, and with grim determination continued its war against the British until they left Palestine in 1947.

When the Stern Gang resumed their campaign of terror in 1944, the Irgun, now under the command of Menachem Begin, also decided to end their truce and declared war on the British.[31] Because both organizations now had a common goal, they easily reached agreement on political and military collaboration.[32] By the beginning of 1946, Irgun strength had grown to three thousand to five thousand men and women, while the Stern Gang numbered approximately 250.[33]

The ending of the war in the Middle East and the continued British insistence on limiting Jewish immigration to Palestine gave the Irgun new life. One critical factor in its comeback was the ability to expand its ranks with Polish Jews who had deserted from General Wladyslaw Anders's Polish army, which had been brought to Palestine by the British. The new volunteers had military training and a burning memory of the loss of family members in the Holocaust.[34] The Irgun carried out dozens of acts of violence and, combined with those perpetrated by the Stern Gang, turned Palestine into a battleground. Between September 1946 and May 1948, for example, the Stern Gang alone carried out over one hundred acts of sabotage against the British in Palestine.[35]

At first the mainstream Jewish community abhorred the violence and had little sympathy for the Stern Gang and the Irgun, but as news of the Holocaust reached Palestine, ordinary people became less inclined to support or cooperate with the British, who continued to bar Jewish refugees from reaching Palestine. Matters became worse as news reached Palestine that spontaneous pogroms had erupted against the survivors of the Nazi death camps in Poland, resulting in thousands of new refugees crowding the displaced persons camps in Europe.[36]

Meanwhile the Stern Gang adopted a new strategy of sending small groups armed with concealed submachine guns and pistols into the streets and opening fire on any passing British troops or police. The British retaliated with a policy of intimidation that included mass arrests, curfews, and the imposition of the death penalty on anyone caught with firearms. These countermeasures were a complete failure; instead of intimidating the Jews, they quickly radicalized almost the entire Jewish community in Palestine. British soldiers were no longer welcome in Jewish towns, and stores refused to serve them.[37]

ELEVEN

By Blood and Fire

"It is not those who can inflict the most, but those who can endure
the most who will conquer."
—*Terrence MacSwiney, Lord Mayor of Cork*[1]

L ord Moyne's house was in Sharia ibn Zanki, an exclusive residential area
in Zamalek, near the Gezira Sporting Club in Cairo. The police guards
who normally protected the British minister-resident worked in eight-hour
shifts, from 8:00 A.M. to 4:00 P.M. However, most Egyptian police officers did
not bother to adhere to the schedule and often let their men work two or three
hours past the allotted time. Four men should have been on duty, but on November 6, 1944, Lord Moyne had, as usual, dismissed his guards early. Major
A. W. Sansom, the officer responsible for counterintelligence and security of
VIPs in Egypt, had repeatedly argued with Moyne about his safety.[2]

"There is no harder job for a security officer than trying to protect a brave
man," writes Sansom.[3] Moyne had fought as a soldier and had been wounded
in the South African War; in the First World War he had taken part in the Gallipoli campaign, as well as in Egypt, where he was awarded the DSO and bar,
together with three mentions in dispatches. According to Sansom, Moyne hated
being cooped up in an office; he was a man of action—an avid traveler to distant and dangerous places and an amateur archaeologist, who found it galling
to suffer the limitations of security on personal movement. He frequently dismissed his guards, refusing to believe that he was in any danger or convinced
he could handle any threat to his life.[4] There had been attempts by Jewish extremists on the lives of British officials in Palestine, but never outside the district
and certainly not in Egypt.

Sometime after 12:45 P.M., despite the searing sun and exhausting heat,
two young men on bicycles arrived at the minister's house and hid in the portico. A few minutes later, Lord Moyne arrived, and the two men leaped out of
the portico, spraying the minister's automobile with fire from their tommy
guns.[5] Lord Moyne's driver tried to grapple with one of the assassins, but he
was cut down. The second man emptied his machine gun into the back seat,
killing Moyne instantly. The two men dropped their weapons, retrieved their

bicycles, and tried to disappear into the morass of Cairo traffic, but to no avail.[6] After a wild chase, Major Sansom and an Egyptian police officer literally smashed into the two cyclists and apprehended them. Except for a few cuts and bruises, the assassins were not hurt.

Both men belonged to the notorious Stern Gang, although their names were not on a list of fifty suspected members of the terrorist organization.[7] One of the assassins, Eliahu Hakim, was a deserter from the British army; the other, Eliahu Beit-Zuri, was a student at Hebrew University.[8] During the course of their interrogation and trial, they showed no remorse but continued to insist that they were soldiers in a war against the British Empire.[9] On March 22, 1945, the two men were executed by hanging, thus inaugurating the body count of martyrs—in the case of Beit-Zuri and Hakim, the process was delayed.

The extremists considered Lord Moyne to be an anti-Semite, a supporter of the 1939 White Paper limiting Jewish immigration, and pro-Arab; as such, the Stern Gang decided to make an example of him. However, the assassination outraged Jewish leaders in the United States and Britain, as well as Jewish communities around the world. Every effort was made to help the British capture the assassins and destroy the Stern Gang, but Britain's sudden moral ascendency was short-lived.[10] The positive British-Jewish relations and cooperation established at the outbreak of hostilities in 1939 did not survive the post–Second World War political changes in London. The election of the Labour Party in Britain and the cancellation of the new government's pledges to eliminate the White Paper and allow the victims of the Holocaust languishing in detention camps in Europe to enter Palestine eliminated any illusions about the future prospects for an Israeli state as long as the British controlled Palestine.[11] This finally extinguished the goodwill engendered by the aftershocks of Lord Moyne's assassination. The Jewish community responded to the new British government's policy with mass demonstrations and passive resistance. However, the British authorities in Palestine mishandled the situation.

Operation Agatha was intended to destroy the Haganah and severely limit the capability of the Jews to wage war against the British army. For a period of two weeks beginning on June 29, 1946, over 100,000 British troops and ten thousand police carried out extensive searches of Jewish towns and settlements, as well as mass arrests of suspected activists, but failed to apprehend the political or military leaders of the Jews. The operation damaged Britain's image in the United States—a critical consideration, given that the British economy and Britain's security needs depended on America—but more significantly it forced the Jewish Agency to change tactics.[12] Even before this, the Haganah had announced on May 12:

> Present British policy . . . is based on an erroneous assumption: Britain, in evacuating Syria, Lebanon, and Egypt [sic], intends to concentrate her military bases in Palestine and is therefore concerned to strengthen her hold over the mandate, and is using her responsibility to the Jewish people as a means to that end. . . . We would therefore warn publicly His Majesty's Government that if it does not fulfill its responsibilities under the mandate—above all with regard to the question of immigration—the Jewish Resistance Movement will make every effort to hinder the transfer of British bases to Palestine and to prevent their establishment in this country.[13]

Until June 1946, the Jewish Agency and its military wings, the Haganah and the Palmach, preferred a strategy of passive resistance and conventional military tactics. This supplemented by a public relations effort aimed at American policymakers, as well as Jewish financial donors in the United States. Furthermore, Zionist leaders like Chaim Weizmann had extensive contacts and personal relationships with the British political establishment and preferred to avoid excessive violence. However, Operation Agatha proved to be a critical milestone. In attempting to emasculate the military capability of the Jewish community, British forces killed and wounded hundreds of innocent bystanders and roughed up thousands of law-abiding Jews.

In the massive sweeps of Jewish cities, the British spared no effort in trying to hunt down anyone who was a member of the Haganah, Palmach, Irgun, or Stern Gang. In Tel Aviv, they combed the city block by block, meticulously examining basements and attics, and ransacking houses, schools, and even hospitals, often breaking the casts of patients suspected of being militants. Such thoroughness earned the British little honor, and ensured the searing hatred of ordinary Jews.[14]

The British actions proved too much for the more moderate leadership of the Jewish Agency. As an organization, it could not afford to follow the extremists; in order to maintain its leadership and coordination of Jewish resistance, it had to lead the battle against the British. Coming in the wake of the immensity of the Shoah, reports of the British interception and occasional sinking of ships carrying Holocaust survivors from Europe finally turned Jewish opinion in general—and specifically in Palestine—against Britain. Many of the immigrants heading for Palestine who were caught by the British ended up interned in camps in Cyprus. The spectacle of Jews behind barbed wire in transit camps, albeit nothing like the Nazi death camps, enraged moderate and radical Zionists alike. These tragic events, coupled with the overt betrayal of the Labour

Party in London and the actions of the British army in Palestine, ultimately radicalized an entire society and brutalized the British army.

The easy success of the British against the conventional forces of the Jewish Agency drove the Jewish military struggle underground. Although Colonial Office officials had argued against a "get tough" policy, which they claimed would only swell the ranks of the Irgun and the Stern Gang, the British army, led by CIGS Field Marshal Viscount Montgomery of Alamein, advocated the use of harsh tactics.[15] Instead of fighting relatively weak and poorly armed Haganah units, the British military now faced an unseen enemy whose hit-and-run tactics against their troops and other acts of sabotage stretched the limits of their capacity to secure Palestine. All past experience of the British in dealing with a Palestinian insurgency was confined to rural areas and derived from operations undertaken against the Arabs in the 1936 uprising. The Irgun and the Stern Gang, on the other hand, had concentrated their efforts almost entirely on an urban environment and were used to wage urban guerrilla warfare. Furthermore, the political section of the Criminal Investigation Department (CID) of the Palestinian police, the primary unit responsible for intelligence, was well staffed with Arabic speakers, but there was a dearth of personnel with facility in Hebrew or Yiddish.[16]

Previous experience in Ireland against the Irish Republican Army, had demonstrated the futility of waging a clandestine war with conventional means against an enemy who struck quickly and just as quickly disappeared into the general population. For example, during the Irish War of Independence (1919–1921), Michael Collins of the IRA organized flying columns of fifteen to thirty men who ambushed British army units and police on solitary country roads or in city alleys; attacked police barracks; and burned down courthouses, tax offices, and coast guard stations. In 1919 alone, the IRA conducted three thousand raids that resulted in the killing of two hundred police and soldiers.[17] Collins also set up a special unit known as the Squad, which included twelve handpicked volunteers who in a single day executed fourteen members of Britain's intelligence service within a half-hour period.[18] The British responded by creating two special counterinsurgency units—the Royal Irish Constabulary Reserve Force (Black and Tans) and the Royal Irish Constabulary Auxiliary Division (Auxies)—with which to terrorize the terrorists.[19]

The Black and Tans and the Auxies undertook a campaign of violence and intimidation that earned them little except odium as brutal thugs. For Collins, the excesses of these counterinsurgency troops proved to be a considerable advantage, as outraged Irishmen swelled the ranks of the IRA, while such atrocities tarnished Britain's image abroad.[20] Despite the lessons of Ireland, the

British also briefly established a special unit in Palestine to fight terrorism with counterterrorism—effectively a halfhearted attempt at torture and assassination that had the same consequences in Palestine as in Ireland. The debilitating effect of such activities on British personnel was underscored by the ending of the otherwise distinguished career of a highly decorated officer, Major Roy Farran, who was accused of killing a young Palestinian terrorist in cold blood.[21]

In February 1947, Brigadier General Bernard Fergusson,[22] deputy inspector general of the Palestine police, organized a special paramilitary unit made up of squadrons (Q Patrols) that included former soldiers of the Special Air Service (SAS) and the SOE who had experience with the use of terror during the Second World War. These Q Patrols undertook "special measures," such as infiltration, kidnapping, and ambush against the terrorists, which were beyond the scope of the regular police and army.[23] Farran himself described the thrill of being part of this new special force when he received his orders:

> In Jerusalem Police Headquarters the brief was explained to us. We would each have full power to operate as we pleased within our own specific areas. We were to advise on defence against terror and to take an active part in hunting the dissidents. . . . It was to all intents and purposes a *carte blanche* and the original conception of our part filled me with excitement. A free hand for us against terror when all others were so closely hobbled![24]

The squads of the special unit moved about in civilian delivery trucks and dressed like ordinary members of the Jewish community. Their primary missions were to set ambushes and to pick up suspected members of the Irgun and the Stern Gang. However, the Rubowitz case compromised the entire operation. In May 1947, Farran was accused of kidnapping and murdering Alexander Rubowitz, a sixteen-year-old member of the Stern Gang.[25]

The abduction of Alexander Rubowitz became linked with Farran through the discovery at the scene of a civilian felt hat with the letters FAR-AN embossed on the sweatband. Although this was the only evidential link with Farran, and witnesses to the abduction of Rubowitz failed to pick Farran out at three identification lineups, the officer remained a suspect.[26] Moreover, because of the sensitivity of public opinion in support of the Jewish situation in Palestine, particularly in the United States, the British high commissioner decided that Farran should be remanded for trial by court-martial on a charge of murder. Farran was placed under house arrest; suspecting that he might be made a scapegoat, he escaped to Syria.[27]

It is not certain whether any assurance was given, but Farran surrendered to the British consul in Damascus ten days later. The court-martial was held in Jerusalem on October 2, 1947. In the absence of any evidence that Rubowitz was actually dead—his body had not been found—together with the failure of the prosecution to link Farran directly with the alleged crime of murder, the court ruled in favor of acquittal. The disappearance of Rubowitz was never solved. Despite this, on returning to England, Farran resigned his commission, but he could not escape the reach of the Stern Gang. In 1948 a parcel arrived at his house; when his brother Rex opened it, the package exploded, killing him instantly.[28]

This was not, however, the first time that frustration, exasperation, and fear had driven the British authorities to extreme measures. The death of Abraham Stern, usually reported as being killed in a gunfight with the police while trying to escape, was in actual fact an execution. The British told representatives of the American OSS in the Middle East that, when the British burst into Stern's safe house, the place was surrounded, and he was unarmed. But when he raised his arms to surrender, the police opened fire and shot him dead. The explanation the British offered to their American counterparts was that Stern was too dangerous to be left alive.[29]

The creation of the Palestine special unit constituted the establishment of a formal means of dealing with terrorists beyond the reach of the conventional police and security services. It operated for less than a month; that was the extent of the use of guerrilla warfare experts in Palestine.

Early in the war, the British had out of necessity turned to using commando raids and combining the clandestine deployment of Special Forces with the resistance organizations fighting the Axis. After the defeat of France and the withdrawal of the British Expeditionary Force from Dunkirk, Churchill had approved the creation of the SOE, an organization that, ironically enough, adopted many IRA tactics and used them to train the resistance organizations that evolved in Axis-occupied Europe. Both Colin Gubbins and J. C. Holland, who created the conceptual and organizational framework of the SOE, had served in Ireland during "the troubles" and had studied the techniques of Michael Collins's IRA for use with the resistance forces in occupied Europe.

Part of the mandate of the SOE was, essentially, to be politically promiscuous and "ready to work with any man or institution, Roman Catholic or masonic, trotskyist or liberal, syndicalist or capitalist, rationalist or chauvinist, radical or conservative, stalinist or anarchist, gentile or Jew, that would help it beat the nazis down."[30] However, although the SOE trained thousands of Jews to prepare for a possible German occupation of Palestine, as well as hundreds of others for clandestine work behind enemy lines in occupied Europe, it was not called upon to play a role in combating Jewish resistance in Palestine. This was despite the fact that, in the spring of 1943, the SOE had anticipated problems in the postwar Middle East and had proposed to use its contacts with such underground organizations to identify and penetrate potential terrorist groups.[31]

In 1945, the SOE was dismantled and only a handful of experts found employment with the Secret Intelligence Service, also known as MI6. The British faced similar difficulties in Greece, Italy, and France in the postwar period, as left-wing resistance organizations instantly transformed themselves into political organizations antithetical to Britain's policy. In these cases as well, the corporate memory that resided with the SOE was lost when the clandestine organization was dismantled after the end of the war. In effect, MI6 took over the task of dealing with the former underground organizations with almost no knowledge, no contacts, and no understanding of the personalities or political aspirations of the resistance in those countries.[32] In Greece, for example, the British military and political authorities contributed to a chain of events that led to a major uprising in Athens, because they had little knowledge of the susceptibilities and complexities of the postwar Greek political landscape.[33]

Under the best of circumstances, urban guerrilla warfare is difficult to counter without the deployment of excessive force and an extensive network of informants and spies. In most cases, the dynamic between resistance movements and counterinsurgency forces results in the resistance's driving the occupation army into making war on the general population. In the process, the resistance achieves three critical objectives: first, it compels a conventional force to vent its frustration against ordinary, usually law-abiding citizens, which has the effect of driving many to join the underground groups out of anger or fear; second, it uses terror to demonstrate that the resistance is in control of the streets and countryside; and third, it creates martyrs. It achieves the first objective by random killing of soldiers and the assassination of senior officers and officials; the second by acts of sabotage against major targets; and the third by inducing the enemy to execute resistance fighters, who are subsequently elevated to the status of national heroes.

Between 1939 and 1946, the British security and intelligence services had successfully identified, arrested, and killed numerous Jewish militants, but after Operation Agatha they faced a new crop of unknown recruits who had joined the clandestine struggle in the interim period.[34] Prior to 1946, the Haganah and the Jewish Agency had, directly and indirectly, assisted the British in rounding up members of the Stern Gang, but this cooperation ceased as a result of British counterinsurgency actions. Another consequence of Operation Agatha was that it brought about an alliance between the Haganah, the Irgun, and the Stern Gang. The collaboration of what used to be termed "terrorists" with the official military arm of the Jewish Agency added credibility to the Irgun and to the Stern Gang. The change of tactics by the established and respected leadership of the Jewish community effectively endorsed and legitimized the clandestine war of terror initiated originally by the Irgun and the Stern Gang.[35]

Furthermore, all attempts at intimidation by the British backfired, because every act of British brutality acquired for the Jewish resistance legions of supporters and thousands of recruits. The British tried imposing long prison sentences, whippings, and executions to combat the "terrorists," but the Stern Gang and the Irgun responded in kind. In one instance, when the British condemned two young members of the Irgun to fifteen years' imprisonment and eighteen lashes, the Stern Gang threatened retaliation. In December 1946, the British had one of the boys whipped, and in response the Stern Gang kidnapped one British major and three NCOs and had them put to the lash.

The British gave in and did not whip the second boy. In April 1947, the British sent to the gallows four Irgun fighters, followed by more executions. Shortly afterward, the Irgun captured two British NCOs and strung them up on a tree.[36] A sense of frustration, helplessness, and rage afflicted the British police and soldiers in Tel Aviv after the two British NCOs were executed, triggering a rampage. By the time order was restored, six Jews had been killed, sixteen wounded, and dozens of Jewish shops burned. British soldiers drove an armored car through a funeral procession; police officers opened fire on a bus, and shot at a crowded café.[37] However, from then until the independence of Israel, the British avoided further executions.

In effect, the underground organizations had taken control of the streets and had successfully challenged the British over the security of Palestine. As every occupation army has discovered—and as subsequent armies usually forget—the battle tips in favor of the force that can guarantee security. Nothing was beyond the reach of the Jewish terrorists, and very quickly Palestine became dangerous for British personnel—death lurked in an ally or on a main street in broad daylight—and safety became an illusion.[38] Although the British could concentrate overwhelming force in a specific city or region, impose curfews, and conduct mass arrests, the Irgun and the Stern Gang cadres simply melted away and struck in another place. Both organizations had gone underground even before the outbreak of the Second World War and avoided the curfews by issuing instructions to regional members to use their own discretion in carrying out operations. The British managed to incarcerate almost 50 percent of the Palmach membership, but this merely left the field open to the more experienced Irgun and Stern Gang to wage a nonconventional battle against a frustrated conventional force.[39]

The assassination of Lord Moyne, the execution of British officers, and killing of ordinary soldiers in Palestine demonstrated that no one was immune from the reach of the urban guerrillas. The Irgun further underscored this on July 22, 1946. On that day, a small group of Irgun fighters disguised as Arabs brought explosive charges in milk churns into the hall outside the Regency Café in the basement of the King David Hotel. That particular part of the hotel, five floors of the south wing, had been appropriated by the British and was used as an administrative headquarters. After the explosives were set, an anonymous woman telephoned the hotel switchboard operator and said that there would be an explosion in a few minutes, and that everyone in the hotel should be evacuated.[40]

Unfortunately, her warning was ignored. At 12:37 P.M., the explosions went off and five floors and twenty rooms were instantly reduced to rubble. Ninety-two Britons, Jews, and Arabs lost their lives. The victims included British military and civilian officials, as well as soldiers, clerks, typists, cleaners, drivers, and messengers. The terrorists' target was the headquarters of the British military administration of Palestine as well as several departments of the Palestine government. Equally significant, the hotel was a symbol of British imperial authority—lamentably for the British it was also the center for their counterintelligence and counterinsurgency operations.[41] By contemporary standards, its devastation and the subsequent loss of life were modest, but the destruction of the hotel effectively crippled the ability of the British security services to participate in the clandestine war being waged by the Jewish resistance.

The Jewish Agency condemned the bombing as "a dastardly crime" perpetuated by a "gang of desperados" and called upon the Jews of Palestine "to rise up against these abominable outrages." This was not mere rhetoric; it was genuine revulsion against the indecent assault of terrorism perpetrated in the heart of Jerusalem. Most of the victims were ordinary men and women—soldiers, innocent Jews, and Arabs—and of those the majority of the dead and wounded were Arabs.[42] The Jewish Agency organized a memorial for the next day, and at 3:00 P.M. on July 23, all work and traffic came to a standstill as people stood for three minutes of silence to mourn the dead.

Again, for a brief moment the British gained the moral high ground, only to squander the opportunity almost immediately. The attack on the King David Hotel and its consequences proved to be a flash in the pan—an instance in which the Jewish leadership had the ability to stay the wave of terrorism that was engulfing all of Palestine.[43] But the British either misunderstood or did not care to differentiate between moderates and radicals. Eight days after the destruction of the King David Hotel, the British isolated Tel Aviv and conducted a four-day house-to-house search that resulted in the arrest of eight hundred Jews, who were subsequently sent to detention camps. None had taken part in the bombing.[44]

The hasty rounding up of Jews was more an act of desperate impotence in the face of a determined and implacable foe than a carefully thought-out operation based on reliable information. It was difficult for the security services to apprehend the terrorists, because it was not easy to penetrate the close-knit organizations of the extreme groups. For example, Eliahu Hakim, one of Moyne's assassins, had been a childhood friend of Amihai Paglin, the chief of operations for the Irgun.[45] After his arrest, despite interrogation and the prospect of death by hanging, Hakim revealed nothing about the Stern Gang or the Irgun.

British public relations suffered another major blow when, shortly after the bombing, a confidential letter written by General Sir Evelyn Barker, C-in-C Palestine, in which he proposed to punish "the Jews in a way the race dislikes—by striking at their pockets."[46] Barker proposed to ban all fraternization between British soldiers and the Jewish community. The letter, written shortly after the blast, became a public relations nightmare for the British and did considerable damage to Britain's image around the world, particularly in the United States, by giving credibility to allegations of anti-Semitism and distracting attention from the King David Hotel tragedy.[47] Although the Haganah terminated its relationship with the Irgun and the Stern Gang as a result of the bombing, the violent tactics of the latter maintained a measure of legitimacy in the Jewish community. Furthermore, the Irgun escalated the number and intensity of its attacks. In addition to new bombings, kidnappings, and retaliatory executions of British soldiers, the Irgun also attempted to assassinate British officials outside Palestine.

The British political and military establishment in London and Jerusalem assumed that they could hold on to Palestine, regardless of the new postwar geopolitical architecture and the emotional and gut-wrenching tragedy of the Holocaust. Furthermore, the British army was ill equipped to fight a war in which there were no set boundaries delineating civilians from combatants. MI6, MI5, and field intelligence failed to appreciate the differences between the conventional military represented by the Haganah, paramilitary units such as the Palmach, and the more radical Irgun and Stern Gang.

The British relied considerably on electronic intelligence (code breaking) with which to identify Jewish members of illegal organizations. One problem with this method was that just about every member of the Jewish community belonged to an underground organization. The British were thus overwhelmed with suspects. Another difficulty was that the Irgun and the Stern Gang, as well as other extreme groups, were small and not easily penetrated by double agents. For example, when splinter members of the Stern Gang known as the Homeland Front assassinated Count Folke Bernadotte on September 17, 1948,[48] British intelligence and security in Palestine had failed to uncover the plot because the splinter group was small and had recently broken off from the Stern Gang. Although the CID was able to infiltrate the Haganah and the Palmach, and had the minutes of executive committee of the Jewish Agency within hours of its meetings, it was unable to penetrate the Irgun or the Haganah.[49] Conversely, the Jewish underground had successfully placed agents in the police and in several departments of the government of Palestine. In 1947, the JIC (Joint Intelligence Committee) in London reflected on the fact that many in the Irgun and the Stern Gang had been trained by MI6 and SOE and were using this tradecraft against the British.[50]

While MI5 was responsible for dealing with the Jewish resistance, MI6 was also operating in Palestine, but it was not charged with gathering intelligence on the radical Jewish organizations. Instead, it was directed to prevent the entry of refugees from Europe. According to Tad Szulc, the Labour foreign secretary Ernest Bevin directed MI6 to implement special operations against the Jews.[51] Until this time, only the SOE had undertaken sabotage, subversion, and assassination operations, while MI6 had always confined its activities to intelligence gathering.

Not surprisingly, MI6 turned to former SOE personnel to carry out a campaign of sabotaging the transportation of refugee Jews to Palestine. In 1941, the SOE had organized special teams to undertake several sabotage missions in the planned invasion of Vichy-controlled Syria, which had included expertise in blowing up ships. The expert chosen to train with the SOE in the techniques of destroying ships and other acts of sabotage was Cathal O'Connor; after the war, MI6 incorporated O'Connor's SOE team into its organization as the Kent Corps Specials.[52]

The mission of the Kent Corps Specials was to prevent ships chartered by the Jewish Agency from reaching Palestine. Generally, the members of this force attempted to sink such ships when they were manned by skeleton crews and anchored outside harbors. In the summer of 1947, the two largest ships procured by the Jewish Agency, the *Pan York* and the *Pan Crescent*, arrived in Marseilles and Venice respectively. The Kent Corps Specials managed to set off an explosion on the *Pan Crescent*, but the Jewish organization Mossad le'Aliyah

Bet (Institute for Illegal Immigration), forerunner of Mossad, managed to have the ship repaired and, along with the *Pan York*, it left for the harbor of Constanza in Romania.[53]

The British considered using their signals intelligence (SIGINT) capability to misdirect the refugee ships by emitting false radio messages and directing them to where they could be intercepted by the Royal Navy. However, it was decided that the Jewish organizations would soon discover this tactic and alter their radio frequencies, thus making it impossible for Britain's SIGINT monitors at Government Communications Headquarters (GCHQ) to track them.[54] Instead, the British stationed four RAF photoreconnaissance squadrons in Palestine, which, in conjunction with SIGINT, led to the interception of seventeen ships in 1946. This provoked new attacks by the Irgun and the Stern Gang and further damaged Britain's image abroad. Most of the ships were not seaworthy, and many of their passengers had to be interned in British camps on Cyprus.[55] This is also what ultimately happened to those aboard the *Pan Crescent* and the *Pan York*. Though seaworthy, they were blockaded by the Royal Navy and escorted to Cyprus, where their fifteen thousand Jewish passengers were discharged and interned on January 1, 1948.[56]

During World War II, many Jewish refugees were able to leave the Balkans with the assistance of American military transport, as well as with the help of operatives dressed as U.S. personnel.[57] During the Axis occupation of the Balkans, the SOE had created escape routes than ran from the Balkans, through Greece, to several of the thousands of Greek islands in the Aegean, and finally to Palestine and Egypt. The purpose of these secret routes was to facilitate the escape of the hundreds of thousands of British soldiers who had been trapped after the withdrawal of the British Expeditionary Force from Greece in April 1941. Several of the SOE operatives were Palestinian Jews who used their wartime expertise to arrange for the smuggling of refugees into Palestine.

British protests to Washington fell on deaf ears. The administration of Harry Truman was not willing to stir public opinion in the United States by being linked to Britain's anti-Jewish policies. Beyond the odium of preventing victims of the Holocaust and the death camps from leaving the shores of a continent that had heaped upon them every imaginable indignity, culminating in mass extermination, there was the issue of the Jewish American vote. Consequently, the British changed tactics and tried to cast the Jewish underground railroad as part of a Soviet plot to flood Palestine with thousands of hard-core communists. Although the specter of an army of Soviet communist Jews arriving in the West as refugees was largely self-delusion on the part of MI6, the Soviet KGB did manage to send several handpicked agents masquerading as refugees.[58]

Overall, British intelligence efforts in Palestine were a dismal failure. Richard Aldrich, in his authoritative study of British and American intelligence during the Cold War, concludes: "Palestine was the intelligence war that Britain lost. The British security forces outnumbered their adversaries by more than twenty to one, a better ratio than Britain enjoyed later in its successful campaign against the guerrillas in Malaya (seventeen to one)."[59]

The British intelligence community, as well as the government, also underestimated the impact of the Holocaust, not just on Jewish communities around the globe, but also on wider public opinion in Europe and the United States. The British embargo preventing Jewish refugees—mostly death camp survivors— from entering Palestine outraged and kept reinvigorating the radical organizations. Meanwhile, ironically, groups such as the Irgun and the Stern Gang were using British-trained Jews against the British forces. For example, in 1941, the British had armed and trained Yaakov Meridor and David Raziel to assassinate the Mufti. Raziel was killed during the unsuccessful operation, but Meridor then became leader of the Irgun and, before the British arrested him again, he recruited the man responsible for setting the charges for the explosions that blew up the King David Hotel.[60] Ultimately, the clandestine war forced the British to withdraw from Palestine and, on May 14, 1948, Israel became a nation-state. The covert field of operations immediately shifted to the Muslim regions of the Middle East and now involved the Americans.

Although the undeclared war in Palestine lasted for only two years, it manifested a microcosm of a never-ending cycle of terrorism and counterterrorism that would bedevil policymakers in Washington and London, along with their intelligence establishments, for decades to come. In May 1948, when Israel became a republic, it subsumed all the existing radical, extremist, terrorist organizations. Some former terrorists returned to civilian life; others found employment in the new Israeli intelligence and security services. After 1948, the terrorists of yesterday were combating the terrorists of tomorrow.

Having faced defeat at the hands of the Israelis in 1948, some Arabs turned to clandestine operations with which to fight the state of Israel, and eventually the British and the Americans too. Unlike former members of the Irgun and the Stern Gang, who could begin new political or professional careers in modern, democratic Israel, their Arab Palestinian counterparts faced a lifetime as professional refugees. Each failure to reclaim Palestine compounded their sense of alienation and betrayal. The loss of Palestine stained the consciousness of generations of Arabs in the Middle East, as well as Muslims in the rest of the world. Many chafed at the inability of the Arabs to defeat Israel, which they linked to the secularism of the Arab state. To many Arabs, occupied Palestine—as they defined Israel—was part of a history of humiliation inaugurated by the demise of the Ottoman Empire and the end of the Sultan-Caliph.

The first Arab-Israeli War in 1948 attracted thousands of Muslim Brothers, who volunteered to fight in Palestine. Although embodying defeat for the Arabs, Palestine became a training ground for radicals and Islamic militants. At the same time, organizations such as the Muslim Brotherhood became the shock troops of the Egyptian government; soon, however, they turned against the secular and bankrupt monarchy of King Farouk. In the kaleidoscope of Middle East politics, secularism, pan-Arabism, and pan-Islam competed relentlessly in a life-and-death struggle for control of the Muslim states. In the period after the Second World War, Arab secularism and nationalism attained a superficial supremacy, which spawned a new set of leaders, whose policies antagonized first the British and later the Americans. The antidote to Arab nationalism was perceived to be Islam, and toward this end the Anglo-American intelligence services were attracted as moths to a flame. In the first decade after the Second World War, the Americans continued the British policy of securing the services of a Muslim strongman—either a religious or secular figure—who could hold sway over the Middle East on behalf of Washington, and at the same time deny the region to the Soviets.

TWELVE

The CIA and Nasser: A Muslim Billy Graham

"Nasser's attempt at the role of a male Cleopatra playing off the
two superpowers and British stubbornness in clinging to the remnants
of empire were bound to bring a clash, and a bad one, though not one
in which we lost, as we did, the confidence of everyone."
—*Dean Acheson*[1]

As early as 1947, the Truman administration believed that Egypt seemed primed for Soviet penetration, unless the United States replaced the decaying British colonial stranglehold on the Middle East with a benevolent American security system. The Americans were convinced that lingering British colonialism, as well as Egypt's post–Second World War slide into chaos, would eventually facilitate communist penetration of the country. These fears were underscored in January 1952, as mass demonstrations swept through the streets of Cairo and Alexandria, reminiscent of the violence in 1882. At that time, the Egyptians had taken to the streets to protest the increasing and pervasive foreign influence that had reduced their country to a client state of Britain and France. Unfortunately, the 1882 riots triggered a chain of events that gave a succession of governments in London cause to transform Egypt into a quasi-British colony.

In 1952, well-organized demonstrations wreaked violence and destruction in response to a British attack on an Egyptian police barracks on January 25. The root cause for the riots was the failure of the British to leave the country after the Egyptian government unilaterally canceled the 1936 Anglo-Egyptian Treaty.[2] The treaty was Britain's legal facade for occupying the Suez Canal Zone and, although the Egyptian government unilaterally annulled the treaty, the British refused to leave. The Suez Canal was just too important to British interests to be left in the hands of the Egyptians—at least that was the thinking in London. Suez had become synonymous with empire; a forlorn notion that still resonated in London's Tory circles, which took heart in the return of Churchill's Conservative government in 1952. The Egyptians did not agree, and they retaliated when British forces remained in place. Over sixty thousand workers left their jobs in the Canal Zone; many carried out acts of sabotage before withdrawing their services, and hundreds volunteered for guerrilla warfare training.

The British were convinced that the Egyptian auxiliary police were responsible for arming and training guerrilla groups. Tensions reached breaking point when rioters shot dead an Irish-born nun after forcing their way into a convent. In retaliation, British troops seized the town of Ismailia, just outside the Canal Zone. On January 25, 1952, British armored forces stormed a police barracks in Ismailia, leaving forty-three dead and many more wounded.[3] The news both enraged and electrified the Egyptians. The next day, Black Saturday, thousands of students in Cairo took to the streets; very quickly they were joined by thousands of cadres from the Muslim Brotherhood as well as from other radical political organizations—including the policemen dispatched to control the crowds. Many from the MB had also taken part in the guerrilla campaign against the British in the Canal Zone between 1951 and 1952. Just for this occasion, the MB had formed a temporary alliance with the Egyptian communists and socialists, and they collaborated to make the demonstrations particularly vicious.[4]

The rioters stormed the streets, focusing their anger on foreigners unlucky enough to be seized by the mobs and on buildings identified with the West. Throughout the day, frenzied demonstrators, along with cool-headed and well-organized professional agitators, torched 475 structures. According to Wesley Adams, second secretary of the American embassy, the mobs concentrated primarily on movie theaters, fashionable restaurants, every liquor store in Cairo, and any foreign establishment they came across, including the Shepheards Hotel and the Turf Club—both grand symbols of British imperialism.[5] In addition, they murdered or maimed any European who inadvertently came across their way, along with innocent Egyptians caught in the foreign establishments under attack. While Cairo burned, Farouk hesitated, hoping to exploit the crisis. After two hours, he ordered the army to restore order. Meanwhile the British had dispatched their own troops, and there was a strong probability that they would clash with Egyptian forces.

Earlier, in late 1951, American policymakers and diplomats had feared that the ongoing dispute between Egypt and Britain would give Moscow a window of opportunity for expanding Soviet influence in the Middle East; the January riot was just such an occasion. Dean Acheson at the State Department and Allen Dulles at the CIA were also convinced that Egypt and Britain were on the brink of war, and that further deterioration of the situation in Cairo would lead to an even greater crisis. Acheson assumed that, if the United States did not

"damp down these fires," it "threatened to involve North Africa in bloody conflict."[6] Acheson adopted a primarily covert approach in dealing with Egypt, to
avoid offending both the British and the Israelis.

Although crypto-diplomacy was not new to international relations, it was
usually conducted by individuals on behalf of states and not by intelligence
services. This new diplomatic role eventually placed the CIA in a position of
not just executing policy (both covert and overt) but also of becoming an instigator of political events—in Egypt and elsewhere. The instrument of this new
policy mechanism was Kermit Roosevelt, grandson of President Theodore
Roosevelt and senior officer in the CIA's Middle East division.

During the Second World War, Roosevelt had served in the OSS and had
been stationed in Cairo to establish an indirect channel to Egypt's government
and monarchy. In October 1951, Acheson placed Roosevelt in charge of a special ad hoc interdepartmental committee to study the situation in Egypt. The
committee eventually concluded: "Our principle should be to encourage the
emergence of competent leaders, relatively well-disposed toward the West,
through programs designed for this purpose, including, where possible, a conscious, though perhaps covert, effort to cultivate and aid such potential leaders,
even when they are not in power."[7]

Roosevelt had come to know Farouk in 1942 as an OSS officer during the
tense days when the British had occupied the palace grounds in Cairo and had
forced the hapless king to purge his government of pro-Axis ministers.[8] At that
time, Roosevelt had established a good relationship with the monarch, despite
meeting under such difficult circumstances. Roosevelt earned Farouk's trust
and became an unofficial advisor to the monarch, while establishing excellent
contacts with the king's immediate entourage. Roosevelt promoted the idea
with Farouk that " 'after the war there could be a New Deal' for Egypt that would
make the king the 'first ruler of a free Egypt in two thousand years.' "[9]

In the late 1940s, Roosevelt arranged for several individuals, mostly from
the Egyptian police services, to be sent to the United States and trained in
fighting communism and subversion.[10] After demobilization, Roosevelt joined
the *Saturday Evening Post* as a correspondent and traveled extensively throughout the Middle East. However, he was brought back to intelligence work in 1950,
and two years later was dispatched to Cairo in order to save Farouk and Egypt.
The State Department had tried to convince the Egyptian government to take
part in the defense of the Middle East through the establishment of the Middle
East Command (MEC), which would also have included the British.

Like them, the Americans believed that Egypt was the natural leader of the
Arab states, and that the Middle East could consequently be brought under a

U.S. security umbrella, thus safeguarding the petroleum routes to and from the Persian Gulf. American interests were focused on securing access to the petroleum-rich Gulf region, as well as on the added urgency caused by the outbreak of the Korean War on June 24, 1950. Coming on the heels of the Greek Civil War (1946–1949), which the Americans believed was caused by Soviet ambitions in the Balkans and in the Eastern Mediterranean, the Korean conflict was further evidence of encroaching communism in the world in general, and in the Middle East in particular.

Even though the plan for the creation of the Middle East Command collapsed because of Egyptian objections, Acheson believed that Egypt could be brought around, if only the country could achieve stability. The U.S. secretary of state was convinced that the volatility of Egypt was the by-product of the corrupt Wafd government, and that Farouk, with American support, could stabilize the country, bringing it to join an Anglo-American alliance. Kermit Roosevelt returned to Cairo in early 1952 and attempted to convince Farouk to reform Egypt's corrupt government.

The American agent planned to orchestrate a peaceful revolution, casting Farouk in the role of an efficient dictator, to replace the corrupt political system. Part of the scheme involved giving money to Farouk with which he was to bribe the Brotherhood into supporting the monarchy. However, in the opaque world of Middle East politics, even a consummate player such as Roosevelt was a neophyte. Farouk took the idea a step further and tried to organize his own coup, by working with the MB to create a fundamentalist Muslim state. Toward this end, the Waqf (Islamic Religious Foundation in Egypt) declared Farouk a descendent of the Prophet Mohammed, with the new name of Al Sayyid Farouk I. The Muslim Brotherhood, for their part, simply took Farouk's American money and used it to establish an alliance with the Egyptian Free Officers, a secret military organization planning to overthrow the monarchy.[11]

After about a month, having finally realized that Farouk was utterly hopeless, Roosevelt returned to Washington. Although the monarch had initially displayed interest and willingness to address the country's problems, he had just as quickly turned his attention to augmenting his own considerable wealth, pornograph collection, and predilection for sexual orgies, while Egypt continued to wallow in corruption. The alternatives were either the austere and xenophobic Muslim Brotherhood or the Free Officers. The U.S. ambassador to Cairo, Jefferson Caffery, was in favor of the Egyptian army's taking power; he argued that the military would be a stabilizing force and, although practically useless in fighting external enemies, it would be able to maintain internal security.[12]

The same rationale had been applied to other crisis-ridden countries, such as post–Second World War Greece, which had appeared to American political leaders and policymakers to be on the brink of a communist takeover.[13] In these cases, the military of the exposed countries offered the best guarantee of keeping the corrupt political establishment in check and the communists at bay. Both in Greece and Egypt, the American tactic was to exploit malleable political figureheads but establish independent channels with the military through the CIA. Eventually Washington lost control over the covert relationships, leaving the CIA to conduct an independent policy toward client states. Not so surprisingly, as events played out in the Balkans, the Middle East, and South America, a military uniform was no guarantee against greed and corruption. Certainly in the case of Egypt, and later Iran, the CIA's support of military strongmen or monarchs contributed to the erosion of the political center, thus leaving the body politic at the mercy of corrupt generals or extreme religious zealots.

By 1952, the U.S. embassy in Cairo had picked up rumors of a pending coup being organized by Egyptian officers. As far as Caffery and Roosevelt were concerned, the Egyptian army offered a better alternative to salvage Egypt from systemic corruption emanating from the palace and the political establishment. Acheson agreed, and Roosevelt set the wheels in motion to find links with the Free Officers, the secret organization committed to the overthrow of the monarchy. Roosevelt sent Miles Copeland, an intrepid irregular CIA officer, to Egypt to seek out these officers and ascertain their intentions with respect to the West, and especially toward the United States.[14] Copeland established contact with intermediaries and eventually with Nasser, the leader of the Free Officers.

In March 1952, Roosevelt paid another visit to Cairo and initiated a series of meetings with Nasser and the Free Officers. According to Copeland, Nasser confirmed for Roosevelt that there would be a coup and asked the American if the United States would abstain from interfering.[15] It was also agreed that that U.S. recognition of the new Egyptian regime would include a private understanding that the "preconditions for democratic government did not exist and wouldn't exist for many years." References to "reestablishing democratic processes" and "truly representative government" would be reserved for public consumption only.[16]

Four months later, on July 23, 1952, Nasser and his Free Officers seized power and abolished the monarchy. The army-dominated Revolutionary Command Council (RCC), headed by Nasser, controlled the new regime; General Mohamed Neguib was installed as president of the Egyptian republic. In actual fact, he remained a figurehead, and Nasser ruled the country from behind the scenes. The speed and efficiency of the coup took most embassies, including the British, by surprise.[17] According to Wilbur Eveland, the U.S. embassy, as well as the CIA, were equally astonished by the coup, and he also claims it was unlikely that Kermit Roosevelt had any role, direct or indirect, in the overthrow of Farouk.[18] Copeland, for his part, states that the CIA station chief in Cairo relied on intelligence almost exclusively from officials and politicians connected with the Farouk regime, and "in fact, the station chief believed right up to the day of the coup that Farouk was following the secret activities of the Free Officers on a day-to-day basis and would lower the boom on them when the strategic moment arrived."[19]

These conflicting claims over what the CIA and the U.S. embassy knew about the coup, and to what degree American officials were involved in the overthrow of Farouk, are not so much contradictory as by-products of the overlapping agencies that loosely constituted the CIA in the early 1950s. Roosevelt and Copeland were members of the Office of Policy Coordination (OPC), an intelligence unit established in 1948 to conduct covert operations at arm's length from the U.S. government. Although its budget and staff came from the CIA, the head of the OPC reported to the secretaries of State and Defense, bypassing the director of the CIA.[20] At best, it was an awkward situation that created serious divisions within the CIA at a time when the White House administration was not certain what direction to give the new agency.

The head of the OPC, Frank Wisner, was a naval officer and wealthy lawyer from Mississippi, well connected to the Washington political establishment. Unlike the career-minded intelligencers of the CIA, Wisner selected the personnel of the OPC from the ranks of Ivy League gentlemen of independent means, along with a handful of eccentrics and mavericks who had served in U.S. intelligence during the Second World War. These differences further expanded and exacerbated the segregation of the OPC from the other directorates of the CIA. For example, the officers of the Office of Special Operations (OSO), the counterpart to the OPC, were professionals of the wartime OSS, along with a few former members of the FBI. Unlike the well-heeled gentleman of the OPC, the rank and file of the OSO, writes Copeland, "lived on their salaries and had modest homes in nearby Virginia."[21] Copeland adds that most members of the OPC belonged to "the Metropolitan Club and/or the Chevy Chase Country Club, and had upmarket homes in Georgetown or Wesley Heights."[22]

As the grandson of a famous president, Kermit Roosevelt was also a member of Washington's privileged class, yet he also belonged to that remarkable group of wartime adventurers that Frank Wisner and Allen Dulles had brought into the OPC who were accustomed to operating on their own initiative with minimal oversight from their immediate superiors. As Evan Thomas observes: "Along with his cousins Archie and Cornelius, Kim Roosevelt formed a kind of cell-within-the cell inside the CIA."[23] While outside the agency, the Roosevelts enjoyed a social primacy that enabled them to access the political establishment on a social level, occasionally bypassing the chain of command.

Roosevelt's home in leafy northwest Washington was just one block away from that of General Walter Bedell Smith, Eisenhower's former chief of staff at SHAEF (Allied headquarters) during the Second World War; Smith was one of the first directors of the CIA and undersecretary of state in the Eisenhower administration. The Roosevelts were also close family friends of Allen and John Foster Dulles, director of the CIA and secretary of state respectively. On more than one occasion, Kermit Roosevelt reported directly to the secretary of state, defense secretary, or even the president himself, over the heads of his immediate superiors.[24] Thomas adds: "When, in those early years, Archie Roosevelt's Lebanese-American wife, Selwa, worried whether she was doing the socially 'right' thing, Archie cut her off. 'Look,' he said. 'What we do is right.'"[25]

Certainly, Kermit Roosevelt exercised considerable latitude in directing America's covert policy in Egypt. Yet his unparalleled access to the U.S. political leadership also meant that Roosevelt did not act on his own but executed the objectives of the current White House administration. In 1952, U.S. policy was to keep Nasser in power and protect him from internal and external enemies preparing to assassinate Egypt's first independent leader in almost two millennia. An integral element of American policy was to establish Nasser as the leader of the Muslim world, and particularly as a reliable American ally. Copeland's succinct description of this policy was to transform Nasser into "a Muslim Billy Graham": one who would use his pulpit to guide that world toward a defensive alliance with the West and away from the clutches of the Soviet Union.[26]

THIRTEEN

The Road to Perdition: The Gehlen Organization

"It was a visceral business of using any bastard
as long as he was anti-Communist."
—*Harry Rositzke*[1]

I n less than one year, the euphoria following the end of the Second World War turned into uncertainty that escalated into Cold War paranoia. Upheavals in Europe, Asia, and the Middle East pointed to Soviet aggression as the culprit. The allies of yesterday quickly became implacable foes and soon stared each other down across an unbridgeable ideological divide that manifested itself in a series of crises. In December 1945, the Italian Communist Party had 1.8 million members and captured 19 percent of the popular vote in Italy's elections; in 1948, the CIA's Office of Special Operations (OSO) had to intervene covertly to prevent the communists from forming a government. The French Communist Party had nearly one million members; in November 1947, at the request of the Cominform (Communist Information Bureau), two million workers went on strike in France, followed by additional strikes in Italy. Civil war broke out in Greece in 1946 and threatened to bring that country into the communist bloc. In the Far East, the Chinese Civil War had also resumed, and in less than three years it brought the communists to victory.[2]

On March 12, 1947, the Truman Doctrine declared America's intentions to checkmate the Soviet Union in Greece, Turkey, and Iran. A year later, in February 1948, the communists took over Czechoslovakia. Four months later, the Soviets blocked rail and land access to Western sectors of Berlin, and the United States undertook a massive airlift to break the Soviet blockade and supply the beleaguered city with food and fuel. In June 1950, North Korean communists overran most of South Korea and threatened to annihilate the U.S. forces trying to defend what was left of the country. To make matters worse, the Soviets had successfully tested their first atomic bomb in 1949, bringing an end to the U.S. nuclear arms monopoly.[3]

The Cold War landscape confronting the United States was, for the most part, terra incognita, with the prospect of a nuclear holocaust looming on the horizon. George F. Kennan's "Long Telegram," dispatched on February 22, 1946, while he was ambassador to the USSR, was the first attempt to provide a comprehensive analysis of Soviet intentions. Kennan's interpretation of Kremlin policy offered a picture of a formidable adversary who viewed the outside world as hostile, which provided justification for Stalin's dictatorship. Whereas the U.S. government had no other intelligence to either support or repudiate Kennan's view, the Soviet Committee for State Security (KGB) immediately provided Stalin with a copy of the telegram.[4] The Truman administration and later that of Eisenhower were desperate for information on the Soviet Union in general and Soviet intentions in particular. However, America's nascent intelligence community remained in the dark, grasping at scraps of information that promised a peek into Moscow's objectives and frantically seeking agents who could prise open the Kremlin's secrets.[5]

One alternative was to look to previous enemies who had had experience in penetrating the Soviet Union. The old and well-tried maxim, "my enemy's enemy is my friend," brought U.S. army intelligence officers, and later the CIA, into occupied Germany to employ former German military intelligence officers and then, through them, former members of the Nazi SS and Gestapo. The catalyst for the CIA's relationship with Hitler's henchmen was Reinhard Gehlen, a German army general in charge of the German armed forces' Eastern Front political and field intelligence organization, Fremde Heere Ost (Foreign Armies East [FHO]), which had focused on gathering intelligence and mounting covert operations against the Soviet Union during World War II.

Toward the end of the war, Gehlen became convinced that, although Germany was going to face defeat in its struggle against communism, that fight would continue under the leadership of the Americans. To participate in this new conflict, as well as to position himself and his organization for a new role in postwar Germany, Gehlen had buried three complete sets of secret documents, including files on Soviet agents who had spied for his organization.[6] Two weeks after the end of the war, Gehlen surrendered to Captain John Boker, an officer in the U.S. Army Counter Intelligence Corps (CIC). For months, Gehlen was treated as just another prisoner of war; only after the Soviets had expressed interest in him did the U.S. Army finally debrief the German spy chief, at the G2 (divisional intelligence) level. During his interrogation, Gehlen offered to gather tactical intelligence for the United States, as well as to reactivate his agents in the Soviet Union and place them at the disposal of the Americans.[7]

The CIC finally became convinced that Gehlen had a great deal to offer and that his organization with its espionage networks, developed in Russia during the war, could be reactivated and made to work for the United States.[8] In August 1945, they brought Gehlen and his closest associates to Washington to continue negotiations. Eventually Gehlen signed an agreement with the Americans that reinvented the remnants of the FHO as the Gehlen Organization—a private intelligence agency working for U.S. Army intelligence.[9] Gehlen and his associates were eventually installed in Pullach, near Munich, in December 1947.

From 1945 to 1947, however, when Gehlen and his associates passed temporarily to the control of the U.S. military, responsibility for dealing with the Germans was given to the OSS Secret Intelligence Branch under the direction of Frank Wisner.[10] It is not certain if Wisner ever met Gehlen in person, although some CIA accounts assert that Allen Dulles sent Wisner, who shortly afterward became head of the Office of Policy Coordination, to make contact with Gehlen.[11] Eventually Wisner, as head of the OPC, would make considerable use of the Gehlen Organization, employing it as a front to sift through the refugee camps for possible volunteers with whom to penetrate the communist bloc. The Gehlen Organization also undertook other less reputable tasks in the Middle East on behalf of the OPC.

In Germany, the Gehlen Organization began searching the displaced persons camps for information and for possible volunteers willing to return to their countries of origin behind the Iron Curtain, to fight the Soviets. At the same time, Gehlen's scouts also enrolled former members of the Nazi intelligence organizations, many of whom were wanted war criminals, although he had promised his American masters that he would not recruit such unsavory individuals. Gehlen's excuse was that the ex-Nazis were valuable intelligence assets who had considerable knowledge on the Soviets. However, the information garnered from these sources was unreliable at best, and before long it proved a useful means for the Soviet intelligence services to penetrate the Gehlen Organization and feed the CIA carefully doctored intelligence. Almost from the moment that the Gehlen Organization was back in business, the Soviet NKVD (forerunner of the KGB) had planted dozens of agents amongst the Russians in the DP camps, who easily slipped into the Gehlen Organization as trusted intelligence assets.[12]

The cost of resurrecting Hitler's FHO was high, both financially and morally. The United States spent over $200 million to maintain approximately four thousand full-time members of the Gehlen Organization, while surrendering the moral high ground by embracing Hitler's former henchmen in the name of fighting communism. The intelligence produced by Gehlen's information factory at

Pullach was fabrication sprinkled with occasional tidbits of tactical data on the Red Army in East Germany. Gehlen's information contributed to the escalating tensions between the Soviet Union and the United States by indicating that the Red Army was poised to overrun Western Europe. Naturally, the perception of a hostile Soviet Union kept Gehlen on the U.S. payroll, while his reports of pending communist aggression found a receptive audience in Washington.

The emerging Cold Warriors and rabid anticommunists found validation in Gehlen's gloomy forecasts. The Pentagon also found Gehlen's affirmation of the Kremlin's warlike posture reassuring and a useful tool in prompting Congress for higher military appropriations. The fabrication of alternative realities was not new for Gehlen; after all, in Nazi Germany he had learned how to accommodate his leader's appetite for such information—Hitler only wanted to know what he wanted to hear.[13] According to Victor Marchetti, the CIA's chief analyst on Soviet capabilities—who made these comments after retirement from the agency—little had changed for Gehlen in his new incarnation as America's spy:

> The agency [CIA] loved Gehlen because he fed us what we wanted to hear. . . . We used his stuff constantly, and we fed it to everybody else: the Pentagon; the White House; the newspapers. They loved it, too. But it was hyped up Russian boogeyman junk, and it did a lot of damage to this country.[14]

However, three years after the end of the war, the work of American military intelligence in Germany began to wind down, while the size and cost of the Gehlen Organization had spiraled beyond the capability of U.S. Army divisional intelligence. After much pressure from the Pentagon, Gehlen and his small of army of spies were passed on to the newly established CIA.[15] Few within the agency, however, were interested in or willing to take responsibility for Gehlen. Richard Helms, the man directly responsible for Gehlen, wrote in his memoirs that, in addition to the moral objections that many in the agency had about working with Gehlen and his less reputable associates:

> CIA officers in Germany were uniformly dismayed by the noisy and insecure activity of the RUSTY [Gehlen Organization] operatives. The intelligence, particularly on East Germany, was valuable, but as seen by our German station, it hardly offset the poor security and discipline of the RUSTY operatives.[16]

Shortly after the CIA assumed responsibility for Gehlen and his agents, the OSO and OPC merged to become the agency's clandestine service. Many in the CIA opposed working with former Nazis, arguing that, once this became known, it would give the Soviets a propaganda bonanza. Others were troubled by the moral ambiguity that filtered U.S. policy toward the ex-Nazis. Officially the Gehlen group was paid to provide the U.S. intelligence service with information about the Soviet Union, but they also worked secretly for the OPC, headed by Wisner. In this capacity, Gehlen's agents helped the OPC mount covert operations and served as the link between that agency and former members of the Sicherheitsdienst (SS Security Service, SD), the Gestapo, and other disgraced elements of the wartime German military-intelligence apparatus.

The rehabilitation of Gehlen and his associates was only a small part of a major program aimed, in the interests of national security, at recruiting German scientists, technicians, and engineers to continue working on the development of rockets and new weapons systems. In the confused and paranoid period that followed the end of the war, the U.S. government believed that the new threat from the Soviet Union outweighed any moral reservations over the employment of Nazis. The transfer of the Nazi scientists to the United States took place under the cover of Operation Paperclip, which in due course facilitated the relocation of over 1,500 Germans and their families.[17] Operation National Interest was another secret maneuver to bypass U.S. laws and acquire the services of Nazis and Nazi collaborators who could be politically useful against the Soviet Union. Among them were Nazi intelligence and security specialists, as well as Nazi collaborators, who quietly moved back into the government services of the Eastern European countries.

In this new kind of Cold War, survival consisted not just in emerging from the bomb shelters in the aftermath of an atomic exchange, but in preventing a communist onslaught from overwhelming the free world. The fear of communism and the mechanics of a Cold War that left little scope for a major military clash, unless both sides were willing to risk a nuclear holocaust, fostered the shadow war of spies and the politics of subversion. Despite the absence of industrial-scale killing, at least in the first decades of the Cold War, successive American governments and the political-military-intelligence establishment in Washington believed that the struggle with the Soviet Union was a matter of survival.

Key to victory was the continuing financial success of the West, which more than rivaled the promise of Soviet collectivist socialism and which relied on unencumbered access to the oilfields of the Gulf states; that meant that

there had to be a strong, unambiguous U.S. policy for the Middle East. However, the political reality of American support for the new state of Israel clashed
with the geopolitical realities of Arab nationalism, backed by petroleum. The
postcolonial world of the Middle East, cluttered with vociferous nationalist
movements and tugged in several directions by an ambitious leadership, offered
considerable opportunity for Soviet penetration. For U.S. policymakers in the
late 1940s, the region was a maze of crosscurrents: national ambitions, religious
zealotry, and conflicting loyalties.

Like the British before them, the Americans attempted to find a single
strongman who could create order out of chaos and preempt Soviet intrigues in
the Middle East. Nasser was a likely candidate—leader of a genuine national
mass movement and head of the largest Arab country, which was emerging as
the leading state in the region. Yet Nasser could not wholeheartedly cast his lot
with the Americans, because the Israeli factor was too great a chasm to overcome. Postwar American administrations, beginning with Truman's, had also
had to tread carefully in an effort to balance support for Israel with the establishment of closer ties with the Arab world. Accordingly, contact with Nasser
evolved on two levels: a formal diplomatic relationship with all its limitations,
and much more substantive links carried on clandestinely through the CIA.
Furthermore, when the CIA could not directly provide certain services required
by Nasser, it was able to use the Gehlen Organization, which could provide the
necessary expertise and personnel, offering the U.S. government the fig leaf of
plausible deniability.

Despite the efforts of the Muslim Brotherhood and other groups hostile to
his regime, Nasser continued to dodge the assassin's bullet. One factor was
luck; however, a more tangible consideration was that Nasser had an exceptionally capable security apparatus, equipped and trained indirectly by the CIA.
The agency's involvement with Nasser was a consequence of the fear of communism that swept across America after the Second World War. The Truman administration, as well as subsequent governments, became interested in Nasser
because of the Suez Canal, the petroleum of the Gulf states, and the fear that
British and French colonialism would pave the way for the Soviet Union to gain
control of the Middle East (1945–1958). After the collapse of the Soviet Union
(1991), the new threat to the Middle East would be seen to be the rapidly expanding influence of political Islam,[18] whereas after the end of the colonial era,
communist penetration of the region remained a fixation with the Americans.

Another critical factor that shaped early American policy toward the Middle East was the foundation of Israel. Although the ramifications of that momentous event grew in intensity over time, it immediately skewed relations

between the United States and the Muslim world. Yet one mitigating factor that elevated the United States above the former European empires was the fact that the Eisenhower administration was clearly opposed to colonialism. In the 1950s, Allen Dulles, the new CIA director, and his brother, John Foster Dulles, the secretary of state, along with numerous congressmen, believed that the Suez Canal in particular had become a symbol of Western imperialism in the Middle East.[19] Such apprehensions had brought the Truman administration, and the early CIA, to consider Nasser a potential bulwark of stability in the region and hence an obstacle to communism.

Thus the CIA's developing relationship with Nasser was part of the United States' evolving security architecture, aimed at containing Soviet expansion. In the early years of the Cold War, the dearth of information on the Soviet Union was hampering American efforts to discern Soviet intentions and to counter Russia's influence around the world. Immediately after the end of the Second World War, the fledgling postwar American intelligence units, mostly remnants of the wartime OSS and CIC, lacked intelligence networks both within and outside the Iron Curtain, and they could barely keep up with Russia's formidable KGB deployed widely across the Cold War battlefields.

Eventually, the bits and pieces of the various ad hoc intelligence units operating in Europe were amalgamated within the CIA. Initially the CIA consisted primarily of the OSO. It had emerged out of the Strategic Services Unit (SSU), which was in turn the remnant of the wartime OSS, concentrating on intelligence gathering. The OPC, on the other hand, was established to undertake clandestine and paramilitary operations. It was created to counter covert Soviet aggression, as well as that of its satellites, and to undertake these tasks with the use of propaganda, economic warfare, sabotage, and subversion, as well as to encourage and support resistance against the communist regimes.[20]

Initially the CIA was itself merely a shell that facilitated salaries, supplied space for offices, and provided other administrative support for its two branches, OSS and OPC, which retained a considerable degree of autonomy and remained distinct from the CIA for several years. Frank Wisner, the first head of the OPC, did not answer to the head of the CIA; in fact, according to Evan Thomas, Wisner had complete autonomy and nominally reported to George Kennan, then head of the State Department Policy Planning Staff. In one respect, the autonomy of the OPC was useful, in that it permitted the administration to invoke the doctrine and distance itself from the more distasteful activities of the new covert directorate. However, the early years of the CIA reflected an institution that was not only less than the sum of its parts, but also honeycombed with further subdivisions of semi-independent units. The OPC, later renamed the Directorate of Operations, branded the CIA as the agency of dirty tricks—an image that continues to dog the organization today.

At first, both the OSO and the OPC desperately needed information and agents, over which they had to compete with friends and enemies alike. Almost before the Second World War was over, the intelligence organizations of the victorious Allies, including the neutrals, began to probe and grope their way around the human wreckage of postwar Europe and Asia in search of potential agents with whom to penetrate the Soviet Union. Among the ruins, CIA officers stumbled into an exotica of strange individuals and shadowy organizations, coughed up by the death throes of old Europe.

The human flotsam of information peddlers and confidence tricksters, along with small armies of self-proclaimed revolutionaries, anticommunists, arms dealers, smugglers, displaced persons, and down-on-their-luck princes and kings, were nothing more than manufacturers of intelligence and proved to be less than useless. American intelligence officials navigating through these hucksters discovered that, no matter how much they paid for secret information, it was invariably unreliable, and with enough cash they could purchase any number of lies or conspiracy theories, almost on demand.[21] Evan Thomas identifies one such example and comments:

> The thirst for intelligence inside the Iron Curtain gave rise to a whole new industry, paper mills churning ever-more fantastic tales of revolt and intrigue in the "denied areas." One U.S.-financed émigré group, known as TsOpe by its Russian initials, even blew up its own headquarters and blamed the KGB. The idea was to show that the Russians really feared TsOpe, and thus Washington should increase its funding.[22]

Many fanciful notions were entertained by American intelligence officers, driven by an almost obsessive determination to unlock the Kremlin's secrets. No idea or plan seemed too crazy; some attempts to create anticommunist forces were downright incredible. For example, the U.S. Army enlisted forty thousand refugees (from the 700,000 in the displaced persons camps) in labor service units to assist with rubble clearance in postwar Germany. Since many of these refugees came from East Germany or countries behind the Iron Curtain, they appeared to be ideal candidates for work inside the Soviet Union.[23]

Wisner used the Gehlen Organization to comb through the labor units, eventually recruiting approximately five thousand volunteers for a "secret army" to be trained as a guerrilla force to invade the USSR after a nuclear war. Others were formed into stay-behind units that would undertake sabotage in the aftermath of a Soviet occupation of Western Europe. Several were selected for secret missions behind the Iron Curtain. For some years, dozens of volunteers were parachuted into the Ukraine and other parts of the Soviet Union either to spy on the Russians or to establish links with the resistance movements that existed mostly in the imagination of men such as Wisner. Many of the volunteers were Ukrainian refugees who had fought for the Nazis in the Second World War, and Wisner deluded himself into believing that these hapless individuals would join groups of indigenous Ukrainians to wage a shooting war in the Carpathian Mountains.[24]

Tragically, the notion of resistance movements fighting Russians was a mirage that consumed the lives of hundreds if not thousands of Eastern European volunteers who had been persuaded to allow themselves to be parachuted into the communist bloc, ending in torture and death. Some of the volunteers had blood on their hands from working with the SS during the war, and undoubtedly rough justice caught up with them. However, many others were just desperate people trying to escape life in the camps, and some were even idealists who, seduced by Wisner's siren song, went blindly to their doom.[25]

The actions of men such as Wisner must be placed in the context of the first decade of the Cold War. He was not a lone Cold Warrior: most of America's political and military leadership was hostage to the notion of an expanding communist empire that threatened to gobble up Europe, the Middle East, and Asia. In the first years following the Second World War, Soviet actions gave every indication to Washington's political and military establishment of aggressive expansionism. Events in Europe and in the Third World, whether instigated by Moscow or not, only served to feed an escalating Cold War paranoia. The absence of any hard intelligence on Moscow's intentions (or spurious information from self-serving sources such as Gehlen) made matters that much more difficult and served to heighten the suspicion that, behind every upheaval, every nationalist movement, and every conflict, there lurked the machinations of monolithic communism.

FOURTEEN

A New Kind of War: Subversive Operations and the CIA

"Whenever we want to subvert a place, the
British own an island within reach."
—*Frank Wisner to Kim Philby*[1]

Almost two weeks after the end of the Second World War in Europe, a Nazi officer in full SS uniform and fully armed, along with two other Germans, walked into U.S. Army headquarters in Salzburg, Austria, to surrender. Prior to his capitulation, Lieutenant Colonel Otto Skorzeny had been on the Allied list of most wanted Nazis but, despite a desperate effort to find him, the Waffen-SS officer remained elusive. Allied-controlled Radio Luxemburg, as well as the local newspapers, had made repeated appeals for his whereabouts, but all to no avail.[2]

In the early days of May 1945, the Allied intelligence organizations were confronting a fantastic but potentially nightmarish scenario. According to fanciful rumors seeping out of the remnants of Nazi Germany, Hitler had prepared an alpine redoubt from which the most fanatical of his troops would fight to the death. In the heady days following the surrender of the German armed forces, the last thing the Allies wanted was to fight an unnecessary protracted battle that would result in needless casualties.[3]

Yet the rumors persisted and, according to speculation from self-deceiving or wishful-thinking Nazi prisoners, Hitler had indeed issued such orders and had selected Otto Skorzeny as the commander of this last hurrah. Viennese-born Skorzeny had been one of Hitler's most intrepid and skillful commandos; his exploits included the audacious rescue of Mussolini from his mountain prison in 1943. Skorzeny and an elite group of commandos swooped down on the prison by glider—an almost impossible feat—and plucked the Italian dictator from his stunned guards. A year later, Skorzeny organized the infiltration of English-speaking Germans behind American lines; during the Ardennes offensive in December 1944, the Battle of the Bulge, they posed as American officers, causing considerable confusion.

On December 19, Skorzeny's notoriety reached new heights when a German air force officer, wearing a U.S. Army uniform, surrendered to the Americans near Liège in Belgium. He informed his interrogators at U.S. First Army HQ that Lieutenant Colonel Otto Skorzeny, with sixty-four German commandos, had crossed the lines in order to assassinate General Dwight Eisenhower, the Supreme Allied Commander, at his headquarters outside Paris.[4] The plot to kill Eisenhower turned out to be a hoax, but during the investigation a joint Anglo-American counterintelligence team came across a Nazi sabotage organization created by Heinrich Himmler, and in the process became convinced of the existence of the so-called alpine redoubt, which would, combined with a guerrilla war, permit the Nazis to hold out against the Allies even after the fall of Germany. According to SHAEF counterintelligence:

> The general consensus was that, after the liberation of Germany, Skorzeny would organize a terrorist campaign to . . . cause political upheaval by assassinations, terrorism, and acts of sabotage at political meetings in a such a manner as to make the blame appear to rest with Left-wing elements and Communists . . . these operations . . . will be directed toward the perpetuation of the Nazi terror with a view to dominating the German population and preventing collaboration with the Allies. The knowledge that there is a Nazi headquarters and the possibility of a Nazi revival would keep alive Nazi doctrines and encourage the formation of autonomous movements throughout Germany.[5]

Because of his many daredevil exploits, as well as his loyalty to Hitler, the Anglo-American counterintelligence team suspected that Skorzeny had been given command of the Nazi alpine redoubt, as well as the post-occupation terror campaign. As far as U.S. Army intelligence were concerned, if they could locate Skorzeny, they could verify whether there was such a hidden Nazi fortress nestled deep in the mountains. True enough, Skorzeny could have easily told them that the idea of a last-ditch defense was only a figment in the imagination of a handful of Nazis who had sought comfort in the mad musings of Hitler's last days. Skorzeny had made a tour of the so-called redoubt and, after discovering it to be a fantasy, had decided to surrender. He made repeated attempts to contact the Americans, but to no avail. He had sent letters to the nearest U.S. headquarters, but they went unanswered. Meanwhile, other American units were searching feverishly for any sign of him.[6]

So, eleven days after the end of the war, Skorzeny, along with one of his staff officers and an interpreter, came down the mountain to present himself to the U.S. Army in Salzburg. Arriving at the first American camp on the outskirts of the city, he identified himself and offered to surrender, but the duty sergeant was not impressed. However, the American informed the Germans that if they were indeed as important as they believed they were, he would provide them with a jeep and a driver, so that they could surrender to divisional headquarters. Once in the city, Skorzeny, still armed, tried again to surrender, but the first U.S. officer he came across, a major, told him to go elsewhere.[7]

Eventually someone realized that this was the infamous Skorzeny, and the comic surrender minuet came to an abrupt end. Subsequently, Skorzeny was treated with appropriate severity, befitting a dangerous prisoner. He was disarmed and stripped to ensure he was not carrying any poison. The SS commando leader was then dispatched with his colleagues to Salzburg, with a military policeman holding a machine gun to his face and was put on display for the media. Forced to sit with his hands tied behind his back, he gave an interview to the Allied press.[8] Skorzeny faced trial on several charges, including wearing an American uniform and using poison bullets. He was acquitted, but the Americans had no intention of letting him go free.

On July 27, 1948, with the assistance of three former SS officers, Skorzeny escaped from Darmstadt Interment Camp. For several years, the ex-commando traveled from Germany to France, Spain, and Syria, setting up ratlines to facilitate the escape of war criminals from Germany, which eventually enabled many unrepentant Nazis—some influential, some not—to find their way to South America and later to the Middle East. For several years, Skorzeny found employment with the Gehlen Organization—he had occasionally worked with Reinhard Gehlen in the last years of the war—until he finally settled in Spain, where he soon established a profitable international engineering consultancy and arms dealing business.[9]

During the 1950s, Skorzeny became a key player in a complex covert operation that brought a mixed bag of former German military officers and Nazi intelligence and security specialists to Egypt. The other player in this clandestine mission was a diminutive Italian-American with a checkered past but very influential friends in the U.S. State Department. Carmel Offie had grown up in a large, poor Italian family in Sharon, Pennsylvania. His parents had immigrated from the vicinity of Naples, and his father worked as a railroad hand in Portage. At the age of seventeen, Offie traveled to Washington and found employment at the Interstate Commerce Commission as a typist and stenographer.[10]

Three years later, in 1931, Offie applied to and was accepted by the State

Department as a clerk. After a short stint in Honduras, he was posted to Moscow at the end of 1934 as confidential secretary to the American ambassador, William C. Bullitt. Offie had a natural disposition to ingratiate himself and swiftly assumed the role of courtier. He became indispensable to the ambassador and undertook all manner of tasks, from professional to personal. Offie was at Bullitt's beck and call almost twenty-four hours a day, and in return the ambassador promoted him to the rank of attaché. Over time, Offie acquired the social graces missing from his background and developed an impressive list of professional and social contacts.

In August 1936, Bullitt was transferred to Paris and brought along his protégé. Burton Hersh describes Offie as: "Bullitt's pet, his performing spaniel, whose moist-eyed deferential efficiency while scampering through his protocol niceties left international society clapping."[11] Thanks to Bullitt's efforts, Offie now became third secretary at the Paris embassy. He excelled as a social butterfly who could charm men and women for Bullitt's benefit. He cultivated a number of people—a skill he perfected over the years—who proved useful in helping him navigate the back stairs of Washington's establishment. For example, he was on excellent terms with Marguerite "Missy" LeHand, President Franklin Roosevelt's private secretary. Occasionally he would send her a variety of gifts ranging from perfume to foie gras. Thus he was able to use Missy as a back channel to Roosevelt and have her give Bullitt's reports top priority, while singing his praises to the president.[12]

After Bullitt fell from Roosevelt's favor and lost the Paris embassy in August 1940, Offie was assigned to the Navy Department, but he continued to serve Bullitt in his spare time. When Bullitt began his campaign to destroy Sumner Welles, it was Offie who distributed handbills on Capitol Hill describing Welles's propositioning of two railroad porters for sexual favors. The scam worked, and Roosevelt had to dismiss Welles, but it did Bullitt little good; the president could not forgive Bullitt for his part in wrecking the reputation of one of his friends.[13] In March 1943, Offie was transferred to the staff of the Allied Advisory Council for Italy. In Europe, he acquired a unique knowledge of the personalities of the governments-in-exile and refugees from Eastern Europe, as well as the dozens of anticommunist groups that had worked for the Nazis and were now offering their services to the Allies.

Carmel Offie's career in the foreign service came to an abrupt end. In 1947, a routine check on a diplomatic pouch in Frankfurt revealed an unauthorized $4,000 in cash from Offie. Further investigation revealed unauthorized traffic in diamonds, black-market rubles, and even three hundred lobsters flown into Frankfurt on a military aircraft. Offie had little choice but to resign from the

State Department, but his many acquaintances pitched in to find him new employment. A few months later, Chip Bohlen, one of Offie's influential patrons, arranged for him to meet Frank Wisner of the newly established Office of Policy Coordination. According to Bohlen, Offie's primary expertise was his extensive knowledge of the Eastern bloc. This was not idle praise; Offie had worked with Allen Dulles in setting up Radio Free Europe and had recruited émigrés from countries occupied by the Soviet Union to broadcast behind the Iron Curtain.[14]

As a result, Wisner took on the disgraced former State Department officer as his personal assistant with responsibility for refugee affairs. As was the case with his previous employers, Offie proceeded to ingratiate himself with Wisner. He took care of Polly, Wisner's wife, as well as his children, and was soon accepted as a trusted member of the family. In addition, Offie became Wisner's social mentor. In the words of James Angleton: "Offie was a world-class sophisticate who could put a stiletto in an opponent and offer him a treatise on the cognac he was serving at the same time."[15]

The former State Department official did indeed have a feel for intelligence work and had learned at an early age to lead a double life. Like the spies he sought, Offie was expert at being all things to all people, while maintaining a secret alter ego. Offie was a homosexual, a circumstance that was lethal to any career in government or private industry in the 1940s and 1950s.[16] This experience, as well as a lifetime of perfecting skillful manipulation, enabled Offie to undertake difficult and covert tasks. At the same time, becoming part of the OPC and working in the shadowy world of spies, double agents, and within flexible moral limits, was a liberating experience for a man who had so much to hide. In the OPC, Offie dropped all attempts to hide that he was gay and had the confidence to live openly as who he was. To a great extent, Offie's newfound freedom was exorcised by the magnitude of the secrets he had to protect.

Carmel Offie and Frank Wisner became close friends. Above and beyond the courtier-master relationship, they also shared a passion for taking on the Soviets. This new epic struggle against communism overshadowed any qualms about the kind of individuals who could be drafted to fight for the greater good. Consequently, in this global contest, Hitler's henchmen, including his handmaidens of death, had to be harnessed in the covert battle of the Cold War. The race was on among the Allies who had fought and defeated Nazi Germany to enlist the services of German scientists and engineers.

Offie became the czar of Operation Paperclip—the covert program that tracked down German rocket specialists and engineers and brought them to the United States—and the deeper Operation Bloodstone, which sought out specific Nazis and wartime collaborators who could be induced, one way or another, to work for the Americans within the Soviet empire.[17] Offie knew that the Nazi collaborators who had survived the liberation of their countries and had quietly slipped back into their former professions were particularly vulnerable to persuasion or blackmail.[18] Others, particularly the Nazis recruited under the auspices of Operation Bloodstone, were brought into the United States and employed as intelligence and covert operations experts. These men and women were not misguided or even opportunistic collaborators who in the name of anticommunism had embraced Hitler's nightmare for Europe: they were high-ranking Nazi intelligence and security specialists on several war crimes lists.

Operation Bloodstone originated primarily in the State Department. On June 10, 1948, the State, Army, Navy, Air Force Coordinating Committee (SANACC) approved the operation, and a month later the Joint Chiefs of Staff expanded the activities of Bloodstone to:

> comprise those activities against the enemy which are conducted by Allied or friendly forces behind enemy lines . . . [to] include psychological warfare, subversion, sabotage, and miscellaneous operations such as assassination, target capture, and rescue of Allied airmen.[19]

In effect, the OPC had come into existence in order to implement covert attacks against the Soviet Union and its allies. One of the OPC's first forays into clandestine paramilitary operations was a disaster. In 1949, representatives of a Polish underground organization called Freedom and Independence (WIN in its Polish acronym) had approached Polish émigrés in London and claimed that they could mobilize an army of guerrilla fighters and overthrow Poland's communist regime.[20]

Initially, the OPC was skeptical, but WIN provided photos of its attacks against military installations and police stations, and even evidence of a pitched battle against Soviet tanks. This was followed by intelligence reports from WIN agents inside the Polish Ministry of Defense that included information on the Red Army's order of battle in Eastern Europe.[21] In November 1950, the OPC signed an agreement with WIN according to which the Polish underground, in return for training, money, personnel, and air drops, would provide espionage and conduct subversive work for the Americans.[22] The Americans also involved MI6, since Britain's spy agency had control over Eastern European émigré groups in London and could activate agents behind the Iron Curtain.[23]

MI6 agreed; unfortunately, however, they sent none other than Kim Philby to Washington to coordinate the Anglo-American guerrilla warfare campaign in Poland. No one knew at the time that Philby was a longtime Russian mole and part of a Soviet deception operation against the West. His opening tactic was to offer the Americans the use of a group of former Nazi counterintelligence officers the British had secretly positioned in Canada. These Germans had employed Polish and other Eastern European informers during the war, and many who had survived had managed to conceal their treason and find employment with the new communist regimes. Consequently, they were vulnerable and could be forced to cooperate with Western agencies under the threat of exposure, which would mean torture and certain death for them. As a result, the ex-Nazi counterintelligence experts were able to provide the CIA with long lists of potential agents.[24]

For eighteen months the CIA poured money and equipment into the Polish resistance, and then things began to go wrong.[25] The intelligence from WIN on the Red Army did not match information from reconnaissance photographs and communication intercepts. Furthermore, some of the agents parachuted into Poland or those activated by the former German counterintelligence experts disappeared after coming into contact with WIN, while the radio communications from others became increasingly suspect. Philby, who had been intimately involved with the program, came under suspicion by MI6, was recalled to London, and was quietly severed from the intelligence service. Finally, in December 1951, the Polish government revealed in a two-hour radio broadcast that WIN had been a deception operation all along. All the agents had been arrested the moment they came into contact with WIN, and the Polish and Soviet intelligence services had benefited greatly from the gold, weapons, and equipment generously provided by the CIA.[26]

A similar situation had developed in Albania. As in the case of WIN, Operation Valuable was a joint OPC-MI6 effort to train expatriate Albanians and return them to Albania to instigate an uprising against the communist regime or at the very least start a long drawn-out guerrilla war. Operation Valuable had originated with the British, who believed that Albania was ripe for counter-revolution. London wanted to punish the communist regime of Enver Hoxha, the dictator of Albania, for supporting the communists in the Greek Civil War (1946–1949). The Greek conflict had cost the British dearly in financial terms and eventually invoked the Truman Doctrine that ended Britain's sphere of influence in southeastern Europe and the Eastern Mediterranean.[27]

Albania was a viable target because of its location. The country had become separated from the Eastern bloc communist territories after the Tito-Stalin split in 1948. In the event of a successful uprising, the Russians would not be able to access Albania by land. Planning for the operation took place later in 1948, and the OPC and MI6 began to scour the DP camps for volunteers. The search produced two hundred Albanian refugees, most of whom were malnourished and in poor health.[28] MI6 trained their volunteers in Malta, while the OPC readied their Albanians in southern Germany. The British proposed to deliver their freedom fighters by sea on the Albanian coast, and the Americans planned to drop theirs by parachute.[29]

The British initiated their part of the operation in October 1949 by arranging for a flotilla of privately chartered boats to land twenty-six volunteers on the Albanian coast. They were ambushed almost immediately. Four were shot, but the rest managed to escape by crossing the mountains into Greece.[30] Several more attempts also met with failure, and by 1951 the British withdrew from the operation, leaving Albania to the Americans.

Earlier, in 1950, while still cooperating with Whitehall, the OPC—on Carmel Offie's initiative—had created Company 400, which included fifty Albanian volunteers. The OPC was in contact with the exiled political wing of the Albanian freedom fighters, the Balli Kombetar (National Front), based in Rome and Athens. MI6 and the OPC, however, could not agree on who should actually lead the Albanian resistance movement. There was considerable wrangling between the Allies and, according to Kim Philby's memoirs, there was some American frustration over the initial British lead in the operations. Philby mentions Wisner complaining, "Whenever we want to subvert a place, the British own an island within reach."[31]

Some of those selected by the Americans and the British had collaborated with the Germans and Italians during the war. One of their protégés, Xhafer Deva, had been Albanian interior minister under the Nazis. He had helped to establish the militarily incompetent yet dreaded 21st Skanderbeg Mountain Division of the Waffen-SS, for which he had recruited ethnic Albanians from Kosovo. On February 4, 1944, Deva had personally supervised a massacre of Albanian resistance fighters by the Gestapo. Another American choice, Hassan Dosti, had been justice minister with the Italian occupation government.[32] When the OPC tried to bring these men to the United States, it faced considerable obstacles, because some of their "guests" were wanted war criminals, and some did not even possess a passport.[33]

Carmel Offie nevertheless managed to convince U.S. Customs and Immigration officials to look the other way, in the national interest. The Albanians traveled to the United States on September 19, 1949, and opened the New York office of the American-backed Free Albania Committee. When the head of the organization died of a heart attack in New York, Offie lobbied hard to have Hassan

Dosti, the former fascist collaborator, replace him. Shortly after he managed to install Dosti as head of the committee, Offie was forced to leave the OPC.

Meanwhile, the OPC proceeded with the infiltration of the Albanian volunteers, but all attempts at transporting them by air or sea ended in tragedy. In one such effort, in June 1951, three groups were dropped by parachute. The first group was annihilated upon landing. The second managed to hide in a house, but they were surrounded by Albanian security forces, who set fire to the place, and all the occupants were burned alive. Of the third group, two were killed, and another two taken into custody. Shortly after, they were placed on trial.[34] The one group of parachutists who managed to survive began transmitting regularly, but it soon became apparent that they were under the control of Albanian state security.[35]

The Americans did have some success in bringing volunteers into Albania using the overland routes from Greece. However, those few Albanian infiltrators who managed to survive confronted a largely hostile population. Most people were too terrified of the Albanian security service to take part in any resistance movement; they were equally afraid of cruel retribution if they did not turn in the freedom fighters.[36] In April 1954, the Hoxha regime held a week-long show trial during which captured infiltrators confessed working for the CIA and made pitiful and futile attempts to plead for mercy. After this debacle, the OPC quietly shut down the Albanian operation.[37]

By 1949, Carmel Offie had become the OPC facilitator of the undesirable leftovers from the Second World War. Thousands of men and women on the wrong side of the new order in Europe and displaced by the new frontiers made ready cannon fodder for the OPC's secret wars, and thus they came within Offie's purview. Effectively, the disparate networks of émigrés, wartime collaborators, and war criminals became the CIA's talent pool for the clandestine war, even after the OPC merged with the agency. At the same time, all covert operations involving the Gehlen Organization, as well as the general use of Nazis, German counterintelligence specialists, and former German military, were routed via Offie.[38] In effect, Offie managed to transpose his flexible morality to OPC policy, and to ameliorate any qualms that his superior, Frank Wisner, may have had about employing war criminals or sending hundreds of men to certain death behind the Iron Curtain.

Ironically, Carmel Offie fell victim to the rabid anticommunist paranoia with which he and Wisner had helped to infect the Washington establishment and the American public. On April 25, 1950, on the floor of the U.S. Senate, Senator Joe McCarthy angrily denounced the subversive activities of certain government employees, although he did not mention Offie by name, and loudly proclaimed that a certain member of the CIA, formerly of the State Department, was a homosexual who spent his time hanging around the men's room in Lafayette Park.[39] Before he was forced to leave the OPC, however, Offie had helped to establish the paradigm for harnessing the services of Nazis, fascists, collaborators, and a variety of émigré groups and desperate volunteers from the DP camps in America's fight against the specter of world communism.

The pattern remained with the CIA, as the agency continued to rely on individuals and groups of radicals and extremists of one kind or another to do its bidding. However, such individuals and organizations often had their own, different agendas. Nazis and fascists, their erstwhile collaborators, fugitive war criminals, and the handful of genuine, self-sacrificing anticommunists were relatively easy to control. Once America's spy agency moved beyond its futile attempts to wage guerrilla warfare in Eastern Europe and the Soviet Union, it encountered new obstacles and troubled waters. While it met with immediate success in Latin and South America, it faced a very different situation in the Middle East. Working with Arab nationalists and Muslim extremists in the name of anticommunism may have served the short-term interests of all the parties concerned, but it also stimulated forces that, once released, ultimately spun out of control.

FIFTEEN

Nasser's Nazis

"We were the reason [Nasser] was out of reach of would be assassins since we had ourselves designed the security arrangements around him."
—*Miles Copeland, CIA*[1]

The thinking in Washington reflected the conviction that the chaos following in the wake of old Europe's decolonization of the Middle East made the region vulnerable to Soviet penetration. The same rationale held true later in the Korean War, and then in Vietnam. The Central Intelligence Agency's initial relationship with the up-and-coming Arab nationalists in Egypt led by Gamal Abdel Nasser and later CIA involvement with the Muslim Brotherhood—and ultimately with the mujahidin in Afghanistan—took place in the context of U.S. fears of communism. The Americans were facing a shooting war in Korea, which had broken out in 1950 and which, unlike the later Vietnam conflict, was a true battlefield confrontation between East and West. Although the Russians did not participate directly in the Korean battles, they openly bankrolled the North Koreans, and later the Chinese, to fight the United States–led United Nations forces.

To counter Moscow's plans for gobbling up the oil-rich states of the Persian Gulf, the Americans looked to embracing a pro-U.S. Middle East strongman who could manage the secular and religious aspirations of Arabs and Muslims respectively. The British had attempted to cast al-Husseini of Mecca in such a role and even Ibn Saud, but neither had found resonance in the Muslim world. Arabia was too sparsely populated and too isolated to lead the Arabs, let alone all Sunni Muslims. Neither the Sharif of Mecca nor the new king of Saudi Arabia could fill the shoes of the Sultan-Caliph—a void that had left the Islamic community rudderless. After the Second World War, Nasser, as leader of the largest Muslim and Arab country, held the promise of rallying the Middle East away from the Soviets; he was indeed the Muslim-style Billy Graham sought by the CIA.[2]

The conundrum facing the Americans was that any relationship with Nasser would not only complicate U.S. support for Israel, but would also run counter to the spirit of the historic Anglo-American alliance. Washington could neither abandon the Israelis for Egypt—a country important to a degree, but not a state with petroleum reserves; nor could they permit their support for Nasser to interfere with the transatlantic special relationship. Consequently, America's links with the Egyptian leader had to be forged in secret and therefore had to be turned over to the CIA. In effect, the Office of Policy Coordination (OPC), and more specifically its Near Eastern Division, suddenly had to assume a covert diplomatic role. And matters became considerably more complicated when Nasser asked Kermit Roosevelt to help him train his military intelligence and internal security services.[3]

The mission had to be conducted covertly, so Allen Dulles turned to the Gehlen Organization and its stable of Nazi intelligence and security specialists for the appropriate know-how. Gehlen recalls that "at the request of Allen Dulles of the CIA, we at Pullach did our best to inject life and expertise into the Egyptian secret service, supplying them with the former SS officers I have mentioned."[4] The Germans had the necessary recent experience in police and security work, as well as in intelligence and counterintelligence operations. They were willing to work cheap and, since most were on several wanted lists, they could be trusted to keep their work secret. Admittedly, most of them were also rabidly anti-Semitic, but that only made them all the more acceptable to Nasser.[5] Unlike the CIA's experiments in Poland, Ukraine, and Albania, the OPC's task in Egypt was not to destabilize the Egyptian government, but to protect Nasser and indirectly enable him to wage relatively harmless, low-intensity warfare against the British.

Gehlen, for his part, attempted to subcontract the entire training mission to Otto Skorzeny, but the former SS commando leader was reluctant to accept, because he did not believe the Egyptians could pay him what he considered himself to be worth. However, Gehlen promised Skorzeny that his salary would be augmented with CIA funds, which would be laundered through the Gehlen Organization. Skorzeny remained skeptical, but "he was approached in a routine manner," relates Miles Copeland, "then at a higher level, then through a personal visit from a certain well known Major General of the American Army, and finally through his father-in-law, Dr. Hjalmar Schacht, Hitler's former Minister of Finance."[6] Because of these entreaties—or more likely because he saw some potential profit—the ever mercenary Skorzeny agreed to help.[7]

Though it is well documented in memoirs, interviews, and autobiographies, the exact trail of the connection between the CIA and Nasser's Nazi advisors has intentionally been rendered obscure. The available CIA documents do not explicitly reveal any direct involvement of the CIA in placing former Nazi officers in Nasser's security apparatus. However, when pieced together, the cumulative evidence is convincing that the agency played a significant role in the process of setting up a new Egyptian intelligence and security service. The secondary literature, mostly by American authors, strongly indicates that a deniable Egyptian operation was launched by Dean Acheson of the State Department and Kermit Roosevelt of the CIA.

The operation was conducted with the connivance of the government of Konrad Adenauer through the agency of the Gehlen Organization (and the West German Bundesnachrichtendienst, the Federal Intelligence Service, BND, which superseded it at Pullach in 1956), and with the purpose of advising the Egyptian leaders on intelligence and security and of recruiting ex-Nazi experts for Egypt. Initially, Skorzeny was brought into the operation, probably by Allen Dulles, who is also said to have supplied the leading intelligence and security professional, Joachim Deumling, although CIA records state that it was the top Nazi boss already in Egypt, Wilhelm Voss, who actually recruited Deumling. Generally, however, it seems likely that most of the Nazis trickled into Egypt individually and in small groups from various sources and by various routes and ratlines: some from West Germany, some from East Germany, some from Spain and Italy, and more than a few from South America, particularly Argentina. Skorzeny most likely facilitated the transfer of only a hundred of these men.

The impression offered by the extant CIA files, whether deliberately or not, is that it was Wilhelm Voss, already in Egypt at the behest of King Farouk since 1951, who recruited many of the Germans; it was Voss who first involved Skorzeny; and it was Voss who was working directly for Adenauer's foreign ministry, which co-opted Reinhard Gehlen. Certainly Voss seems to have always had a direct line to Bonn, to do his own recruiting, and to circumvent Bonn's diplomatic representatives in Cairo.

In the early 1950s, CIA records begin to track the backgrounds and current activities of various former Nazis, many of whom had moved to the Middle East and were now acting as security advisors to local governments and running sidelines in the arms trade and weapons smuggling. In some cases, the CIA seems to have been testing the grounds for establishing contact with these individuals, in order to gain inside information about Middle East governments. In other cases, the CIA had reason to believe that these former Nazis were already in the pay of the Eastern bloc, and hoped to turn them into double agents.

From available American documents and secondary sources, it appears that the CIA successfully used the cover of the Gehlen Organization (and later the BND) to avoid direct involvement with the actual placement of German advisors in Egypt. Later, however, the CIA established direct links with these former Nazis, once they had arrived in Egypt. As Timothy Naftali states:

> the extent of Gehlen's recruitment of former officers of the SD [the intelligence service of the SS] and Gestapo . . . was widespread. At least one hundred of Gehlen's officers and agents had served with the SD or the Gestapo, and the number may in fact be significantly higher—some of those hired had participated in the worst atrocities committed by the Nazi regime.[8]

The CIA records show that there was consistent and close contact between the agency and the Gehlen Organization or BND.[9] Members of these organizations are frequently cited as sources for intelligence reports, and are also used as intermediaries with former Nazis whom the Americans were interested in recruiting. In these reports Zipper is the code name for the Gehlen Organization and Upswing is the code name for the BND.[10]

The CIA did not introduce all the former German military and security personnel to Egypt, for some of the Germans, like Wilhelm Voss, had arrived prior to 1953 at the invitation of King Farouk. One of the first groups to arrive, numbering about thirty officers, was led by General Wilhelm Fahrmbacher and six aides in 1950.[11] Most were overt career soldiers hired by Farouk, who had always had a soft spot for the German Afrika Korps, to replace the British military mission, which had left Egypt in 1947. Economic, industrial, and administrative experts followed shortly and were joined, in turn, by missile and aircraft engineers, and other weapons scientists.

While some of the German specialists were, like Fahrmbacher, essentially military men, there was also a hard core of odious and considerably less reputable Nazis. Skorzeny's work for the CIA expanded the number of malevolent Nazis in Egypt by recruiting a cross section of former SS, Waffen-SS, Gestapo, and Sicherheitsdienst (SS Security Service, SD) members, together with virulently anti-Semitic propagandists from Joseph Goebbels's information ministry, as well as former medical officers, administrators, and guards from the death camps of the Holocaust, who were recruited to construct and run desert concentration camps for Nasser that held the Egyptian leader's enemies.

This list of fascist misfits and malcontents included approximately one hundred "advisors" dredged from their hideouts in Germany, South America, and Spain. They made their way to Egypt along the ratlines operated by various neo-Nazi and escape organizations. Some of the recruits prominent in this rogues' gallery of war criminals included, to name but a few, SS Major General Hermann Lauterbacher, gauleiter of Hannover and former deputy leader of the Hitler Youth, tried for war crimes and discharged on a technicality, sent by Gehlen to Egypt as BND liaison officer; Professor Johannes von Leers, vicious anti-Semite and senior official in Goebbels's propaganda ministry, said to have been recommended by the Mufti, whom he knew well in Berlin; his close associate, SS Lieutenant Franz Bünsch, best known for his pornographic work, co-authored with Adolf Eichmann, *The Sexual Habits of the Jews*, who served in Eichmann's Jewish Affairs section at the Reichssicherheitshauptamt (SS headquarters, RSHA) and who proposed setting up for Nasser a grandiose global intelligence network staffed by Egyptians and ex-Nazis from all over the world; and SS Colonel Sepp Tiefenbacher, Himmler's personal chief of security and friend of the Mufti, who was to become Wilhelm Voss's faithful assistant in Cairo.[12]

Skorzeny did not spend much time in Egypt; it seems his role in the training mission was to recruit the initial group, but not to direct the program. The man who most likely took charge of the German intelligence and security advisors was a very senior Nazi indeed: SS Lieutenant General Wilhelm Voss, a close friend of both Himmler and Heydrich, and one of the bearers of the elite SS death's-head ring, worn by only a very few of Himmler's innermost circle of associates. Voss, a university-educated economist and brilliant accountant, was effectively in sole charge of the entire wartime Czechoslovak economy, while also functioning as director general of the huge Skoda plant in Pilsen, where very secret weapons (jets, rockets, nuclear bombs, and antigravitational devices) were under development in the latter stages of the war. In February 1945, Voss was relieved of his post and was in command of an SS combat unit (although he denied this) when the U.S. Army captured him and, after interrogation, turned him over to the Czechs. Although he was indicted as a war criminal and destined for execution, the Czechs mysteriously returned him to the Americans.[13]

Voss testified on behalf of the U.S. prosecution in several war crimes trials and subsequently lived, mostly under house arrest, at Rottach on the Tegernsee, conveniently near the Gehlen Organization at Pullach. According to a CIA daily log, Voss was an important contact for Gehlen and, perhaps at his behest, left for Egypt in 1951.[14] According to the British embassy in Cairo, Voss presided over all the Nazi fugitives, saboteurs, and "bad hats" in Egypt.[15] His official position in Egypt was special advisor to the Ministry of National Production. So it seems likely that Skorzeny's role in the CIA-sponsored training mission to Egypt was merely that of recruiter, whereas Wilhelm Voss was the onsite director of operations, who also recruited technical specialists himself.[16]

One key member of the Nazi training mission was SS (SD) Lieutenant Colonel Dr. Joachim Deumling, a police professional and the senior intelligence and security specialist among the Germans. Deumling had been a typical German student from a middle-class family who had found in the Nazi movement an opportunity to pursue a professional career. In 1937, while working as an SS officer in the Hannover Gestapo, he completed his education and received a law degree. Two years later, he was able to advance to the elite of the SD at SS headquarters in Berlin and was placed in charge of the Polish Desk.[17]

In July 1941, he became head of the Oppeln Gestapo, but shortly after he was transferred back to Berlin and given responsibility for the Office of Polish Affairs within Germany. Significantly, his immediate superior was SS (SD) Colonel Erwin Weinmann, a trained physician who was responsible for the mass murder of Ukrainian Jews in 1942–1943. But something went wrong for Deumling,[18] and in the spring of 1943 he was dismissed from his post in Berlin and transferred to the command of an SS death squad in northern Yugoslavia: Einsatzkommando (Operational Task Squad, EK) 10B, which was part of Einsatzgruppe (Operational Task Force, EG) E (Croatia).[19]

In December 1944, Deumling was seriously wounded, and for the remainder of the war he was confined to a military hospital. After the German surrender in May 1945, he was interned by the Americans but managed to escape and, using a false name, worked as a laborer near Braunschweig for the next couple of years. Sometime in 1948–1951, he also found employment with a British army auxiliary organization and as a legal advisor in an insurance company.[20] Most likely, Wilhelm Voss recruited him through the Gehlen Organization. To reach Egypt, Deumling, expert in such matters of course, took extraordinary security precautions to avoid detection by the British. Finally, although his departure for Egypt was delayed because of a broken leg, he arrived in Cairo with his wife and three daughters in February 1954.[21]

During his two years in Egypt, Joachim Deumling passed himself off as a Ministry of Social Affairs employee working for the Ministry of Health or as directly employed by the Ministry of Social Affairs. Meanwhile, his official title was "Intelligence Advisor to the Director of Military Intelligence, Egyptian Army," although his actual work seems to have been conducted in the Ministry of the Interior. SS (SD) Colonel Leopold Gleim, former head of the Gestapo in Poland, another police professional, served as Deumling's right hand in Egypt and helped him on the security aspects of his work. The CIA file on Deumling makes note of the fact that Deumling "was active in the collection and evaluation of information," that he "had no contact with the remaining German experts in Egypt (General Fahrmbacher Group)," and that "his activities were severed from the group and kept secret."[22]

Deumling's "real job" is described as "the organization of intelligence and a central security agency similar to his former German organization."[23] In effect, Deumling's accomplishment in Cairo was reorganizing the Egyptian intelligence service along the lines of the RSHA, although Miles Copeland claims that it was modeled after the CIA.[24] However, if the Egyptian intelligence agency used the CIA organization for a blueprint, it stands to reason that officers from the American spy service would have guided the work of Deumling.

Although the CIA's Deumling file suggests that the agency did not have contact with him during his time in Egypt, it does include sufficient details to indicate that the Americans were keen to have him work for them. One June 1958 memorandum asks its recipient to "inform UPSWING [BND also Gehlen] we have requirements which [we] would like [to] levy via UPSWING if subject [Deumling] willing to cooperate. Would appreciate UPSWING making recruitment effort soonest and advise us results." This request was passed along, and Gehlen replied that they did not intend to recruit Deumling, as he was considered "unreliable." Earlier that same month, the CIA had been informed by "Winterstein" that "the BND has had operational interest" in Deumling but that "no contact exists nor does he think intelligence exploitation possible." This turn of events left the CIA in a difficult position, as they did not feel that German intelligence was being honest about their own connection to Deumling. Gehlen had admitted that Deumling was of operational interest to them.

In early June, Gehlen requested "no further contact by AIS," but were "apparently willing to service KUBARK [CIA Headquarters] requirements." In response to this, the CIA planned to pass requests from the assistant chief of staff for intelligence [ASCI] as CIA HQ requests, in order that Upswing (Gehlen) would respond to them.[25] At the request of the ASCI, military intelligence approached Deumling on May 18, with the intent of debriefing him regarding Soviet backing of Egyptian intelligence service training and operations against the United States and NATO in Egypt. Deumling refused, and resented the contact having been made. However, it was felt that Deumling might reconsider the request if it came from CIA headquarters.[26]

Although Deumling's file does not refer to interactions between him and the CIA during his time in Egypt, it does make it clear that Deumling had done intelligence work for Gehlen and/or the CIA at some time before 1958. As of June 1958, Deumling "had rejected all proposals for continued intelligence work with UPSWING (Gehlen) or any other service."[27]

Aside from any contact the CIA may have had with Deumling in Egypt, his file indicates that they were gathering information on Deumling from a "trusted source who is an ex-German Abwehr officer in Cairo."[28] Nine years later, on June 26, 1967, Deumling's Nazi past caught up with him. Along with Bernhard Baatz, Emil Berndorff, and a few other former RSHA officers, Deumling was arrested as an alleged war criminal. All were imprisoned in Berlin and charged in the so-called RSHA Trial. According to the charges, Deumling, as former head of the Polish Desk, was guilty of having assisted in the murder of 150 people by drafting and issuing state police decrees that sanctioned the bad treatment of Polish workers and prisoners of war, as well as the carrying out of executions. Ultimately, he was implicated in the killing of 3,823 people, but he was released (because of a technicality) in December 1968. He died in February 2007 at the age of ninety-seven.[29]

One of the most contentious activities engaged in by Nazi officers who provided their services to the Egyptians was the guerilla training of Muslim Brotherhood paramilitary squads. Despite the presence of highly questionable Nazi elements in Egypt, and in defiance of evidence to the contrary, German diplomats insisted that the "nearest approach made to guerilla training is the formation and instruction of a regular Egyptian unit of paratroops by a Major Mertins."[30]

In 1953, the British saw German air force Major Gerhard Mertins, a former airborne combat engineer and sabotage expert, as the key "renegade" German officer whose presence in Egypt was detrimental to British interests. While even the British viewed the other advisors as somewhat cooperative with the West German government, which was trying to ensure that the German officers did not engage in anti-British activity in Egypt, Mertins was thought to be heavily involved in training the MB squads. Some other German advisors were also thought to be involved in similar activities, but their names were not known to the Foreign Office.[31] German advisors such as Mertins were ostensibly training the Egyptian government's legitimate Liberation Battalions; despite careful attempts to obscure the reality of the situation, the archival record reveals quite a different story.

In December 1952, General Neguib announced his intention of forming an official organization of the Arbeitsdienst (labor service) type, which would be aimed at providing discipline and employment to students, and which would include a paramilitary wing, the Liberation Battalion. As the Liberation Battalion training camps were established, a highly publicized recruitment campaign was launched.[32] Throughout 1953, varying reports reached the outside world about how these camps were being organized and run, and about who was being trained in them. Although the success of the recruitment drive was debatable, information came in that attendance at the government training camps had definitely been poor, though it was improving. "It is nevertheless very unlikely that more than about 10,000 men in all have received training in the camps." Significant, however, was the fact that "of these . . . possibly as many as 6,000 have been members of the Moslem Brotherhood who have taken advantage of the training offered in Government-organized camps without in any way transferring their allegiance to the Liberation Rally from the squads of the Moslem Brotherhood."[33]

Members of the MB were indeed participating in the government camps. After the January 1952 coup, existing guerrilla organizations were disbanded. Nevertheless, the MB, which had a wealth of experience in underground warfare, remained intact, and, by the end of 1952, it was known that these squads had resumed training.[34] Until early June 1953, the MB's paramilitary wing, the IEM Kateibas, had run their own camps and used their own instructors. After that, the training was brought, at least partially, under the control of the Egyptian government and conducted by Egyptian army officers in army camps.[35] From this point onward, MB members generally attended the Liberation Battalion camps for initial training.

The MB, however, maintained its own secret training camps for the "final preparation" of its members.[36] These camps were known to recruit within the universities and were organized into three categories: unattached men, men with dependents but no children, and men with no dependents. "The most dangerous assignments will be allotted to men in the first category, who may well act as 'suicide' squads."[37] The suicide attackers that were anticipated by the British were expected to come from the ranks of the MB.[38] The Brotherhood's squads were thought to be better staffed and trained, and of higher morale than the government units. It was estimated that, in addition to the existing squads, approximately eight thousand men had been trained in the Brotherhood's own camps, and were not yet formed into squads.[39]

The German advisors were certainly involved in training at the government camps, but their presence seems to have been much stronger in the exclusive MB camps, as well as in the Liberation camps that had been set aside for the training of MB members.[40] A British report of May 1953 notes evidence of "considerable assistance" being given the Brotherhood's paramilitary arm (IEM Kateibas) by German advisors, while the same advisors had not played a direct part in training at the government camps. It went on to state:

> In particular a great deal of attention has been paid to [training] in explosives, demolition, sabotage, etc. which will be a feature of IEM

operations. IEM Kateibas are being trained by expert German advisors for specialist sabotage tasks. Such targets as filtration plants, 9 BAD, armouries, Main HQs and communication centres are likely to be the object of carefully timed and planned sabotage operations for which specific training and even rehearsals have been undertaken with meticulous German thoroughness.[41]

A later report noted:

> There has certainly been considerable German influence if not assistance in training. This has given rise to increased attention being paid to and probably more effective techniques in the use of explosives, sabotage and in mobile Commando type operations. Such assistance is probably more apparent at IEM than at Liberation unit establishments.[42]

Beyond the level of simple training, there were "indications of considerable German influence and even of the possibility of German leadership in Guerilla fighting."[43] Some reports insisted that a large proportion of the Egyptian population was likely armed and trained in the use of weapons, and that "extensive and coordinated attacks by German trained Liberation units are likely" in the event of conflict. Though Egyptian army officers in plainclothes or in IEM or Liberation unit uniforms would lead most of these attacks, the British assumed that larger attacks might even be led by the Germans.[44]

The MB's squads were not only being trained separately in unique tactics; they remained ideologically separate from the government units. In Lord Hankey's view, the MB would not cooperate with the Liberation forces in a clash with foreign forces. He noted that the Brotherhood as an organization remained detached from the troubles in 1951 and stated his opinion that "it is unlikely that they would now agree to pick the chestnuts of the C.R.C. out of the fire."[45] It was noted that the Brotherhood remained a "more formidable proposition" than the regular Liberation Battalions, particularly as they had "been able to take advantage of training in Government camps without losing their identity."[46] This state of affairs had been engineered by the CIA, but it was also a portent of the very dangerous environment they were helping to build. As a result, the MB's IEM Kateibas were established as the most highly trained and powerful paramilitary force in Egypt. Their isolation from the Liberation Battalions had been encouraged.

The British were anxiously observing the German advisors in Egypt, concerned that they might be encouraging or abetting anti-British activity. In 1953, they made contact with General Fahrmbacher's deputy, General Oskar Munzel, a former panzer commander in the Western Desert under Rommel. Munzel provided the British military attaché with information about the German personnel, and, as the West German government had done, reassured the British that the advisors were not involving themselves in politics that would disadvantage the British.[47] The British, however, had information to the contrary. In June 1953, in response to a parliamentary question, the government composed a draft that stated they were aware that the German advisors in Egypt had been involved in the training of guerrillas. This draft also noted that the German government had sent a representative to Egypt, despite having no direct control over these advisors who had been recruited unofficially by the Egyptians.[48]

This representative, Helmut Allardt, a West German career diplomat, subsequently denied that the Germans were engaged in activities injurious to the British, and advised against their removal. All of this information was then deleted from the approved draft, which stated simply that the West German chancellor had promised an investigation, despite the fact that the technicians had been recruited directly by the Egyptians. In response to a specific question about the training of guerrillas, the government-approved draft stated: "I have seen many reports about their activities. I should prefer not to go into detail pending the results of the investigation." This revision was made in order to save the West German chancellor embarrassment.[49]

The British were well aware that MB squads were being trained in guerrilla tactics, that "Mertins has been doing [this] on the side," and that "he is not the only one."[50] In fact, British intelligence had a significant amount of information about guerrilla training. A note on a Foreign Office file from August 1953 refers to the training of MB sabotage squads by the German advisors. "No doubt Mertins is in charge of this. I understand we have asked the German government to get him removed," writes Sir Reginald J. Bowker. During this period, the Foreign Office had the impression that the majority of the advisors—with Mertins as one definite exception—had a British-friendly attitude in their dealings with the Egyptian government, and that for this reason were not training Egyptians in guerrilla warfare.[51] Even given the knowledge that the Foreign Office had of these activities, it remains possible that they knew little in comparison to the covert British intelligence services, such as MI6.

This was just one of the many problems spawned by resorting to war criminals as part of the U.S. covert relationship with Nasser. The actions of the CIA in Egypt certainly worked against Britain, America's closest ally, and at the same time helped Soviet intelligence. A number of the Nazis recruited to work for Nasser were certainly also double agents or had at some time been under the control of the Soviet KGB. Yet neither the CIA nor Gehlen had paid much attention to the background of the Nazi recruits for Egypt.

For example, the fact that Wilhelm Voss, after his initial surrender to the Americans in 1945, was also in Russian and Czech captivity but was never tried or sentenced by either authority, and was subsequently returned to the Americans, suggests that he may have been played back to the West by the East as a mole or a double agent. The additional fact that he first appeared in Egypt accompanied by Czech assistants, and that he subsequently recruited Czech personnel, reinforces this view, as does the fact that the first prominent personality to be recruited by Voss—the rocket scientist Rolf Engel—was a known communist.[52]

Another example was Gerhard Mertins himself. After leaving Egypt, Mertins became one of the world's most powerful dealers and shippers of surplus German arms (MEREX Corporation). The British were probably well aware in 1956 of Mertins's clandestine connections with the BND and of his possible double-dealings with Moscow, which made him even more of a destabilizing presence among the MB guerrillas, whom he may even have been supplying with weapons.[53]

Of course, the Soviets did not rely solely on the Nazis in Egypt for intelligence on Nasser and the CIA. One of the best agents of Soviet intelligence was Ze'ev Avni (born Wolf Goldstein). Avni was an economist and master of several languages. He had spent the Second World War in Switzerland, where he was recruited by Soviet military intelligence, the GRU. In 1948, he immigrated to Israel and found employment in the Israeli Foreign Ministry. In 1952, he was posted to Brussels as commercial attaché, as well as security officer. He used his new position to gain access to the Israeli embassy safe, and he photographed its contents for his Soviet masters. While in Brussels, Mossad also recruited him, and he used his fluent German to pose as a German businessman. At this time he was transferred from the GRU to the KGB. Using his cover as a German businessman, he penetrated the ranks of the Nazis working for Nasser and indirectly for the CIA. Avni also passed on to the KGB the Mossad ciphers, thus enabling the Soviet spy agency to break the codes of the Israeli secret service. In 1956, he was caught and sentenced to fourteen years in prison.[54]

Undoubtedly, Moscow used Avni's information on Nasser's Nazis to keep a wary eye on those Germans already in the service of the KGB and to acquire information on the rest, in order to enlist new agents by various means of coercion. For the Americans, the use of Nazis was the beginning of a policy that called for the deployment of anyone or any organization that could be identified as anticommunist. Nasser himself fulfilled that role for a few years; after he abandoned the covert relationship with the United States and turned to the Soviets for support, the CIA reversed gears and sought to undermine the Egyptian "Muslim Billy Graham." Once again, the old maxim, "my enemy's enemy is my friend," underwrote the CIA's war against Nasser. In this case, harnessing the forces of Islam through the MB to counter Arab nationalism led by Nasser served as the harbinger of a dangerous and futile U.S. policy toward the Middle East.

SIXTEEN

A Legacy of Coups: Anglo-American Intervention in Syria

An elderly man approached a soldier who was sitting on a tank.
"What is going on my son?"
"Hush" said the soldier, signaling the old man to silence.
"This is an Inkilab [coup d'état]!"
The puzzled man responded, "Okay . . . but, what is an Inkilab?"[1]

At half an hour before midnight on March 29, 1949, the commander-in-chief of the Syrian army, Colonel Husni Zaim, dispatched military units to arrest members of Syria's government. Army detachments swooped in to gather "marked" officials, seal off streets, cut off communications, and close the Syria-Lebanon border. At 6:00 A.M. on March 30 a curfew was implemented; by morning, the takeover was complete, and the sounds of army boots echoed through the streets of Damascus. A statement issued by radio introduced the new regime and outlined Zaim's message to the country and to the world. Resonating with affected seriousness the announcer proclaimed: "Impelled by patriotic zeal, we have been forced to overthrow the former Government. We are not driven by ambition, but only by the desire to create a really democratic state." The revolt, Zaim insisted, was "purely local and has no foreign implications."[2]

The suggestion that a change of power in Syria had no foreign implications was laughable. Syria's geography straddled a strategic zone—an ideal land route for transporting oil, the country shared borders with several key Middle East states, including Israel, the ongoing flash point for the region. As a result, Syria's allies had a vested interest in who held power in Damascus. For this reason, the coup in March 1949 had not only foreign implications, but also certainly direct foreign involvement via the CIA.

From the 1500s to 1918, Syria, as well as neighboring Lebanon, Jordan, and Palestine, did not exist as states, but were administrative units of the Ottoman Empire. During the First World War, Britain proposed the creation of an independent Arab state to secure the allegiance of the Hashemite Sharif Hussein of Mecca and by extension the loyalty of the Arabs in the Ottoman Empire. Not long after, the British also offered Palestine as a Jewish national home. The British, in effect, betrayed both Hussein and Arab nationalism. The 1916 Sykes-Picot Agreement between Britain and France called for the postwar award of Syria and Lebanon to the French and designated Palestine as an international zone under a British mandate. Despite Syrian and Palestinian appeals to Woodrow Wilson's policy of self-determination, the Americans failed to support the creation of independent Arab states, and after the war the Middle East was divided more or less according to the terms laid out in the Sykes-Picot Agreement. Lebanon emerged as a state within Syria and in 1926 France made Lebanon a separate entity, thus setting in place Syria's subsequent and relentless intervention in Lebanon, whereupon all regimes in Damascus remained committed to the notion that Lebanon was part of Greater Syria.

France had established a presence in the region before the war by forming alliances with minorities in Syria and the region, claiming the right to protect the Maronite Christians, who had established links with the French during the First Crusade. Despite this historical connection, France's mandate over Syria and Lebanon was rife with repression that provoked rebellions by the native groups. It was not until the end of the Second World War that Syria finally gained independence from France.[3] The end of the war also brought about the reluctant fulfillment of the Balfour Declaration, when the United Nations created a Jewish state in Palestine—the defining moment in Syrian history.

Syria today is a complex mix of religious, cultural, social, and political factions, many of which are embroiled in a historical struggle for dominance and even survival. Entrenched divisions in the region have deepened and warped over time, manipulated by domestic and foreign elements, in the quest for financial, political, and ideological preeminence. For decades, the struggle for oil, the conflict over Israel, and Cold War rivalry effectively drove Western foreign policy in the Middle East. During the Cold War, the states of the Middle East tried to avoid officially linking their fortunes to either the West or the Soviet Eastern bloc and many preferred to remain neutral. Neutrality, however, was not palatable to Britain and the United States or to the Soviet Union. As a result, the British, Americans, Israelis, and Soviets waged a clandestine proxy war in Syria to control the region.

The fear of a communist-dominated Middle East forged Western strategic thinking, as well as the Arab nationalist movement acting as a vehicle for Moscow's agenda. Although Arab nationalism is often associated with the Egyptian leader Nasser, its roots are in early-twentieth-century Syria. The movement originated with Syrian students influenced by Arab history in the American University of Beirut and by the efforts of the Ottoman Empire to suppress Arab

culture. Gradually, the concept of Arab culturalism transformed into the demand for an independent Arab nation along with a revival of Arabism.[4] Because the Arab world is composed of a spectrum of religions and spiritual
sects, Arab unity implicitly meant a unity across religious boundaries. But at
the same time, the mosaic of Arab religious, cultural, and minority groups was
vulnerable to manipulation and exploitation by foreign powers.

Like the British before them, the CIA and other U.S. intelligence agencies
co-opted political movements and dissident factions across the Middle East who
could be helpful to the West, pitting them against those who posed a threat to
American interests. In response to the twin evils of communism and Arab
nationalism, Western powers turned to extreme religious groups, who inher-
ently opposed both the atheist ideology of the Soviets and the secularism of
Arab nationalism. The Muslim Brotherhood was one such group, armed and
funded by the West to counter Arab nationalism and Soviet influence.

In the 1930s Syrian students who had attended the Al-Azhar University in
Cairo brought the Muslim Brotherhood back with them to Syria.[5] The Muslim
Brotherhood's political wing operated for some time in Damascus and Aleppo
as the Islamic Socialist Front. But after 1945, the organization adopted the
name Muslim Brotherhood to represent themselves in their political activities.
Remarkably the Muslim Brothers managed to unnerve both the British and the
Syrian communists. According to one Foreign Office report, the Muslim Brothers
were described as "a Marxist drink in a Moslem cup."[6] Meanwhile the Syrian
Communist Party branded the Muslim Brotherhood as the "British Brethren."[7]
Regardless of these sentiments, in 1950 the Foreign Office was very concerned
about links between the Muslim Brotherhood in Syria and Soviet communism.[8] However, the Muslim Brothers found the United States a lesser evil than
the communists, while the Americans had few compunctions working with a
militant Islamic organization.

The Brotherhood was one of many overt and covert organizations that
found in Syria a convenient clandestine battleground. Prior to the end of the
Second World War, for example, Syria and Lebanon had become bases for rival
terrorist groups, some pro-Zionist, others pursuing an anti-Zionist policy. By
1943, the Jewish Agency and Haganah had created an intelligence service in
Syria and Lebanon. The American Office of Strategic Services monitored this
group, gathering information on those involved and following their activities.[9]

In the postwar years, the Americans and the British took a particular interest in Polish refugee groups that were building up terrorist cells in the region. American counterintelligence and British intelligence began collecting
information on these Polish refugee groups, which, in turn, had links to the

Irgun.[10] By the 1950s, Lebanon even housed neo-Nazi organizations, such as the BDO (a German nationalist organization comprised of ex-Nazis), whose members hid in Beirut and became involved in Syrian political activities.[11]

Throughout the 1950s furthermore, Damascus served as an organization center for ongoing subversive struggle against Israel. In 1955, Egyptian army officers approached Syrian military intelligence asking for names of Palestinian terrorists living in Syria the Egyptians could deploy against Israel along the Jordan border. The operation was backed by Saudi Arabia, and planned in the Saudi embassy in Damascus, under the supervision of Jamal al-Hussein, a Palestinian activist, brother of Amin al-Husayni, and the founder of the Palestine Arab Army.[12] Recruits also came from supporters of Amin al-Husayni in Jordan, and the Mufti himself acted as a major organizer from his usual base in Cairo. The Mufti was rumored to be behind an extensive terrorist network, though the organization was not currently active either due to lack of funds or because its members were waiting for the right moment. Temporarily out of favor with Nasser's government due to his links with Muslim Brotherhood, the Mufti was once again welcome in Cairo, because the Egyptians believed that they could use his network to create trouble for Israel.[13]

The Foreign Office was well aware of Egypt's use of Palestinian refugees for espionage operations against Egypt, but the British avoided cautioning the Syrian government, for fear of damaging relations with Damascus.[14] In the early 1950s, the British were treading delicately in the highly unstable world of Syrian politics. The Foreign Office representative in Damascus complained of Britain's "negative" policy toward Syria, while the Cairo office stressed the importance of maintaining good relations with the Arab world as a whole. The Foreign Office argued that current British assurances regarding the maintenance or curtailing of Israeli borders were not enough.[15] The British were trapped into placating the Syrian regime because they knew that Syria, like other "neutral" Middle Eastern states, could turn to other friends. The most obvious of these was the Soviet Union; but the British were also worried about their competitive allies, the Americans. Throughout the 1940s and 1950s, the Foreign Office frequently warned London that any policy moves that upset the Arab world would simply invite Washington to replace Britain in the region.[16]

America's relationship with the Middle East began well into the twentieth century with Syria as the primary springboard of U.S. intervention in the region. Prior to the First World War, the United States had little interest in the Middle East.[17] However, by the 1920s, with the consumption of oil dramatically increasing at home, the Americans began to challenge Britain's exclusive control over the petroleum reserves of the Middle East. American investments in the Middle East petroleum expanded throughout the 1930s and 1940s, and at the end of the Second World War the security of the region was a major strategic concern for the United States. The topography of Syria was ideal for the efficient and inexpensive transportation of petroleum. Syria is situated between the Persian Gulf and the Mediterranean, making the country an ideal route for an oil pipeline, which can replace the long sea journey around Saudi Arabia to the Suez Canal. In 1949 the Trans-Arabian Pipeline Company (Tapline) had a deal in place with the Syrian government, and the oil pipeline was operating by 1950. Tapline was a subsidiary of the Arabian-American Oil Company (Aramco), which, in turn, was a subsidiary of the California-owned Texaco.[18]

Following the end of the Second World War, the United States emerged as a major player in the Middle East. After 1945, the Americans established their own intelligence networks and the State Department began receiving regular reports on key regions of the Middle East from the Office of Strategic Services, Special Intelligence.[19] The cover for American intelligence operatives was to pass as members of the Foreign Economic Administration (FEA) and in State Department posts in capitals throughout the Middle East.[20]

As the Cold War rivalry between the West and the Eastern bloc expanded, both British and American intelligence feared that Syria would become a Soviet satellite.[21] These concerns intensified after the construction of the pipeline and the growing Syrian dependence on Soviet arms and money.[22] By the late 1940s, the situation continued to deteriorate because Syria, the Americans were convinced, housed "a surprising array of left-wing political organizations, including the Arab world's most active communist party."[23] Indeed, by the 1950s, Soviet influence expanded dramatically in Syria and the KGB was well established in Damascus.[24] The Soviets, for their part, catered to Syrian needs and during the 1948 Arab-Israeli War, for example, provided them with weapons. The Arab-Israeli War, in fact, became a major source of discord between the United States and Syria, and it did not escape Washington's notice that, the more alienated Syria became from the Americans, the closer Damascus moved toward Moscow.[25] In response, London and Washington began considering the use of a covert strategy to implement anticommunist measures in Syria, and by the end of the decade the intelligence services of both countries were planning a regime change in Damascus.[26]

Meanwhile the country itself was struggling. The Arab-Israeli War of 1948 had followed immediately on the tails of the Second World War.[27] The army blamed Syria's defeat on the government, accusing them of being ill prepared. The military was further enranged by Faysal al-'Asali, a right-wing member of

Parliament, who publicly insulted the weak performance of the army. Some historians feel that these attacks led directly to the upcoming Zaim coup.[28] Thus began a trilogy of coups, which created a tremendous degree of socio-political instability in the young state and brought about widespread corruption.

The aftershocks of Syria's losses in the Arab-Israeli War of 1948 eventually led to the resignation of the elected Nationalist/Populist government. Not long after, in March 1949, Zaim, then the Army chief of staff, overthrew the interim government.[29]

Colonel Zaim's ascent to power followed a series of meetings with CIA agent Stephen Meade. In March, Meade reported Zaim's request that "U.S. agents provoke and abet internal disturbances . . . essential for coup d'état or that U.S. funds be given him for this purpose."[30] It is not possible to confirm that this money was provided, but contact between the CIA and Zaim increased considerably leading to the coup.[31] Miles Copeland, formerly a CIA agent, has outlined how he and Stephen Meade backed Zaim, and American archival sources confirm that it was during this period that Meade established links with extremist right-wing elements of the Syrian army, who ultimately carried out the coup.[32]

The CIA was also involved with the installment of Colonel Adib Shishakli, in the final coup of 1949. Zaim had been an excellent ally of the United States. After he seized power, he outlawed the Syrian Communist Party, made peace agreements with Israel and Turkey, and offered a home to Palestinian refugees. But unfortunately his tenure as head of Syria was short-lived. Zaim was murdered in August 1949 and replaced by Colonel Sami Hinnawi. Despite American fears, there is no evidence of actual Soviet involvement; Hannawi had no particular partisan political leanings and mainly opposed Zaim's erratic and high-handed rule.[33] Hannawi was a colonel who commanded the main army units in southern Syria. There are allegations that Iraq had backed the coup partly because they did not like Zaim's pro-Egypt policy and responded to Hannawi's call for Syrian-Iraqi unity. The Iraqis certainly had contact with Hannawi along with others in the Syrian army, and one of the conspirators, Lieutenant Fadlallah Abu Mansur, later claimed that Iraq was directly involved.[34]

The new Syrian strongman restored the communists, hinted at renewed hostility with Israel, and proposed to unite Syria with Iraq. The Americans were anxious to forestall Hannawi and to act quickly before the Soviets intervened. Miles Copeland had found the aspiring leader, Shishakli, to be "a likeable rogue" and arranged for him to receive American financial and military aid.[35] Shishakli took control of the government in December 1949 and cooperated with the Americans with respect to the oil pipeline and Israel. He remained in power for four years. Despite the fact that the Americans found his efforts against communism insufficient, Shishakli's pro-West policies eventually became a source of public anger. Consequently, army officers, lead by Lieutenant Colonel Adnan Malki, overthrew him in February 1954.[36]

The interim government that followed the 1954 Syrian coup was a major threat to Washington and London. Furthermore, the pro-Western opposition faced considerable internal resistance, while the army itself was divided into left- and right-wing camps. Informants told their British contacts that there was no chance of a regime change without external help, preferably from Iraq. According to them, Iraq would have support of tribes in the north, along the Turkish border, as well as some of the tribes and army factions in the south through contacts in Saudi Arabia. British and Turkish embassy staff held several discussions over the Syrian situation, while the Foreign Office mulled over the fact that one or two possible candidates for Syrian dictator were in prison.[37]

At the same time, the CIA's Allen Dulles noted in 1955 that Syria was "ripe for a military coup d'état."[38] In 1956, the Americans toyed with Operation Straggle, a scheme to back the Syrian Social Nationalist Party (SSNP),[39] a right-wing party friendly to the United States, so that it would overthrow the Malki regime. This plan was scrapped because the CIA feared that the SSNP would fail. Another critical factor was just as Straggle was about to commence the Suez Crisis exploded, further negating the prospects for an American coup in the Middle East.

After the dust settled over the Suez Crisis, London and Washington then initiated a new joint Anglo-American operation to topple the Syrian regime. Operatives of the Near Eastern Division of the CIA led by Kermit Roosevelt and its counterpart headed by Sir George Young, the deputy director of the British Secret Intelligence Service, lobbied right-leaning members of the Syrian army to plan a coup, while the CIA provided hundreds of thousands of Syrian pounds in backing the new operation. The plan called for instability within Syria and along its borders. British and American intelligence operatives would encourage internal rebellion by the Muslim Brotherhood, while staging "Syrian" attacks in Jordan and Iraq. This seeming aggressive activity on the part of Syria would then permit the United States to invoke the Eisenhower Doctrine and provide aid for Iraq to invade Syria.[40]

It is not surprising that the Muslim Brotherhood were to be the foot soldiers in the plot. In the mid-1950s, the British and Americans were enjoying a renaissance in their relations with the Brotherhood, linked by their bitter opposition to Nasser. Egypt's Nasser had cracked down harshly on the Brotherhood in 1954, imprisoning and killing many of its members. Some fled to Syria, others found refuge and support in Saudi Arabia. In addition to direct contacts with the Muslim Brotherhood, the Americans also supported Saudi efforts that facilitated the Brotherhood's terrorist activities across the Middle East.[41]

As the coup evolved, the Brotherhood had another reason to assist the British; prior to the January 1957 elections, the Ba'ath Party (a Syrian secular and nationalist organization) and the Muslim Brotherhood parted ways and soon became implacable enemies.[42] The initial rift was almost certainly caused by the growing relationship between Syria's Ba'ath Party and Egypt's Nasser, which became official by early 1957. The Ba'athists in Syria had spearheaded a successful campaign for Syro-Egyptian union (which was to come to fruition in 1958). However, Nasser was a bitter enemy of the Muslim Brothers, who were certain that a harsh fate awaited them in the case of a united Syria and Egypt.[43]

Despite the political and public relations disaster of the Suez Crisis, or rather because of it, the Americans opted to continue to use covert operations in order to intervene in the Middle East, instead of the high-handed approach of the British-French-Israelis in Egypt. Perhaps the Eisenhower administration believed that an American-financed coup would be less abhorrent than military invasion or held the conviction that the CIA would not fail. Regardless of these or any other considerations, the January 1957 Syrian elections heightened Washington's and London's fears over Syria's progressive tilt to the Soviets and accelerated plans to overthrow the Damascus regime.

The left swept to power in Syria under the Popular Progressive Front, an alliance of Communists, Ba'athists, and nationalists. The election results underlined the abilty of the army and of the leftist groups to dominate Syria.[44] The new government excluded rightist elements in general and shut out political figures who had been friendly to the West. The level of paranoia increased rapidly and the British government in London was subjected to frantic political reports from the Foreign Office that identified several major Syrian political figures as potential threats to Britain and the United States, but these men later fell victim to assassination.[45] When the Ba'ath Party swept to power, the Brotherhood, like the Americans and the British, but with dramatically divergent motives, were anxious to be rid of the new regime.

During the 1950s Syria was rife with rumors and accusations of Western interference in Syrian politics; exploiting this atmosphere of impending coup in the early morning of August 12, 1957, government agents arrested hundreds of suspects. A few months later a trial was held in Damascus during which the accused were charged with plotting to overthrow the government with support from Iraq, the United States, and Britain. Iraq, under Nuri Said, was alleged to have instigated the coup plans, which included a plot to assassinate Khalid Bik-dash, the communist leader, followed by the killing of the Ba'ath Party leader; Salah al-Bizri, the chief of the Syrian general staff; and 'Abd al-Hamid Sarraj, the head of Syrian military intelligence.

Making matters worse, Washington's old friends, the SSNP, were heavily implicated in the plot thus indirectly linking the Americans.[46] Shishakli, the charges stated, had been approached by Iraqi officials at a meeting in Geneva in early 1956 after which he made a visit to Paris. In April of 1956, Adib Shishakli and his brother, Salah, who was also involved in the coup, were transported from Paris to Lebanon on a British cargo ship. Beirut was used as a base for planning the coup and the Shishaklis held meetings at a house near the British embassy.[47]

The plot uncovered in August 1957 was a variation of Operation Wappen, devised by the CIA and the SIS in 1956. A major player was Rocky Stone of the CIA. From the time that Stone had arrived in Syria as CIA station chief in Damascus in April, he had set out to work on making contacts and cultivating officers in the Syrian army. But just as Stone finally got to the point of handing over the large funds being provided by the CIA to the Syrian officers, his contacts went on national television and denounced him as a spy.[48]

The plot was organized on three levels. The SSNP was responsible for training paramilitaries, Iraq had agreed to supply arms and money, and a political group was being groomed within the Syrian government.[49] In addition to the Muslim Brotherhood, the CIA enlisted the help of a variety of extreme and militant Islamic groups that included the Islamic Society for the Salvation of the Homeland from Russian Oppression and the [Secret] Society for the Liberation of the Usurped Land to lay the groundwork for the coup.[50] Arms were smuggled into Syria from Iraq, Jordan, and Turkey and distributed to plotters inside Syria, as well as to the Druze and Massa'id tribes.[51]

A camp near Beirut, most likely Beit Mery, was used to train members of the SSNP and many of them were treated at the American University Hospital in Beirut.[52] Once all preparations were complete and sufficient arms secured, the signal for the coup was to be given during the Voice of Britain over the Near East Broadcast station, which was operated by British intelligence. The assassinations were then to take place, and one cell was to occupy the city of Homs and another Hama to complete the overthrow of the government.[53] One of the proposed victims, Sarraj, had been targeted by the Britain. In March 1957, the Foreign Office, along with the SSNP, were pressuring Sarraj to accept the post of military attaché in Cairo. Communist and socialist factions protested against the removal of Sarraj. An assassination attempt had been made on him the previous year and Syrian intelligence had blamed the Israeli Mossad, but British Foreign Office documents openly comment on the need to eliminate Sarraj, as well as the other two high-profile alleged targets of the plot.[54]

The Syrian government accused British and American intelligence services of hatching this plan from its early stages. There was ample evidence. Many of the accused were found in possession of large amounts of money, American cigarettes, and other goods the Syrian authorities claimed were given to them by Western backers. British agents had been seen in tribal areas in the months leading up to the planned coup.[55] The allegations were reported in the Western press: the Americans had offered between $300 and $400 million, and assigned Stone to carry out the scheme. The Associated Press reported that, upon revelation of the plot, Shishakli was whisked away to Beirut in an American diplomatic car.[56] He was sentenced to death in absentia by the Syrian court. Afterward he returned to Brazil, where he had been living prior to the plot. On September 27, 1964, Nawaf Ghazaleh, a Syrian Druze, assassinated Shishakli in Brazil.[57]

The disastrous failure of the 1957 plot along with the revelations of the Syrian court shredded America's reputation and drove many local groups to seek support and protection from the Soviets.[58] A similar debacle in Iraq further eroded the influence of the United States and exposed the British and Americans as feeble coup organizers. The CIA had been in collusion with the royalist government in Iraq, and was taken by surprise when it was suddenly overthrown. Iraqi officers led by Abdul Karim Qasim toppled the Hashemite monarchy; the new regime withdrew from the Baghdad Pact, the Central Treaty Organization, and established friendly relations with the Soviet Union. Equally embarrassing, the Qasim government published documents that laid out the full extent of the CIA plot against Syria.[59]

In the fallout of the Syrian debacle, the Foreign Office reported that Rocky Stone and two other American contacts had been expelled from Syria.[60] The ensuing trial and its associated publicity further eroded the reputation of the United States as well as that of Great Britain. Subsequently, for years rumors of new plots and military interventions continued to be linked to the British and Americans. In the fall of 1957, Syrians spotted American soldiers mixed in with Turkish troops along the Syrian-Turkish border.[61] The atmosphere of suspicion and paranoia made it very easy for the Soviets to implement their schemes in the region.

In the mid-1960s, the Soviets launched Operation Pulya (Bullet). Pulya was designed to "expose" a new CIA plot against the Ba'athist regime. This, however, was a disinformation campaign, in which Soviet contacts provided names and details of "spies" and "traitors" (some information was true and some was false) to the Syrian government. A member of the Soviet embassy even placed a call to a pro-American officer in the Syrian army, pretending to be a friend, warning him that he was about to be exposed as an American contact. The officer, in a panic, asked whether he should go into hiding or seek asylum in the U.S. embassy. Naturally, his telephone was tapped; this was as good as a confession and the officer was exposed as an American agent—there are no records attesting to his ultimate fate. As a result of Operation Pulya, some CIA agents and their contacts were eliminated, further straining U.S.-Syrian relations and pushing Damascus closer to the Soviets.[62]

In the aftermath of the 1957 crises, British officials were alarmed by the breakdown of American and British covert operations, particularly with respect to countersubversion. A briefing note for Harold Macmillan's visit to Washington explained the drawbacks of American intelligence:

> On the British side there is a fairly expert staff covering the Foreign Office, M.I.6, the Information Research Department, and to an increasing degree the Ministry of Defence (and Service Departments), the Colonial Office and the Commonwealth Relations Office. . . . On the American side the organisation is not so tight and the co-ordination between the State Department and the C.I.A. is not complete. Neither side trusts the other.
>
> There is a need on both sides for better forecasting of possible trouble spots, quicker provision of the type of intelligence required to launch counter-subversive operations, and above all quicker financial and logistical provision of military and other supplies for all these operations. . . .
>
> . . . Working Groups must be attended by suitably high-level people who can speak authoritatively on policy and operational matters and they must meet at frequent intervals. In the case of the Lebanon the Working Group met but State Department representation was inadequate.[63]

However, Anglo-American machinations in Syria accomplished little except to pave the way for a strong Soviet presence in Damascus. Remarkably, the Soviets, like the Americans, decided that religious groups were the best mechanism by which to gain influence in Syria. Soviet infiltration took the form of Eastern Orthodox missions to Syria and financial support awarded to religious groups in Syria. A Soviet Eastern Orthodox mission led by the Bishop of Moscow arrived in Syria for a month-long visit in May 1957 as the guest of the Damascus Orthodox Patriarchate. A Soviet "cultural mission" of six people also visited during the same period. The Patriarch of Antioch arrived in Moscow in November 1957 and in the course of the visit Alexei, the Russian Patriarch, stressed to the Syrian cleric that the friendship of the Soviet Union helped to preserve Syrian independence. Offers of money and support were also made to the Greek Orthodox Church in Syria; in a countermove the British launched plans for the Church of England to forge ties with churches in the region.[64]

In February 1958, Shukri al-Quwatli and Gamal Abdel Nasser joined Syria and Egypt into the United Arab Republic. This union lasted until September 1961, when a fresh military coup, in which the CIA was rumored to be involved, terminated the United Arab Republic.[65] The officer behind the coup was Lieutenant Colonel 'Abd-ul-Karim an-Nahwali, who belonged to a social and religious circle that had a direct link to the Muslim Brotherhood. Following the 1961 regime change, the Brotherhood regained its legitimacy and increased its membership in Syria. This, however, did not prevent the success of the Ba'athist coup of March 1963, which was carried out by the National Council of the Revolutionary Command (NCRC), essentially made up of Syrian military officers.[66] In February 1966, however, yet another army coup removed President Amin Hafiz and other members of the NCRC, and abolished the provisional constitution that had been in effect since 1964. The new regime referred to itself as Ba'athist, but claimed to be returning to a purer Ba'athist form of government.

The 1960s were marked by riots and conspiracies instigated by the Muslim Brotherhood against the Ba'athist regime. The Brotherhood's resistance was driven by objections to the secular ideology of the Ba'ath Party, the economic policies of the government, and by fear of communism. The urban small merchants and artisans, whom the Brotherhood supported, comments Hanna Batatu, "viewed the 'socialism' of the [current regime] as a weapon by which the more conscious segments of the long neglected and long suppressed rural people sought revenge against the main cities."[67] The fear of communist infiltration increased in February 1967, when a leftist military coup brought in a Moscow-friendly regime. The new government accepted financial aid from the Soviets and in return allowed the Syrian Communist Party to rebuild. This regime, under Salah Jadid, was seriously undermined by the June 1967 Six Day War with Israel in which the Syrian army was poorly armed and suffered major losses.[68] Almost everyone blamed the government and it was not long before another coup installed a new regime in Damascus.

In November 1970, Hafiz al-Asad deposed Jadid. Unlike the traditional ruling bodies of Syria, Asad (and Jadid) came from the Alawi minority. The Alawis are an offshoot of Shiite Islam and had historically been excluded from military and political positions of prominence in Syria. Yet, for reasons that remain a matter of debate, members of the Alawi sect had not only joined the Ba'ath Party and but also flourished.[69] Unlike Jadid, who avoided Alawis while in power, Asad staffed the high command and the senior intelligence posts with Alawi officers. Regardless of his Alawi origin, Asad proceeded with extreme caution, establishing up to fifteen separate intelligence and security services, which employed thousands of staff and a small army of informants.[70]

The Muslim Brotherhood had backed Asad against Jadid, because Jadid had experimented with socialist programs, which the Brotherhood and their supporters, the urban artisans and small merchants, fiercely opposed. Some younger members of the Brotherhood objected to supporting any Ba'athist faction and moved to Jordan, where they joined the Palestinian Fatah. Those who remained in Syria faced little opposition or persecution from Asad.[71] But the Brotherhood's relationship with Asad came under considerable strain after 1973 and the Brothers soon turned against the Syrian dictator.

Asad's introduction of a secular constitution in 1973 was the first point of friction.[72] The fragile friendship came to an end when the Syrian's regime moved against the Palestinians in the Lebanese Civil War. In 1976, the Syrian army assisted the Phalange massacre of Palestinians at the Tal az-Za'tar camp in Lebanon. During the same period, the Brotherhood observed that Sunni Muslims were being deliberately excluded from positions of power in Asad's regime. Although Sunni Muslims were well represented in the more visible elements of the government, the real power, according to Batatu, was held "by Asad and the leaders of three intelligence apparatuses and of two crucial heavily armed units which underpin the whole structure."[73]

In 1976, the Brotherhood began a campaign to overthrow Asad and establish Sunni Muslim rule over Syria. An assassination campaign began to target Ba'athist military officers and Alawi politicians. In June 1979, Brotherhood members locked a building at a Syrian military school and slaughtered the imprisoned trainees with automatic weapons and firebombs, killing eighty-three. The Brotherhood then attempted to assassinate Asad in 1980 and, in November 1981, killed two hundred people with a car bomb in Damascus.[74]

The Muslim Brothers were not acting alone. In 1983, Asad signed a friendship pact with the Soviet Union, and the CIA, once again, turned to the Muslim militants for help. While there is no documented evidence that the Americans directly funded the Brotherhood throughout the 1980s, there is little doubt that Israel and Jordan backed the group from the late 1970s. The Jewish state and secular Jordan, while not obvious allies of the Brotherhood, supported them as a counterbalance to the Asad regime and the PLO, the Palestine Liberation Organization. The CIA was well aware of the Israeli and Jordanian assistance to the Brotherhood, but did not discourage it. As the Near East chief of the Bureau of Intelligence and Research explained: "We knew about the Muslim Brotherhood . . . a lot more than what was in the papers. We looked benignly upon it. We knew it was risky, but life is risky."[75] The American ambassador to Syria put it even more cynically: "I don't think it bothered us too much that they were causing problems for Asad."[76]

Once the Muslim Brotherhood became linked to Western interests, the KGB decided to eliminate the organization in Syria. The instrument of the Muslim Brothers' destruction was Rift'at al-Asad, the younger brother of the Syrian dictator. In 1971 the KGB had cultivated Rif'at because as the commander of the Syrian army's prestigious Defense Brigades he had at his disposal the most effective force in the country.[77] The KGB also made contact with two terrorist organizations in the 1970s: the Democratic Front for the Liberation of Palestine, which was under the leadership of a Greek Orthodox individual, and the Popular Front for the Liberation of Palestine—General Command. This latter was a splinter group from the PFLP, of which Carlos the Jackal was a member, to work against the Muslim Brothers and the British and Americans.

The KGB supplied the terrorist organizations with money and arms while they exploited Rift'at's love of luxury. Unlike his reclusive and austere elder brother, Rif'at had acquired a taste for foreign travel and Western luxuries and had exploited his position to accumulate a small fortune. Under his direction, the Defense Brigades held a weekly market in Damascus to sell black-market goods smuggled in from Lebanon. Rif'at was often referred to as the "King of the Oriental Carpets" due to the frequent confiscations of these items by his personal Lebanese militia, disparagingly called the Pink Panthers.[78] Not surprisingly, it was Rif'at al-Asad who led the crackdown on the Muslim Brotherhood. In February 1982, Rift'at's Defense Brigades carried out a bombardment of Hama, a city of 180,000 where Brotherhood-inspired riots had taken place. The assault lasted for three weeks, ultimately killing between ten thousand and 25,000 militants and civilians.[79]

Driven by fear of Soviet penetration of Syria, Western intelligence services strengthened extremist groups and inadvertently created a culture of conspiracy theories that played into the hands of the KGB. The Soviet intelligence service took advantage of the prevailing fear of Western intervention by fabricating CIA plots aimed at overthrowing the Asad regime. This hardened the Syrian dictator's obsession with his personal security. As a result, Asad was protected by a presidential guard of over twelve thousand, backed by no fewer than fifteen intelligence and security services with personnel of fifty thousand along with a greater number of informants.[80] After decades in which Syria was splintered by coups and countercoups, Asad had "coup-proofed" Syria.[81]

Both the CIA and the SIS repeatedly ignored reports from Western observers and even from their own officers in the field, reassuring them that Syria was not about to "go red." Patrick Seale challenged the assumption that Syria had ever been at serious risk of becoming a Soviet satellite, concluding that "the CIA messed up in the region."[82] CIA agents, such as Robert Baer, tried to convince his superiors that supporting the Muslim Brotherhood in Syria was a serious and dangerous policy, but were told "the Muslim Brotherhood isn't a target for us."[83]

SEVENTEEN

America's Eyes in the Middle East: The CIA and Israeli Intelligence

"I know of no country that has given such public recognition
to a foreign intelligence officer."
—*William Hood (on Israeli honors for James Jesus Angleton)*[1]

Despite differences of opinion over policy with parts of the Middle East, Britain remained a close ally of the United States. However, Israel's secret service, Mossad, became the primary source of intelligence for the CIA on the region, as well as on Eastern bloc countries and the Soviet Union. In his history of the CIA, Tim Weiner comments: "The channel [Mossad] produced much of the agency's intelligence on the Arab world, but at a cost—a growing American dependence on Israel to explain events in the Middle East. The Israeli perspective colored American perceptions for decades to come."[2]

The architect of this relationship was James Jesus Angleton, the CIA's head of counterintelligence and the one-man liaison with Israel.[3] Angleton's relationship with Israel cannot be defined in stark black-and-white terms—pro-Israel and pro-Zionist, certainly not in the absolute conviction of someone like Orde Wingate, but in subtle shades of gray. Angleton was committed to the Israeli-American alliance but suspicious of Jewish organizations in the United States as well as of Jewish individuals both in and out of the CIA. He backed a CIA operation to buy a Washington garbage company that collected trash from the Israeli embassy and the office of B'nai B'irth, and took it to the agency for sorting and analysis.[4]

Yet for over three decades, Angleton was the closest ally of Israel in Washington; even before 1948, Angleton had close ties to clandestine Jewish organizations. Israeli sentiments for this secretive American intelligence officer are on public display. Just north of Jerusalem, along the Jerusalem—Tel Aviv highway, a series of stones has been inscribed to serve as a memorial for Israeli war heroes who have made the ultimate sacrifice for their country. One of these stones is reserved for the memory of James Angleton. Inscribed on the stone in English and Hebrew: "James Jesus Angleton. 1917–1987. In memory of a Good Friend."[5] A similarly dedicated stone is on a hill overlooking the Jaffa Gate, near the King

David Hotel in Jerusalem, bearing the inscription, in English, Hebrew, and Arabic: "In memory of a dear friend James (Jim) Angleton."[6] The latter was unveiled in a special ceremony where many former and current members of Israel's intelligence community were present to reminisce on the life of their greatest American ally.[7]

Angleton's relationship with Israeli intelligence organizations dated back to the Second World War when, as an OSS (the Office of Strategic Services—America's first clandestine service) officer, he had worked with underground Jewish networks in Italy. After the war, Angleton was the official liaison with all the Allied secret services and the exclusive conduit for information from Israel's intelligence community.[8]

One of Angleton's close friends described the importance of this position:

> That's the job that was so sensitive . . . and that's the one that you don't read about. While he was liaising with everyone, he was getting them to do favors for either the CIA—things the CIA didn't want to carry out directly; like they've never killed anyone, right?—or for his own agenda. Even on a more mundane level, he could use his contacts with Israeli intelligence, which he kept to himself, as authority for whatever line he was trying to push at the CIA. You know, "My Israeli sources tell me such and such," and no one was going to contradict him, since no one else was allowed to talk to Israeli intelligence. I always had the impression that he used the Israelis in this way, getting them to say that the Russians had not really broken with the Chinese or whatever. They would be perfectly happy to do him the favour. On top of all that he felt that he was getting the benefit of Israeli networks and connections all over the place, not just in the Communist bloc.[9]

A former colleague of Angleton explained Angleton's interest in his work:

> Jim believed that the real exercise of power in and between countries occurs through networks of leaders. This was the importance of the liaison unit. It operated outside of the normal channels, which really irritated people like the State Department at times. A lot of it went back to relationships formed during and just after World War II. He cultivated these people, whether they were in or out of government.[10]

James Jesus Angleton was the prime mover that helped forge the relationship between the CIA and Israeli intelligence. The alliance began May 1951, when Angleton arranged for Prime Minister David Ben-Gurion to meet with Walter Bedell Smith, the director of the CIA at the time, and who later that year hosted the mastermind of the Israeli intelligence community, Reuven Shiloah (formerly Zaslany), to draft the first formal U.S.-Israel intelligence sharing arrangement.[11] Contrary to popular belief, this agreement was initially only in verbal form with no written contract.[12] Angleton's first trip to Israel took place in October of that year—the beginning of an annual pilgrimage that would continue throughout his career.[13]

Angleton's attitude toward Israel had been shaped by the Holocaust and was also influenced by the success of the Jewish secret networks. After recruitment by the counterintelligence section of the OSS in 1943, he served for a short time in Britain but spent most of the war in Italy. Among his best sources were Palestinian-Jewish agents who after the end of the war in Europe managed to smuggle thousands of their persecuted European cousins to Palestine through escape networks in Italy.[14] Although later he was integral to the 1951 CIA-Mossad agreement, Angleton feared that the influx of Soviet bloc immigrants into Israel would carry with it spies seeking to penetrate the West.[15] Soviet agents did indeed join the waves of immigrants, but a great number defected, were unmasked, or proved unable to function in any significant strategic employment after arrival in Israel.

It was Soviet policy in 1947 that Israel become an ally of the Soviet Union in order to counter American attempts to use the Israeli links with the Jewish community in the United States. It became the strategy of the KGB to ensure that large numbers of its agents were among the Soviet Jews permitted to leave for Israel. The most successful of the first generation of Soviet agents infiltrated into Israel was the epidemiologist Avraham Marcus Klingberg, who in 1948 was recruited to work on chemical and biological weapons. Later, Klingberg was one of the founders of the Israeli Institute of Biological Research in Ness Ziona (southeast of Tel Aviv). Remarkably he remained a successful agent of the Soviet Union for thirty-five years. Another example was that in the period 1947–1950, thirty-six of the Jews who immigrated to Israel from Bulgaria were operatives of the KGB. In 1953, the Israeli security service, Shin Bet, caught two Israeli members of the Knesset, Yaakov Riftin and Moshe Sneh, passing information on Israel's foreign policy to the Soviet embassy.[16] Both were members of Mapam, Israel's Marxist-Zionist party, and the information passed on to the Soviets reinforced Moscow's suspicions of the special nature of the Israeli-American relationship. And in the 1950s the KGB had penetrated the Mossad itself through the services of Ze'ev Avni, an Israeli diplomat and agent of Mossad.

Just about the time of Avni's capture, the KGB recruited Yisrael Beer, a professor of military history at Tel Aviv University and a military commentator and lieutenant colonel in the Israeli Defense Forces (IDF) reserves. Beer became a close friend of Shimon Peres, then deputy minister of defense. Until Beer was unmasked as a Soviet agent, he was able to provide his masters with Peres's secret attempts in 1957 to obtain assistance from West Germany and purchase refurbished German submarines. Beer most likely leaked the information to the media and the subsequent public outcry almost caused David Ben-Gurion to resign. Shortly afterward, in 1961, he was caught and one year later sentenced to seventeen years in prison, but died after four years of incarceration.[17]

Although none of the Soviet Jews or Israelis recruited in the 1960s achieved anything as valuable as Avni and Beer, Angleton remained cautious about the vulnerability of Israel's population of immigrants whose backgrounds could not be traced behind the Iron Curtain. A report from the British embassy to the Foreign Office underscored these concerns, warning:

> the perpetual problem of security which Israel by its very nature is bound to face . . . [is that] it is a country of immigrants about whose origins and past in many cases nothing is known except for what they themselves reveal. It has been pointed out that hundreds of people in responsible positions in theory offer the same kind of risk as Beer.[18]

Despite the apparent liability, neither Angleton nor most of the senior leadership of the CIA could afford to ignore Israeli intelligence assistance. Mossad collected a great deal of intelligence on the Warsaw Pact powers from the steady stream of Jewish refugees making their way to Israel and forwarded it to Washington through Angleton.[19] When Nikita Khrushchev, the leader of the Soviet Union made his speech condemning Stalin's excesses before the Twentieth Congress of the Communist Party of the Soviet Union in February 1956, Mossad was able to deliver a copy to Angleton in April 1956, who passed it on to a grateful Allen Dulles.[20]

Victor Grayevski, a Polish Jew and journalist with a strong sense of Zionism, had managed to obtain an unofficially reproduced copy of the speech from a secretary in the office of the head of the Polish Communist Party, Edward Ochab. Rather than sell the speech to the Americans or another Western power, Grayevski chose to give the copy to Israel as a gift.[21] Grayevsky allowed an Israeli diplomat to photograph all fifty-eight pages before returning the copy. When the speech landed on the desk of Ben-Gurion a few days later, he called an emergency meeting with his top officials and made the decision to hand over the speech to the CIA, thus cementing the U.S.-Israeli alliance and forging closer ties with America's intelligence agency.[22] The Israelis had acted just in the nick of time, as Frank Wisner, the CIA's deputy director for plans, had acquired his own copy of the speech from the French.[23]

It was not a one-way street, however. According to Mohamed Heikal, Angleton passed back vital information that assisted the Israelis in developing an atomic program, and at the very least he was a strong and influential voice backing Israel in Washington.[24] Heikal was a close associate of Nasser and had little love for Angleton or Israel, but it is certain that the zealous head of the CIA's counterintelligence gave Mossad something in exchange. Michael Holzman, in a recent biography of Angleton, poses an intriguing scenario:

> One monument set up by the Israelis after Angleton's death, then, the public monument might be taken to memorialize his long operational relationship with the Israeli intelligence services. The other, the more obscurely situated monument, perhaps could be taken as memorializing, in part, a quite specific service to Israel that was performed by Angleton: his help with the Israeli atomic bomb.[25]

Holzman's assertion is not entirely implausible if taken in the context of the Cold War. Above everything else, Angleton was an implacable foe of communism and it was not unreasonable for him, or any of the administrations he served, to fear a Soviet strike against Israel. Under such circumstances passing nuclear weapons technology would have been part of America's strategy of deterrence and not necessarily the sole act of a pro-Israeli Angleton.

If Angleton did not give the Israelis vital American scientific secrets, at the very least he must have used his considerable influence inside the CIA on behalf of the Jewish state. Furthermore, the sensitivity of the Truman White House to the Jewish vote was another factor in American policy toward the Middle East. On the other hand, the Eisenhower administration, which succeeded that of Truman, initially tried to secure alliances with Arab states and was not inclined to support Israel, but this policy changed after a few years.[26]

Although Angleton emerged as Israel's chief ally in Washington, it did not prevent the Israelis from trying to manipulate the CIA's counterintelligence chief. In 1956 a dispatch from the military attaché at the American embassy in Tel Aviv reported that Israel had mobilized its reserves. Kermit Roosevelt gave similar information to Dulles. Another warning came from London and

Robert Amory, the CIA's deputy director for intelligence, predicted the attack would happen within twenty-four hours.[27]

Allen Dulles called a meeting of the CIA's Watch Committee, and it met an hour later in Dulles's office. Amory recalled:

> At that moment James Angleton suddenly burst out of a bathroom that connected Allen's office and the deputy director's office next door. We used it to keep people visiting the director from meeting each other outside. You wouldn't want the head of Pakistani intelligence to meet his Indian counterpart on the way out, for instance. Anyway, Angleton comes bursting in and says "I can discount what Amory is saying. I spent last night with our friends and they have assured me that they are just carrying out protective measures against the Jordanians." Well, I got mad at that. I said to Allen, "The taxpayer lays out $16,000 a year to me as your deputy director for me to give you the best intelligence based on the evidence available. Either you believe me or you believe this co-opted Israeli agent here," and I pointed at Angleton.[28]

It was possibly the harshest thing that Amory could have said about Angleton in the presence of the head of the CIA. Nevertheless, Dulles put his faith in Angleton and when Israel attacked Egypt, on October 29, 1956, Dulles called the invasion merely a probing action. But it soon became apparent that the Israelis were moving against Egypt, and Dulles and the CIA were caught unaware. Angleton was embarrassed when Israel proceeded to invade the Sinai and seize the Suez Canal as part of its tripartite plot with Britain and France. One of Angleton's colleagues remarked, "The Israelis could get away with lying to Jim that once. I don't think they did it again."[29] However, according to Rhodri Jeffrey-Jones, "There has been considerable speculation about this presumed intelligence failure. For example, some accuse James Angleton . . . of suppressing some indications of the attack because he sympathized with its objectives, while others report that he was furious at being kept in the dark by his Israeli friends. But there is some doubt as to whether the CIA was, in fact, caught unaware."[30]

This was not the first occasion in which the American-Israeli alliance was strained. During the period of 1952–1953 the FBI determined that Mossad and Aman (Israel's Military Intelligence Directorate) were conducting espionage activities on American soil. Elyashiv Ben-Horin, an Israeli diplomat, was discovered trying to recruit Arab diplomats to spy on their countries. Though this was standard practice for Israeli intelligence agents in Western capitals, it did not sit well with their American hosts. The Israeli operation achieved debacle-like proportions when the Jordanian military attaché pretended to accept recruitment but reported Mossad's activities to the FBI. An FBI surveillance team later saved the Jordanian from a gun-wielding Ben-Horin after the attaché provoked him into an argument at a restaurant. Ben-Horin was expelled from the country and was barred from returning to the United States until years later, despite his successful career as a diplomat, including a term as ambassador to Germany. The FBI also suspected Colonel Chaim Herzog, Israel's military attaché to Washington, of attempting to steal defense technology, but as evidence against him was weak and his term at the embassy was coming to a close, no action was taken.[31] Upon his return to Israel he was promoted to the rank of general and appointed chief of Aman.

From the beginning of the intelligence cooperation agreement, Angleton had been meeting regularly with Memi de Shalit, Israel's unofficial and only semi-involved intelligence officer in Washington in 1951. Shalit was made official liaison to the CIA, and he developed a long-lasting friendship with Angleton, with whom he shared the same birth date, December 9 (the two would exchange birthday cards for decades). "Jim impressed me," Shalit reminisced, "he seemed detached and acted with great caution and circumspection." Shalit held most of his meetings with Angleton at his house on Massachusetts Avenue, and sometimes in restaurants. He recalls his meetings: "He came, two or three times a week, to my house in the early evening, and often stayed until the early hours of the morning. It happened more than once that his wife, Cecilia, phoned at about 4:00 A.M. to find out whether the meeting was still going on."[32]

Despite its early tensions, however, by 1953 the covert alliance between the two countries had settled into a productive and reciprocal relationship, and Angleton's meetings with Shalit began to yield results. Angleton had the occasional requests and sometimes favors that the CIA was not able to secure. As Shalit recalled, "Once he asked us if we could get him gold coins. For them [the CIA], getting gold coins was not an easy affair. It was very easy for us. We got them from friends in Europe and passed them on to the Americans [with which to pay their agents behind the Iron Curtain]."[33] On another occasion, Angleton inquired if Israeli intelligence could find work for the musician wife of a Soviet defector, in order to keep the man happy and talking. He wanted Mossad to ask a favor from a well-known Jewish violinist on the international concert circuit to hire the woman, but despite Israeli efforts, the violinist found the defector's wife unskilled. In return, the CIA helped Israel by giving them intelligence equipment: bugs, radio receivers, and transmitters to be installed at the Syrian border in order to transmit false information. The CIA also hosted Israeli intelligence personnel for training at Langley.[34]

The general framework of the alliance was simple: in exchange for intelligence on the Soviet bloc, Israel's intelligence community received training and technology.[35] The intelligence that Israel provided included a range of subjects on the Soviet Union. A top secret Shabak program to debrief the constant flow of immigrants to Israel from the Soviet bloc yielded vital information on topics from military installations to economic conditions and the morale of Soviet citizens. As Teddy Kollek recalled,

> our people talked with immigrants, translated what they told us into English and passed the material on to the Americans. The CIA was interested in any crumb of information from the East Bloc, from the price of bread and train timetables, to the description of the lines of people that were waiting to get into the food shops.[36]

Kollek estimated that one quarter of all information on the Soviets that the Americans acquired throughout the 1950s was from Israel intelligence sources.[37] To show their gratitude, the CIA hosted a number of senior Israeli intelligence officers in 1952 for a training course on modern intelligence and espionage techniques.[38] The Israelis even received help from former Nazi intelligence chief Reinhard Gehlen, in his capacity as head of the BND. After the Sinai War in 1956, the BND provided training and assisted in infiltrating Israeli agents. The Germans also offered the Israelis expert advice on the organization and development of intelligence services.[39]

However, the primary relationship was with the United States and the Israelis shared the spoils with their friends in the American intelligence establishment. On August 16, 1966, Israeli intelligence managed to obtain a Soviet MiG-21 and offered it to its allies in the CIA. The Americans were surprised and delighted by the opportunity to obtain detailed insight into the capabilities of Soviet bloc air forces. The operation originated in late 1964, when an Iraqi Jewish merchant, "Yosef," informed Israeli officials that his girlfriend's sister was married to an Iraqi air force pilot named Munir Radfa, who had an interest in defecting with his MiG because he was frustrated over the discrimination he faced as a Christian. Radfa was worried for his family and he knew that they would surely face punishment or even death at the hands of Iraq's security service. With extensive planning and help from Kurdish guerrillas, the Israelis managed to smuggle Radfa's family out of Iraq. Thus Radfa took off one morning from Iraq and landed his MiG in Israel. He and his family were settled under a new name and likely still live somewhere in Israel.[40]

On another occasion, Israel supplied the United States with an entire Soviet radar station, which the Israelis had captured from the Arabs a few months following the Sinai War. Earlier, the CIA had asked their Israeli counterparts to send samples of Soviet military hardware that had been captured by the IDF.[41] In September 1969, Israeli commandos raided an Egyptian radar post across the Gulf of Suez and stole an entire radar station—the most advanced in Soviet technology. The station was airlifted by four helicopters and then flown in parts to the United States for closer examination. The radar was the same model as that which was in use by North Vietnamese forces and it provided invaluable assistance to the American forces fighting in Vietnam.[42]

There were other, lesser coups that served American as well as Canadian interests. For example, Israeli intelligence was able to unmask a Soviet mole in the Royal Canadian Mounted Police. In 1959, Roy Guidon had been posted as an intelligence officer in the Canadian embassy in Moscow. Guidon tried in vain to initiate a number of affairs with women at the embassy, which brought him to the attention of the Soviet intelligence. The KGB, consequently, concocted a honey trap in the form of a young and beautiful agent who called herself Larissa Fedorovna Dubanova. The KGB arranged for Guidon to meet Dubanova in an apparent coincidence at the Bolshoi Ballet and the two carried on an affair for several months, until she informed him that she was pregnant. After a hasty illegal wedding, arranged by the KGB, Guidon was coerced into supplying the Soviets with Canada's diplomatic codes and even bugged his embassy, all under the threat of never seeing Dubanova again. Guidon continued to spy for the Soviets after his transfer to Washington, in exchange for infrequent visits with his wife—who did not give birth to any child after allegedly having an abortion. Guidon was unmasked after being transferred to the Canadian embassy in Tel Aviv, where Shabak had tapped his telephone, as was the case with most other foreign diplomats in Israel. Israeli intelligence informed MI6 after overhearing Guidon's careless conversations with his Soviet handler, and the British, in turn, shared the information with the RCMP, who lured Guidon home on a pretext and arrested him. He avoided trial and imprisonment in exchange for his full confession and cooperation.[43]

When Israeli intelligence managed to unmask the true identity of Kim Philby, the most famous Soviet mole in Britain's Secret Intelligence Service, MI6, it eventually paved the way for improving relations between London and Tel Aviv. Kollek had met Philby at the CIA's Langley headquarters when the

Israeli intelligence officer first met Angleton and at the time had warned Angleton of Philby's left-wing sentiments, which surfaced when the two were ac-
quainted in Austria in the 1930s (a part of his past that Philby had concealed
from his MI6 employers). Israeli intelligence also received information from a
British Jewish woman, whom Philby had unsuccessfully tried to recruit into
Soviet intelligence during the 1940s. The woman was visiting Israel in 1961 and
had let the information slip at a cocktail party. Though these warnings went
unheeded, after Philby defected, the warning from Israeli intelligence nevertheless impressed Maurice Oldfield, at that time deputy chief of MI6, and Peter
Wright, deputy head of MI5. This new appreciation of Israel's intelligence capabilities led to the signing of a formal British-Israeli intelligence sharing agreement similar to that of the United States.[44]

Relations with Israel's intelligence community required a particular protocol. John Hadden had been posted as the Tel Aviv CIA station chief in 1963 and
acquired a degree of expertise in the counterintuitive and complex skill of what
liaising with Israeli intelligence entailed. Hadden described the Israeli-American
intelligence as a far cry from the "card game" of tit-for-tat exchanges between
friendly intelligence services such as with those of the British or the West Germans, which would eventually conclude with everyone giving each other what
they wanted. The meetings with the Israelis, according to Hadden, were "crazed."
Hadden recalls being subjected to the usual forty-five-minute diatribe wherein
the Israelis issued a litany of the grievous threats to Israeli security and a cata-
logue of the military and intelligence material that they required to overcome
those threats. "Christ!" Hadden remembers in frustration, "there you were in
your chair and they were shouting way over behind you! Absolutely outrageous!
They were asking for the goddamned moon!"[45]

Hadden's method for dealing with the Israelis, which he advised Angleton
and other American negotiators to adopt, was to listen respectfully and take
careful notes, then speak for forty-five minutes on the American position without allowing any interruption. During this time the Americans would ignore
everything that the Israelis had said and do their best to be equally outrageous.
Then both sides could slowly relax into an agreement. While some American
negotiators were left infuriated by the Israeli rants and monologues, Hadden
was simply amused and advised his colleagues: "Just hold on to your hat and
take the ride!"[46]

Hadden also recommended to his successor at the CIA Tel Aviv posting to
"learn Hebrew. Your professional peers will be afraid of you, but ordinary Israelis will speak more freely. And that is what matters for intelligence men." He
urged CIA officers not to fall into the trap of other U.S. diplomats, who adored

Israelis and their country and found themselves unable to stand up to them. Hadden added:

> No matter what you really feel, you're going to get absolutely no-where unless you're one of their friends. . . . You are going to be worth-less to the United States government if you don't reserve some part of your brain to be friendly and share their interests. When you're in Hamburg, you sail. When you're in Austria, you ski. When you're in Israel, you dig.[47]

Indeed, he would suggest to CIA officers posted in Israel to take up archaeology, noting that Israelis are obsessed with their past. But he warned that the Tel Aviv posting was a career-wrecker, because work in Israel precluded working in an Arab country. He added that that they should be prepared for a long stay, as "it's going to take you more than two years for the Israelis to realize that you're not working for Saudi intelligence." And while most Israelis are talkative, the same cannot be said for their intelligence agents: "The Mossad and [Aman] aren't going to treat you as an ally, even if you do get some Israelis to accept you as part of the family." Hadden described Israel as neither allied territory like Britain nor enemy territory like East Germany.[48] Finally, he lamented that there was not much to do intelligence-wise in Tel Aviv since "Washington was only interested in fighting the Russians," and the small number of Soviet spies in Israel had been "completely bottled up by Israeli counter-intelligence."[49]

The alliance between American and Israeli intelligence went far beyond the exchange of technological and tradecraft favors. Israel, on the request of the CIA, served as the "hands-off" trainer and arms dealer for supporting some of the world's most brutal, yet America-friendly, regimes. In the course of Operation KK Mountain during the 1960s, the Israelis received $10 to $20 million per year of funds to carry out missions that were too sensitive for the CIA or any other intelligence agency of the United States.[50] Part of these missions included Israeli training for the military and secret police of various African and South American countries as well as to the death squads of the Medellín Cartel, which prior to its destruction was the largest drug cartel in the world.[51]

The precursor to these training operations was the training and arms that Israel and the United States provided to the armed forces and security apparatus of the Shah of Iran. In a secret CIA review written in 1976 and captured by Iranian students during the Khomeini revolution, the CIA reported:

A formal trilateral liaison called the Trident Organization was established by Mossad with Turkey's National Security Service (TNSS) and Iran's National Organization for Intelligence and Security (SAVAK) in late 1958 . . . the Trident Organization involves continuing intelligence exchange plus semi-annual meetings at the chief of service level.[52]

Prior to this alliance, which included Turkey, Israel and Iran had an ongoing relationship. In 1950, Israel essentially purchased de facto diplomatic recognition from the Shah for $400,000. A mutual exchange of services began in 1954 in which Iran traded petroleum in exchange for Israeli expertise in intelligence, defense, and domestic security.

The Shah's regime viewed Israel as a gateway to the West. According to Chaim Herzog, at the time head of Aman, the Shah believed that every Israeli was a link to Washington. David Kimche, a former high-ranking Mossad officer and former chief of the Israeli Foreign Ministry, recalls, "If there'd be any anti-Iranian article in any newspaper in the United States or even in Europe, the Shah would call us and say, 'Why did you allow this to happen?' We would in vain plead innocence, saying that we don't control the whole or world media, we don't control the banks as some people think we do."[53]

Not long afterward, the Israeli security services served as a conduit and proxy for the CIA in order to create for the Shah an effective intelligence and security service. Consequently, the CIA created SAVAK in 1957 with the active assistance of Germany and Israel.[54] SAVAK was organized in several sections: the Second Department dealt with foreign intelligence, the Seventh analyzed intelligence, the Eighth carried out counterintelligence operations, while the Third was charged with internal security. It was the Third Department, with its reputation for brutality, where the CIA made use of Israel's expert training. The CIA has denied having taught SAVAK about torture, claiming that the Israelis were the ones who worked on the "hard stuff."

The Mossad-SAVAK relationship originated in the fall of 1957 in Rome, when Isser Harel, formerly of Mossad, met the first head of SAVAK, General Taimour Bakhtiar.[55] A little later Bakhtiar met with Ya'acov Zur, Israel's ambassador to France, in September 1957. The Iranian general, speaking on behalf of the Shah, suggested cooperation and an exchange of political viewpoints between the two countries. In October, Bakhtiar and Harel met again in Rome and agreed to more in-depth strategic cooperation. Iranian and Israeli relations became more intimate after the overthrow of the Iraqi monarchy by Abdul

Karim Qasim, which led to Iraq leaving the Baghdad Pact and allying itself with Nasser.[56] Then, in 1960, the head of Aman, General Chaim Herzog, arrived for his first visit in Tehran and suggested that the two countries exchange military attachés. The Shah agreed and Ben-Gurion appointed Ya'acov Nimrodi.[57]

Nimrodi was a perfect choice for the position. The corpulent officer was a former Shai (the precursor of Israel's Military Intelligence Directorate) agent and fluent in Farsi and Arabic. Nimrodi lived in Tehran for thirteen years and has warned, "When one day we shall be permitted to talk about all that we have done in Iran, you will be horrified. . . . It is beyond your imagination." Nimrodi hardly kept a low profile, but rather loudly demonstrated his power and influence, printing visiting cards with the title "Israeli Military Attaché," and holding court with Iran's top officials.[58] Meanwhile in Israel, Iranian military and intelligence officers were often spotted throughout the 1960s and barely managed to keep a low profile as they received their training.[59]

In a 1975 interview with the Arabic-language Paris newspaper *El-Mustaqbal* the Shah personally admitted to the arrangement with Israel and complained that Nasser's hostility toward Iran left him little choice. He revealed that Iran and Israel shared intelligence evaluations and exchanged information pertaining to Palestinian terrorist activities as well as information on Iranian trainers at PLO bases in Lebanon. The two SAVAK (National Intelligence and Security Organization) officers, Generals Hashemi Manucher and Ali Parvaresh, admitted in their 1979 trial that they had disclosed the location of Palestinian bases in Lebanon to their Israeli allies. In addition to intelligence cooperation, Israel trained around four hundred Iranian pilots, paratroopers, and artillery operators, as well as supplied the Shah with large numbers of arms.

The Israel-Iran alliance ended with the 1979 Iranian Revolution, when the theocracy headed by the Ayatollah Ruhollah Khomeini replaced the monarchy and declared its implacable hostility toward Israel and the West. Despite this dramatic shift in Iranian policy, Israel and the United States would resume their military support of Iran during the mid-1980s in response to the specter of an Iraq victory in the Iran-Iraq War.

In the meantime, an extensive purge of Iran's military, political, and civil service establishment followed the revolution. The security services were not exempt, but although the higher-ranking officers of SAVAK were executed, along with those officers implicated in the torture and execution of those who had been opposed to the Shah, particularly those from SAVAK's infamous Third Department.[60] However, according to an interview with Eliezer Tsafrir, the former chief of Mossad's Iran station, those officers in the middle and lower ranks of SAVAK continued their work in VAVAK—the new ministry of intelligence in post-revolution Iran—and in SAVANA, the post-revolution intelligence service. These Mossad-trained experts were vital in maintaining a high standard of proficiency for the post-revolution Iranian intelligence community.[61] Whether out of fear for their lives or out of more casual pragmatism, the former SAVAK officers decided to work for the new regime and brought with them the skills and training they had gained from Mossad and the Israeli military. When the Islamic Revolutionary Guard Corps, Pasdaran, and Iranian intelligence helped to establish Hizbullah (Party of God) in Lebanon, following the Israeli invasion in 1982, they trained their new Lebanese proxy to use Israeli weapons and Israeli intelligence tradecraft against Israel, according to the interview with former Mossad officer Eliezer Tsafrir.[62]

Both in the cases of Egypt and Iran, America's intelligence establishment enabled successive administrations in Washington to engage in secret diplomacy and wage a clandestine war against the Soviets in the Middle East. A major partner in this effort was Israel and, ironically, a range of radical organizations motivated by political Islam. On many occasions militant Muslims employed the intelligence tradecraft that the CIA and Mossad had so carefully, and secretly, transferred to individuals and organizations committed to the destruction of the state of Israel and the defeat of the United States. Yet, in the context of the Cold War, America's primary objective in the Middle East was to stymie Arab, Iranian, and South Asian nationalism from serving the interests of the Soviet Union by exploiting the role of Islam in the Muslim world.

EIGHTEEN

The Iranian Jihad

"I owe my throne to God, my people, my army—and to you."
—*Shah Mohammad Reza Pahlavi to Kermit Roosevelt*[1]

For a short period of time, Nasser was the Arab leader who held promise for contributing to American security in the Middle East. However, in the early 1950s, communism and nationalism assumed center stage in the domestic and foreign policy of the United States. Although the McCarthy anticommunist hysteria was beginning to wane in 1953, the Eisenhower administration was predisposed to suspect and fear Moscow. In particular, John Foster Dulles, the new secretary of state, believed that radical nationalism paved the way for communist penetration of the Third World. Dulles reported to the Senate that: "Whether it is in Indo-China or in Morocco or Egypt or Arabia or Iran . . . the forces of unrest are captured by the Soviet Communists."[2]

The fact that Eisenhower had surrendered foreign affairs to Dulles, and that Dulles's brother, Allen, became director of the Central Intelligence Agency, gave these comments considerable potency, as they underscored America's foreign policy. Despite these comments and his assurances to the Senate that he would extricate the nationalist gateways of communism, at first glance it appeared that John Foster Dulles could not quite make up his mind whether the United States was to become a force of change in the Middle East or a guarantor of the colonial assets of the old regimes. On the one hand, the secretary supported Nasser's nationalization of the Suez Canal (July 1954), opposed French colonialism in North Africa (1955), and countered the Anglo-French-Israeli attempt to seize the canal in 1956. On the other, he endorsed the Anglo-American coup against the Mossadeq government in Iran to uphold British oil interests. These policies were not so much contradictory as guided by the principle of self-interest in the face of a potential communist onslaught.

Dulles's Cold War anticommunism and "with-us-or-against-us" policy placed the United States in an ideological straitjacket. Against this background, Nasser's increasing role in the Nonaligned Movement and the Egyptian leader's decision to purchase arms from the Soviet Union (via Czechoslovakia) in 1955 set the United States on a collision course with Egypt.[3] Dulles made several attempts to woo Nasser back into the American fold, and particularly to join MEDO (Middle East Defense Organization), but the Egyptian leader declined and instead recognized communist China.[4]

Nasser also snubbed Dulles's attempts to mediate between Israel and Egypt. In 1954, the State Department produced Alpha, a secret proposal whereby Israel would surrender large tracts of territory in exchange for Egyptian nonbelligerency. But Nasser's meteoric rise in the Arab world made it difficult for him to compromise on the soon-to-be intractable Palestinian-Israeli issue and, after stalling, he declined.[5] A second peace plan, Gamma, fared no better, after which the secretary lost all patience with Nasser and authorized Operation Omega, with the objective of overthrowing the Egyptian government by all means except war. The plan called for denying Egypt funding for building the Aswan Dam, and it included a provision for promoting King Saud of Saudi Arabia as an Islamic "pope."[6]

Effectively, American policymakers gave up on Nasser as a modern-day Caliph who could unite the Muslims and lead them away from communism; instead they demonized him as if he were some kind of Saddam Hussein. Only, instead of harboring weapons of mass destruction, Nasser was cast as the peddler of Soviet infiltration in the Middle East. Islam became the bulwark against the Soviets since it had no possible affinity with Marxism, and devout Muslims could be counted on to shun godless Moscow's encroachments. Accordingly, along with supporting the Saudis and other conservative regimes in the Middle East, such as Iran, Jordan, Pakistan, and Turkey, the U.S. government turned to the Muslim Brothers to fight Nasser and oppose communism throughout the region.

American political officials had first established contact with Hassan al-Banna in the late 1940s in Cairo and in Jeddah. According to Herman Eilts, at the time a young diplomat in Saudi Arabia, the U.S. embassy in Cairo:

> had regular meetings with Hassan al-Banna at the time, and found him perfectly empathetic. We kept in touch with them [the Muslim Brothers] especially for reporting purposes, because at the time the Muslim Brotherhood was one element that was viewed as potentially politically important. I don't think we were alarmed by them, though there was concern when the Brotherhood's Secret Apparatus assassinated the prime minister [Mahmud Nokrashy Pasha of Egypt]. We were concerned about stability, primarily, and our judgment was that the assassinations were worrying but they did not forecast serious political instability.[7]

Every indication from the pronouncements of the Muslim Brotherhood reinforced the organization's commitment to anticommunism, further endearing it to the United States. In an interview with *Al-Mari*, Judge Hassan al-Hudaibi, supreme guide of the Muslim Brotherhood, stated, "communism denies all religions, contradicts the fundamentals of Islam and undermines its moral and social systems." In the same interview, he underlined his conviction that "Islam is the strongest bulwark against communist ideologies."[8]

After the death of al-Banna, his son-in-law, Said Ramadan, had begun to play a prominent role in the leadership of the Brotherhood and became an important contact with the Americans. In September 1953, Ramadan attended the Colloquium on Islamic Culture co-sponsored by Princeton University and the Library of Congress. However, funding for the guests from the Middle East originated from the International Information Administration, a branch of the State Department, and was taken over shortly after by the U.S. Information Agency, which was linked to the CIA.[9]

During the nine-day conference, Ramadan slipped into Washington and had a photo opportunity with Eisenhower. Robert Dreyfuss, who has chronicled Ramadan's participation in the colloquium, makes the case that there is circumstantial evidence that the CIA had set up the event in order to cultivate Ramadan as an agent.[10] According to Sylvain Bensson's article in *Le Temps* of Geneva, in the 1960s the Swiss authorities believed that Ramadan was an intelligence agent of the British and the Americans, as well as the Swiss.[11] Certainly Ramadan's subsequent career as a roving ambassador on behalf of the MB in the cause of political Islam might have given him considerable opportunity to report on developments to his handlers, but it is not likely. It is not difficult to surmise that the CIA made an effort to recruit him, and that Ramadan went along to the degree that it suited the interests of the MB. In other words, it was a mutual exploratory endeavor, but what each side got out of it is not known.

After Nasser outlawed the MB and imprisoned thousands of its members, the survivors found refuge in Saudi Arabia. King Saud tried to exploit the Brotherhood's antipathy for Nasser in his struggle with the Egyptians over leadership of the Arab world. But the Brothers in Saudi Arabia joined up with local extremists and helped to radicalize the next generation of Muslim zealots. It is ironic that today's adherents of political Islam, whether intellectual activists, militants fighting in the mountains of Afghanistan, or urban guerrillas ratcheting up the level of terrorism in the cities, were exported to the United States via the schools of radicalism staffed in part by Muslim Brothers. Indeed, the CIA's flirtation with political Islam in their struggle against Nasser or against the Soviets in Afghanistan earned the United States little gratitude among most Muslims.

The list of grievances against the Americans in the Middle East is long and begins less with the U.S. recognition of Israel in 1948 than with the coup against Iran's Mohammad Mossadeq, followed by blanket U.S. support for virtually every corrupt and repressive regime in the region.[12] The Anglo-American coup against the secular government of Iran succeeded because Kermit Roosevelt was able to tap into the well of discontent harbored by Iran's religious establishment. A key ally of convenience for the CIA operation in Iran was Ayatollah Kashani. Although the ayatollah was initially a supporter of Mossadeq, he had turned against the premier because he resented his power, and the ayatollah became open to American approaches, in order to achieve a better advantage. Roosevelt's agents advised the CIA officer that Kashani's participation in the coup could be purchased, so he handed over to one of the ayatollah's confidants the sum of $10,000.[13]

Kashani was fiercely anti-Western and despised liberal ideas, holding the conviction that Muslims should only obey secular laws that were in harmony with the Islamic legal tradition of sharia. He supported Mossadeq only because the religious leader hated the British more and wanted Iran to achieve complete independence, so that it could eventually join a pan-Islamic federation. Kashani marshaled his religious followers, who took to the streets to support Mossadeq, just as he and other religious leaders would later inflame them against the premier.[14] Like the Americans, the ayatollahs hated communism and resented Mosaddeq's political alliance with Iran's Communist Party.

The Anglo-American coup succeeded in the short term, because Roosevelt and his agents harnessed the influence of the religious establishment, bought the media, and managed to generate large demonstrations, creating the impression that there was mass opposition to Mossadeq. A key factor in the coup was the ability of Roosevelt's Iranian agents to mobilize the bazaar, with its complex layers of businessmen, mullahs, small shopkeepers, carpet dealers, spice merchants, magicians, beggars, artists, scribes, professional rabble-rousers, and not least of all, storytellers. Remarkably, Roosevelt turned the stories of Mossadeq against the premier and in favor of the Shah. It was a Pyrrhic victory, albeit one that kept the Iranian monarch in power for a quarter of a century. Twenty-six years later, the Ayatollah Khomeini was able to harness the power of public opinion, as well as the bazaar, against the Shah and in 1979 seized power in Iran.

Ayatollah Ruhollah Musavi Khomeini, the dour cleric who led the Iranian Revolution, cast himself as the avenger of the humiliations that the West had for more than a century inflicted on the Muslims of the Middle East. Unlike Ataturk or Nasser, who embraced secularism to counter the power of the West, Khomeini looked to the past and brought about an Islamic revolution. The

Ayatollah walked through history; he brought down the Iranian monarchy, but at the same time ignited mass opposition to Western ideas and practices in the Muslim world. Khomeini's victories legitimized Islam as a source of power and reinvigorated the notion of religion as the arbiter of all aspects of life.

On November 4, 1979, around three hundred to five hundred students successfully attacked and captured the U.S. embassy in Tehran. Fifty-two American diplomats were taken hostage and held for the next 444 days. The United States appeared helpless and impotent. Khomeini gave the students his full support and reveled in President Jimmy Carter's dilemma. The hostage taking was a crisis in the United States, but a unifying factor in Iran. The militancy of the students precluded any prospect of the establishment of a moderate government. Khomeini's power was further enhanced when an American rescue attempt on April 24, 1980, ended in disaster.

Khomeini's revolution had a limited shelf life outside the bounds of the Shiite Muslim world. Yet this did not deter the new regime in Tehran from attempting to project Iran's influence in the region. In a Sunni-dominated Muslim world only Lebanon offered an ideal base for Khomeini's brand of Islam to spread in the Middle East. Lebanon was fertile ground because it has had a long history as home to a complex mix of religious sects with unique loyalties to different strains of Islam as well as Christianity.

During the Crusades, the Lebanese Christian Maronites threw in their lot with the West and when the Christian warriors were driven from Lebanon, the Maronites retreated into the northern mountains where many of the original villages remain to this day.[15] Through this experience they learned that "responsibility for their own existence," writes Robert Fisk, "lay exclusively in their own hands, that their ultimate fate depended solely upon their own determination and resources. It was a characteristic that they were to share with all the minorities of Lebanon; and later with the Israelis."[16]

From the early modern period, foreign powers realized that they could exploit the region and pursue their own goals there by manipulating particular religious groups. Traditionally and because of religious affinity, the French favored the Maronite Christians, the Russians the Orthodox Christians, and the British supported the Druze by default. Consequently, the Western powers were thus able to intervene in the country under the guise of protecting their religious allies. According to Tom Russell, "This insertion of foreign interests occurred in the course of a protracted shift of power in the Mt. Lebanon area from Druze to Maronites and contributed to the tensions among the various communities and ruling clans."[17]

In 1860, a major war between the Druze and the Christians in Lebanon gave the French the opportunity to intervene ostensibly to protect the Maronite community. In 1920, France was given its share of the Middle East with a mandate for Lebanon and Syria. Shortly after, the French created the state of Greater Lebanon, but Lebanon became a separate entity from Syria in 1926.[18]

During the Second World War, Vichy forces held the country until the British and Free French invasion in 1941. Lebanon gained independence in 1943 and French troops finally withdrew in 1946. The 1943 "national pact" organized the Lebanese government along religious lines. Russell adds, "It gave Christians a 6–5 advantage in parliament and major government posts, including the officer corps. The president must be a Maronite, the prime minister a Sunni, the speaker of parliament a Shi'a."[19]

Despite this agreement and the attempt to create a balance of power for the three primary religious groups, Lebanon was permanently altered by the creation of Israel in 1948 and the arrival of 120,000 Palestinian refugees.[20] The presence of such a large disgruntled refugee community in Lebanon engendered the creation of militant Palestinian groups that periodically attacked Israel from across the Lebanese border.

Another factor that destabilized Lebanese society was that for most of the Cold War, Lebanon, like Syria, was neutral and contested middle ground, over which the West and the Soviets battled to control Arab nationalism. In this context, Lebanon acted as a hub and propaganda platform for the Americans and Soviets throughout the Cold War.[21] Throughout the latter half of the twentieth century, Lebanon also became home not only to major Palestinian militant groups, but a variety of rival terrorist groups, exploited as secret forces by the Cold War rivals.

Ultimately, the multiple layers of competing ideologies, rivalries, and private militias fragmented Lebanon and made it ideal for Iranian penetration. The Iranians began by providing funds and military training to radical Shiite groups in the surrounding region. A camp was established close to Khomeini's home, in which terrorists were given weapons training and prepared to conduct suicide attacks. In addition to Lebanon, Khomeini's shock troops also reached Bahrain, Kuwait dictator, Saudi Arabia, and Iraq.[22]

In early 1982, Iraq's Saddam Hussein ordered the assassination of Shlomo Argov, the Israeli ambassador to London. This act, he had hoped, would be blamed on the PLO, which would in turn cause Israel to invade Lebanon. When Israel invaded Lebanon, Iran would then divert some of the troops poised to invade Iraq. The plan did not work quite as Saddam had expected. Israel did indeed invade Lebanon, on June 6, 1982. Khomeini reacted as expected, but only dispatched one thousand Revolutionary Guards to Lebanon. The Iranians established a base in the Bekaa Valley where they already had extensive networks with extreme groups.[23]

The main Shiite militia in Lebanon at this time was AMAL (Battalions of the Lebanese Resistance), a primarily secular group, fighting for economic and social rights. Many who began their militant careers under the umbrella of AMAL later broke away to form more hard-line fundamentalist organizations. The Iranians organized training centers and intelligence networks, and supplied them with weapons and money to form the resistance against the Israeli forces. The Lebanese Hizbullah was originally created not as an independent force in and of itself, but as a coordinating body to oversee the activities of all the pro-Iranian splinter groups working in Lebanon. According to Kenneth Pollack:

> Through it all, Iran was the principal moving force behind Hizballah, providing it with an organizational structure, training, material support, moral guidance, and often direction.... Indeed, the Hizballahis and Iranians have always been on the same ideological page.[24]

Hizbullah did not remain a mere oversight committee, but quickly developed into a major force in Lebanon. In 1983, Iran through the Hizbullah challenged the United States in the Middle East. On October 23, 1983, Hizbullah suicide bombers killed 241 U.S. marines and fifty-eight French paratroopers in Beirut. The American investigators did not identify the two men who drove bomb-laden trucks into the U.S. Marine barracks and French battalion headquarters; but Islamic Jihad claimed credit and stressed that it had been Lebanese Muslims who carried out the act and not Iranians or Palestinians. Earlier that year, Hizbullah had gutted American intelligence in Lebanon when on March 16 the Shiite militants kidnapped William Buckley, the CIA station chief in Beirut, undermining the ability of the United States to conduct a covert war in the Middle East. Although Islamic Jihad claimed to have executed the American CIA officer on October 4, 1985, he had actually died in captivity of pneumonia-like symptoms on June 3 of that year.[25]

The mishandling of covert support for the mujahidin in Afghanistan, where the United States paid for the arms and training that made the Islamic victory possible, compounded the U.S. failure in Iran and Lebanon. The stories in the bazaar lauded the mujahidin but continued to revile the Americans. Had Khomeini been a Sunni Muslim, he could have dreamed of assuming the mantle of Caliph. He may have inspired millions of Muslims, but his Shiite faith prevented him from any claim to lead all of Islam.

And so, all America's attempts to establish the king of Saudi Arabia, the strongman of Egypt, or even the Shah of Iran as a new Caliph, like those of the British before them, amounted to nothing. Certainly any attempt at finding a new Saladin to lead Islam into the future remained a dream in the sand. This tapestry of deceit and manipulation of religion and nationalism served only to reawaken militant Islam. Across the Muslim world the concept of political Islam took hold and the contagion of extreme Islamic practices spread to the Muslims of Central and Southeast Asia. Almost overnight the crisis of the Middle East became inexplicably bound with the regional paranoia and fears of South Asia and backed by the prospect of nuclear weapons.

NINETEEN

Espionage, Religion, and War in the Northwest Frontier

"All of the nightmares of the twenty-first century
come together in Pakistan."
—*Bruce Riedel*[1]

The small dinghy gently lodged against the shore of Mumbai's fisherman's colony on that fateful Wednesday evening around 9:15 and a group of ten young men disembarked. They moved silently, mimicked by the long shadows cast by the moonlit night. Bharat Tamore, a solitary figure on the beach that night, who came across the group, recalled that when he inquired what they were doing on the beach the men claimed to be students. When Tamore inquired further, the men replied "that they were tense, and that they did not need any more tension." Afterward they made their way to Mumbai, determined to wreak havoc on India's economic capital.[2]

The plan was simple. The terrorists, in teams of two, equipped with AK-47 assault rifles and 350 rounds of ammunition, descended to the center of the city and began to kill as many people as possible. At the targeted hotels, restaurants, and other public places, when circumstances permitted, they checked the identity of the prospective victims and summarily executed anyone with an American or British passport. For three days (November 26–29, 2008), the terrorists held the center of Mumbai hostage and indulged in an orgy of death that resulted in the murder of 164 civilians and Indian military personnel and left 293 wounded. By the third day, India's security forces had killed nine and captured one of the terrorists.

For a few days, Indian government officials threatened hostilities against Pakistan, which they alleged to be the source of the terrorists. Gradually, grudgingly, New Delhi accepted that Pakistan's government was not behind the attack. However, an even darker truth soon unfolded: the killers were the foot soldiers of an Islamic terrorist organization, Lashkar-e-Taiba, that was, in turn, a creature of Pakistan's Inter-Services Intelligence (ISI). Despite the shock of the Mumbai killings, the Indian government allowed itself to be convinced that the regime in Islamabad was not directly accountable for the terrorists—at least not on this occasion.

The bloody journey to Mumbai began in 1947 with the partition of India and the creation of Pakistan and was egged along with fear, hatred, and war that has dogged the relations of the two states for half a century. This strife was, in turn, a legacy of the British Raj. For decades, the British kept control of their colony in South Asia by deliberately stoking religious rivalry that pitted Hindus, Muslims, and Sikhs against each other in a classic policy of divide-and-rule. This cynical colonial policy was particularly useful in the Northwest Frontier of the empire, where the British had to defend the most direct invasion route to India and safeguard against foreign intrigue among the unruly tribes of the region.

The Northwest Frontier in particular has a unique place in the history of British intelligence, and intelligence activities in the region have contributed greatly to the evolution of extremist political Islam. During the course of the nineteenth century, the Northwest Frontier became a training ground for the British, where they conducted special operations and espionage against the Russian empire during the course of the Great Game. Although individual British officers undertook a variety of covert missions in the region, formal intelligence organizations did not begin to operate in the Northwest Frontier until the middle of the nineteenth century.

In 1846, Colonel Sir Henry Lawrence, Britain's political agent in the Northwest Frontier, recommended the formation of a special force that was established as the Indian Corps of Guides. Lawrence required such a unit to help him maintain British control over the Punjab, and he insisted that the Guides be recruited from the local tribes. An 1852 report noted: "The Corps has been composed of the most varied elements; there is scarcely a wild or warlike tribe in Upper India, which is not represented in its ranks. . . . It is calculated to be of the utmost assistance to the Quarter-Master-General's Department as intelligencers, and most especially in the escort of reconnoitering officers."[3] British liking for Northwest Frontier recruits eventually influenced the organization and development of the Indian and Pakistani armed forces.

From the late nineteenth century onward, it became British policy to enlist Indian soldiers from the so-called martial races of the Northwest Frontier. Lord Roberts, who became commander-in-chief of the British Indian army in 1885, was one of the primary architects of the mythology of the "martial races." According to Roberts, the northern region of India was populated by "warlike and hardy races," while the south was composed of "effeminate peoples."[4] After the British conquered India, they deliberately kept the northern areas un-industrialized and under-educated, to protect their recruiting base and keep the "martial races" from engaging in peaceful pursuits and occupations. Even within the region itself, the British sought recruits in the most rural parts, avoiding the larger villages and towns.[5] In addition to the notion of traditional warriors, the British deliberately kept the Indian army segmented, isolating groups from particular regions within the larger military formations, and keeping them moving around the country to prevent them from forming "local" ties.[6]

As a result of the "martial races" recruitment policy, a disproportionate number of South Asian soldiers and officers were recruited among Muslims and Sikhs. Because these groups were kept together, the soldiers established strong bonds of loyalty based on religious lines. After Pakistan's creation in 1947, successive Pakistani governments, closely linked with the military, continued to recruit from the same geographical regions, following the British strategic policy of cultivating the "martial races."

During the 1980s, for example, three quarters of the Pakistani army was recruited from three districts in the Punjab and two in the Northwest Frontier Province—areas that collectively represent only 9 percent of the population.[7] Some of these army recruits also served in Pakistan's intelligence service, and the fact that they had family and tribal ties in the troubled northwest region of Pakistan created a unique relationship for Pakistan's intelligence establishment with the Northwest Frontier. In the early 1980s, for example, General Akhtar Abdur Rahman was the director of ISI and, like many Pakistani officers, was a Pashtun from Peshawar on the Afghan frontier. In 1987, General Hamid Gul, a devout Muslim from the Punjab with close ties to the Saudis, replaced Rahman as head of the ISI. Both men owed their appointments to Muhammad Zia-ul-Haq, Pakistan's dictator after 1977, who also came from the Punjab.[8]

In the 1990s, General Naseerullah Babar, the guiding hand for Prime Minister Benazir Bhutto's Afghanistan policy—some argue that he was the mastermind behind the creation of the Taliban—was also a native Pashtun from the Northwest Frontier region.[9] After he retired from the army, Babar served as minister of the interior between 1994 and 1997, during Bhutto's second term as prime minister. Indeed, the Indian subcontinent has a unique place in the history of the British and Pakistani intelligence services. Certainly, today the region is a critical battleground between political Islam and the West, while Pakistan's ISI remains a covert ally of the Muslim extremists in order to further Pakistani strategic and security interests in South Asia.

The Great Game, the competition for control over Central Asia, between the British and Russian empires, was waged almost exclusively in the shadows.[10] Spies, double agents, subversion, terror, psychological warfare, sabotage, and assassination became essential elements of the Russo-British conflict in the region. The stakes were high, and the clandestine war consumed the lives of British and Russian officers who undertook secret and dangerous missions in the name of emperor or czar. Rudyard Kipling's tales were not only good yarns, but also offered romanticized vignettes of the Anglo-Russian rivalry that inspired generations of young men.

Although Arthur Conolly, an intelligence officer in the East India Company's 6th Bengal Light Cavalry, coined the term "Great Game" it was Kipling who made the phrase popular with the publication of his novel *Kim* in 1901.[11] The novel also served as source of inspiration for Harold Adrian Russell Philby, whose father gave him the nickname "Kim" because of his affinity for the boy-spy in the novel.[12] Kim Philby was born in India and became one of the most notorious and successful moles of the twentieth century, spying on behalf of the Soviet KGB while rising through the ranks of Britain's secret service.[13]

To some degree, the use of intelligence and covert operations in Central Asia and northern India was the result of necessity, topography, and opportunity. The great distances and the long border with the Russian empire (depending on the period, from one thousand to two thousand miles in length), as well as the rugged Northwest Frontier of India and Central Asia, forced the British and Russian authorities to undertake exploration of the uncharted areas, organizing surveys, reconnaissance, and mapmaking in order to establish control over the region. In addition, the territories of a variety of tribal chiefs, emirs, and a host of petty kings lay across strategic lines of communication, spurring an Anglo-Russian race for the allegiance of these local potentates.

British officers and civilian adventurers, as well as natives in the employ of the government of India or the army, served as soldiers in the undeclared war. Both sides had to tread carefully because even simple diplomatic missions, intended to secure the allegiance of a local ruler, could result in charges of espionage, with deadly consequences. One such example was the cruel fate of Lieutenant Colonel Charles Stoddart, who like other unfortunate officers became a casualty of the Great Game.

In 1838 Stoddart traveled to Bokhara on a mission to secure the freedom of a number of Russian slaves and to offer the ruler of the place Britain's protection. The British feared that the Russians would exploit the slaves as a pretext to annex Bokhara. Unfortunately the local emir, Nasrullah Khan, suspected that espionage was the officer's real intention; equally the emir took offense at

Stoddart's failure to show appropriate respect. The British officer was oblivious to the etiquette of the place by failing to dismount from his horse before entering the city, as well as ignoring the traditional niceties of flattery and gift exchange.[14]

After a couple of days Stoddart was arrested, shackled, and thrown into Bokhara's prison. Perhaps prison is too generous a designation for the facility: it was basically a twenty-one-foot hole lined with the bones and flesh of previous inmates, as well as a home to armies of rodents and several varieties of insect. To add insult to injury, the emir compelled Stoddart to convert to Islam or face execution.[15]

For the next four years, the emir took pleasure toying with Stoddart. On some occasions the hapless English officer was removed from the hole to more pleasant confinement in the city and then, on the whim of the emir, tossed back. The emir's mood—and Stoddart's situation—fluctuated depending on the victories or defeats of the British army in Central Asia. A second British officer, Arthur Conolly (the first to use the term "Great Game"), made his way to Bokhara in 1841 to rescue Stoddart, but he too was apprehended, and both men spent a few months in the filthy hole before they were beheaded in a public execution sometime in June of 1842.[16]

A year later, the Reverend Joseph Wolff, appalled at the indifference of the British government to the plight of the two officers, decided to mount his own rescue operation. After many misadventures, which included being abandoned by his guides, Dr. Wolff eventually stumbled into Bokhara, only to find that the emir still harbored suspicions about British visitors. The poor man was also accused of espionage and tossed into the infamous prison. Fortunately the Shah of Persia intervened, and Wolff was set free.[17] Wolff was fortunate, unlike Stoddart and Conolly, because neither the British army nor the civilian leadership in India or London had had the foresight to establish a professional intelligence service with appropriately trained personnel.

In 1879, the Indian army finally got around to organizing its own intelligence department with a complement of five officers (two were assigned only part-time duties) and several native clerks and cartographers. The tasks of the new unit were military intelligence on the order of battle of the Russian army and the potential threat to India in a future conflict; but also to spy on nationalists and religious movements. As well, frontier officers continued to collect political intelligence and lead covert forays in enemy and neutral regions for the Political Department of the Indian Government.[18] In Britain, as well as in India, the British continued to reject the notion of combining the intelligence work of military units with an agency committed to espionage.

During the nineteenth century, the Indian civil service, the Foreign Department, the Survey Department, and—most importantly—the British-staffed Indian army were primarily charged with intelligence duties. By the 1870s, British authorities in London were convinced that the Russians were planning an invasion of South Asia, and that they did not have the means of gaining intelligence on Afghanistan—the traditional invasion route to India. Thomas Fergusson, a specialist in the early history of British military intelligence, writes: "Although the Indian Army was still without its own intelligence branch in the summer of 1878 . . . the War Office Intelligence Branch was not attempting to collect information inside India on its own. Practically all of the intelligence about India reached the War Office and the Branch via the India Office."[19] Not long afterward, in 1878, an Intelligence Branch was added to the Indian army that, adds Fergusson, "could pull together and report on vast quantities of information acquired not only by the Indian Army units throughout the subcontinent, but also by other branches of the Indian government, sources to which the Intelligence Branch in London had at best only indirect access."[20]

In 1904, in response to increased terrorist activities in South Asia, the British created the Department of Central Intelligence (DCI) to monitor the movements of extremists. The new intelligence establishment included religious sections organized to penetrate and influence the various religious communities in the Raj. The primary task of the religious sections was to undermine the rise of Hindu, Sikh, and Muslim independence movements. In order to implement this policy of divide-and-rule, the Indian Intelligence Bureau recruited native officers from the respective religious communities, who developed skills at manipulating religion to suit British colonial interests.[21]

In time, the British realized that Muslim groups throughout South Asia identified with Islam rather than with secular nationalist movements. The British concluded that Islam could be used to counterbalance the much larger Hindu community and stem the accompanying tide of Indian nationalism. As long as the Hindus, Sikhs, and Muslims of South Asia remained antagonistic, the British could rule the Indian subcontinent with only limited forces. Winston Churchill on February 2, 1940, described the Hindu-Muslim feud as the "bulwark of British rule in India" and added that, were it to be resolved, the peaceful coexistence of these groups would result in "the united communities joining in showing us the door."[22]

In addition to fostering Hindu-Muslim rivalry to undermine the development of a powerful nationalist movement, the British also tried to use Islam to counter the spread of communism. One of the early British intelligence agents to focus on Islamist movements in India was Norman Napier Evelyn Bray. Bray had a remarkable career as an Indian army officer, special intelligence operative, SIS officer, multilinguist, and critic of T. E. Lawrence. He was also the author of several biographical and historical works and later served in the Royal Air Force. In the 1930s, he fell on hard times: he was suspected of fascist sympathies and accused of arms smuggling.

Bray's career in intelligence work began in the early 1900s, when he was recruited by Sir Charles Cleveland, director of Criminal Intelligence in India, to trace the roots of Muslim unrest in South Asia. During the course of his investigations, Bray became familiar with the pan-Islamic movement in the Middle East, as well as with various influential Muslims in the region and in South Asia.[23]

In 1916, the colonial authorities in India became aware of an organization named the Army of God or *Al Junad Al Rabbania*, which called for a united Islamic front against the British. Instead of confronting these Muslim radicals, Bray launched his own campaign, fronted by key Muslim leaders, and attempted to undermine the Islamic movement from within the Muslim community. Bray also visited Ali bin Hussein, King of Hejaz and Sharif of Mecca, with the intention of uniting Muslims in India, Persia, and Afghanistan under the banner of the Arab Revolt.[24] A year later, Bray submitted a report to the Foreign Office on the "Muhammedan Question," in which he warned that Germany, Turkey, Japan, and Russia were actively involved in attempts to use pan-Islamic movements as a means of destabilizing the British Empire's large Muslim population.[25] Bray added, "it wasn't simply a matter of 'sincere Mohammedans' wanting independence but of 'thousands of . . . fanatics running before they can walk.' Otherwise, unless measures were taken to sever its membranes, it would become 'a real and pressing danger . . . as a weapon in the hands of a future enemy'."[26]

The strategy that would work, Bray insisted, was not suppression of Muslim radicals or of the pan-Islamic movement itself, but rather the implementation of Britain's own propaganda campaign, legitimized by Sharif Hussein, who was already a British ally and the recipient of generous military assistance. Bray felt that Hussein's Arab Revolt provided an alternative outlet for the holy war that he saw brewing in Arabia, Persia, Afghanistan, and the northwest.[27] For the duration of the war, the British continued to fear German, Ottoman, and—after 1917—Soviet manipulation and intrigue aimed at the pan-Islamists, while overlooking the rise of Arab nationalism.[28]

In the 1920s, Britain's Interdepartmental Committee on Bolshevism, led by Bray, continued warning of "Bolshevik" interference in India via the Northwest Frontier.[29] Regardless to what degree these suspicions were true, his superiors, including Churchill, were easily convinced, because the historic rivalry with Russia made such threats credible and because they were convinced that nationalism and religion provided the most serious challenge to the British Empire. Looming large in the context of these fears was the emergence of the Soviet Union—a potential ally to the dozens of nationalist and pan-Islamic movements stirring in the British Empire after the First World War.

In this climate of imperial paranoia, exploiting pan-Islamist movements offered a method of countering the perceived twin evils of communism and nationalism. To some degree, this was the legacy of men such as Bray, who saw Bolsheviks lurking at the frontiers of the British Empire and who had promoted the notion that Islam was the antidote to those evils. Such concepts not only influenced British policy in the interwar period, but also guided the British intelligence community in South Asia during the Second World War. The idea that Islam could be co-opted to serve state interests would eventually leave a dangerous legacy, not only to the Pakistani government, army, and intelligence establishment, but also to the United States.

The stakes were high in South Asia, because Britain's economic and strategic stature relied on the Raj. In the nineteenth century and the first half of the twentieth, the Middle East and Eastern Mediterranean were vital to British interests, insofar as these regions could be used to secure the sea and land routes to India. British strategic priorities in the interwar period (1919–1939) envisaged the Middle East as a staging area for military resources that would be rushed to South Asia in the event of war with the Soviet Union or Japan.

Yet British intelligence in South Asia was for, the most part, organized to deal with the internal threats of nationalism and religious movements rather than with threats from outside the empire. In India, according to one expert, Richard Aldrich, the British Secret Intelligence Service (SIS) was "effective, if narrowly focused . . . designed to address internal threats from nationalists, communists or other types of 'agitators.' "[30]

It was the outbreak of the Second World War that forced the British to shift their intelligence priorities in South and Central Asia and co-opt Islam as an ally in the new global conflict. During the war, British intelligence in India was the responsibility of the SIS (under its cover name of Interservice Liaison Department [ISLD]) and of the Special Operations Executive (SOE), in addition to local intelligence units, including the Indian Intelligence Bureau.[31] Unlike the traditional intelligence services, the SOE was a secret organization created in July 1940, specifically in response to the war and to the German occupation of Europe (and later parts of Asia). In this respect, the SOE was established with a single purpose—to fight the Axis—and did not share the SIS's anticommunist and antinationalist legacy. The long-standing colonial tilt of British intelligence in India came to an end, as the SOE concentrated on defeating the Axis, rather than the long-term preservation of the empire. Consequently, the SOE worked covertly with communist and extreme Muslim groups, to check the efforts of the Japanese in South Asia.[32]

As early as 1939, Japan had implemented an intensive propaganda effort aimed at instigating rebellion among the officers and men of the Indian army. The campaign targeted nationalists in India, and it tried to cultivate a pan-Asian nationalist movement to challenge British and Western colonialism.[33] In December 1941, the Japanese, with the collaboration of radical Indian nationalists, created the Indian National Army (INA). This force was recruited from Indian civilians in Malaya and from Indian soldiers who had been taken prisoner after the fall of Singapore in 1942. Some of these recruits joined the INA to escape the terrible conditions of the prisoner of war camps, but many more took up arms with the Japanese in reaction to the perceived racism of the British colonialists in Asia.[34]

In addition to trying to exploit Indian nationalism, the Japanese also launched a pro-Islamic propaganda campaign in Malaya, in order to persuade local Muslims to raise Islamic armies against the British, but did not achieve any significant results.[35] In response to the potentially serious threat posed by the defection of Indian soldiers to Japan, a dedicated department was formed by British intelligence. The new organization was placed under the British India Command's Psychological Warfare Section and was overseen in part by Major General Walter J. Cawthorn, who was later to establish the ISI in Pakistan.[36] By 1943, this unit had overtaken all the activities of the Indian Psychological Warfare Section, which broadcast anti-Japanese propaganda through the Far Eastern Bureau.[37] Picking up the threads of Bray's legacy, Cawthorn and British officers in the Indian army expanded contacts with Islamists as part of the ongoing British strategy to exploit Muslim groups against Japanese-supported Indian nationalists, as well as against the Indian National Congress.

The efforts of British intelligence were not the predominant reason for Japan's failure to sway the direction of the war. The Muslim League in India, in contrast to the predominantly Hindu Indian National Congress, steadfastly supported the British war effort. Mohammed Ali Jinnah, leader of the Muslim League and future father of the Pakistani state, felt it was not in the interests of the Muslims for the British to leave India until the creation of Pakistan, because Indian Muslims would be left in a hostile Hindu state.[38] Yet the creation of Pakistan was not considered by many Islamic leaders to be in the interests of the Muslim community. Regardless of how India would be partitioned, large numbers of Muslims would be left to languish in a predominantly Hindu state.

In the meantime, the Congress Party was refusing to cooperate with Britain's war effort unless independence was immediately granted. Indian leaders were encouraging resistance within India aimed at draining resources the British badly needed to fight the war. Dharmindra Gaur, who had served with the SOE during the Second World War, recalled how Britain's SOE used both Jinnah and the Muslim League to create a buffer against Indian nationalists. Gaur alleges that Churchill was greatly concerned about the formation of a national government in India and that the British armed the Muslim League for this purpose.[39]

In August 1942, riots engulfed several cities and villages in India, partly as a result of Gandhi's call for civil disobedience and partly in reaction to the defeat of Britain's armies in Asia at the hands of the Japanese. Confounding the British authorities was the fact that at the root of the unrest was an unorganized popular movement beyond the control of any particular organization or individual.[40] By imprisoning India's leaders in June 1942, the British had created a leadership vacuum that, for a period of time, had left the nationalist movement without direction and control.

The Second World War not only changed the British relationship with South Asia, but it also ushered the Americans into the complex layers of religion and nationalism in the region. Following in the steps of the British, the Office of Strategic Services (OSS), roughly the American equivalent to the SOE, pursued a long-term policy of cultivating Islam.[41] By June 1944, General William Donovan, head of the OSS, was prepared to implement a pro-Islam policy and. According to Richard Aldrich, his plan was triggered by interest in the Arab Gulf states and his desire to build up "some very much undercover 'intelligence' in Saudi Arabia, perhaps under the pretense of some large archaeological mission."[42] Donovan assigned Major Carlton S. Coon—an anthropologist, Arabist, and specialist in North Africa and the Middle East—to plan this project. Later in 1944, after an extensive tour of the region, Coon concluded that intelligence gathering should not only be limited to Saudi Arabia but had to encompass the Muslim world as a whole, with Saudi Arabia acting as a gateway to the Muslim Middle East and Muslim South Asia.[43] Even before the end of the war, the Americans had reached the same conclusion as the British that the Middle East was inextricably tied to South Asia with respect to Islam. Unfortunately, this lesson was forgotten before and after the Soviet invasion of Afghanistan.

With the creation of the Muslim state of Pakistan in 1947, the British had to reinvent their policy toward South Asia.The special relationship formed between Jinnah and the British during the Second World War extended into the postwar period. The British government and its intelligence establishment felt more comfortable forming close connections with Pakistan than with India, which was still believed to be anti-British and to harbor communist connections. While the British were keen to have Pakistan on their side, they were not interested in establishing an equal relationship. Two issues arose immediately between Britain and Pakistan: how much intelligence the British should share with Pakistan and what assistance London was willing to provide in the establishment of Pakistan's intelligence infrastructure. Although there was extensive representation of British staff in senior positions in the Pakistan civil and military services, concerns lingered over security in Pakistan, specifically about the risk of intelligence leaks and communist infiltration.

During 1947 and 1948, the British Joint Intelligence Committee determined that British information was safer in Pakistani hands than it would have been with India. This faith in Pakistan was, for the most part, the legacy of India's Muslims—Jinnah's Muslim League in particular—with the British during the Second World War. In London, Pakistan was also considered more reliable, in part because of the extensive presence of British officers in senior positions. The majority of officers in senior posts in Pakistan—particularly in the Ministry of Defense and the military—were still British. For the British, this arrangement was essential (the Pakistani prime minister also agreed that it was beneficial for the country) in order to share confidential and sensitive information with Pakistan.[44] Pakistanis, as a whole, were also believed to be not as antagonistic toward Britain than was the case with Indian nationals.

Although Pakistan was generally seen as less problematic than India, many observers felt that security measures in Pakistan's institutions were inadequate and that the "oriental mind" would not lend itself to "view the problem [of security] as seriously as is done elsewhere."[45] Concerns about communist elements in India and Pakistan also remained. For example, in 1946–1947 certain information had been leaked to communist groups in India, and the leak was believed to have been through a communist cell in the Indian military, which was assumed still to exist.[46]

After April 1948, the British treated Pakistan as nominally a Category A country; thus it could receive information up to "Top Secret," but with restrictions placed on American-source information. In reality, Pakistan was being provided with very little information. This was a strategic practice that had been applied in India before the creation of Pakistan and was carried over to

Pakistan. By the spring of 1948, however, Pakistan had a large number of liaison officers in London, so it was no longer possible to maintain this deception.

Shortly afterward, the British reassessed Pakistan's position and shifted their policy with respect to intelligence sharing. Pakistan was to be downgraded to Category B, which meant it could receive information up to the level of "Confidential": in effect, this adjustment matched policy with actual practice. The Pakistanis were informed that this downgrade was due to the fact that their security arrangements were not adequate and that Pakistan's "political associations" were still undecided. But they were not told that American-source information could not be shared without American approval, which was unlikely in the case of Pakistan.[47]

Not everyone in the British camp had such reservations about Pakistan's reliability. Cawthorn, who was later to participate in the establishment of the ISI, defended the Pakistani military and governmental institutional security measures, insisting that the individual Pakistani was every bit as patriotic and security-minded as an Englishman. Security, he argued, was excellent in Pakistan, because of the potential threat of an Indian invasion.[48] Cawthorn also commented on "the political solidarity resulting from practically one hundred percent adherence to a common religious faith."[49] However, he was concerned that, while Pakistan had a benevolent attitude toward Britain, this was endangered by Britain's unwillingness to share intelligence openly, especially on India, and by restrictions on the training of Pakistani intelligence officers. Cawthorn and others argued that Pakistan was vital to Britain strategically, since it offered the British a base for defending the Indian Ocean. In addition, Pakistan offered special opportunities for the collection of intelligence. Particularly, as Cawthorn pointed out in a report to the Chiefs of Staff, "Pakistan as a Moslem state on the flank of the Middle East Moslem block and of Afghanistan and Persia obviously possesses considerable political potential in relation to British interests in the Middle East."[50]

Eventually, the intelligence apparatus that the British helped to establish in Pakistan was extracted from the British intelligence structure in India. An Intelligence Bureau that paralleled MI5[51] was set up in Pakistan in 1948, partly staffed by British personnel. The Intelligence Bureau was modeled on the Muslim section of the former Intelligence Bureau in India (formerly based in Delhi) and incorporated the intelligence body that had responsibility for the Northwest Frontier, Afghanistan, and Persia. A Frontier Bureau was also created to cover East Pakistan and similar organizations set up in Peshawar and Quetta.[52]

TWENTY

Pakistan's Inter-Services Intelligence and Organized Terror in South Asia

"They are our people: they are not our enemies."
—*ISI officer referring to the Taliban in the Northwest Frontier region*[1]

The Pakistani Intelligence Bureau remains in existence to this day and is now charged with overseeing politicians, political activists, and foreign intelligence agents.[2] The bureau now monitors certain international situations: in particular, nationals of countries that are considered "hostile" to Pakistan. However, in 1948, the Inter-Services Intelligence Directorate was established for the purpose of addressing foreign threats.[3] Quickly the ISI emerged as Pakistan's predominant intelligence organization and not long afterward became covertly involved in religious and political affairs.

Its first director was Brigadier Saiyid S. Hamid, formerly military secretary in India, who upon the creation of Pakistan became the director of the Pakistan National Guard.[4] Cawthorn, deputy chief of staff of the Pakistan army, as well as secretary of the Pakistan Joint Services Commanders' Committee, oversaw the organization and early operations of the ISI.[5] It was not uncommon for British officers to have served with both the Indian and Pakistani armed forces. Cawthorn had been with the Indian army for thirty years, receiving his commission during the First World War.[6] In the 1920s, he was attached to the 16th Punjab Regiment and between 1930 and 1935 saw active and covert service in the Northwest Frontier, subsequently being posted to the War Office in London.[7] However, it was Cawthorn's experience in the Northwest Frontier that prepared him for intelligence work.

In the 1930s, British intelligence was active in the Northwest Frontier; intelligence officers had been working with tribal groups in that area to counter communist influence and infiltration in the region.[8] Cawthorn's own service in the Northwest Frontier gave him considerable experience in intelligence work that he would later put to good use in the newly formed Pakistan. Undoubtedly he brought to the Pakistan intelligence service his contacts in the Northwest Frontier and forged new links for the ISI with the tribal groups of the region.

The ISI included all the Pakistani military intelligence organizations, which became part of an interservices body headed by a single director, who was advised and overseen by the Joint Service Commanders' Committee and by its secretary, Cawthorn, in particular.[9] However, each of the armed services continued to maintain separate intelligence directorates, while working closely with the ISI.[10] In April 1949, in a somewhat less restrictive environment than had existed the year before, the Joint Intelligence Committee of the British Chiefs of Staff arranged for British departments to forward relevant intelligence and information to the ISI.[11]

More than in any other issue, Pakistan was interested in British intelligence with regard to India. In the postwar period, Pakistan had to confront the considerably larger and more powerful Indian state. The 1947 war between Pakistan and India over Kashmir further underscored the fact that conventional warfare ultimately gave India the military advantage. Furthermore, the frontiers of the Pakistani state provided narrow strategic depth—effectively Pakistan's forces had limited space to fall back on if an invasion by the Indian army could not be stopped at the frontier. In response to this strategic limitation, Pakistan adopted covert and unconventional warfare operations in both Kashmir and India. Covert tactics and the use of nonattributable clandestine organizations freed the Pakistani state from any commitment to treaty obligations, but relied on the establishment and maintenance of a large intelligence service.

This was the beginning of a perfect arrangement: although a cease-fire had been agreed to by Pakistan and India in 1948, individual militants were neither party to it nor officially under the control of the Pakistani government.[12] For half a decade, the ISI assisted Islamic terrorist groups and supported a variety of radical religious organizations, as part of the grand design to further Pakistan's interests in Kashmir and bleed the Indian army through an endless guerrilla war.[13] The dispute over the Kashmir region has not only remained one of the most pervasively contentious and destructive issues plaguing India and Pakistan, but has also acted as a key ingredient in Pakistan's becoming a breeding ground for political Islam and Muslim militancy.

In the period following the creation of Pakistan in 1947, the British Dominion Office paid close attention to the role of religion and reported that Islam was the most powerful political mechanism for unity in the region. Pakistan lacked a cohesive national identity, and the British concluded that religion could form the binding ties for the new state, particularly since Islam was what distinguished Pakistan from India, a powerful and significantly larger neighbor. To this end, the British government encouraged Pakistani politicians to use religious rhetoric and appeal to Islam, yet reports filed by the Dominion Office in 1948 sound slightly alarmed, describing a "fanatical" populace, inflamed by Islam above all other social or political concerns.

All the same, while the Dominion Office described the general population as mindless fanatics, they felt assured by the leadership they had helped bring to power—primarily by Jinnah and Liaquat Ali Khan—that Pakistan would remain under secular control. These leaders, British officials assumed, would merely feign religiosity in order to enlist Islam for political ends.[14] As one report observed: "Religion has proved its worth as a potent political weapon, and it is one which may be required again."[15] Not for the first time, the British perceived a situation in which religion could be used as a vehicle for secular agendas.

As early as the 1950s, Pakistan's military had become the most powerful force in the country, and when they seized political control they adopted an Islamic facade and used it as a manipulative device. In 1958, Ayub Khan instituted a military dictatorship in Pakistan. Although it is not entirely clear what information or involvement the British had about his coup, they believed that the United States had backed Ayub Khan in overthrowing the government.[16] Officials at the British Dominion Office appeared to be satisfied with Ayub and his attitude toward Islam; some of them felt "it was primarily political—he saw it as a counterbalance to Indian challenges, but did not hold 'narrow orthodox views.'"[17]

Ayub was given conditional praise for his speeches that stressed the threat of communism to Islam in the spring of 1959. This focus on Islam was acceptable to the British and the Americans because Ayub's rhetoric also included a general criticism of dogmatism. "The miracle of Islam," said Ayub, "was that it destroyed idolatry, and the tragedy of the Muslims is that they rendered religion into the form of an idol." Ayub was lauded, of course, because his speeches denigrated communism, holding it up as the enemy of Islam. Civilian groups were also felt to be espousing a satisfactory vision of the role of Islam; Maulana Perwez, director of the Quranic Research Centre in Lahore, was said to express an "American style" democratic understanding of Islam.[18]

Throughout the late 1950s, the British continued to gather intelligence on the influence of Islam in Pakistan as a "research" interest. In the period leading up to the 1958 coup by Ayub Khan, British agents in Pakistan watched and established contacts with religious groups, which they thought could provide useful information or influence amidst the prevailing political uncertainty. One group under observation by the British Dominion Office in the mid-1950s was Jamaat-e-Islami (JI), an Islamist group characterized by its British onlookers as extremely right-wing and anticommunist. Abul Ala Maududi created the JI in

India in 1941. It was an Islamic orthodox organization and was established in part as an opponent to the Muslim League, which was seen as both pro-British and pro-secular. The JI was against the formation of an Islamic state in the 1940s, although it became the most outspoken agitator for a strict Islamic legal and political system after Pakistan achieved independence.[19] Maududi himself had been influenced by Saudi theologians and had close contact with the Saudis before the creation of Pakistan.[20]

The JI had been outlawed in 1954 after being accused of planning a coup, leading student unrest in Lahore, and receiving funds from foreign groups hostile to the Pakistani government. In 1958, the Dominion Office reported that the JI had considerable influence, but not enough to overthrow the regime. Reports compared the JI to the Egyptian Muslim Brotherhood, although no link was established between the two organizations beyond the JI's criticism of the Egyptian government's persecution of the Brotherhood.[21] The JI came to attention of the British again in 1964, when they regained legal status after the Supreme Court ruled against the Pakistani government. At this time, the JI was reported to be extremely anticommunist and to oppose the Kashmiri independence movement.[22]

By this time the British were mere observers of events in Pakistan. In the 1950s, the Americans had joined the British and had become involved with both Pakistani politics and the Pakistani army. After the arrival of the Americans, British influence in the country declined quickly, and Washington replaced London as Pakistan's patron and ally. Pakistani leaders made the adjustment easily and exploited Pakistan's geopolitical and religious credentials to maintain the relationship with the Americans and pursue a forward policy in Afghanistan.

Pakistan was seen as being in the unique position of having an ostensibly Islamic government, which in fact was sympathetic to the West, and "whose Islamic faith was . . . often not more than skin deep," while being populated by devout Muslims who could be recruited to combat communism with Islam.[23] By 1952–1953, the rise of Arab nationalism and the threat of Iran nationalizing its oil industry increased American interest in Pakistan. In 1952, Secretary of State John Foster Dulles floated the idea of a "Northern Tier" of linked Islamic states, including Iran, Pakistan, and Turkey, as a defense zone against Soviet encroachment.[24] The United States also launched various economic assistance programs in Pakistan during the 1950s, which were seen by some as fronts for political and social intervention.[25]

In effect, Pakistan became a strategic necessity for the United States, because it occupied a key geographical position, situated between the Middle East and South Asia. Furthermore, the Soviet relationship with India drastically limited Soviet influence in Pakistan. Andrei Gromyko, the Soviet foreign minister, complained of the "insidious [Western] web into which Pakistan fell almost at the onset of her existence as an independent state."[26] The new Pakistan emerged as a frontline state in the Cold War and a strategic partner of the United States from 1947 to 1989.

By the middle of the 1950s, the Pakistani army had entered into a closer relationship with the United States, primarily because of Pakistan's membership in the Baghdad Pact, which later became the Central Treaty Organization (CENTO).[27] Despite the upheaval that followed the partition of India, the creation of Pakistan in 1947 offered the British and later the Americans a unique advantage in the region. The new country was located in a critically vital zone, controlled by cooperative leaders and administered along ostensibly Islamic grounds. Unlike India, whose nonaligned policy and friendship with the Soviet Union annoyed and alarmed Washington, Pakistan remained a steadfast ally of the United States. In addition, the Americans had a poor impression of India and Hinduism. Politically, India was undesirable because the Soviets were well embedded in the Congress.[28] The Americans also viewed Hinduism as backward-looking and passive. In contrast, monotheistic Islam seemed much closer to Christianity, and Pakistan's leaders appeared "much more vigorous, energetic, forthright, and warlike, in short more manly."[29]

During this period, the Pakistani military began to shift from its British roots, as a new generation of Pakistani officers was trained in Pakistan within the framework of American military doctrine.[30] This change was also accompanied by the attitudes of some officers, who adopted an inflated estimate of their own and Pakistan's martial qualities and assumed that one Pakistani soldier equaled ten or more Indians. This perception was, of course, related to the "martial races" ideology employed by the British in India.[31] The emphasis on the unique qualities of the Pakistani army resulted in equal emphasis on the Islamic quality of the armed forces.

Religion became a critical element in the identity of the Pakistani army, since, as member of the various "martial races," the military was ethnically diverse and, except for Islam, indistinguishable from the Indian army. Although the Pakistani army is not thought to have taken a broad turn toward political Islam prior to the 1970s, the focus on Islam in connection with militarism laid the ground for later developments in the relationship between political Islam and the Pakistani army. The officers of the ISI were no exception. Domestic and international events in the 1970s expanded the organization's contacts with political Islam and to radical Muslim groups in Afghanistan.

Although Muhammad Zia-ul-Haq is the Pakistani leader primarily responsible for increasing the power of the ISI, Zia's predecessor, Zulfikar Ali Bhutto, also played an important role in bolstering the ISI and militant Islam. Bhutto made alcohol illegal and Friday a holiday. He also declared that the Ahmediyya sect, which most Muslims considered heretical, was non-Muslim. This action was most helpful to the monopoly of extremist groups in Pakistan and a concession that the JI had long demanded, but which no other leader had been willing to grant.[32] Bhutto was motivated to take such actions, at least in part, by security concerns about Afghanistan. From 1947 onward, Pakistan's military had adopted the strategy that Afghanistan was the key to redressing Pakistan's lack of strategic depth. Some believed that since invaders of India historically came through Afghanistan, Pakistan's defense could only be guaranteed by the integration of the two states, but for many a friendly and pro-Pakistan Afghanistan was far more realistic.

This notion of unification held little appeal for some Afghans, who had a sense of distinct ethnic and racial identity, but was attractive to the Pashtuns, whose tribe straddles Pakistan's northwest and Afghanistan. On the other hand, the prospect of a merger with Pakistan did appeal to Afghans committed to Islam—Almost from the inception of Pakistan, Pakistani politicians and generals remained fixated on the threat of Indian intervention in Afghanistan and the possibility that India could exploit Afghanistan to attack Pakistan. Accordingly, by the 1960s, the ISI was encouraging militant Islamic Pakistani groups to cultivate similarly minded organizations in Afghanistan.[33] Under Bhutto, Pakistani intelligence began providing arms to Afghan exiles and instigating tribal uprisings, with the aim of keeping India out of Afghanistan and from eventually absorbing the Afghan state.[34]

The use of covert operations and instigating insurgencies in Kashmir reinforced this strategy, particularly after the 1965 Pakistan-India War, when Islamabad discovered the limits of the alliance with the United States. After the outbreak of hostilities, the Americans decided to impose an embargo against both Pakistan and India. Pakistan relied almost exclusively on weapons and other military supplies from the United States, and the embargo undermined the ability of the Pakistani army to defeat India—at least that was the conclusion drawn in Islamabad. Three years earlier, the administration of John F. Kennedy had tried to improve relations with India, a move that had incited considerable outrage; and, although little was achieved, the Pakistanis opened discussions with China and Russia. The Russians did supply Pakistan with some weapons, but not enough to replace those provided by the United States. Although there had been no large-scale uprisings to coincide with the outbreak of hostilities in 1965, the ISI continued to encourage the organization of an anti-India guerrilla movement.[35]

In 1970, civil war broke out in Pakistan, with the eastern segment fighting to break away from Pakistan.[36] One outcome of this conflict, in which India aided the separatists, was that Bhutto greatly increased the ISI's budget. Significantly, some of the funding came from the United States, because the Americans had a particular interest in aiding Pakistan during the subsequent India-Pakistan confrontation of 1971. Richard Nixon and his administration believed that it was vital to show the international community—and China in particular (a staunch supporter of Pakistan)—that the United States supported its strategic partners in times of crisis. The White House assumed that India was determined to humiliate Pakistan over Bangladesh and that, toward this end, they had concluded a de facto alliance with the Soviets.

Thus the administration, over the strong objections of the State Department, ordered a diplomatic tilt toward Pakistan, to prevent the dismemberment of Pakistan and to demonstrate to China that the Americans would resist any Soviet-backed military intervention.[37] The Saudis also backed Muslim Pakistan. Although covert warfare had been used in the 1947–1948 and 1965 conflicts with India, the ISI promoted full-scale insurgency in the 1970–1971 Pakistani Civil War.[38] Islamist guerrilla armies were recruited to carry out operations in Bangladesh—a fully Islamic country. Most of these men came from carefully selected Bengali militant religious groups.[39] Increased support from Pakistan, as well as from the United States and Saudi Arabia, during the 1970–1971 war gave the ISI greater domestic authority and an enlarged network of contacts in militant Islamic guerrilla groups. As a result, the ISI was in a position to intervene covertly in Pakistani politics, religion, and society.[40]

In July 1977, Zia deposed Bhutto and instituted a military dictatorship in Pakistan that lasted for eleven years. This coup had the support of the White House, which wanted a stable Pakistan, regardless of the cost and consequences. The Americans felt that Zia was in a position to stabilize not only Pakistan, but also the entire region, including Afghanistan.[41] Despite Bhutto's earlier use of religious extremists to control Pakistan, it was Zia's regime that completed the transformation of the ISI into a political weapon and enhanced its relationship with militant Islamists. The ISI and its Islamist colleagues established a strong hold over Pakistani politics and over large segments of society. They infiltrated universities and the media and assisted in organizing terrorist groups for action abroad and at home. Through the ISI, the JI established links with the United States and the Saudis.[42] However, both the Saudis and Americans remained uneasy with the Pakistani Islamic organization.

Through the ISI, Zia used Islamic parties like the JI to counter opposition to the military dictatorship and to undermine political opponents. Zia increased support to the JI and helped to spread the influence of the organization into Afghanistan. Thanks to Zia's patronage, the JI, which had previously received less than 5 percent of the vote in free elections, grew in power and influence throughout the 1970s.

Any qualms in Washington over the legitimacy of Zia's regime evaporated with the Soviet invasion of neighboring Afghanistan in 1979. The ensuing jihad against the Soviets created the ideal circumstances for Pakistan to intervene directly in Afghanistan—only this time with the connivance of the United States. The ISI promoted the Afghan War as a battle against heathen communists and recruited fighters from across the Arab states, South Asia, and the Middle East. The ISI helped the JI form connections in Afghanistan, where they assisted the ISI in building up Islamist militant movements.[43]

The director of the ISI, General Akhtar Abdur Rahman established the Afghan Bureau of the ISI, which collaborated with American intelligence agencies and was, in turn, supplied with American and Saudi arms and funding. Zia did not want to openly oppose the Soviets, so the "secretive and aloof" ISI covertly channeled the U.S. and Saudi funds to the fighters.[44] Under the scheme, funding went through the ISI to the mujahidin, while the government denied involvement.[45] Aid was concentrated on Islamist resistance groups similar to the JI.[46] While the CIA wanted to provide aid directly to field commanders among the mujahidin, the ISI insisted on working through religious parties.[47] This arrangement worked well for Zia and the ISI, who used the American largesse to fund groups in Afghanistan that were ideologically suited to Pakistan's interests. In the long run, the Afghan War experience solidified Pakistan's—specifically the ISI's—links with Islamic militants both in Afghanistan and Pakistan, and underscored the value of covert warfare as the primary means of fighting India.[48]

The power and influence of the ISI within Pakistan has continued to grow in recent years, as their connections to radical Islam have increased. The triangular link between the Pakistan government, the ISI, and the radical mujahidin continued under Benazir Bhutto, who came to power in December 1988. General Hamid Gul, who was director general of the ISI under Bhutto, spoke openly in a 2008 interview of her ties to—and support of—"jihadis."[49] Bhutto's government was directly involved in infiltrating Taliban members into Afghanistan in the 1990s, while Bhutto claimed that Pakistan was merely returning Afghan refugees to their homeland. Without ISI support, the Taliban could not have made the gains they did in Afghanistan during the early 1990s.[50]

Meanwhile, after the defeat of the Soviet Union in Afghanistan, Washington essentially turned a blind eye to the region until the events of 9/11, when Pakistan once again became an integral part of the Anglo-American relationship with Islam.

During this period, several key members of General Pervez Musharraf's military regime who came to power in 1999, including Musharraf himself, had served in the ISI.[51] In fact, Musharraf succeeded in taking over Pakistan with the assistance of Mahmood Ahmed, the director of the ISI, who was able to bring over to Musharraf key senior officers of the Pakistani army.[52] Significantly, the Pakistani officer corps has become increasingly linked to Islamic groups. Ahmad himself, almost immediately after the coup, rediscovered his Islamic roots and became a devout Muslim, as well as an enthusiastic supporter of the Taliban and the fundamentalist Islamic groups fighting in Kashmir.

As head of the ISI and a key member of the ruling junta, Ahmad not only had control over clandestine operations but also of Pakistan's foreign policy, in effect making a sham of Musharraf's antiterrorist protestations.[53] George Tenet, director of the CIA, recalls that at a luncheon meeting with Ahmad, the Pakistani intelligence chief, "the guy was immovable when it came to the Taliban and al-Qa ida."[54] Ahmad also met with congressmen on Capitol Hill just as reports were reaching Washington that aircraft had struck the Twin Towers in New York and the Pentagon. Not long afterward, Musharraf replaced Ahmad as head of the ISI as a sop to the Americans and to show that Pakistan was ready to join America's war against terrorism; little actually changed. The fact that Washington believed Musharraf is indicative of the difficulties that confronted the Americans when dealing with South Asia. Musharraf had to balance considerable pressure from the administration of George W. Bush with the trend in the Pakistani officer corps toward Islam.

Almost a decade earlier, increasing numbers of senior Pakistani officers had begun to turn to Islam and Islamic organizations. Nineteen retired Pakistani army officers were present at a 1991 JI convention, and it became common for ISI officers to take part in JI politics after retirement, including joining militant Islamic groups.[55] Furthermore, the ISI itself has been accused of wide-ranging terrorist activities in recent years, including the Daniel Pearl murder, scores of assassinations within Pakistan, the bombing of a church in Islamabad, and recently the attacks in Mumbai. According to one expert, Tariq Ali, many of these actions were intended to punish Pakistani leaders for "betraying" the Taliban after 9/11 and as a warning to the Pakistan government not to bow too far to Washington's demands.[56] Despite the accusations, it is unlikely that the SIS orchestrated these attacks—most likely it was radical groups over which the ISI has limited control.

The ISI has also been directly involved with the reorganization and ongoing support of the Taliban. The ISI provided the Taliban with access to food, medical supplies, the ability to raise funds (through private sources), and with intelligence information and strategic advice in their key battles. It even helped them negotiate deals with local commanders and warlords. Although many organizations had sprouted in Afghanistan to fight the Soviets and vie for control of the country in the aftermath of the Soviet defeat, the Taliban emerged as the most successful. As a result, the ISI abandoned the other mujahidin groups in Afghanistan in favor of the Taliban. The ISI could not have undertaken such a significant policy without the connivance of the Pakistani government. Remarkably, Pakistan's commitment to the Taliban was not expanded by a pro-Islamist such as Zia, but came about after the election of Benazir Bhutto, a woman with ostensibly liberal credentials, from a cosmopolitan family, and with a Western education. But as Rasul Bakhsh Rais comments, "she had no control over Pakistan's policy toward Afghanistan."[57]

The pro-Taliban policy of various Pakistani regimes is driven by a combination of factors: the sentiments of Pakistani Pashtuns, the influence of the militant Islamic establishment, and the ISI. The strongest backing for the Taliban comes from ethnic Pashtun tribal and regional leaders. After 2001, the bonds with the local tribal leaders became even closer when the U.S. Army forced the Taliban out of Afghanistan. As part of their campaign to ingratiate themselves with the Pashtuns of Pakistan, both the Taliban and al-Qaeda encouraged their commanders to marry into the families of the local tribal heads. In the words of Graham Fuller, former CIA station chief in Kabul:

> The Taliban represent zealous and largely ignorant mountain Islamists. They are also all ethnic Pashtuns. Most Pashtuns see the Taliban—like them or not—as the primary vehicle for restoration of Pashtun power in Afghanistan, lost in 2001. Pashtuns are also among the most fiercely nationalist, tribalized and xenophobic peoples of the world, united only against the foreign invader. In the end, the Taliban are probably more Pashtun than they are Islamist.[58]

Religion is a considerable factor and a critical part of the Taliban's survival. The Deobandis of the Jamiat Ulema-e -Islam (JUI),[59] as well as most of the other organizations that make up the Deobandi movement and the madrassa (religious schools) network, are closely bound to the Taliban.[60] Like the JI, the JUI accepts the notion of ethnicity and devotion to Islam and gets involved in Pakistani politics. It has taken part in Pakistan's election process, and in 1993–1996 had been part of Benazir Bhutto's coalition government. But, regardless of religious affinity, according to a war office report, "deep down there was a common ethnic factor binding all these elements."[61] Certainly the Pakistani officer corps, as well as the ISI, includes Pashtuns from Pakistan's northwest provinces—a legacy of the "martial races" concept that continues to dominate the Pakistani armed forces.

Ostensibly, the ringmaster of Pakistan's covert and overt policies toward Afghanistan and India is the ISI. Yet the ISI is not a rogue element, but rather represents the cream of Pakistan's officer corps, and has a thorough understanding of the Northwest Frontier better than any other organization locally or abroad. Rasul Bakhsh Rais argues that it is unlikely that the ISI could advance a separate agenda outside the political and military Pakistani leadership. Whenever circumstances in Afghanistan—or elsewhere in the region—threaten Pakistan's interests, the ISI has carried the burden of using clandestine means to meet the challenge.

In the heady months and years following the defeat of the Soviet Union in Afghanistan, America's interest in Pakistan began to wane, and eventually the region simply dropped out of Washington's field of vision. Occasionally, Pakistan and India came into sharp focus, particularly when both countries achieved nuclear weapons capability. But beyond imposing economic sanctions on both countries in retaliation, America's political leadership remained uninterested in South Asia. The Pakistani officer corps felt betrayed and abandoned by the Americans; Washington's lack of interest in Pakistan's security problems in the region compounded the deteriorating relationship between the former allies. Following the defeat of the Soviet Union in Afghanistan, the Pakistanis had even tried to establish a friendly government in Kabul, or at the very least one that would keep India out of Afghanistan.[62]

But by 1992, the interim government in Kabul had become hostile to Pakistan and thus might potentially deny Pakistan's access, through Afghanistan, to the new Islamic republics of Central Asia. Making matters worse, the Pakistani government feared that the new administration in Afghanistan might be open to overtures from India and might ultimately compromise Pakistan's influence in the region. There was also—however remote—the possibility that the Afghanistan regime might even lay claim to Pakhtunistan in northwestern Pakistan. These fears were realized as India's presence (especially the Indian intelligence service) in Afghanistan has expanded dramatically. Moreover, Pakistan had become increasingly isolated since the administration of Bill

Clinton continued to impose harsh economic sanctions on the country, while establishing friendly relations with India.[63] Under these circumstances, it became critical for Pakistan to control the political situation in Afghanistan. According to Lawrence Ziring:

> The ISI therefore developed a strategy that not only undermined the secular Afghan government, but also nourished the Afghan Islamist movement. The key ISI decision . . . was the formation of the Taliban and its recruitment of Pakistanis as well as Afghans. By 1993 the Tehrik-i-Taliban was a formidable force with direct ties to the Pakistan army.[64]

In 1995, when the Taliban called for support from Pakistan's religious schools, they received an enthusiastic response, but it was the ISI that continued to control the ongoing recruitment and training of militants and their subsequent dispatch to Afghanistan.[65] Ultimately, the Taliban fulfilled Pakistan's requirements for Afghanistan. Fuller emphasizes that "Pakistan will therefore never rupture ties or abandon the Pashtuns, in either country, whether radical Islamist or not. Pakistan can never afford to have Pashtuns hostile to Islamabad in control of Kabul, or at home."[66]

The ISI's support of the Taliban and other extremist groups like Lashkar-e-Taiba has enhanced the reach of political Islam which has emerged as a major sociopolitical factor in Pakistan. In fact, the ISI—created by the British and nurtured by the Americans and the Saudis—has become, for better or for worse, part of Pakistan's social and political evolution. The Mumbai massacre in 2008 has demonstrated that extreme Islamic organizations and terrorist groups easily slip beyond the control of the ISI. Although militant Muslim groups have not penetrated the ISI, it is clear that the Pakistani intelligence establishment has become a fellow traveler of political Islam.

NOTES

A Note on Sources

1. Matthew M. Aid, "The Secret Reclassification Program," *Organization of American Historians Newsletter* 34 (May 2006), http://www.oah.org/pubs/nl/2006may/aid.html (accessed December 2, 2009).
2. Ibid.
3. Richard J. Aldrich, "Did Waldegrave Work? The Impact of Open Government upon British History," *Twentieth Century British History* 9, no. 1 (1998), http://tcbh.oxfordjournals.org/cgi/reprint/9/1/111 (accessed December 2, 2009).
4. Ibid.

PROLOGUE: • *Stories from the Bazaar*

1. The bazaar (or *souk* in Arabic) is a marketplace that also accommodates social, cultural, religious, and political centers of activity. In this respect the bazaar is reminiscent of the ancient Athenian *agora*, which served as the hub for Greek society and remained as a meeting place until the middle of the twentieth century. However, in the Middle East the bazaar also fulfills the role of political forum. According to Mahmoud Abdullahzadeh, "The Political Significance of the Bazaar in Iran," in *Technology, Tradition and Survival: Aspects of Material Culture in the Middle East and Central Asia*, ed. Richard Tapper and Keith McLachlan (London: Frank Cass, 2002), 234–35, the bazaar has also served as an effective vehicle for communication and social mobilization.
2. In a broad sense the principle of *taqiyah* (a form of deception, secrecy, caution, and precaution), particularly in Shiite Islam, was acceptable historically in times of duress. Specifically, *taqiyah* was applied in the precautionary denial of religious belief in the face of potential persecution. Although not exclusive to them, it was originally practiced by Shiite Muslims who had been subjected to persecution by Sunnis. See "Taqiyah," *The Oxford Dictionary of Islam*, ed. John L. Esposito (Oxford: Oxford University Press, 2003), 314. According to Bernard Lewis, *The Assassins: A Radical Sect in Islam* (London: Weidenfeld & Nicolson, 2001), 25, *taqiyah* denotes an Islamic doctrine of dispensation that absolves the believer from fulfilling certain obligations of religion.

3. Daniel Pipes, *The Hidden Hand: Middle East Fears of Conspiracy* (New York: St. Martin's Press, 1996), 110.

4. Ibid.

5. Akbar S. Ahmed, *Living Islam: From Samarkand to Stornoway* (London: Penguin, 1995), 76); quoted in Carole Hillenbrand, *The Crusades: Islamic Perspectives* (Edinburgh: Edinburgh University Press, 1999), 590.

6. Amin Maalouf, *The Crusades Through Arab Eyes*, trans. Jon Rothschild (London: Al Saqi, 1984), 265.

7. Spies or any combatants out of uniform have few or no rights and were often executed or tortured with impunity.

8. The mosque is one of the sacred focal points for pilgrims to the annual Hajj and can accommodate close to 300,000 people. At the center of its courtyard, which is forty acres in size, is the Kaba, a cube-shaped structure always covered by a black cloth embroidered in gold. Muslims believe that Abraham built this to honor God and that Mohammad in A.D. 630 cleansed it of idols. Over 2 million pilgrims each year conduct their prayers and rituals at this site.

9. Madawi al-Rasheed, *A History of Saudi Arabia* (Cambridge: Cambridge University Press, 2002), 144.

10. Ibid.

11. The Mahdi is the Islamic messiah who is supposed to appear at the end of the new century.

12. Peter W. Wilson and Douglas F. Graham, *Saudi Arabia: The Coming Storm* (New York: M. E. Sharpe, 1994), 58, add that it is still debatable whether Qahtani was actually proclaimed Mahdi by Utaibi.

13. "Khomeini on Mecca Attack," *FBIS Middle East Report*, 21 November 1979, in Yaroslav Trofimov, *The Siege of Mecca: The Forgotten Uprising in Islam's Holiest Shrine and the Birth of Al-Qaeda* (New York: Doubleday, 2007), 275.

14. One hundred thirty-seven American diplomats and marines were trapped in the embassy. Two marines were killed, as well as an American pilot and two Pakistani embassy staff.

15. According to Wilson and Graham, *Saudi Arabia*, 58, the Ulema took one day and a half to formulate a judgment. One report in *Time* magazine ("Sacrilege in Mecca," *Time*, 3 December 1979) claimed it took the Ulema eight hours, while a second report filed one week later (*Time*, 10 December 1979) said the ruling was issued on the third day of the siege.

16. Stephen Schwartz, "Is Saudi Arabia Holy Soil?," *Think Israel* (September–October 2004), http://www.think-israel.org/schwartz.saudiarabia.html. The Wikipedia entry "Juhayman al-Otaibi" (http://en.wikipedia.org/wiki/Juhayman_al-Otaibi) claims that General Zia-ul-Haq, at the time directing the Pakistani army, captured the

mosque with the assistance of French paratroopers, while another *Wikipedia* entry, "Grand Mosque Seizure" (http://en.wikipedia.org/wiki/Grand_Mosque_Seizure), states that it was French GIGN counterterrorist commandos who took part in the fighting.

17. Robert Fisk, *The Great War for Civilization: The Conquest of the Middle East* (London: Fourth Estate, 2005), 1046–1047. Fisk comments that the rebels were electrocuted "Saddam style."

18. Trofimov, *Siege*, 192.

19. Although some writers, like John K. Cooley, *Unholy Wars: Afghanistan, America and International Terrorism* (Sterling, VA: Pluto, 2000), 83, 85–86, 195, 204, have claimed there have been assertions that the CIA and/or other agencies of the U.S. government directly trained Arab mujahidin, including Osama bin Laden, there is little evidence to support this, according to Peter L. Bergen, *Holy War, Inc.: Inside the Secret World of Osama bin Laden* (New York: Free Press, 2001), 64–67. Instead, America's contact with Arab mujahidin was indirect. U.S. aid in the form of training, weapons, and funding was funneled through Pakistan's ISI agency.

20. Saudi Arabia agreed to match U.S. funding for the mujahidin, and Egypt permitted the U.S. Air Force to use Egypt as a base from which it shipped to Pakistan tons of weapons and equipment. Even the Chinese contributed $600 million to the cause. Furthermore, Egypt's government of Anwar al-Sadat trained members of the Muslim Brotherhood for the jihad in Afghanistan. In the first years, in order to avoid any links with the United States, the CIA secured weapons from the First and Second World Wars, stockpiled in countries such as Egypt, India, and China. By 1985, sixty thousand tons of equipment was made available in Pakistan. See John Prados, *Safe for Democracy: The Secret Wars of the CIA* (Chicago: Ivan R. Dee, 2006), 471–72, 488; and Robert Dreyfuss, *Devil's Game: How the United States Helped Unleash Fundamentalist Islam* (New York: Metropolitan, 2005), 274–75.

21. George Crile, *Charlie Wilson's War: The Extraordinary Story of the Largest Covert Operation in History* (New York: Atlantic Monthly Press, 2003), 201. The British Secret Intelligence Service (SIS) and Special Air Service (SAS) were also able to send teams into Afghanistan. This direct contact was invaluable to the United States, because neither the CIA nor any other American agency was permitted to send men into Afghan territory.

ONE • *Assassination*

1. Anthony Nutting, *No End of a Lesson: The Story of Suez* (London: Constable, 1967), 34–35.

2. Robert St. John, *The Boss: The Story of Gamel Abdel Nasser* (New York: McGraw-Hill, 1960), 179–80.

3. The only casualties were a Sudanese minister and a lawyer from Alexandria, who were cut by the shattered glass.

4. St. John, *The Boss*, 181. Cf. Richard P. Mitchell, *The Society of Muslim Brothers* (Oxford: Oxford University Press, 1969), 151.

5. Mitchell, *Muslim Brothers*, 150.

6. Beyond Eden's general antipathy to Nasser, certain events, such as the nationalization of the Suez Canal, would send him off in a murderous frenzy. Even unrelated and smaller instances that underlined the decline of British influence in the Middle East would convince Eden that Nasser was the culprit. On March 1, 1956, King Hussein of Jordan dismissed Sir John Glubb, the commander of the Arab Legion, a Jordanian unit commanded by British officers. Eden took this as an insult to Britain and vowed to punish Nasser, although the latter had nothing to do with the affair. It was at this time that Eden blasted his deputy foreign minister Anthony Nutting about Nasser, screaming over the phone to him, "I want him destroyed, can't you understand?" See Stephen Dorril, *MI6: Inside the Covert World of Her Majesty's Secret Intelligence Service* (New York: Free Press, 2000), 612.

7. Certainly the British embassy emphasized Nasser's stipulation that, despite the purges of the Muslim organization, there were still many Brothers free in Egypt (Cairo to Foreign Office, VG 1015/45, FO 371/183884, The National Archives of the United Kingdom [TNA]).

8. Dorril, *MI6*, 613–14.

9. One French plan involved sending a commando team on rubber boats from the French embassy to destroy the Egyptian Revolutionary Command building on the northern tip of Gezira Island, but the attempt was aborted. See Mohamed H. Heikal, *Cutting the Lion's Tail: Suez Through Egyptian Eyes* (New York: Arbor House, 1987), 154n1.

10. Peter Wright, *Spy Catcher: The Candid Autobiography of a Senior Intelligence Officer* (Toronto: Stoddart, 1987), 160–62.

11. According to Heikal, *Lion's Tail*, 215n1, the Egyptian security service also received information about three British subjects who had been sent to Cairo to make another assassination attempt, but the mission was aborted, or they got cold feet.

12. John Keay, *Sowing the Wind: The Seeds of Conflict in the Middle East* (New York: Norton, 2003), 436. The Israelis also tried poison to eliminate the Egyptian leader. About this time they recruited a Greek waiter employed by Groppi, the presidential catering service, to sprinkle poison in Nasser's coffee. Fortunately for the Egyptian leader, the would-be assassin became so nervous that his hand shook uncontrollably, and he broke down and confessed (Heikal, *Lion's Tail*, 215n1).

13. Dorril, *MI6*, 631; Eric Downton, *Wars Without End* (Toronto: Stoddart, 1987), 229, 341.

14. Keith Kyle, *Suez* (London: Weidenfeld & Nicholson, 1991), 218–91. Swinburn and James Zarb, an employee of Marconi in Cairo and a British subject, were released under a general amnesty in 1959 (Dorril, *MI6*, 631n84).

15. Dorril, *MI6*, 631; Yaacov Caroz, *The Arab Secret Service* (London: Corgi, 1978), 23.

16. Kyle, *Suez*, 218; Dorril, *MI6*, 631–32.

17. Dorril, *MI6*, 631.

18. Scott Lucas and Alistair Morey, "The Hidden 'Alliance': The CIA and MI6 Before and After Suez," in *American-British-Canadian Intelligence Relations, 1939–2000*, ed. Maurizio Ferrera and Martin Rhodes (London: Frank Cass, 2000), 108.

19. Heikal, *Lion's Tail*, 151n3. Heikal suggests that the intent was to re-create the conditions of 1882, during which Egyptian riots in Alexandria that resulted in the killing of Europeans and the destruction of property gave the British an excuse to land troops and eventually dominate Egypt (see also Chapter 4).

20. Caroz, *Arab Secret Service*, 21–22; Richard Deacon, *"C": A Biography of Sir Maurice Oldfield, Head of MI6* (London: Futura, 1984), 110–11.

21. Dorril, *MI6*, 653.

22. Caroz, *Arab Secret Service*, 22n.

23. Dorril, *MI6*, 603.

24. Tom Bower, *The Perfect English Spy: The Unknown Man in Charge During the Most Tumultuous Scandal-Ridden Era in Espionage History* (New York: St. Martin's Press, 1995), 231; Dorril, *MI6*, 603.

25. Xan Fielding, *One Man in His Time: The Life of Lieutenant-Colonel N. L. D. ("Billy") McLean, DSO* (London: Macmillan, 1990), 104–5.

26. Caroz, *Arab Secret Service*, 24.

27. According to Kyle, *Suez*, 149, Khalil revealed that Saudi money was involved, but few details or the exact amount.

28. Kyle, *Suez*, 149; Dorril, *MI6*, 659.

29. Lucas and Morey, "Hidden 'Alliance,'" 101.

30. Like with Nasser, an unpopular treaty, in this case the Sinai Treaty between Israel and Egypt (March 26, 1979), triggered the assassination of Sadat on October 6, 1981. As early as February 1981, Egyptian security became aware of the plot to kill Sadat after arresting a member of Egyptian Islamic Jihad, and in September Sadat had ordered the round-up of over 1,500 suspected Islamic radicals, including Jihad members, along with feminists, Coptic Christian clergy, university professors, journalists, and members of various student groups. The arrests were a part of a major crackdown on all radical Islamic organizations, including student movements. Another factor was Sadat's role in the aftermath of the assassination

attempt against Nasser. Sadat had presided as a judge and had helped to convict Muslim Brothers, who were sentenced to death or imprisonment. According to Gilles Kepel, *Muslim Extremism in Egypt: The Prophet and the Pharaoh*, trans. Jon Rothschild (Los Angeles: University of California Press, 1984), 192, the assassin, Khalid al-Islambuli, killed Sadat at the peak of the president's unpopularity.

31. "The Man Behind Bin Laden," *The New Yorker*, 16 September 2002.

32. Kepel, *Muslim Extremism*, 192–93.

33. Adeed Dawisha, *Arab Nationalism in the Twentieth Century: From Triumph to Despair* (Princeton: Princeton University Press, 2003), 284.

TWO · *The Mahdi*

1. Alan Furst, *The World at Night* (New York: Random House, 1996), 9.

2. Charles Royle, *The Egyptian Campaigns, 1882–1885: And the Events Which Led to Them*, 2 vols. (London: Hurst & Blackett, 1886), 89. Royle estimates the mob to have reached approximately 2,000–2,500.

3. The more malicious of the rioters studded them with nails for greater effect.

4. Ibid.

5. Royle, *Egyptian Campaigns*, vol. 2, 88, states that on June 8, Bedouin were observed storing their rifles in various locations throughout the city.

6. During the course of the riot, about one hundred Bedouin proclaimed their loyalty to Tawfik the Dervish Pasha, the sultan's representative. See "The Crisis in Egypt: Serious Riots in Alexandria," *The Times*, 11 June 1882; Royle, *Egyptian Campaigns*, vol. 2, 182.

7. Royle, *Egyptian Campaigns*, vol. 1, 94.

8. Ibid., 97

9. Ibid., 54–55.

10. A. J. P. Taylor, *The Struggle for Mastery in Europe, 1848–1918* (Oxford: Clarendon Press, 1965), 272–73. Taylor argues that initially the French were not interested, but they were equally determined to deny the territory to the Italians. According to Luigi Albertini, *The Origins of the War of 1914*, trans. and ed. Isabella M. Massey, vol. 1 (London: Oxford University Press, 1952), 29, a major political and cultural figure in Italy in the early twentieth century, the prime mover behind the annexation of Tunisia, was Otto von Bismarck, who believed that French hostility toward the German empire could be diverted to North Africa.

11. Thomas Pakenham, *The Scramble for Africa: The White Man's Conquest of the Dark Continent from 1876 to 1912* (New York: Random House, 1991), 121.

12. Christina P. Harris, *Nationalism and Revolution in Egypt: The Role of the Muslim Brotherhood* (The Hague: Mouton, 1964), 45.

13. Harris, *Nationalism*, 44–45; the note was delivered to the Egyptian government on January 8, 1882.

14. The letter reached Gladstone via Blunt, who had received a translated version from Jean Sabunji. on 2 July 1882 in W. S. Blunt, *Secret History of the British Occupation of Egypt: Being a Personal Narrative of Events* (London: Unwin, 1907), 371–74.

15. Nineteenth-century Sudan also included the present-day Sudan, Somalia, Eritrea, and Ethiopia.

16. The "Expected One" (or the "Guided One") is the prophesied redeemer of Islam, who will remain on earth for seven, nine, or nineteen years (depending on the interpretation) before the Day of Judgment. Sufi and Shiite Islam accept the concept, but for Sunnis it never became a formal doctrine, and it is neither endorsed nor condemned. However, according to Edward Mortimer, *Faith and Power: The Politics of Islam* (New York: Vintage, 1982), 54, it has gained a strong hold on the imagination of many ordinary, self-described "orthodox" Sunni, thanks to Sufi preaching.

17. William L. Cleveland, *A History of the Modern Middle East* (San Francisco: Westview, 1994), 117–18.

18. Rudolf C. Slatin, *Fire and Sword in the Sudan: A Personal Narrative of Fighting and Serving the Dervishes, 1879–1895*, trans. F. R. Wingate (London: Arnold, 1896), 126, 132, 141.

19. Khartoum held sixty thousand inhabitants and was defended by a garrison of two thousand men. See Dominic Green, *Three Empires on the Nile: The Victorian Jihad, 1869–1899* (New York: Free Press, 2007), 150.

20. Gordon had to arrange transportation for approximately fifteen thousand civil servants, soldiers, and their families by boat to Egypt (Green, *Three Empires*, 152).

21. Paul Kennedy, *The Realities Behind Diplomacy: Background Influences on British External Policy, 1865–1980* (Glasgow: Collins, 1981), 88.

22. The scramble for Africa, inaugurated by the conference, delineated the spheres of influence that apportioned the region to the European powers.

23. Menelik II, ruler of Shewa, an independent kingdom of Ethiopia, made himself emperor of Ethiopia with the support of the Italians. On May 2, 1889, the Italians forced him to sign a treaty that effectively turned Ethiopia into an Italian protectorate, with the establishment of a colony in Eritrea. In 1893, Menelik repudiated the treaty, and the Italians attempted to reestablish control, only to face a humiliating defeat at the battle of Adowa on March 1, 1896, which resulted in the death of seven thousand Italian soldiers and the capture of another three thousand.

24. Kassala was captured by the Mahdi army in 1885 and then by the Italians in 1897.

25. Robert Gascoyne-Cecil, Marquess of Salisbury, became leader of the Conservatives in 1881, following the death of Benjamin Disraeli, and prime minister in

1886. Except for three years (1892–1895), he remained head of the government until 1902.

26. Taylor, *Struggle for Mastery*, 367.

27. Cleveland, *Modern Middle East*, 102.

THREE · *The Eclipse of Imperial Islam*

1. Joseph Heller, *British Policy Towards the Ottoman Empire, 1909–1914* (London: Frank Cass, 1983), 39.

2. The Caliph was head of a governing institution that was both state and church. As Bernard Lewis explains in *What Went Wrong?: Western Impact and Middle Eastern Response* (Oxford: Oxford University Press, 2002), 114, the Caliph "was himself neither a jurist nor a theologian, but a practitioner of the arts of politics and sometimes of war."

3. Philip Mansel, *Constantinople: City of the World's Desire, 1453–1924* (London: John Murray, 1995), 414.

4. From Mehmed II until the resignation of Mehmed VI in 1924, the Ottoman Sultans had claimed the title of Caliph. However, according to Caroline Finkel, *Osman's Dream: The Story of the Ottoman Empire, 1300–1923* (New York: Basic, 2006), 111, until Selim I, the Ottoman Sultans used the title in a rhetorical sense rather than in a political-legal assertion of sovereignty over the Muslim community. Finkel adds that by the eighteenth century stories emerged, although there is no credence to them, that there was an actual transfer of power to Selim from the last Mamluk Caliph. In the Shiite interpretation of Islam, descent from Mohammed originates from his son-in-law Ali, who is regarded as the first imam. In the Shiite doctrine, the imams have a special religious role, divine inspiration passed on from Mohammed, that the Sunni Caliphs did not possess. See Cleveland, *Modern Middle East*, 34–35.

5. Andrew Mango, Ataturk: *The Biography of the Founder of Modern Turkey* (New York: Overlook, 2000), 403. The sultanate was abolished two years earlier on November 1, 1922.

6. From the Turkish-language memoirs of Ismet Inönü, quoted in Mango, *Ataturk*, 403.

7. Gilles Kepel, *Jihad: The Trail of Political Islam*, trans. Anthony F. Roberts (Cambridge: Harvard University Press, 2002), 43.

8. Shiite Muslims, however, did not acknowledge any Sunni Caliph. Indeed the succession of the Caliphate is at the heart of the Shiite-Sunni schism. See also Vali Nasr, *The Shia Revival: How Conflicts Within Islam Will Shape the Future* (New York: Norton, 2006), 40–43.

9. The Turkish parliament under the direction of Mustapha Kema (Ataturk) formally ended the Caliphate on March 3, 1924. The day after the law was passed, the governor and police chief of Istanbul informed the last Caliph, Abdulmecit, that he had to leave immediately. The Ottoman Empire had officially come to an end on November 1, 1922, when the Turkish Grand Assembly in Ankara abolished the sultanate. The last Ottoman sovereign, Mehmed VI Vahdettin, departed Istanbul on November 17, 1922, with the assistance of the British. In a less than dignified manner the last Sultan escaped from his palace smuggled in an ambulance for transport to Malta on the British battleship *Malaya*. He finally settled on the Italian Riviera. For further details, see Mango, *Ataturk*, 364–65.

10. In the 1920s the Khilafat Movement sprang up throughout the British colonial territories in Asia to defend the Ottoman Caliphate. It was particularly effective in British India, where it formed a rallying point for Indian Muslims and was one of the many anti-British political movements to secure widespread support. For a few years it worked in alliance with Hindu communities and was supported by Gandhi, who was a member of the Central Khilafat Committee. The movement came to an end in 1924, after the British incarcerated most of the leadership, and several parts broke off to establish their own organizations. See Ali Rahnema, ed., *Pioneers of Islamic Revival* (London: Zed, 2005), 100–102.

11. Brynjar Lia, *The Society of the Muslim Brothers in Egypt: The Rise of an Islamic Mass Movement, 1928–1942* (Reading: Ithaca, 1998), 80.

12. According to Finkel, *Osman's Dream*, 492, after the losses from the Treaty of Berlin, three-quarters of the empire's population was Muslim.

13. Ibid.

14. S. Tufan Buzpinar, "The Hijaz, Abdulhamid II and Amir Hussein's Secret Dealings with the British, 1877–1880," *Middle East Studies* 31, no. 1 (January 1995): 99–123, 105–6, 110–16.

15. The Hashemite clan traces its ancestry to Hashim ibn Abd al-Manaf, the great-grandfather of the Prophet Mohammed.

16. Although the other three schools of Sunni Islam—Shafi'i, Hanbali, and Maliki—had maintained the Arab prerequisite of the Caliphate, they had not opposed the Ottoman claim. See Finkel, *Osman's Dream*, 494.

17. Buzpinar, "Secret Dealings," passim.

18. F. A. K. Yasamee, *Ottoman Diplomacy: Abdulhamid II and the Great Powers* (Istanbul: Isis, 1996), 89.

19. According to Yasamee, Hussein's death was not a coincidence. The assassin, despite torture, did not reveal his motives for killing the Emir, nor if he was acting on behalf of anyone else. Buzpinar, "Secret Dealings," 118–19, comments that the evidence is inconclusive whether Abdulhamid was behind the assassination. The

Sultan, though, was fully aware of the Emir's secret dealings with the British. Furthermore, Buzpinar adds, Abdulhamid's fears over conspiracies with respect to the Arab provinces breaking away had been raised by warnings from Layard, the British ambassador to Istanbul. Layard informed Abdulhamid that there was a secret society in Arabia dedicated to this end, as well as to the overthrow of the Sultan himself.

20.   David Fromkin, *A Peace to End All Peace: The Fall of the Ottoman Empire and the Creation of the Modern Middle East* (New York: Avon, 1989), 97.

21.   Hew Strachen, *The First World War*, vol. 1, *To Arms* (Oxford: Oxford University Press, 2001), 651.

22.   Fromkin, *Peace*, 97.

FOUR • *Jihad for All Occasions*

1.   C. S. Jarvis, *Three Deserts* (London: John Murray, 1941), 5. At the time, Jarvis was a major in the British army and posted to the Libyan Desert during the First World War. Later he served as governor of the Sinai Peninsula.

2.   Urguplu Hayri Bey, the Sheikulislam, was Mufti of Istanbul, but in 1540 Suleyman elevated the Mufti to the role of head of the Ottoman religious establishment and supreme cleric of the empire.

3.   Accordingly it was translated into Arabic, Farsi, Urdu, and Yaaric. The fatwa was a legal opinion; in this case, five fatwas were presented in the form of elaborate questions with a simple affirmative or negative answer. See Rudolph Peters, *Islam and Colonialism: The Doctrine of Jihad in Modern History* (The Hague: Mouton, 1979), 90–91.

4.   Mango, *Ataturk*, 136.

5.   Ulrich Trumpener, *Germany and the Ottoman Empire, 1914–1918* (Princeton: Princeton University Press, 1968), 117.

6.   The details, as well as a cogent argument with respect to the failure of the jihad, are to be found in Gottfried Hagen, "German Heralds of Holy War: Orientalists and Applied Oriental Studies," *Comparative Studies of South Asia, Africa and the Middle East* 24, no. 2 (2004): 145. Mango, *Ataturk*, 136, also cites Eshref Kushchubashi, a leading member of Enver Pasha's Special Organization, who commented that the proclamation of jihad was received coolly in Istanbul and added that there would be even less enthusiasm in other parts of the Muslim world.

7.   Hagen, "German Heralds," 145.

8.   Ibid.

9.   Trumpener, *Germany*, 112.

10.   Tilman Lüdke, *Jihad Made in Germany: Ottoman and German Propaganda and Intelligence Operations in the First World War* (Münster: LIT, 2005), 48.

11. Ibid., 50. Abdulhamid was the last Sultan to rule with absolute power. He was exiled to Salonica, but after the city fell to the Greek army in 1912, Abdulhamid was brought back to Istanbul and held under house arrest at the Beylerbeyi Palace. He spent the last few years of his life studying, carpentering, and writing his memoirs, until his death on February 10, 1918.

12. Albert Hourani, *Arabic Thought in the Liberal Age, 1798–1939* (London: Oxford University Press, 1962), 51. Hagen, "German Heralds," 51, points out that, in addition to Sharif Hussein's making claims on the Caliphate, Abbas Hilmi, the Khedive of Egypt, attempted to have himself proclaimed Caliph before the outbreak of the First World War.

13. Peters, *Islam*, 90–94.

14. Ibid., 94.

15. Tripolitania, Cyrenaica, and Fessan are modern Libya.

16. Jarvis, *Three Deserts*, 4–5.

17. Ibid., 24.

18. R. H. S. Crossman and Michael Foot, *A Palestine Munich* (London: Victor Gollancz, 1946): quoted in Arthur Koestler, *Promise and Fulfilment: Palestine, 1917–1949* (London: Macmillan, 1949), 50. The Anglo-American Report was issued by the Anglo-American Committee of Inquiry established by the U.S. and British governments to look into the plight of post–Second World War Jewish refugees in Europe. The committee recommended that 100,000 of these refugees be admitted to Palestine.

19. Crossman's experience with the British civil service is chronicled in *The Diaries of a Cabinet Minister: Richard Crossman* (New York: Henry Holt, 1976), upon which the popular BBC comedy series *Yes, Minister* was based; not surprisingly, every effort was made by the Whitehall establishment to stop its publication.

20. Gail Minault, *The Khilafat Movement: Religious Symbolism and Political Mobilization in India* (New York: Columbia University Press, 1982), 2 and passim.

21. Ibid., 2.

22. Kepel, *Jihad*, 57.

23. Sayyid Qutb (1906–1966) and Mawlana Mawdudi (1903–1979), both Sunnis and major figures in the pan-Islamic movement, and Ruhollah Khomeini (1902–1989), a Shiite cleric, also subscribed to the concept of Islam as a political force. See Kepel, *Jihad*, 23.

FIVE · *A New Caliph*

1. John Buchan, *Greenmantle* (London: Nelson, 1916), 16.

2. Mecca was occupied by only 1,400 Turkish soldiers, the bulk of the garrison having

been withdrawn to Taif, the summer station of the Hejaz, to spare them from the summer heat that reached 45 degrees Celsius.

3. R. L. Bidwell, ed., *The Arab Bulletin: Bulletin of the Arab Bureau in Cairo* (Gerrards Cross: Archive Editions, 1986), vol. 1, bulletin 21, 258.

4. *Ibid.* According to George Antonius, one report claimed that Zia Bey said: "The Arabs are in revolt, and it is said that they have declared their complete independence." To which Hussein replied: "I have also heard that they want their independence. I shall certainly do all I can about it." See George Antonius, *The Arab Awakening: The Story of the Arab National Movement* (Safety Harbor, FL: Simon, 2001), 196n2. Originally published in 1939 by J. B. Lippincott.

5. The Arabs simultaneously laid siege to all the Turkish garrisons and barracks but only with rifle fire, since they lacked artillery. The fighting lasted for three days, after which the smaller Turkish posts surrendered, but the main barracks and the fort of Jiad held out for three weeks and only capitulated when the British brought up Egyptian artillery units from the Sudan (Antonius, *Arab Awakening*, 195).

6. Hussein's sons Feisal and Ali, supported by a couple of tribes, raised the revolt on June 5, 1916.

7. Fromkin, *Peace*, 219.

8. After several informal contacts through go-betweens, Hussein entered into formal negotiation in the summer of 1917. The outcome of these discussions came after an exchange of letters, four from each side, between the Sharif and Sir Henry McMahon, Kitchener's successor as high commissioner in Cairo. The letters reveal that deception colored all aspects of the agreements, and after the war both sides repudiated the hollow promises and commitments engendered by expediency. For the text of the letter, see J. C. Hurewitz, *Diplomacy in the Near and Middle East: A Documentary Record*, vol. 2 (Princeton: Van Nostrand,1956), 13–17.

9. Fromkin, *Peace*, 218–19. According to Bruce Westrate, *The Arab Bureau: British Policy in the Middle East, 1916–1920* (University Park: Pennsylvania State University Press, 1992), 15, in January 1915, Hussein's son Ali had discovered a plot outlining a Turkish plan to depose him.

10. Fromkin, *Peace*, 217.

11. Joshua Teitelbaum, *The Rise and Fall of the Hashimite Kingdom of Arabia* (London: Hurst, 2001), 47.

12. Dennis P. Hupchick, *The Balkans: From Constantinople to Communism* (New York: Palgrave, 2002), 321. In the first Balkan War, the empire lost Western Thrace, Macedonia, and Albania; in the war with Italy, the Sultan was forced to surrender Libya.

13. The CUP also merged with the secret military society based in Thessalonica,

whose officers would eventually dominate the empire (Finkel, *Osman's Dream*, 504–5).

14. Bismarck was not indifferent to the outcome of the Eastern Question—the consequence following the disintegration of the Ottoman Empire—on several occasions he had encouraged France and Austria-Hungary to seek colonies among the Sultan's provinces and advised the British to annex Egypt. However, the imperial chancellor was equally reluctant for the Ottomans to become too dependent on Russia. See Yasamee, *Ottoman Diplomacy*, 73–75.

15. Peter Hopkirk, *On Secret Service East of Constantinople: The Great Game and the Great War* (London: John Murray, 1994) 17.

16. The Baghdad Railway included the newly built Orient Express line and was intended to run from Koyna in Turkey to Baghdad, and then on to Basra. Although the British government welcomed the proposed railway, British financiers were against it and organized public opinion to oppose the project. Because of this, the Baghdad Railway became a source of friction not only between Britain and Germany but also with Russia, since it would challenge Russia's influence in the Caucasus and in northern Persia. In 1911 and 1913, Russia and Britain reached separate settlements with Germany. The Baghdad Railway Company relinquished operations in southern Mesopotamia to the British and gave the Russians a monopoly over railways in northern Persia. French financial investment in the project also helped the achievement of a compromise (Strachan, *First World War*, vol. 1, 33).

17. Hopkirk, *Secret Service*, 23–24; Taylor, *Struggle for Mastery*, 383.

18. Hopkirk, *Secret Service*, 24.

19. Mohs, *Military Intelligence*, 14–15.

20. Antonius, *Arab Awakening*, 140.

21. Teitelbaum, *Hashimite Kingdom*, 41, states that the British ambassador to the court of the Sultan was instrumental in getting Hussein appointed as Sharif of Mecca.

22. According to Teitelbaum, *Hashimite Kingdom*, 68–69, before Abdullah left for Cairo, he confided to the French consul that he was disgusted with the Ottomans, and that he planned to give up his seat in the Ottoman parliament.

23. Abdullah used the pretext of going to Cairo in order to improve the traveling conditions of the annual pilgrimage to Mecca and in order to sound out the British. See Westrate, *Arab Bureau*, 14.

24. The Hejaz Railway was a narrow-gauge railway built mostly by the Ottomans with German advice and support; it ran from Damascus to Medina. The railway reached Medina on September 1, 1908, the Sultan's anniversary.

25. Cited in Mohs, *Military Intelligence*, 15.

SIX · *Middle East Delusions: The Great Arab Revolt*

1. Elie Kedourie, *In the Anglo-Arab Labyrinth: The McMahon-Husayn Correspondence and Its Interpretations, 1914–1939* (Cambridge: Cambridge University Press, 1976), 108.

2. The description of the surrender of the British forces at Kut is based on Russell Braddon, *The Siege* (New York: Viking, 1969), passim.

3. This is only an approximate number; according to Kitchener's speech in the House of Lords, the total of those who surrendered was six thousand Indian and 2,970 British troops.

4. Unlike the Western practice of hanging a person by snapping the neck, the Ottoman mode of execution relied on choking the victim at the end of a rope.

5. The British Army doctors suspected enteritis, cholera, or even poisoning.

6. Around thirteen thousand Allied troops survived at the time of surrender, of these, 70 percent of the British and 50 percent of the Indian troops died of disease or were killed by the Ottomans.

7. The battle of Gallipoli took place at the Gallipoli Peninsula in present-day Turkey, west of the Dardanelles, from April 25, 1915, to January 9, 1916. The British lost 21,255 killed and 52,230 wounded. In addition, 145,000 British troops became ill from enteric fever, dysentery, and diarrhea. Other Commonwealth casualties (Australian, New Zealand, Newfoundland, and Indian troops) included 11,702 killed and 28,060 wounded. The French suffered ten thousand killed and seventeen thousand wounded.

8. Hussein explained to the Turkish authorities was that a jihad supported by Mecca would result in the British blockading the Red Sea and causing great hardship to its inhabitants.

9. Islamic juridical opinion in Egypt and India declared that it was incumbent upon Muslims to obey the British (Finkel, *Osman's Dream*, 529).

10. Despite British efforts to discourage the practice, Indian Muslims made considerable donations to the railway project, regardless of the fact that most of them reached Mecca after a voyage by sea. In 1990, contributions amounted to 417,000 Turkish lira; between 1903 and 1908 they climbed from 651,184 to 1,127,894 lira. The railway carried approximately thirty thousand pilgrims per year. See Kemal H. Karpat, *The Politicization of Islam: Reconstructing Identity, State, Faith and Community in the Late Ottoman State* (Oxford: Oxford University Press, 2001), 255.

11. Lowell Thomas produced a show, *The Last Crusade*, part documentary and part lore, that played to large audiences in New York and London. In 1924, *The Last Crusade* was published as a book entitled *With Lawrence in Arabia* (New York: Century, 1924).

12. H. V. F. Winstone, *The Illicit Adventure: The Story of Political and Military Intelligence in the Middle East from 1898 to 1926* (London: Jonathan Cape, 1982), 247–48.

13. The creation of the Arab Bureau in 1916 came after Sir Mark Sykes returned from a major tour of almost six months in 1915 to the Balkans, the Persian Gulf, Egypt, and India to discuss the future of the Near and Middle East with British officials in the regions. Part of his soundings included the idea of establishing a bureau to take over the administration of Arab affairs. Sykes came under considerable opposition from various quarters, including the viceroy of India, who believed that the new organization would encroach on his areas of jurisdiction. See also Fromkin, *Peace*, 170–71, and Westrate, *Arab Bureau*, 27–32.

14. But the compromise to establish the Arab Bureau was necessary, not only to appease the fears of the viceroy of India, but more importantly those of the India Office, the Foreign Office, and other agencies of British foreign policy.

15. In early February 1916, both the French and British cabinets approved the Sykes-Picot Agreement, which was then brought to Moscow in April, and the process was completed on May 1916. The region was divided into areas of direct British and French rule, and others defined as zones of influence. The Syrian littoral, as well as southeastern Turkey and Lebanon, came under direct French administration, while the interior of Syria, together with northern Mesopotamia around Mosul, was decreed a zone of influence. Britain was allocated control of areas roughly comprising today's Jordan, southern Mesopotamia (including Basra and Baghdad), and a small area around Haifa, to allow access to a Mediterranean port. Jerusalem and the holy places came under an international administration, but Britain would retain the ports of Haifa and Acre. The rest, including most of Arabia, was to be placed under an international administration that would include representatives of the Sharif of Mecca. In exchange for agreeing to the Anglo-French partition of the Middle East, Russia was to acquire Constantinople, the Straits, and the Ottoman Armenian provinces.

16. "Extracts from a Report on Feisal's Operations, 30 October 1916," *Arab Bulletin*, vol. 1, bulletin 31, 465.

17. Malcolm Brown, ed., *T. E. Lawrence in War and Peace: An Anthology of the Military Writings of Lawrence of Arabia* (London: Greenhill, 2005), 61. Originally published in Arnold W. Lawrence, ed., *Secret Despatches from Arabia* (London: Golden Cockerel Press, 1939).

18. Antonius, *Arab Awakening*, 248.

19. Efraim Karsh and Inari Karsh, *Empires of the Sand: The Struggle for Mastery in the Middle East, 1789–1923* (Cambridge: Harvard University Press, 1999), 231, argue that the Sykes-Picot Agreement constituted recognition, by the Entente powers, of the Arabs' right to self-determination. Alan Palmer, *The Decline and Fall of the*

Ottoman Empire (New York: Barnes & Noble, 1992), 236, writes that the agreement amplified, clarified, and complemented McMahon's proposals rather than invalidated them.

20. Regardless of his other recorded comments, T. E. Lawrence described the Sykes-Picot Agreement in *Seven Pillars of Wisdom: A Triumph* (New York: Penguin, 1962), 282–83, as a fraud and claimed that he "vowed to make the Arab revolt the engine of its own success . . . and vowed to lead it so madly in the final victory that expediency should counsel to the Powers a fair settlement of the Arab's moral claims." Elie Kedourie, *The Chatham House Version and Other Middle Eastern Studies* (London: Weidenfeld & Nicolson, 1970), 24, cites Gilbert Clayton, expressing his disquiet and dissatisfaction at the outcome of the Sykes-Picot Agreement.

21. Westrate, *Arab Bureau*, 205.

22. In 1909, Arab officers in the Ottoman army in Istanbul founded al-Ahd (The Covenant). A year earlier, two Arab students in Istanbul established another secret society, al-Fatat. The full name was Jamiyyat al-Umma al-Arabiyya al-Fatat (The Society of the Young Arab Nation). The program of both societies was to enhance the status of Arabs in the Ottoman Empire, but after the outbreak of war they decided to seek independence. See Eliezer Tauber, *The Arab Movements in World War I* (London: Frank Cass, 1993), 2–3.

23. Initially, the societies had approached Ibn Saud, but he declined. See Tauber, *Arab Movements*, 61.

24. "Statement by Captain X," Cairo, 12 September 1915, FO 882/15, TNA.

25. Tauber, *Arab Movements*, 73.

26. The McMahon letter of October 24, 1915, was most significant in that it promised British support for Arab independence and accepted Hussein's delineation of the borders of the proposed state. This letter and the rest of the McMahon correspondence remain controversial, as the British commitments are in dispute. In the letter, McMahon writes: "Subject to the above modifications [referring to parts of Syria that would be excluded from the new Arab state] Great Britain is prepared to recognize and support the independence of the Arabs in all the regions within the limits demanded by the Sharif of Mecca." McMahon's language was generally evasive. Although he conceded Arab independence, he stressed that British officials would be needed to organize the administration of Arab countries. See Hurewitz, *Diplomacy*, vol. 2, 14–15. Fromkin, *Peace*, 183, rightly points out that, under those circumstances, the Arab states would be British protectorates.

27. Tauber, *Arab Movements*, 76. Tauber provides a complete breakdown of the membership of the societies, as well as their participation in the revolt. He indicates that al-Fatat had a membership of thirty-seven before the war, with another seventy-eight during the conflict; al-Ahd included fifty-four before 1914, while an

additional fifty-seven signed up during the course of World War I. Only forty-six of them took part in the fighting (twenty-nine from al-Fatat and seventeen from al-Ahd). See also Tauber, *Arab Movements*, 113.

28. Tauber, *Arab Movements*, 221–22.

29. On the various scholarly interpretations of Arab nationalism and its relationship to the Great Arab Revolt, see Dawisha, *Arab Nationalism*, 30–40. Also, on the Islamic character of Arab nationalism, see Efraim Karsh, *Islamic Imperialism: A History* (New Haven: Yale University Press, 2006).

30. Jeremy Wilson, *Lawrence of Arabia: The Authorised Biography of T. E. Lawrence* (New York: Atheneum, 1990), 404.

31. The Bolsheviks published the Sykes-Picot Agreement in *Izvestia* and *Pravda* on November 23, 1917. Three days later, on November 26, the *Manchester Guardian* published it in English.

32. On these debates, see Karsh, *Islamic Imperialism*, 127–30, 130n10.

33. Antonius, *Arab Awakening*, 267.

34. Regardless of the small number of activists in the Arab secret societies, those Arabs who joined the British leaders in the war had the opportunity to take part in the debates over the future of the Middle East, and a few had the opportunity of gaining experience in the government within the British mandate administrations (Dawisha, *Arab Nationalism*, 41).

SEVEN • *Spies, Adventurers, and Religious Warriors*

1. Koestler, *Promise and Fulfilment*, 50.

2. Charles Allen, *God's Terrorists: The Wahhabi Cult and the Hidden Roots of Modern Jihad* (London: Little, Brown, 2006), 244–45.

3. Ibid., 245.

4. Ibid., 246.

5. Winstone, *Illicit Adventure*, 143.

6. Ibid., 149.

7. Ibid., 151.

8. Ibid., 152.

9. Ibid., 153. According to Allen, *God's Terrorists*, 247–48, Shakespear was observing the battle when Ibn Saud's infantrymen near him ran away, leaving him to face a party of Ibn Rashid's cavalry. Shakespear, however, was not manning the gun but held his ground on the summit of the dune and defended himself with his revolver.

10. The Secret Service Bureau was created in 1909 "to take charge of all matters relating to intelligence gathering." In 1916, the bureau was renamed the Directorate of

Military Intelligence and was divided into two sections: MI5 dealt with internal security and counterintelligence, while MI6 was responsible for overseas espionage and eventually became the SIS. In popular literature the current SIS is still referred to as MI6. See Nigel West, *MI5: British Security Service Operations, 1909–1945* (London: Triad Granada, 1983), 38.

11.   Winstone, *Illicit Adventure*, 9.

12.   Philby had also been an officer in the countersedition section of the Indian Police Special Branch.

13.   From 1904 to 1913, Cox had been the political resident in the Persian Gulf of the government of India. Cox appointed Philby head of the financial department of the British administration in Mesopotamia.

14.   The other Englishman was Captain Forster Sadler of the 47th Regiment. In 1819, Sadler was sent from India to secure the assistance of Ibrahim Pasha to put down piracy in the Persian Gulf. At that time Ibrahim was busy, on behalf of the Ottoman Sultan, destroying the Wahhabi rebellion led by Ibn Saud's forefathers. See Elizabeth Monroe, *Philby of Arabia* (Reading: Ithaca, 1973), 53.

15.   Quoted in Allen, *God's Terrorists*, 254.

16.   Albert Hourani, *A History of the Arab Peoples* (New York: Warner, 1991), 319. This was a factor in Ibn Saud's decision to destroy the more radical Wahhabi tribesmen, since he was afraid that the British would intervene to stop the Wahhabis from raiding Iraq and Syria. See Allen, *God's Terrorists*, 255.

17.   On November 7, 1918, four days before the Armistice, Britain and France had issued the Anglo-French Declaration to the Arabs, essentially granting them self-determination but no single sovereign state. Philby viewed this as another betrayal that, along with the Balfour Declaration and the Sykes-Picot Agreement, negated the British promise of a single unified Arab nation as the reward for the Arabs having fought for the Allies.

18.   Iraq, carved out of the region of Mesopotamia by Winston Churchill when he was Colonial Secretary, with advice from T. E. Lawrence, was essentially the three former Ottoman provinces of Basra, Baghdad, and Mosul.

19.   Eliezer Tauber, *The Formation of Modern Syria and Iraq* (London: Frank Cass, 1995), 315.

20.   Ibid., 207.

21.   Fromkin, *Peace*, 449.

22.   H. V. F. Winstone, *Gertrude Bell* (London: Jonathan Cape, 1978), 207.

23.   Ibid.

24.   Margret MacMillan, *Paris 1919: Six Months That Changed the World* (New York: Random House, 2003), 397. According to MacMillan, between 1909 and 1919, British petroleum imports quadrupled, and most of the increase came from out-

side the British Empire (from the United States, Mexico, Russia, and Persia). MacMillan adds that the British navy was arguing, without further evidence, that the Iraqi oilfields were the largest in the world. See MacMillan, *Paris 1919*, 395–96.

25. Gertrude Bell, *Review of the Civil Administration of Mesopotamia* (London: HMSO, 1920): quoted in Georgina Howell, *Gertrude Bell: Queen of the Desert, Shaper of Nations* (New York: Farrar, Straus & Giroux, 2006), 329.

26. Howell, *Gertrude Bell*, 320. The population of Iraq in 1920 was approximately 50 percent Shiite, 25 percent Sunni, and the rest included smaller minorities of Jews and Christians. A further complication was that half of the population was Arab; the rest included Kurds, Assyrians, and Persians. MacMillan, *Paris 1919*, 398.

27. As was the case with Philby, the government of India employed Wilson. During the interwar years he maintained his colorful career. He worked in business, and in 1933 he was elected a member of Parliament. At the outbreak of war in 1939, he volunteered for the Royal Air Force as an air gunner; he was shot down over France on May 31, 1940.

28. Tauber, *Formation*, 317

29. Monroe, *Philby of Arabia*, 99–100.

30. Ibid., 105.

31. Ibid., 125.

32. Philby converted to Islam in 1930.

33. He began as an ardent Christian, became an atheist and socialist at Cambridge University, and after his conversion to Islam he was named Abdullah by Saud. See Monroe, *Philby of Arabia*, 152–53; Daniel Yergin, *The Prize: The Epic Quest for Oil, Money, and Power* (New York: Free Press, 1991), 287.

34. Philby provided the scientific name for the Arabian woodpecker (*Desertipicus* [now *Dendrocopos*] *dorae*), as well as naming a subspecies of owl (*Otus scops pamelae*). He named most of his birds after women he admired.

35. Monroe, *Philby of Arabia*, 127; Allen, *God's Terrorists*, 249.

36. Kim Philby, *My Silent War: The Autobiography of a Spy* (New York: Modern Library, 2002), 131–32; originally published in 1968.

37. Yuri Modin, "On Kim Philby," in ibid., i.

38. John le Carré, "On Kim Philby," in ibid., i.

39. Cited in Yergin, *Prize*, 286.

40. Monroe, *Philby of Arabia*, 133.

41. SOCAL was owned by John D. Rockefeller, which made him one of the richest men in the world. In 1911 the United States ruled that SOCAL was a monopoly and had to be broken up into thirty-four companies. Today ExxonMobil represents a major part of the original company.

42. Thanks to Philby's intervention and Ibn Saud's need for funds, SOCAL acquired the rights to excavate for oil.

43. In return for the concessions, SOCAL agreed to pay the Saudis £35,000 in gold as a down payment, £30,000 in the form of a loan, and £5,000 as an advance royalty. Eighteen months later, SOCAL would provide a second loan of £20,000. The loans were to be repaid out of future petroleum royalties. See Yergin, *Prize*, 291.

44. Ibid., 290–91.

45. In 1949, the Saudi share of oil revenue was $39 million. See ibid., 446–47.

46. Monroe, *Philby of Arabia*, 269–71.

EIGHT • *Absolute Faith: The Muslim Brotherhood and the Politics of Intelligence*

1. Spoken in response to his sister's pleas to appeal his death sentence and accept Nasser's proposed mercy shortly before his execution. See Lawrence Wright, *The Looming Tower: Al-Qaeda and the Road to 9/11* (New York: Vintage, 2006), 31.

2. Artemis Cooper, *Cairo in the War, 1939–1945* (London: Hamish Hamilton, 1989), 4.

3. Wright, *Looming Tower*, 36

4. Ibid., 37.

5. Qutb's brother, Muhammad, has tried to claim that the jihad espoused in the writings of Sayyid emphasized the intellectual and moral efforts of Muslims to defend their faith rather than violence. See Charles Tripp, "Sayyid Qutb: The Political Vision," in Rahnema, *Pioneers*, 177.

6. Kepel, *Muslim Extremism*, 34.

7. Gilles Kepel, *The War for Muslim Minds: Islam and the West*, trans. Pascale Ghazaleh (Cambridge: Harvard University Press, 2004), 78–83, 174–75.

8. Kepel, *Muslim Extremism*, 39.

9. Ibid., 40. Qutb enrolled at the Colorado State College of Education and earned a master's degree.

10. Ibid., 40–44; Tripp, "Sayyid Qutb," 158.

11. Robert Irwin, "Is This the Man Who Inspired Bin Laden?," *The Guardian*, 1 November 2001.

12. Robert Baer, *Sleeping with the Devil: How Washington Sold Our Soul for Saudi Crude* (New York: Three Rivers, 2003), 127.

13. Rashid Khalidi, *The Iron Cage: The Story of the Palestinian Struggle for Statehood* (Boston: Beacon, 2006), xxii; Dreyfuss, *Devil's Game*, 79.

14. Baer, *Sleeping*, 99.

15. See Chapter 12.

16. Banna founded the MB in the city of Ismailia with six workers of the Suez Canal Company.

17. Lia, *Society*, 41; Mitchell, *Muslim Brothers*, 9.

18. Kepel, *Jihad*, 27.

19. Dawisha, *Arab Nationalism*, 102.

20. The mandate for Palestine was awarded by the League of Nations to the British in July 1922. The actual document was internationally recognized by the Great Powers of the day. The mandate for Palestine included the entire text of the Balfour Declaration and, like the Balfour Declaration, did not make any references to the Arabs in Palestine. For details of the establishment of the mandate, see Khalidi, *Iron Cage*, 32.

21. Benny Morris, *1948: A History of the First Arab-Israeli War* (New Haven: Yale University Press, 2008), 12, writes that the outbreaks of 1920, 1929, and 1936–1939 grew progressively more lethal and more extensive.

22. Al-Husseini came from a prominent and influential Jerusalem family. After the First World War, he found employment as a clerk with Gabriel Haddad, a Christian-Arab advisor to Ronald Storrs, the military governor of Jerusalem. In 1919, when Haddad was transferred to Damascus and assumed the position of commissioner of public safety, al-Husseini followed along and soon became involved with the Arab nationalists supporting Feisal's claim to the crown of Syria. After Haddad was transferred to London, al-Husseini returned to Palestine and helped organize demonstrations in Jerusalem in support of Feisal and shortly after against the Jews. The demonstration of April 4, 1920, led to a wave of violence with both Jewish and Arab fatalities. The British were taken by surprise by the intensity of the Arab protests and tried to arrest the ringleaders, including al-Husseini. See Philip Mattar, *The Mufti of Jerusalem: Al-Hajj Amin al-Husayni and the Palestinian National Movement* (New York: Columbia University Press, 1988), 15–17.

23. The British administration in Palestine appointed a Muslim committee of notables to elect the Mufti of Jerusalem. Four candidates were selected and the committee had to choose three with the largest number of votes. Al-Husseini was effectively eliminated (Mattar, *Mufti*, 25).

24. David G. Dalin and John F. Rothmann, *Icon of Evil: Hitler's Mufti and the Rise of Radical Islam* (New York: Random House, 2008), 21.

25. Ibid. In 1918, according to Kedourie, *Chatham House*, 63, Richmond was languishing in the Imperial War Graves Commission when he was transferred to Jerusalem, thanks to Storrs.

26. Dalin and Rothmann, *Icon of Evil*, 21.

27. Kedourie, *Chatham House*, 65.

28. Mattar, *Mufti*, 24–26, points out that there is no documentary evidence to support Kedourie's assertion that Richmond's intervention influenced Samuel.

29. The Husseini family claimed descent from Arab aristocracy back to the time of Mohammed and, with few interruptions, had held the position of Mufti since the seventeenth century (Mattar, *Mufti*, 24).

30. Mattar, *Mufti*, 27.

31. Khalidi, *Iron Cage*, 56.

32. Harris, *Nationalism*, 178–79; Mitchell, *Society*, 16.

33. Dawisha, *Arab Nationalism*, 108.

34. On one occasion Western and Middle East radicals even collaborated on a joint operation. On June 27, 1976, two Palestinians from the Popular Front for the Liberation of Palestine—External Operations (PFLP—EO) hijacked Air France Flight 139 with two Germans, Wilfried Böse and Brigitte Kuhlmann, of the German Revolutionäre Zellen (RZ).

35. Harris, *Nationalism*, 179.

36. The proposal called for the division of Palestine into three parts: the British would retain the religious section, including Jerusalem and Bethlehem; there would be a Jewish state in Galilee; and the rest of Palestine was to be united with Transjordan in a single state ruled by Britain's protégé Abdullah bin al-Hussein.

NINE · *The British-Jewish Military Alliance*

1. Mark Twain, *The Innocents Abroad* (Mineola, NY: Dover, 2003), 559.

2. Kathleen Christison, *Perceptions of Palestine* (Berkeley: University of California Press, 1999), 17.

3. Wingate had a reputation as an eccentric. He often wore an alarm clock around his wrist, which would go off, and he walked around with a raw onion hung around his neck, which he would bite into for a snack. Occasionally, he strolled around without any clothing. In Palestine, for example, recruits were used to seeing him step out of the shower wearing nothing but a shower cap and while continuing to scrub himself with a shower brush barking orders. See Charles McMoran Wilson, *Churchill: Taken from the Diaries of Lord Moran* (Boston: Houghton Mifflin, 1966).

4. Tom Segev, *One Palestine Complete: Jews and Arabs Under the British Mandate* (New York: Henry Holt, 1999), 429.

5. Liddell Hart to Churchill, 11 November 1938, 80/69/5, Haganah Archive.

6. John Bierman, *Fire in the Night: Wingate of Burma, Ethiopia, and Zion* (New York: Random House, 1999), 64–66.

7. Trevor Royle, *Orde Wingate: Irregular Soldier* (London: Weidenfeld & Nicolson, 1995), 98.

8. Ibid.

9. The pipeline was completed in 1935 by the British Iraq Petroleum Company.

10. Mordecai Naor, *Lexicon of the Haganah Defence Force* (Tel Aviv: Ministry of Defence, 1992), 140.

11. Gudrun Kramer, *A History of Palestine: From the Ottoman Conquest to the Founding of the State of Israel* (Princeton: Princeton University Press, 2002), 291.

12. In 1929, major clashes between Jews and Arabs over the use of a gender partition and the presence of tables and chairs by the Wailing Wall shattered the temporary peace of the 1920s. Tensions were further fueled by a variety of conspiracy theories claiming that the Jews were planning to rebuild the Temple of Solomon. During one week of fighting, over 250 people were killed, including 133 Jews and 116 Arabs, as well as 580 injured. See Kramer, *Palestine*, 232.

13. Khalidi, *Iron Cage*, 57–58, argues that the British had only recognized the Jews as a political or national entity and thus intended to divide, distract, and divert Palestinian Arabs so they would not unite as a national entity against the mandate.

14. Benny Morris, *Righteous Victims: A History of the Zionist-Arab Conflict, 1881–2001* (New York: Vintage, 1999), 128.

15. Kramer, *Palestine*, 271.

16. On April 25 members of the political parties formed the Arab Higher Committee, chaired by the Mufti.

17. Khalidi, *Iron Cage*, 65–73.

18. Morris, *Righteous Victims*, 131–32; Kramer, *Palestine*, 274.

19. However, the primary motive of these Arab leaders was economic. The outbreak of the Spanish Civil War had eliminated the competition for Palestinian citrus fruits, and the harvest was approaching. Under the new circumstances, prices had soared. See Kramer, *Palestine*, 278.

20. Ibid., 280–81.

21. Ibid., 276.

22. Morris, *Righteous Victims*, 144–45.

23. Haggai Eshed, *Reuven Shiloah—The Man Behind the Mossad: Secret Diplomacy in the Creation of Israel*, trans. David and Leah Zinder (Portland: Frank Cass, 1997), 32.

24. One such commander was Yitzhak Sadeh, who later became commander of the Palmach; others were Moshe Dayan and Yigal Allon. See Samuel Katz, *Israeli Elite Units Since 1948* (Oxford: Osprey, 1988), 3.

25. Yitzhak Sadeh also selected the best fighters of the Nodedot and other combat units at the Haganah's disposal to create the Haganah's first commando unit, its Plugot Sadeh, or FOSH. As *sadeh* is also the Hebrew word for field, this unit could be named "field companies," as well as "Sadeh's companies." It comprised a semiautonomous strike force that would, by 1938, command over 1,500 well-trained fighters, who conducted lightning raids against hostile Arab targets. See Katz, *Elite*, 3.

26. Bierman, *Fire*, 83.

27. Ibid., 86.

28. Ibid., 90.

29. Ibid., 98.

30. Despite this friendly-fire debacle, the action was a major success. At least nine Arab rebels were killed with two of the dead and five of the wounded attributed to the SNS. Wingate's own estimates put the numbers at fifteen killed and at least twenty wounded. Wingate was awarded the DSO for his actions. See: Bierman, *Fire*, 98–103.

31. Ibid., 107, 115–17.

32. Ibid., 108.

33. Ibid., 125.

34. John Masters, *The Road Past Mandalay* (New York: Bantam, 1979), 217–29.

35. Eshed, *Shiloah*, 42–43.

36. Ian Black and Benny Morris, *Israel's Secret Wars: The Untold History of Israeli Intelligence* (London: Hamish Hamilton, 1991), 35.

37. Jacques Derogy and Hesi Carmel, *The Untold History of Israel* (New York: Random House, 1979), 50.

38. Eshed, *Shiloah*, 45.

39. Sherut Yediot (SHAI), Information Service, was the primary intelligence-gathering apparatus of the Jewish community from the mid-1930s until the establishment of the Israel state in 1948, at which point it was assimilated into the Israeli intelligence community.

40. Eshed, *Shiloah*, 48.

41. The Hebrew term for such undercover soldiers is *mista'aravim*, based on the verb "to become" and *aravim* (Arabs). The term was revived during the Intifada to refer to undercover Special Forces units operating in the occupied Palestinian territories. Those units have been active until today, and the term remains in use.

42. Eshed, *Shiloah*, 47.

43. Black and Morris, *Secret Wars*, 32–33. Reuven Zaslany (later Reuven Shiloah, after he Hebraized his name post-1948) was an intelligence expert for the Jewish Agency's Political Department and their chief liaison officer with British security. He also organized the Yishuv's first intelligence network, SHAI.

44. Eshed, *Shiloah*, 48.

45. Hermione Ranfurly, *To War with Whitaker: Wartime Diaries of Countess Ranfurly, 1939–45* (London: Heinemann, 1994), 76.

46. Black and Morris, *Secret Wars*, 52.

47. Eshed, *Shiloah*, 52.

48. Derogy and Carmel, *Untold History*, 53.

49. Katz, *Elite*, 5.

50. Ibid.

51. Derogy and Carmel, *Untold History*, 57.

52. Katz, *Elite*, 5.

53. Moshe Dayan in Eshed, *Shiloah*, 53.

54. Eshed, *Shiloah*, 54.

55. Ibid., 55.

56. A Jew and a Zionist, he would later change his name to Abba Eban and immigrate to Israel, where he would become Israel's ambassador to the United Nations and eventually foreign minister.

57. Derogy and Carmel, *Untold History*, 52–53.

58. Ibid., 57.

59. Eshed, *Shiloah*, 56.

60. At Cairo MI9 there was, besides Simmons, another veteran of Palestine from the days of the Arab Revolt: Brigadier Dudley Clark.

61. Ha'Mossad le'Aliya Bet (Institute for Immigration B) was a special clandestine organization within the Haganah, formed in 1939 to facilitate illegal immigration in violation of the 1939 White Paper quotas on the permissible number of Jewish immigrants to Palestine. Though its networks were largely inactive during the war, they remained in place and went into operation again at the war's end.

62. Originally 250 Palestinian Jews had volunteered, and 170 received training for the mission. See Eshed, *Shiloah*, 59–68.

63. Ibid., 54–55.

TEN • *Kill the Mufti: Politics and Blowback*

1. 7 October 1940, 367/31, FO 371/32900, TNA.

2. Mattar, *Mufti*, 95. According to an intelligence report from the British military attaché, based on information received from the Turkish general staff on May 3, 1940, the Mufti's organization in Baghdad had received a large sum of money, presumably from the Germans, with instructions to begin the rebellion by assassinating British, French, and friendly Arab officials (Military Attaché Ankara to C-in-C Middle East, 3 May 1940, E1940, FO 371/24568, TNA).

3. C-in-C Middle East to War Office, 1 October 1940, E2802/448/93, FO 371/24558, TNA; Martin Gilbert, *Finest Hour*, vol. 6 of *Winston S. Churchill* (London: Heinemann, 1983), 1079, 1124.

4. Mattar, *Mufti*, 95.

5. Specifically the Mufti's chief political opponent, Raghib al-Nashashibi. The Nashashibi family were historical rivals of the Husseinis for the leadership of the Arabs in Palestine.

6. Leo Amery to Secretary of State, 5 October 1940, E2762/367/31, FO 371/24568, TNA.

7. Secretary of State to Leo Amery, 10 October 1940, E2762/367/31, FO 371/24568, TNA.

8. 10 October 1941, E2762/367/31, FO 371/24568, TNA.

9. 17 October 1940, E2900/367/31, FO 371/24568, TNA.

10. 18 November 1940, E2900/367/31, FO 371/24568, TNA.

11. Foreign Office minutes, 18 November 1940, E2900/367/31, FO 371/24568, TNA.

12. Ibid.

13. Yitshaq Ben-Ami, *Years of Wrath, Days of Glory: Memoirs from the Irgun* (New York: Speller, 1982), 245–46, claims that it was David Raziel's idea to kidnap or eliminate the Mufti. The word used in his memoirs was to "acquire" the Mufti. He also adds that the British in Habbaniya had difficulty in obtaining Arab dress for the Irgun commandos. The Irgun (Hairgun HaTzva'i HaLe'umi BeEretz Yisra'el or National Military Organization in the Land of Israel) was one of three paramilitary organizations, along with the Stern Gang and the Palmach, that originated out of the Haganah (Jewish Defense Organization). The members of the Irgun broke away from the Haganah because they decided to retaliate against the Arab revolt of 1936–1939, whereas the Haganah had adopted a policy of defense. See Y. S. Brenner, "The Stern Gang, 1940–1948," in *Palestine and Israel in the 19th and 20th Centuries*, ed. Elie Kedourie and Sylvia G. Haim (London: Frank Cass, 1982), 114.

14. Wavell was confronted by multiple threats: the German Afrika Korps in the Western Desert, the British withdrawal from mainland Greece, and the immediate threat to Crete, as well as the real possibility that a hostile government in Iraq could cut off oil supplies and expose his eastern flank to German infiltration from Vichy-controlled Syria. He tried to transfer the Iraq problem to India Command, but Churchill insisted that Wavell undertake the relief of the British forces in Iraq, because it was quicker and closer to bring reinforcements from Palestine. See Victoria Schofield, *Wavell: Soldier and Statesman* (London: John Murray, 2007), 183–84.

15. Ben-Ami, *Years of Wrath*, 246–46; J. Bowyer-Bell, *Terror out of Zion* (London: Avon, 1997), 70.

16. William Seymour, *British Special Forces: The Story of Britain's Undercover Soldiers* (Toronto: Grafton, 1985), 152.

17. As reich protector (governor) of Bohemia and Moravia, Heydrich suppressed the black market, increased food rations and pensions, and introduced unemployment insurance. On the other hand, anyone linked with the resistance movement or the black market faced torture and execution. Under Heydrich's administration, Czechoslovakia was pacified and industrial output went up. Because of his success in Prague, Hitler was considering making him governor of Paris. When

British intelligence became aware of this, they decided that Heydrich had to be stopped before he had a similar impact on France and eventually all occupied Europe.

18. Heydrich died of his wounds one week later on June 4, 1942. As a consequence, approximately thirteen thousand people were arrested, deported, imprisoned, or killed by the SS. On June 10, 1942, all males over the age of sixteen in the village of Lidice, twenty-two kilometers northwest of Prague, and another village, Ležáky, were executed. All houses and buildings in the two villages were burned and the ruins leveled. For a detailed account of the Heydrich assassination and its consequences, see Callum MacDonald, *The Killing of SS Obergruppenführer Reinhard Heydrich* (New York: Free Press, 1989).

19. According to a poll commissioned by the American consulate in Jerusalem at the beginning of the war, 88 percent of Palestinian Arabs favored Germany and only 9 percent Great Britain. See Morris, *1948*, 21.

20. 21 March 1940, 28 March 1940, 29 May 1940, and 11 September 1940, HS 3/201, TNA.

21. Morris, *1948*, 28.

22. Morris, *1948*, 28; Franklin Lindsay, *Beacons in the Night: With the OSS and Tito's Partisans in Wartime Yugoslavia* (Stanford: Stanford University Press, 1993), 361n.

23. Lindsay, *Beacons*, 361n.

24. C. M. Keble to Lord Moyne, 16 January 1943, 89637/537/1817, HS 3/209, TNA.

25. Morris, *1948*, 29.

26. Ronald W. Zweig, *Britain and Palestine During the Second World* War (London: Royal Historical Society, 1986), 165n68.

27. Howard M. Sachar, *A History of Israel: From the Rise of Zionism to Our Time* (New York: Knopf, 2007), 247; Brenner, "Stern Gang," 115.

28. Sachar, *History of Israel*, 247.

29. Morris, *1948*, 29.

30. Ben-Ami, *Years of Wrath*, 295.

31. Brenner, "Stern Gang," 121. According to a report from MI6, passed on to Washington (21 February 1944, HNO 867108, NARA), the Irgun would destroy property but not resort to assassination, whereas the Stern Gang would easily resort to murder.

32. 28 March 1946, KV 5/30, TNA.

33. During the same period, the Haganah had a field army of sixteen thousand, while the Palmach included approximately six thousand men and women. Both organizations could draw on more recruits from a static force of forty thousand based in rural and urban areas (Colonial Office, "Palestine: Statement of Information Relating to Acts of Violence," KV 5/30, TNA).

34.   Sachar, *History of Israel*, 266.

35.   Brenner, "Stern Gang," 134; Colonial Office, "Palestine: Statement of Information Relating to Acts of Violence," KV 5/30, TNA.

36.   In 1946, over ninety thousand Jews left Poland; along with 25,000 from the Balkans, they increased the number of refugees in the West German DP camps to 250,000. See Sachar, *History of Israel*, 264.

37.   Brenner, "Stern Gang," 123.

ELEVEN · *By Blood and Fire*

1.   MacSwiney said this during the course of his hunger strike following his imprisonment as a member of the IRA. MacSwiney died in Brixton Prison of malnutrition as a result of a seventy-three-day hunger strike on October 24, 1920.

2.   A. W. Sansom, *I Spied Spies* (London: Harrap, 1965), 168–70.

3.   Ibid., 167.

4.   Ibid.

5.   In another account, Moyne and his driver were killed with three bullets, each fired in rapid succession. See Thurston Clarke, *By Blood and Fire: The Attack on the King David Hotel* (New York: Putnam, 1981), 44–45.

6.   Sansom, *Spies*, 180.

7.   Ibid., 177.

8.   Brenner, "Stern Gang," 124.

9.   According to a report from the Special Investigation Branch dated November 13, 1944, the British authorities in Egypt feared that indigenous troops would see the assassins as heroes and possibly emulate their actions (CO 732/88/32, TNA).

10.   The Jewish Agency ordered the Haganah to track down the members of the Stern Gang and also to help the British authorities apprehend them. As a result, 279 members of both the Stern Gang and the Irgun were apprehended by the British, with the help of the Haganah. See Christopher Sykes, *Crossroads to Israel* (Cleveland: World, 1965), 257.

11.   Brenner, "Stern Gang," 131. In Israeli accounts.

12.   Ben-Ami, *Years of Wrath*, 376; Morris, *1948*, 35; Brenner, "Stern Gang," 132.

13.   Quoted in Sachar, *History of Israel*, 264–65.

14.   Sachar, *History of Israel*, 265.

15.   Richard J. Aldrich, *The Hidden Hand: Britain, America and Cold War Secret Intelligence* (New York: Overlook, 2002), 261.

16.   Ibid., 259.

17.   Mathew Carr, *The Infernal Machine: A History of Terrorism* (New York: New Press, 2007), 60.

18. Peter Taylor, *Provos: The IRA and Sinn Fein* (London: Bloomsbury, 1997), 21.

19. Ibid., 20. The Black and Tans earned their curious nickname from their hastily assembled uniforms, consisting of surplus dark police tunics and surplus British army khaki trousers, resembling the colors of a famous pack of Irish foxhounds: the Scarteen Black and Tans.

20. In one such operation, a unit of Black and Tans captured several IRA at Kerry Pike near Cork and proceeded to cut off the nose of one man, the tongue of another, smashed the skull of a third, and cut out the heart of the fourth unfortunate victim. (Ibid).

21. Sykes, *Crossroads*, 308. Farran, whose decorations included the DSO and the MC with two bars, subsequently emigrated to Canada, where he became a successful provincial politician and cabinet minister.

22. Fergusson, formerly Wavell's ADC in Palestine, was no stranger to special operations: he had commanded a Chindit unit (16th Infantry Brigade) in the Burmese jungle and had ended the war as director of combined operations, in operational command of Britain's commandos and other Special Forces.

23. "Roy Farran (Obituary)," *Daily Telegraph*, 5 June 2006.

24. Roy Farran, *Winged Dagger: Adventures on Special Service* (London: Collins, 1970), 348.

25. Aldrich, *Hidden Hand*, 263.

26. Ibid. Farran confessed, but his written account of the events was ruled inadmissible.

27. "Major Roy Farran (Obituary)," *The Times*, 6 June 2006.

28. Ibid.

29. Robert Kumamoto, *International Terrorism and American Foreign Relations* (Boston: Northeastern University Press, 1999), 17.

30. M. R. D. Foot, *S.O.E. in France: An Account of the Work of the British Special Operations Executive in France, 1940–1944* (London: HMSO, 1966), 13–14. The curious use of lowercase letters is to be found in the original text.

31. 89846, HS 7/269, TNA.

32. André Gerolymatos, *Guerrilla Warfare and Espionage in Greece, 1940–1944* (New York: Pella, 1992), 335–36.

33. André Gerolymatos, *Red Acropolis, Black Terror: The Greek Civil War and the Origins of Soviet-American Rivalry* (New York: Basic, 2004), passim.

34. In 1946, British code breakers successfully monitored communications between the Jewish Agency in Palestine and their representatives in London and Paris. As a result, the British security services were able to arrest 2,650 men and fifty-nine women. See Ben-Ami, *Years of Wrath*, 375–76.

35. Brenner, "Stern Gang," 132.

36. The Irgun also booby-trapped the bodies, resulting in further British casualties. See ibid., 137–38.

37. Aldrich, *Hidden Hand*, 262.

38. As early as 1946, British military security in Palestine correctly surmised that the Stern Gang had adopted new tactics of terror by indiscriminately ambushing and killing British personnel as part of the organization's plan of assassinations ([1] 1282, KV 5/30, TNA).

39. In January 1947, the British security services estimated that the Irgun and Stern Gang included approximately 474 members (or suspected members) and were able to identify the country of origin for only 129 of them. The majority came from Russia (13), Poland (51), and Palestine (24); the rest originated from Czechoslovakia (9), Austria (8), Romania (7), Germany (7), Lithuania (4), Bulgaria (2), Hungary (1), Egypt (1), Turkey (1), and Iran (1). However, they were not able to identify the origin of the other 345 members (H. J. Seager to S. H. E. Burley, 6 November 1947, KV 5/38, TNA).

40. Clarke, *Blood and Fire*, 211.

41. Aldrich, *Hidden Hand*, 261.

42. Clarke, *Blood and Fire*, 250.

43. The Haganah had approved the attack but later requested a postponement. See Clarke, *Blood and Fire*, 45, 144.

44. Ibid., 251.

45. Ibid., 40.

46. Sykes, *Crossroads*, 301.

47. Clarke, *Blood and Fire*, 251–52.

48. Bernadotte was killed because he was perceived to favor the Arabs. See Brenner, "Stern Gang," 137.

49. One difficulty was that both the Irgun and Stern Gang were organized in small, self-contained cells. The members of the cells did not use their real names or address so if one were arrested he could do little to help the authorities. See Aldrich, *Hidden Hand*, 258.

50. Final, Possible Future of Palestine, 9 September 1947, JIC(47)5(0), IOR/L/WS/1/1162, India Office Records (IOR), British Library (BL).

51. Tad Szulc, *The Secret Alliance: The Extraordinary Story of the Rescue of the Jews Since World War II* (London: Macmillan, 1991), 48–50.

52. Dorril, *MI6*, 547.

53. Jon Kimche and David Kimche, *The Secret Roads: The "Illegal" Migration of a People, 1938–1948* (London: Secker & Warburg, 1954), 161.

54. Illegal Immigration to Palestine, 9 September 1947, LCS (47) 5, CAB 81/80.

55. Roy C. Nesbit, *Eyes of the RAF: A History of Photo-Reconnaissance* (Kettering: Sutton, 1996), 267–68.

56. Dorril, *MI6*, 549.

57. Ibid., 548.

58. The British intelligence and security services generated several reports indicating that the Stern Gang, the Irgun, and even the Haganah were in contact with the Soviets or were receiving funds from them (KV 5/39, TNA).

59. Aldrich, *Hidden Hand*, 257.

60. Clarke, *Blood and Fire*, 43.

TWELVE · *The CIA and Nasser: A Muslim Billy Graham*

1. Dean Acheson, *Present at the Creation: My Years in the State Department* (New York: Norton, 1969), 567.

2. Under the terms of that arrangement the British had the right to maintain military bases and collect tolls from ships, which, in turn, were guided by English and French pilots, all constant reminders of Egypt's subservient status.

3. Heikal, *Lion's Tail*, 25.

4. Harris, *Nationalism*, 187, 192, also comments that some observers claim the communists were primarily responsible for the organized violence.

5. Matthew F. Holland, *America and Egypt: From Roosevelt to Eisenhower* (London: Praeger, 1996), 24.

6. Acheson, *Creation*, 565–66.

7. Holland, *America and Egypt*, 23; Lucas and Morey, "Hidden 'Alliance,'" 97.

8. At 9:00 P.M. on February 4, 1942, the British high commissioner, Sir Miles Lampson, flanked by a detachment of British officers and a column of tanks and armored personnel carriers, compelled Farouk to accede to their wishes.

9. Holland, *America and Egypt*, 24.

10. Heikal, *Lion's Tail*, 50n2.

11. Holland, *America and Egypt*, 26.

12. Ibid., 25.

13. Ibid. On the U.S. role in the Greek Civil War, see Gerolymatos, *Red Acropolis*.

14. The primary source for the CIA's role in Egypt, as well as in Syria, is much maligned former CIA officer Miles Copeland. His three memoirs, *Game of Nations: The Amorality of Power Politics* (New York: Simon & Schuster, 1969); *The Real Spy World* (London: Weidenfeld & Nicolson, 1974); and *The Game Player: Confessions of the CIA's Original Political Operative* (London: Arium, 1989), offer an intriguing and detailed insight into CIA operations. I agree with Lucas and Morey, "Hidden 'Alliance,'" 118n44, that documentary evidence, including archival records in Washington and London, verify most of Copeland's version of events. Scott and Morey comment that his works have been "treated with skepticism by some historians," in

part "because of his tendency to exaggerate his role in events" and by "the campaign of the Agency to discredit Copeland through 'information' to trusted contacts." Clearly, a major obstacle in intelligence history is the ability of the intelligence organizations to practice deception against historians, as well as against their enemies.

15. Copeland, *Game Player*, 153–54.

16. Ibid., 154.

17. Michael Holzman, *James Jesus Angleton, the CIA, and the Craft of Counterintelligence* (Amherst: University of Massachusetts Press, 2008), 161, suggests that Roosevelt's directorate had backed the Free Officers and later organized Nasser's security forces.

18. Wilbur Crane Eveland, *Ropes of Sand: America's Failure in the Middle East* (New York: Norton, 1980), 97n.

19. Copeland, *Game Player*, 156.

20. Initially, the CIA was established in 1947 to collect and analyze information gathered through espionage, as well as from open sources, and report to the National Security Council (NSC). Its operational arm was the OSO, a remnant of the Strategic Services Unit (SSU), which, in turn, was a leftover from the OSS. However, the secretaries of state, defense, or, for that matter, the NSC did not want the CIA to be engaged in covert action, and even though the OSO was designed for this purpose, the OPC was established to undertake clandestine operations. See Evan Thomas, *The Very Best Men: The Daring Early Years of the CIA* (New York: Simon & Schuster, 1995), 29.

21. Copeland, *Game Player*, 112–13.

22. Ibid.

23. Thomas, *Very Best*, 108.

24. Kermit Roosevelt, *Countercoup: The Struggle for the Control of Iran* (New York: McGraw-Hill, 1979), 3–4.

25. Thomas, *Very Best*, 108–9.

26. Copeland, *Game of Nations*, 198.

THIRTEEN · *The Road to Perdition: The Gehlen Organization*

1. Harry Rositzke, fomer head of CIA secret operations inside the Soviet Union, quoted in Christopher Simpson, *Blowback: The First Full Account of America's Recruitment of Nazis and Its Disastrous Effect on the Cold War, Our Domestic and Foreign Policy* (New York: Macmillan, 1988), 159.

2. Mao Zedong proclaimed the establishment of the People's Republic of China in May 1949.

3.   In 1950, the United States had 369 operational bombs, and the Soviet Union, five. See Niall Ferguson, *The War of the World: Twentieth-Century Conflict and the Descent of the West* (New York: Penguin, 2006), 597.

4.   John Lewis Gaddis, *The Cold War: A New History* (New York: Penguin, 2005), 29–30.

5.   In October 1944, Churchill and Stalin worked out the so-called Percentages Agreement that divided the Balkans into British and Soviet spheres of influence. President Franklin D. Roosevelt was not pleased with the notion of spheres of influence dividing parts of Europe. However, in December 1944, when the Greek communists attempted to take over the country and fought the British, only the Soviet press did not condemn Churchill's actions. Stalin kept his part of the bargain. Yet, after the death of Roosevelt in April 1945 and the defeat of Churchill at the polls in July of that year, Stalin's ability to keep a bargain was lost on the new political leadership in London and Washington. Indeed, a certain degree of opportunism and territorial security guided the Soviet dictator's policies after 1946, rather than a commitment to world communism. On the Percentages Agreement, see Gerolymatos, *Red Acropolis*, 125–28, 206–7; on Stalin's foreign policy, see Vladislav Zubok and Constantine Pleshakov, *Inside the Kremlin's Cold War: From Stalin to Khrushchev* (Cambridge: Harvard University Press, 1996), chapter 2.

6.   Reinhard Gehlen, *The Service: The Memoirs of General Reinhard Gehlen*, trans. David Irving (New York: World, 1972), 111.

7.   Richard Helms, *A Look over My Shoulder: A Life in the Central Intelligence Agency* (New York: Ballantine, 2003), 84.

8.   Gehlen, *Service*, 107–8; Joseph J. Trento, *The Secret History of the CIA* (New York: Prima, 2001), 22–23.

9.   According to Trento, *Secret History*, 29, Gehlen and his group remained on an army base near Washington, D.C., for ten months; according to Richard Helms, *Look*, 88–89, Gehlen and his associates stayed only a few weeks.

10.   R. Harris Smith, *OSS: The Secret History of America's First Central Intelligence Agency* (Guilford, CT: Lyons, 2005), 220.

11.   Gehlen, *Service*, 116; Trento, *Secret History*, 23.

12.   Simpson, *Blowback*, 52–56.

13.   Ibid., 60–65.

14.   Marchetti interview in Simpson, *Blowback*, 65.

15.   A formal agreement of cooperation took effect in June 1949. See Prados, *Safe*, 51.

16.   Helms, *Look*, 88.

17.   Details concerning Operation Paperclip can be found in the Records of the Office of the Secretary of Defense, RG 330, U.S. National Archives and Records Administration (NARA).

18.   "Political Islam" describes the role of a wide rage of moderate to radical religious

organizations and institutions that have emerged in the twentieth and twenty-first centuries, sometimes in opposition to colonialism, secular regimes, and outright dictatorships.

19. Yergin, *Prize*, 481

20. Thomas, *Very Best*, 29–30.

21. Tim Weiner, *Legacy of Ashes: The History of the CIA* (New York: Doubleday, 2007), 17, writes that Richard Helms, head of the OSO and later CIA director, determined that at least half the information on the Soviet Union and its Eastern European satellites was useless.

22. Thomas, *Very Best*, 36. The acronym stands for Tsentralnogo Obedineniia Politicheskikh Emigrantov iz SSSR (Central Association of Political Emigrants from the Soviet Union); it was based in Munich.

23. Ibid., 25, 36. They included Ukrainians, Czechs, Poles, Hungarians, and Russians; most had fought against the Red Army in German uniform and had sought refuge in the West.

24. Ibid., 36.

25. On the Nazi collaboration of the volunteers, see Burton Hersh, *The Old Boys: The American Elite and the Origins of the CIA* (New York: Scribner's, 1992), 274–77.

FOURTEEN • *A New Kind of War: Subversive Operations and the CIA*

1. Philby, *Silent War*, 154.

2. Charles Whiting, *Skorzeny: The Most Dangerous Man in Europe* (Conshohocken, PA: Combined, 1972), 96–97.

3. Glenn B. Infield, *Skorzeny: Hitler's Commando* (New York: Military Heritage Press, 1981), 78.

4. Heron [Stuyvesant Wainwright, Jr.] to Berding, SCI Headquarters, 12 AG, 20 December 1944, Box 89, Entry 139, RG 226, NARA.

5. SHAEF, Counter Intelligence War Room London, "The German Intelligence Service," April 1945, William J. Donovan Collection, Military History Institute, Carlisle, PA.

6. Infield, *Skorzeny*, 122.

7. Whiting, *Skorzeny*, 97; Infield, *Skorzeny*, 123.

8. Whiting, *Skorzeny*, 97, claims Skorzeny's hands were manacled behind his back, but Infield, *Skorzeny*, 126, insists that he could not have appeared before the media with his hands tied.

9. According to Infield, *Skorzeny*, 155–56, Gehlen organized Skorzeny's escape.

10. Hersh, *Old Boys*, 42.

11. Ibid., 62.

12. Ibid., 66.

13. Ibid., 151–52.

14. Trento, *Secret History*, 47.

15. Ibid., 47–48.

16. Ibid., 47.

17. Operation Paperclip was also sponsored by the Joint Intelligence Objective Agency, established as a subcommittee of the Joint Intelligence Committee of the Joint Chiefs of Staff in 1945. Approximately 1,500 German scientists, engineers, technicians, and their families were recruited. For complete details, see the Records of the Office of the Security of Defense, RG 330, NARA.

18. Trento, *Secret History*, 51–52.

19. 2 August 1948, JSPC 862/3, NARS, RG 319, NARA.

20. The information about WIN's existence comes from Joseph Sienko, a former member of the Polish resistance; see Thomas Powers, *The Man Who Kept the Secrets* (New York: Knopf, 1979), 41. Sienko brought the news to Lieutenant General Wladyslaw Anders, the commander of the Polish army-in-exile, and claimed that WIN had five hundred members, along with twenty thousand sympathizers and another 100,000 ready to fight the communists; see Harry Rositzke, *The CIA's Secret Operations: Espionage, Counterespionage, and Covert Action* (Boulder, CO: Westview, 1988), 168–71.

21. Edward J. Epstein, *Deception: The Invisible War Between the KGB and the CIA* (New York: Simon & Schuster, 1989), 34.

22. Hersh, *Old Boys*, 279.

23. Epstein, *Deception*, 34.

24. Ibid., 34–35.

25. Over a period of almost two years, the CIA supplied $1 million in gold sovereigns, as well as radios and other equipment. See Hersh, *Old Boys*, 279.

26. Epstein, *Deception*, 39.

27. Aldrich, *Hidden Hand*, 160–61.

28. Ibid., 161–62.

29. Ibid., 162.

30. Ibid., 163; Hersh, *Old Boys*, 270.

31. Philby, *Silent War*, 154.

32. The British choice to be head of the Albanian government-in-exile, Major Abas Kupi, had also resorted to collaboration with the Axis in order to protect himself against the communist partisans. See Aldrich, *Hidden Hand*, 162.

33. Prados, *Safe*, 61.

34. Ibid.

35. Aldrich, *Hidden Hand*, 164.

36. Ibid.; Philby, *Silent War*, 156.

37. Prados, *Safe*, 64.

38. Hersh, *Old Boys*, 269.

39. U.S. Congress, Congressional Record, 25 April 1950.

FIFTEEN • *Nasser's Nazis*

1. Copeland, *Game Player*, 165.

2. See Chapter 12.

3. Copeland, *Game of Nations*, 103.

4. Gehlen, *Service*, 260.

5. Simpson, *Blowback*, 249.

6. Copeland, *Game of Nations*, 104.

7. Ibid.

8. Timothy Naftali, "Reinhard Gehlen and the United States," in *U.S. Intelligence and the Nazis*, ed. Richard Breitman et al. (Cambridge: Cambridge University Press, 2005), 377.

9. Naftali's review of the CIA files pertaining to some of the Nazi advisors in Egypt leaves him with the view that there was no direct link between the advisors and the CIA. This view, however, is based on the fact that the CIA files do not explicitly acknowledge such a connection. It is quite possible, however, that the absence of this information demonstrates nothing more than the CIA's censorship of its own files. Naftali does not present any evidence from the files that constitutes a denial of CIA involvement, and he notes that requests for access to further CIA documents regarding Skorzeny have been denied. See Naftali, "Gehlen," 417n166.

10. See various documents regarding the attempted recruitment of Deumling in Box 13, Entry ZZ-18, RG 263, NARA.

11. Cairo Embassy to African Department, 6 February 1953, V6703174, FO 371/102869, TNA.

12. See CIA Name Files Issue 1:32-2000/06/07 and Issue 2:45-2002/A/11/2, RG263, NARA (Lauterbacher); Issue 1:32-2000/06/07, RG263, NARA (Leers); Issue 1:51-2000/07/04 and Issue 2:52-2002/A/11/3 RG263, NARA (Tiefenbacher). For more about Bünsch, see Copeland, *Game of Nations*, 154–56.

13. The most informative British archival records regarding Voss are FO 371/102869, FO 371/108489, and FO 371/118975, TNA; the relevant U.S. records are CIA Name Files Issue 1:53-2000/07/04, and Issue 2:53-2002A/11/3, RG263, NARA.

14. It is equally likely that he was invited to Egypt by King Farouk. According to Lewis A. Frank, "Nasser's Missile Program," *Orbis* 11, no. 3 (Fall 1967): 746–57, "In 1951 a

small team headed by the World War II German armaments expert, Dr Wilhelm Voss, was asked by King Farouk's government to develop a small-caliber rocket and an arms industry for modern warfare."

15. Copeland, *Game of Nations*, 87–88; Aide-memoire from Belgian counselor, JE1202/13, FO 371/102869, TNA; African Department to Cairo Embassy, 1 April 1954, JE1203/4, FO 371/108489, TNA.

16. Voss unilaterally obtained the services of some important German technical and scientific experts, who seem to have constituted his recruiting priority. See JIC Summary, Ministry of State to Prime Minister, 30 April 1953, PM/MS/53/93, PREM 11/391, TNA.

17. The British records on Deumling are flimsy; for instance, see P. A. Wilkinson, Bonn Embassy to T. W. Garvey, Cairo Embassy, 20 March 1956, JE1194/4, FO 371/118975, TNA, which notes that "the Americans here ... expressed particular interest in Daimling [sic]." By contrast, the relevant U.S. records are relatively extensive; see CIA Name Files Issue 1:10-2000/06/04, and Issue 2:13-2002/A/10/3, RG263, NARA.

18. A former subordinate states that Deumling may have been removed from office and transferred to the death squad because he entered into some kind of unauthorized negotiations with Polish leaders. The same source also describes Deumling as "only a lukewarm Nazi." See CIA Name Files Issue 1:10-2000/06/04, RG263, NARA.

19. Michael Wildt, *Generation des Unbedingten: Das Führungskorps des Reichssicherheitshauptamtes* (Hamburg: Hamburger Edition, 2003), 934.

20. P. A. Wilkinson, Bonn Embassy to T. W. Garvey, Cairo Embassy, 6 April 1956, JE1194/6, FO 371/118975, TNA.

21. According to an unidentified source dated July 7, 1954, Deumling "was recruited by Wilhelm Voss in November or December of 1953." See CIA Name Files Issue 1:10-2000/06/04, RG263, NARA.

22. Memo, ca. 1954, Box 13, Entry ZZ-18, RG 263, NARA.

23. Report on "Activities of German Experts in Egypt," 21 October 1954, Box 13, Entry ZZ-18, RG 263, NARA.

24. Copeland, *Game of Nations*, 81.

25. Munich to Director, 29 May 1958, Box 13, Entry ZZ-18, RG 263, NARA.

26. Frankfurt to Director, 27 May 1958, Box 13, Entry ZZ-18, RG 263, NARA.

27. Memorandum, June 1958, Box 13, Entry ZZ-18, RG 263, NARA.

28. Report on "The German Advisory Group in Egypt," ca. 1954, Box 13, Entry ZZ-18, RG 263, NARA.

29. Wildt, *Generation*, 738–39, 828–30, 934–35.

30. "Egyptian Soldiers Learn the German Way," *Daily Telegraph*, 17 July 1953, JE1202/16, FO 371/102869, TNA.

31. Minutes, August 1953, JE1202/15, FO 371/102869, TNA.
32. Hankey to Salisbury, 20 July 1953, JE1202/15, FO 371/102869, TNA.
33. Ibid.
34. Ibid.
35. JE1202/15, FO 371/102869, TNA.
36. "Egyptian Para-Military Forces," HQBTE Report, August 1953, JE1202/24, FO 371/102869, TNA.
37. HQBTE Report, May 1953, JE1202/15, FO 371/102869, TNA.
38. Hankey to Salisbury, 20 July 1953, JE1202/15, FO 371/102869, TNA.
39. Ibid.
40. "Egyptian Para-Military Forces," HQBTE Report, August 1953, JE1202/24, FO 371/102869, TNA.
41. HQBTE Report, May 1953, JE1202/15, FO 371/102869, TNA. "9 BAD" was 9th Base Ammunition Depot, Royal Army Ordnance Corps (RAOC), which was permanently situated near the village of Abu Sultan.
42. "Egyptian Para-Military Forces," HQBTE Report, 24 August 1953, JE1202/24, FO 371/102869, TNA.
43. Ibid.
44. Hankey to Salisbury, 20 July 1953, JE1202/15, FO 371/102869, TNA.
45. Ibid.
46. Ibid.
47. Cairo Chancery to African Department, 6 February 1953, JE1202/2, FO 371/102869, TNA.
48. Draft response to parliamentary question, 17 June 1953, JE1202/12, FO 371/102869, TNA.
49. Ibid.
50. Minutes, August 1953, JE1202/15, FO 371/102869, TNA.
51. Ibid.
52. According to Ambassador Caffery's dispatch, Voss himself brought up the fact that there were rumors circulating to the effect that he was a communist. Voss remarked that this was obviously impossible since the Russians were responsible for the loss of his wife and sons during the war. He mentioned the terrible conditions prevailing in east Germany as compared to the favorable situation in western Germany; in this respect Voss seemed to be under no illusions about the Russian regime in the Eastern Zone. But perhaps sensing McCarthyist American suspicions, Voss may simply have been issuing preemptive denials. See Memorandum of Conversation with Dr. Wilhelm Voss, 24 June 1953, 2905, Attachment to Embassy Despatch 2276, 28 April 1953, CIA Name File, Issue 2: 53-2002A/11/3, RG263, NARA.

53. See Heinz Vielain, *Waffenschmuggel im Staatsauftrag: Was lange in Bonn geheim bleiben musste* (Herford: Busse Seewald, 1986), passim; Martin A. Lee, *The Beast Reawakens* (New York: Routledge, 2000), 184.

54. Christopher Andrew and Vasili Mitrokhin, *The World Was Going Our Way: The KGB and the Battle for the Third World* (New York: Basic, 2005), pp. 226–27.

SIXTEEN • *A Legacy of Coups: Anglo-American Intervention in Syria*

1. A commonly repeated anecdote about the dawn of March 29, 1949, when Colonel Zaim seized control of Syria. Sami Moubayed, "Keeping an Eye on Syria: March 29, 1949," *Mideastviews: Middle East Analysis by Sami Moubayed*, 29 May 2009, http://www.mideastviews.com/articleview.php?art=387.

2. "Army Coup in Syria: Government Overthrown," *Sunday Morning Herald*, 31 March 1949; "Syria Army Takes Over Government: Leaders Ousted in Bloodless Coup d'Etat," *Evening Independent*, 30 March 1949.

3. Bonnie F. Saunders, *The United States and Arab Nationalism* (Wesport, CT: Praeger, 1996), 4; Patrick Seale, *The Struggle for Syria* (London: I. B. Tauris, 1985), 15.

4. Dreyfuss, *Devil's Game*, 47; Saunders, *Nationalism*, 2.

5. Hanna Batatu, "Syria's Muslim Brethren," *MERIP Reports*, no. 110 (November–December 1982): 12–20, 34, 36; Dreyfuss, *Devil's Game*, 47–48, 199.

6. FO 370/2719, TNA.

7. FO 371/82792, TNA.

8. Ibid.

9. Indices to Series 16, 36433C, Box 351, Entry 14, RG 226, NARA.

10. Folder 8, Box 125, Entry 99, RG 226, NARA.

11. KV 2/1970, TNA.

12. The British Foreign Office was in contact with Jamal al-Hussein in 1957. At that time, the Mufti was providing them with reports on the internal situation in Syria. See FO 371/128226, TNA.

13. VR1092/120-121, VR1092/123-124, VR1092/129-130, FO 371/115899, TNA.

14. VR1092/144, VR1092/149, FO 371/115900, TNA.

15. FO 371/82800, TNA.

16. E1284, FO 371/45542, TNA.

17. Saunders, *Nationalism*.

18. Ibid., 5–7.

19. Folder 8, Box 125, Entry 99, RG 226, NARA.

20. Folders 09271-6, 09290, 09302, Box 195, Entry 210, RG 226, NARA.

21. The British Foreign Office, however, saw the Syrian Kurds as a far smaller problem than the Iraqi and Iranian Kurds.

22. Saunders, *Nationalism*, 7.

23. Douglas Little, "Cold War and Covert Action: The United States and Syria, 1945–1958," *Middle East Journal* 44, no. 1 (Winter 1990): 52.

24. FO 371/128226, TNA.

25. Little, "Cold War," 54.

26. FO 371/82792, TNA.

27. The army ultimately failed in its assault on Israel, although Syria did gain some territory beyond its original borders, which was to become an ongoing source of tension between Syria and Israel. This newly acquired territory was converted into a demilitarized zone by the United Nations, but was gradually acquired by Israel over the coming years.

28. Seale, *Struggle*, 41–43.

29. Saunders, *Nationalism*, 10–11.

30. Meade to G-2, 18 March 1949, 350 Syria, Damascus Post Files, Box 49, RG 84, NARA, quoted in Little, "Cold War," 56.

31. Little, "Cold War"; Saunders, *Nationalism*, 11–12; 27.

32. Miles Copeland, *Game of Nations*; Stephen Meade to G-2 (Intelligence), 3 December 1948, 350 Syria, Damascus Post Files, Box 49, RG 84, NARA.

33. Saunders, *Nationalism*, 11.

34. However, there is no known documented evidence that the Iraqis were involved. See Seale, *Struggle*, 73–74.

35. Weiner, *Legacy*, 159.

36. Little, "Cold War"; Saunders, *Nationalism*, 11–12; 27.

37. FO 371/128222, TNA.

38. Weiner, *Legacy*, 159.

39. Also referred to as the Parti Populaire Syrien (PPS) or Parti Sociale Nationaliste Syrien (PSNS).

40. Weiner, *Legacy*, 159–60; Saunders, *Nationalism*, 48–51.

41. Dreyfuss, *Devil's Game*, 126–27.

42. FO 371/128222, TNA.

43. Seale, *Struggle*, 310–12.

44. FO 371/128224, TNA.

45. FO 371/128220, TNA.

46. Saunders, *Nationalism*, 41.

47. FO 371/128220, TNA.

48. Matthew Jones, "The 'Preferred Plan': The Anglo-American Working Group Report on Covert Action in Syria, 1957," *Intelligence and National Security* 19, no. 3

(Autumn 2004): 401–15; Andrew Rathmell, *Secret War in the Middle East: The Covert Struggle for Syria, 1949–1961* (London: I. B. Tauris, 1995); and Weiner, *Legacy*, 159–60.

49. FO 371/128221, TNA.

50. FO 371/128221, FO 371/128231, TNA.

51. Atrash, minister of state, investigated these activities and allegedly ignored General Sir John Glubb's smuggling of arms from Jordan to Druze tribes.

52. FO 371/128220, FO 371/128221, TNA.

53. FO 371/128220, TNA.

54. FO 371/128222, TNA.

55. FO 371/128220, TNA.

56. "U.S. Accused of Syrian Coup Attempt," *The Age*, 14 August 1957.

57. Ghazaleh sought revenge for the bombardments of Jabal Druze in 1954. While in power, Shishakli had cracked down on all opposition, including on the Druze minority on Jabal Druze mountain, who had been planning a coup in coordination with Jordan. Shishakli had ordered the shelling of the Druze areas.

58. Weiner, *Legacy*, 161–63.

59. Ibid., 162.

60. FO 371/128226, TNA.

61. FO 371/128233, TNA.

62. Andrew and Mitrokhin, *World*, 196.

63. PREM 11/2324, TNA, quoted in Richard J. Aldrich, *Espionage, Security and Intelligence in Britain, 1945–1970* (Manchester: Manchester University Press, 1998), 212–13. The "working groups" referred to were responsible for coups. See Dorril, *MI6*, 656–58.

64. FO 371/128268, TNA.

65. Ibid.

66. Batatu, "Brethren," 18.

67. Ibid.

68. The Six Day War, between the Israeli army and Syria, Egypt, and Jordan, ended with the Israelis gaining control of the Sinai Peninsula, the Gaza Strip, the West Bank, East Jerusalem, and the Golan Heights.

69. Daniel Pipes has surveyed some of the scholarship on this issue. The core debate focuses on whether the Alawis made a sectarian and strategic effort to infiltrate the ranks of the Ba'ath Party. See Daniel Pipes, "The Alawi Capture of Power in Syria," *Middle Eastern Studies* 25, no. 4 (October 1989): 429–50.

70. Andrew and Mitrokhin, *World*, 197–99.

71. Batatu, "Brethren," 19.

72. Dreyfuss, *Devil's Game*, 199–205.

73. Batatu, "Brethren," 12–20, 34–36.

74. Dreyfuss, *Devil's Game*, 199–205.

75. David Long, interview with Robert Dreyfuss, April 2004, in Dreyfuss, *Devil's Game*, 202.

76. Talcott Seelye, interview with Robert Dreyfuss, June 2004, in Dreyfuss, *Devil's Game*, 203.

77. Andrew and Mitrokhin, *World*, 198–200.

78. Ibid., 200.

79. James Kelly and William Stewart, "Syria: The Proud Lion and His Den," *Time*, September 5, 1983. The CIA is alleged to have backed Muslim Brotherhood activity during this time. See Dreyfuss, *Devil's Game*, 202–5.

80. Andrew and Mitrokhin, *World*, 199.

81. Baer, *Sleeping*, 93.

82. FO 371/170603, TNA.

83. Baer, *Sleeping*, 95–97.

SEVENTEEN • *America's Eyes in the Middle East: The CIA and Israeli Intelligence*

1. William Hood, "Angleton's World," in *Myths Surrounding James Angleton: Lessons for American Counterintelligence*, ed. William Hood et al. (Washington, D.C.: Consortium for the Study of Intelligence, 1994), 10.

2. Weiner, *Legacy*, 123.

3. Eveland, *Ropes*, 95; William Colby and Peter Forbath, *Honorable Men: My Life in the CIA* (New York: Simon & Schuster, 1978), 365, 367.

4. Holzman, *Angleton*, 154.

5. Andrew Cockburn and Leslie Cockburn, *Dangerous Liaison: The Inside Story of the U.S.-Israeli Covert Relationship* (Toronto: Stoddart, 1991), 15.

6. Appendix 21 of Eshed, *Shiloah*.

7. Dan Raviv and Yossi Melman, *Every Spy a Prince* (Boston: Houghton Mifflin, 1990), 91.

8. Gordon Thomas, *Gideon's Spies: The Secret History of the Mossad* (New York: St. Martin's Press, 2007), 37. William Colby, the CIA director who eventually forced Angleton to retire, wrote that Angleton had been one of the CIA's earliest contacts with Israeli intelligence, but this was a highly personal and special relationship. See Colby and Forbath, *Honorable Men*, 365.

9. Cockburn and Cockburn *Dangerous*, 42–43.

10. Ibid., 43.

11. Black and Morris, *Secret Wars*, 169.

12. Yossi Melman and Dan Raviv, *Friends in Deed: Inside the U.S.-Israeli Alliance* (New York: Hyperion, 1994), 61.

13. Cockburn and Cockburn, *Dangerous*, 41; Melman and Raviv, *Friends*, 63.

14. Raviv and Melman, *Spy*, 78.

15. Ibid.

16. Riftin served on the Knesset Foreign Affairs and Security Committee. See Andrew and Mitrokhin, *World*, 225.

17. Ibid., 229.

18. Tel Aviv Embassy to Foreign Office, 17 April 1961, FO 371/1546, TNA.

19. John Ranelagh, *The Agency: The Rise and Decline of the CIA* (New York: Simon & Schuster, 1978), 286; Hersh, *Old Boys*, 359.

20. The Israelis acquired a copy from one of their agents in Poland. See Hersh, *Old Boys*, 381.

21. Melman and Raviv, *Friends*, 67.

22. Ibid., 68.

23. Cockburn and Cockburn, *Dangerous*, 63.

24. Heikal, *Lion's Tail*, 86.

25. Holzman, *Angleton*, 163–64.

26. Sachar, *History of Israel*, 312, 460–61; Christison, *Perceptions of Palestine*, 67, 96–99. Eisenhower was not so much pro-Arab and later pro-Israel as anticommunist. The fear of Soviet influence in the region colored his administration's policy toward the Middle East. See Christison, *Perceptions*, 98–99.

27. Holzman, *Angleton*, 162.

28. Cockburn and Cockburn, *Dangerous*, 65.

29. Ibid., 67.

30. Rhodri Jeffrey-Jones, *The CIA and American Diplomacy* (New Haven Yale University Press, 1989), 108–9.

31. Melman and Raviv, *Friends*, 64.

32. Ibid., 62–63.

33. Ibid., *Friends*, 65.

34. Ibid., 66.

35. Eshed, *Shiloah*, 167.

36. Melman and Raviv, *Friends*, 62, 169.

37. Ibid., 62.

38. Black and Morris, *Secret Wars*, 169.

39. Ibid., 162.

40. Ibid., 207–9.

41. Melman and Raviv, *Friends*, 89.

42. Ibid., 154.

43. Raviv and Melman, *Spy*, 93–94.

44. Ibid., 91–92.

45. Interview with Hadden, in Melman and Raviv, *Friends*, 127–29.

46. Ibid.

47. Ibid.

48. Ibid., 126.

49. Ibid., 123–25.

50. Cockburn and Cockburn, *Dangerous*, 100–101.

51. Ibid., 212–15.

52. Ibid., 100.

53. Ibid., 100–102.

54. Samuel Segev, *The Iranian Triangle* (New York: Free Press, 1988), 31. The entire Iranian security apparatus had significant foreign organizers. In their trial in 1979 following the revolution, two senior SAVAK officers, Generals Manucher Vajdi and Reza Parvaresh, revealed that the United States, Britain, Israel, and Germany had helped establish SAVAK and the Iranian army. See Segev, *Triangle*, 43.

55. Cockburn and Cockburn, *Dangerous*, 103–4.

56. Segev, *Triangle*, 32–35.

57. Ibid., 39.

58. Ibid., 104–6.

59. Raviv and Melman, *Spy*, 82.

60. Cockburn and Cockburn, *Dangerous*, 103.

61. Shay Shaul, *The Axis of Evil: Iran, Hizballah and the Palestinian Terror* (New Brunswick, NJ: Transaction, 2005).

62. Interview with Eliezer Tsafrir on November 26, 2009, Ramat Ha Sharon, Israel. Tsafrir is a former Shabak and Mossad senior officer, and the prime minister's advisor on Arab affairs. He served as head of Mossad stations in Iraqi Kurdistan, Iran, and Lebanon. He was head of the Mossad station in Iran between 1987 and 1979. He has published two books on his experiences: *Satan gadol, satan katan* [Big Satan, Small Satan: Revolution and Escape in Iran] (Tel Aviv: Maariv 2002) and *Plonter* [Labyrinth in Lebanon] (Tel Aviv: Yediot, 2006).

EIGHTEEN · *The Iranian Jihad*

1. Roosevelt, *Countercoup*, 199.

2. Cited in Michael B. Oren, *Power, Faith, and Fantasy: America in the Middle East, 1776 to the Present* (New York: Norton, 2007), 510–11.

3. Hersh, *Old Boys*, 395.

4. The U.S. foreign policy establishment considered plans to replace Britain as the preeminent power in the Middle East. Paul Nitze, then head of the U.S. Policy Planning Staff, proposed the creation of a Middle East Defense Organization that would protect the Suez Canal and provide military security to the petroleum-producing regions and the Northern Tier countries of Iran, Pakistan, and Turkey.

5. Nasser refused to sign on to MEDO until the United States could convince the Israelis to stop raiding Egyptian territory (Oren, *Power*, 513–14).

6. Ibid., 514

7. Dreyfuss, *Devil's Game*, 66.

8. Foreign Service Dispatch, *Al Misri*, 18 August 1953.

9. Dreyfuss, *Devil's Game*, 76.

10. Ibid., 76–77.

11. Sylvain Besson, "When the Swiss Protected Radical Islam in the Name of Reasons of State," *Le Temps*, 26 October 2004, quoted in Dreyfuss, *Devil's Game*, 79.

12. A great deal has been written about the coup in Iran, including publication of the actual operation: Donald Wilber, *Overthrow of Premier Mossadeq of Iran, November 1952–August 1953* (Nottingham: Spokesman, 2006). See also Roosevelt, *Countercoup*, passim. For the British perspective, see C. M. Woodhouse, *Something Ventured: The Autobiography of C. M. Woodhouse* (London: Granada, 1982), passim. Woodhouse was Roosevelt's MI6 counterpart.

13. Mark J. Gasiorowski, "The 1953 Coup d' Etat Against Mosaddeq" in *Mohammad Mosaddeq and the 1953 Coup in Iran*, ed. Mark J. Gasiorowski and Malcolm Byrne (Syracuse: Syracuse University Press, 2004), 254, argues that it is not certain whether Kashani received the money or, if he did receive it, whether he proceeded to organize demonstrations. Ayatollah Behbahani, however, played a key role in organizing the demonstrations against Mossadeq on August 19, 1953.

14. Stephen Kinzer, *All the Shah's Men: An American Coup and the Roots of Middle East Terror* (Hoboken, NJ: John Wiley, 2003), 75–76.

15. Robert Fisk, *Pity the Nation: The Abduction of Lebanon* (New York: Thunder Mouth, 2002), 55

16. Ibid.

17. Tom Russell, "A Lebanon Primer," *MERIP Reports*, no. 133 (June 1985), 17–19.

18. Fisk, *Pity*, 55–57.

19. Russell, "Primer," 17.

20. Ibid.

21. FO 371/142062, TNA.

22. Dilip Hiro, *The Iranian Labyrinth: Journeys Through Theocratic Iran and Its Furies*

(New York: Nation, 2005), 346; Kenneth M. Pollack, *The Persian Puzzle: The Conflict Between Iran and America* (New York: Random House, 2004) 198–205.

23. Pollack, *Puzzle*, 199–200.

24. Ibid., 201.

25. U.S. Security Council, "U.S./Iranian Contacts and the American Hostages," NSC Chronology of Events, 17 November 1986.

NINETEEN • *Espionage, Religion, and War in Northwest Frontier*

1. Bruce Riedel, "Pakistan and Terror: The Eye of the Storm," *The ANNALS of the American Academy of Political and Social Science* 618, no. 1 (2008): 31.

2. "Mumbai Terror Attacks: Nightmare in the Lap of Luxury," *The Observer*, 30 November 2008.

3. Thomas G. Fergusson, "Army Annual Inspection Report, 1852" in *British Military Intelligence, 1870–1914: The Development of a Modern Intelligence Organization* (Frederick, MD: University Publications of America, 1984), 135–36; WO 4/171, WO 6/138, WO 40/10, TNA.

4. Shuja Nawaz, *Crossed Swords: Pakistan, Its Army, and the Wars Within* (Oxford: Oxford University Press, 2008), 11, quoting Frederick Sleigh Roberts, *Forty-one Years in India: From Subaltern to Commander-in-Chief*, vol. 2 (London: Bentley, 1897), 442.

5. Nawaz, *Swords*, 11–13.

6. WO 33/36, TNA.

7. At present there are more Sikhs in the Indian army than Muslims, although the Sikhs represent 4 percent of the population and Muslims 12 percent. See Stephen P. Rosen, *Societies and Military Power: India and Its Armies* (Ithaca: Cornell University Press, 1996), 217.

8. Steve Coll, *Ghost Wars: The Secret History of the CIA, Afghanistan and Bin Laden, from the Soviet Invasion to September 10, 2001* (New York: Penguin, 2004), 64, 174–75.

9. Rasul Bakhsh Rais, *Recovering the Frontier State: War, Ethnicity, and State in Afghanistan* (New York: Lexington, 2008), 71.

10. The traditional period of Anglo-Russian rivalry in Central Asia dates from the Russo-Persian Treaty of 1813 to the Anglo-Russian Convention of 1907. After the Bolshevik Revolution of 1917, the competition between the two powers declined. During the Soviet occupation of Afghanistan and the U.S. support of the mujahidin, a new Great Game emerged that has continued between the Russian Federation and the United States.

11. Conolly had made reference in a letter to a friend of taking part in "a great game, a noble game" in Central Asia. After his death, the letters passed to the historian Sir John Kaye, who introduced the term "Great Game." See Karl E. Mayer and Shareen B. Brysac, *Tournament of Shadows: The Great Game and the Race for Empire in Central Asia* (Washington, D.C.: Counterpoint, 1999), xxiii; and Peter Hopkirk, *The Great Game: The Struggle for Empire in Central Asia* (New York: Kodansha International, 1992).

12. Philip Knightley, *The Master Spy: The Story of Kim Philby* (New York: Knopf, 1989), 24.

13. In 1949, Philby was British liaison officer in Washington with the CIA and the FBI, part of a career path that was preparing him to become head of the British Secret Service (Knightley, *Master Spy*, 1). For more about Kim Philby's father, Harry St. John Philby, see Chapter 7.

14. Robert Johnson, *Spying for Empire: The Great Game in Central and South Asia, 1757–1947* (London: Greenhill, 2006), 84.

15. Johnson, *Spying*, 85.

16. Conolly believed he would check the Russian annexation of Central Asia by uniting all the Khanates (local rulers), and when that mission failed, he went on to rescue Stoddart (Johnson, *Spying*, 86).

17. Mayer and Brysac, *Tournament*, 122–32. Hopkirk, *Great Game*, 1, begins his study of the Great Game with the execution of the two British officers and remarks that today tourists arrive at a bus stop located in a square that was once the place of execution. The remains of the two men lie in unmarked graves under the square. Hopkirk also adds that Captain Arthur Conolly coined the phrase the "Great Game."

18. The Intelligence Bureau was established in 1885. See Hopkirk, *Great Game*, 422–23.

19. Fergusson, "Report," 63. India was officially assigned to Section D during this time.

20. Ibid., 85.

21. Husain Haqqani, *Pakistan: Between Mosque and Military* (Washington, D.C.: Carnegie Endowment for International Peace, 2005), 20; Johnson, *Spying*, 127.

22. Piers Brendon, *The Decline and Fall of the British Empire, 1781–1997* (London: Jonathan Cape, 2007), 382.

23. John Fisher, *Gentleman Spies: Intelligence Agents in the British Empire and Beyond* (Stroud: Sutton, 2002), 107–8.

24. Ibid., 108–10.

25. Ibid., 112.

26. Ibid.

27. Later Bray recommended the centralization of intelligence collection, counterintelligence, and the foundation of a religious school by Sharif Hussein in Mecca. See Ibid., 112–13.

28. In the immediate postwar period and through most of the 1920s, British intelligence officials could not agree on the extent or significance of pan-Islam, either in the Middle East or in South Asia. See Martine Thomas, *Empires of Intelligence: Security Services and Colonial Disorder After 1914* (Berkeley: University of California Press, 2008), 75.

29. Fisher, *Spies*, 125.

30. Richard J. Aldrich, "Britain's Secret Intelligence Service in Asia During the Second World War," *Modern Asian Studies* 32, no. 1 (February 1998): 184.

31. Both SIS and SOE had been based elsewhere in Asia prior to the fall of Singapore in 1942, at which time they were moved to India. The SIS had maintained a base in Asia before the war, but it had been neglected. The SOE, which was not established until during the war, established a strong presence in the region and in some cases overtook the SIS in efficiency and achievement.

32. The SOE in South Asia was designated as the "Oriental Mission" and later became the "India Mission," or Force 136.

33. Japanese intelligence officers established direct links with Pritam Singh's Indian Independence League, with Captain Mohan Singh, and later with the well-known nationalist Subha Chandra Bose.

34. Christopher Bayly and Tim Harper, *Forgotten Wars: The End of Britain's Asian Empire* (London: Penguin, 2007), 19.

35. Louis Allen, "Japanese Intelligence Systems," *Journal of Contemporary History* 22, no. 4 (October 1987): 547–62. Muslim officers who joined the INA did so less out of any nationalist or religious conviction than to protect their men from the horrors of the Japanese prisoner of war camps. Others joined in order to restrict Japanese involvement or to sabotage the INA from within. See also Christopher Bayly and Tim Harper, *Forgotten Armies: The Fall of British Asia, 1941–1945* (New York: Allen Lane, 2004), 256.

36. Richard J. Aldrich, *Intelligence and the War Against Japan* (Cambridge: Cambridge University Press, 2000), 159.

37. Ibid., 163.

38. Akbar Ahmed, *Jinnah, Pakistan and Islamic Identity: The Search for Saladin* (London: Routledge, 1997), 82.

39. Dharmendra Gaur, *Behind the Enemy Lines* (New Delhi: Sterling, 1975).

40. Bayly and Harper, *Armies*, 247.

41. Aldrich, *Intelligence*, 134.

42. Ibid., 307.

43. Ibid.

44. DEFE 11/31, TNA.

45. CAB 159/6, Part 2, TNA.

46. CAB 158/3, TNA.

47. Ibid.

48. DEFE 11/31, TNA.

49. Ibid.

50. Ibid.

51. Britain's security and counterintelligence service.

52. DEFE 11/31, TNA.

TWENTY • *Pakistan's Inter-Services Intelligence and Organized Terror in South Asia*

1. Graham Usher, "Taliban v. Taliban," *London Review of Books* 31, no. 7 (9 April 2009).

2. According to PakistaniDefence.com, a news media Web site committed to independent research on the social, economic, environmental, political, and military components of global security, http://www.pakistanidefence.com/Info/Intelligence .html (accessed 7 May 2009).

3. A Joint Counter-Intelligence Bureau was also formed in late 1948/early 1949, tasked with ensuring service security; it was headed by the British officer. See Political Intelligence, India: Disclosure of Information, 3 parts, WS 17079/3-5, IOR/L/WS/1/1074, BL.

4. During Hamid's visit to London in December 1949, he stated that the ISI had been in existence for ten months, which would mean its establishment in February 1949 (see CAB 159/6, Part 2, TNA); however, Brigadier J. F. Walter, DSO, visited Hamid at ISI headquarters in Karachi in October 1948, reporting that the ISI was then in the early stages of development (see WO 208/4961; CAB 159/6 Part 2; and WO 208/4961, TNA). Hamid's full name is found in the July 1948 Strategic Intelligence Digest report on Pakistan, which lists Hamid as the director of the Pakistan National Guard (see WO 208/4960 and WO 208/4961, TNA).

5. CAB 159/6, Part 2, TNA.

6. WO 208/4960, TNA.

7. Peter Hohnen, "Cawthorn, Sir Walter Joseph (1896–1970)," *Australian Dictionary of Biography*, vol. 13 (Melbourne: Melbourne University Press, 1993), 392–93.

8. See weekly reports of the India Office Political and Secret Department, IOR, BL.

9. When a Joint Counter-Intelligence Bureau was planned, to be placed within the ISI, it was felt that a British officer should be put in charge of creating and controlling it. The head of this unit would "have full access to the Civil Intelligence Bureau and its activities." It is not clear from the documents summarized here whether or not a British officer was put in charge of this position (DEFE 11/31,

TNA). Until the division of Pakistan from India, counterintelligence was organized under the Intelligence Bureau in New Delhi and under Provincial CIDs; it was assumed by the Joint Intelligence Committee that this system was still in place in both India and Pakistan in the spring of 1948. At that time, the JIC had no security liaison officer in place in Karachi as they did in New Delhi. See CAB 158/3, TNA.

10. WO 208/4961, TNA.

11. CAB 159/5, Part 1, TNA.

12. Jessica Stern, "Pakistan's Jihad Culture," *Foreign Affairs* 79, no. 6 (November–December 2000): 117–18.

13. After the creation of Pakistan in 1947, the Muslim states of the British Raj had the choice of joining Pakistan or India. Although the majority of the Kashmir and Jammu population followed the Islamic faith, the maharaja, the historic ruler of the state, preferred India. His decision, as well as the borders established for the two new states, has never been accepted by Pakistan.

14. DO 142/345, TNA.

15. Ibid.

16. Tariq Ali, *The Duel: Pakistan on the Flight Path of American Power* (New York: Scribner, 2008), 50. Most records currently accessible from this period derive from the Dominion Office, and as always it is entirely possible that the "right arm" of the British government was blissfully unaware of what the "left arm" of intelligence was up to in Pakistan.

17. Outside the—at least nominally—religious realm, the president held the "right" attitude toward dangerous figures like Nasser; he personally disliked him and approached him with caution. See DO 35/8962, TNA.

18. Ibid.

19. Pooja Joshi, *Jamaat-i-Islami: The Catalyst of Islamization in Pakistan* (New Delhi: Kalinga, 2003), 15–21; Ali, *Duel*, 23.

20. The Jamaat-Ulema-e-Islam (JUI) has also become a powerful player in Pakistan and Afghanistan. They too have a Wahhabi background and basis, and fall within the Deobandi tradition, which was seen as the "home of Sunni orthodoxy in prepartition India." See Ali, *Duel*, 23.

21. DO 35/5154, TNA.

22. DO 196/418, TNA.

23. See Rizwan Hussain, *Pakistan and the Emergence of Islamic Militancy in Afghanistan* (Farnham: Ashgate, 2005), 69, who also cites Miles Copeland, *Game of Nations*, 58.

24. Hussain, *Emergence*, 59.

25. Hamza Alavi describes U.S. involvement in an allegedly bogus food crisis in Pakistan in the early 1950s, which led to a change in power that favored the U.S. government. See Hamza Alavi, "Pakistan-US Military Alliance," *Economic and Political Weekly* 33, no. 25 (20–26 June 1998): 1554.

26. Andrei Gromyko, *Memories* (London: Hutchinson, 1989), 246–47. Gromyko's frustration with Pakistan is underlined by the revelations of Soviet intelligence operations in the Third World included in the documents smuggled to the West by the former KGB archivist Vasili Mitrokhin. Except for some minor intelligence activities and subversive operations, Soviet intelligence made few inroads in Pakistan, See Andrew and Mitrokhin, *World*, 341–68.

27. The Central Treaty Organization, originally known as the Middle East Treaty Organization or the Baghdad Pact, was adopted by Iran, Iraq, Pakistan, Turkey, and Britain in 1955. The pact was a cooperative and noninterventionist agreement, designed to protect the Middle East's Northern Tier from a Soviet invasion.

28. Andrew and Mitrokhin, *World*, 341.

29. George C. Herring, *From Colony to Superpower: US Foreign Relations Since 1776* (Oxford: Oxford University Press, 2008), 680–81.

30. Stephen P. Cohen, *The Idea of Pakistan* (Washington, D.C.: Brookings Institution, 2004), 102.

31. Ibid., 103.

32. Ali, *Duel*, 107. Under Bhutto, the ISI also established an "election cell," which menaced voters and rigged results. Bhutto's religious posturing deeply altered Pakistan's political integrity.

33. Haqqani, *Pakistan*, 165–67.

34. Ali, *Duel*, 119.

35. Haqqani, *Pakistan*, 265; Victoria Schofield, *Kashmir in Conflict: India, Pakistan and the Unfinished War* (London: I. B. Tauris, 2000), 113; Herring, *Colony*, 712–13. According to Arif Jamal, *Shadow War: The Untold Story of Jihad in Kashmir* (Brooklyn, NY: Melville House, 2009), 86–87, between 1965 and 1971 there were eighty underground cells established in the valley of Kashmir, some of which were working with the ISI.

36. The separatist movement was successful, and the country now known as Bangladesh was formed in 1971 from what had been East Pakistan.

37. Henry Kissinger, *Years of Renewal*, vol. 3 (New York: Simon & Schuster, 1999), 82.

38. Cohen, *Idea*, 100.

39. Ibid., 105.

40. Ibid., 100.

41. Ali, *Duel*, 113–19.

42. Ibid., 23, 123.

43. Cohen, *Idea*, 195; Hussain, *Emergence*, 249.

44. Ali, *Duel*, 119; Lawrence Ziring, *Pakistan at the Crosscurrent of History* (Oxford: Oneworld, 2003), 180.

45. Stephen Tanner, *Afghanistan: A Military History from Alexander the Great to the Fall of the Taliban* (Cambridge: Da Capo, 2002), 250.

46. Ziring, *Crosscurrent*, 177.

47. Tanner, *Afghanistan*, 254. After Zia's death in 1988, the CIA managed to gain the right to distribute arms into the field. However, the ISI and Saudi Arabia continued to manipulate the scene by providing their own aid selectively. See Tanner, *Afghanistan*, 274.

48. Even prominent U.S. politicians have been willing to concede the damage done by U.S. policies during the Afghan War. In a 2008 panel discussion, Richard Armitage, former deputy secretary of state, openly said that the United States knew what the impact of their actions during the war would be in Pakistan. "In other words they knew perfectly well that they had handed the country to religious groups and the ISI." See Ali, *Duel*, 251.

49. Ibid., 137, quoting from "Get America Out of the Way and We'll Be Okay," interview with Harinder Baweja, *Tehelka Magazine*, 2 February 2008.

50. Ali, *Duel*, 136–37, 142.

51. Hussain, *Emergence*, 249.

52. George Tenet, *At the Center of the Storm: My Years at the CIA* (New York: HarperCollins, 2007), 142.

53. Ahmed Rashid, *Descent into Chaos* (New York: Viking, 2008), 24.

54. Tenet, *Center*, 141.

55. Cohen, *Idea*, 112.

56. Ali, *Duel*, 149–50.

57. Rais, *Recovering*, 71.

58. Graham E. Fuller, "Obama's Policies Making Situation Worse in Afghanistan and Pakistan," *Huffington Post*, 6 September 2009, http://www.huffingtonpost.com/graham-e<->fuller/global-viewpoint-obamas-p_b_201355.html.

59. Assembly of Islamic Clergy.

60. Most of the Taliban rank and file have passed through the Deobandi madrasas in the Northwest Frontier province and Balochistan. See "Pakistan: Madrasas, Extremism and the Military," *ICG Asia Report*, no. 36 (29 July 2002); "Pakistan: Karachi's Madrasas and Violent Extremism," *ICG Asia Report*, no. 130 (29 March 2007); and Rais, *Recovering*, 72.

61. Rais, *Recovering*, 71.

62. Another critical consideration was that Islamabad had to be seen to support Afghan Pashtuns for the benefit of the Pakistani Pashtuns, and also because the non-Pashtuns had found support from India, Iran, and Russia. See Rashid, *Descent*, 25.

63. Ibid., 26.

64. Ziring, *Crosscurrent*, 283.

65. Tanner, *Afghanistan*, 282.

66. Fuller, "*Policies*."

BIBLIOGRAPHY
UNPUBLISHED SOURCES

British Library (BL), London
INDIA OFFICE RECORDS
IOR/L/WS/1/1074; IOR/L/WS/1/1162.

The Haganah Archives, Tel Aviv
80/69/5.

The National Archives of the UK, Kew, Surrey (TNA)
RECORDS OF THE CABINET OFFICE
CAB 81/80; CAB 158/3; CAB 159/5; CAB 159/6.
RECORDS OF THE COLONIAL OFFICE
CO 732/88/32.
RECORDS OF THE DOMINIONS OFFICE
DO 35/5154; DO 35/8962; DO 142/345; DO 196/418.
FO 370/2719; FO 370/82792; FO 371/1546; FO 371/24558; FO 371/24568;
FO 371/32900; FO 371/45542; FO 371/82800; FO 371/102869;
FO 371/108489; FO 371/115899; FO 371/115900; FO 371/118975;
FO 371/128220; FO 371/128221; FO 371/128222; FO 371/128224;
FO 371/128226; FO 371/128233; FO 371/128268; FO 371/170603;
FO 371/183884.
RECORDS OF THE MINISTRY OF DEFENCE
DEFE 11/31.
RECORDS OF THE PRIME MINISTER'S OFFICE
PREM 11/391.
RECORDS OF THE SPECIAL OPERATIONS EXECUTIVE (SOE)
HS 3/201; HS 3/209; Hs 7/269.

RECORDS OF THE SECURITY SERVICE (MI5)

KV 2/1970; KV 5/30; KV 5/38; KV 5/39.

RECORDS OF THE WAR OFFICE

WO 4/171; WO 6/138; WO 33/36; WO 40/10; WO 208/4960; WO 208/4961.

US National Archives and Records Administration,
College Park, Maryland (NARA)

RECORDS OF THE CENTRAL INTELLIGENCE AGENCY (RG 263).

RECORDS OF THE FOREIGN SERVICE POSTS OF THE
DEPARTMENT OF STATE (RG 84).

RECORDS OF THE OFFICE OF THE ARMY STAFF GROUP (RG 319).

RECORDS OF THE OFFICE OF THE SECRETARY OF DEFENSE (RG 330).

RECORDS OF THE OFFICE OF STRATEGIC SERVICES (RG 226).

PUBLISHED SOURCES

Abdullahzadeh, Mahmoud. "The Political Significance of the Bazaar in Iran." In *Technology, Tradition and Survival: Aspects of Material Culture in the Middle East and Central Asia.* Edited by Richard Tapper and Keith McLachlan. London: Frank Cass, 2002.

Acheson, Dean. *Present at the Creation: My Years in the State Department.* New York: Norton, 1969.

Ahmed, Akbar S. *Jinnah, Pakistan and Islamic Identity: The Search for Saladin.* London: Routledge, 1997.

———. *Living Islam: From Samarkand to Stornoway.* London: Penguin, 1995.

Aid, Matthew M. "The Secret reclassification Program." Organization of American Historians Newsletter 34 (May 2006).

Alavi, Hamza. "Pakistan-US Military Alliance." *Economic and Political Weekly* 33, no. 25 (20–26 June 1998).

Albertini, Luigi. *The Origins of the War of 1914.* Translated and edited by Isabella M. Massey. 3 vols. London: Oxford University Press, 1952–1957.

Aldrich, Richard J. "Britain's Secret Intelligence Service in Asia During the Second World War." *Modern Asian Studies* 32, no. 1 (February 1998).

———. "Did Waldegrave Work? The Impact of Open Government upon British History." *Twentieth Century British History* 9, no. 1 (1998).

———. *Espionage, Security and Intelligence in Britain, 1945–1970.* Manchester: Manchester University Press, 1998.

———. *The Hidden Hand: Britain, America and Cold War Secret Intelligence.* New York: Overlook, 2002.

———. *Intelligence and the War Against Japan.* Cambridge: Cambridge University Press, 2000.

Ali, Tariq. *The Duel: Pakistan on the Flight Path of American Power.* New York: Scribner, 2008.

Allen, Charles. *God's Terrorists: The Wahhabi Cult and the Hidden Roots of Modern Jihad.* London: Little, Brown, 2006.

Allen, Louis. "Japanese Intelligence Systems." *Journal of Contemporary History* 22, no. 4 (October 1987): 547–62.

al-Qalanisi, Ibn. *The Damascus Chronicle of the Crusades.* Translated by H. A. R. Gibb. London: Luzac, 1967.

al-Rasheed, Madawi. *A History of Saudi Arabia.* Cambridge: Cambridge University Press, 2002.

Andrew, Christopher M. *Secret Service: The Making of the British Intelligence Community.* London: Heinemann, 1985.

Andrew, Christopher, and Vasili Mitrokhin. *The World Was Going Our Way: The KGB and the Battle for the Third World.* New York: Basic, 2005.

Antonius, George. *The Arab Awakening: The Story of the Arab National Movement.* Safety Harbor, FL: Simon, 2001.

"Army Coup in Syria: Government Overthrown." *Sunday Morning Herald,* 31 March 1949.

Baer, Robert. *Sleeping with the Devil: How Washington Sold Our Soul for Saudi Crude.* New York: Three Rivers, 2003.

Batatu, Hanna. "Syria's Muslim Brethren." *MERIP Reports,* no. 110 (November–December 1982).

Bayley, Christopher, and Tim Harper. *Forgotten Armies: The Fall of British Asia, 1941–1945.* New York: Allen Lane, 2004.

———. *Forgotten Wars: The End of Britain's Asian Empire.* London: Penguin, 2007.

Bell, Gertrude. *Review of the Civil Administration of Mesopotamia*. London: HMSO, 1920.

Ben-Ami, Yitshaq. *Years of Wrath, Days of Glory: Memoirs from the Irgun*. New York: Speller, 1982.

Bergen, Peter L. *Holy War, Inc.: Inside the Secret World of Osama bin Laden*. New York: Free Press, 2001.

Bidwell, R. L., ed. *The Arab Bulletin: Bulletin of the Arab Bureau in Cairo*. 4 vols. Gerrards Cross: Archive Editions, 1986.

Bierman, John. *Fire in the Night: Wingate of Burma, Ethiopia, and Zion*. New York: Random House, 1999.

Black, Ian, and Benny Morris. *Israel's Secret Wars: The Untold History of Israeli Intelligence*. London: Hamish Hamilton, 1991.

Blunt, W. S. *Secret History of the British Occupation of Egypt: Being a Personal Narrative of Events*. London: Unwin, 1907.

Bower, Tom. *The Perfect English Spy: The Unknown Man in Charge During the Most Tumultuous Scandal-Ridden Era in Espionage History*. New York: St. Martin's Press, 1995.

Braddon, Russell. *The Siege*. New York: Viking, 1969.

Brendon, Piers. *The Decline and Fall of the British Empire, 1781–1997*. London: Jonathan Cape, 2007.

Brenner, Y. S. "The Stern Gang, 1940–1948." In *Palestine and Israel in the 19th and 20th Centuries*. Edited by Elie Kedourie and Sylvia G. Haim. London: Frank Cass, 1982.

Brown, Malcolm, ed. *T. E. Lawrence in War and Peace: An Anthology of the Military Writings of Lawrence of Arabia*. London: Greenhill, 2005.

Buchan, John. *Greenmantle*. London: Nelson, 1916.

Buzpinar, S. Tufan. "The Hijaz, Abdulhamid II and Amir Hussein's Secret Dealings with the British, 1877–1880." *Middle East Studies* 31, no. 1 (January 1995).

Caroz, Yaacov. *The Arab Secret Service*. London: Corgi, 1978.

Carr, Matthew. *The Infernal Machine: A History of Terrorism*. New York: New Press, 2007.

Christison, Kathleen. *Perceptions of Palestine: Their Influence on U.S. Middle East Policy*. Berkeley: University of California Press, 1999.

Clarke, Thurston. *By Blood and Fire: The Attack on the King David Hotel*. New York: Putnam, 1981.

Cleveland, William L. *A History of the Modern Middle East.* San Francisco: West-view, 1994.

Cockburn, Andrew, and Leslie Cockburn. *Dangerous Liaison: The Inside Story of the U.S.-Israeli Covert Relationship.* Toronto: Stoddart, 1991.

Cohen, Stephen P. *The Idea of Pakistan.* Washington, D.C.: Brookings Institution, 2004.

Colby, William, and Peter Forbath. *Honorable Men: My Life in the CIA.* New York: Simon & Schuster, 1978.

Coll, Steve. *Ghost Wars: The Secret History of the CIA, Afghanistan and Bin Laden, from the Soviet Invasion to September 10, 2001.* New York: Penguin, 2004.

Cooley, John K. *Unholy Wars: Afghanistan, America and International Terrorism.* Sterling, VA: Pluto, 2000.

Cooper, Artemis. *Cairo in the War, 1939–1945.* London: Hamish Hamilton, 1989.

Copeland, Miles. *Game of Nations: The Amorality of Power Politics.* New York: Simon & Schuster, 1969.

———. *The Game Player: Confessions of the CIA's Original Political Operative.* London: Arium, 1989.

———. *The Real Spy World.* London: Weidenfeld & Nicolson, 1974.

Crile, George. *Charlie Wilson's War: The Extraordinary Story of the Largest Covert Operation in History.* New York: Atlantic Monthly Press, 2003.

"The Crisis in Egypt: Serious Riots in Alexandria." *The Times,* 11 June 1882.

Crossman, R. H. S. *The Diaries of a Cabinet Minister: Richard Crossman.* New York: Henry Holt, 1976.

Crossman, R. H. S., and Michael Foot. *A Palestine Munich.* London: Victor Gollancz, 1946.

Dalin, David G., and John F. Rothmann. *Icon of Evil: Hitler's Mufti and the Rise of Radical Islam.* New York: Random House, 2008.

Dawisha, Adeed. *Arab Nationalism in the Twentieth Century: From Triumph to Despair.* Princeton: Princeton University Press, 2003.

Deacon, Richard. *"C": A Biography of Sir Maurice Oldfield, Head of MI6.* London: Futura, 1984.

Derogy, Jacques, and Hesi Carmel. *The Untold History of Israel.* New York: Random House, 1979.

Disraeli, Benjamin. *Contarini Fleming: A Psychological Romance*. London: John Lane, 1927.

Dorril, Stephen. *MI6: Inside the Covert World of Her Majesty's Secret Intelligence Service*. New York: Free Press, 2000.

Downton, Eric. *Wars Without End*. Toronto: Stoddart, 1987.

Dreyfuss, Robert. *Devil's Game: How the United States Helped Unleash Fundamentalist Islam*. New York: Metropolitan, 2005.

Epstein, Edward J. *Deception: The Invisible War Between the KGB and the CIA*. New York: Simon & Schuster, 1989.

Eshed, Haggai. *Reuven Shiloah—The Man Behind the Mossad: Secret Diplomacy in the Creation of Israel*. Portland: Frank Cass, 1997.

Esposito, John L., ed. *The Oxford Dictionary of Islam*. Oxford: Oxford University Press, 2003.

Eveland, William Crane. *Ropes of Sand: America's Failure in the Middle East*. New York: Norton, 1980.

Fairlie, J. A. "The Economic Effects of Ship Canals." *Annals of the American Academy of Political and Social Science* 11 (January 1898).

Farran, Roy. *Winged Dagger: Adventures on Special Service*. London: Collins, 1970.

Ferguson, Niall. *The War of the World: Twentieth-Century Conflict and the Descent of the West*. New York: Penguin, 2006.

Fergusson, Thomas G. "Army Annual Inspection Report, 1852." In *British Military Intelligence, 1870–1914: The Development of a Modern Intelligence Organization* (Frederick, MD: University Publications of America, 1984).

Fielding, Xan. *One Man in His Time: The Life of Lieutenant-Colonel N. L. D. ("Billy") McLean, DSO*. London: Macmillan, 1990.

Finkel, Caroline. *Osman's Dream: The Story of the Ottoman Empire, 1300–1923*. New York: Basic, 2006.

Fisher, John. *Gentleman Spies: Intelligence Agents in the British Empire and Beyond*. Stroud: Sutton, 2002.

Fisk, Robert. *The Great War for Civilization: The Conquest of the Middle East*. London: Fourth Estate, 2005.

———. *Pity the Nation: The Abduction of Lebanon*. New York: Thunder Mouth, 2002.

Foot, M. R. D. *S.O.E. in France: An Account of the Work of the British Special Operations Executive in France, 1940–1944*. London: HMSO, 1966.

Frank, Lewis A. "Nasser's Missile Program." *Orbis* 11, no. 3 (Fall 1967): 746–57.

Fromkin, David. *A Peace to End All Peace: The Fall of the Ottoman Empire and the Creation of the Modern Middle East*. New York: Avon, 1989.

Fuller, Graham E. "Obama's Policies Making Situation Worse in Afghanistan and Pakistan." *Huffington Post*, 6 September 2009, http://www.huffingtonpost.com/graham -e-fuller/global-viewpoint-obamas-p_b_201355.html.

Furst, Alan. *The World at Night*. New York: Random House, 1996.

Gabrieli, Francesco. *Arab Historians of the Crusades*. Translated by E. J. Costello. Berkeley: University of California Press, 1969.

Gaddis, John Lewis. *The Cold War: A New History*. New York: Penguin, 2005.

Gasiorowski, Mark J. "The 1953 Coup d' Etat Against Mosaddeq." In *Mohammad Mosaddeq and the 1953 Coup in Iran*. Edited by Mark J. Gasiorowski and Malcolm Byrne. Syracuse: Syracuse University Press, 2004.

Gaur, Dharmendra. *Behind the Enemy Lines*. New Delhi: Sterling, 1975.

Gehlen, Reinhard. *The Service: The Memoirs of General Reinhard Gehlen*. Translated by David Irving. New York: World, 1972.

Gerolymatos, André. *Espionage and Treason: A Study of the Proxenia in Political and Military Intelligence Gathering in Classical Greece*. Amsterdam: J. C. Gieben, 1986.

——. *Guerrilla Warfare and Espionage in Greece, 1940–1944*. New York: Pella, 1992.

——. *Red Acropolis, Black Terror: The Greek Civil War and the Origins of Soviet-American Rivalry*. New York: Basic, 2004.

Gilbert, Martin. *Finest Hour*. Vol. 6 of *Winston S. Churchill*. London: Heinemann, 1983.

Green, Dominic. *Three Empires on the Nile: The Victorian Jihad, 1869–1899*. New York: Free Press, 2007.

Gromyko, Andrei. *Memories*. London: Hutchinson, 1989.

Hagen, Gottfried. "German Heralds of Holy War: Orientalists and Applied Oriental Studies." *Comparative Studies of South Asia, Africa and the Middle East* 24, no. 2 (2004): 145–162.

Haqqani, Husain. *Pakistan: Between Mosque and Military*. Washington, D.C.: Carnegie Endowment for International Peace, 2005.

Harris, Christina P. *Nationalism and Revolution in Egypt: The Role of the Muslim Brotherhood*. The Hague: Mouton, 1964.

Haswell, Jock. *British Military Intelligence*. London: Weidenfeld & Nicolson, 1973.

Heikal, Mohammed H. *Cutting the Lion's Tail: Suez Through Egyptian Eyes*. New York: Arbor House, 1987.

Heller, Joseph. *British Policy Towards the Ottoman Empire, 1900–1914*. London: Frank Cass, 1983.

Helms, Richard. *A Look over My Shoulder: A Life in the Central Intelligence Agency*. New York: Ballantine, 2003.

Herring, George C. *From Colony to Superpower: US Foreign Relations Since 1776*. Oxford: Oxford University Press, 2008.

Hersh, Burton. *The Old Boys: The American Elite and the Origins of the CIA*. New York: Scribner's, 1992.

Hillenbrand, Carole. *The Crusades: Islamic Perspectives*. Edinburgh: Edinburgh University Press, 1999.

Hinsley, F. H., and others. *British Intelligence in the Second World War: Its Influence on Strategy and Operations*. Vol. 1. London: HMSO, 1979.

Hiro, Dilip. *The Iranian Labyrinth: Journeys Through Theocratic Iran and Its Furies*. New York: Nation, 2005.

Hohnen, Peter. "Cawthorn, Sir Walter Joseph (1896–1970)," *Australian Dictionary of Biography*. Vol. 13. Melbourne: Melbourne University Press, 1993.

Holland, Matthew F. *America and Egypt: From Roosevelt to Eisenhower*. London: Praeger, 1996.

Holzman, Michael. *James Jesus Angleton, the CIA and the Craft of Counterintelligence*. Amhest: University of Massachusetts Press, 2008.

Homer. *The Odyssey*. Translated by Robert Fagles. New York: Penguin, 1996.

Hood, William. "Angleton's World." In *Myths Surrounding James Angleton: Lessons for American Counterintelligence*. Edited by William Hood et al. Washington, D.C.: Consortium for the Study of Intelligence, 1994.

Hopkirk, Peter. *The Great Game: The Struggle for Empire in Central Asia*. New York: Kodansha International, 1992.

———. *On Secret Service East of Constantinople: The Great Game and the Great War*. London: John Murray, 1994.

Hourani, Albert. *Arabic Thought in the Liberal Age, 1798–1939*. London: Oxford University Press, 1962.

———. *A History of the Arab Peoples*. New York: Warner, 1991.

Howell, Georgina. *Gertrude Bell: Queen of the Desert, Shaper of Nations*. New York: Farrar, Straus & Giroux, 2006.

Hupchick, Dennis P. *The Balkans: From Constantinople to Communism*. New York: Palgrave, 2002.

Hurewitz, J. C. *Diplomacy in the Near and Middle East: A Documentary Record*. 2 vols. Princeton: Van Nostrand, 1956.

Hussain, Rizwan. *Pakistan and the Emergence of Islamic Militancy in Afghanistan*. Farnham: Ashgate, 2005.

Infield, Glenn B. *Skorzeny: Hitler's Commando*. New York: Military Heritage Press, 1981.

Irwin, Robert. "Is This the Man Who Inspired Bin Laden?" *The Guardian*, 1 November 2001.

Jamal, Arif. *Shadow War: The Untold Story of Jihad in Kashmir*. Brooklyn, NY: Melville House, 2009.

Jarvis, C. S. *Three Deserts*. London: John Murray, 1941.

Jeffrey-Jones, Rhodri. *The CIA and American Diplomacy*. New Haven: Yale University Press, 1989.

Johnson, Robert. *Spying for Empire: The Great Game in Central and South Asia, 1757–1947*. London: Greenhill, 2006.

Jones, Matthew. "The 'Preferred Plan': The Anglo-American Working Group Report on Covert Action in Syria, 1957." *Intelligence and National Security* 19, no. 3 (Autumn 2004): 401–15.

Joshi, Pooja. *Jamaat-i-Islami: The Catalyst of Islamization in Pakistan*. New Delhi: Kalinga, 2003.

Karabell, Zachary. *Parting the Desert: The Creation of the Suez Canal*. New York: Knopf, 2003.

Karpat, Kemal H. *The Politicization of Islam: Reconstructing Identity, State, Faith and Community in the Late Ottoman State*. Oxford: Oxford University Press, 2001.

Karsh, Efraim. *Islamic Imperialism: A History*. New Haven: Yale University Press, 2006.

Karsh, Efraim, and Inari Karsh. *Empires of the Sand: The Struggle for Mastery in the Middle East, 1789–1923*. Cambridge: Harvard University Press, 1999.

Katz, Samuel. *Israel Elite Units Since 1948*. Oxford: Osprey, 1988.

Keay, John. *Sowing the Wind: The Seeds of Conflict in the Middle East*. New York: Norton, 2003.

Kedourie, Elie. *Afghani and 'Abduh: An Essay on Religious Unbelief and Political Activism in Modern Islam*. London: Frank Cass, 1966.

———. *The Chatham House Version and Other Middle Eastern Studies*. London: Weidenfeld & Nicolson, 1970.

———. *In the Anglo-Arab Labyrinth: The McMahon-Husayn Correspondence and Its Interpretations*. Cambridge: Cambridge University Press, 1976.

Keegan, John. *The Price of Admiralty: The Evolution of Naval Warfare*. New York: Viking Penguin, 1988.

Kelly, James, and William Stewart. "Syria: The Proud Lion and His Den." *Time*, 5 September 1983.

Kennedy, Paul. *The Realities Behind Diplomacy: Background Influences on British External Policy, 1865–1980*. Glasgow: Collins, 1981.

Kepel, Gilles. *Jihad: The Trail of Political Islam*. Translated by Anthony F. Roberts. Cambridge: Harvard University Press, 2002.

———. *Muslim Extremism in Egypt: The Prophet and the Pharaoh*. Translated by Jon Rothschild. Los Angeles: University of California Press, 1984.

———. *The War for Muslim Minds: Islam and the West*. Cambridge: Harvard University Press, 2004.

Khalidi, Rashid. *The Iron Cage: The Story of the Palestinian Struggle for Statehood*. Boston: Beacon, 2006.

Kimche, Jon, and David Kimche. *The Secret Roads: The "Illegal" Migration of a People, 1938–1948*. London: Secker & Warburg, 1954.

Kinzer, Stephen. *All the Shah's Men: An American Coup and the Roots of Middle East Terror*. Hoboken, NJ: John Wiley, 2003.

Kissinger, Henry. *Years of Renewal*. Vol. 3. New York: Simon & Schuster, 1999.

Knightley, Philip. *The Master Spy: The Story of Kim Philby*. New York: Knopf, 1989.

———. *The Second Oldest Profession: The Spy as Bureaucrat, Patriot, Fantasist and Whore*. London: Andre Deutsch, 1986.

Koestler, Arthur. *Promise and Fulfilment: Palestine, 1917–1949*. London: Macmillan, 1949.

Kramer, Gudrun. *A History of Palestine: From the Ottoman Conquest to the Founding of the State of Israel*. Princeton: Princeton University Press, 2002.

Kumamoto, Robert. *International Terrorism and American Foreign Relations, 1945–1976*. Boston: Northeastern University Press, 1999.

Kyle, Keith. *Suez*. London: Weidenfeld & Nicolson, 1991.

Lawrence, Arnold W., ed. *Secret Despatches from Arabia*. London: Golden Cockerel, 1939.

Lawrence, T. E. *Seven Pillars of Wisdom: A Triumph*. New York: Penguin, 1962.

le Carré, John. "On Kim Philby." In Kim Philby, *My Silent War: The Autobiography of a Spy*. New York: Modern Library, 2002.

Lee, Martin. A. *The Beast Reawakens*. New York: Routledge, 2000.

Lewis, Bernard. *The Assassins: A Radical Sect in Islam*. London: Weidenfeld & Nicolson, 2001.

———. *What Went Wrong?: Western Impact and Middle Eastern Response*. Oxford: Oxford University Press, 2002.

Lia, Brynjar. *The Society of the Muslim Brothers in Egypt: The Rise of an Islamic Mass Movement, 1928–1942*. Reading: Ithaca, 1998.

Lindsay, Franklin. *Beacons in the Night: With the OSS and Tito's Partisans in Wartime Yugoslavia*. Stanford: Stanford University Press, 1993.

Little, Douglas. "Cold War and Covert Action: The United States and Syria, 1945–1958." *Middle East Journal* 44, no. 1 (Winter 1990).

Lucas, Scott, and Alistair Morey. "The Hidden 'Alliance': The CIA and MI6 Before and After Suez." In *American-British-Canadian Intelligence Relations, 1939–2000*. Edited by Maurizio Ferrera and Martin Rhodes. London: Frank Cass, 2000.

Lüdke, Tilman. *Jihad Made in Germany: Ottoman and German Propaganda and Intelligence Operations in the First World War*. Münster: LIT, 2005.

Maalouf, Amin. *The Crusades Through Arab Eyes*. Translated by Jon Rothschild. London: Al Saqi, 1984.

MacDonald, Callum. *The Killing of SS Obergruppenführer Reinhard Heydrich*. New York: Free Press, 1989.

MacMillan, Margaret. *Paris 1919: Six Months That Changed the World*. New York: Random House, 2003.

"Major Roy Farran (Obituary)." *The Times*, 6 June 2006.

"The Man Behind Bin Laden." *The New Yorker*, 16 September 2002.

Mango, Andrew. *Ataturk: The Biography of the Founder of Modern Turkey*. New York: Overlook, 2000.

Mansel, Philip. *Constantinople: City of the World's Desire, 1453–1924*. London: John Murray, 1995.

Masters, John. *The Road Past Mandalay*. New York: Bantam, 1979.

Mattar, Philip. *The Mufti of Jerusalem: Al-Hajj Amin al-Husayni and the Palestinian National Movement*. New York: Columbia University Press, 1988.

Mayer, Karl E., and Shareen B. Brysac. *Tournament of Shadows: The Great Game and the Race for Empire in Central Asia*. Washington, D.C.: Counterpoint, 1999.

Melman, Yossi, and Dan Raviv. *Friends in Deed: Inside the U.S.-Israeli Alliance*. New York: Hyperion, 1994.

Michaud, Joseph F. *History of the Crusades*. Translated by W. Robson. 3 vols. London: Routledge, 1852; repr., New York: AMS, 1973.

Minault, Gail. *The Khilafat Movement: Religious Symbolism and Political Mobilization in India*. New York: Columbia University Press, 1982.

Mitchell, Richard P. *The Society of Muslim Brothers*. Oxford: Oxford University Press, 1969.

Modin, Yuri. "On Kim Philby." In Kim Philby, *My Silent War: the Autobiography of a Spy*. New York: Modern Library, 2002.

Mohs, Polly A. *Military Intelligence and the Arab Revolt: The First Modern Intelligence War*. New York: Routledge, 2008.

Monroe, Elizabeth. *Philby of Arabia*. Reading: Ithaca, 1973.

Morris, Benny. *1948: A History of the First Arab-Israeli War*. New Haven: Yale University Press, 2008.

———. *Righteous Victims: A History of the Zionist-Arab Conflict, 1881–2001*. New York: Vintage, 1999.

Mortimer, Edward. *Faith and Power: The Politics of Islam*. New York: Vintage, 1982.

Moubayed, Sami. "Keeping an Eye on Syria: March 29, 1949." *Mideastviews: Middle East Analysis by Sami Moubayed*, 29 May 2009. http://www.mideastviews.com/articleview.php?art=387.

"Mumbai Terror Attacks: Nightmare in the Lap of Luxury." *The Observer*, 30 November 2008.

Naftali, Timothy. "Reinhard Gehlen and the United States." In *U.S. Intelligence and the Nazis*. Edited by Richard Breitman et al. Cambridge: Cambridge University Press, 2005.

Naor, Mordecai. *Lexicon of the Haganah Defence Force*. Tel Aviv: Ministry of Defence, 1992.

Nasr, Vali. *The Shia Revival: How Conflicts Within Islam Will Shape the Future*. New York: Norton, 2006.

Nawaz, Shuja. *Crossed Swords: Pakistan, Its Army, and the Wars Within*. Oxford: Oxford University Press, 2008.

Nesbit, Roy C. *Eyes of the RAF: A History of Photo-Reconnaissance*. Kettering: Sutton, 1996.

Nutting, Anthony. *No End of a Lesson: The Story of Suez*. London: Constable, 1967.

Oren, Michael B. *Power, Faith, and Fantasy: America in the Middle East, 1776 to the Present*. New York: Norton, 2007.

Painter, Sidney. "The Third Crusade: Richard the Lionhearted and Philip Augustus." In *A History of the Crusades*. Edited by Robert Lee Wolf and Harry W. Hazard. Vol. 2, *The Later Crusades 1189–1311*. Madison. University of Wisconsin Press, 1969.

Pakenham, Thomas. *The Boer War*. New York: Avon, 1979.

———. *The Scramble for Africa: The White Man's Conquest of the Dark Continent from 1876 to 1912*. New York: Random House, 1991.

"Pakistan: Karachi's Madrasas and Violent Extremism." *ICG Asia Report*, no. 130 (29 March 2007).

"Pakistan: Madrasas, Extremism and the Military." *ICG Asia Report*, no. 36 (29 July 2002).

Palmer, Alan. *The Decline and Fall of the Ottoman Empire*. New York: Barnes & Noble, 1992.

Parritt, B. A. H. *The Intelligencers: The Story of British Military Intelligence up to 1914*. Ashford: Intelligence Corps Association, 1971.

Paul, Jim. "Insurrection at Mecca." *MERIP Reports*, no. 91, "Saudi Arabia on the Brink" (October 1980).

Peters, Edward, ed. *The First Crusade: The Chronicle of Fulcher of Chartres and Other Source Materials*. 2nd ed. Philadelphia: University of Pennsylvania Press, 1998.

Peters, Rudolph. *Islam and Colonialism: The Doctrine of Jihad in Modern History*. The Hague: Mouton, 1979.

Philby, Kim. *My Silent War: The Autobiography of a Spy*. New York: Modern Library, 2002.

Pipes, Daniel. "The Alawi Capture of Power in Syria." *Middle Eastern Studies* 25, no. 4 (October 1989): 429–50.

———. *The Hidden Hand: Middle East Fears of Conspiracy*. New York: St. Martin's Press, 1996.

Pollack, Kenneth M. *The Persian Puzzle: The Conflict Between Iran and America*. New York: Random House, 2004.

Powers, Thomas. *The Man Who Kept the Secrets*. New York: Knopf, 1979.

Prados, John. *Safe for Democracy: The Secret Wars of the CIA*. Chicago: Ivan R. Dee, 2006.

Rahnema, Ali. *Pioneers of Islamic Revival*. London: Zed, 2005.

Rais, Rasul Bakhsh. *Recovering the Frontier State: War, Ethnicity, and State in Afghanistan*. New York: Lexington, 2008.

Ranelagh, John. *The Agency: The Rise and Decline of the CIA*. New York: Simon & Schuster, 1978.

Ranfurly, Hermione. *To War with Whitaker: Wartime Diaries of Countess Ranfurly, 1939–1945*. London: Heinemann, 1994.

Rashid, Ahmed. *Descent into Chaos*. New York: Viking, 2008.

Rathmell, Andrew. *Secret War in the Middle East: The Covert Struggle for Syria, 1949–1961*. London: I. B. Tauris, 1995.

Raviv, Dan, and Yossi Melman. *Every Spy a Prince*. Boston: Houghton Mifflin, 1990.

Riedel, Bruce. "Pakistan and Terror: The Eye of the Storm." *The ANNALS of the American Academy of Political and Social Science* 618, no. 1 (2008).

Roberts, Frederick Sleigh. *Forty-one Years in India: From Subaltern to Commander-in-Chief*. Vol. 2. London: Bentley, 1897.

Roosevelt, Kermit. *Countercoup: The Struggle for the Control of Iran.* New York: McGraw-Hill, 1979.

Rosen, Stephen P. *Societies and Military Power: India and Its Armies.* Ithaca: Cornell University Press, 1996.

Rositzke, Harry. *The CIA's Secret Operations: Espionage, Counterespionage, and Covert Action.* Boulder, CO: Westview, 1988.

"Roy Farran (Obituary)." *Daily Telegraph,* 5 June 2006.

Royle, Charles. *The Egyptian Campaigns, 1882–1885: And the Events Which Led to Them.* 2 vols. London: Hurst & Blackett, 1886.

Royle, Trevor. *Orde Wingate: Irregular Soldier.* London: Weidenfeld & Nicolson, 1995.

Runciman, Steven. *The First Crusade and the Foundation of the Kingdom of Jerusalem.* Vol. 1 of *A History of the Crusades.* Cambridge: Cambridge University Press, 1989.

Russell, Tom. "A Lebanon Primer." *MERIP Reports,* no. 133 (June 1985).

Sachar, Howard M. *A History of Israel: From the Rise of Zionism to Our Time.* New York: Knopf, 2007.

"Sacrilege in Mecca." *Time,* 3 December 1979.

Sansom, A. W. *I Spied Spies.* London: Harrap, 1965.

Saunders, Bonnie F. *The United States and Arab Nationalism.* Wesport, CT: Praeger, 1996.

Schofield, Victoria. *Kashmir in Conflict: India, Pakistan and the Unfinished War.* London: I. B. Tauris, 2000.

———. *Wavell: Soldier and Statesman.* London: John Murray, 2007.

Schwartz, Stephen. "Is Saudi Arabia Holy Soil?" *Think Israel* (September–October 2004), http://www.think-israel.org/schwartz.saudiarabia.html.

Seale, Patrick. *The Struggle for Syria.* London: I. B. Tauris, 1985.

Segev, Samuel. *The Iranian Triangle.* New York: Free Press, 1988.

Segev, Tom. *One Palestine Complete: Jews and Arabs Under the British Mandate.* New York: Henry Holt, 1999.

Seymour, William. *British Special Forces: The Story of Britain's Undercover Soldiers.* Toronto: Grafton, 1985.

Shaul Shay. *The A&B of Evil: Iran, Hizballah and the Palestinian terror New Brunswick NJ: Transaction, 2005.*

Simpson, Christopher. *Blowback: The First Full Account of America's Recruitment of Nazis and Its Disastrous Effect on the Cold War, Our Domestic and Foreign Policy.* New York: Macmillan, 1988.

Slatin, Rudolf C. *Fire and Sword in the Sudan: A Personal Narrative of Fighting and Serving the Dervishes, 1879–1895.* Translated by F. R. Wingate. London: Arnold, 1896.

Smith, R. Harris. *OSS: The Secret History of America's First Central Intelligence Agency.* Guilford, CT: Lyons, 2005.

St. John, Robert. *The Boss: The Story of Gamel Abdel Nasser.* New York: McGraw-Hill, 1960.

Stern, Jessica. "Pakistan's Jihad Culture." *Foreign Affairs* 79, no. 6 (November–December 2000).

Storrs, Ronald. *Orientations.* London: Nicholson & Watson, 1943.

Strachan, Hew. *To Arms.* Vol. 1 of *The First World War.* Oxford: Oxford University Press, 2001.

Sykes, Christopher. *Crossroads to Israel.* Cleveland: World, 1965.

"Syria Army Takes Over Government: Leaders Ousted in Bloodless Coup d'etat." *Evening Independent,* 30 March 1949.

Szulc, Tad. *The Secret Alliance: The Extraordinary Story of the Rescue of the Jews Since World War II.* London: Macmillan, 1991.

Tanner, Stephen. *Afghanistan: A Military History from Alexander the Great to the Fall of the Taliban.* Cambridge: Da Capo, 2002.

Tauber, Eliezer. *The Arab Movements in World War I.* London: Frank Cass, 1993.

———. *The Formation of Modern Syria and Iraq.* London: Frank Cass, 1995.

Taylor, A. J. P. *The Struggle for Mastery in Europe, 1848–1918.* Oxford: Clarendon Press, 1965.

Taylor, Peter. *Provos: The IRA and Sinn Fein.* London: Bloomsbury, 1997.

Teitelbaum, Joshua. *The Rise and Fall of the Hashimite Kingdom of Arabia.* London: Hurst, 2001.

Tenet, George. *At the Center of the Storm: My Years at the CIA.* New York: HarperCollins, 2007.

Thomas, Evan. *The Very Best Men: The Darling Early Years of the CIA.* New York: Simon & Schuster, 1995.

Thomas, Gordon. *Gideon's Spies: The Secret History of the Mossad.* New York: St. Martin's Press, 2007.

Thomas, Lowell. *With Lawrence in Arabia.* New York: Century, 1924.

Thomas, Martine. *Empires of Intelligence: Security Services and Colonial Disorder After 1914.* Berkeley: University of California Press, 2008.

Trento, Joseph J. *The Secret History of the CIA.* New York: Prima, 2001.

Tripp, Charles. "Sayyid Qutb: The Political Vision." In *Pioneers of Islamic Revival.* Edited by Ali Rahnema. London: Zed, 2005.

Trofimov, Yaroslav. *The Siege of Mecca: The Forgotten Uprising in Islam's Holiest Shrine and the Birth of Al-Qaeda.* New York: Doubleday, 2007.

Trumpener, Ulrich. *Germany and the Ottoman Empire, 1914–1918.* Princeton: Princeton University Press, 1968.

Tsafrir, Eliezer. *Big Satan, Small Satan: Revolution and Escape in Iran.* Tel Aviv: Maariv 2002.

Turner, Barry. *Suez 1956: The Inside Story of the First Oil War.* London: Hodder & Stoughton, 2006.

Twain, Mark. *The Innocents Abroad.* Mineola, NY: Dover, 2003.

Tyerman, Christopher. *God's War: A New History of the Crusades.* Cambridge: Harvard University Press, 2006.

"U.S. Accused of Syrian Coup Attempt." *The Age*, 14 August 1957.

U.S. Congress. Congressional Record. 25 April 1950. Washington, D.C.

Usher, Graham. "Taliban v. Taliban." *London Review of Books* 31, no. 7 (9 April 2009).

Vaglieri, Laura Veccia. "The Patriarchal and Umayyad Caliphates." In *The Cambridge History of Islam.* Edited by Ann K. S. Lambton, P. M. Holt, and Bernard Lewis. Vol. 1, *The Central Islamic Lands.* Cambridge: Cambridge University Press, 1970.

Vagts, Alfred. *The Military Attaché.* Princeton: Princeton University Press, 1967.

Vielain, Heinz. *Waffenschmuggel im Staatsauftrag: Was lange in Bonn geheim bleiben musste.* Herford: Busse Seewald, 1986.

Weiner, Tim. *Legacy of Ashes: The History of the CIA.* New York: Doubleday, 2007.

West, Nigel. *MI5: British Security Service Operations, 1909–1945.* London: Triad Granada, 1983.

———. *MI6: British Intelligence Service Operations, 1909–1945.* London: Weidenfeld & Nicolson, 1983.

Westrate, Bruce. *The Arab Bureau: British Policy in the Middle East, 1916–1920*. University Park: Pennsylvania State University Press, 1992.

Whiting, Charles. *Skorzeny: The Most Dangerous Man in Europe*. Conshohocken, PA: Combined, 1972.

Wilber, Donald. *Overthrow of Premier Mossadeq of Iran, November 1952–August 1953*. Nottingham: Spokesman, 2006.

Wildt, Michael. *Generation des Unbedingten: Das Führungskorps des Reichssicher-heitshauptamtes*. Hamburg: Hamburger Editon, 2003.

Wilson, Charles McMoran. *Churchill: Taken from the Diaries of Lord Moran*. Boston: Houghton Mifflin, 1966).

Wilson, Jeremy. *Lawrence of Arabia: The Authorised Biography of T. E. Lawrence*. New York: Atheneum, 1990.

Wilson, Peter W., and Douglas F. Graham. *Saudi Arabia: The Coming Storm*. New York: M. E. Sharpe, 1994.

Winstone, H. V. F. *Gertrude Bell*. London: Jonathan Cape, 1978.

———. *The Illicit Adventure: The Story of Political and Military Intelligence in the Middle East from 1898 to 1926*. London: Jonathan Cape, 1982.

Woodhouse, C. M. *Something Ventured: The Autobiography of C. M. Woodhouse*. London: Granada, 1982.

Wright, Lawrence. *The Looming Tower: Al-Qaeda and the Road to 9/11*. New York: Vintage, 2006.

Wright, Peter. *Spy Catcher: The Candid Autobiography of a Senior Intelligence Officer*. Toronto: Stoddart, 1987.

Yasamee, F. A. K. *Ottoman Diplomacy: Abdulhamid II and the Great Powers*. Istanbul: Isis, 1996.

Yergin, Daniel. *The Prize: The Epic Quest for Oil, Money, and Power*. New York: Free Press, 1991.

Ziring, Lawrence. *Pakistan at the Crosscurrent of History*. Oxford: Oneworld, 2003.

Zubok, Vladislav, and Constantine Pleshakov. *Inside the Kremlin's Cold War: From Stalin to Khrushchev*. Cambridge: Harvard University Press, 1996.

Zweig, Ronald W. *Britain and Palestine During the Second World War*. London: Royal Historical Society, 1986.

ABBREVIATIONS AND ACRONYMS

ADC	Aide-de-camp
AIS	Allied Information Services
AMAL	Harakat Amal (Lebanese Resistance Detachments)
ANA	Arab News Agency
APOC	Anglo-Persian Oil Company
ARAMCO	Arabian-American Oil Company
ASCI	Assistant Chief-of-Staff for Intelligence
BAD	Base Ammunition Depot
BBC	British Broadcasting Corporation
BDO	Bund deutscher Offiziere (Federation of German Officers)
BEF	British Expeditionary Force
BL	British Library
BND	Bundesnachrichtendienst (Federal Intelligence Service)
BTE	British Troops Egypt
CENTO	Central Treaty Organization
CIA	Central Intelligence Agency
CIC	Counter Intelligence Corps
CID	Criminal Investigation Department
CIGS	Chief of the Imperial General Staff
C-in-C	Commander-in-Chief
Comintern	Information Bureau of the Communist and Workers' Parties
CP	Communist Party
CPSU	Communist Party of the Soviet Union
CRC	Council of the Revolutionary Command
CUP	Committee of Union and Progress
DAK	Deutsches Afrikakorps (German Africa Corps)
DCI	Department of Central Intelligence
DMI	Director(ate) of Military Intelligence

DP	displaced person(s)
DSO	Distinguished Service Order
EEC	European Economic Community
EG	Einsatzgruppe (Operational Task Force)
EK	Einsatzkommando (Operational Task Squad)
FBI	Federal Bureau of Investigation
FEA	Foreign Economic Administration
FFI	Freedom Fighters of Israel (Stern Gang)
FHO	Fremde Heere Ost (Foreign Armies East)
FO	Foreign Office
FOSH	Plugot Sadeh (Field Companies)
G2	Divisional Staff Intelligence Officer
GCHQ	Government Communications Headquarters
Gestapo	Geheime Staatspolizei (Secret State Police)
GIGN	Group d'Intervention de la Gendarmerie Nationale
GRU	Glavnoje Razvedyvatel'noje Upravlenije (Main Intelligence Directorate)
HMG	His/Her Majesty's Government
HQ	headquarters
HQBTE	Headquarters, British Troops Egypt
IA	Indian Army
IB	Intelligence Bureau
IEM	Ikhwan el Muslimeen (Muslim Brotherhood)
ICG	International Crisis Group
IDF	Israeli Defence Force
INA	Indian National Army
IOR	India Office Records
IRA	Irish Republican Army
ISI	Inter-Services Intelligence
ISLD	Inter-Services Liaison Department
IZL	Irgun Zvai Leumi (National Military Organization)
JAE	Jewish Agency Executive
JI	Jamaat-e-Islami
JIC	Joint Intelligence Committee

JUI	Jamaat-Ulema-e-Islam
KGB	Komityet Gosudarstvennoy Bezopasnosty (Committee for State Security)
KSA	Kingdom of Saudi Arabia
MB	Muslim Brotherhood
MC	Military Cross
MEC	Middle East Command
MEDO	Middle East Defense Organization
MERIP	Middle East Research and Information Project
MI5	Military Intelligence Dept. 5 (Colloquial designation for the Security Service)
MI6	Military Intelligence Dept. 6 (Colloquial designation for the Secret Intelligence Service)
MI9	Military Intelligence Dept 9 (Colloquial designation for POW Escape and Evasion Department)
MP	Member of Parliament
NARA	National Archives and Records Administration
NATO	North Atlantic Treaty Organization
NCO	Non-commissioned officer
NCRC	National Council of the Revolutionary Command
NKVD	Narodnyy Komissariat Vnutrennikh Del (People's Commissariat for Internal Affairs)
NSA	National Security Agency
NSC	National Security Council
ODESSA	Organisation der ehemaligen SS-Angehörigen (Organization of Former Members of the SS)
OPC	Office of Policy Coordination
OSO	Office of Special Operations
OSS	Office of Strategic Services
PFLP	Popular Front for the Liberation of Palestine
PFLP-EO	Popular Front for the Liberation of Palestine— External Operations
PLO	Palestine Liberation Organization
PPS	Parti Populaire Syrien

PS	Palestine Scheme
PSNS	Parti Social Nationaliste Syrien
RAF	Royal Air Force
RAOC	Royal Army Ordnance Corps
RCC	Revolutionary Command Council
RCMP	Royal Canadian Mounted Police
RSHA	Reichssicherheitshauptamt (SS Headquarters)
RZ	Revolutionäre Zellen (Revolutionary Cells)
SANACC	State, Army, Navy, Air Force Coordinating Committee
SAS	Special Air Service
SAVAK	Sazeman-e Ettela'at va Amniyat-e Keshvar (National Intelligence and Security Organization)
SAVAMA	Sazman-e Ettela'at va Amniat-e Melli-e Iran (Ministry of Intelligence and National Security of Iran)
SEATO	Southeast Asia Treaty Organization
SD	Sicherheitsdienst (SS Security Service)
SHAEF	Supreme Headquarters Allied Expeditionary Force
SHAI	Sherut Yediot (Information Service)
SIGINT	signals intelligence
SIS	Secret Intelligence Service (MI6)
SNS	Special Night Squads
SOCAL	Standard Oil of California
SOE	Special Operations Executive
SS	Schutzstaffel
SSNP	Syrian Social Nationalist Party
SSU	Strategic Services Unit
SVR	Sluzhba Vneshney Razvedki (Foreign Intelligence Service)
Tapline	Trans-Arabian Pipeline Company
TNA	The National Archives
TNSS	Turkish National Security Service
TSOPE	Tsentralnogo Obedineniia Politicheskikh Emigrantov iz SSSR (Central Association of Political Emigrants from the Soviet Union)
UK	United Kingdom

UN	United Nations
US	United States
USSR	Union of Soviet Socialist Republics
VEVAK	Vezarat-e Ettela'at va Amniat-e Keshvar (Iranian Ministry of Intelligence and Security)
WIN	Wolnosc i niezawislosc (Freedom and Independence)
WP	Warsaw Pact

CHRONOLOGY

THE WEST		THE EAST
	1090	Hashshashin established by Hasan-I Sabbah
	1095	First Crusade begins
	1098	Massacre of Ma'arra
	1099	Jerusalem falls; First Crusade ends
	1147	Second Crusade begins
	1149	Second Crusade ends
	1187	Third Crusade begins
	1192	Third Crusade ends; Conrad of Montferrat assassinated
	1202	Fourth Crusade begins
	1204	Fourth Crusade ends; Constantinople sacked
Magna Carta is signed	1215	
	1217	Fifth Crusade begins
	1221	Fifth Crusade ends
Birth of Saint Thomas Aquinas	1225	
	1228	Sixth Crusade begins
	1229	Sixth Crusade ends
Inquisition is established	1232	
	1244	Siege of Jerusalem
	1245	Fall of Jerusalem
	1248	Seventh Crusade begins
	1254	Seventh Crusade ends
	1261	Constantinople reclaimed by the Byzantines
	1270	Eighth Crusade

THE WEST		THE EAST
	1271	Ninth Crusade begins
	1272	Ninth Crusade ends
Papacy begins residency at Avignon	1309	
Hundred Years War begins	1337	
The Black Death spreads across Europe	1347	
Start of the Great Schism in the Roman Catholic Church	1378	
Council of Constance ends the Great Schism	1417	
Habsburg Dynasty begins	1438	
Hundred Years' War ends	1453	Fall of Constantinople to the Ottomans under Mehmed II; end of the Byzantine Empire
Gutenberg Bible printed	1455	
Columbus lands in the New World; Catholics conquer Granada and establish Spanish nation; Spanish Moors begin to abandon Islam	1492	
Moors expelled from Portugal	1496	
Moors expelled from Spain	1502	
Martin Luther posts his 95 Theses in Wittenberg	1517	
	1540	Sheikulislam named spiritual leader of all Ottoman Muslims
Defeat of the Spanish Armada	1588	
Last remaining Moriscos expelled from Spain	1616	

THE WEST		THE EAST
Thirty Years' War begins	1618	
Thirty Years' War ends	1648	
American Declaration of Independence	1776	
Treaty of Paris	1783	
French Revolution begins	1789	
Napoleon Bonaparte seizes power	1799	
Habsburg Dynasty ends	1806	
War of 1812	1812	
	1813	Russo-Persian Treaty; Great Game begins
Congress of Vienna convenes; Treaty of Ghent	1814	Congress of Vienna
Battle of Waterloo	1815	
	1819	Sadler crosses Arabia
Napoleon Bonaparte dies	1821	
Queen Victoria crowned	1838	
	1841	Straits Convention becomes effective
	1842	Stoddart and Conolly executed by Nasrullah Khan
	1843	Wolff released by Nasrullah Khan
Year of Revolution in Europe	1848	
Crimean War begins	1853	
Crimean War ends	1856	
	1857	Indian Mutiny begins; Indian Army formed
	1858	East India Company dissolved; Government of India Act enters into force

THE WEST		THE EAST
American Civil War begins	1861	
American Civil War ends	1865	
	1869	Suez Canal opens
France loses Franco-Prussian War	1871	
Congress of Berlin	1878	
	1879	Ismail Pasha abdicates
	1882	Alexandria riots
	1883	Battle of Tel-el-Kebir
	1885	Fall of Khartoum, Gordon killed; Intelligence Bureau established in India by Sir Charles MacGregor
	1889	Committee of Union and Progress founded in the Ottoman Empire
	1896	Menelik II defeats Italians at Adowa
Boer War begins	1899	Kitchener takes Khartoum
Queen Victoria dies	1901	
Boer War ends	1902	
Directorate of Military Intelligence abolished	1904	
	1907	Anglo-Russian Convention; Great Game ends
	1908	CUP takes power in the Ottoman Empire
Secret Service Bureau established	1909	
Assassination of Franz Ferdinand leads to First World War	1914	Sultan-Caliph proclaims *jihad*
	1915	McMahon-Hussein correspondence begins; Armenian Genocide

THE WEST		THE EAST
	1916	Arab Revolt begins; Sykes-Picot Agreement; British surrender at Kut and are defeated at Gallipoli; Arab Bureau created
Balfour Declaration; Bolshevik Revolution begins	1917	St. John Philby crosses Arabia
First World War ends	1918	Arab Revolt ends
Treaty of Versailles; Irish War of Independence begins	1919	
	1920	Haganah created
Ireland partitioned	1921	
Mussolini achieves power in Italy; Irish Civil War begins; Irish Free State established	1922	Transjordan created as Hashemite kingdom; Ottoman sultanate abolished
Irish Civil War ends	1923	Turkey becomes a republic; Ottoman Empire ends; Britain assumes control of Palestine mandate
	1924	Ataturk abolishes caliphate
	1928	Al-Banna founds Muslim Brotherhood
Wall Street Crash; Great Depression begins in United States	1929	
	1931	Irgun established
	1932	Iraq gains independence; Ibn Saud proclaims Kingdom of Saudi Arabia
Adolf Hitler becomes German chancellor	1933	SOCAL signs oil agreement with Saudi Arabia
Spanish Civil War begins	1936	Mufti-incited Arab Revolt begins in Palestine
	1937	Peel Commission proposes Palestinian partition

THE WEST		THE EAST
Germany annexes Austria	**1938**	Oil struck in Saudi Arabia
Spanish Civil War ends;	**1939**	Arab Revolt ends
Germany invades Poland;		
Second World War begins		
Battle of Britain	**1940**	Stern founds Freedom Fighters of Israel (Stern Gang)
Germany invades Soviet Union; United States enters war after Japanese attack on Pearl Harbor	**1941**	Rashid Ali coup fails in Iraq; Allies occupy Iran; Ali and the Grand Mufti flee to Germany; Haganah creates Palmach
Heydrich assassinated	**1942**	Germans defeated at El Alamein
German surrender at Stalingrad; Red Army wins battle of Kursk; Allies invade Sicily and Italian mainland	**1943**	Afrika Korps and Italians surrender to Allies
Allies invade Normandy	**1944**	Lord Moyne assassinated
Nazi death camps liberated; Second World War ends; Special Operations Executive disbanded; FDR dies; Truman becomes president; Churchill loses election	**1945**	Atom bombs dropped on Japan
Greek Civil War begins; Kennan's "Long Telegram."	**1946**	King David Hotel bombing
Truman Doctrine proclaimed; CIA formed; Gehlen establishes Pullach HQ	**1947**	Jerusalem riots; Farran trial; end of British Palestine Mandate; Pakistan gains independence
Apartheid becomes law in South Africa	**1948**	State of Israel created; Arab-Israeli War begins; Bernadotte assassinated; Irgun, Stern Gang, and all other paramilitaries disbanded; Jinnah dies; ISI created

THE WEST		THE EAST
Greek Civil War ends; NATO established; Soviet Union tests A-bomb	**1949**	Liaqat Ali Khan assassinated; Mao proclaims People's Republic of China; Stern Gang granted amnesty
	1950	Korean War begins
Acheson convenes ad hoc Egypt committee	**1951**	
Britain tests Atom bomb; United States tests Hydrogen bomb and launches first nuclear sub	**1952**	Free Officers overthrow Farouk; Revolutionary Command Council governs Egypt
Eisenhower becomes president; Stalin dies; Khrushchev succeeds him; Beria executed	**1953**	Korean War ends; France withdraws from Indo-China; Mossadeq ousted in Iran (Operation Ajax); MI6 recruits Khalil
	1954	Nasser becomes Egyptian president; first attempt on Nasser's life; Algerian war of independence begins; SEATO is established
Warsaw Pact and non-aligned movement established; Pentagon announces plan to develop ICBMs; Eden becomes prime minister	**1955**	St. John Philby leaves Saudi Arabia; Baghdad Pact among anticommunist states; Soviet aid to Syria begins
Khrushchev attacks Stalin in CPSU speech and de-Stalinization begins; Hungarian Revolution crushed by Red Army	**1956**	Hussein of Jordan dismisses Glubb Pasha; Arab News Agency raided; Nasser vows to reconquer Palestine; Suez crisis begins; Britain and France invade Egypt; Israel takes Sinai; Pakistan becomes an Islamic republic

THE WEST		THE EAST
Eden resigns; Macmillan becomes primne minister; Gromyko becomes Soviet foreign minister; Treaty of Rome signed; Soviet Union launches *Sputnik*	**1957**	Suez crisis ends with Israeli withdrawal from Sinai; Suez Canal reopened; Vietnam insurgency begins
EEC founded	**1958**	United Arab Republic created with Nasser as president; Iraq and Jordan unite; Qassim assumes power in Iraq; Soviet aid to Iraq begins; Ayub Khan takes over Pakistan
Castro takes over Cuba; CENTO established; Khrushchev meets Mao	**1959**	Vietnam War begins
Mau Mau uprising ends in Kenya; U2 spy plane shot down; Eichmann abducted in Argentina by Israel; Khrushchev pounds shoe on UN podium; JFK wins election over Nixon	**1960**	Malayan insurgency ends; OPEC formed
JFK becomes president; Bay of Pigs invasion fails; Berlin Wall constructed; Vietnam War begins; Eichmann sentenced to death in Israel	**1961**	United Arab Republic collapses
Eichmann hanged; Cuban missile crisis	**1962**	Algeria gains independence; civil war begins in Yemen
JFK assassinated; LBJ becomes president; Kim Philby given asylum in Moscow; the Profumo affair scandalizes Britain	**1963**	Baathists come to power in Syria and Iraq

THE WEST		THE EAST
Brezhnev succeeds Khrushchev; China tests A-bomb; Wilson defeats Hume at the British polls and forms a Labour government	**1964**	Founding of the Palestinian Liberation Organization in Cairo
Churchill dies; Heath becomes Tory leader	**1965**	US airborne troops and marines deployed in Vietnam; Pakistani troops enter Indian Kashmir
Prime Minister Verwoerd of South Africa assassinated; British Soviet spy George Blake escapes from prison and reaches Moscow; Ronald Reagan elected governor of California	**1966**	Kosygin invites Indian and Pakistani prime ministers to Moscow, and peace is achieved; Indira Ghandi becomes prime minister of India.; Sayyid Qutb executed; Baath Party takes over Syria; China's Cultural Revolution begins
Che Guevara executed in Bolivia	**1967**	Moshe Dayan becomes Israeli minister of defence; Six Day War; Israel captures the Golan Heights and the West Bank; War of Attrition begins
Prague Spring crushed by Warsaw Pact forces; Robert Kennedy and Martin Luther King assassinated; Pierre Trudeau becomes Canadian prime minister; beginning of The Troubles in Northern Ireland	**1968**	Saddam Hussein becomes vice president of Iraq; My Lai massacre in Vietnam
Nixon becomes president; Apollo 11 moon landing	**1969**	Arafat becomes head of Palestinian Liberation

(Continued)

THE WEST		THE EAST
		Organization; Gaddafi takes over Libya, seeks Soviet aid
Nuclear Non-Proliferation Treaty signed; Heath replaces Wilson as British prime minister	**1970**	War of Attrition ends; Nasser dies; Sadat takes over Egypt; Black September in Jordan
Construction of the World Trade Center completed; Australia and New Zealand withdraw their forces from Vietnam	**1971**	Assad becomes Syrian president; Aswan Dam completed with Soviet aid; United Arab Emirates established in the Persian Gulf; East Pakistan gains independence from Pakistan and becomes Bangladesh
The Watergate burglaries; Black September terrorists murder eleven Israeli athletes at Munich Olympics	**1972**	Lod Airport massacre; Nixon visits China; Ali Bhutto becomes president of Pakistan; Pakistan and India sign Simla Agreement
Allende ousted by Pinochet in Chile	**1973**	Yom Kippur War
Nixon resigns in disgrace	**1974**	PLO represents Palestine at United Nations; Turkish invasion of Cyprus
Helsinki Final Act signed	**1975**	Fall of Saigon; Vietnam War ends; Cambodian genocide begins; Lebanese Civil War begins
Harold Wilson finally resigns; James Callaghan takes over No. 10 Downing Street; Soweto riots in South Africa; United States' bicentennial celebrations	**1976**	Hijacking of AF139; Israeli counterterrorist rescue mission at Entebbe, Uganda; Mao dies; Pol Pot becomes prime minister of Kampuchea; North and South Vietnam unite

THE WEST		THE EAST
Jimmy Carter becomes president; mid-air collision over Tenerife kills 583 people; Trans-Alaska pipeline opened; *Concorde* begins regular supersonic transatlantic flights	**1977**	Zia-ul-Haq ousts Bhutto and takes over Pakistan; Likud, led by Menachem Begin, win Israeli election; Sadat visits Israel; SEATO dissolved
Mass suicide by cultists at Jonestown, Guyana	**1978**	Operation Litani, successful Israeli intervention in Lebanon; Begin and Sadat sign Camp David Accords; 2 million demonstrate in Tehran against the Shah; communists take over Afghanistan
USA and China open diplomatic relations; Margaret Thatcher becomes British prime minister; Mountbatten assassinated by IRA Provos; Pope John Paul II visits his native Poland; Sandanistas assume power in Nicaragua	**1979**	Sinai treaty; Egypt recognizes Israel; Soviet Union invades Afghanistan; Shah leaves Iran, Khomeini assumes power, and Tehran hostage crisis begins; Islamic fundamentalists attack and occupy Mecca Grand Mosque; Saddam Hussein takes over Iraq; Zia-ul-Haq has Bhutto executed; Pol Pot regime collapses in Cambodia; 200,000 Chinese troops invade northern Vietnam but are forced to withdraw with severe losses
Marshal Tito dies; Pierre Trudeau returns as Canadian leader; Special Air Service squad successfully storms the Iranian Embassy in London, after its occupation by	**1980**	Iran-Iraq War begins; Israel and Egypt establish diplomatic relations; Muslim Brotherhood assassination attempt on Assad fails; Shah dies in Cairo; Canadian diplomats facilitate escape of American diplomats from

(Continued)

THE WEST		THE EAST
Iranian-born terrorists; Polish Solidarity union is established		Tehran; commando mission to rescue the 52 hostages fails
Reagan becomes president; Poland's last communist ruler, General Jaruzelski, assumes power; both Reagan and the Pope wounded by gunmen in separate incidents; Mitterand becomes French president	**1981**	Sadat assassinated; Mubarak becomes Egyptian president; Tehran hostages released; Israel bombs Beirut
Falklands War between Britain and Argentina; Andropov succeeds Brezhnev	**1982**	Israel invades Lebanon; Hama Massacre; Sabra and Shatila Massacres
Reagan proposes "Star Wars"; Thatcher wins huge landslide victory in aftermath of Falkands War; Soviet fighter downs South Korean airliner in Soviet air space; military rule ends in Argentina	**1983**	United States embassy and marine barracks bombings in Beirut
Chernenko succeeds Andropov; Reagan calls for ban on chemical weapons; over the next two years Palestinian terrorist attacks on Western targets by Abu Nidal and others reach their height	**1984**	US marines withdraw from Lebanon; CIA Beirut station chief William Buckley kidnapped by Islamic Jihad and murdered; Iran accuses Iraq of using chemical weapons

THE WEST		THE EAST
Reagan sworn in for second term; Gorbachev becomes Soviet leader	**1985**	Israel withdraws troops from Lebanon and bombs PLO headquarters near Tunis
Iran-Contra affair causes scandal in Washington; Air India 182 blown up over the Atlantic; Swedish prime minister Olaf Palme assassinated; disco bombed in West Berlin by Libyan terrorists; Chernobyl nuclear disaster	**1986**	United States bombs Libya
	1987	First Intifada begins
Gorbachev initiates *perestroika* (restructuring) in Soviet Union; Libyan terrorists destroy PanAm jumbo jet over Lockerbie, Scotland	**1988**	Zia-ul-Haq dies in air crash; Benazir Bhutto becomes prime minister of Pakistan; Iran Air Flight 655 shot down by U.S. Navy accidentally
Bush Sr. becomes president; Hungarian border opened; Solidarity wins Polish elections; Berlin Wall falls; Velvet Revolution in Czechoslovakia; Ceaușescu toppled and executed in Romania; United States invades Panama	**1989**	Iran-Iraq War ends; *fatwa* issued by Ayatollah Khomeini concerning Salman Rushdie's British publication of *The Satanic Verses* in 1989; Khomeini dies; Soviet Union withdraws from Afghanistan; *mujahideen* factions start fighting; Tiananmen Square demonstrations in Beijing
Germany re-unified; Mandela released; Major succeeds Thatcher as British prime minister	**1990**	First Intifada ends; Lebanese Civil War ends; Iraq invades Kuwait; launch of Operation Desert Shield; North and South Yemen unite. Benazir Bhutto dismissed in Pakistan; Nawaz Sharif takes over and Shariah law is incorporated into legal code

THE WEST		THE EAST
Yeltsin becomes Russian president; USSR and Yugoslavia collapse; former Soviet republics and satellite states gain independence; Warsaw Pact dissolved; KGB is transmuted into SVR	**1991**	The first Gulf War; sanctions imposed on Iraq; former Soviet republics in central Asia gain independence
Apartheid ends, and the United States lifts sanctions against South Africa	**1993**	Oslo Accords signed; Sharif is replaced by Benazir Bhutto in Pakistan
Bill Clinton becomes president	**1993**	
Nelson Mandela becomes president of South Africa; Rwandan Genocide takes place; First Chechen War begins	**1994**	Jordan recognizes Israel
Sarin gas attack on Tokyo subway injures over 5,000; massive bomb destroys Oklahoma City federal building; over 8,000 Bosniaks massacred by Serbs at Srebrenica	**1995**	Yitzhak Rabin assassinated in Tel Aviv
First Chechen War ends; massive Irish Republican Army bomb devastates Manchester city centre	**1996**	Taliban seize power in Afghanistan; Benazir Bhutto dismissed for a second time in Pakistan; Khobar Towers bombing in Saudi Arabia
Tony Blair becomes British prime minister; Princess Diana dies in Paris car crash	**1997**	Nawaz Sharif returns to power in Pakistan

THE WEST		THE EAST
Clinton-Lewinsky scandal breaks in Washington; Clinton is later impeached and cleared; United States embassy bombings in Tanzania and Kenya	1998	Pakistan becomes a nuclear power; Osama bin Laden issues *fatwa* declaring holy war on all Jews and "crusaders."
Kosovo conflict culminates in NATO bombing of Serbia; Second Chechen War begins; Putin succeeds Yeltsin	1999	Hussein of Jordan dies; Musharraf seizes power in Pakistan
Russian submarine *Kursk* sinks in Barents Sea; Serb president Milosevic ousted; Hillary Clinton elected senator; "dot.com bubble" bursts	2000	Second Intifada begins; Assad Sr. dies and is succeeded by his son; Al Qaeda bombs USS *Cole* in Aden
Bush succeeds Clinton as president; 9/11 Al Qaeda attack on World Trade Center and the Pentagon; Al Qaeda shoe bomber fails to detonate device on flight from Paris to Miami	2001	Sharon becomes Israeli prime minister; NATO invades Afghanistan; Taliban ousted from power; Pakistani gunmen attack Indian parliament
Britain celebrates Queen's Golden Jubilee; Bush creates Department of Homeland Security	2002	Daniel Pearl kidnapped, tortured, and murdered in Karachi; Bali nightclub bombing

THE WEST		THE EAST
Space shuttle disintegrates during reentry; last flight of *Concorde*; Libyan Lockerbie bomber sentenced to a minimum term of 27 years	**2003**	United States invades Iraq, withdraws troops from Saudi Arabia; Saddam Hussein captured; Riyadh compound bombings trigger harsh Saudi response involving mass arrests; Libya admits to building a nuclear bomb; Musharraf escapes two assassination attempts within two weeks
Jihadis bomb Madrid commuter railways; Blair visits Libya in recognition of Qaddafi's dismantling of Libyan WMD program; George Tenet resigns as CIA head and Colin Powell as Secretary of State; Reagan dies; Chechen terrorists take hostages at North Ossetian school with bloody outcome	**2004**	Abu Ghraib prisoner abuse shocks West and East; Singh becomes Indian prime minister; Karzai wins Afghan elections; United States consulate in Jeddah attacked; tsunami hits southeast Asia
Bush inaugurated for second term; John Paul II dies; Cardinal Ratzinger elected pope; *jihadis* bomb London underground and bus; Provisional IRA formally ends terror campaign; Danish newspaper publishes controversial caricatures of Mohammed	**2005**	King Fahd of Saudi Arabia dies; Ahmadinejad elected president of Iran; Saddam Hussein goes on trial; bombings in Amman; Iranian Hercules crashes into 10-storey Tehran apartment block; Shakidor Dam bursts

THE WEST		THE EAST
Aircraft terrorist plot discovered in UK leads to greatly increased preflight security measures; Pope criticizes Islam, provoking mass protests; global housing bubble peaks and bursts; subprime lending triggers beginning of global financial crisis	**2006**	Israel-Lebanon conflict; Sharon suffers massive stroke; Olmert becomes Israeli prime minister; Saddam Hussein executed; Al Qaeda's Iraq leader Zarqawi killed in air raid; "Islamic State of Iraq" set up by insurgents; Mecca stampede kills 362 *Hajjis*; Ahmadinejad affirms Iranian enriched-uranium production and hosts "International Conference to Review the Global Vision of the Holocaust"
Wildfires break out throughout Greece; Putin announces resumption of Russian strategic bomber patrols	**2007**	Musharraf proclaims state of emergency in Pakistan; Benazir Bhutto assassinated
Fidel Castro resigns; brother Raul is elected Cuban president; Medvedev becomes Russian president; Putin is nominally his prime minister; alleged war criminal Karadzic arrested in Belgrade; South Ossetia War breaks out; Somalian piracy intensifies; global financial crisis pushes Iceland to the brink	**2008**	Taliban attempt on Karzai's life; Musharraf resigns from presidency of Pakistan and is succeeded by Asif Ali Zardari, Benazir Bhutto's widower; Israeli attacks against Gaza; Terorists attack Mumbai
Barack Obama succeeds George W. Bush as president;	**2009**	Israel invades Gaza, then withdraws; financial crisis

(Continued)

THE WEST	THE EAST
Russia in energy dispute with Ukraine; Icelandic economy collapses; devastating bush fires in Australia; H1N1 ("swine flu") virus reaches pandemic proportions; Britain releases Lockerbie bomber to Libya on compassionate grounds	threatens apparently solvent Dubai; widespread protests in Iran after Ahmadinejad rigs re-election; Sri Lankan civil war ends; Uyghurs and Han Chinese clash in western China

DRAMATIS PERSONAE

ABDUL AZIZ IBN SAUD - (1876–1953) ruler and first monarch of Saudi Arabia, who founded the Kingdom of Saudi Arabia as a unified nation in 1932. When oil was struck in 1938, his closest advisor and chief negotiator was **Harry St. John Philby**, father of **Kim Philby**.

ABDULHAMID II - (1842–1918) 34th Sultan of the Ottoman Empire from 1876 until deposed in 1909; the last sultan to rule with absolute power.

ABDULLAH I - (1882–1951) Emir and King of Transjordan (1921–1949) and of Jordan (1949–1951), second son of **Hussein bin Ali**. Abdullah worked closely with **T. E. Lawrence** during the Arab Revolt (1916–1918). Shot dead by a Palestinian gunman in Jerusalem while attending prayers with his grandson, who succeeded him as king.

ABDULMECIT II - (1868–1944) last Caliph of the Ottoman dynasty (1922–1924). Nominally crown prince when the sultanate was abolished in 1922, he was elected Caliph by the Turkish National Assembly.

DEAN ACHESON - (1893–1971) secretary of state under President Truman (1949–1953).

WESLEY ADAMS - (n.d.) Second secretary of the U.S. embassy in Cairo.

KONRAD ADENAUER - (1876–1967) German statesman, conservative politician, and first chancellor of the Federal Republic of Germany (West Germany) (1949–1963).

AGRIPPINA THE YOUNGER - (15–59) fourth wife of Emperor **Claudius** and mother of **Nero**; a beautiful woman with political ambitions and a ruthless streak. Executed by her son, although the various historical accounts of how and why she died differ significantly.

MAHMOOD AHMED - Pakistan Army officer and Director General of the Pakistani ISI who helped bring **Pervez Musharraf** to power.

HAFEZ AL-ASAD - (1930–2000) Former Syrian Air Force fighter pilot who was President of Syria for three decades from 1971.

RIFAAT AL-ASAD - (1937–) Younger brother of **Hafez al-Asad** and former commander of the Syrian Defense Brigades, who played a key role in his brother's takeover of executive power in 1970.

HASSAN AL-BANNA - (1906–1949) Egyptian social and political reformer, founded the Muslim Brotherhood, one of the largest and most influential twentieth-century Muslim revivalist organizations.

SALAH AL-BIZRI - (n.d) Chief of the Syrian General Staff.

ALEXANDER I - (1777–1825) favorite grandson of **Catherine the Great**, ruled Russia during the Napoleonic Wars. An interesting man during his lifetime, his possibly staged death from typhoid fever remains shrouded in mystery, and the location of his body unknown. Godfather to Queen **Victoria,** who was christened "Alexandrina Victoria" in his honor.

ALEXANDER II - (?–1073) born Anselmo da Baggio, known mainly for his tolerant attitude toward unrepentant Jews and for endorsing William the Conqueror's invasion of England in 1066, which helped the Normans pacify the English clergy.

HAROLD ALEXANDER - (1891–1969) British Army officer, commander of British forces in the Middle East (1942–1943); later became the last British governor general of Canada (1946–1952).

MUHAMMAD SHARIF AL-FARUQI - (1891–1920) Arab staff officer in the Ottoman army who played a pivotal role in events leading up to the Arab Revolt by either unintentionally or deliberately misinforming the British as to the extent of Arab preparedness to rise against the Turks.

RASHID ALI AL-GAYLANI - (1892–1965) pro-Nazi politician and former prime minister who mounted an abortive anti-British coup in Iraq in 1941, with support from the Mufti, **Hajj Amin al-Husseini**. After escaping to Tehran, he finally reached Berlin, where he spent the remaining war years under Hitler's protection.

HASSAN AL-HUDAIBI - (n.d.) Judge and supreme guide of the Muslim Brotherhood.

HAJJ AMIN AL-HUSSEINI - (1895–1974) Mufti of Jerusalem and militant leader of Palestinian nationalism during the British mandate and one of the modern Arab world's most controversial figures, who at times cooperated with the British, but who was pro-Nazi and spent most of the Second World War in Berlin.

ALI BIN HUSSEIN - (1879–1935) King of Hejaz and Grand Sharif of Mecca (1924–1925), and later regent of Iraq; eldest son of **Hussein bin Ali**.

MAHMUD ABD AL-LATIF - (n.d.) Muslim Brother who made an attempt on **Nasser**'s life in 1954, for which he was condemned to death and hanged.

HASHIM IBN ABD AL-MANAF - (n.d.) Great-grandfather of the Prophet **Mohammed**

RAGHIB AL-NASHASHIBI - (1881–1951) Palestinian politician, mayor of Jerusalem, and the Mufti's chief rival.

ABDULLAH AL-QAHTANI - (?–1979) co-leader of the 1979 seizure of the Grand Mosque of Mecca, proclaimed by his brother-in-law, **Juhaiman al-Utaibi**, to be the Mahdi, and killed during the two-week battle that ensued.

SHUKRI AL-QUWATLI - (1891–1967) President of Syria from 1943–1949 and 1955–1958.

MUHAMMAD ANWAR AL-SADAT - (1918–1981) 3rd president of Egypt, closely associated with **Nasser,** whose policies he initially embraced but later abandoned by reintroducing a multiparty system. In 1978, together with Menachem Begin of Israel, received the Nobel Peace Prize for negotiating peace between their countries, a move that was to prove hugely unpopular in the Islamic world.

JUHAIMAN AL-UTAIBI - (1936–1980) former Saudi National Guard soldier and militant Wahhabi Islamist who led over 1,000 men in the takeover of the Grand Mosque of Mecca in 1979, after which he was beheaded, along with 66 other insurgents. Justified his action by claiming that the Saudi leadership had lost its legitimacy through corruption and imitation of the West. He was married to the sister of fellow insurgent **Abdullah al-Qahtani**, whom Utaibi had claimed was the Mahdi before seizing the mosque.

MUHAMMAD IBN ABD-AL-WAHHAB - (1703–1792) influential Sunni scholar from Nejd (central Saudi Arabia). Although he never specifically called for a separate school of Islamic thought, it is from al-Wahhab that the term Wahhabism was coined to designate the ultraconservative form of Islam observed predominantly in Saudi Arabia.

HELMUT ALLARDT - (1907–1987) West German career diplomat and jurist, who investigated the situation with German advisors in Egypt in 1953 and submitted a whitewash report.

YIGAL ALLON - (1918–1980) Israeli politician, Palmach commander, and general in the IDF.

JULIAN AMERY - (1919–1996) British army officer and politician, militantly anticommunist and strongly supportive of Eden's policy over Suez. Son of **Leo Amery**, he was married to **Harold Macmillan**'s daughter and was a close friend of **Billy MacLean**.

LEO AMERY - (1873–1955) politician, journalist, and mountaineer, a school acquaintance of **Winston Churchill**, with whom he was associated throughout his career, although they frequently disagreed. Father of **Julian Amery**.

ROBERT AMORY - (1915–1989) Harvard University law professor who became CIA Deputy Director of Intelligence in 1952.

WLADYSLAW ANDERS - (1892–1970) Free Polish army officer who in 1941 led an army of Polish and Jewish soldiers (and many civilians) out of the Soviet Union into the Middle East, where they were retrained and formed the 2nd Polish Corps in the Italian campaign under Anders's command. Later C-in-C of all Free Polish forces.

L. Y. ANDREWS - (n.d.) District commissioner of Galilee killed by Arab extremists in 1937.

CECILIA ANGLETON - (n.d.) Wife of **James Jesus Angleton.**

JAMES JESUS ANGLETON - (1917–1987) career intelligence officer and head of CIA counterintelligence operations for over two decades (1954–1975).

AHMAD ARABI (URABI) - (1841–1911) Egyptian army officer who led the Urabi Revolt of 1879 against the Khedive and Turkish influence in the Egyptian military. Finally defeated by the British at the battle of Tel el-Kebir in 1882, after which he spent many years in exile in Ceylon (Sri Lanka).

TUVYA ARAZI - (n.d.) Yishuv intelligence officer in Syria and Lebanon.

SHLOMO ARGOV - (1929–2003) Israeli ambassador to the UK whose assassination was ordered by **Saddam Hussein.**

MUSTAPHA KEMAL ATATURK - (1881–1938) Turkish army officer, revolutionary statesman, and founder and 1st president of the Republic of Turkey from 1923 until his death. Subscribed to the ideals of the Enlightenment and sought to transform the remnants of Ottoman Turkey into a modern, secular democracy.

ZE'EV AVNI - (1920–2007) Israeli diplomat who operated in the 1950s as a KGB mole in Mossad. He was caught in 1956 and imprisoned.

GUS AVRAKOTOS - (1938–2005) Greek-American CIA case officer who was principally involved in organizing and arming the Afghan mujahidin in their struggle against the Soviet Union.

ABDULLAH YUSUF AZZAM - (1941–1989) highly influential Islamic scholar and theologian; taught and mentored **Osama bin Laden;** assassinated in Pakistan.

BERNHARD BAATZ - (1910–1978) SS officer indicted for war crimes in Poland, together with **Joachim Deumling** and others, in the so-called RSHA Trial in 1967–1968.

NASEERULLAH BABAR - (1928–). Pakistani Army officer who served as **Benazir Bhutto**'s interior minister 1993–1996. and who is thought by some to have been the mastermind behind the Taliban.

ROBERT "BOB" BAER - (1952–) American author and former CIA field officer in the MiddleEast.

KHALID BAKDASH - (1912–1995) Syrian Communist Party leader from 1936 until his death.

TAIMOUR BAKHTIAR - (1914–1970) Iranian general and ruthless founding head of SAVAK 1958–1961, assassinated by a SAVAK agent while hunting in Iraq.

ARTHUR BALFOUR - (1848–1930) prime minister of the U.K. (1902–1905); later as foreign secretary authored the Balfour Declaration of 1917, which supported the establishment of a Jewish homeland in Palestine.

EVELYN BARKER - (1894–1983) British Army officer and commander of British forces in the Palestine mandate from 1946 to 1947; miraculously survived many attempts on his life by the Irgun and the Stern Gang, even after he left Palestine.

WALTER BEDELL SMITH - (1895–1961) U.S. Army officer, chief of staff during **Eisenhower**'s tenure at SHAEF, ambassador to the Soviet Union (1946–1948), and director of the CIA (1950–1953).

YISRAEL BEER (BAR) - (1912–1966) Israeli army officer and professor of Military History at Tel Aviv University who was a close friend of **Shimon Peres** but also a Soviet agent. He was convicted of espionage in 1961 and died in prison.

MENACHEM BEGIN - (1913–1995) Israeli politician and head of the Irgun (1943–1948); later prime minister (1977–1983).

ELIAHU BEIT-ZURI - (1922–1945) member of the Stern Gang, hanged in Cairo for the assassination of **Lord Moyne**.

GERTRUDE BELL - (1868–1926) archaeologist, linguist, writer, photographer, traveler, political analyst, and colonial administrator; as Arab Bureau liaison officer she became a friend of **T. E. Lawrence**, an associate of **Percy Cox**, and field controller of **Harry St. John Philby**. Bell was partly if not largely responsible for the birth of the Iraqi nation.

DAVID BEN-GURION - (1886–1973) a passionate Russian Zionist who emigrated to Palestine in 1906; was the first prime minister of Israel 1948–1953 and 1955–1963. After retirement from politics, he lived the rest of his life on a kibbutz in the Negev desert.

ELYASHIV BEN-HORIN - (n.d.) Israeli diplomat who tried to recruit Arabs in the United States as Israeli espionage agents.

FOLKE BERNADOTTE - (1895–1948) Swedish diplomat assassinated by the Stern Gang while on a U.N. assignment in Jerusalem.

EMIL BERNDORFF - (1892–1968) SS officer indicted for war crimes in Poland, together with **Joachim Deumling** and others, in the so-called RSHA Trial in 1967–1968.

ERNEST BEVIN - (1881–1951) British Labour leader, politician, and statesman best known as Britain's wartime minister of labour and postwar foreign secretary. Bitterly opposed to violent Zionist dissidents, like the Irgun and the Stern Gang, and advocated for an independent Arab Palestinian state.

BENAZIR BHUTTO - (1953–2007) Harvard and Oxford-educated prime minister of Pakistan for two terms (1988–1990 and 1993–1996) and eldest daughter of **Zulfikar Ali Bhutto**. Al-Qaeda claimed responsibility for her assassination.

ZULFIKAR ALI BHUTTO - (1928–1979) Berkeley and Oxford-educated foreign minister, president, and prime minister of Pakistan between 1963 and 1977 and father of **Benazir Bhutto**. Sentenced to death and executed under the regime of his successor, military dictator **Muhammad Zia-ul-Haq**.

SAYYID HUSSEIN BIN ALI - (1854–1931) Sharif and Emir of Mecca (1908–1917); King of Hejaz (1917–1924, abdicated).

OSAMA BIN LADEN - (1957–) Saudi-born founder of the jihadist organization al-Qaeda, generally considered responsible for worldwide terrorist activities including the destruction of the World Trade Center in New York on September 11, 2001.

OTTO VON BISMARCK - (1815–1898) Prussian and German statesman known as the "Iron Chancellor" who succeeded in unifying Germany, which had hitherto consisted of hundreds of autonomous principalities and free cities; after unification, Germany became one of Europe's Great Powers and began seeking its "place in the sun," which had the ultimate effect of uniting the other Great Powers (with the exception of Austria-Hungary) against it.

BOHEMOND I - (1058–1111) led the First Crusade (1095–1099), capturing Antioch in 1098 and establishing a Frankish (Norman) monarchy there, which outlasted Norman rule in Europe.

CHARLES "CHIP" BOHLEN - (1904–1974) career diplomat and Soviet expert, served as U.S. ambassador to the Soviet Union (1953–1957). Did not get along well with **John Foster Dulles**.

JOHN BOKER - (n.d.) CIC (Counter Intelligence Corps) officer to whom **Reinhard Gehlen** surrendered in 1945.

SUBHA CHANDRA BOSE - (1897–1945) Indian politician and leader of the pro-Nazi Indian National Army (INA).

WILFRIED BÖSE - (1949–1976) Member of the West German left-wing terrorist group Revolutionäre Zellen (RZ), killed in 1976 in the famous Israeli raid on Entebbe airport,

Uganda. Along with **Brigitte Kuhlmann**, one of two German and six Palestinian hijackers of an Air France flight from Tel Aviv via Athens to Paris.

REGINALD J. BOWKER - (n.d.) British diplomat.

NORMAN N. E. BRAY - (1885–1962) Indian Army and RAF officer, intelligence officer, historian, and biographer.

JOHN BUCHAN - (1875–1940) colonial administrator, intelligence officer, politician, and novelist; as Lord Tweedsmuir became 15th governor-general of Canada in 1935.

WILLIAM FRANCIS BUCKLEY - (1928–1985) U.S. Army officer and CIA station chief in Beirut, kidnapped by Hezbollah in 1984 and later executed by Islamic Jihad.

WILLIAM C. BULLITT - (1891–1961) brilliant, wealthy U.S. diplomat, journalist, writer, and outspoken anticommunist and antifascist. FDR made him the first U.S. ambassador to the Soviet Union in 1933.

FRANZ BÜNSCH - (n.d.) Anti-Semitic Nazi propagandist and expert on "Jewish affairs"; worked as part of **Nasser**'s anti-Zionist propaganda apparatus.

GEORGE H. W. BUSH - (1924–) 41st president of the United States (1989–1993).

GEORGE W. BUSH - (1946–) 43rd president of the United States (2001–2009).

JEFFERSON CAFFERY - (1886–1974) U.S. career diplomat, ambassador to Egypt (1949–1955).

CARLOS THE JACKAL - Alias of **Ilich Remírez Sánchez** (1949–), convicted Venezuelan Marxist terrorist and murderer, in 1997 jailed for life in France. He is since said to have converted to Islam.

CARMEL OFFIE - (n.d.) Confidential secretary to and close associate of William C. Bullitt. Left State Department in disgrace in 1947 and joined the OPC (Office of Policy Coordination), where he became a close friend of Frank Wisner and ran Operations Paperclip and Bloodstone.

LORD CARODON - See **Hugh Mackintosh Foot.**

JIMMY CARTER - (1924–) 39th president of the United States (1977–1981).

CATHERINE THE GREAT - (1729–1796) minor Prussian princess who ruled Russia as Catherine II for 34 years during a period of significant growth in Russian influence, culture, and territory. Subscribed to the ideals of the Enlightenment and had a reputation as a patron of the arts, literature, and education. Is also reputed to have had many lovers.

WALTER J. CAWTHORN - (1896–1970) Deputy Chief of Staff of the Pakistan Army, as well as Secretary of the Pakistan Joint Services Commanders' Committee, who established the ISI.

AUSTEN CHAMBERLAIN - (1863–1937) statesman, politician, and recipient of the Nobel Peace Prize for his part in the negotiations over the Locarno Pact of 1925.

WINSTON CHURCHILL - (1874–1965), prime minister of U.K. during the Second World War, held many political offices between 1910 and 1955, always retaining enormous influence even when out of office.

CLAUDIUS I - (10 B.C.–54) **Nero**'s stepfather, he ruled the Roman Empire from A.D. 41 until his death, which may have been natural or by assassination. An able administrator who endowed Rome and the provinces with many fine public works; a prolific author of histories and other books, regrettably none of which has survived.

ILTYD NICHOLL CLAYTON - (1886–1965) British Army officer and head of British military intelligence in Cairo early in the Second World War. Subsequently served as advisor on Arab affairs to the British government.

GILBERT CLAYTON - (1875–1929) British Army officer, Arab Bureau officer, and colonial administrator. While colleagues and subordinates such as **T. E. Lawrence** achieved worldwide fame, the confidential nature of Clayton's successive offices necessarily obscured the importance of his achievements. Clayton's premature death during a polo match cut short a distinguished career of great promise.

CLEOPATRA VII PHILOPATOR - (69–30 B.C.) Hellenistic pharaoh who ruled Egypt from 51 B.C. until her death. Famous for her political skill, great beauty, and disingenuous liaisons with two famous Romans: Julius Caesar and Mark Antony.

CHARLES CLEVELAND - (1866–1929) Legendary head of the Indian secret service, with a brilliant mind, a larger-than-life physique, and a matching personality. Recruited **Norman N. E. Bray.**

WILLIAM JEFFERSON "BILL" CLINTON - (1946–) 42nd President of the United States from 1993 to 2001.

WILLIAM COLBY - (1920–1996) career intelligence officer and director of the CIA (1973–1976).

MICHAEL COLLINS - (1890–1922) Irish revolutionary leader, politician, and IRA director of intelligence, shot and killed during the Irish Civil War.

ARTHUR CONOLLY - (1807–1842) Indian Army officer, intelligence officer, explorer, and writer who completed many reconnaissance missions in Central Asia during the Great Game (he probably invented the term) and who, like **Charles Stoddart**, was captured and executed by **Nasrullah Khan**.

CONRAD OF MONTFERRAT - (ca.1145–1192) one of the leaders of the Third Crusade (1189–1192); became king of Jerusalem and was famously assassinated by the Hashshashin. Married **Isabella I of Jerusalem** after her scheming mother had forced her to separate from her loving but unambitious husband, **Humphrey of Toron**.

CONSTANTINE THE GREAT - (272–337) first Christian Roman emperor; proclaimed religious tolerance throughout the empire and made Constantinople the capital of Byzantium.

CARLTON S. COON - (1904–1981) U.S. anthropologist and OSS officer involved in North African espionage and the smuggling of arms to French resistance groups in German-occupied Morocco under the guise of anthropological fieldwork.

MILES COPELAND - (1916–1991) musician, businessman, and career intelligence officer; one of the original OSS (Office of Strategic Services) counterintelligence officers in the Second World War; later participated in major CIA political operations from the 1950s through to the 1980s.

PERCY COX - (1864–1937) Indian Army officer and diplomatist; closely associated with **Gertrude Bell**; replaced **Sir Arnold Wilson** as administrator of Iraq.

RICHARD CROSSMAN - (1907–1974) socialist politician, author, and editor of the *New Statesman*; a leading Zionist and anticommunist.

EFRAIM DAFNY - (n.d.) First Jewish volunteer from Palestine to parachute into Yugoslavia in March 1943.

ALBERT D'ÁIX - (n.d.) Chronicler of the First Crusade (1095–1099) on whose writings **William of Tyre** based much of his Crusade history.

MOSHE DAYAN - (1915–1981) Israeli general and Palmach commander, who became defense minister and foreign minister of Israel.

VALÉRY GISCARD D'ÉSTAING - (1926–) 20th president of France (1974–1981).

JOACHIM DEUMLING - (1910–2007) SS (SD) and Police lieutenant colonel and indicted war criminal; the foremost intelligence and security expert in **Nasser**'s Egypt.

XHAFER DEVA - (1904–1978) Albanian interior minister during the Nazi occupation.

BENJAMIN DISRAELI - (1804–1881) Tory statesman and literary figure, served twice as

British prime minister between 1868 and 1880, known for his rivalry with **William Gladstone** and warm friendship with Queen Victoria.

WILLIAM DONOVAN - (1883–1959) U.S. Army officer, establishment lawyer, and intelligence officer, nicknamed "Wild Bill," who headed the Office of Strategic Services (OSS), forerunner of the CIA, during the Second World War.

HASSAN DOSTI - (1894–1991) Albanian justice minister during the Italian occupation.

LARISSA DUBANOVA - (n.d.) Alias of KGB agent who ensnared Royal Canadian Mounted Police officer **Roy Guidon** in a honey trap.

ALLEN DULLES - (1893–1969) lawyer, diplomat, and career intelligence officer; rose to become the first civilian director of the CIA (1953–1961). Younger brother of **John Foster Dulles**.

JOHN FOSTER DULLES - (1888–1959) secretary of state under Eisenhower (1953–1959). Older brother of **Allen Dulles**.

ABBA (AUBREY) EBAN - (1915–2002) Israeli diplomat and politician, and former South African Army officer who served in Palestine as liaison officer between the Special Operations Executive (SOE) and the Haganah.

ANTHONY EDEN - (1897–1977) controversial British prime minister (1955–1957) whose reputation rests largely on his highly skilled performance as **Churchill**'s foreign secretary before and during the Second World War and was severely damaged by his conduct of the Suez campaign in 1956.

HERMANN EILTS - (1922–2006) U.S. ambassador to Saudi Arabia and Egypt; worked with **Sadat** throughout the Camp David Accords.

DWIGHT EISENHOWER - (1890–1969) U.S. Army officer (Supreme Allied Commander [Europe] in the Second World War) and 34th president of the United States (1953–1961).

ROLF ENGEL - (1912–1993) celebrated German rocket scientist who worked at Skoda with **Wilhelm Voss** during the war on liquid and solid fuel rockets and later developed missiles for **Nasser**.

ENVER PASHA - (1881–1922) also known as Ismail Enver, the most famous of the "Three Pashas" who ruled the Ottoman Empire during the Balkan Wars and the First World War (the others were Talat Pasha and Cemal Pasha).

JOHN EWART - (1861–1930) War Office director of military operations and intelligence; a keen supporter of establishing a Secret Service Bureau before the First World War.

WILHELM FAHRMBACHER - (1888–1970) German army officer and one of **Rommel**'s top generals; headed the first contingent of German military advisors to Egypt (1950–1959).

JOHN FARMER - (n.d.) Wartime SOE (Special Operations Executive) officer and career SIS (Secret Intelligence Service) officer.

FAROUK I - (1920–1965) penultimate king of Egypt and Sudan, succeeding his father, Fuad I, in 1936; deposed by the Free Officers revolt and exiled in 1952.

ROY FARRAN - (1921–2006) British army officer, politician, farmer, and author who served in the SAS (Special Air Service) during the Second World War and in Palestine after the war, where he encountered major difficulties with the Stern Gang, ultimately emigrating to Alberta, Canada, where he became a prominent provincial cabinet minister (1971–1979).

FAYSAL BIN ABDUL AZIZ - (1903–1975) king of Saudi Arabia from 1964 until his death; third son of **Abdul Aziz ibn Saud**. Assassinated by his half-brother's son, who was deemed insane but was nevertheless found guilty of regicide and beheaded.

FEISAL I - (1883–1933), king of Iraq from 1921 until his death; third son of Sharif **Hussein bin Ali**. During the Arab Revolt in the First World War, closely supported by **T. E. Lawrence**, and subsequently by **Gertrude Bell**.

BERNARD FERGUSSON - (1911–1980) British army officer who was assistant inspector-general of the Palestine police force (1946–1947). Later governor-general of New Zealand (1962–1967), like his father and both his grandfathers before him.

J. B. FLUX - (n.d.) First secretary for commercial affairs at the British embassy in Cairo, where he began service in 1919. One of two British diplomats (the other was **J. G. Gove**) expelled from Egypt by **Nasser** for their alleged involvement in espionage at the time of the ANA raid and arrests in 1956.

HUGH MACKINTOSH FOOT - (1907–1990) **Lord Carodon,** Britain's last governor of Cyprus.

FREDERICK II - (1194–1250) unlike the militaristic German emperor Frederick I Barbarossa, Frederick II was an enlightened Sicilian who ruled as emperor for thirty years until his death, living mostly with his mother in Palermo as an avid patron of the arts. Despite papal opposition, he led the Sixth Crusade (1228–1229) to the Holy Land, which ended in a bloodless victory, ten years of peace, and considerable Muslim discontent.

GRAHAM E. FULLER - (n.d.) U.S. State Department and CIA officer for 27 years, including a term as CIA station chief in Kabul, Afghanistan, now affiliated with Simon Fraser University as an adjunct history professor.

MAHATMA GANDHI - (1869–1948) political and spiritual leader of India, who pioneered the concept of nonviolent civil disobedience, which ultimately led India to independence.

ROBERT GASCOYNE-CECIL - (1830–1903), Marquess of Salisbury, foreign secretary under **Benjamin Disraeli,** and prime minister of the U.K. for over thirteen years between 1885 and 1902.

DHARMINDRA GAUR - (n.d.) Indian Special Operations Executive (SOE) officer during the Second World War.

NAWAF GHAZALEH - (n.d.) Syrian Druze who assassinated **Adib Shishkali** in 1964.

REINHARD GEHLEN - (1902–1979) German army officer and military intelligence chief on the Russian Front during the Second World War, after which he became head of West German intelligence until 1968.

WILLIAM GLADSTONE - (1809–1898) four times Liberal prime minister of U.K. between 1868 and 1894, nicknamed the GOM (Grand Old Man); famous for his political and personal rivalry with the Tory **Benjamin Disraeli** and his tense relationship with Queen Victoria.

LEOPOLD GLEIM - (n.d.) Former SS colonel who worked in Egypt as **Joachim Deumling**'s assistant and security expert.

SIR JOHN GLUBB - (1897–1986) British Army officer who commanded the Transjordanian Arab Legion (1939–1956). Better known as Glubb Pasha.

CHARLES GORDON - (1833–1885) British Army officer and colonial administrator, known variously as "Chinese Gordon" (he commanded a Chinese army brilliantly in the 1860s), "Gordon Pasha" (he was governor of Sudan), and "Gordon of Khartoum," where he was killed in close combat with the Mahdi's warriors.

J. G. GOVE - (n.d.) Head of the visa section at the British embassy in Cairo. One of two British diplomats (the other was **J. B. Flux**) expelled from Egypt by Nasser at the time of the ANA raid and arrests in 1956.

BILLY GRAHAM - (1918–) U.S. Christian (Baptist) evangelist with universal charismatic appeal.

VICTOR GRAYEVSKI - (n.d.) Polish Zionist journalist who covertly supplied Israel with a copy of **Nikita Khruschev**'s anti-Stalin speech in 1956.

GREGORY VII - (1020–1085) born Hildebrand of Soana, canonized in 1728 as Saint Gregory, one of the great reformers of the papacy.

EDWARD GREY - (1862–1933) statesman, diplomat, and ornithologist; foreign secretary for eleven continuous years (1905–1916): an unbroken record.

ANDREI GROMYKO - (1909–1989) Soviet foreign minister (1957–1985) and Chairman of the Supreme Soviet until 1988, when he was succeeded by Mikhail Gorbachev.

COLIN GUBBINS - (1896–1976) British Army officer and SOE (Special Operations Executive) director of operations and training, the prime mover of SOE during the Second World War; described as one of the war's unsung heroes.

ROY GUIDON - (n.d.) Soviet mole in the RCMP unmasked by Israeli intelligence.

WALTER GUINNESS - (1880–1944) Anglo-Irish politician and businessman who, as **Lord Moyne**, was assassinated in Cairo by the Stern Gang.

HAMID GUL - (1936–) Pakistan Army officer and Director General of the Pakistani ISI under **Benazir Bhutto**, Gul was a devout Muslim from the Punjab with close ties to the Saudis.

GABRIEL HADDAD - (n.d.) Christian Arab advisor to **Ronald Storrs**.

JOHN HADDEN - (n.d.) CIA station chief in Tel Aviv.

ELIAHU HAKIM - (1925–1945) member of the Stern Gang, hanged in Cairo for the assassination of **Lord Moyne**.

SAIYID S. HAMID - (n.d.) Former Indian Military Secretary and Director of the Pakistan National Guard, who became the first director of the Pakistani ISI.

NICK HAMMOND - (1907–2001) Special Operations Executive (SOE) liaison officer with the Arab Platoon in Palestine.

MAURICE HANKEY - (1877–1963) Royal Marines officer and civil servant, cabinet secretary for twenty-six years (1912–1938); highly respected official, Hankey also undertook, as a very young subaltern, unofficial and unpaid intelligence work, an activity he maintained to the end of his public life and beyond.

ISSER HAREL - (1912–2003) Mossad officer who later became director 1952–1963.

BASIL LIDDELL HART - (1895–1970) British soldier, journalist, and military historian. Hart was knighted in 1966.

HASAN-AS-SABAH - (1056–1124) Persian Nizari-Ismaili (Shia) missionary who founded the quasi-religious political cult of the Hashshashin (Hashishiyan), who were trained to assassinate Sunnis.

URGUPLU HAYRI BEY - (n.d.) Sheikulislam (Muslim Patriarch) of the Ottoman Empire and minister of religious affairs under the Committee of Union and Progress (or Young Turk) regime of 1913–1918. Father of Ali Suat Hayri Urguplu, who served briefly as Turkish prime minister in 1965.

MOHAMED HEIKAL - (1923–) leading Egyptian journalist, former editor of the Cairo newspaper *Al-Ahram*; longtime friend of **Nasser** and **Sadat**.

RICHARD HELMS - (1913–2002) naval officer and director of the CIA (1966–1973) who served in the OSS (Office of Strategic Services) during the Second World War and ran OSO (Office of Special Operations) operations in Austria, Germany, and Switzerland immediately after the war.

HENRY II OF CHAMPAGNE - (1166–1197) one of the leaders of the Third Crusade (1189–1192); succeeded **Conrad of Montferrat** as King of Jerusalem and married **Conrad**'s widow, **Isabella I of Jerusalem**, only eight days after the Hashashshin assassination.

OTTO VON HENTIG - (1886–1984) German diplomat who achieved fame during the First World War for his mission to Afghanistan in 1915 and who functioned as a Middle East expert in Ribbentrop's Foreign Office during the Second World War.

HERACLIUS - (575–641) Byzantine emperor of the Roman Empire, thought to be the first to engage the Muslims.

AUBREY HERBERT - (1880–1923) diplomat, traveler, and intelligence officer who worked for the Arab Bureau and was a friend of **T. E. Lawrence**, **Sir Mark Sykes,** and **John Buchan**. An extremely adventurous man, despite being nearly blind from birth.

CHAIM HERZOG - (1918–1997) Israeli military attaché in Washington, who was twice head of Israeli military intelligence (Aman) 1948–1950 and 1959–1962. Herzog later served as president of Israel for ten years (1983–1993).

REINHARD HEYDRICH - (1904–1942) German SS officer who from 1941 governed what remained of Czechoslovakia (Reich Protectorate of Bohemia and Moravia) while remaining in charge of the Berlin HQ of the SS (Reich Security Main Office). He was attacked by Czech partisans on May 27, 1942, and fatally wounded. The Nazis avenged Heydrich's death by annihilating the Bohemian villages of Lidice and Lezaky.

HEINRICH HIMMLER - (1900–1945) immensely powerful Nazi politician and Reichsführer-SS, C-in-C of the SS, who oversaw all Nazi police and security forces (1929–1945) and coordinated the Nazi genocide, presiding over concentration camps, extermination camps, death squads, and a vast business empire.

SAMI HINNAWI - (1898–1950) Syrian Army colonel who seized power in Syria in 1949 only to be displaced by **Adib Shishakli** and murdered in Lebanese exile.

ADOLF HITLER - (1889–1945) Austrian-born politician and genocidal fascist dictator of Germany from 1933 until his suicide who plunged the world into the conflagration of the Second World War.

J. C. HOLLAND - (1897–1956) British Army officer and expert on irregular warfare who is credited with inventing the concept of the commando and who helped **Colin Gubbins** organize and operate the Special Operations Executive SOE during the Second World War.

WILLIAM HOOD - (1920–) journalist, novelist, and former OSS counterintelligence officer with **Allen Dulles** in Switzerland, who later became a close friend of and deputy to **James Jesus Angleton** at the CIA.

ENVER HOXHA - (1908–1985) Marxist-Leninist-Maoist ruler of Albania from 1944 until his death who for forty years effectively sealed his country off from the rest of Europe.

HUMPHREY OF TORON - (1166–1197) first husband of **Isabella I of Jerusalem** with whom he grew up as a child and whom he married when she was eleven years old.

SADDAM HUSSEIN - (1937–2006) notoriously brutal Ba'athist ruler of Iraq who aggressively resisted foreign intervention in the Middle East and advocated for Palestinian independence. Tried, convicted, and hanged for ordering the mass killing of Shiites in 1982.

HUSSEIN BIN TALAL - (1935–1999) became king of Jordan in 1952 and succeeded in guiding his country through four decades of Arab-Israeli conflict, mostly in the context of the Cold War.

HUSSEIN BIN ALI - (1854–1931) Hashemite Grand Sharif of Mecca, ruled Hejaz as part of the Ottoman Empire until 1924, when he was defeated by **Abdul Aziz ibn Saud** and abdicated all his titles in favor of his eldest son, Ali.

MUHAMMAD AHMAD IBN ABD ALLAH - (1844–1885), otherwise known as the Mahdi, Ahmad proclaimed himself the prophesied redeemer of Islam and in 1881 led a bloody and victorious jihad against the Egyptians (and British) in Sudan. Thirteen years after his death, what was left of his army was annihilated by the British at the battle of Omdurman.

KHALID IBN MANSUR IBN LUWAY - (n.d.) Fiercely independent Wahhabi Sharif of Khurma (Hejaz), an important Saudi trade center, who generally supported **Abdul Aziz ibn Saud** in his struggles with the Hashemites, but on his own terms.

ABDULLAHI IBN MUHAMMAD - (1846–1899), otherwise known as the Khalifa, an able general who succeeded Muhammad Ahmad ibn Abd Allah (the Mahdi) in 1885. After his defeat by the British at the battle of Omdurman, he was pursued and killed by Wingate's troops at Umm Diwaikarat.

IBN RASHID - (1900–1920) Saud bin Abdul Aziz was Emir of Hail from age ten and constantly in conflict with **Abdul Aziz ibn Saud**, whom he never succeeded in defeating militarily. After Rashid's assassination by a cousin, **Abdul Aziz ibn Saud** married two of his wives, one of whom gave birth to the future King Abdullah of Saudi Arabia.

ISMET INÖNÜ - (1884–1973) Turkish army officer, prime minister, and 2nd president of the Turkish Republic, also known as Milli Sef (National Chief).

ISABELLA I OF JERUSALEM - (1172–1205) described as "exceedingly fair and lovely," she married four times, her second, third, and fourth husbands, all kings of Jerusalem, were **Conrad of Montferrat**, **Henry II of Champagne**, and Amalric II.

ISMAIL PASHA - (1830–1895), also known as Ismail the Magnificent; Khedive of Egypt and Sudan from 1863 to 1879, when he was removed by the British and the French.

IVAN THE TERRIBLE - (1530–1584) first czar of Russia was intelligent and devout but mentally unstable. Despite the mistranslated epithet associated with his name ("Fearsome" would be more accurate), he was not a particularly cruel ruler but tended to bully his subjects and was given to terrifying outbursts of apoplectic rage. His death is mysterious; it is possible that he was poisoned by Boris Godunov, who became czar fourteen years later.

SALAH JADID - (1926–1993) Syrian general and Baathist politician who became de facto head of the Syrian government for four years until deposed in 1970.

CLAUDE JARVIS - (1879–1953) British Army officer, colonial administrator, and orientalist who served in Egypt and Palestine during the First World War, later becoming a legendary governor in Libya and Sinai with an intimate knowledge of Bedouin customs and law. He was also a prolific author and gifted painter.

MOHAMMED ALI JINNAH - (1976–1948), politician and statesman, leader of the Muslim League and founder of the state of Pakistan.

ABOL-GASHEM KASHANI - (1882–1962) Iranian Shiite ayatollah and populist politician.

JOHN KAYE - (1814–1876) Indian Army officer, colonial administrator, novelist, and military historian who was partly responsible (as well as **Rudyard Kipling**) for popularizing **Arthur Conolly**'s term the "Great Game."

GEORGE F. KENNAN - (1904–2005) U.S. diplomat, political scientist, and historian who dispatched his "Long Telegram" from Moscow to Washington in 1946 highlighting the expansionist nature of Soviet foreign policy and the need for its strategic containment.

KHALID BIN ABDUL AZIZ - (1912–1982) king of Saudi Arabia from 1975 until his death, he was easygoing and apolitical, and willingly allowed his ultimate successor, Fahd, to govern the country. Died of a heart attack.

MAHMUD KHALIL - (n.d.) Head of Egyptian air force intelligence recruited by the SIS (Secret Intelligence Service) as a double agent in an attempt to topple **Nasser** and restore the Egyptian monarchy.

AYUB KHAN - (1907–1974) Pakistan Army commander and first military ruler of the country (1958–1969).

LIAQUAT ALI KHAN - (1896–1951) lawyer, politician, and right-hand man of **Mohammed Ali Jinnah**, who become the first prime minister of Pakistan from 1947 until his assassination.

HUSSEIN KHAYRI - (n.d.) King **Farouk**'s deputy head of Egyptian military intelligence.

RUHOLLAH MUSAVI KHOMEINI - (1902–1989) Iranian politician, scholar, religious leader, and political leader of the 1979 revolution that overthrew the Shah.

DAVID KIMCHE - (1928–) British-born Israeli diplomat and writer who was a Mossad intelligence officer and became DG of the Israeli foreign ministry under **Menachem Begin.**

NIKITA KHRUSHCHEV - (1894–1971) first secretary of the Soviet Communist Party and Soviet premier (1953–1964) at the height of the Cold War. A reformer who, despite his abrasive, pugnacious personality and international saber rattling, effectively de-Stalinized the Soviet Union and introduced a more liberal agricultural, industrial, and foreign policy regime.

RUDYARD KIPLING - (1865–1936) author, poet, and Nobel laureate, one of the most popular writers of late-nineteenth/early-twentieth century English literature, whose principal subject was the British Empire in all its aspects.

HORATIO KITCHENER - (1850–1916) soldier, diplomat, and statesman, famous for his decisive victory over the Mahdi at the battle of Omdurman in 1896, but later notorious for his brutality during the Boer War.

ABRAHAM MARCUS KLINGBERG - (1918–) Epidemiologist who was a Soviet agent in Israel sentenced in 1983 to twenty years' imprisonment for espionage.

ARTHUR KOESTLER - (1905–1983) prolific Hungarian-British author of political commentary and fiction, whose life was controversial and troubled, and whose various causes included communism, anticommunism, and Zionism.

THEODOR "TEDDY" KOLLEK - (1911–2007) Austrian-born, pro-British Israeli agent who worked for the British Security Service (MI5) and knew **Kim Philby**. He became a successful politician and was mayor of Jerusalem for twenty-eight years.

BRIGITTE KUHLMANN - (1947–1976) Member of the West German left-wing terrorist group Revolutionäre Zellen (RZ), killed in 1976 in the famous Israeli raid on Entebbe airport, Uganda. Along with **Wilfried Böse,** she was one of two German and six Palestinian hijackers of an Air France flight flying from Tel Aviv via Athens to Paris.

ABAS KUPI - (n.d.) British choice to be head of the Albanian government-in-exile; Nazi collaborator during the Second World War.

ESHREF KUSHCHUBASHI - (1873–1964) Leading member of **Enver Pasha**'s secret service.

MILES LAMPSON - (1880–1964) British career diplomat who served for many years in Egypt and the Sudan (1934–1946), ultimately as high commissioner and ambassador.

HERMANN LAUTERBACHER - (1909–1988) Nazi gauleiter and deputy head of the Hitler Youth who later became **Reinhard Gehlen**'s liaison officer with the Nazi diaspora in **Nasser**'s Egypt.

HENRY MONTGOMERY LAWRENCE - (1806–1857) British artillery officer and political agent to the Governor-General for the North West Frontier. Killed at the Siege of Lucknow during the Indian Mutiny.

T. E. LAWRENCE - (1888–1935) British army officer and Arab Bureau intelligence officer, famous as Lawrence of Arabia for his liaison role during the Arab Revolt of 1916–1818.

AUSTEN LAYARD - (1817–1894) archaeologist, diplomatist, and politician. Layard was British ambassador to the Ottoman Empire (1877–1880).

MARGUERITE "MISSY" LEHAND - (1898–1944) private secretary to Franklin D. Roosevelt and his close companion for many years.

TOM LITTLE - (1911–1975) head of the Arab News Agency (ANA), correspondent for *The Economist* and *The Times,* and senior SIS (Secret Intelligence Service) officer in Cairo.

JOHN BRUCE LOCKHART - (1914–1995) intelligence officer, educator, and rugby player, who succeeded **Kim Philby** as liaison officer in Washington, where he successfully repaired much of the damage done to the "special relationship" by Philby; later he was responsible for SIS operations in the Middle East at the time of the Suez Crisis.

FRANCIS B. LOOMIS - (1861–1948) U.S. newspaperman, diplomat, and public servant who served as foreign trade advisor to Standard Oil.

JOSEPH MCCARTHY - (1908–1957) U.S. politician who achieved notoriety as an obsessive investigator of suspected communists during the 1950s. His career was ultimately ruined after being formally censured by the U.S. Senate, and he died of alcoholism, aged only forty-eight.

FITZROY MACLEAN - (1911–1996) SAS (Special Air Service) officer, diplomatist, politician, adventurer, and writer, whose possible covert work as a British agent is to this day fiercely denied by those who knew him well. Not to be confused with **Billy McLean**.

HAROLD MACMILLAN - (1894–1986) British prime minister (1957–1963) whose warm friendship with **Eisenhower** helped him repair Anglo-American relations after the Suez Crisis. "Supermac," as he was known, was **Julian Amery**'s father-in-law.

TERENCE MACSWINEY - (1879–1920) Irish politician, writer, and lord mayor of Cork, who died on hunger strike while serving a two-year term for sedition in Brixton Prison, thus becoming an IRA martyr.

MAKARIOS III - (1913–1977) Archbishop and Primate of the Cypriot Orthodox Church and 1st/4th president of the Republic of Cyprus.

ADNAN MALKI - (1918–1955) Deputy Chief-of-Staff of the Syrian Army who led a coup in Syria in 1954 and was assassinated the following year.

FADLALLAH ABU MANSUR - (n.d.) Junior officer involved in the **Hannawi** coup in Syria.

MAO ZEDONG - (1893–1976) military and political leader of People's Republic of China from its establishment in 1949 until his death.

VICTOR MARCHETTI - (1930–) U.S. soldier who joined the CIA in 1955 and became a Soviet expert, rising to the position of chief Soviet analyst and assistant to **Richard Helms**, before resigning in 1969, after which he became one of the agency's fiercest and most outspoken critics.

CHARLES MARTEL - (688–741) Frankish ruler and brilliant general, known as "The Hammer," whose victory at the battle of Tours in 732 arguably prevented the spread of Islam north from Spain.

MAWLANA MAWDUDI - (1903–1979) influential Sunni Pakistani journalist, theologian, and political philosopher.

NEIL "BILLY" MCLEAN - (1918–1986) British Army officer, intelligence officer, and politician who became a close personal and political friend of **Julian Amery,** fellow SOE officer in wartime Albania. His main interest was in international affairs; after the war he roamed the globe on many trips as a semiofficial or unofficial power broker, negotiator, and representative of British interests. Not to be confused with **Fitzroy Maclean**.

HENRY MCMAHON - (1862–1949) diplomat who served as the high commissioner in Egypt from 1915 to 1917 and is best known for the McMahon-Hussein correspondence concerning the future political status of the Arab lands under the Ottoman Empire.

STEPHEN MEADE - (n.d.) CIA agent in Syria.

MEHMED II - (1432–1481) Sultan of the Ottoman Empire for a short time from 1444 to 1446, and later from 1451 to 1481.

MEHMED V RESHAT - (1844–1918) 35th Sultan of the Ottoman Empire from 1909 until his death shortly before the Ottoman downfall. Had no real power, but did declare jihad against the Allies in 1914.

MEHMED VI VAHDETTIN - (1861–1926) 36th and last Sultan of the Ottoman Empire, reigning from 1918 to 1922.

MENELIK II - (1844–1913) emperor of Ethiopia from 1889 until his death.

YAAKOV MERIDOR - (1913–1995) Israeli politician and head of the Irgun (1941–1943).

GERHARD MERTINS - (1919–1993) Former Luftwaffe Special Forces officer and sabotage expert who trained guerrilla squads for the Muslim Brotherhood in Egypt and later became one of the world's biggest arms dealers.

KLEMENS VON METTERNICH - (1773–1859) Austrian diplomat, politician, and statesman, Prince Metternich became a major figure of his era, associated primarily with the Congress of Vienna (1814–1815), which he chaired and which effectively redrew the European map after the defeat of **Napoleon Bonaparte**.

VASILI MITROKHIN - (1922–2004) Former KGB officer and archivist who, after the fall of the Soviet Union, brought to the West an extensive body of secret archival material covering clandestine Soviet activities dating back to before the Second World War.

YURI MODIN - (1922–) KGB case officer who controlled the "Cambridge Five," including **Kim Philby**, from 1944 to 1955.

BERNARD "MONTY" MONTGOMERY - (1887–1976) British army officer, brilliant but abrasive Anglo-Irish general who aggressively reversed German fortunes at the battle of El Alamein in 1942 and expelled the Axis forces from North Africa.

MOHAMMED MOSSADEQ - (1882–1967) Iranian statesman and prime minister who was forcibly removed from office in 1953 by a CIA-backed coup.

LORD MOYNE - See **Walter Guinness**.

OSKAR MUNZEL - (1899–1992) Former German Afrika Korps panzer general who served as **Wilhelm Fahrmbacher**'s deputy in postwar Egypt.

PERVEZ MUSHARRAF - (1943–) Pakistani general who was Chief of Army Staff 1998–2007 and 10th President of Pakistan 2001–2008.

NAPOLEON BONAPARTE - (1769–1821) Corsican artillery officer during the French

Revolution who rose to become one of history's greatest military commanders, ruling over most of Europe, and establishing the Napoleonic Code, which formed the foundation of the modern French state. Ironically, he is said to have spoken French with a heavy Italian accent and never learned French spelling.

NAPOLEON III - (1808–1873) colorful nephew of **Napoleon Bonaparte**, educated in Switzerland and Germany, Louis-Napoleon, as he was known, led until middle age the lascivious life of a footloose, unmarried political adventurer, living in many places (including the United States and Britain) until he was finally elected president of France in 1848 and became emperor four years later. After his humiliating defeat in the Franco-Prussian War of 1870, he was exiled to Britain where he died, in severly reduced circumstances.

NASRULLAH KHAN - (n.d.) Emir of Bukhara from 1826 to 1860, notorious for cruelly executing British envoys **Charles Stoddart** and **Arthur Conolly** in 1842.

GAMAL ABDEL NASSER - (1918–1970) 2nd president of Egypt (1956–1970) led the Free Officers' coup of 1952, which overthrew King **Farouk I** and ushered in a period of nationalization, industrialization, pan-Arab nationalism, and Cold War brinkmanship.

MOHAMED NEGUIB - (1901–1984) Egyptian army officer and leader of the Free Officers, became 1st President of Egypt (1953–1954) when the republic was constituted after the revolution of 1952 had deposed King **Farouk I**. **Nasser** ultimately forced Neguib's resignation and placed him under house arrest for eighteen years.

NERO - (37–68) given name Lucius, he ruled the Roman Empire from A.D. 54 until his suicide in the face of execution at the hands of a military coup. While there is clear evidence that he persecuted the Christians and had his own mother, **Agrippina**, executed, some modern historians consider depictions of him as a cruel, insane despot to be exaggerated.

WILLIAM NICHOLSON - (1845–1918) British Army officer who, before being appointed chief of the Imperial General Staff (1908) and promoted to field marshal (1911), served for a while as an intelligence officer, becoming director general of mobilization and military intelligence in 1901.

ARTHUR NICOLSON - (1849–1928) diplomat and politician, whose overseas postings included Tehran, Constantinople, and Tangiers. Father of the diplomat Harold Nicolson.

PAUL H. NITZE - (1907–2004) ranking Washington official who helped shape U.S. Cold War defense policy during several presidencies.

ANTHONY NUTTING - (1920–1999) diplomat, politician, and writer who resigned from the **Eden** government in 1956 over British policy on Suez, thereby terminating his political career.

EDWARD OCHAB - (1906–1989) Head of the Polish Communist Party.

MAURICE OLDFIELD - (1915–1981) British counterintelligence officer who had close ties with **James Jesus Angleton** and ultimately became "C" (head of the British Secret Intelligence Service [MI6]) in 1973.

OMAR THE GREAT - (581–644) second Sunni Caliph, regarded as one of the four *Rashidun* (righteously guided Caliphs).

AMICHAI PAGLIN - (1922–1978) Chief of operations of the Irgun who helped plan the bombing of the King David Hotel in 1946.

ANTHONY PALMER - (n.d.) British Special Operations Executive (SOE) officer who commanded Haganah special forces during the Second World War in Palestine.

REZA PARVARESH - (n.d.) Iranian SAVAK officer.

DANIEL PEARL - (1963–2002) American-Jewish journalist kidnapped, tortured, and beheaded by al-Qaeda terrorists in Pakistan.

ROBERT PEEL - Headed the Peel Commission of 1936–1937, formally known as the Palestine Royal Commission, formed to investigate the causes of unrest among Palestinian Arabs and Jews and to propose changes to the mandate for Palestine following the outbreak of the 1936–1939 Arab Revolt.

SHIMON PERES - (1923–) Polish-born Israeli leftist politician and former senior Haganah officer, who has served Israel as cabinet minister, prime minister, and president (with interruptions) for over forty years.

DORA PHILBY - (n.d.) Wife of **Harry St. John Philby**, after whom he named a species of owl.

H.A.R. "KIM" PHILBY - (1912–1988) British intelligence officer and NKVD/KGB mole, the Third Man of the Cambridge Five (Maclean, Burgess, Philby, Blunt, and Cairncross). Son of **Harry St. John Philby**.

HARRY ST. JOHN PHILBY - (1885–1960) Arabist, explorer, and British colonial office intelligence operative who became famous as an international writer and explorer and who acted as advisor to **Abdul Aziz ibn Saud**, playing a dominant role in the Saudi oil negotiations with the Americans that ultimately brought wealth to the kingdom . . . and to Philby. He converted to Islam in 1930 and became known as Sheikh Abdullah. Father of notorious KGB mole **Kim Philby**.

PHILIP OF DREUX - (1156–1217) warlike Bishop of Beauvais; cousin of **Philip Augustus** and second cousin of **Conrad of Montferrat**; lifelong enemy of **Richard the Lionheart(ed)**, and a leading French participant in the Third Crusade (1189–1192).

PHILIP AUGUSTUS - (1165–1223), also known as Philip II of France; co-led the Third Crusade (1189–1192) with **Richard the Lionheart(ed)** and the elderly Frederick (Friedrich I) Barbarossa.

FRANÇOIS GEORGES-PICOT - (1870–1951) Co-signatory of the Sykes-Picot Agreement of 1916 with **Sir Mark Sykes**, which provided for the annexation of Ottoman Arab lands and their incorporation into the British and French empires.

JOHN POLLOCK - (n.d.) Cairo Special Operations Executive (SOE) chief.

ABDUL KARIM QASSEM - (1914–1963) nationalist Iraqi Army officer who seized power in 1958 and ruled as prime minister until his assassination.

MUHAMMAD QUTB - (1919–) Islamic author, scholar, and teacher resident in Mecca and best known as the younger brother of the Egyptian Islamist thinker **Sayyid Qutb**, and a supporter and promoter of his older brother's ideas after his brother was executed by the **Nasser** government.

SAYYID QUTB - (1906–1966) Egyptian author, Islamist, and the leading intellectual of the Muslim Brotherhood in the 1950s and 1960s. Older brother of **Muhammad Qutb**.

BURHANUDDIN RABBANI - (1940–) Afghan Islamic theologian and mujahidin commander (former president of the Afghan Northern Alliance), now head of the Afghan Jamaat-e Islami party.

MUNIR RADFA - (1934–1998) Iraqi Air Force pilot who defected to Israel in his MIG-21 fighter in 1966.

AKHTAR ABDUR RAHMAN - (1928–1988) powerful Director General of the Pakistani ISI who established the ISI Afghan Bureau. Rahman was a Pashtun from Peshawar on the Afghan frontier and also a close friend of CIA director William Casey.

SAID RAMADAN - (?–1995) Influential son-in-law of **Hassan al-Banna**, who left Egypt to live in Saudi Arabia and Switzerland, where he founded an Islamic think tank in Geneva known as the Islamic Center.

RASHID-AD-DIN SINAN - (?–1194) one of the leaders of the Syrian wing of the Hashshashin sect, known as "The Old Man of the Mountain" (Sheikh-al-Jabal); arranged the assassination of **Conrad of Montferrat** in 1192, possibly at the behest of either **Saladin** or **Richard the Lionheart(ed)**.

DAVID RAZIEL - (1910–1941) head of the Irgun (1938–1941) and one of its first members.

ALEXANDER REYNOLDS - a (n.d.) British former resident of Egypt, tried in absentia by Nasser for espionage in 1957, together with **George Rose**, **John Stanley**, and **George Sweet**.

RICHARD THE LIONHEART(ED) - (1157–1199), also known as Coeur de Lion, Richard I of England; one of the leaders of the Third Crusade (1189–1192) took over virtually sole command after the departure of **Philip Augustus**, scoring major victories against Saladin. Essentially French, the third son of Henry II of England, Normandy, and Anjou, and Eleanor of Aquitaine, who had earlier launched the disastrous Second Crusade (1147–1149), he spent only six months of his entire reign in England, yet enjoyed immense popularity there.

ERNEST T. RICHMOND - (1874–1974) Rabidly anti-Semitic, pro-Mufti member of the British High Commissioner for Palestine's Secretariat, rumored to have been the homosexual partner of **Ronald Storrs** and sometimes described as the "godfather of Palestinian terrorism."

YAAKOV RIFTIN - (1907–1978) Israeli Marxist Knesset member who passed information to the Soviet Union.

FREDERICK SLEIGH ROBERTS - (1832–1914) distinguished Anglo-Irish general, he won the Victoria Cross as a young subaltern during the Indian rebellion of 1857 and later rose to command the Indian Army.

JOHN D. ROCKEFELLER - (1839–1937) U.S. industrialist and philanthropist; founded Standard Oil in 1870.

ERWIN ROMMEL - (1891–1944) German army officer, also known as the "Desert Fox," commanded the German Afrika Korps in the Western Desert and subsequently German forces in occupied France. Forced to commit suicide after the July 20, 1944, bombing attempt on Hitler's life.

ARCHIE ROOSEVELT - (1918–1990) Cousin of **Kermit Roosevelt**

CORNELIUS ROOSEVELT - (1915–1991) Cousin of **Kermit Roosevelt**

FRANKLIN D. ROOSEVELT - (1882–1945) 32nd president of the United States (1933–1945).

KERMIT ROOSEVELT - (1916–2000) CIA political intelligence officer and Middle East specialist; best known for his leading part in the overthrow of Mossadeq in Iran (1953). Grandson of **Theodore Roosevelt**.

SELWA ROOSEVELT - (n.d.) **Archie Roosevelt**'s Lebanese-born wife.

THEODORE ROOSEVELT - (1858–1919) 26th president of the United States (1901–1909). Grandfather of **Kermit Roosevelt**.

GEORGE ROSE - (n.d.) British former resident of Egypt, tried in absentia by Nasser for espionage in 1957, together with **Alexander Reynolds**, **John Stanley**, and **George Sweet**.

HARRY ROSITZKE - (1911–2002) Head of CIA secret operations inside the USSR.

FORSTER SADLER - (n.d.) British Army officer who in the nineteenth century was the first explorer to cross the central Arabian Peninsula.

NURI SAID - (1888–1958) Iraqi politician who served seven terms as prime minister. He attempted to flee the country after the republican revolution, disguised as a woman, but he was captured and killed.

SALADIN - (1138–1193) Kurdish Muslim Sultan of Egypt and Syria who opposed the Third Crusade (1189–1192).

LORD SALISBURY - See **Robert Gascoyne-Cecil**.

HERBERT SAMUEL - (1870–1963) British diplomat, politician, and Zionist, high commissioner for Palestine (1920–1925).

ILICH RAMÍREZ SÁNCHEZ - See **Carlos the Jackal**.

A. W. SANSOM - (n.d.) British army security intelligence officer and chief of field security in Cairo during the Second World War.

ABD AL-HAMID SARRAJ - (1925–) pro-**Nasser** Syrian Army officer, politician, and head of Syrian military intelligence.

SAUD IBN ABDUL AZIZ - (1902–1969) eldest surviving son of **Abdul Aziz ibn Saud**, ruled Saudi Arabia from 1953 until 1964.

HJALMAR SCHACHT - (1877–1970) aristocratic German banker and economist; served briefly as a Nazi minister and president of the Reichsbank, although he never joined the Nazi Party. Both during and after the war, he was always closely associated with his son-in-law, **Otto Skorzeny**.

PATRICK SEALE - (n.d.) Sometimes controversial British journalist, author, and Middle East expert.

SELIM I - (1465–1520) also known as "the Grim" or "the Brave," Sultan of the Ottoman Empire from 1512 to 1520.

WILLIAM H. SHAKESPEAR - (1871–1915) Indian army officer, explorer, photographer, and diplomatist, the first Westerner to meet **Abdul Aziz ibn Saud**, with whom he formed an enduring friendship, dying with Ibn Saud's forces at the battle of Jarab.

MEMI DE SHALIT - (1921–2007) Washington-based Israeli liaison officer to the CIA and friend of **James Jesus Angleton**.

REUVEN SHILOAH - (1909–1959) Close friend of **Ben-Gurion** and mastermind of the

Israeli intelligence community, he was the first director of Mossad (1949–1952). He was born Zaslanski, which he later shortened to Zaslani and often substituted with the codename Shiloah.

ZEEV SHIND - (n.d.) Senior commander of Mossad LeAliyah Bet.

ADIB SHISHAKLI - (1909–1964) Syrian military leader and president 1953–1954, assassinated in Brazilian exile.

SALAH SHISHAKLI - (n.d.) Co-conspirator and brother of Syrian dictator **Adib Shishakli**.

PRITAM SINGH - (?–1942) Prominent anti-British Indian expatriate nationalist who led the Indian community in Indonesia and participated in both the Indian and the Indonesian struggle for independence. Killed in an air crash.

MOHAN SINGH - (1909–1989) Anti-British founder and commander, with Axis sanction and support, of the First Indian National Army (First INA), consisting largely of Sikh volunteers captured by the Japanese in Malaya. Later worked with Nazi sympathizer and fellow nationalist **Subhas Chandra Bose** to establish the Indian National Army (INA), which fought fiercely against Allied forces in Burma in 1944–1945.

WALTER BEDELL SMITH - (1895–1961) U.S. general and diplomat, "Beetle" Smith served successively as **Eisenhower**'s chief of staff, ambassador to the Soviet Union, and CIA director.

MOSHE SNEH - (1909–1972) Polish-born Israeli physician and Marxist politician who passed information to the Soviet Union.

ANTHONY SIMMONDS - (n.d.) Head of MI9 for Southern Europe who served with **Orde Wingate.**

GJERGJ KASTRIOTI SKANDERBEG - (1405–1466) the "Dragon of Albania," an Albanian national hero after whom a Waffen-SS division was named.

OTTO SKORZENY - (1908–1975) Viennese engineer and Waffen-SS Special Forces commander in the Second World War; later became an international arms dealer and facilitator for fugitive war criminals. Married to **Hjalmar Schacht**'s daughter.

SAINT SOPHRONIUS - (560–638) Orthodox Patriarch of Jerusalem.

JOSEF STALIN - (1878–1953) Communist Party leader and dictator of the Soviet Union from 1922 until his death. Ethnic Georgian known for his courageous, steadfast leadership of Russia in the Second World War, yet also for his unpredictability and dispassionate cruelty on a massive scale.

JOHN STANLEY - (n.d.) Cairo representative of the Prudential Assurance Company, tried in absentia by Nasser for espionage in 1957, together with **Alexander Reynolds**, **George Rose**, and **George Sweet**.

ABRAHAM STERN - (1907–1942) founder and leader of the Stern Gang, which he organized when the Irgun, of which he was a member, combined with the Haganah to fight the Nazis, a move he could not support.

CHARLES STODDART - (1806–1842) British Army officer, diplomat, and agent in Central Asia during the Great Game who, like **Arthur Conolly**, was captured and executed by **Nasrullah Khan**.

ROCKY STONE - (n.d.) CIA station chief in Damascus, publicly denounced as a spy.

RONALD STORRS - (1881–1955) British army officer and official in the British Foreign and Colonial Office who held several important posts, including governor of Jerusalem. Described by **T. E. Lawrence** as "the most brilliant Englishman in the Near East."

SULEYMAN I - (1494–1566) also known as "Suleiman the Magnificent"; 10th and longest-reigning Sultan of the Ottoman Empire (1520–1566). It was his armies that were checked at the Siege of Vienna in 1529, thus preventing the Ottomans from advancing into northern Europe.

GEORGE SWEET - (n.d.) a British Briton former resident of Egypt, tried in absentia by Nasser for espionage in 1957, together with **Alexander Reynolds**, **George Rose**, and **John Stanley**.

JAMES SWINBURN - (n.d.) Business manager of the Arab News Agency (ANA), which was an SIS (Secret Intelligence Service) cover operation, convicted of espionage and imprisoned by **Nasser**, together with **James Zarb**, in 1957.

MARK SYKES - (1879–1919) British military intelligence officer, traveler, and political advisor, whose name will always be associated with the Sykes-Picot Agreement of 1916, co-signed with French diplomat **François Georges-Picot**, which apportioned postwar spheres of interest in the Ottoman Empire to Britain, France, and Russia.

TAWFIK (TEVFIK) PASHA - (1852–1892) son of **Ismail Pasha**; Khedive of Egypt and Sudan from 1879.

GEORGE TENET - (1953–) CIA director for seven years (1997–2004), whose role in the WMD controversy and the lead-up to the 2003 U.S. invasion of Iraq remains unclear.

LORD TERRINGTON - See **C. M. "Monty" Woodhouse**.

LOWELL THOMAS - (1892–1981) U.S. writer, broadcaster, and traveler best known as the man who made **T. E Lawrence** famous as "Lawrence of Arabia."

JOSEF "SEPP" TIEFENBACHER - (n.d.) SS officer who was **Himmler**'s personal chief of security and served as personal assistant to **Wilhelm Voss** in Egypt.

JOSIP BROZ TITO - (1892–1980) Marxist ruler of federal Yugoslavia (1943–1980). Originally led the communist partisans in the Second World War, after which he resisted Stalin, maintained Yugoslav nonalignment, and kept the lid on ethnic tensions.

CHARLES TOWNSHEND - (1861–1924) British Army officer who led and lost the crack 6th Indian Division on the disastrous first British expedition against Baghdad during World War I, culminating in the siege of Kut. After his return to England, he died in poverty and disgrace.

HARRY TRUMAN - (1884–1972) 33rd President of the United States (1945–1953).

ELIZIER TSAFRIR - (n.d.) Chief of Mossad's Iran station.

MARK TWAIN - (1835–1910) Nom-de-plume of Samuel Langhorne Clemens, famous American author and humorist.

YAAKOV TZUR - (1937–) Israeli ambassador to France who negotiated with Iranian General **Bakhtiar** in 1957.

URBAN II - (1042–1099) born Otto de Lagery, a protegé of **Gregory VII**, he initiated the First Crusade (1095–1099) to wrest the Holy City from the occupying Seljuk Turks. Died two weeks after the fall of Jerusalem, but before hearing the news.

MANUCHER VAJDI - (n.d.) Iranian SAVAK officer.

VICTORIA - (1819–1901) ruled the British Empire as constitutional monarch for 63 years and became the most important symbolic figure of her time.

WILHELM VOSS - (n.d.) SS lieutenant general, economist, and close intimate of **Himmler** and **Heydrich**; administrative leader of the Nazi diaspora in **Farouk**'s and **Nasser**'s Egypt (1951–1956).

ARCHIBALD WAVELL - (1883–1950) British Army officer, commander of British forces in the Middle East (1939–1941).

ERWIN WEINMANN - (n.d.) SS officer and nonpracticing physician; Joachim Deumling's immediate superior at SS headquarters in Berlin. Supposedly killed in action near Prague in 1945, but actually fled to Egypt and became advisor to the police in Alexandria, where he became a permanent resident.

CHAIM WEIZMANN - (1874–1952) Zionist leader and 1st president of Israel from 1949.

Sumner Welles - (1892–1961) career diplomat and key official in the FDR administration. Forced out of public life in 1943 by a sex scandal. Said to have played a key role in conceiving the U.N.

Kaiser Wilhelm II - (1859–1941) grandson of Queen **Victoria** and last German emperor and king of Prussia, who ruled from 1888 until his abdication in 1918, when he was exiled to Doorn, Netherlands. Never formally relinquished his titles and always hoped to return to Germany.

William of Tyre - (1130–1185) Archbishop of Tyre and chronicler of the Crusades and medieval history.

Arnold Wilson - (1884–1940) Indian army officer, served in Persia; publicly known for his role as colonial administrator of Mesopotamia during and after the First World War, after which he joined the management of the Anglo-Persian Oil Company (APOC). Killed in action as an RAF air gunner over Dunkirk.

Woodrow Wilson - (1856–1924) 28th president of the United States (1913–1921).

Reginald Wingate - (1861–1953) British general and colonial administrator, right-wing, anti-Zionist, pro-Arab brother of **Orde Wingate**.

Orde Wingate - (1903–1944) Brilliant but eccentric British pro-Zionist commander of the Israeli Special Night Squads (SNS). He also distinguished himself as a special-forces commander in East Africa and Burma. Much younger brother of Sir **Reginald Wingate**. Killed in an aircraft crash aged only 41.

Frank Wisner - (1909–1965) U.S. Navy officer, lawyer, and intelligence officer; served in the OSS during the Second World War, became CIA director of plans (head of Office of Policy Coordination) during the 1950s. A manic-depressive, he committed suicide three years after being forced to retire from the CIA.

Polly Wisner - (n.d.) Wife of **Frank Wisner**.

Joseph Wolff - (1795–1862) German Jewish-Christian missionary and orientalist; journeyed to Bukhara in 1843 in search of the British officers **Charles Stoddart** and **Arthur Conolly**, narrowly escaping death himself at the hands of **Nasrullah Khan**.

Garnet Wolseley - (1833–1913) British army officer who, toward the end of his distinguished military career, was given command of the British forces in Egypt and led them to defeat **Ahmad Arabi** at the battle of Tel el-Kebir in 1882.

C. M. "Monty" Woodhouse - (1917–2001) aristocratic British artillery officer, brilliant scholar, diplomat, and politician who served with the Special Operations Executive

(SOE) during the Second World War in Greece. In 1998 he inherited the family title, becoming **Lord Terrington** for the last three years of his life.

PETER MAURICE WRIGHT - (1916–1995) British scientist and Security Service (MI5) counterintelligence officer, who befriended **James Jesus Angleton,** and who fiercely argued that former MI5 director general Sir Roger Hollis was a Soviet mole.

GEORGE KENNEDY "GK" YOUNG - (1911–1990) British journalist, diplomat, and merchant banker who studied at various foreign universities, served with the British Secret Intelligence Service (MI6) during the Second World War, and ultimately became deputy director general in 1959. After retirement in 1961, Young was involved in extreme right-wing British politics.

HUSNI ZAIM - (1897–1949) Commander-in-Chief of the Syrian Army who became military president of the country in 1949 after a bloodless coup. His moderate rule only lasted a few months, after which he was overthrown by **Adib Shishakli** and Sami Hinnawi and was executed.

JAMES ZARB - (n.d.) Maltese owner of a porcelain factory, convicted of espionage and imprisoned by **Nasser**, together with **James Swinburn**, in 1957.

MEHMED ZIA BEY - (n.d.) Ottoman army major in command of Ottoman forces in Mecca during the 1916 attack by Bedouin tribesmen.

MUHAMMAD ZIA-UL-HAQ - (1924–1988) Pakistani army officer, president, and military ruler of Pakistan (1977–1988); killed in a mysterious aircraft crash, along with the U.S. ambassador and several generals.

INDEX

THE
Second
Objective

THE
$\mathfrak{S}$ECOND
OBJECTIVE

Mark Frost

HYPERION

New York

Library of Congress Cataloging-in-Publication Data
Frost, Mark
    The second objective / Mark Frost. — 1st ed.
        p. cm.
    ISBN 1-4013-0222-X
    ISBN-13 978-1-4013-0222-1
    1. Eisenhower, Dwight D. (Dwight David), 1890–1969—Assassination attempts—Fiction.
2. Attempted assassination—Fiction.   3. World War, 1939–1945—Commando
operations—Fiction.   4. Ardennes, Battle of the, 1944–1945—Fiction.   I. Title.

PS3556.R599S43 2007
813'.54—dc22   2006043683

Hyperion books are available for special promotions and premiums. For details contact
Michael Rentas, Assistant Director, Inventory Operations, Hyperion, 77 West 66th Street,
12th floor, New York, New York 10023, or call 212-456-0133.

Design by Renato Stanisic
Endpaper map by Laura Hartman Maestro

FIRST EDITION

10 9 8 7 6 5 4 3 2 1

FOR LYNN

THE
SECOND
OBJECTIVE

The Wolf's Lair, Rastenburg, East Prussia
OCTOBER 22, 1944

At half past midnight, Lieutenant Colonel Otto Skorzeny left the command bunker. He walked alone down the corridor outside, buried twenty feet belowground, bleak with artificial light. The poorly ventilated air still smelled of musty concrete and earth. The Führer had named his new field headquarters, one of ten structures linked by underground passages, *Die Wolfsschanze*: The Wolf's Lair. To Skorzeny, in that moment, it felt more like a tomb.

Skorzeny stared at the medal he held in his hand, the German Cross rendered in gold. He had just received the Reich's highest decoration for his most recent paramilitary operation, a bloodless coup that replaced the regent of Budapest with a Fascist cipher. Only a year before, Skorzeny had rocketed to fame after his first triumph, the daring rescue of Italian dictator Benito Mussolini from imprisonment on a remote Italian mountaintop. He had since led his personally trained special forces brigade on half a dozen other suicidal assignments, and was known and feared throughout Europe as "Hitler's commando."

The order he had just received made those missions seem like a training exercise.

Madness. This is madness.

The staff told him afterward that no one had seen the Führer in such a positive mood for months. He seemed at last to have shaken

off the ill health and depression that had beset him after the nearly successful attempt on his life by a cadre of aristocratic German officers in July.

The amphetamines must be working, thought Skorzeny, who was burdened by few illusions about Adolf Hitler or any other human being.

The Führer's enthusiasm appeared unhinged from reality. In less than six months the German Army had been driven back from the shores of Normandy to their own borders. With the Soviets advancing from the east, and the Allies preparing to attack from the west, most military leaders privately believed the war was already lost. All that remained for the Wehrmacht was a brutal, grinding defensive collapse toward Berlin.

But as his empire crumbled around him, Hitler now proposed to mount the most ambitious offensive of the entire war. He had just outlined for Skorzeny his secret plan for a savage counterattack against the Western Allies. He would hurl all his remaining divisions at a lightly defended section of Belgium and Luxembourg. Entitled Operation Autumn Mist, the attack was designed to drive a wedge of steel between the American and British armies all the way west to the Atlantic. If they succeeded in cutting off the British north of Antwerp and trapped them in a second Dunkirk, the Führer believed that the English would sue for peace, and that the Americans would have no stomach for invading Germany on their own. Only then could he turn his entire war machine loose on Russia and destroy the Bolshevik menace he considered the one true enemy of Western civilization.

Genius shares a common border with insanity, thought Skorzeny. *Since I've last seen him he's crossed over.*

Skorzeny waited for the rant to end. Hitler put both hands on the table and sagged forward. His skin looked jaundiced under the room's sickly fluorescents. He inhaled deeply, spittle collecting at the sides of his mouth. As he raised his left hand to brush back an unruly forelock of hair, Skorzeny saw that it shook with a violent, involuntary tremor. The Führer took a few steps toward him with a shuffling gait, an old man's walk, his hand searching for support. In moments all his vitality had drained away, leaving this brittle husk.

Yes, amphetamines. Time for another dose.

On instinct Skorzeny reached out a hand. Hitler gripped the blond giant's immense right forearm and seemed to gather strength from it. Or perhaps this weakness was a ploy to elicit Skorzeny's sympathy. In either case, it stirred awake his loyalty to the man who had lifted him from obscurity to glory.

"How may I help?" asked Skorzeny.

When he learned what his own role was to be in Operation Autumn Mist, Skorzeny couldn't speak.

He was to raise a new brigade from throughout the German armed forces to take part in the invasion: two thousand men with one specialized ability in common. None could know the true nature of their mission until the night before they embarked. They were to be sworn to a blood oath under pain of death, trained in secrecy, turned into an effective commando unit, and sent to fulfill an objective that would mean almost certain death.

In six weeks' time.

That wasn't all. From within that brigade he was to select another group of men, no more than twenty of the most qualified he could find.

They would be given a second objective.

Grafenwöhr, Bavaria, Germany
NOVEMBER 3, 1944

ernie Oster arrived in Nuremberg after traveling through
the night alone on a passenger train. He carried classified,
stamped orders handed to him the previous day by his commanding officer in Berlin. He had been told to pack nothing and
change into civilian clothes before soldiers escorted him directly
from that meeting to the train. After showing his papers to the SS officers at Nuremberg Station, he was led into an empty holding area
and left there without explanation. At noon, after a dozen other men
had joined him in isolation, they were loaded into the back of a
blacked-out transport truck.

They were ordered to keep silent. The men exchanged only wary
looks and nods. None of his fellow passengers wore uniforms either,
but Bernie surmised from their appearance and manner that they
were all soldiers or sailors. Sitting alone in a corner, he chain-smoked
cigarettes, wondering where the other men had come from, what they
all had in common. His CO had given him no details during his briefing, only that Bernie had "volunteered"—without being offered the
choice—for a special assignment that required immediate transfer.
Fifteen hours and hundreds of kilometers later, he found himself in a
part of Germany he'd never seen before.

Soon after they started driving, the most agitated passenger

blurted the questions they were all thinking: "What are we doing here? . . . What do they want with us?"

Bernie didn't answer. The risk that any of these other men could be an SS plant, placed among them to monitor their conversations—or provoke them by asking those same questions—was too great. He already had reason enough to fear for his life. Perhaps these other men did as well; none of them answered.

Peeking through a seam in the canvas, Bernie saw they were on a highway moving through stark gray countryside—bare trees, fallow fields, barren wilderness. Halfway through their second hour, they turned onto a remote road threading through a dark wood. Half a mile on, they approached the entrance to an elaborate compound, surrounded by steel-framed gates and barbed-wire fences that stretched into the trees as far as the eye could see.

It looked like a prison camp. Guards in unfamiliar uniforms patrolled the parapets and blockhouses above the walls. Machine guns had been placed on the towers, their barrels pointed to the interior. His stomach turned over.

So that's it. I've been found out.

The truck braked to a stop just short of the gates. The back canvas parted and two armed guards waved the passengers out at the point of a bayonet, their eyes flinching at daylight after the long, dark ride. An SS officer waited to escort them through the open gates. Bernie noticed that the guards on the walls and towers all had broad Slavic features. He heard an exchange between two of them in some unfamiliar, guttural language. The gates clanged shut behind them. Bernie wondered if these walls had been put up to keep others out or to keep them in.

The compound appeared to have been built for military purposes. He could see deep tank tracks in the mud, an artillery range in the distance. The guards led them into a low, empty barracks built from freshly cut logs, where sandwiches and bottles of beer had been set out for them. They sat on crude wooden beds and ate in silence as the guards watched. After a brief rest, they were led, one by one, to another cabin that Bernie could see through a window across

the compound. None of them returned. Bernie was one of the last men summoned.

Two SS officers, a lieutenant and a captain, waited behind a desk in the building's only room, facing a single empty chair. Black-jacketed SS grenadiers stood sentry at the door, holding MP40 submachine guns.

The lieutenant ordered Bernie to empty his pockets on the table, including his military identity card, traveling papers.

"Your paybook, as well," said the lieutenant.

He collected the items in an envelope and put the envelope in a desk drawer. Without them, Bernie knew that as far as the army was concerned, he no longer existed. His heart thumped in his chest, and he was sure that the fear he'd been struggling to suppress showed on his face. He'd been dreading a moment like this for months: discovery, torture, execution.

The captain didn't look up at him once from his notes while the lieutenant ordered him to sit and began asking questions, in German, reading from a dossier.

"Private First Class Bernard Oster."

"Yes, sir."

"What is your unit?"

"The 42nd *Volksgrenadier* Division, sir. Mechanized Brigade."

"Your duties there?"

"I'm a mechanic in the motor pool, sir. Attached to central command headquarters in Berlin. I take care of the officers' cars."

"Is that your only responsibility?"

Here it comes, thought Bernie.

"No, sir. For the last month I've worked in the radio room. As a translator."

The lieutenant showed something on the dossier to the captain. He looked up at Bernie for the first time. A slender man in his early thirties, with slicked black hair and steel-gray eyes that stared through Bernie like an X-ray. He gestured to his lieutenant: *I'll take it from here.*

"You were born in the United States," said the captain, in crisp English.

"Yes, sir," said Bernie, trying not to look surprised.

"Your parents emigrated there in the early 1920s, after the last war. Why?"

"As I understand, there was little or no work in Germany then," said Bernie. "Economic hardship."

"Your father is an industrial chemist. He worked for Pfizer, on Long Island."

"That's right."

"And you were raised and educated in New York."

"Brooklyn. Yes I was, sir."

"When did your family return to Germany?"

"In 1938. I was fourteen."

"Why?"

Bernie hesitated. "For the same reason we left in the first place. My father lost his job in the Depression. He had no way to support his family. As a scientist and a German citizen, he got an offer from the new government to go home and work here."

The captain betrayed no reactions. Judging from the man's shrewd manner, he knew the answer to every question he was asking. His steady, unblinking gaze sent waves of fear through Bernie. When the SS took an interest in someone, he had a way of disappearing, even if he had nothing to hide. Bernie felt sweat dripping down under his arms.

"Your father works for IG Farben, in Frankfurt," said the captain.

"Yes, sir."

"Has he ever discussed his work with you?"

Is that what this is about? My father? Not what happened in Berlin?

"No, sir. I believe it is classified."

"You began military service sixteen months ago," said the captain. "When you turned eighteen. You made no attempt to enlist prior to that."

"I was still in school, sir—"

"Nor were you ever a member of the *Hitlerjugend*."

The captain's eyes bored into him. Bernie felt rattled to his core, certain the man could read the thoughts he tried to keep from his mind. Did he know that within months of returning to Nazi Germany, his father had been warned by his bosses at IG Farben that if he ever

tried to leave, his family would be killed? Or that Bernie's own hatred of the Nazis had only grown greater after he was drafted? He'd come to Germany against his will, with an American teenager's skepticism intact, immune to the Nazis' nationalist fantasia. With their fixation on pomp and ritual, he'd thought them coarse and buffoonish. Then he and his family had watched in horror as they brought Europe to its knees.

Bernie's mind raced to the one question that mattered: Did this man know that when they learned about his language skills and moved him to the radio room, Bernie had twice altered his translation of intercepted American intelligence reports about troop movements, trying to mislead his superiors about their intent? Fighting his own private resistance, probably ineffectual, certainly reckless. He'd waited a month before trying again, sure they were watching him. His second attempt had come just a week ago.

Had they only been waiting for him to stick his neck out again? Why else would they have brought him here?

"I was older than the compulsory age when we returned from America," said Bernie. "My father wanted me to finish my education."

The captain stood up and walked around the table. "Why has your father never joined the National Socialist Party?"

"I'm afraid you'd have to ask him, sir—"

"Is he a patriotic man?"

"He's always thought of himself as a German first. That's why he came home when he had the chance—"

The captain pulled his pistol and held it firmly to Bernie's forehead. "And how do you think of yourself, Private?"

Bernie swallowed before answering. "As my father's son."

"You are an American citizen."

"I have dual citizenship, German and American."

"And if you had to choose?"

"I've never been given a choice—"

"I'm giving you one now."

Bernie never took his eyes away from the captain's, convinced that the slightest slip would make him pull the trigger. "Speak with my commanding officers if you think my allegiance is in question."

The captain kept staring at him. Bernie remained at attention, eyes forward, trembling.

"We have spoken with them. Isn't there anything else you wish to tell me?"

Bernie looked right at him. "No, sir."

Another moment, then the captain lowered the pistol and holstered it. Bernie had passed the test. His knees nearly buckled.

"You've volunteered to become part of a new brigade. English is a requirement. Yours is excellent, for obvious reasons. Is it safe to say you also have knowledge of American culture? Movie stars. Baseball. Current events."

"I've been away for six years, sir."

"You read newspapers, don't you? America is still of interest to you. You can answer the question honestly, son; it's only natural. It was your home for fourteen years."

Bernie saw the trap beneath the question, and asked neutrally, "Why, sir?"

"Your experience can be of value during our training. We may call upon your expertise in this area."

"I'll help any way I can, sir."

"I am Captain Stielau. You will report directly to me. You look relieved."

"Do I? I suppose I am, sir."

Stielau seemed amused by Bernie's reaction, then turned to his lieutenant: "Category One."

The lieutenant wrote Bernie's name on a roster with four columns. Bernie saw that his was the first name in the first column.

"May I ask the purpose of our new brigade, sir?"

"Yes," said Stielau.

Bernie hesitated. "What is the purpose of our new brigade, sir?"

"I said you could ask. I didn't say I would tell you. You're dismissed, Private Oster."

2

Grafenwöhr
NOVEMBER 1944

ernie tried to bury his fear by losing himself in the camp's routine. Over two thousand men from every corner of the Reich arrived during the following week. Bernie helped conduct their initial interviews, asking questions to determine their level of competence in English, both speaking and comprehension. They were then classified into four categories. One: fluency in English and working knowledge of American slang. Two: fluency without knowledge of specific American idioms. Three: general comprehension and the ability to conduct limited conversations. Four: restricted comprehension, men who had studied English in school without real-world application.

Bernie quickly realized that most of the "volunteers" had vastly overstated their abilities. By the end of the week, as the last men arrived, he had picked fewer than twenty to join him in Category One. Fifty went into Category Two. The third category had about one hundred men in it, and the fourth another two hundred. As for the rest, over two-thirds of the men who had been summoned to *Grafenwöhr*, their English was limited to single-word responses. Bernie barracked with the rest of the Ones and Twos; Threes and Fours occupied separate quarters across the yard, and the rest stayed on the far side of the compound.

The men were issued neutral olive-green uniforms without insignia. All previous ranks were erased, and officers received no preferential treatment. They dined together in the same large mess hall, eating meals that far surpassed normal army fare. Contact with friends or family was forbidden. Every man signed an oath of silence, and letters home had to pass a censor's strict review. Medicine and prescription drugs were dispensed freely to prevent illness, since no one was allowed out of camp to see a doctor. This taut atmosphere fueled rumors and speculation about their brigade's reason for being, which flew through the camp, mutating on a daily basis. Their true purpose remained a mystery.

They heard their first explanation when Bernie and the rest of the brigade were called one day at dawn to a general assembly in the compound. Captain Stielau addressed them. They were now part of the 150th Panzer Brigade, he said, operating under the command of Colonel Otto Skorzeny. The mention of his name sent a ripple through the yard; he was without rival the most notorious figure in the German armed forces. Stielau told them their mission was called "Operation *Greif*," and they were being trained to defend Cologne when the Allies attacked across the Rhine. It sounded plausible, but Bernie found it impossible to reconcile with what they were being taught.

Their training began each morning with English lessons, focusing on American slang, and tutoring to eliminate native accents. Bernie helped craft a crash course on American culture, using newspapers, magazines, sports sections, and comic strips. Tests were given each day to drill this information into long-term memory. The men were ordered to use only English; anyone heard speaking German was disciplined with solitary confinement.

Each afternoon they were put through Skorzeny's commando training: demolition, communications, reconnaissance, special weapons, light artillery, night fighting in both urban and forest environments, hand-to-hand combat. They were schooled in map reading, the basics of movement under combat conditions, camouflage techniques, and communications. They were taught how to drive and service captured American jeeps, scout cars, half-tracks, and tanks. Each

man in Categories One and Two was issued an M1 rifle. Ammunition was too scarce for target practice, but they learned to carry, field strip, and maintain their rifles as rigorously as any GI.

After dinner they gathered in the mess hall to listen to U.S. Armed Forces Radio. Beer was served and they were encouraged to sing along with the popular songs of American recording artists. On some nights they watched American films, in English, with orders to observe and mimic the actors' mannerisms. Seeing these familiar faces again, the first Hollywood stars he'd seen in years, made Bernie desperately homesick. His dread about what Skorzeny was really preparing them for grew with each passing day; only exhaustion kept it from overwhelming his mind.

At the end of the second week, the fluent English speakers, about eighty men, were placed directly under the command of Captain Stielau. Except for meals, they now spent their days apart from the others, and their language training intensified. Whenever shipments of new Allied material arrived—uniforms, boots, weapons—Stielau's men received it first. Bernie believed that the future objectives of the two groups, whatever they might be, had begun to diverge.

Bernie met one other American-born man in Category One, a U.S. Army deserter named William Sharper. He had served in the American Army until after the invasion of Normandy. Sharper took a lead role during training, teaching the men specific GI behaviors; the way they slouched, chewed gum, how to rip open a pack of cigarettes with a thumbnail, and the fine art of swearing. Bernie stayed clear of him, disturbed by the violence he saw in the man's eyes. A handful of others were former members of the German diplomatic corps who had learned English serving in foreign embassies. The rest came from the merchant marine, itinerant seamen who at some point had worked on American or English ships. One was a former porter on the *Queen Mary*. Their isolation, intense physical training, and the airtight atmosphere of secrecy brought them quickly and closely together as a unit.

At the start of the third week, each man in Bernie's unit was assigned an American name. American dog tags were issued bearing these names, along with a new rank, and they were ordered to refer to

one another only by these new names and ranks. They were told to create and memorize a fictional American history: place of birth, family members, education, hometown history, favorite pets, girlfriends left behind, baseball teams, local geography. Bernie decided the only way to create a life story he could remember under pressure was to keep it as close as possible to his own. A New Yorker from Brooklyn, the son of immigrant parents, he became Private James Tenella.

That Tuesday Bernie was summoned to the interview cabin. A new arrival sat joking with Stielau's lieutenant, waiting to go through the evaluation process. Unlike the hundreds who'd preceded him, he still wore his German uniform: the crisp black tunic of a *Waffen*-SS lieutenant. He was in his mid to late twenties, wiry, compact, with close-cropped blond hair and a ready, dazzling smile.

Stielau's lieutenant waved Bernie into the room: "Private Tenella, meet our latest arrival, SS *Unterstürmführer* Erich Von Leinsdorf."

Von Leinsdorf stood up to shake his hand, and looked him in the eye. "A pleasure. They tell me you may be able to iron the starch out of my plummy Mid-Atlantic tones."

Von Leinsdorf spoke perfect English, with a crisp upper-class British accent.

"Whatever it takes, sir," said Bernie.

Stielau's lieutenant handed Bernie the clipboard and left the room. Von Leinsdorf perched on the edge of the table and opened a sterling silver cigarette case engraved with his initials.

"I suppose I'll have to start smoking Lucky Strikes," he said. "No more English Players for me."

Von Leinsdorf torched his cigarette with a matching silver lighter and smiled again. He smoked like a movie star, or someone who had studied movie stars smoking. Despite his easygoing charm, Bernie felt a visceral wariness of the man. He seemed to take up more space than he physically occupied. The superior airs seemed characteristic for someone from his class, but Bernie was reacting to something starker than the aristocratic "Von" in his name. He pulled back the chair Von Leinsdorf had been using and sat down facing him.

"How was your trip?" asked Bernie.

"Appalling," he said with a smile, making no effort to keep the conversation going.

"Where'd you come in from, Lieutenant?"

"Where are *you* from, if you don't mind my asking? Your English is astonishing."

"I'm from New York. Brooklyn."

"Is that a fact? How fascinating. Born and bred?"

"That's right. How about you?"

"Munich, but as you may have gathered, I spent my formative years in England. Father was in the diplomatic corps, stationed to the embassy in London. We went over in twenty-eight. I was ten at the time. Father enrolled me at Westminster, public school. All those incestuous aristocratic family trees, it's a breeding ground for degenerate half-wits. So in I waltzed from the hinterlands, armed only with my meager schoolboy English. Bit of a wonder I survived."

"Hope the education was worth it."

"Oh, I got an education, all right. Where were you at ten, Brooklyn?"

"Fifth grade. PS 109."

"Of course you were. How charming."

"So you spoke only English in school?"

"Not just in school, old boy. At home, in the park, in the bath with my proper English nanny. Even family dinners. Father didn't want any guttural German consonants ruffling the feathers of our hosts."

"When did you come back to Germany?"

"Once the unpleasantness broke out, the tea bags ushered us straight to the door. Imagine my father's disappointment. He'd spent the better part of his life trying to penetrate this ironclad veil of courtesy. He never realized that's the reason for their obsession with manners: a coat of paint covering a hatred of all things foreign. And they seem so polite until you get to know them." Von Leinsdorf flashed a smile, stood up, and walked to the window. "So we both came back to Germany at the same age. Strange, feeling the outsider in your own country, isn't it?"

You don't know the half of it, thought Bernie.

"Where the devil are we, by the way? I was hoping I might be headed to Berlin. Has anyone told you what this is about?"

"Not a word," said Bernie.

"Very hush-hush all this, isn't it? Have they tipped their hand about what we're doing here, Brooklyn?"

"All they told us is that this guy Colonel Skorzeny's running the show."

Von Leinsdorf spun around. "Skorzeny? Otto Skorzeny?"

"That's what they said."

"Have you seen him? Has he been here?"

"No. Why?"

"I tried to transfer into his commando unit last year—"

"Where you been stationed?"

"Dachau," he said casually, flicking his cigarette.

Bernie had heard about the Munich suburb the SS used as a training center. Lurid stories about their concentration camp had been circulating through Berlin, but he knew better than to ask. He'd learned never to ask an SS man anything.

"I'm going to write up this report that your English is first rate," said Bernie. "They'll probably put you in Category Two."

Von Leinsdorf leaned over to glance at Bernie's notes. "That sounds suspiciously like a demotion. Why not Category One?"

"That's only for guys who come in knowing a lot of American slang."

"But you could teach me, couldn't you?"

"If that's what they want—"

"It's what *I* want," said Von Leinsdorf, sharply. He softened his tone and turned the charm back on. "Just between us, old boy, I hate thinking I'm not good enough for the top category. Sheer vanity, really."

"It's not up to me."

"I'm not asking for much. Wouldn't want the officers to think you're reluctant to help a fellow soldier. All this cloak and dagger, they must be watching you more closely than the rest of us. I'm sure they'd take a dim view of wobbly loyalties."

Bernie smiled, trying not to let him see that he'd even heard the threat. "I'll try to help you out, sure, what the fuck."

"What the fuck?"

"Most popular word in the GI language. Fuck this, fucking that. Fucking camp—"

"Fucking Krauts—"

"Now you're cooking with gas."

"What the fuck does that mean?"

"Means you're on the money, on the beam, moving down the right track."

"Right. So, Category One, then. I'll make it up to you, Brooklyn, see that you're assigned to my squad. We should fucking stick together, don't you think?"

"Sure, what the fuck."

Both men laughed. Bernie couldn't help liking the man, in spite of his initial reservations.

"What took you so long getting here?" asked Bernie. "They brought the rest of us in two weeks ago, you don't mind my asking."

"Haven't a clue. I assume it was some bureaucratic foul-up."

"A snafu."

"Pardon?"

"It's a whatchamacallit, a word you make from initials, an acronym? Situation Normal: All Fucked Up."

"Yes, brilliant. Snafu, indeed. The thing is, Brooklyn, I only heard about this two days ago. We were near the end of a major project, so they couldn't bear to part with me."

"At Dachau."

"That's right," said Von Leinsdorf, smiling as he lit another cigarette.

"So did you finish it? Your project?"

"A ways to go yet. Afraid they'll have to carry on without me."

Von Leinsdorf motioned with his head for Bernie to follow, and they walked into the darkening evening, back toward the dining hall. Von Leinsdorf tossed away his half-smoked cigarette and asked Bernie for one of his Lucky Strikes.

"Do you mind?" he asked. "I should get used to these."

"Help yourself."

Von Leinsdorf pulled the cigarette from the pack with his lips and torched it. "What do we call these? Smokes?"

"Smokes, nails," said Bernie.

"Nails?"

"Coffin nails. Sticks, butts."

Von Leinsdorf nodded, then lit and studied his cigarette. "So what are they training us for, Brooklyn? I get a different answer from everyone."

"They say we're going to defend Cologne when the Allies invade—"

"Come on, that's pure codswallop. All this trouble just to have us dig and wait for Patton to cross the Rhine? This is a Skorzeny mission. Hitler's commando. Start with the name: Operation *Greif*— the griffin. You remember what it looks like? Half German eagle, half Allied lion. Our purpose is in that image. We're going to cross the line disguised as an American brigade, a surprise attack. Something to shock the world."

"Maybe you're right," said Bernie, trying to sound casual as he heard his worst fear realized.

"I'm sure of it. And I've got a good idea what our target might be."

Bernie's eye caught a metallic flash of light above them in the darkness, from a guard tower directly above the courtyard.

"Somebody's up there," he said.

Von Leinsdorf turned to look. A tall, sturdy officer in uniform leaned forward, lighting a cigar, his face visible in the flame of the lighter a soldier held for him.

"It's him," said Von Leinsdorf.

"Who?"

"Skorzeny's here."

Grafenwöhr
NOVEMBER 20, 1944

The entire 150th Panzer Brigade was called into the commons at six-thirty A.M., before the morning meal. Bernie, Von Leinsdorf, and the rest of Captain Stielau's commando group stood in the first two rows facing the dining hall as a light mist fell from an overcast sky. Five minutes later the brigade snapped to attention as the camp's brass marched out ahead of Colonel Skorzeny. He wore his dress uniform but no overcoat, unlike the rest of the officers, and a confident smile that seemed oblivious to bad weather and any other adversity. Skorzeny stopped and surveyed his men for nearly a minute, studying faces, before he uttered a word. The Iron Cross hung at his throat, between the lightning SS runes and insignia of rank on his high, stiff collar. His bright eyes and sharp features suggested to Bernie the image of a hyper-intelligent fox.

"We are not here to turn you into soldiers," he said in English, his voice ringing out over the yard. "That was someone else's job. If they failed, there's nothing we can do for you now. Nor is there time to train you properly as commandos; the urgency of our mission is too great. It is the responsibility of every man to do the best he can with what we give you. Your principal weapons will be intelligence, ingenuity, and cunning.

"What I do expect from you is this: the willingness to change

your entire pattern of behavior. Nationality, race, and culture are qualities you express unconsciously in your basic instincts, habits, and attitudes. They are much more deeply ingrained in your mind and body than you know. As far as the outside world is concerned, these qualities, these 'German characteristics,' have to change if you have any hope of surviving what lies ahead. It is no use dressing you in olive green and teaching you American slang if you click your boot heels and snap to attention like a Prussian grenadier the first time one of their officers barks out an order."

He gave a comic, self-deprecating demonstration, like one of the boys in the ranks. A big laugh spread through the assembly. Bernie glanced over at Von Leinsdorf, standing down the row. He watched Skorzeny with almost religious rapture. Skorzeny smiled and waited for the laughter to subside with the polished air of a comedian.

He's got them in his hands. They're ready to die for him right now.

"No similar operation of this size has ever been attempted in the history of warfare. I won't minimize the dangers you face. But I assure you the Führer has entrusted us with a responsibility on which the future of our country depends. You have his full support and absolute confidence. I know in my heart that you will not let him, or Germany, down. The rest is up to God and chance. Heil Hitler!"

Skorzeny turned with a click of his heels and marched away, his adjutant and officers falling into step behind him. He radiated command and iron confidence, tempered by empathy for his troops and self-deprecating humor. Von Leinsdorf and the others around him glowed with patriotic zeal; they looked ready to burst into song.

Skorzeny watched the brigade's military division go through maneuvers that morning on the training ground. Two captured American Sherman tanks and twelve German Panthers, which had been retrofitted to resemble Shermans, rumbled through their paces. In the afternoon, Stielau's commando company conducted a sabotage demonstration, blowing up a mock bridge ahead of schedule against a running clock. Skorzeny appeared pleased with their performance.

. . .

When Skorzeny returned to the officers' quarters for the evening, his adjutant was waiting for him outside. "Sir, a lieutenant from the commando company has requested a word with you."

"I don't have time for that now."

The adjutant lowered his voice. "He is SS. From a diplomatic corps family."

Skorzeny looked past him into the next room, where a young, upright man with close-cropped blond hair waited.

"All right, leave us," said Skorzeny.

Skorzeny walked in to join the man, who snapped to attention and saluted. "*Unterstürmführer* Erich Von Leinsdorf, sir. It is an honor to meet you."

"What can I do for you, Lieutenant?"

"Sir, as a fellow SS officer, I take the liberty of speaking directly. The wildest rumors are circulating through camp regarding the mission. Once the men learned you were in charge, imaginations ran riot."

"Give me an example," said Skorzeny.

"We are going to rush across France to liberate our trapped garrison at Brest. Some have us crossing the Channel to invade London. There's even one that claims we're to cross the Atlantic by submarine and attack Roosevelt in the White House."

Skorzeny shook his head, amused. "And what do you think, Lieutenant?"

"I believe I know the real objective of the 105th Panzer Brigade, sir."

The man radiated such conviction that for a moment Skorzeny wondered if his seconds had disobeyed orders and taken him into their confidence. Skorzeny poured a drink, stood in front of the fire, and listened as Von Leinsdorf explained his theory. Hiding his astonishment at what the man told him, Skorzeny rolled the brandy in the snifter, a grand master with his hand poised over a suddenly useful pawn. He said nothing when Von Leinsdorf finished, letting him squirm.

"I will share this much with you," said Skorzeny finally. "The Führer has given us a specific military objective, the details of which I am not at liberty to disclose."

"I understand, sir," said Von Leinsdorf.

"He also gave us a second objective," said Skorzeny, moving closer. "No one else knows about it, not even your superior officers. Never mind how, but you've hit on it exactly. Let me tell you my problem, Lieutenant."

Von Leinsdorf tensed. "I didn't mean to cause any trouble—"

Skorzeny held up a hand for silence. "For some time I have been looking for an officer capable of leading this phase of the operation. I've found my man."

"I'm honored, sir."

"Choose a few others from your company. The best English speakers, three men, each qualified to lead a small squad. Do any come to mind?"

"Yes, sir."

"Take them into your confidence, but without the particulars we've discussed. Have each of these men assemble his own four-man team. Then consider this objective carefully and work out the tactical details yourself."

"What guidance can you give me, sir?"

"None. The rest is up to you. I don't like to limit a talented young officer's initiative. In the meantime, to help morale, introduce a rumor of our own into camp. Three American commandos were recently captured wearing German uniforms near Aachen. They were given safe passage back across the American line by the SS a few days later."

"Is that true?"

"Of course not. They were shot immediately." Skorzeny opened the door for him. "We'll meet again on the eve of the attack and finalize your plan. Good luck to us all."

"You may count on me, sir." Von Leinsdorf saluted, spun on his heel, and exited the room. Skorzeny's adjutant entered moments later.

"Bring me that man's dossier," said Skorzeny. "Ask Captain Stielau to come in."

Skorzeny watched the fire as he waited, and felt the threads of three different fabrics bind into one satisfying whole. The adjutant and Stielau returned together. Skorzeny quickly scanned Von Leinsdorf's dossier, while Stielau stood by.

"How did he end up here? His father was one-quarter Jewish."

"Yes, on the mother's side. According to Party standards that still made him half-caste, *Mischlinge*."

"And he was Ambassador Ribbentrop's right-hand man in London at the time?" asked Skorzeny. "I remember hearing about this. A minor scandal."

"Ribbentrop shipped him off to an obscure post in Sweden. The mother took ill, went home, and died shortly after. When the father committed suicide a few months later, the boy, Erich, became a ward of the state."

"How did he kill himself?"

"The rope. A coward's death. Fit for a Jew."

Skorzeny read something in the file. "Erich found the body."

"Yes. He was sent back to Germany, and enrolled in the *Hitlerjugend*. He so excelled in every youth program they put him in—the Hitler School, the Political Institute—that he was transferred to the *Ordensburgen*. It's for only the most fanatical young National Socialists. Intense physical discipline, military instruction, education in the racial sciences, and the Jewish question—all under SS."

"In spite of his Jewish blood."

"The mother's line was pure Aryan, so he's only one eighth, slightly more than twelve percent. In special cases one can argue the Aryan blood is more dominant. For all that, he seems determined to eradicate his father's heritage. The lieutenant's creativity at Dachau has been nothing less than astonishing."

Skorzeny knew about the extermination program at Dachau and other death camps, but offered no comment. Senior officers working at a remove from the Final Solution never discussed what they knew in any way that required expressing an opinion. Stielau interpreted his silence as disapproval.

"In any case, since he is of such concern to you," said Stielau, "we'll have the man executed tomorrow."

"No, Stielau, you miss my point entirely. He's perfect."

"If I may ask, in what way, sir?"

"It's all very well to send our little brigade across enemy lines. If the stars align, and we catch them napping, there's even a slight chance we might succeed."

"Sir, I think you're discounting a very good chance we might change the course of the war—"

"I appreciate your enthusiasm, Captain Stielau, and your devotion to our cause. But realism is the harshest discipline. The longer view suggests that a bleak future awaits us all, regardless of our interim efforts."

Stielau said nothing, and Skorzeny instantly regretted his frankness.

"We are soldiers, nevertheless," said Skorzeny, closing Von Leinsdorf's dossier. "We play the hand we are dealt. And this man could turn out to be a wild card."

Bernie saw the change in Von Leinsdorf as soon as he returned to the barracks. A hard set in his eyes, jaw taut. He recruited his first two squad leaders that same night: a fellow SS officer, *Unterstürmführer* Gerhard Bremer, and an Army Intelligence translator named Karl Heinz Schmidt. Bernie watched these conversations take place. When Von Leinsdorf returned to his bunk, Bernie asked what was going on but got no answer. *He's following new orders*, thought Bernie. *From Skorzeny himself*.

Von Leinsdorf recruited his third squad leader the next morning, the former American Army sergeant William Sharper. After four years as a GI in North Africa and France, Sharper had deserted to the Wehrmacht three months earlier after beating his superior officer half to death during a barracks poker game. He'd spent those months in the custody of German Intelligence, before being cleared and released for this mission. Von Leinsdorf sized up Sharper as a working-class hooligan, more suited to life as a Nazi storm trooper than in the conformist U.S. Army. He authorized each of the three men to recruit his own four-man squad. When Karl Schmidt pressed

for details about this "second objective," Von Leinsdorf said it had to remain classified until the night before the mission.

That night Von Leinsdorf asked Bernie Oster to join his squad, along with a middle-aged merchant seaman named Marius Schieff and a former bank clerk from Vienna named Gunther Preuss, both Category Two men. Von Leinsdorf told them nothing about what the new assignment involved, but it was clear to Bernie that his status within the brigade had changed for the worse. He no longer feared discovery for what he'd done in Berlin. The path Von Leinsdorf was leading him down now felt far more dangerous.

A week before the launch, Otto Skorzeny attended a final briefing with the Army General Staff at the Reich Chancellery in Berlin. Skorzeny walked through his brigade's role in the invasion, and they agreed on procedures to protect his commandos from German attack. His disguised American tanks would bear two yellow triangles within the unit insignia stenciled onto their armor. If any regular Wehrmacht and commando units met on the battlefield during daylight, the men of Operation *Greif* were to remove their American helmets and hold them over their heads. At night, when encountering regulation German forces, they were to use pistol-fired flares, known as Verey lights, to reveal their identities.

Skorzeny was told that weather forecasts for their target day appeared favorable, calling for heavy cloud cover that neutralized Allied air superiority. All signals were go.

The counteroffensive into Belgium and Luxembourg known as Operation Autumn Mist would begin at dawn on December 16.

4

Grafenwöhr
DECEMBER 10, 1944

hortly after dark on December 10, the men of Operation *Greif* left their camp at Grafenwöhr and loaded onto a special transport train. Bernie saw that the cars had been camouflaged to resemble a shipment of Christmas trees being delivered to troops along the Western Front. Their vehicles, freshly painted and accessorized as American, were loaded on covered flatbeds at the rear of the train. Outfitted in their GI uniforms, Skorzeny's men were not allowed to leave the crowded boxcars during the two-day journey. A Gestapo detachment came on board to protect the train and deflect questions from outsiders about its secret manifest. Bernie knew the heavily armed Gestapo was also there to prevent any of the brigade from deserting.

The 150th Panzer Brigade detrained just before midnight on December 12 near an infantry training grounds at Wahn, southwest of Cologne, where they quartered for the night. To avoid contact with regular Wehrmacht units, they remained confined to the buildings throughout the following day. That night, under blackout conditions, the brigade convoyed in their own vehicles to the town of Münstereifel, twenty miles closer to the Belgian border. Stielau's commando group continued ten miles farther west, near the town of Stadtkyll. During that trip, camouflage netting slipped from a half-track in front of Bernie's transport, revealing its

white five-pointed Allied star. A Wehrmacht patrol tried to intercept what appeared to be a column of American vehicles. They were taken into custody by the Gestapo escort and weren't seen again.

The commandos spent the rest of the night around a remote forester's cottage, organizing into their patrol units and receiving fuel, ammunition, and last-minute supplies. As dawn approached, Bernie could make out the vast bunkers and ramparts of the German Western Wall. Since their arrival at Wahn, he had caught glimpses around the border of a massive Wehrmacht buildup that dwarfed their brigade.

At six A.M., Otto Skorzeny arrived and the company assembled outside the cottage. The only soldier present in German uniform, Skorzeny ordered them to circle around him, informally, in the American manner. He told them their appearance and manners reflected a complete and convincing transformation: They were GIs now. Shivering in the frigid predawn air, Bernie learned for the first time the full scope of Operation Autumn Mist, and their own primary objective. Not as bad as he'd feared, but he knew Von Leinsdorf had something far worse in store. Skorzeny tried to rally them with stories of the German Army's long history of successes in the Ardennes, and how thinly it was now held by the Allies. He told them to be prudent about their use of gasoline, to scrounge any they could while in the field. They were to avoid at all costs any hostile engagement with the enemy.

"Every patrol must remain in radio contact with our corps command," said Skorzeny. "Our mission depends on the intelligence you provide. Make note of everything you see and hear. Trust your training. Take no unnecessary risks."

One man asked the question that was on all of their minds: "Will they treat us as spies if we're captured?"

"I have consulted with experts on international law. If you are captured, we believe that if you wear your German uniform underneath, or change into it beforehand, you will be granted the same protection as any other prisoner of war."

Before they had time to question that, Skorzeny wished them luck and shook every man's hand. Following behind him, his adjutant handed every commando a silver Zippo lighter. Bernie noticed it

gave off a faint smell of bitter almonds. They were told each lighter contained a glass vial of hydrocyanic acid, and that the poison could be used offensively to subdue an opponent. The implication that they were expected to use it on themselves in the event of capture was inescapable.

Skorzeny called Captain Stielau and Lieutenant Von Leinsdorf into the cottage. He asked to hear a summary of Von Leinsdorf's plan for executing the Second Objective, listened quietly, made suggestions but appeared satisfied with his overall strategy. He asked Von Leinsdorf to call in the squad leaders he had selected. Skorzeny chatted briefly with each man, addressing them only by their adopted American names.

Skorzeny's adjutant presented each squad leader with a packet of specially forged documents, including U.S. Army ID cards, high-level American security passes, letters of transit, and detailed maps of various cities in France. They were also given a cache of customized weapons, explosives, and ammunition prepared at Skorzeny's request by the Technical Criminal Institute of Berlin. These included piano wire garrotes, concealed knives, and a new technology: a metallic silencer that attached to the end of their American officer's handgun. He then drew their attention to a map of the Belgian border his adjutant laid out on the table.

"Your squads will be the first to cross, through these gaps in their line," said Skorzeny, showing points of infiltration. "Begin your reconnaissance assignments. Your reports will be vital to us during the early hours. Avoid capture at any cost."

Then Skorzeny for the first time detailed their second objective. When he finished, no one broke the silence. From their shocked reaction Skorzeny knew that Von Leinsdorf had followed orders and refused to discuss the mission with them.

"Sir, at what point are we expected to attempt this?" asked Karl Schmidt.

"I will explain when the colonel leaves," said Von Leinsdorf to silence him.

"I would prefer to hear the colonel's views firsthand," said a defiant Schmidt.

"Your orders are perfectly clear," said Skorzeny. "For the next

two days, reconnaissance and support for the invasion. At midnight on the seventeenth, regardless of whether or not our brigade has reached its first objective, proceed with the second."

"What should we tell the men in our squads?" asked Schmidt.

"Tell them nothing," said Skorzeny. "Until you have to."

"That was my advice as well," said Von Leinsdorf, making clear his irritation.

"What kind of support will we have from the rest of our brigade?" asked Schmidt.

"That depends on the progress of the entire offensive," said Skorzeny. He gestured to his adjutant to pack up, eager to leave.

"No more questions," said Von Leinsdorf.

"But should we expect them, sir?" asked Schmidt, ignoring Von Leinsdorf. "Is anyone else involved or are we acting alone?"

"If all goes according to plan," said Skorzeny, "help will be waiting when you near your target."

"How much help?" asked Schmidt.

"A fifth squad," said Von Leinsdorf.

"There, you see?" said Skorzeny with a smile. "Support will be there when you need it the most. On the other hand, as I always tell my men, expect nothing and you won't be disappointed."

Skorzeny wished them luck and walked out toward his waiting transport, followed by his adjutant. Their vehicle was parked on the edge of a clearing, near where the commandos' twenty American jeeps were being serviced and fueled. The paint on the jeeps' unit insignia was still drying.

"Keep no records of that meeting," said Skorzeny firmly to his adjutant. "As far as Autumn Mist is concerned, it never occurred."

Skorzeny climbed into the transport where his bodyguards waited and drove off to the north.

In the cottage, standing over the various maps of Belgium and France on the table, Von Leinsdorf walked them one last time through their first two days. "On the seventeenth I'll contact each of you by radio. If you don't hear from me, assume we are going ahead and work your way south. We'll stage the operation from here, on the evening of the nineteenth."

He pointed to a prominent old cathedral city, an hour and a half northeast of Paris.

"We need a place to meet," said Von Leinsdorf. "Any suggestions?"

"I was stationed there for a couple weeks," said William Sharper, the American.

"In which army?" asked Schmidt.

"Fuck you, Schmidt. There's an old movie house here, on an old square on the east bank of the canal," said Sharper, pointing to the area. "The Wehrmacht showed films during the Occupation. GIs are using it now."

"Mark it on your maps. Meet at this cinema between nine P.M. and midnight on the nineteenth," said Von Leinsdorf. "Wait no longer than that. Even if you're the only squad, move forward on your own initiative."

Von Leinsdorf shook each man's hand before they all exited the cottage and went their separate ways. He placed a hand on Schmidt's shoulder, holding him back.

"I realize that in our former positions we hold equal rank," said Von Leinsdorf, once they were alone. "And that you've held yours slightly longer than I have mine."

"That's correct."

"Be that as it may, Colonel Skorzeny has put me in charge of this mission. I take that responsibility seriously. If you ever question my authority again, I'll kill you."

Von Leinsdorf stared at Schmidt until he recognized the terror he had over the years grown so accustomed to seeing in weaker men's eyes, then walked outside.

The men of his squad, Bernie Oster, Marius Schieff, and Gunther Preuss, were waiting for him near their own jeep, loading in supplies.

"Good news, gentlemen," said Von Leinsdorf. "We're going across tonight."

5

Northeast Belgium
DECEMBER 14, 1944, 8:40 P.M.

Shivering under a sky thick with stars, three GIs manning the Frontier Control Station lit a fire in a discarded oil drum, in violation of blackout orders. Their tin-roofed hut offered no relief from the arctic air riding in behind a storm front. Winter hadn't officially arrived, but the season's first storm had dropped six inches of snow the night before. Although they were less than four miles from the German border, and occasionally heard engines gunning in that direction, only sporadic skirmishing had broken the calm during the weeks they'd been stationed there. So each night after dark they lit a fire behind their hut and took turns warming their hands, while the others sat inside, playing cards by the light of a Coleman lantern.

They were green recruits—a sergeant and two privates—drafted in the last six months and hastily trained. Their 99th Infantry Division had deployed in the Ardennes only a month before, thrown in beside new units too raw for combat and veterans too beaten down for more. The men's regiment, the 394th, had dug in along a twenty-mile perimeter that paralleled the Belgian-German border, a craggy, forested gap between two mountainous ridges. Stationed at thousand-yard intervals, the soldiers of the 394th spent their days and nights in bone-chilling foxholes, staring at a silent forest, protected from the elements only by rough ceilings of pine branches.

By comparison these three men of Rifle Company F, Squad "D," had drawn a plush assignment, guarding this checkpoint on an old logging road a mile north of the village of Elsenborn. Ten miles to the rear their base camp offered hot meals and showers, Hollywood movies, and touring swing bands that played weekly USO dances swarming with grateful Belgian girls. A conviction had spread through their barracks that the war was all but over. A month of frigid nights hunkered down in the Losheim Gap seemed an easy way to work off your part in the war effort. They might even sail home without firing a shot in anger.

"Sarge," said Private Anderson, from behind the blockhouse.

"What is it?" answered Mallory from inside.

"Something coming."

Headlights washed over the blockhouse window. Sergeant Vincent Mallory of South Boston grabbed his Garand M1 carbine, and Private Jack Ellis followed him out the blanket hanging over the open doorway. Private First Class Chick Anderson stationed himself at the gate beside the striped wooden arm that crossed the dirt road.

A single vehicle drove toward them from the direction of Kalterherberg, a crossroads four miles north, near the German border. Mallory recognized the round headlights and straining gearbox; a Willys Jeep, pack mule of the American Army. He stepped forward and waved the lantern, flagging them down. Ellis readied his rifle and flanked his sergeant in the road ten yards ahead of the gate.

The jeep slowed as it approached. Top down, windscreen flipped up. A GI in the front passenger's seat stood up and frantically waved his arms at Mallory.

"What the fuck—where the hell is this?"

When the jeep stopped a short distance away, Mallory could see that the GI wore a private's stripe. Skinny, agitated, barely out of his teens, black curly hair peeking out from a helmet shoved back on his head. The driver beside him kept his head down, eyes straight ahead on the road.

"Where you coming from?" asked Mallory.

"Jesus, I got no idea—we been driving around out here for I don't know how fuckin' long—how long, Lieutenant?"

He turned to an officer behind him in the backseat. Mallory swung the lantern around.

Four men in the jeep.

The lieutenant with the bar on his collar leaned forward: compact, blond, good-looking, mid-twenties, a confident big-man-on-campus smile.

"And he's supposed to be our fucking navigator," said the lieutenant. "Show him our pass, dummy."

"All fucking night like this," said the jittery private, handing over their trip ticket to Mallory, then turning to Ellis. "You got any smokes, buddy?"

Mallory read the trip ticket, which looked in order, then scanned the unit markings stenciled on the jeep's hood. "You fellas are a long way from Twelfth Army, sir."

"Tell me about it," said the lieutenant, a slight Southern twang in his voice. "We left HQ in Luxembourg eight hours ago. Supposed to hook up with the 106 in Vielsalm at eighteen hundred."

Mallory handed back the pass as he watched the fourth man, in the back beside the lieutenant, unfold a large map.

"You overshot it, sir," said Mallory. "Vielsalm's twenty miles southwest of here."

"That's fuckin' beautiful news," said the private, as Ellis handed him a cigarette. "I tried to tell you, sir, we should've turned left about two hours ago— Hey, thanks, man; you got a match?"

"You don't want to light that here, son," said Mallory.

"Right, shit, what am I thinking?" The private stuck the cigarette behind his ear; Mallory noticed his hands were shaking.

"Probably don't want to be running your headlights either," said Mallory. "Didn't they give you blackouts?"

"Is that why you stopped us, Sergeant?" asked the lieutenant.

"This is a roadblock, sir. We've got orders to stop everybody."

"Well, I'm glad you did. Maybe you can give Private Knucklehead here some pointers on reading a map."

"If I ever get it back— Would you please let me see that?" the private pleaded with the fourth man, who had just flicked on a flashlight, buried his face in the map, and showed no interest in handing it over.

"You're coming from the direction of the Kraut line," said Mallory.

"No shit," said the private. "Why do you think we turned around? You could smell the fuckin' Wiener schnitzel."

"Kind of unusual to see four men in a jeep," said Mallory.

"We're escorting Captain Conway here," said the lieutenant, nodding to the man beside him. "New intelligence officer for the 106."

"Captain." Mallory saluted the man, who didn't respond, still shining his flashlight over the map, looking for something.

"Aren't you supposed to ask me for the password, Sergeant?" asked the blond lieutenant.

"That's right. If we're not sure of the men."

"So what do you do if somebody doesn't know it? I mean, Christ, I don't know it myself."

"Don't worry about it. Password's 'Betty Grable.' They'll ask you for it at the next roadblock outside the village."

"I want to ask these guys a *question*—would you please give me that back, sir?" said the private to the intelligence officer.

Thinking the kid seemed a little out of line talking like that to an officer, Mallory signaled Anderson to raise the gate. In his peripheral vision Mallory noticed that the jeep's driver had no unit insignia on the shoulder of his field jacket.

"So what unit you guys with anyway?" Mallory asked the driver. "Hey, buddy?"

The driver turned toward him but didn't answer. The man looked older than he expected, lined and weathered, forty if he was a day. He smiled and nodded at Mallory, but it seemed like a rehearsed response, furtive and uncomprehending.

This guy's not right, whispered some primal instinct.

Mallory felt a surge of adrenaline kick in. His index finger reconnected with the trigger of his M1.

"We're Field HQ, Radio Company," said the blond lieutenant,

smiling again. "Could I trouble you to give us a hand reading our map?"

The driver gave an awkward wave and turned away from Mallory, training his eyes straight ahead again. In one smooth move the lieutenant stood up in the back and snatched the map from the private's hand just as he wrested it away from the intelligence officer.

"No problem, sir. You know, our radio's on the fritz," said Mallory, moving no closer to the jeep. "Maybe one of you could take a look at it?"

"We're already running pretty late—"

"Sure it'll just take a second, sir. Get it working, we could hail the 106 for you, let 'em know where you're at."

Neither man moved as the lieutenant looked down at Mallory for a long moment; then he smiled again. "Private Tenella, grab your kit."

The lieutenant slipped over the edge of the jeep, landed like a cat, and stopped to fold the large map down to a manageable size. Mallory tried to catch Ellis's eye, but he was helping the private fish out some tools from the back of the jeep.

"Betty Grable," said the lieutenant, shaking his head, as he passed Mallory, headed for the blockhouse. "What'll they think of next?"

"I don't know. Can you believe that bombshell married Mickey Rooney?" asked Mallory.

"I heard it, but I don't believe it," said the lieutenant.

Mallory ran a last visual check on the driver, who was rummaging for something on the front seat. His finger firmly on the trigger, Mallory raised the muzzle toward the lieutenant's back as he turned to follow him, when the man pivoted in his direction.

All Mallory saw was the map, taut in front of his face, moving straight at him. A muffled pop, and the lines and shades of Belgium burst inward. The first bullet caught Mallory under the right ear, shattering his jaw, glancing off the bone, and tearing through the other side of his mouth. Choking on blood and shattered teeth, he dropped his rifle and was reaching for his throat when Von Leinsdorf fired again, catching him in the right shoulder, spinning him around.

The intelligence officer, Gunther Preuss, stood up and hit Private Ellis in the face with the flashlight. Bernie dropped his toolbox and backed away from the jeep.

The driver vaulted out of the jeep and ran toward Anderson at the gate.

Preuss jumped down after Ellis from the jeep, a knife in his hand. They landed with a heavy thud, Ellis underneath giving a groan as Preuss's full weight compressed him.

Anderson turned at the gate to see the driver with a machine pistol in his hand, ten feet away, closing fast. Anderson raised his rifle. They fired simultaneously: Anderson squeezed off two shots; the driver emptied his magazine.

Von Leinsdorf fired once more at Mallory as he toppled over, then turned casually away as if bored with a conversation. Preuss had his knife buried in Ellis's ribs, bearing down on him, using his left hand to push the barrel of Ellis's rifle away from his chest. Grunting with effort, Ellis stubbornly held the gun with both hands, trying to inch a finger toward the trigger. Eyes wild, Preuss looked up at Bernie, standing a few feet away.

"Das Gewehr!" he said. *"Erhalten das Gewehr!"*

Bernie didn't move. Von Leinsdorf marched over, pointed the pistol, with a long steel cylinder attached to the muzzle, at Ellis's head, and fired twice. Once the American went slack, Preuss slapped the rifle away and rolled off the body, breathing heavily.

Bernie felt shock stun his system. He'd never seen anyone die before. He couldn't think; he couldn't move.

"What the fuck?" whispered Bernie. "What the fuck?"

"Get hold of yourself," said Von Leinsdorf; then he turned to Preuss and pointed. "Drag the bodies into those woods."

Von Leinsdorf jogged back toward the gate. Private Anderson lay dead, sprawled facedown in the dirt, bleeding from half a dozen wounds. The driver—merchant seaman Marius Schieff, from Rostock—had propped himself up against the base of the gate, pistol still in hand, looking down at a dark stain spreading across his field jacket.

Von Leinsdorf knelt down beside him and spoke to him gently. "Marius? How bad is it? Can you walk back to the line?"

Schieff smiled grimly. "Walk five miles?"

"We can't turn back, my friend," said Von Leinsdorf.

"*Ich weisse,*" said Schieff. "Go on, leave me here, maybe someone finds me—"

Von Leinsdorf stood up and without hesitating fired twice into Schieff's head at close range. He unscrewed the silencer as he glanced into the guardhouse, then holstered the weapon and walked back to the jeep. Gunther Preuss was already on his feet, grunting with effort as he dragged Ellis's body toward the nearby woods. Bernie hurried toward Von Leinsdorf.

"Jesus Christ, what the fuck did you do?"

"I told you to be quiet. Collect their tags, get the bodies off the road—"

"You know the orders, god damn it, we're not supposed to engage, somebody must've heard those shots—"

Von Leinsdorf walked past him to Mallory's body, flicked open his lighter, and fired up a Lucky Strike as he looked at the dead American. "Who's married to Betty Grable?"

"Betty Grable, the movie star? Fuck if I know—"

"Mickey Rooney?"

"No, it's not him—wait a minute, let me think a second—it's that bandleader, Harry James—what difference does it make?"

"I gave him the wrong answer. He was about to do something heroic." Von Leinsdorf picked up Mallory's legs and glared at Bernie. "Are you just going to stand there, Brooklyn?"

Bernie grabbed Mallory's arms, and they carried him toward the woods. "But how did you know that? How could you possibly know that?"

"There's no radio in the shed," said Von Leinsdorf.

Gunther Preuss, the overweight former bank clerk from Vienna, stomped past them on his way from the woods back toward the guard gate.

"*Was sollten wir mit Schieff tun?*" asked Preuss.

"Take his papers, empty his pockets, put him with the others," said Von Leinsdorf.

"*Kann ich seine Aufladungen nehmen?*"

"For Christ's sake, Preuss, the body's not even cold—"

"Mine . . . they fit no good," said Preuss elaborately.

"That the best you can do?" asked Bernie. "You sound like fucking Frankenstein."

"Then take one of the American's boots," said Von Leinsdorf.

"*Danke, Unterstürmführer—*"

"And speak English or keep your mouth shut, you fat, fucking, useless piece of shit."

Preuss dropped his shoulders and broke into a harried trot. Von Leinsdorf looked over at Bernie, with a sly smile. "What do you think? My slang is improving, yes?"

Bernie glared at him. "You said 'kit.' "

"What about it?"

"It's not a 'kit,' it's a toolbox."

"You're right," said Von Leinsdorf. "Kit's British. Fuck all."

"And you're on Preuss's case? You're fuckin' nuts, you know that?"

Von Leinsdorf laughed, blew smoke, enjoying himself. Twenty yards into the woods, they dropped Mallory's body beside Ellis under a thick stand of evergreens. A gust of wind stirred the branches overhead, dropping clots of wet snow on them.

"Why'd you have to kill Schieff?" asked Bernie.

"He was gut shot, he wouldn't have lasted an hour—"

"We could've treated him, taken him for help—"

"He knew the risks. Besides, you heard what our friendly sergeant said back there," said Von Leinsdorf, tapping Mallory's boot with his. "Americans ride three men to a jeep. You'd think our fearless leaders might have picked up that little detail, eh, Brooklyn?"

Von Leinsdorf leaned down, opened their shirts, and slipped the dog tags off Mallory and Ellis.

"Cover the bodies," he said, tossing the tags to Bernie. "Take their ID, jackets, weapons, anything else we can use. You're driving."

Bernie caught the tags and dropped them into his pocket. His nightmare had come to life; American blood on his hands. Four men

dead in less than five minutes. And Von Leinsdorf seemed to like it. He was practically humming as he walked away. But how long now before they became the hunted?

He saw Mallory's foot twitch once as he rifled through the man's field jacket. He leaned down and realized Mallory was still breathing.

Once Von Leinsdorf was out of sight, Bernie took a sulfa packet, bandages, and an ampule of morphine from his pocket, and knelt down beside the gravely wounded sergeant.

6

arl Grannit leaned out the window of the engine car and looked back along the length of the U.S. Army transport train, eleven freight cars trailing behind them as they rounded a broad turn. He gazed out at the smooth moonlight glancing off the Meuse River as it flashed through the trees, then at his watch under the bare bulb of the cab. He shoveled more coal into the firebox while he waited for his engineer to finish a call on the radio, talking to dispatch.

"How close are we?" asked Grannit, over the roar of the engine, when the call ended.

"Four miles," said the engineer. "Next station's Clermont."

"What about our backup?"

"Says they're all in place. Ready to go."

"Famous last words," said Grannit.

"Think they're gonna make a move, Earl?"

"I'll take a look."

Grannit swung outside on the handrail, found his footing, and inched back along the ledge rimming the coal car. He stepped across to the first freight car, climbed the ladder to the roof, set himself, and looked ahead down the tracks. He could already make out the Clermont station lights piercing the night in the distance. Then he spotted a crossing in the foreground, where two cars were flashing

their headlights toward the oncoming train. The engine had already started to slow; he heard the whining steel grind of the brakes.

At least half a mile short of the station.

"Shit. Shit, shit."

By the time Grannit worked his way back to the engine car, the train had nearly come to a complete stop.

"That was the signal, wasn't it?" asked the engineer, looking wide-eyed. "I was supposed to stop, right?"

"Yeah, Ole," said Grannit. "You were supposed to stop."

Four men were moving toward them alongside the tracks from the crossroads, flashlight beams zigzagging. Grannit grabbed a lantern and jumped down to meet them.

"Hey, how's it going there?" said the man leading the way.

The others behind him hung back. Two wore trench coats with raised collars, peaked hats silhouetted black against the sky. Officers.

The advance man stepped into the light of Grannit's lantern. He was short, energetic, pounding a wad of gum, the flat rasp of Jersey or Philly in his voice. Grannit eyed his insignia; corporal, battalion quartermaster's staff.

"Eddie Bennings, Company C," he said, offering a glad hand. "You new to the unit?"

"Just last week. Me and Ole," said Grannit.

"Welcome to the 724. Let me tell you something, pal: You landed in clover. You been to our billet in Paris yet?" Grannit shook his head. "You'll see. They don't call us the 'million-dollar outfit' for nothing, know what I'm saying?"

"We heard some talk."

"So they put you on the milk run up from Matelot, huh?" Bennings waved to the officers, letting them know he had the situation under control. They headed back to the cars.

"Who's the brass?" asked Grannit.

"Interested parties. We look out for each other in the 724. What the Frogs call 'es-pree de corpse.' I'll explain the drill—what's your name?"

"Earl Grannit. Like I said, that's Ole. Ole Carlson."

"Okay, Earl, there's a side rail coming up on your right about a

hundred yards. We'll switch you over. Take the whole rig onto that side rail. Uncouple the stock you're carrying after car eight then head into the station."

"Just leave 'em?"

"Right. We'll take it from there."

"What if the depot asks questions, the end of our run?"

"That ain't gonna be a problem—"

"We come in three cars light they might—"

"I'm telling you, they won't have a problem," said Bennings. "You're covered, okay? This ain't our first clambake."

Earl Grannit toed the dirt for a second, thinking it over. "So what's our end, Eddie?"

"Listen to you, all business all of a sudden. This ain't gonna take long. We'll hook up on the platform after; you'll make out. Piece a cake. Easy as Betty Crocker."

"Everything after car eight."

"You got it, pally," said Bennings, patting him on the arm and shaking his hand again. He shoved a roll of twenties wrapped around a couple packs of Chesterfields into Grannit's shirt pocket and handed him a box of cigars. "That's just a taste. Wait'll you see the setup in Paris. The 724 takes care of its own, my friend. Our guy Jonesy'll ride in with you, make sure everything's square."

Bennings bounded away down the tracks after the officers. Grannit heard their cars starting up. The fourth man from the cross-road, Jonesy, a hulking, beady-eyed noncom, walked after Grannit toward the engine. Grannit swung back up into the cab ahead of him and stashed the contraband goods in the tender.

"You get all that?" asked Earl quietly.

"The PX cars," said Ole Carlson.

"You signal the station?"

"They're at least five minutes away."

Jonesy climbed up into the cab behind them. Grannit turned to him.

"Ole," said Grannit. "Jonesy."

Carlson nodded, friendly, ready to shake hands. Jonesy stuck a toothpick in his mouth, and put a hand on his hip, showing the

holstered, pearl-handled .45 on his belt. Making it clear he wasn't there to chitchat.

"Let's take her in," said Grannit.

Ole Carlson engaged the throttle and eased the train forward at five miles an hour. They passed Corporal Bennings, standing by the switch at the crossroads. He gave a jaunty little wave as they rolled past him onto the side rail. Grannit leaned out of the cab and checked the stock behind them, signaling Carlson to brake again once the last car cleared the main track.

"You want to let the station know we're delayed?" asked Grannit.

Carlson had picked up the transmitter, when two more GIs walked out of the shadows near the engine car, carrying Thompson machine guns. Jonesy grabbed the handset from Carlson and hung it back up.

"Let 'em worry," said Jonesy. "Let's get it done."

Grannit jumped down and headed back along the train. Jonesy followed him a few paces back. A dozen other uniforms stepped out of the woods around them, converging on the end of the train. Two five-ton cargo trucks pulled up alongside the last few cars, men rolling up their canvas backing, ready to load in.

Like vultures, thought Grannit. *Like they can smell it.*

The first eight cars carried artillery ordnance. They'd been told exactly where the commissary cars started. By the time Grannit reached the coupling, the crew had already pried open the locks and thrown back the sidings. They swarmed inside, foraging through the boxes and crates, looking for cigarettes, liquor, chocolate, soap, coffee. Designated for front-line battalions, this cargo, Grannit knew, would disappear by daybreak into the burgeoning black markets of Paris and Brussels. In the last few months thousands of Allied soldiers had deserted to join this gold-rush racket, siphoning off army supply trains, selling to the French, Belgians, even stranded Krauts with cash. Once the American Army marched into Paris, the situation spiraled out of control. Fortunes were being made. The high-end players were said to be living in style on the Left Bank, like Al Capone and Dutch Schultz. By December over 40 percent of the luxury goods landing at Normandy, the staples of corps morale, never made it to the front-line soldier.

From what Grannit saw in front of him, an entire U.S. railway battalion had been infected, swarming over this train like locusts, their officers standing by to supervise. He'd witnessed enough human imperfection that few variations on the tune surprised him, but this put a fist in his stomach.

Grannit pulled out a heavy coupling jack wedged into the freight car's slats. As he inserted the jack into the joint to uncouple the cars, the train's steam whistle blew: three short bursts, then three long, three short.

Ole sending an SOS. If they were paying attention, their backup at the station would double-time it down the tracks.

Grannit looked over at Jonesy. He had turned around, staring back at the engine, trying to decide what that whistle signified, whether he should worry or not.

Grannit covered the five steps between them and tomahawked Jonesy in the back of his knee with the coupling jack. He buckled and dropped to one knee. Grannit caught him with a second shot on the crown of the right shoulder, paralyzing his gun arm before he could reach his holster. Grannit shoved him and Jonesy hit the ground, whimpering in pain, trying to roll off the damaged shoulder. Grannit pulled Jonesy's Colt and knelt down on top of him, grabbing his neck, driving a knee into the big man's kidney.

"Stay down, Jonesy," he said.

"Fuck, what'd you hit me for?"

"You're under arrest, you dumb shit. Put your hands in front of you and your face in the dirt or I'll blow your head off."

Jonesy complied. Grannit slipped a homemade sap out of his pocket—a black dress sock filled with twelve-gauge shot—and cracked him behind the ear. Jonesy went limp. Grannit stood up and turned toward the PX cars. The train whistle hadn't appeared to alarm the scavengers, and none of them had seen him take Jonesy down in the dark, but more than a few glanced his way. He spotted the two officers he'd seen earlier with Eddie Bennings beside the cargo trucks, looking a lot more concerned.

Grannit walked straight at them, holding the gun at his side. As he got close, the two officers and Bennings headed for their car,

parked nearby. When the engine started, Grannit raised the .45 and shot out the left front tire. The concussion cut through the night. He reached the driver's side, smashed the window with the barrel of the Colt, reached in, and yanked the keys out of the ignition. The man behind the wheel, a captain, looked at him, red-faced and indignant, and made a feeble swipe at Grannit's hand.

"What the hell you think you're doing, soldier?"

Grannit grabbed the captain by the collar, pulled his head out the window, and shoved his neck against the edge of the roof, knocking off his hat. By now he had the whole unit's attention, soldiers coming toward him with weapons drawn, others scattering. Eddie Bennings scrambled out of the backseat, staring at Grannit like he'd seen a ghost.

"Easy, Earl, buddy—" said Eddie.

Grannit jammed the Colt in the captain's cheek and spoke right into his ear. "Name and rank."

"Captain John Stringer."

"Captain, tell your boys to drop everything and lie down where they're standing, right now."

"Who the fuck are you?"

"Military Police, CID." Stringer didn't respond, eyes wide. Grannit leaned in closer. "Criminal Investigation Division."

"What the fuck is that?"

"Bad news for Company C." Grannit spotted Bennings in the corner of his eye, edging away. "Get on the ground, Eddie—all you 'million dollar' sons of bitches!"

Grannit fired a shot in the air and two more at the nearest cargo truck, shredding a tire and blowing off the driver's side mirror. Eddie hit the ground, and most of the others around him followed suit. A few sprinted for the woods.

He heard MP whistles trill in the distance, and heavy footsteps, twenty men running toward them on cinders. Ole and their backup.

"Can't we work something out here?" asked Stringer.

"Sure," said Grannit. "How about twenty years?"

Elsenborn, Belgium
DECEMBER 14, 9:30 P.M.

Betty Grable," said Erich Von Leinsdorf.

The young MP manning the heavily fortified checkpoint just outside the village gave a cursory glance at the three men in the jeep.

"Can I see your trip ticket, sir?" he asked.

"Of course."

Von Leinsdorf tapped Bernie Oster on the shoulder. He handed over a flawless forgery of an American military road pass, detailing their itinerary from Luxembourg City to Vielsalm. A smudged thumbprint obscured the ink around the day, date, and authorizing stamp.

The MP held it under his flashlight, trying to make it out. "You're from Twelfth Army HQ?"

"That's right," said Bernie.

"I don't mean to be an asshole, but we're running an errand for old man Bradley," said Von Leinsdorf. "It's time sensitive."

"Go on through," said the MP, handing back the pass.

"Have a good night," said Von Leinsdorf.

Bernie dropped the jeep into gear and drove past a sandbag installation protecting an unmanned .50-caliber machine gun and an M-10 tank destroyer. The one-lane village crawled with rowdy

GIs, more than a few of them drunk. The snow had turned to slush, and Bernie slowed behind two men weaving down the middle of the road, dragging a freshly cut fir behind them toward a brightly lit tavern in the center of the town, soldiers crowding the door.

"Can we stop to eat?" asked Preuss.

"You can't honestly be that stupid, can you?" said Von Leinsdorf. "Put some distance between us and that checkpoint."

Bernie slammed on the brakes as another GI wandered right in front of the jeep. He carried an open wine bottle and banged on the hood as they jerked to a halt a few feet away.

"Hey, watch it!" the man said.

Bernie waved apologetically. The soldier staggered around the jeep and hung on the passenger side, leaning in to talk to Preuss.

"You hear the latest fuckin' morale booster?" the American asked, "Frankie Frisch, Mel Ott, buncha hotshot ballplayers and some tootsie from the movies, what's her name, that Kraut broad—"

"Marlene Dietrich," said Von Leinsdorf.

"That's the one. Driving all around, visiting wounded and shit—"

Bernie leaned across the front seat, trying to get the drunk to focus on him instead of Preuss. "Mel Ott, how about that? We gotta get a move on now, buddy—"

The drunk leaned in closer toward Preuss, who had a witless smile frozen on his face. Bernie caught a glimpse of Von Leinsdorf drawing his pistol and holding it against the back of Preuss's seat. Ready to shoot if he gave them away.

"But y'know what that means, don't you?" said the drunk. "Letting big shots so close to the line? Means the fuckin' Krauts are done. Kaput."

"Don't be so sure," said Bernie.

"Any luck the turkey shoot's over by Christmas and we're on a gut bucket home. Cheers, buddy."

The drunk offered his bottle to Preuss. Preuss stared at him blankly. Von Leinsdorf leaned forward and grabbed the bottle.

"To Christmas in Connecticut," he said, and took a hearty swig.

"Yes, sir, Lieutenant," said the drunk, trying to straighten as he realized he was talking to an officer. "Didn't see you there."

Von Leinsdorf handed back the bottle. The drunk saluted him, and nearly fell on his ass. Von Leinsdorf watched the drunk stagger away, then looked at the boisterous soldiers stacked outside the noisy tavern, most with open bottles in hand.

"There's your civilian American Army, Brooklyn," said Von Leinsdorf. "Stinking drunk, in uniform, within sight of the front. Bloody amateurs."

The two soldiers finally dragged the fir tree off the road, pausing to toast the three men in the jeep with their bottle.

"Merry Christmas, assholes!" they said.

"Bottoms up, fuckers," said Von Leinsdorf quietly.

"Up your bottoms!" Preuss said to them, half-standing in his seat.

Von Leinsdorf shoved Preuss back in his seat. "I ought to just shoot you right now."

Bernie looked over at Gunther Preuss, his face like putty, panting for breath, mopping the sweat off his forehead in twenty-degree weather. Von Leinsdorf gave Bernie an exasperated glance and Bernie knew they were thinking the same thing: *This shithead's going to get us killed.*

"Hey, you picked him," said Bernie.

"In camp, the model soldier. In the field: a nitwit." Von Leinsdorf cuffed the back of Preuss's head and slid down into his seat. "Get us the hell out of here."

Five miles down the road they crossed the Warche River and entered Butgenbach. For the first time since they'd crossed the Allied lines, their wheels hit two-lane pavement. This town, much larger than Elsenborn, was all buttoned up, not a soul on the streets. A heavy fog crept in, enshrouding the empty streets. A few dim lights glowed through it from the row of tidy businesses they passed.

"These signs are in German," said Bernie.

"This *is* Germany," said Von Leinsdorf. "Over eight hundred square miles. Don't you know your history?"

"It's not my neighborhood," said Bernie.

"This was never part of Belgium; they just gave it to them. Versailles, 1920. Reparations, that was the polite word. A proud moment for the West, putting the Hun in his place. They carved up the German empire like birthday cake. Here. The Saar to France, the Polish corridor, the Southern Tyrol. Crippled our economy and punished a race of innocent people for the crimes of a corrupt monarchy. The Allies' idea of fair play." He gauged Bernie's reaction. "Wasn't this in your American schoolbooks, Brooklyn?"

Bernie let that go. "They still speak German?"

"That's right. When we took it back in 1940, they lined the streets and cheered that they were part of the fatherland again."

"Yeah? What'd they say when the Americans took it back? Heil Roosevelt?"

Bernie glanced back in the mirror at Von Leinsdorf, who couldn't keep the superior smirk off his face.

"Irony. You're aware that's a well-known Jewish trait, Brooklyn."

Bernie didn't answer. Halfway through the town, they dead-ended into the International Highway that ran due west from the German border. Von Leinsdorf signaled Bernie to pull over, then stood in the backseat, surveying both ways down the empty road.

"The panzers will drive straight through here," he said. "Fifty miles from the border to the river and nothing in our way but a rabble of drunken fraternity boys. By God, the plan will work."

Not if I have anything to say about it, thought Bernie.

"So we keep going?" he asked.

"The next village," said Von Leinsdorf.

Three miles west they entered the town of Waimes. Von Leinsdorf signaled Bernie to slow down. He took out his officer's notebook and paged through it.

"What are we looking for?" asked Bernie.

"There's a curfew," said Von Leinsdorf. "We can't stay on this road too late."

"*Ich bin hungrig,*" said Preuss, the first words he'd uttered since Elsenborn.

"I didn't hear that," snapped Von Leinsdorf.

"I have hungry," said Preuss.

"I *am* hungry," said Bernie, correcting him.

"Yes. Me also," said Preuss.

"Speak German again," said Von Leinsdorf, "and I'll feed you your own leg."

Von Leinsdorf scanned the buildings as they continued through the encroaching fog. A lettered sign in the shape of an oversized pink pig loomed out of the mist on the right. Von Leinsdorf told Bernie to pull over beside the butcher's shop beneath it. Preuss looked up at the sign and his mood brightened.

"We eat now," he said.

Von Leinsdorf banged on the front door. Bernie peered through the front display window. A massive shape carrying a lantern appeared inside and moved behind the door.

"We close," said a woman's voice.

"*Das Phoenix steigt. Der Pfeil fliegt,*" said Von Leinsdorf.

The Phoenix rises. The Arrow flies.

The woman shuffled to the window and held up the lantern to look at them. She stood over six feet tall, wrapped in a cheap housecoat. Bernie shrank back on instinct as she appeared in the light.

Her enormous head looked oblong, misshapen, and her skin was flushed with ragged scarlet patches—a peasant's face, absent a healthy glow of outdoor labor. Bright, small eyes peered out from beneath a thick ridge of simian bone. A fringe of lank, mousy brown hair hung down in greasy clumps. Her tongue darted out between thick sensual lips as she sized them up. With a sidestep she vanished again, and the door opened.

"*Gekommen,*" she said.

"Park the jeep around back," said Von Leinsdorf to Bernie.

Von Leinsdorf and Preuss followed her into the shop. A smell of onions and fried meat wafted off her. With every step waves of cascading fat shimmied down her upper back. She led them through a storeroom behind the sales counter, into a small abattoir with a

stained concrete floor. Two bare bulbs provided the only light. A butchered animal carcass hung from a steel hook suspended on a chain connected to a bolt in the ceiling. Judging by the shape, Von Leinsdorf thought it might be a dog. A sharp scent of blood and offal thickened the air. The woman turned sideways to wedge her girth behind the cutting block. She opened a hidden hatch in the wall, then slid out a small shelf revealing a crystal wireless shortwave radio.

"Für zu verwendende Sie," she said to Leinsdorf.

"Please, fräulein, may we speak English?" asked Von Leinsdorf, indicating Preuss. "My friend needs the practice."

"The *Amis* come here, but never find this radio," she said. "I speak with my contact every day. They tell me you come."

"Good; that's what they were supposed to do. The *Abwehr* was also supposed to leave a package for us here. Do you have it with you?"

"No package. No one comes."

"Did they contact you about it?"

"No. No *Abwehr* comes. The *Amis* take all the food, from all the village. They leave me nothing." She picked up a large meat cleaver from an array of cutting instruments on the chopping block, which was covered with a mass of some half-minced internal organ. "They don't tell me you dress like the *Amis*."

The cleaver posed both a question and a threat. Von Leinsdorf tried to keep her focused on him, and not Preuss.

"And you mustn't tell anyone either, fräulein," said Von Leinsdorf, turning on an authoritative charm. "It is fräulein, isn't it?"

The big woman blushed, the scarlet patches on her cheeks glowing like embers. "Frau. Frau Escher."

Bernie entered the house through the back after parking the jeep and came face to face with Frau Escher, clutching the meat cleaver.

"Whoa, what the fuck," said Bernie.

Von Leinsdorf signaled Bernie to stay calm. "What is your Christian name, my dear?"

"Lisolette," she said, smiling coquettishly.

"What a pretty name. And might I ask, where is Herr Escher?"

"German Army. Four years. I see him last time two years."

After a while looking at her, he probably ran all the way to the Russian Front, thought Bernie.

"Four years without your husband is a terrible sacrifice," said Von Leinsdorf. "We're proud of you, working for our cause, giving us information with your radio. Risking your life during this American occupation. You've done a great service for your country."

She blushed again. "So kind of you to say."

Bernie couldn't tell if she was crazy or just simple. Maybe it was both.

"Another favor, Frau Escher," said Von Leinsdorf. "We were told you could give us something to eat. And shelter for the night."

"I would be happy," she said; then she frowned and re-gripped the cleaver. "But why you dress like the *Amis*?"

"A top secret assignment," said Von Leinsdorf. Then whispering: "On orders from the Führer himself."

"No."

"I swear to you, it's true."

"*Mein Gott.* I go now. You eat."

Frau Escher laid down the cleaver, flashed a travesty of a schoolgirl smile at Von Leinsdorf, and waddled into the front room. Von Leinsdorf signaled the others to follow, while he turned to the radio. He fingered the tuning knobs; their slotted grooves were slippery with clotted animal fat.

Disgusted, Von Leinsdorf took out his handkerchief and wiped off the knobs. He dialed in the frequency for their corps command post, twelve miles east of the border. He spoke in prearranged code, broadcasting less than a minute, letting headquarters know they were safely across. He made it clear their other jeep squads should steer clear of the Elsenborn logging road, but made no mention of the shooting at the checkpoint. He also let them know the package they'd expected to find from the *Abwehr* in Waimes had not arrived. After a pause, the dispatcher told him to return to the butcher shop the next day and try again.

Report of their success encouraged Colonel Skorzeny to step up deployment of their remaining commando squads. Before dawn, nine more advance teams of Operation *Greif* would infiltrate the American line.

Then there would be only twenty-fours hours until it began.

8

Shortly after Earl Grannit and Ole Carlson arrested Captain John Stringer and his squadron of thieves near the Clermont station, two platoons of MPs raided the 724th's barracks at Liège and dropped a net over the rest of C Company. MPs herded the suspects into the ballroom of the Hotel Britannique. Set on top of a ridgeline to the north of the Losheim Gap, this marshy plateau around Spa had been uninhabitable until the Romans discovered natural thermal baths percolating up from under the barren sulfuric soil. Over the centuries, as the city of Spa grew to accommodate the well-heeled travelers who came to bask in those beneficial waters, the name became the generic term for all such pleasure-seeking temples. Since early October, Spa's ornate nineteenth-century resorts had all been commandeered by First Army.

When he arrived at the hotel, Grannit was pleased to see over ninety anxious GIs cooling their heels in the ballroom. The two officers, and three others who'd been hauled in from the barracks, including the battalion commander, had been confined to private rooms upstairs. Grannit and Carlson filled out their paperwork in the hotel's ornate lobby, smoked cigarettes, and ordered coffee and sandwiches from the kitchen, while they waited for their superiors and counterparts in Army Intelligence to arrive.

"What the heck is this, Spam?" asked Carlson, scrutinizing the contents of his sandwich.

"Pâté," said Grannit.

Carlson kept staring at it. "Sure looks like Spam."

"I'm pretty sure they use some of the same parts."

"Of what?"

"Of whatever goes into Spam. Pig, cow," said Grannit, taking another big bite.

Eyeing the meat spread suspiciously, Ole took an exploratory sniff.

"It's not going to bite back, Ole."

"Smells iffy," said Carlson.

"You eat Spam, don't you?"

"Sure. Spam's great. Breakfast, lunch, and dinner. Fourteen different ways."

"Trust me on this," said Grannit. "Whatever parts of those pigs or cows that's in Spam? What's in here is from higher up."

Ole put the sandwich back together, took a small, cautious bite, and rolled it around in his mouth for a while.

"You're right, Earl," said Carlson. "That is a whole lot tastier than Spam."

They'd only been partnered a few weeks. Carlson had been an insurance investigator and volunteer fireman back home in Sioux Falls. Grannit liked how that prepared him for both the quick, unpredictable action and the crushingly dull aftermath of police work. Ole had gone through training as an MP before being transferred to CID, where he specialized in forgery and document work, the area of insurance fraud that he'd trained in. Ole was religious, always went to chapel on Sundays, and said his prayers but never threw it at you. He liked Ole for his flat, halting Midwestern voice, too, his blond brush cut on a head like a shot put, and his straight-ahead nature.

"Man, I like this French coffee," said Carlson. "Got some hair on it. Makes you want to stand up and say hello."

"That's Belgian coffee," said Grannit.

Ole just nodded. He watched two uniformed MPs lead another

group of GI suspects through the lobby. "You gonna handle interrogating these boys?"

"Many as they'll let me," said Grannit.

"That the kind of thing you do back in New York, Earl?"

"That's right, Ole."

"Thieves and murderers and rapists—"

"We didn't turn anybody away."

"Man oh man oh man. Life in the big city." Ole pondered for a moment. "Could I watch you interrogating these fellas?"

"That's not up to me," said Grannit.

"I figure I could pick up a lot from that. About detective work and what have you."

"Nothing personal, okay? This ain't night school. Just keep your eyes open and don't pass up an opportunity to shut the hell up. What you do with it after is your business."

"Sure, okay," said Carlson. "I can tell you're mad, though. Makes me mad, too, these railroad bums. Thinking about what they did."

"Don't lose any sleep over it."

Grannit finished his sandwich, stretched out on the sofa, pulled his hat down over his eyes, and folded his arms. Carlson had watched him do this before, grabbing short bursts of shut-eye, and figured it for an old detective's trick, catnapping when he got the chance. Ole decided to give it a try and squirmed to get comfortable in the big overstuffed chair. Grannit cocked open an eye and watched Ole decide whether or not he should park his muddy boots on a heavy gilded table. Then he got up, spread out an edition of *Stars and Stripes* on the table, sat back down, and eased one boot down and then the other on the folded page.

Grannit pulled his hat back down. There was the occasional shit about Ole that drove him nuts, too.

A young captain and lieutenant from Army Intelligence showed up at five in the morning, throwing their weight around, while their adjutants ran around for coffee and donuts. When they started bitching about how hard they were going to have to work to keep

the whole stinking Railway Battalion story out of the *New York Times*, Grannit turned over a table in their laps.

"We just broke the biggest criminal case of the war trying to solve a front-line morale problem, so I don't give a fuck it's a public relations headache for some rear-echelon horse's ass. You got that?"

Grannit's superiors from CID showed up in time to hear that and let it drop that Lieutenant Grannit had fifteen years in NYPD robbery-homicide. The hotshots from Intelligence seemed eager to tidy up their paperwork and hit the road.

At daybreak, over breakfast, the CID prosecutors laid out what they hoped to hear from these suspects before their courts-martial. Grannit liked what he heard about due process in a military tribunal: They required less burden of proof during wartime, which meant no lawyering bullshit from defendants' counsel. But Supreme Command wanted this mess scooped up and thrown out with the trash, and no ink spilled in the press with the war headed into the final innings. Home-front spirits were riding high, and nobody wanted to spoil Mom and Pop's Sunday dinner dwelling on the sordid details about these greedy, thieving pricks.

"How we going to do that, Earl?" they asked.

"You need confessions," said Grannit.

"What we're hearing so far," said one of the senior MPs, "is that none of 'em wants to cooperate."

None of them had a solution. Grannit held back, reminding himself that CID was a brand-new unit, less than four months in the field, organized to handle major felony crimes committed by GIs against fellow soldiers or civilians. With such limited time to get on its feet, they'd barely had a chance to print manuals, let alone train their personnel. To keep peace at home when the war broke out, Uncle Sam handed every working American cop a draft exemption. Grannit had tried to enlist during the first weeks of the war, but NYPD brass said he was too valuable to let go. Twenty-seven months and one pricey midtown lawyer later, he had argued his way off the force and into the army without forfeiting his pension. The next day

they shipped him to the new Criminal Investigation Division training base in Michigan.

His superiors had never worked a day in civilian law enforcement. They were career soldiers in the Military Police, straight as their standard-issue neckties. You wanted traffic control in a crowded staging area, a fight in a dockside bar suppressed, or chain of custody maintained on prisoners of war? That played to the MPs' strengths— logistics, discipline, and security; all beat-cop talents—but they were ill equipped for felony detective work. In less than a week the men trying to run CID realized Grannit knew more about organizing a criminal investigation force than they did. The railroad case had taken six weeks to crack, and Grannit had quarterbacked the effort. Now they were waiting for him to send in the next play.

"What you got here is a massive racketeering operation," said Grannit. "Organized crime, like we had on the Brooklyn docks."

"You work those cases?"

"A couple."

"How'd you break 'em?"

"Hook a small fish. Small fish gives up a bigger fish. Roll 'em over like that all the way up the line."

"HQ needs this to go away today," said the senior CID man.

"Then for starters," said Grannit, "let me talk to 'em."

Grannit strolled through the holding area in the ballroom, studying faces. He picked out six men, including Corporal Eddie Bennings. They were hustled upstairs to the fourth floor and tossed into a room. Grannit had some MPs empty out the furniture, turn off the heat, and open the windows to the balcony. He let the suspects stew for an hour in the freezing cold, with orders to keep silent. The first time the MPs outside heard one of them say a word, they marched in and took away their matches and cigarettes. Whenever one of them dozed off, the MPs kicked him awake.

Two hours later, Grannit walked into the hotel room, followed

by the three biggest MPs in the unit, swinging their nightsticks. Grannit wore a brown civilian suit with no badge or insignia. He explained to the prisoners that during the next fifteen minutes they were each going to write and sign a confession detailing their involvement in the battalion's black-market activities. He set paper and pens down in the middle of the floor and lit a cigarette. The six men looked at him and one another, but no one moved toward the pens.

Grannit finished his cigarette, walked over to the toughest-looking guy in the group, slammed his head into the wall, and went to work on his kidneys. By the time he finished, the man was urinating on himself and four of the other five suspects had pens in their hands. Each was escorted to a separate, heated room down the hall, where they were told a hot meal and a cocktail of their choice would be served as soon as they finished their confessions.

Grannit stayed in the cold room with Eddie Bennings, the one man who hadn't picked up a pen.

"You're not going to write a statement?"

"Fuck you," said Bennings.

Grannit ordered the other MPs out of the room and lit another cigarette.

"I know you from someplace, Eddie?"

"Where the fuck would I know you from?"

"You ever been fingerprinted in a New York police station? Done any time? Eduardo DiBiaso, that's the name you were born with, isn't it?"

"Where'd you get that?"

"Right here on your paperwork, Eduardo. Why is that, you change it for the draft board to get the stink of garlic off you? Or were you dodging a warrant?"

Bennings narrowed his gaze, working hard to show how little he cared. Grannit had known this pissant had a rap sheet the moment he laid eyes on him, strictly small potatoes, a wannabe who'd clocked enough time around the mob to lose his moral compass.

"You got a wife and kids back home, Bennings?"

"I got a wife."

"That where you're sending the money? Home to the wife?" No response. "Which makes her an accessory after the fact. We could go after her, too. Send the NYPD to her door. What's her taste been so far, five thousand? Ten?"

"I got nothing to say till I talk to a lawyer."

"Lawyer? Where the fuck you think you are, Hoboken? There's no justice system here. There's no neighborhood capo back home taking care of the family 'cause you kept your mouth shut. Military courts don't work that way. This ain't some penny-ante beef, pinching rum off the back of a Seagram's truck. These are war crimes, pal. People go to jail for life or face a firing squad. We got you on ice. You don't play ball, you're never gonna see your wife again."

"Bullshit."

"And once word gets around how you guys ripped off our troops in the field? Life in the brig is gonna be some hard fucking time."

The first crack showed in Eddie's practiced tough-guy facade. "What about it?"

"We know you got a relationship with the officers running this show. You brought some experience from home; they trust you 'cause you got things done. You're a key man for them. You want to tell me anything different?"

Eddie didn't.

"Help us put those big shots in the pokey and the system's gonna treat you better. That's common sense. Your boys are soldiers, not gangsters, so nobody's coming back at you if you roll over, you might not even stand trial. A slap on the wrist, maybe. They transfer you into another unit with no jail time."

"What, so I can get killed on the front line? Thanks but no thanks."

"Okay, Eddie. So we'll go with choice number three."

Grannit stubbed out his cigarette, grabbed Eddie by the collar and wrist, and marched him through the balcony doors.

"What's that? What the fuck you doing?"

"I turn my back for a split second, you were so despondent you

threw yourself over the rail. Tragic waste of life. No death payment, no gold star in the window, no folded flag for the missus—"

"Wait a second, wait a second—"

"You don't think I'm pissed off enough? I'd be doing a favor for everybody in your life you're going to fuck over if you live through this—"

Eddie grabbed hold of the wrought iron balcony with both hands for dear life as Grannit muscled him to the edge.

"Okay, okay, I'll write it, I'll write it, I'll cooperate—"

"You sure about that?" Grannit yanked hard on his arms.

"I'm sure, I'm sure, Jesus Christ!"

Grannit let him drop to the floor of the balcony, panting like a puppy, slick with sweat.

"Fifteen minutes," he said, and walked out of the room.

By six o'clock that night the urge to confess had spread through the 724th like old-time religion. Whenever Earl Grannit returned to the ballroom, he found more willing volunteers to take upstairs. He'd seen this before, panic spreading through a pack of crooks on some silent animal wavelength. By midafternoon, he no longer needed to speak to suspects personally and handed them off to teams of junior CID officers like Ole Carlson, who needed the experience. As confessions piled up on their desks, the Army Intelligence men in charge felt as if they'd witnessed Grannit turn water into wine.

The CID brass organized dinner for their investigators that night in the hotel's private dining room. Grannit made it clear he didn't want anybody making too big a deal, but there was no doubt about who they were celebrating. CID had cracked its biggest case of the war, and Earl Grannit made it happen.

During the main course, a radio message came into the communications center downstairs for CID's commanding officer. Three GIs from the 394th stationed at a checkpoint outside a small village called Elsenborn fifteen miles due east had gone AWOL overnight. Local MPs were on their way to investigate, so the

radio operator didn't feel it was important enough to interrupt the dinner.

An hour later, the radio man burst into the room during coffee and dessert with a second dispatch: The missing men's bodies had been found in the woods a mile outside of town.

9

The Road to the Meuse, Belgium
DECEMBER 15, 7:00 A.M.

The three other commando teams working under Erich Von Leinsdorf crossed into Belgium before midnight and passed through American lines without incident. Gerhard Bremer's team spent the night with a family of German sympathizers in the town of St. Jacques. American deserter William Sharper's team, posing as a forward recon unit for Fifth Army, reached their safe house in Ligneuville. Karl Schmidt's team lost their way, fell in behind a convoy of American vehicles heading west, then peeled off after midnight and spent the remainder of the night hidden in a forest. All three teams were up and on the road, heading west, before first light.

Von Leinsdorf's squad spent the night on the floor in the parlor of Frau Escher's apartment over her butcher shop in Waimes. Bernie Oster drifted between sleep and consciousness, disturbed by a persistent vision of their fleshy hostess storming into the room with her meat cleaver while they slept. Every time a floorboard groaned, a blast of adrenaline went off in his gut like a firecracker. By five A.M. Bernie couldn't lie still any longer and went downstairs to piss.

The woman was already working at the bench in the shop's back room. He could see her distorted shadow splashed against the far wall and heard the rough rasp of a bone cutter. He stepped quietly outside into the frigid morning air, his feet crunching on a crust of muddy

frost. Their jeep sat just around the corner. The International High-way stretched out in front of him. The impulse to bolt hit him so hard he couldn't catch his breath.

But which way should he run? Back toward the German line, into the teeth of the offensive that was about to be unleashed? Not as long as Erich Von Leinsdorf had access to a radio; they'd shoot him as a deserter, or take him for a GI and kill him on sight. Maybe if he lay low for a day and changed into civilian clothes, he could slip across once the attack began. But the odds of making his way home to Frankfurt without papers or travel passes were low. He tried to put the thought from his mind, but after months of Allied carpet bombing, for all he knew his parents were already dead.

No, he should head deeper behind the American line, try to hook up with one of their units, and tell them the Krauts were about to invade. Would they buy it? Wasn't that what they'd trained him for these last three months? To pass as an American? In his heart of hearts, in his mortal soul, he was still a kid from New York who wanted his old life back. But what if he broke down under questioning, and the truth came out?

Who was he kidding? Betting his life on the mercy of the U.S. Army with the Germans about to rain holy hell down on them? He'd be court-martialed and shot in no time flat. So how could he warn them without dying for it?

One other way occurred to him. They had stashed their regulation Wehrmacht gear in four jerricans strapped to the jeep. He could take off in the jeep, change into his German uniform, then walk west waving a white flag and surrender as a deserter who'd just come across the lines. Tell them everything he knew about the coming attack, and live out what was left of the war as an Allied prisoner. That was his best chance, but only until zero hour. As soon as bullets started flying, his bargaining chip lost its value. But did he know enough about the offensive beyond what his own brigade was doing? His knowledge about even that was sketchy; Von Leinsdorf had kept them in the dark.

His mind raced back and forth, stuck on a final question: Was it

worth the risk of giving Erich Von Leinsdorf a reason to hunt him down?

"Did she feed you breakfast?"

He turned sharply. Von Leinsdorf stood six feet behind him.

Jesus, I didn't even hear him coming.

Bernie worked to keep the traitorous thoughts he'd been dancing with off his face. Von Leinsdorf took a piss, supremely casual, a cigarette on his lip.

"Fuck no," said Bernie. "Not after that dinner she fed us. Bet my left nut this fucking village is missing some cats."

Von Leinsdorf chuckled, and buttoned his pants back up. "Go tell Preuss we're leaving."

"She said the Americans took all her food? Jesus, how fat was she before the war started?"

"Get Preuss."

Bernie worried for a moment that the man had read his mind.

"What, you don't want to see her again either?"

"Fuck no," said Von Leinsdorf, and smiled slyly.

He found Preuss hunched over the table in the kitchen, greedily scarfing down a thin fried egg and another plate of sausages from Frau Escher's display case of mystery meats. The woman sat on a stool in the corner polishing Preuss's new GI boots.

"Well, ain't this a cozy picture of domestic bliss," Bernie said.

Preuss looked up at him, half-chewed food in his mouth, slack-jawed and clueless. Frau Escher offered Bernie a plate for himself, but his stomach turned at the thought of it. He pulled Preuss out the back door, still carrying his boots, to where Von Leinsdorf had backed up their jeep.

The woman waved from her doorway as they drove off. Preuss waved back. Bernie saw her wiping her eyes with a handkerchief.

"She's set her cap for you, Preuss," said Von Leinsdorf.

"Cap? What is this?" asked Preuss.

"She's in the market for a husband."

"You want to fill that position, Preuss?" asked Bernie.

"I like her cooking," said Preuss.

Bernie meowed like a cat.

"Here pussy, pussy, pussy," said Von Leinsdorf. "Here pussy, pussy, pussy."

"I don't appreciate," said Preuss, turning red. "I don't appreciate."

Bernie and Von Leinsdorf broke out laughing.

The highway filled with routine morning traffic as they traveled west. Allied security loosened, and the road took on the look and feel of an ordinary day; citizens going about their business, soldiers minding theirs. They passed a major crossroads outside Malmédy, then worked southwest through Stavelot to the bridges over the Ambleve River at Trois-Ponts. The Ambleve was the last geographic obstacle before the ground graded down toward the Meuse River valley. Bernie watched Von Leinsdorf make coded entries in his notebook, detailing each defensive position they passed. The deeper they drove, the more encouraged Von Leinsdorf became; the Allies had no idea what was about to hit them.

By late afternoon, as daylight faded, they drew within sight of the Meuse River and the bridge at Amay. They pulled off the road on a steep bluff above the river, into a stand of woods. Heavy clouds rolled in as they made camp, a new weather system lowering the ceiling and reducing visibility, exactly as forecast. Allied aircraft would be neutralized by those skies, attack planes and reconnaissance alike. Preuss broke out packets of American K rations they'd taken from the dead GIs. Bernie activated their field transmitter, adjusting the antennae until he secured a signal. Preuss came over to show him one of the K rations.

"Look here," said Preuss. "Can you believe this?"

"It's just a slice of cheese, Preuss."

"No, look, it have bacon in it," he said, pointing to the cheese, then taking a bite. "Real bacon. Here, try."

Bernie took a bite to humor him. The cheese was hard, dry, and bland as wax, but carried an insistent odor of rancid pork.

"That's okay, Preuss."

"An army which can do this," said Preuss, shaking his head in admiration. "Cheese *mit* bacon."

Von Leinsdorf climbed a nearby embankment, unfolded a map, and studied the bridge below through field glasses. Light traffic, half of it American military, flowed in both directions. Sandbags surrounded an antiaircraft gun emplacement and a single machine gun on the eastern shore, manned by what looked like a single platoon. He saw no forces at all on the western shore. Bernie joined him, while Preuss sat a short distance away with a pad and pen. Trained as the reconnaissance officer for their squad, he began sketching in details of the bridge on a hand-drawn map.

"That's why we're here?" asked Bernie. "That bridge?"

"Our first objective," said Von Leinsdorf. "We take and hold it, and two others between here and Namur, before the Americans can destroy or defend them."

"Just me, you, and lard-butt over there."

"The entire commando company. Tomorrow, after our recon. Bremer, Schmidt, and Sharper's teams are scouting the other two."

Bernie thought about it for a moment. "You said first objective."

"Did I?"

"Does that mean there's a second one?"

Von Leinsdorf didn't look at him. Bernie felt him hiding something, and tried again.

"All those crazy stories flying around camp. We went through all that training just to take a few bridges and sit on our hands?"

"What are you asking?"

"You know what I'm asking," said Bernie. "Are we supposed to do something else?"

Again Von Leinsdorf kept quiet.

"Doesn't take a genius to figure it out," said Bernie, trying to keep the alarm from his voice. "Skorzeny gave you another assignment. You picked the other squads."

"What if he did?" said Von Leinsdorf.

"Then come on, at least tell me what it is."

Von Leinsdorf bent over the radio to transmit a coded report of their progress.

"When our tanks cross this bridge," said Von Leinsdorf, "all that stands between them and the coast at Antwerp is seventy miles of

open highway. Once they're past here, we move on to something else. And that's all I can say."

He stared at Bernie, hard, then turned back to the radio.

Okay, asshole, thought Bernie. *Keep your secret. But I'm going to find out what it is.*

East of Elsenborn
DECEMBER 16, 1:00 A.M.

"Their relief detail showed up as scheduled at fourteen hundred hours yesterday afternoon," said the MP, "but the squad's position couldn't be immediately ascertained."

"You mean they weren't here," said Grannit.

"That's correct, sir."

The MP walked Grannit from the jeep toward the cinder-block guardhouse. The young soldier—too eager to please—had been first on the scene with jurisdiction ever since he'd arrived a few hours ago. Once the bodies were discovered, a crowd had descended. Grannit could already see they'd made a hash of it, two dozen soldiers trampling the crime scene. What was left of the snow had melted into thick slurry and frozen again during the night. Grannit picked up a stick and ran it along the ground.

"What's your name, son?"

"Chester Brosh, sir."

"Chester, take a deep breath, blow your whistle, and get that giant cluster fuck over here behind this line I'm drawing," said Grannit.

"Right now, sir?"

"Yes, right now."

Chester blew his whistle. It took five minutes to clear traffic in front of the blockhouse. Grannit had the drivers line up all the vehicles in a semicircle and turn on their headlights. Once the blockhouse was lit up and secure, he walked around and studied the scene from different angles, knelt down to look at some tire tracks, pointed out

areas he wanted Ole and the other MPs to comb over, then told Chester to lead him to the bodies.

Grannit used a flashlight to follow the ground toward the woods as they walked. Under a dense copse of fir trees, many of the branches still laden with snow, three bodies lay next to one another. They were stiff with cold and rigor mortis. Each had been stripped of his jacket and dog tags. One was missing his boots.

"Anybody ID these men?" asked Grannit.

"Guys from their squad say this is Private Anderson and that's Private Ellis," said Brosh, pointing to the man without boots. "They had a third man out here with them, Sergeant Mallory, but we can't find him."

"So who the hell is this guy?"

"They didn't know him, sir."

Grannit looked at the third man. Near forty. Weathered, wind-burned face and a working man's hands. He studied the man's right hand, then examined his wounds. A single shot, left torso, with a large exit wound through the back, probably a rifle round. Double-tap gunshot wound to the head, small-caliber, close-range, the same as Ellis. He had a small tattoo on his right shoulder, a nautical an-chor and rope. Grannit looked into the man's mouth, then took out a plastic bag and secured it around the man's right hand.

Grannit lit a cigarette and settled back on his haunches. All three men had been killed out by the road; then, judging by the boot prints, they were dragged back here by three fellow GIs. As he ex-amined the ground, he noticed another faint drag line in the dirt moving away from this spot deeper into the woods. He followed it with his flashlight. About fifty yards into the trees the beam flashed on another pair of combat boots. Grannit pulled his pistol and hur-ried toward them.

A fourth man had dragged himself away from the others. He had scooped out a shallow depression to keep himself warm, and cov-ered himself with downed branches, which Grannit hurriedly tossed aside. The soldier still wore his field jacket and lay on his side, curled up, unconscious. Grannit felt for a pulse.

"This man's still alive," said Grannit.

A medic summoned to the scene covered him in blankets and pumped four units of blood into Sergeant Mallory as they drove him to a field hospital ten miles away in Malmédy.

At five in the morning Grannit completed his sweep of the checkpoint. The other soldiers hadn't been any help, but Ole Carlson collected eight shell casings from around the guard gate, six small-caliber and two copper-jacketed M1 rounds. Ten yards short of the gate, where Grannit found tire tracks in the mud, he turned up three more pistol rounds. Grannit also bagged a broken cigarette, a Lucky Strike, unsmoked. He pinpointed a number of bloodstains—one on the base of the road gate itself—and a few more footprints, all of them regulation GI combat boots.

Before they took the bodies away, Grannit asked the medic to have the hospital remove any bullets before they were turned over to a graves detail. He needed them for forensics, and if it wasn't too much to ask, he also wanted autopsies. The medic said he'd try, and told him to come by the field hospital later that morning when they'd have a clearer picture of Sergeant Mallory's condition. Grannit agreed. If Mallory made it, Grannit wanted to be there when he came around.

Ole Carlson brought him a cup of coffee from a supply wagon and they stood near the blockhouse, stamping their feet to stay warm.

"What do you think happened, Earl?" asked Carlson.

"They drive up in a Willys out of the north, down the logging road. Pull up short of the gate. The detail's playing cards inside; they step out to question them. Whatever the beef was, it starts here, next to the jeep. Mallory, Ellis, and the third man are tapped by the same shooter. Somebody else kills Anderson over by that gate. The third man's hit first by a second shooter, in the chest, with an M1. Then he was shot in the head afterward like the others. The third man's the only one of them who discharged his pistol."

Carlson stared at him with his mouth open. "Geez, you think he killed the other two?"

"No, Ole," said Grannit patiently. "He got shot the same as Ellis, right? In the head."

"Right."

"I think the third guy ran toward the gate and shot Anderson—he's got six small-caliber rounds in him—and Anderson shot him back with the M1. Won't know for sure till I see the bullets, if they don't fuck that up at the hospital, which is a big if."

"Okay," said Carlson. "So we got GIs shooting GIs. Maybe it's a robbery. Maybe the parties knew each other. Maybe the killers drove out here to settle some score, or a gambling debt—"

"Facts first, theories later." Grannit stepped forward, setting the scene. "Our third man came in on the jeep with three others. One of those men is the main shooter."

"They shoot 'em, drag the bodies, dump 'em in the woods, and just drive off?"

"That's right. With one of 'em wearing a new pair of boots," said Grannit. "Ask the MPs in Elsenborn if any jeeps came through there last night that fit the profile. See if any infantry dug in around here heard anything. The trail's already cold."

Carlson hurried off toward the other MPs. Soldiers carried the bodies by him on three stretchers, covered by ponchos. Grannit asked them to hold up. He uncovered the third man, looked at the tattoo on his arm again and the dental work in his mouth. Then he examined his boots. He wore them without leggings, against dress regulations, but not unheard of in the field. Reaching inside, he found a small photograph tucked in the calf of the man's right boot and held it up to his flashlight. A casual Kodachrome snapshot with scalloped edges, probably taken with a Brownie, of a woman in her mid-thirties standing on a dock near a waterline. An ordinary brunette in a swimsuit, overweight, her arms folded self-consciously across her middle, forcing a smile for the camera. Bright midday sun overhead, shining in the woman's eyes, causing her to squint.

The man's wife or girlfriend at some vacation spot, probably the last one they spent together. A row of buildings lined the shore to the right, a couple of street vendors visible in soft focus behind her. The developer's stamp on the back was slightly smudged, but it

looked like "August 1944." Grannit kept looking at it. Something about the photograph felt wrong, although he couldn't put his finger on why.

Grannit shined the flashlight on the face of his watch: 5:30. Daylight wouldn't break for another hour. He caught a flicker of bright light out of the corner of his eye to the east, miles in the distance. As he looked up, more pinpricks of intense light blossomed, like an immense panel of flashbulbs going off. The thick cloud cover on the eastern horizon began to glow as if a full moon had just lit up the sky.

It occurred to him in that split second that the last few hours had passed silently, none of the distant small-arms fire you heard this close to the front. Not even a dog barking.

Grannit ran toward the ring of vehicles, calling for Carlson, looking for their jeep. He jumped in behind the wheel, shouting at Ole to get in—

Just then a roar like a hundred distant thunderstorms filled the night from the east, shattering the silence with a series of cascading booms that stepped toward them in intensity.

Then the barrage hit and obliterated time.

The first fourteen-inch shells whistled overhead and crashed through the highest trees. A shower of others landed and detonated across a thousand-yard range, shaking the earth in a continuous shudder. Grannit saw a string of explosions and flame rising to the east, closer to the border, lines of trees uprooting in eruptions of fire. High above, at a piercing frequency above the rumbling artillery, he heard the deadly whine of V1 missiles. On top of that, screaming engines of aircraft flying low, headed west, emitting a sonic roar unlike any planes he'd ever heard before. White blossoms, small solid clouds, hundreds of them, mushroomed in the gray clouds above. It took a moment for Grannit to register that he was looking at a sky full of parachutes.

Carlson jumped into the jeep as Grannit stepped on the gas. As they skidded onto the road, a shell landed where Grannit had been standing thirty seconds earlier and demolished the cinder-block guardhouse.

10

rich Von Leinsdorf's squad had been on the road for three hours, working their way back from the Meuse, when they heard the artillery barrage begin in the east. Von Leinsdorf patted Bernie on the shoulder as he drove, and showed him the time: Operation Autumn Mist had begun exactly on schedule. With the offensive under way, their task on its first day was to disrupt the American reaction. Moving east, they had already reversed or removed half a dozen road signs at key intersections to confuse Allied troops who would soon be swarming toward the invading forces. They also severed three telephone and telegraph trunk lines between Spa, Liège, and the American Front.

Bernie huddled over the wheel, unable since hearing about it the night before to shake the idea of a "second objective" out of his head. They were trying to injure or kill more Americans, and it made him sick. The thought of what Von Leinsdorf would do to him if he tried to interfere paralyzed him.

The barrage from the east ended abruptly at 0630 hours. Bernie knew that was the signal for the three army groups to begin their advance into Belgium and Luxembourg. If all went according to plan, German paratroopers and assault squads would already be swarming through the Losheim Gap, ripping holes in the Allies' defenses, opening the way for the tanks.

A light appeared on the road ahead of them as they entered a clearing. Bernie slowed when he caught sight of it. The overcast sky had begun to turn gray with the approach of dawn, and he could make out what looked like a farm boy standing by the side of the road, swinging a lantern. The boy waved at them and stepped into their path.

"Keep your distance," said Von Leinsdorf.

Bernie stopped the jeep about fifty feet in front of the boy. He waved his hands again and walked toward them.

"American?" the boy shouted. "American?"

"Whoa, hold up there. What do you want, kid?" asked Bernie.

"American, yes?"

"That's right. What do you want?"

The boy glanced nervously to his left, toward a tangled, over-grown hedge to the right of the jeep. Something rustled in those branches. Von Leinsdorf grabbed his rifle and dropped down in the seat.

"Drive, drive!" he shouted.

Bernie stepped on the gas and ducked, just as a rifle barrel pointed at them out of the dense branches. He heard two loud booms. The jeep fishtailed in the mud then righted itself and skidded forward. The boy on the road pulled out a pistol and pointed it at the wind-screen, but the jeep's right front fender clipped him on the leg, spun him around, and knocked him to the ground before he could fire. Von Leinsdorf came up from the floor of the backseat firing an M1, emptying an entire clip at the brush behind them.

"Stop!"

Bernie slammed on the brakes. Von Leinsdorf jumped out of the jeep and ran toward the trees, slamming another clip into the rifle.

"Get the boy!" he shouted.

Bernie pulled his pistol and jumped down, crouching low around the jeep. The boy on the ground was writhing in pain, whimpering, trying to reach the pistol lying a few feet from him in the snow. Bernie hurried over and kicked the gun out of his reach. The boy glared up at him, pain and raw hatred contorting his face.

"*Amis*, fuck you!"

"Easy," said Bernie. "Take it easy, you little shit. You all right?"

The boy spat at him.

"*Ami*, I hate fucking *Amis*," he said. "Fuck you."

Von Leinsdorf came around the hedge dragging a second boy by the collar, carrying an old shotgun. He manhandled him to the ground next to the first boy. As he went down, the boy's coat came off in Von Leinsdorf's hand. Something he saw made him laugh.

"What's so funny?" asked Bernie.

Von Leinsdorf moved and Bernie saw that the boy wore a red armband with a Nazi swastika around his left arm. Bernie stripped the coat off the wounded boy on the ground; he was wearing a swastika as well.

"God damn," he said. "Fucking Hitler Youth."

"I told you this was more Germany than Belgium." Von Leinsdorf spoke to the boys in German. "*Meine kleine Hitlerjugend*. So tell me, you pick up a signal the invasion is about to begin and try to pick off some Americans with your father's bird gun, *nicht wahr?*"

The boys stared at him in shock. Von Leinsdorf broke down the ancient double-barreled shotgun and popped out the spent shells.

"You are German?" asked the second boy, in broken English.

"That's right. Not that we don't appreciate your enthusiasm," said Von Leinsdorf, "but you nearly shot my head off."

"Are you really soldiers?" the wounded boy asked.

"What are you, the village idiot?" asked Bernie.

"Where's your father?" asked Von Leinsdorf. "In the army?"

"He was killed. In Russia."

"He'd be proud to know his son is a patriot. Even if you don't know which side to shoot at."

They heard a rumble of heavy vehicles rolling up behind them along the same road. Headlights flashed through the woods. Von Leinsdorf yanked the wounded boy to his feet.

"Go home, get the hell out of here," he said. "Those are real Americans coming now."

"You better think twice before taking any more potshots if you want to live till dinner," said Bernie.

The second boy put an arm around his injured friend and helped him limp toward the trees.

"And don't forget your blunderbuss," said Von Leinsdorf, hurling the old gun after them. The boy picked it up and they helped each other stumble out of sight.

Bernie and Von Leinsdorf hurried back to the jeep and saw Gunther Preuss slumped forward in the backseat. He turned to look at them, a pinched, fearful hangdog stare. His left hand gripped his right shoulder, blood seeping between his fingers.

"Oh shit," said Bernie.

"It's nothing," said Preuss. "It's nothing, Erich, I swear."

"Let me see," said Von Leinsdorf.

He pried Preuss's hand away from the wound. The uniform was shredded across his unit patch, the flesh of his shoulder peppered with shot. Other pellets had sprayed him across the neck and the right side of the face. All three areas were bleeding copiously.

"God damn it," said Leinsdorf.

"Please, Erich," said Preuss, tears running down his face. "Don't kill me. Don't kill me."

Bernie could see Von Leinsdorf weighing the odds, and his hand moved toward his pistol.

"It's not that bad," said Bernie.

"Get out of the jeep," said Von Leinsdorf.

"I can patch him up," said Bernie. "It's not going to kill him, he won't slow us down—"

"Out of my way. Preuss, get down—"

Von Leinsdorf reached for Preuss. Bernie grabbed his hand.

"Don't do it."

"Let go of my hand, Brooklyn—"

Before they started to struggle, both men were caught in the convoy headlights; eight vehicles—jeeps, transport trucks, and a towed antitank gun—turned into the clearing behind them. Von Leinsdorf shook off Bernie's grip and stepped toward the oncoming vehicles waving his arms. Bernie could see a platoon of rifle infantry hunched in the trailing canvas-backed trucks.

The lead jeep pulled up alongside Von Leinsdorf. An American captain in the backseat stood up.

"What's the holdup?" asked the captain.

"Somebody fired on us when we drove in," said Von Leinsdorf. "One of my guys is hit."

"Let's take a look at him," the captain said, then turned and called to the rear. "Get a medic up here!" A man jumped out of one of the transports and jogged toward their jeep. "Was it Krauts?"

"We couldn't see. We returned fire, I think they moved off—"

"You a recon unit?"

"That's right, sir."

"Well, don't go after 'em, all hell's broke loose up ahead—"

"We heard shelling. What's going on?"

"Who the hell knows? We're getting reports they started coming at us in force soon as that artillery knocked off. Radio's saying there's Kraut paratroopers up along the ridgeline—"

"No shit—"

"We've got units strung out all along this road; everybody's ass is hanging out. They want us to hook in and form a line at Malmédy—"

The medic opened his haversack and stepped up on the jeep's sideboard to take a look at Preuss. Bernie hovered next to him.

"He can't even talk," said Bernie. "Think he's hit pretty bad."

Taking his cue from Bernie, Preuss rolled his head back, moaning as the medic ripped the arm of his jacket down and probed the wound. Preuss didn't respond to any of the medic's questions; Bernie answered in his place.

"We heard they might try a spoiling attack," said Von Leinsdorf.

"Hell, you hear those planes overhead, the V1s? They're throwing the works at us. It's no fucking spoiling attack—"

"He needs a field hospital," said the medic, sifting a packet of sulfa powder onto Preuss's shoulder.

"We were on our way to Vielsalm," said Von Leinsdorf.

"Screw that, I'm overriding it, you're coming with us," said the captain. "Two hundred ninety-first Combat Engineers. Got orders

to drag every able body we can muster in there. Fall in behind me, Lieutenant. We're about five miles from Malmédy."

The medic jumped into the jeep beside Preuss, unrolling a bandage. Bernie looked for guidance at Von Leinsdorf, who nodded at him to climb in. Bernie steered their jeep into line behind the captain and they continued down the road.

"One hell of a morning, huh?" said the medic to Von Leinsdorf.

"You said it, pal."

Malmédy, Belgium
DECEMBER 16, 6:30 A.M.

Earl Grannit's jeep covered the mile back to Elsenborn at top speed, dodging through a moving wall of vehicles as the artillery barrage continued behind them. The village was in an uproar, hungover soldiers roused from sleep running in every direction. Frantic citizens clogged the roads, belongings in hand, evacuating to the west. Grannit pulled up next to the checkpoint at the edge of town, waved over one of the young MPs trying to control the traffic spilling in from the east, and flashed his CID credentials.

"Were you on duty here night before last, son?" asked Grannit.

"I guess I was, sir," said the MP.

"A jeep came through, sometime between nine and midnight, three men. Anything come to mind?"

"Coulda been ten like that, sir."

"I'm only looking for one. Think about it. Something stand out?"

Another shell burst, closer to the village, less than a hundred yards from where they were parked. The MP ducked down; Grannit didn't flinch. "Yeah, maybe. There was one came through from Bradley's headquarters, Twelfth Army. Seemed like they were a little off course."

"Who was in it?"

"Couple of officers. A lieutenant, I think, that's who I talked to. They had a private driving."

"Was their pass in order?"

"I think it was."

"Where were they headed?"

"Somewhere south of here."

"You get any names?"

"Sorry, Lieutenant, that's all I remember." Another shell exploded, even closer, and the MP ducked again. "Jesus, what the hell's happening?"

"There's a war going on," said Grannit.

He steered them past the checkpoint, getting bogged down in traffic and mud on the main road halfway through the village.

"I never been shelled before," said Carlson. "You been shelled before?"

"No. I'd say once is enough."

"Yeah, I don't need to go through that again."

"Next chance you get at a radio, call Twelfth Army," said Grannit, "see if they've got any patrols in this sector answers to that description."

Carlson wrote it down.

"Where we headed, Earl? We going after them?"

"Has our job changed in the last ten minutes?"

"I guess not."

"These are wrong guys, Ole."

"Okay, so we're going after 'em. So where we going?"

"You remember the location of that field hospital where they took Sergeant Mallory?"

Carlson searched his notebook. "I think I wrote it down."

"It was Malmédy, wasn't it?"

Just as Carlson found it in the book. "Sixty-seventh Evac."

67th Evacuation Hospital, Malmédy
DECEMBER 16, 8:00 A.M.

When the artillery barrage began at dawn, no one at the hospital paid it much mind: By the time it ended an hour later, shells had started to land near Malmédy, word came in that the Germans had punched a hole through the American line, and paratroopers had been spotted

79

on the ridge less than three miles away. The operating theater, which had been running at less than a third of capacity during the recent lull, was put on full alert.

A wave of ambulances arrived within minutes—front-line soldiers with blunt trauma and shrapnel wounds. Many had suffered puncture wounds when shells shattered the trees, firing splinters in every direction. A number of civilians were injured when a rocket hit near the town's medieval Catholic cathedral after morning mass, knocking down a wall and ringing the bells.

Earl Grannit and Ole Carlson entered the large tent complex on the outskirts of Malmédy just after 7:30 A.M. They moved past a crowd of wounded GIs stacked in the prep area, located the surgery ward, and found the senior nurse on duty, Dorothy Skogan, working in postop recovery. Grannit showed his credentials and asked about Sergeant Vincent Mallory. Skogan didn't know the name, but recognized him from Grannit's description.

She told them Mallory had arrived earlier that night, without dog tags, just after 3:00 A.M., accompanied by a medic and a pair of MPs. He had been shot three times and his complicated surgeries lasted over two hours. By the time they finished, the soldier had stabilized, his severe blood loss restored by transfusion. The surgery team had just wrapped out of the OR when the bombs started flying.

"What's his condition?" asked Grannit.

"Critical but stable. Severe blood loss, shock and hypothermia. Gunshot wounds to the right shoulder, left hip. His jawbone's shattered, most of his teeth fractured."

"Is he conscious?"

"No. Won't expect him to be for hours, if then."

"Well. We really need to talk to him."

"That may be difficult, Lieutenant. The bullet tore up his tongue, and we had to wire what was left of his jaw to a plate. I didn't even know his name until you just told me; he didn't have his tags."

Grannit looked at Carlson, frustrated. He quickly told her that Mallory had been shot and left for dead with three other men for over twenty-four hours before they'd found him. "Anything strike you as unusual about him?"

"When I was prepping him, I found an empty ampule of morphine in his field jacket. There was sulfa on all three wounds. I found bandages compressed against the wounds on his hip and shoulder that stopped him from bleeding out."

"So the medics took care of him during transport," said Grannit.

"No, that's my point. The medic in the ambulance said that's how they found him."

"We're the ones who found him," said Grannit, puzzled.

"And you didn't notice this?"

"No. You're saying somebody gave him first aid before we got there?" asked Grannit.

"That's what the medic said," she replied. "I don't think the sergeant was in any shape to do it himself, do you?"

They had reached Mallory's cot in the recovery tent. His lower face and neck were encased in a yoke of bandage, an IV drip fed his arm, oxygen tubes straddled his nose. His face looked swollen as a football. Skogan wrote Mallory's name on a strip of tape and fixed it to his cot.

"Least we know his name now," she said. "He was lucky that bullet hit him in the jaw. It was headed toward his brain."

"You didn't happen to save the bullets, did you?"

"We're a little busy right now."

"It's important. Ole'll give you a hand," said Grannit.

"Where you from, Dorothy?" asked Carlson, as he walked away with her.

"A long way from here, kiddo," she said. "Madison, Wisconsin."

"No kidding. I'm from Sioux Falls."

Grannit moved to take a closer look at Mallory. He studied the angle of the wounds, visualizing him back at the checkpoint, trying to re-create the encounter.

He was behind you. You turned and he fired point-blank. He thought the first shot took you out. The second and third were afterthoughts, as you fell. Then he got distracted by the other men and assumed you were dead. He killed Private Ellis, while the second shooter took care of Anderson. Then he killed the second shooter, his own man.

Why?

Because he was hit. Private Anderson returned fire and shot him before he went down. Chest wound from an M1. Possibly fatal, but not right away. So our man didn't want to take a chance and leave one of his own behind.

Two head shots. No hesitation. Kills his own man. They toss his body next to the other vics, take all their tags, placing a big bet nobody would notice this stranger among them. Drive on to Elsenborn.

Two officers, one private driving the jeep. One lieutenant who does the talking, and probably the shooting. All the way from Twelfth Army, Bradley's HQ in Luxembourg, almost a hundred miles south.

So who treated Mallory's wound before we got there?

Grannit shook his head to stay awake and rubbed a hand over his eyes, waves of fatigue washing through him. He'd been gunning for forty-eight hours straight; it was a sudden struggle to keep his thoughts on track.

Fuck it. The trail was cold. Now the Krauts launch this offensive. That tipped over the fucking applecart. No chance he'd ever get to the bottom of this now.

The idea burned a hole in him. He never let go of a case while he was on the job. Why should it be any different over here? Because life was cheaper? Did that make these murders any less important?

Vince Mallory lying there, hanging by a thread, his life shattered. Somebody did this to him. Find out who.

No excuse not to finish the job. He'd made that promise a long time ago, and backed it up ever since.

His mind kept working through the fatigue. *Don't let go. There's more to this than you can see.*

He needed coffee. He went to look for some.

Captain Hardy of the 291st Engineer Combat Battalion led his small convoy into Malmédy at 7:45 A.M. They found the tent complex of the 67th Evac Hospital on the outskirts of town. Bernie pulled up outside next to a line of ambulances. Hardy stopped his jeep alongside them and barked directions.

"Get your man squared away. Our rally point's near the cathedral on the eastern approach."

"We'll be there," said Von Leinsdorf, snapping a salute.

Hardy's jeep pulled away. The medic helped Bernie guide Preuss down from the back of their Willys.

"We'll get him inside," said Bernie. "Thanks for your help."

The medic swung onto the back of one of the convoy trucks as it drove off. Preuss stumbled and Von Leinsdorf grabbed his other arm. They propped him up between them, through the traffic congesting the front of the tent. Preuss moaned, half-conscious, in a morphine haze.

"What the hell do we do?" asked Bernie.

"We can't leave him here," said Von Leinsdorf. "For obvious reasons."

Two nurses stationed at the entrance trotted out to help.

"Where's he hit?" one of them asked.

"Right shoulder," said Von Leinsdorf.

"Bring him this way."

Holding Preuss between them, they followed the nurses into the tent, then set him down on a stretcher in a waiting area overflowing with wounded. A passing nurse kneeled down to take a look at Preuss just after he hit the canvas.

"He's had first aid already," said Dorothy Skogan.

"Medic gave us a hand on the way in," said Von Leinsdorf. "What's the procedure?"

"We'll take him, but there's going to be a wait. There's a lot of wounded ahead of him."

She stood up briskly and moved on. A young, moonfaced MP with a blond brush cut walked after her, and took a passing glance at Von Leinsdorf and Bernie. Von Leinsdorf met his eye, deep concern evident on his face, which the MP, Ole Carlson, took for worry over their wounded friend. Preuss moaned again, drifting in and out of the morphine clouds, head rocking from side to side.

"*Schiesse . . . Schiesse . . .*"

Bernie knelt down next to Preuss and laid a hand over his mouth. "Easy, easy, don't talk."

"He'll come out okay, buddy," said Carlson.

"Thanks," said Bernie, lowering his head.

Carlson walked away following the nurse. Von Leinsdorf knelt beside Bernie.

"Take his tags," said Von Leinsdorf.

"What?"

"Put these on him," he said, slipping another set of dog tags from his pocket. "Take his ID and anything else that could tie him to us."

Bernie reached into Preuss's shirt and yanked off his tags as Von Leinsdorf stood watch. Bernie slipped the second set of tags into Preuss's pocket, then pulled his forged ID card out of his jacket.

"Where's his lighter?" asked Von Leinsdorf, as he tucked the card away.

"How should I know?"

"Find it."

Bernie realized what he was asking. "I'm not doing that."

"Then wait outside."

"I know what you want it for; I'm not letting you do that—"

A young admitting nurse with a clipboard walked up to them. "I need some information before we take him to the ward."

Von Leinsdorf reached past Bernie into Preuss's pocket, fished out the tags they'd just put there and handed them over. "He's not with our unit. We were driving by, he flagged us down and passed out in the jeep, so we brought him in."

The nurse examined the tags and wrote down the name. "Sergeant Vincent Mallory."

"See, we didn't even know his name," said Von Leinsdorf, continuing to rummage through Preuss's pockets. "Maybe we can find something else to help you." He fished out a silver Zippo lighter and a pack of cigarettes. "Don't suppose he'll be needing these for a while, huh?"

"You don't know anything else about him?"

"You know as much as we do," said Von Leinsdorf, pocketing the lighter.

The nurse printed the name on a strip of white tape and attached it to the stretcher. "You did a good thing just getting him this far." She signaled a couple of orderlies, who lifted Preuss's stretcher and carried him toward an adjoining tent.

"Where you taking him?" asked Bernie.

"To prep him for surgery. If you don't know this guy, there's no reason to wait, it's going to be a while."

The nurse moved off, following the stretcher.

"Shit. He's going to come out of it and start crying for his *Mutter*," said Von Leinsdorf.

"Let's get out of here."

Von Leinsdorf looked around, thinking, before he answered.

"Wait here," he said.

Von Leinsdorf followed Preuss into the next tent. As he entered, he picked up a clipboard hanging next to a bulletin board, pretending to study it as he tailed the stretcher. The orderlies set Preuss down in the busy prep center, where two dozen wounded lay waiting, separated by screens, attended by an assembly line of nurses and orderlies.

Standing near a busy nurses' station by the entrance to the operating theater, Von Leinsdorf watched them strip off Preuss's jacket and shirt and plug him into an IV. Moments later, Von Leinsdorf buried his face in the clipboard when Dorothy Skogan walked up to the desk with Ole Carlson and a supervising orderly.

"I don't have time for this shit now," said the orderly.

"He just wants the bullets we pulled from the maxillofacial we did this morning," said Dorothy.

"We got a hundred people shot to shit, what's the rush?" asked the orderly.

"Criminal investigation," said Carlson, showing his badge. "There's a harder way to do this, you want to give that a try?"

The orderly sighed. "Patient's name?"

"Mallory, Vincent Mallory. He was brought in late last night."

Von Leinsdorf was about to move toward Preuss when he heard that name, and stopped to listen.

"Where is he now?"

"He's in recovery. I've got to get back to work," said Dorothy.

"That's fine, I can take it from here," said Carlson. "Thanks for your help, Dorothy."

Skogan left for the operating theater. The orderly sifted through a pile of paperwork on the desk, looking for Mallory's.

"Your chances ain't good. We usually toss everything when we scrub down," said the orderly.

"Anything you give us is really appreciated," said Carlson, smiling patiently.

Neither of them noticed Von Leinsdorf walk out of the prep tent. He stopped a passing nurse to ask: "I'm looking for a man from my unit just came out of surgery, where would he be?"

She directed him outside to an adjoining tent. Von Leinsdorf carried the clipboard with him, sloshed through the mud, and parted the flaps of the recovery tent. Quieter in here, fewer lights, sharp contrast to the chaos in the OR. Patients rested on cots in cubicles created by curtains. Two nurses moved from one man to the next, making notations, monitoring medication. Von Leinsdorf slipped on a white coat, kept his focus on the clipboard, and drew no attention as he walked by. He glanced in each cubicle he passed, reading the names on strips of white tape attached to the foot of their cots.

He found Mallory's name but didn't recognize the man on the cot as the sergeant he had shot at the checkpoint. His face was bloated by surgery and covered with bandages. Another man stood to the right of the cot, arms folded, looking down at Mallory. Broad shoulders, rangy, weathered—a "tough customer" was the slang that came to Von Leinsdorf's mind. The man wore a regulation uniform with no insignia. That may have been the privilege of an officer, but this one had the leathery aura of a seasoned noncom. Von Leinsdorf walked past the cot, stepping in to look at a patient two beds down.

Von Leinsdorf pieced together a scenario: Someone found Mallory where they'd left him in the woods. Alive, against all odds. He might have talked about the shooting but his condition suggested otherwise. Von Leinsdorf had learned as much as anyone alive would ever want to know about the nuances of dying. He knew exactly how to gauge death's approach, when it was ready to make its final embrace.

This man was hanging by a thread. A whisper would nudge him into its arms.

The man standing over Mallory rubbed his face and headed for

the exit. They nearly collided; Von Leinsdorf let him pass. As soon as the man left, Von Leinsdorf stepped back to Mallory's cot and took Preuss's Zippo lighter from his pocket. Opening a pocketknife he pried away the wick and flint and removed a small glass vial from the cavity. He used the knife to cut a slit in the IV bag attached to Mallory's arm. Snapping the head off the vial, he poured the clear contents through the slit into the bag. A nurse walked into the ward. He pocketed the empty vial and walked away without looking back. Stepping out of the tent, he dropped the vial and crushed it into the mud.

A minute later Grannit walked back into the tent with a cup of coffee, saw the man's legs bucking and kicking, his arms twitching, head whipping from side to side, his breathing rapid and labored. He called out for the nurses and used all his weight to restrain Mallory on the cot. The man's eyes opened, the pupils fixed and unseeing. Bright cherry-red blood streamed from his nose and mouth. By the time a trauma team arrived, Mallory's limbs had gone rigid and he had stopped breathing. Grannit stepped back and let them work.

Bernie sat on his helmet beside a Christmas tree near the entrance of the admitting tent. Every time an officer passed, he agonized about whether he should take him aside and identify Von Leinsdorf as a spy. Once they had the German in custody, he might be able to blend into the chaos and fade away. But the thought of a second objective held him back. Von Leinsdorf wouldn't crack even if they tortured him, of that he was sure; he'd sneer at a firing squad while they tied the blindfold on. Bernie didn't know how many others in their brigade had been assigned this second objective, so unless he found out what it was, he couldn't do a thing to stop it. Until then he needed Von Leinsdorf alive and in the clear. But how many others would he kill before then? That was the equation he had to live with. Now that the attack had started, trying to surrender would only get himself shot. He kept his head down, picked up a newspaper, and tried to shrink into the corner.

It was the American service paper, *Stars and Stripes*. His eye was drawn to a headline on the front page.

ALLIES BOMB IG FARBEN

German Industrial Giant Near Frankfurt Hit Hard
Daylight Raid Leaves Nazi War Machine Reeling

His father still worked at IG Farben. He'd had no contact with his family since leaving for Grafenwöhr in October, at which point both his parents were alive. That suddenly seemed in doubt.

Bernie's gaze drifted to the improvised Christmas tree, gauze serving as tinsel, surgical clamps and scissors hung like ornaments. The meager attempt at holiday cheer, his own peril, and the growing crowd of wounded arriving for treatment brought him to the verge of tears. A nurse's aide offered him a cup of coffee. He declined, and his forlorn look drew her sympathy.

"Hard being away from home this time of year, isn't it?" she asked.

He looked up at her. She was a plain girl, early twenties, with crooked teeth and a one-sided smile.

"I guess you could say that," said Bernie.

"I love Christmas. Never spent one like this before. Where you from?"

"Brooklyn," he said, surprised when it came out of his mouth.

"Really? We sailed out of the Brooklyn yard on our way over a few weeks ago. You'll be happy to know it's still there. I'm from Wichita. That's a long way from New York. Might even be farther away from it than where we are now."

"I don't think you can get any farther away than this."

"Don't worry now, you'll be going home soon," she said.

She patted him on the back. Her kindness made it hard for him to say anything more. He spotted Von Leinsdorf coming toward him through the room, wearing a doctor's white coat, and stood up.

"Get in the jeep," said Von Leinsdorf. "Keep the engine running."

"Where are you going?"

"Make sure you're pointed toward the road," he said, taking off the coat and heading back toward the prep tent.

"I want an autopsy," said Grannit. "I need to know what killed him."

"Could have been any number of things," said the surgeon who'd worked on Mallory, not eager to oblige. "Postoperative trauma, delayed reaction to anesthesia—"

"His original wounds were enough to kill him," said a second doctor.

"We were told he'd come through that surgery, that he'd recover," said Grannit.

"The truth is, Lieutenant, these things aren't predictable," said the surgeon. "We see it every hour of every day. Each man has a different breaking point. Sergeant Mallory reached his."

Grannit looked at the weary doctors in their blood-soaked gowns—decent men, trained to heal, not kill. He could hardly expect a different reaction: What was one more dead soldier? After watching so many young men lose their lives, what else could they do but turn up their hands?

A passing nurse overheard the name. "Did you say Mallory?"

"That's right," said Grannit."

"But he hasn't even gone into surgery yet."

"Yes he did, he was postop."

"When did they operate?"

"Last night when he came in."

"But I just admitted him fifteen minutes ago."

"What's the first name?" asked the surgeon, looking at the chart. "We can't be talking about the same Mallory."

"First name's Vincent," said Grannit. "Vincent Mallory."

"Sergeant Vincent Mallory, that's him," said the admitting nurse. "I just took the information off his tags—"

"Where is he now?"

"In the prep tent."

"Show me," said Grannit.

They hurried toward the tent, burst through the flaps, and searched down the busy rows, the doctors following.

"Did he come in alone?" asked Grannit.

"No, a couple of soldiers brought him in—"

The admitting nurse pulled back the curtain isolating his cubicle. Gunther Preuss lay on the cot, an IV in his arm, bright red blood sliding from his mouth and nose, his body racked with convulsions.

The nurse and doctors hurried to the patient's side, calling for help. Grannit caught movement out of the corner of his eye. An officer in uniform walking against traffic out of the tent at a rapid pace. Grannit took off after him, pulling his Colt, holding it aloft so people would notice.

"Out of the way!"

The crowd parted, some hitting the floor in alarm. The officer heard the shouts and, without looking back, sprinted out the front of the tent. Grannit hurdled a cot, bowled over a couple of soldiers, and jammed his way out after him.

A jeep was pulling out of the parking area, wheels skidding in the mud. Two men on board. Grannit saw the officer he'd followed haul himself into the front seat as it slipped away. The glint of silver bars on his collar. A lieutenant. No stripes on the driver's jacket, a private.

Grannit gave chase to the edge of the parking area, aiming the pistol but unable to sight a clear shot. He waved down a motorcycle dispatcher, flashed his badge to the driver, then yanked him off the bike when he slowed and jumped on. Jacking the bike around, he downshifted to gain torque in the mud and slid onto the narrow road heading into Malmédy. He spotted the jeep a quarter of a mile ahead crossing a small bridge into town. Grannit downshifted again and opened the throttle.

"Keep going," said Von Leinsdorf to Bernie. "Head southeast."

"What happened? Where's Preuss?"

"Just do as I tell you," said Von Leinsdorf, glancing behind them.

Bernie whipped the jeep around the town center, a welter of narrow, ancient streets, avoiding collisions, wheeling around obstacles, ignoring traffic signs. The sidewalks were packed with citizens carry-

ing suitcases and bags, pushing carts full of possessions, fleeing from the German advance. Twice he narrowly missed civilians who darted suddenly into the street, one carrying a bright green parrot in a cage. As they reached a narrow bridge leading out of town, they came face-to-face with an American half-track headed the other way. Bernie steered to the right without slowing and accelerated past it, only inches to spare, the jeep's right fender sending up sparks as it scraped against the stone wall.

Behind them, Grannit dodged through oncoming traffic, weaving around slower cars and trucks. Crossing the first bridge into town, he veered into an intersection and nearly collided with a stalled wagon. Turning hard right, he jumped the bike up onto a sidewalk, leaned on the horn, and shouted for people to clear out of his way. He skirted a group of Allied soldiers organizing a defense along the town's eastern perimeter on the near side of a second bridge. Halfway across the bridge, he slammed on the brakes when a column of American vehicles barreled into the village. Grannit stood up on the bike, looked ahead, and caught sight of the jeep across the bridge, moving down a long straightaway into the country. Some MPs jumped out of a jeep to set up a roadblock and direct traffic. Grannit shouted at them, showed him his badge.

"Clear this bridge, god damn it!"

The MPs waded into traffic and cleared a path for him. Soldiers riding into the village shouted at Grannit that he didn't want to head that way. Paratroopers had taken the towns to the east, and columns of panzers were coming up behind them.

As their jeep cleared the outskirts of town, Bernie steered onto the shoulder. American military vehicles crowded the westbound side of the road, carrying soldiers on hoods of jeeps and hanging off the sides of trucks. The men wore the haunted look of battle fatigue and many were wounded. Bernie could hear the boom of artillery and the rattle of small arms to the east. Von Leinsdorf lit a cigarette and couldn't keep a smile off his face.

"Quite a sight, Brooklyn," said Von Leinsdorf. "Your amateur American Army. What did I tell you? Retreat's too dignified a word—they're bugging out after only four hours."

Bernie didn't respond, alarmed by an image he was picking up in the rearview mirror.

The moment the MPs opened a path, Grannit muscled the bike across the bridge, accelerating through the gearbox as he roared past the retreating American column. He caught sight of the jeep again, at the top of a rise less than a mile ahead, where the road headed into a stretch of gently rolling hills. He tried to coax more speed out of the jeep as they crested another hill.

"Somebody's following us," he said.

Von Leinsdorf looked back and saw the motorcycle clear the hill behind them. He picked up his rifle. When they reached the top of the next rise, the bike had closed the gap to less than half a mile.

"Who is it?" asked Bernie.

"I don't know. Maybe we forgot to pay our bill at the hospital," said Von Leinsdorf, screwing a telescopic sight onto the rifle. "Pull over at the bottom of the next hill."

When they reached the base of the hill, Bernie pulled off the road onto a hidden drive that led to a farmhouse in a stand of pines. Once they were out of sight, he cut the engine. Dust settled. Over the country silence, they could hear the buzz of the approaching motorcycle. Von Leinsdorf steadied the barrel of the rifle on the back of the windscreen and waited. The buzz grew louder. He looked down the sight, settling the crosshairs on the peak of the hill.

Bernie swiveled around when he heard a clatter of breaking dishes from inside the farmhouse. The face of a GI appeared in a window, then the door swung open; a group of six young soldiers hurried toward them.

"Jesus Christ, get out of sight," said one of them. "What the hell are you doing?"

Von Leinsdorf took his eye off the sight and looked over, annoyed.

"They're right on top of us, get out of sight!"

A rumble shook the earth, along with it the high-pitched whine of steel grating on steel. On the far side of the woods to the east three Panther tanks appeared and wheeled to a stop on the summit of the next hill, straddling the road. Walking alongside and behind them, in skirmish formation, were a column of black-jacketed soldiers. On

their collars Bernie saw the double-lightning insignia of the SS *Panzergrenadiers.*

Aboard the bike, Grannit hit the top of the incoming hill and skidded to a halt when he saw the tanks astride the next rise, a quarter of a mile in front of him. Behind them, stretching as far as he could see, was a solid column of soldiers, mounted artillery, and half-tracks filled with infantry. In a hollow below and to the right he spotted the jeep he'd been chasing. A squad of GIs was trotting toward it from a nearby stone farmhouse.

Von Leinsdorf found Earl Grannit in his sights as he crested the hill, and nestled him right in the center of the crosshairs. As he was about to fire, Bernie grabbed the barrel, yanking it off target.

"I think that's one of ours, Lieutenant," he said, for the benefit of the approaching GIs.

Von Leinsdorf glared at him but didn't respond. Bernie refused to let go of the rifle.

"You don't want the Krauts to know we're down here, do you?"

The soldiers from the farmhouse reached the side of their jeep. They were all Bernie's age or younger, frightened and confused.

"You got to get us out of here," one of them said.

"Who the fuck are you?" snapped Von Leinsdorf.

"Rifle company, 99th Infantry," said their sergeant. "We were mining a logging road near the Skyline Drive. Krauts started coming out of the woodwork. Our jeep got hit. We've been dodging 'em for hours, trying to get back to our line."

"They're all over the fuckin' place," said another. "What the hell are we supposed to do, Lieutenant?"

One of the young Americans, wearing a bandage on a leg wound, started crying. They all looked to Von Leinsdorf for guidance, like a lost pack of Boy Scouts. Von Leinsdorf could barely conceal his disgust.

"They haven't spotted us yet," said Bernie. "Hop on, we'll make a run for it."

The six GIs crowded into the backseat and jumped onto the running boards as Bernie turned the engine over.

Looking down into the valley, Grannit saw the officer he'd been

chasing since the hospital stand up in the jeep and hold up his rifle. The man met his eye and waved jauntily, just as the jeep turned and headed onto a dirt road behind the farmhouse.

As Grannit turned back to the hill, a turret on one of the tanks turned in his direction. He spun the bike around and accelerated down the hill back toward Malmédy, just as the first tank round came whistling over his head and exploded off to the side of the road.

67th Evacuation Hospital
DECEMBER 16, NOON

The naked body of Gunther Preuss lay on a stainless steel countertop behind curtains near the back of the surgery tent, a makeshift morgue. Vincent Mallory's corpse, already examined, lay on a second counter, covered with a bloodstained sheet. Earl Grannit had persuaded the head surgeon he'd spoken with earlier to examine both men's bodies. While the doctor opened them up, Grannit sat off to the side and lit a cigar to kill the stench, a technique he'd learned during visits to the New York City morgue.

After making his way back to the hospital, Grannit had sought out a senior combat officer and given him a detailed report about the German battalion he'd seen on the road east of Malmédy. Returning to his own assignment, he found that Ole had secured the scene, quarantined evidence before it got tossed, and collected statements from witnesses. Among the evidence, Grannit took particular interest in the two plastic IV bags. Both had been cut open in identical fashion.

The doctor called Grannit over and pointed out unnaturally bright pink mucous membranes lining the man's exposed throat and lungs. Even over the cigar, Grannit noticed a faint odor of bitter almonds emanating from the body.

"They were both poisoned," said the doctor. "Some toxin caused the hemorrhaging that destroyed all this soft tissue."

"What do you think it was?"

"Judging from the smell, if I recall my rudimentary chemistry correctly, hydrocyanic acid. Prussic or cyanide."

"Something you could pour into an IV bag," said Grannit.

"Comes in liquid form. It's a clear substance, so nobody'd notice."

"How big a dose?"

"Wouldn't take more than a few drops—don't get too close with that cigar smoke, Lieutenant, or you're gonna get a nasty taste in your mouth; that stuff forms a bad compound with tobacco."

Grannit stood back. "You keep that here in the hospital?"

"No, we do not, sir." The doctor snapped off his gloves and looked at him sharply. "You're a cop, aren't you? Back home."

"That's right."

"You like to tell me what's going on? We don't have enough carnage, some sick son of a bitch has to come into my hospital and kill wounded soldiers? Why in the hell should that happen?"

"I'll have to get back to you."

"I'm going back to work," said the surgeon. "They're saying we got big trouble out there. That what you saw?"

"Trouble doesn't cover it."

"There's talk we might have to pull out of here, if the damn army doesn't chase its tail around before they're on top of us. My staff can't save lives in a German prison camp."

The doctor left him alone with the bodies. Grannit set the cigar down and took a close look at the false Vincent Mallory. A second soldier with no ID killed in two days. Wearing a captain's bars. Soft hands, a wedding ring. A new pair of boots, taken off one of the dead GIs at the checkpoint.

This was that second officer the MP spotted in the jeep at Elsenborn.

So why'd you kill this one, Lieutenant? He gets tagged along the way to wherever you're going, all of a sudden he's expendable, too? A superior offi-

*cer? This wasn't a fatal wound like your other man—buckshot in his shoul-
der and neck—but still you took him out.*

*Then why run the risk of taking him to a hospital? If you wanted him
dead, why bring him here when you could just shoot him by the side of the
road?*

*Unless you were still after the real Mallory. Is he what brought you
here, you needed to finish the job? But how could you have known he survived Elsenborn? The way you left him, what were his chances? And why
would you give this other man of yours his tags unless you thought the real
Mallory was dead?*

*Because the sergeant's surviving was a loose end you didn't realize
you'd left hanging until you got here, when your friend checked in wearing
Mallory's tags. Once you were inside, you found this out and killed them
both.*

He could leave the why for later. Grannit had seen the man
who'd done this. The blond lieutenant. Standing in that jeep, waving
at him.

*Five murders in two days. A killer with the nerve to cut open Mallory's
IV and pour that poison into him, then do the same to his own man on his
way out before Mallory was even dead.*

Grannit's eye was drawn to a magnifier mounted on a stand attached to the autopsy table, and he remembered the photograph
he'd found in the other man's boot. That led him back to this man's
boots, sitting under the table. He searched through them, found
nothing inside; then, following a hunch, he pulled his knife and
pried away at the heels.

The right heel came away in his hand. Hidden inside he found a
folded piece of paper. On it was a hand-drawn map of a river and a
bridge crossing, detailing access roads on both sides and defensive
emplacements. A few words had been scribbled hastily in the margins,
but Grannit couldn't make them out. Arrows pointed to two other
bridges, on either side, that were only sketched in, without detail.

Ole Carlson hurried into the tent, excited, holding up a plastic
bag. "It took some doing but I found 'em, Earl. These are the bullets
from Mallory. The real Mallory, not the fake Mallory."

"I get it, Ole."

Carlson's eyes settled at the body on the table and turned away as if he'd been hit in the stomach, blood draining from his face. He opened his eyes and was looking straight down at Mallory on the other table. "Oh Lord."

"You all right there, Ole?"

"Not so good, actually."

"Close your eyes and breathe."

"I would, but the smell is sort of a problem."

"Can't help you there," said Grannit.

Grannit put the spent shells under the magnifier. One was badly damaged, little more than a shapeless lump, probably the shot that shattered Mallory's jaw. The others were pistol rounds, and at first glance he knew they were .45s from a Colt, a U.S. officer's sidearm. But they also bore peculiar rifling, as if they'd passed down an unusually long barrel.

"They pulled some buckshot from the fake Mallory there," said Carlson, trying not to retch, keeping his eyes off the bodies. "Kind of strange, isn't it? Who the heck is using shotguns out there? It ain't duck season, I know that much. Dang, that smell could take down a bull."

"You want a cigar or something?"

"No, thanks, a cigar would definitely make me puke."

Grannit pulled out the photograph he'd found on the first John Doe and held it under the magnifier.

"Anyway, I finally got through to Twelfth Army," said Carlson. "The phone lines are down; they think that's the Krauts' doing, so I got through to Twelfth Army dispatch on the radio. Krauts are coming at 'em down there, too—"

"Did you ask about the patrol?"

"Yeah. The Twelfth has no record of any patrol in this sector answering that description."

"There's a reason for that," said Grannit.

"What is it?"

Grannit waved Carlson over to look at the photograph of the woman at the seaside scene under the magnifier.

Among the structures lining the dock behind her was a civic office building, probably the port's customs house. Carved into the stone entablature over its entrance, in the center of a laurel wreath clutched in the talons of the German imperial eagle, was an elaborate swastika.

"Because they're Krauts," said Grannit.

12

Dwight Eisenhower was nursing a same-day champagne hangover. His valet, an ex-bellhop named Mickey McKeough, had married his Women's Army Corps sergeant girlfriend that morning in the gilded Louis XIV chapel of the Trianon Palace Hotel on the grounds of the Versailles compound. Eisenhower told a friend that the diminutive bride and groom looked cute enough to decorate the top of their own cake. The reception went into the early afternoon, and when the bubbly ran out they dipped into the general's private wine cellar. With only nine days left until Christmas and the front firmly in Allied control, few of the overworked staff at Supreme Headquarters of the Allied Expeditionary Forces needed an excuse to let off steam, but wishing Mickey and his wife well was better than most.

General Eisenhower had a more personal reason for indulging himself. A cable had arrived that morning informing him that President Roosevelt had placed his name in nomination before Congress for the post of General of the Army. This new rank would bring with it a fifth star and sole authority over the Allies' entire armed forces in Europe. That much power had not been conferred on one soldier since the First World War. After sixteen years as a desk-bound major, Eisenhower had risen from lieutenant colonel to the army's highest rank in a little over three years. The affable fifty-four-year-old

Kansan had planned a private dinner that night to celebrate with some drinking buddies, among them one of his best friends and colleagues, General Omar Bradley. Bradley had arranged for a bushel of Ike's favorite oysters to be flown in from the Normandy coast. Given their recent successes in the field, for the first time in two years, Eisenhower felt he could allow the weight of the war to slip slightly off his shoulders.

Eisenhower, Bradley, and four staff officers were in the Clemenceau Ballroom of the Trianon Palace at Versailles, which they used as their tactical map room. They were halfway through a relaxed meeting about how to speed up training and delivery of replacement soldiers from the States. Eisenhower drank coffee, chain-smoked, popped a handful of aspirin, and ate a big lunch, trying to negotiate away his headache from the morning's champagne before the evening's Scotch. He was already on medication for high blood pressure and stress. His left knee, sprained two months earlier and slow to recover, ached with the arrival of an early winter cold front. Outside, heading into the shortest days of the year, the sky was already beginning to darken.

The meeting was interrupted by the arrival of a brigadier general, deputy to Eisenhower's chief intelligence officer, British Brigadier General Kenneth Strong. The man appeared grim and called Strong out of the room. Eisenhower saw the same look on Strong's face when he returned, and asked him to share what he'd learned. Strong moved to one of the large maps that adorned the walls.

"We're getting fragmented reports that the enemy counterattacked this morning across a broad front," said Strong. "Here, in the Ardennes, First Army sector, all the way down into Luxembourg."

Eisenhower looked to Bradley, whose headquarters were in Luxembourg City. "What do you know about this?"

"I was in Spa with General Hodges yesterday, but I didn't see any of this myself," said Bradley.

"Didn't you hear anything, Brad?"

"Some early reports came in as we were leaving. My first thought

was it's just a spoiling attack. That's what I still think. They're trying to disrupt our move across the Rhine."

Eisenhower stood up to join them at the map and pointed at the Losheim Gap. They called this sector the "Ghost Front," for it had seen no heavy action since Hitler's panzer blitz to Paris four years earlier. Eisenhower also knew that this same sleepy seven-mile corridor had served as the fast lane for Germany's first-strike invasions of France in 1914 and 1870. Concentrating their effective forces to the north and south after pushing the Germans out of France, the Allies had rolled the dice that in winter the harsh terrain and broken roads of the thinly held Ardennes offered no strategic advantage or tactical temptation to the reeling Nazi army.

"We're spread pretty thin in here, aren't we, Brad?"

"Four divisions."

"Fairly green, aren't they?"

"Two of them are replacements. The others we've pulled off the line after heavy action."

"So it's half nursery, half old folks' home."

"That's the risk we've taken."

"How many divisions have they committed; do we have a count?"

"Not yet," said Strong. "But Jerry's put together a steady buildup on the other side of the Siegfried, as many as ten divisions already—"

"And intelligence always indicated that was purely defensive, in anticipation of our moving against them," said Bradley, slightly irritated.

"Well, it isn't defensive now."

"This has to be a local attack, to distract us from Patton's move into the Rhine."

They had all been stunned by the news, but Eisenhower was the first to recover. His headache was gone, swept away by alarm and clarity. "This is our weakest point. Why would they hit our weakest point in force?"

"I don't know the answer," admitted Bradley. "He's not after a terrain objective. That ground doesn't mean anything."

"This is no spoiling attack. Not with those kind of numbers."

"Then what kind of attack is it?" asked Bradley.

"I don't know yet, Brad, but we're not going to wait to find out.

First Army doesn't have any reserve; they've caught us with our pants down."

"I'm sure Hodges would've let us know by now—"

"Maybe he can't. Mobilize 7th Armored out of Holland, get them moving toward Spa by morning. And I want three more divisions on stand-by to support this sector until we get it sorted out," said Eisenhower. "What's available to us?"

"We've got the 82nd and 101st bivouacked near Reims," said Strong.

"They're still being refitted," said Bradley.

"Cancel all leaves, get 'em back in camp and ready to move in twenty-four hours," said Eisenhower. "Patton'll have to give us one of his for the third."

"That's going to hurt his move across the Saar," said Bradley. "George isn't going to like it."

"George isn't running this damn war," said Eisenhower.

They wouldn't learn until the following day that General Courtney Hodges, commander of First Army, headquartered in Spa, had been trying since early morning to alert Allied headquarters in Versailles that German forces were rolling over his forward positions.

His phone lines had all been cut.

The foul weather hovering over the Ardennes worsened during the night. Cold winds pushed through a front with heavy cloud cover that discharged sleet storms and sporadic snow. Across the Channel, all of England remained socked in as well, grounding Allied fighters and bombers that might have blunted the initial German advance. C-47 transports were unable to take off from British bases, denying reinforcements and fresh supplies to the troops under siege throughout the expanding front.

By dawn the disjointed communications received by Supreme Allied Command had coalesced into an alarming realization that the weakest sector in their front line was under assault from thirty-six divisions, over half a million men, the largest German offensive of the entire war.

13

Bernie powered the jeep along a logging road into the cover of a nearby forest. Hearing more German troops headed their way, he pulled off the road and the six young soldiers of the 99th Infantry covered the jeep with evergreen branches downed by an artillery barrage. Bernie, Von Leinsdorf, and the Americans waited in silence as the forward line of German infantry and scout cars swept past them, visible twenty yards away on the edge of the woods. Von Leinsdorf had to order the agitated engineers to stay down and keep silent. Those were battle-ready German veterans; if these green kids drew fire, they were all dead. Once the Germans passed—Von Leinsdorf identified them as a reconnaissance company—they climbed back on the jeep and cautiously drove deeper into the woods to the east.

An hour after dark they came across an abandoned woodcutter's cabin. Bernie parked the jeep in a small shed out back and shut the doors. Inside, they pulled the curtains to black out the one-room cabin, lit a kerosene lamp, and settled in for the night. Bernie helped tend the injured GIs with the jeep's med kit. The crump of artillery, rockets flying overhead, and the crackle of small arms continued through the night. The riflemen shared their K rations, eaten cold. Von Leinsdorf learned as much as he could from the Americans about their company and its movements during the

last day. It was clear the German attack had taken the Allies completely by surprise.

Von Leinsdorf assigned a sentry rotation for the platoon, to get them through what remained of the night. The first man stood his post at the door while the rest bunked down around the room. Von Leinsdorf asked the platoon sergeant for a look at their maps, which he spread out on the room's crude table. Von Leinsdorf held the lamp close and tried to pinpoint their position.

One of the American kids, a baby-faced private, crawled over next to Bernie and offered him a smoke, then lit it for him, cupping his hand to hide the flame.

"You're from New York, ain'tcha?" the kid asked.

"Yeah."

"Thought so. Heard it in your voice. Me too. Charlie Decker."

"Jimmy Tenella," said Bernie.

"Pleased to meetcha, Jimmy. I'm from the Bronx, Grand Concourse up near Van Cortlandt Park?"

"Yankees fan?"

"Only since birth."

"I'm from Brooklyn."

"Dem bums. Too bad for you." They shook hands awkwardly. "So how long you been over here, Jimmy?"

"Too long," said Bernie. He noticed Von Leinsdorf watching them from across the room.

"You in the first wave? Since D-day, huh?"

"Feels like longer."

"Wow. We been here three weeks. Fresh off the banana boat," said Charlie, trying to sound hardened and indifferent. "I graduated high school six months ago. I never been anywhere before."

"You're someplace now."

"You guys know how to handle yourselves. You've seen the hellfire and brimstone, am I right?"

Bernie looked at him. "I've seen a few things."

"You probably went through basic, too. They hardly gave us any training. Then they stick us out here, saying we won't even see any action? I don't even have the right socks."

Charlie smiled and slowly shook his head. With his unlined face and wide eyes, he seemed eerily matter-of-fact about their predicament. Bernie felt an urgent impulse to get away from him.

"You got a girl back home, Jimmy?"

"No, not really. You?"

"Ann Marie Possler. Real sweet kid. I got a letter from her the other day. Finally wrote her back last night." He took an envelope out of his jacket, smiling as he looked at it. "She's in Queens. I'd like you to get this to her."

"Just keep your head down, you'll be okay."

"I'm going to die today."

Bernie didn't know what to say, but the hollow look on Charlie's face put a chill through him. *Maybe he knows. Maybe he's right.*

"See, a guy like Bobby Dugan"—Charlie pointed at the wounded soldier across the room—"he catches some shrapnel today, falls all to pieces? He's gonna grow old and die in bed." He nodded at two more of his men. "Rodney and Patchett. They're not gonna see home again either."

"Come on, knock it off, how could you know that?"

"I've heard the words of the Prophet. Even a heart of stone can be turned into a heart of flesh, if you don't reject the teaching. The new covenant will be unbreakable. It will be written on the heart. Redemption is at hand."

Charlie held the envelope out to him. Bernie saw the madness in his eyes.

"Say but the word, cleanse your soul of sin, and you shall be healed, and you shall have new life," said Charlie, and then without changing expression: "Just make sure this gets into the mail for me, okay?"

"Sure thing, Charlie." Bernie took the letter and stuck it in his pocket. "I'll take care of it."

"You got a Bible, Jimmy?"

"Not on me."

"I'd like you to have mine. Here, take it."

"Why don't you hang on to it."

"You mail the letter," said Charlie, lying back down on his bedroll. "I got a good feeling about you."

Bernie walked away from him and stood by the door, trying to shake the kid's voice out of his head. When Von Leinsdorf finished at the table, he joined Bernie outside for a smoke. The air was dead still, a frozen pool. They moved out of earshot from the cabin. A thick fog crept in and snow fell silently around them.

"Have you talked to these guys?" whispered Bernie. "At least one of 'em's a fucking lunatic."

Von Leinsdorf looked at his watch. "We have to be somewhere in a few hours."

"Where, for what?"

"To pick up something we need."

"Is this about the bridge, or the other thing?"

Von Leinsdorf glared at him. "The other thing. And they're not coming with us."

"Leave 'em here. Tell 'em we're going for help—"

"I'm not asking for suggestions." Von Leinsdorf loaded a fresh clip into his pistol.

"So wave down one of our patrols, identify ourselves—we've got signals for that, right? Let 'em surrender."

Von Leinsdorf chambered a round. "You're getting sentimental on me, Brooklyn."

"Look, they don't have any idea who we are or what we're doing. What can they say that could give us any trouble? You don't have to kill them."

"If you're not willing to help, I'll do it myself."

They heard the cabin door swing open behind them. One of the riflemen walked outside to take a piss. Von Leinsdorf raised the gun on instinct. The man in his sights wasn't looking their way and gave no indication that he knew they were there. Bernie stepped between Von Leinsdorf and the target.

"I need to know what the fuck we're doing here," whispered Bernie. "What are we picking up?"

"Security passes. From the *Abwehr*."

Bernie's heart jumped at the mention of the German secret intelligence organization. "Why didn't they give 'em to us before we left?"

"They were supposed to be with that fat woman the night we came across. They'll be there now."

"What the fuck do we need 'em for?"

"I can't tell you any more," said Von Leinsdorf. "Are you going to help or wait out here?"

"We can't shoot 'em. What if there's a patrol in the area?"

Von Leinsdorf answered by taking the silencer out and screwing it on the pistol.

Bernie saw the rifleman go back inside. "At least let 'em fall asleep first. It'll be easier then."

"Not if there's two of us." Von Leinsdorf saw the look on his face and relented. "All right. We'll wait till they're asleep."

Bernie followed him back inside. He told the soldier at the window to catch some rest, that he'd take the last watch. The American joined his friends on the floor. Three were already sleeping; the other two were playing cards by the light of the lantern. Bernie looked at Von Leinsdorf. Both men lit cigarettes and waited.

As snow accumulated outside, the fog reduced their field of vision to less than twenty yards, a white void surrounding the cottage. The first hint of dawn was in the sky before the soldiers finally turned off the lamp and lay down. Von Leinsdorf drew his pistol and signaled Bernie. Bernie picked up a rifle sitting by the door and looked down at Charlie Decker lying asleep at his feet.

You could shoot Von Leinsdorf instead, he thought.

No. Not without knowing what his mission was first. But he couldn't shoot these GIs either.

Von Leinsdorf pointed his pistol at the first man's head. Bernie heard something outside and waved his hand to stop him. He cracked open the window and gestured Von Leinsdorf over.

The faint sputter of motorized diesels. Moments later, they both heard faint shouts coming toward them in the distance. Charlie Decker woke when he heard the voices and saw Bernie and Von Leinsdorf at the window.

"Who is it?" asked Charlie. "Who's out there?"

Von Leinsdorf gestured urgently for quiet. They waited. More shouts, closer, then the squeak of footsteps running in the snow

outside. A few isolated gunshots, then bursts of automatic fire. The rest of the soldiers woke in the room behind them. Then came the unmistakable grinding of heavy gears. Bernie recognized the distinctive rumble; German tanks were moving their way.

"They're ours," said Bernie to Von Leinsdorf, before he could censor himself.

Thinking he meant Americans, Charlie Decker threw open the front door and ran outside before Bernie could stop him.

"Hey! Hey, guys! Hey, we're Americans! We're over here!"

From somewhere in the fog a stream of .50 bullets chunked across the front of the cabin, cutting down Charlie Decker at the door, ripping open his chest. He fell back through the doorway, dead before he hit the floor at Bernie's feet. Everyone inside scrambled for cover. Bernie looked down at Decker, a faint smile on the kid's face, as his eyes glassed over.

Moments later, GIs slashed out of the fog right in front of the cabin, a platoon in headlong retreat, most without weapons, running for their lives. A tank shell hit the cottage with a massive, dull thud, but didn't detonate, a hissing dud, the tip of its nose poking out between logs. At the sight of it, two of the riflemen broke out the back door, out of their heads with fear. Heavier gunfire erupted, bullets piercing the wattled walls of the building. Screams issued from behind the building.

Von Leinsdorf and Bernie dove to the floor as more bullets whistled overhead. The wounded American kid crawled against the rear wall and began screaming for his mother as more rounds kicked through the room.

Bernie crawled to the open door and pushed it almost shut. A ghostly line of German paratroopers in white parkas and winter camouflage emerged from the fog, submachine guns firing. From behind them, the muzzle of a white panzer appeared, and then, moments later, the hulking body of the tank, painted a ghostly white, drove into the clearing. Von Leinsdorf crawled over to Bernie.

"I told you we should have fucking killed them," he said in Bernie's ear.

The panzer rolled toward the cottage as paratroopers trotted past

the building, picking off survivors running ahead of them. Von Leinsdorf crawled to the wounded American boy and held a hand over his mouth. Pressed against the base of the wall, the last two riflemen looked to Von Leinsdorf for orders, close to cracking, ready to bolt like the others. He gestured at them to stay put.

Bernie saw the parka of a German soldier who was peering in through the cottage window. He pressed his face forward trying to see through the crude glass and his breath condensed on the pane. The Americans huddled directly under the window below him, unseen, terrified. Von Leinsdorf kept his hand clamped over the wounded GI's mouth, pulled his knife, and held it to his throat. A moment later the German soldier moved away. Bernie raised onto his knees to peer out the same window. What he saw coming drove him to dive down away from the wall.

The barrel of the panzer's cannon smashed through the window, penetrating halfway across the room. It paused for a moment and then swung violently to the right, toppling furniture, knocking over shelves. Bernie flattened himself against the wall closest to the tank, away from where the machine gun was mounted. He heard the engine engage as the barrel swung back to the left. Muffled shouting issued from inside the tank. Someone reloaded the machine gun.

The Americans panicked and ran for the back door. Bernie turned in time to see Von Leinsdorf cut the throat of the wounded GI. He heard the crew in the tank crank another shell into the chamber, and sprinted for the door as the cannon fired. The shot blew away the back wall of the cottage just as Bernie and Von Leinsdorf hurled themselves out the doorway. Bernie felt the concussion ripple through his body from behind, and the crack of the explosion deafened him.

Bernie landed facedown in the snow. He turned and looked up, groggy, lost in a white, silent world. His senses haywire, he staggered to his hands and knees, trying to remember where he was. A shrill, bell-like tone screamed out of the deep silence and pierced his mind. He felt someone grabbing for him, tugging him to his feet by the sleeve—Von Leinsdorf—then pulling him into the fog. Bernie saw the spinning tracks of the panzer, reversing away from the shattered cottage wall. A boot landed in the snow near him, with a leg still in it.

He felt something wet on his face, wiped at it, and his hand came away smeared with blood, the bright red shocking amid all the white.

They lurched into the fog, Bernie trailing Von Leinsdorf, trying to keep him in sight. He knew he was shouting, but he couldn't hear his own voice. Von Leinsdorf vanished ahead of him in the fog. Bernie turned his head to look for him, and a tree hurtled at him out of the white. He had no time to stop or change course—a low-hanging branch clotheslined him across the neck and everything went black.

14

Malmédy
DECEMBER 17, 8:00 A.M.

The order came down from First Army headquarters in Spa shortly after 7:30 A.M. to abandon the 67th Evacuation Hospital. The situation to the east had grown steadily worse during the night, as waves of new wounded continued to arrive, overwhelming the facility. Confirmation that *Waffen*-SS panzer divisions were moving toward Malmédy hastened the decision to withdraw; stories about their atrocities to female prisoners preceded them. Doctors and nurses were ordered to drop everything and take only what they could carry. The hospital's chief surgeon asked a skeleton staff of five volunteers to stay behind and tend the few men who were too critically wounded to transport. Every nurse in the ward raised her hand, so they had to choose by drawing lots.

Earl Grannit and Ole Carlson had worked through the night on a borrowed typewriter, piecing together the investigation until they'd condensed it to five pages. After placing repeated calls on deteriorating phone lines to Spa and Liège, Grannit finally got through to a reconnaissance officer at First Army headquarters shortly after dawn.

"There's a hundred damn rivers in this part of Belgium," said Grannit. "We're trying to figure out which one we're looking at here."

After describing in detail the map of the river he'd found in the

boot of the dead German, Grannit held on the line while the officer consulted his charts.

"Sounds like the Meuse," said the officer. "There's three bridges southwest of Liège at Engis, Amay, and Huy."

"How far apart are they?"

"They're all within twenty miles of each other. You got any maps with you?"

Carlson handed him one, folded to that section of the river. "I'm looking at it. What's their tactical significance?"

The officer thought for a moment. "If Jerry's looking to get across the Meuse, that'd be a damn good place to try—"

"How so? What good does it do them to cross that far south?" asked Grannit.

The line crackled and went dead. Grannit jiggled the receiver but couldn't reestablish the connection. Another shell exploded nearby outside. Ole ducked instinctively, but Grannit didn't move, lost in thought.

"Earl?"

"Let's go," he said finally, heading outside. "Bring the maps."

A fleet of trucks and ambulances lined up behind the tents to convoy patients and staff back toward Liège. V1 rockets and German planes continued to scream westward above the clouds overhead. Red crosses were being hastily painted on the canvas tops of the transports, as the staff hoped to ward off attack from the air.

Grannit climbed behind the wheel of their jeep, and they fought their way out of the congestion surrounding the hospital. He headed west, dodging around a brigade of American armor moving toward Malmédy. Their CO, standing up in a Willys at the rear of the column, shouted at them for directions. Grannit pointed them toward Malmédy, moved the jeep off to the shoulder, and kept driving.

"I was thinking, shouldn't we tell somebody what we know?" asked Carlson.

"What do we know, Ole?"

"You know, about the Krauts and the murders and—" Ole stuttered for a moment.

"And what?"

"I don't know what. But somebody at HQ ought to hear about this."

"We tried, Ole. Nobody's answering the god damn phone."

"Well, we should just drive over there."

"They've got their hands full. For all we know they're not even there anymore."

"But these guys are killing GIs, Earl."

"There's a lot of that going around today."

"But they're Krauts—"

"I know that, Ole, and you know that, and we're gonna tell 'em soon as we know what the hell they're doing here. That's our job now. Make sense of it first."

Grannit swerved as another shell landed by the side of the road.

"Everybody's got their job today and we got ours, okay? And, by the way, mine doesn't include having to cheer you the fuck up," said Grannit.

Baugnez Crossroads, Belgium
DECEMBER 17, 1:00 P.M.

"Private Tenella! Private Tenella!"

Bernie came to lying on the worn wooden floor of a small café. An American sergeant was staring down at him, holding his dog tags in one hand, shaking him by the shoulder with the other. The man's voice sounded muffled, as if Bernie had cotton stuffed in his ears. It took him a moment to connect himself to the name the man was using. He tried to answer, but his own voice came out as a dry croak he couldn't hear. His throat throbbed where he'd collided with the tree, and his head pulsed in painful disjointed rhythms. He felt a bandage on his forehead as he sat up and looked around.

At least thirty other GIs were huddled nearby in the room, crouched or sitting. None carried weapons. Two American medics moved from man to man, tending to the injured. Bernie thought he recognized some faces, then looked at their shoulder patches and

realized they were part of the same unit they'd ridden into Malmédy with only the day before, the 291st Combat Engineers. Then Bernie saw the half dozen black-jacketed SS grenadiers holding submachine guns near the door. Their commanding officer, a tall, whip-thin captain, stood nearby, jabbering angrily at a middle-aged male civilian.

"Where are we?" Bernie asked in a harsh whisper.

"Who the fuck knows?" said the sergeant. "Keep it down. You gotta keep quiet, for Christ's sake, you were moaning so loud. They just beat the piss out of a guy for less."

"How'd I get here?"

"We found you in the woods, 'bout half a mile back, and carried you in." Bernie had to concentrate, reading the man's lips to understand him. "We were about to saddle up when this big column of Kraut tanks rolls up on us so fast we couldn't even put up a fight."

"You seen my lieutenant? I was with somebody—"

"Sorry. Just you and a bunch a dead GIs, kid. Keep your voice down. I can hear you just fine."

Bernie noticed the attention of the other prisoners in the room drifting toward the door. The SS captain was shouting at the civilian, who had his hands up, flinching at every word. He wore a white shirt and stained white apron. Bernie guessed he owned the café. The captain pulled his handgun and pistol-whipped the man across the face, knocking him to the ground. He covered his head with his hands, pleading for his life. The captain twisted the barrel of the gun into his ear, toyed with shooting him but didn't. He shoved the man to the floor with his boot, then turned to his soldiers and barked a series of orders.

The SS men at the door fanned out toward the prisoners, gesturing with their guns. *"Raus! Raus! Ausenseite!"*

The GIs stumbled to their feet and pressed together as a unit toward the front door. Swept up with the men around him, Bernie tried to maneuver near one of the grenadiers to try to say something in German, but he couldn't get close enough. Even if he'd caught the man's attention, what would he say? All he had with him was

American identity papers. He didn't know if any other divisions involved in the invasion even knew about their brigade. Without Von Leinsdorf to back him up, what if they didn't believe him?

The SS men herded the GIs outside. A main highway passed in front of the café, intersecting with a smaller road that fed down from the north around a tight corner. Both arteries were jammed with German military vehicles—artillery, rocket launchers, tanks, scout cars, troop transports—entire armored divisions pouring in from the north and east. Two SS officers stood at the intersection, shouting frantically, trying to direct the columns as they merged toward the west. The traffic stretched out in either direction as far as the eye could see.

In a meadow to the east of the café, just south of the main road, stood a larger group of American prisoners, over fifty of them bunched together in the trampled snow and dead grass, under heavy Wehrmacht guard. Bernie and the GIs from the café were funneled down into the meadow to join them, forming a solid mass. German soldiers riding along the road shouted curses and laughed at the Americans as they passed. When one of the massive German Tiger tanks slowed to negotiate the sharp turn, an officer—Bernie thought he was a general—stood on the turret of his tank and called out to the prisoners in crisp English.

"How do you like us now, *Amis*? It's a long way to Tipperary, boys!"

The other SS men riding on the general's tank roared with laughter and gave the Americans mock salutes as they drove past the clearing. A burly American sergeant standing in front of Bernie raised his middle finger at them, which only made the Germans laugh harder.

"Nice to know they took care of that little morale problem they been having since we kicked their ass in France," said the GI defiantly, moving toward the road and shouting after them. "We'll see you again, you Prussian pricks! Go shit in your hat!"

Some of his buddies stepped in front of him to head the man off and shepherd him back into the crowd. Bernie didn't like any part of what he felt brewing. The Germans were riding on a belligerent high that felt reckless and unpredictable. He worked his way to the

southern edge of the crowd, away from the road, and looked back toward the café.

Bernie thought he spotted a green American field jacket among the black-shirted soldiers. He took a few steps closer. When the SS blocking his view shifted, he realized that Von Leinsdorf was standing next to them. He had his American helmet propped against his hip, talking to two SS officers. The two men laughed at something he said; Von Leinsdorf clearly hadn't had any trouble explaining his identity.

Bernie took a few steps toward the café, waving his arms at Von Leinsdorf. He raised his helmet over his head, their brigade's signal to alert other German divisions, and tried to call out, but he couldn't make himself heard above the traffic from the road. Two Wehrmacht soldiers stepped toward him as soon as he moved out of the cluster in the meadow. He showed his helmet and raised it even further as he continued toward them, hoping they knew the signal.

"*Ich bin deutsch! Ich bin ein deutscher Soldat!*" he said as loudly as he could.

Von Leinsdorf never looked in his direction. Bernie saw Erich and the officers shake hands and part. The SS captain issued a fresh set of orders to the grenadiers around him. They hurried toward the meadow, while the captain followed Von Leinsdorf back into the café. Bernie pointed after Von Leinsdorf as the two guards closed in on him.

"*Der ist mein dominierender Offizier! Ich muß mit ihm sprechen!*"

The first soldier speared him in the stomach with the butt of his rifle, doubling him over. The second man struck him a glancing blow behind the ear. Bernie hit the ground and covered his head.

No other blows fell. He thought for a moment that he'd gotten through. When he chanced a look up, the soldiers had turned back toward the road. The SS grenadiers from the café entered the meadow, shouting orders to every soldier in the area. The two privates dragged him back to the main body of prisoners, dropping him near the perimeter.

Bernie heard the sound of breaking glass from the café, and moments later flames sprouted from the windows. The SS captain pushed the café owner ahead of him out the front door, shoving him to the ground, kicking him, pistol in his hand again.

The grenadiers from the café waved down two troop transports. They pulled to the side, out of the flow of traffic. A dozen heavily armed *Waffen*-SS jumped down from the back of the trucks, listened to the grenadiers, and then spread out along a fence that ran the full length of the meadow. Bernie heard a loud crack. He looked back over to the café; the owner was loping down the street, comically unsteady on his feet. The SS captain fired his pistol at him a second time, laughing, shooting for sport rather than trying to hit the man in earnest. Bernie didn't see where Von Leinsdorf had gone, but he was no longer in sight.

The Americans in the meadow shifted restlessly in place. Bernie could smell the bloodlust in the air, and when the SS men turned to face them, he knew exactly what was coming. He backed slowly away from the rear edge of the group, the mass of prisoners between him and the guards near the road. Then he bent low and sprinted straight for the line of trees behind the meadow, fifty feet away.

One of the *Waffen*-SS standing along the road stepped forward, pulled his handgun, and fired three shots point-blank at an American private in the front rank of the crowd. The GI fell to the ground, clutching his chest in surprise, crying out for help.

Time seemed to slow; no one on either side moved. The prisoners around the man stepped back in horror and watched him drop.

Bernie dug in his feet to gain traction with every step, as if he were running in place, his legs heavy and unresponsive. As the first fatal shots cut sharply through the meadow, all he could hear was his own labored breathing. The logic of what the SS was about to do hit him in an oblique flash of intuition.

They don't want prisoners. They're moving forward too fast. They don't want anything to slow them down—

The meadow filled with bullets. Machine guns opened up all along the edge of the road. Gunners on top of half-tracks turned their barrels into the meadow and fired away. As the first rows of

prisoners went down, the stunned Americans behind them scattered in all directions, but the relentless fire from the SS grenadiers covered every angle. Cries of anguish and terror rose from the field as panic spread. Many tried to follow Bernie toward the woods but couldn't catch him. Only a handful covered more than twenty paces before they were cut down, blood splattering the snow. A few close to the front line never even moved, but helplessly stood their ground; some fell to their knees and prayed while they waited to die.

Bernie reached the tree line. Bullets nicked the trunks and naked branches around him, buzzing like hornets. He didn't know if any of the shooters had him in their sights, but he didn't dare look back, plunging into denser stands of evergreens until he was gasping for air. He didn't stop for half a mile, when the enfilade behind him finally ended.

Bernie fell to his hands and knees. All he heard from the meadow now were single shots and occasional bursts. The SS killers were walking in among the bodies, finishing off survivors. He turned back and held perfectly still, but he couldn't see or hear anyone moving through the woods behind him.

The snow was deeper here, slanting drifts of cold, fresh powder. Bernie's body began to shake uncontrollably, chilled to his core, on the brink of going into shock. He pushed his back against a tree, wrapped his arms around his middle, and tried to breathe deeply. His feet and hands felt numb; his ribs ached where the soldiers had clubbed him. Some deep animal instinct told him he had to keep moving or his body might shut down. He willed himself forward, the trail of footprints behind him his only point of reckoning.

It began to snow again, flurries thickening to a heavy shower. He darted through the woods for another mile, until he heard traffic and caught sight of another road and tried to get his bearings. A steady line of German vehicles moved along it, heading right to left; if they were going west, he was facing north. Farther down the road to the right he saw the edge of a small village. He kept going inside the tree line until he could see the first buildings more clearly.

The town looked deserted. A few houses had been hit by shells. One structure was still burning. A vague idea drove him—that he could crawl into an abandoned basement, find some warmth and maybe something to eat—but he knew he couldn't chance crossing the road in daylight. Just then the dull drone of a plane passed overhead, slower and lower than any he'd heard all day.

Moments later, a shower of paper fluttered down around him. He looked up, as hundreds of white pages descended like oversized snowflakes. He plucked one out of the air as it neared him, held it up in front of his face, and willed his eyes to focus.

It was an illustrated leaflet, written in English. It featured a line drawing of two handsome, tuxedoed men, with their arms around three sexually exaggerated women in evening gowns and jewelry carrying open bottles of champagne. Next to these decadent figures, and oblivious to them, three American GIs stood over the dead body of another soldier in the snow. The title underneath the drawing read: YOUR FIRST WINTER IN EUROPE.

"EASY GOING HAS STOPPED" read the headline to the flyer.

Perhaps you've already noticed it: The nearer you get to the German border, the heavier your losses.
Naturally. They're defending their own homes, just as you would.
Winter is just around the corner, hence diminishing the support of your Air Force. That places more burdens on the shoulders of you, the infantry.
Therefore, heavier casualties.
You are only miles from the German border now.
Do you know what you're fighting for?

Bernie laughed bitterly. The absurdity of it lifted enough of the weight he carried that somehow he felt he could keep going. There were at least two hours of light left, and he prepared to settle in among a stand of trees to wait. His vantage point gave him a view

down the main street of the village. He couldn't understand why it looked familiar.

He found himself staring for almost thirty seconds at something hanging from one of the buildings that he knew he should recognize, before he remembered where he'd seen it before.

A sign in the shape of a large pink pig.

15

arl Grannit pulled out the German's hand-drawn map and compared it to the bridge crossing in the town of Engis, but it didn't match the picture. He climbed back in the jeep, where Ole Carlson waited, and continued along the road fronting the east bank of the Meuse.

"There's another bridge ten miles south," said Carlson, who had been studying their regulation map. "Town's called Amay."

They had made slow progress west on the roads out of Malmédy that morning, which were choked with Allied vehicles. At every checkpoint, they encountered GIs who knew less than they did, and who held them up with questions about the German offensive. Coherent orders had yet to filter down from First Army headquarters to company levels. The officers they ran into were acting solely on their own authority, without any overview of the field. There was no consensus at ground level about what the Krauts were up to, where their attack was headed, or how the Allies were going to respond.

As they rounded a turn in the river and the nineteenth-century stone bridge at Amay first came into sight, Grannit ordered Carlson to stop the jeep. He pulled out the hand-drawn map again, and compared it to the scene in front of them.

"This is it," said Grannit.

Carlson craned out of his seat to look. "Think the Krauts are here already?"

"I don't know, Ole. Let's drive up and ask."

"But what if they've taken the bridge already?"

"Then we'll ask in a more subtle way."

They found a platoon of GIs manning an antiaircraft battery on the eastern approach to the two-lane bridge. A single .50-caliber machine gun and some sandbags completed its defenses, another match to the map. Grannit waved over the sergeant in charge as they drove up in front of the bridge. Grannit showed his credentials and asked the sergeant what orders he'd received since the offensive began.

"Stay on alert," said the sergeant, his cheek plumped with a wad of tobacco. "Increase patrols. Company said they were sending reinforcements, but we ain't seen squat. Thought that might be you."

"What's the new vice president's name?" asked Carlson.

"What?"

"The new vice president. What's his name?"

"What do you want to know for?"

"I just want to know," said Carlson, his hand on the butt of his pistol.

"Harry S Truman, from my home state of Missouri," said the sergeant, spitting some tobacco. "What the hell's wrong with you, son?"

"I think he's okay, Earl," said Carlson.

"Thanks, Ole."

Grannit told the sergeant what they'd run into at Malmédy. Other men from the platoon drifted forward to listen. He skimped on detail, but it was still the most news they'd had since the attack began.

"What's backing you up on the other side of the river?" asked Grannit.

"Backing us up? Not a damn thing. Everything's supposed to be in front of us. We're it, brother."

"So what's over there?"

"Cows, dairy farms, and a shitload of pissed-off Belgians."

"Where's this road lead?"

"Once you're across, about fifteen miles west it ties into their main highway. Straight shot from there to Brussels, about forty miles, then another thirty to Antwerp."

Grannit held the hand-drawn map out to the sergeant. "You have any idea what angle you'd have to be looking at your bridge to draw this?"

"Up on that bluff, most likely," said the sergeant, pointing to some low hills to the east. "Where'd you get this?"

Grannit ignored the question. "Any jeeps come through here the last two days with guys saying they're from Twelfth Army?"

The sergeant canvassed his platoon. "Don't ring a bell, Lieutenant."

Grannit looked up toward the hill behind them. "Your boys know the way up there?"

"Sure, we patrol it all the time." The sergeant ordered one of his men into the jeep with Grannit and Carlson. "Duffy'll take you up."

It took ten minutes up a steep dirt switchback road to reach the summit. Grannit climbed out and walked along the ridge until he found an opening in the trees that offered a view down at the bridge. He compared it to the map. The angles and perspectives matched perfectly. Grannit signaled to Ole and the private.

"Spread out and search this area," he said.

A short distance away, Carlson found some tire tracks that had pulled off the road. They followed them fifteen yards into the woods and in a small clearing found the remains of a campsite: discarded K-ration wrappers, a few soggy cigarette butts. Grannit examined them.

Lucky Strikes. The brand he'd found at the Elsenborn checkpoint, smoked down to the nub.

"They were here," said Grannit. "Before the attack even started. That's the reason for the American uniforms, that's why they came over the line. They sent teams in to scout these bridges."

"Why's that?"

"Because this is where they're headed. They don't give a damn about Malmédy or Liège or Spa—"

"Earl—"

"This isn't about taking back ground or engaging us where we

stand. They're going to cross this river and drive straight for the coast—"

"Hey, Earl," said Carlson. "There's a jeep coming down the river road."

Carlson handed Grannit his field glasses. He steadied them on Carlson's shoulder, found the road, then picked out a Willys heading south, slowing as it approached the checkpoint at the bridge.

There were four men in the jeep.

Grannit ran for their own jeep, shouting for the others to follow.

Waimes, Belgium
DECEMBER 17, 4:30 P.M.

Traffic slowed as daylight began to fail, German vehicles passing now in clusters instead of a steady stream. Bernie could see their oncoming headlights splash across the side of a barn at the corner just before they turned right and exited the village. He waited until the barn went dark, then burst out of the trees toward the road. The barn lit up again just before he reached the front of the pavement. Ten seconds to cross over and reach the shadows behind the barn.

The approaching vehicle leaned around the corner at high speed before he was halfway across. Bernie picked up his pace, cleared the far side, and sprinted for the barn. The headlights swept across him just as he flattened his back against the wall, but the German scout car shooting past him down the road never hesitated. He caught his breath, then crept along the dark side of the barn toward the edge of town.

He heard footsteps crunching in the snow, voices speaking German just around the corner, and he froze in place. Two soldiers walked around the building ahead of him, rifles on their shoulders. Bernie was about to step out and speak to them in German when he saw the double-lightning insignia of the SS on their collars. Images of the shooters who'd gone to work in the meadow flooded his mind. He leaned back into the dark and waited for them to pass out of sight.

He crept cautiously down an alley in the failing light until he found Frau Escher's butcher shop. He tried the back door, but it was locked, and he saw no lights inside. Bernie moved around the side until he found a narrow casement window at ground level that fed down into the cellar. He leaned down, broke the pane with his elbow, brushed the splinters out, reached in to undo the lock, and lifted the frame. He lay down on his belly and shimmied backward into and through the opening, feeling for the ground inside with his feet.

When he dropped to the floor, Bernie pulled out his lighter, turned up the wick, and waited for his eyes to adjust to the faint, flickering light. He was in a storage room with a dirt floor, and a pile of firewood and a variety of cans, boxes, and tools stacked against the walls. He moved to the room's only door, opened it quietly, and stepped into a short hallway covered with filthy, chipped linoleum.

On the left, a steep flight of open stairs without a banister led up to the first floor and ended at a door. A second door was straight ahead of him at the end of the hall he was in. In the gloom of the basement he could see at least one other door, possibly to a closet. He started up the stairs. They creaked loudly under his feet. As he was about to reach the door at the top, he heard something move in the room at the end of the hallway down below.

Bernie stopped midstep, held his breath, and listened. A few moments later he heard the sound again. A slight rustling, some substantial mass shifting in place against the floor. It sounded heavy and alive. An animal most likely. Maybe she kept livestock down here. He remembered the unidentifiable carcass he'd seen earlier hanging in the woman's abattoir. He tried to erase that picture from his mind as he reached for the doorknob.

A low, keening moan issued from the room down below and sent chills crawling across the back of his neck. Startled, Bernie turned toward the sound; the flame wavered in the air, burning his hand, and he dropped the lighter. It clattered through the gap between the stairs; the flame went out as it fell from sight, and the basement plunged into absolute darkness.

The sound again. He realized that his first instinct had been

wrong; it wasn't an animal. A terrible sound of pain and despair—only a human voice could express such suffering.

Bernie stopped in place, trying to orient himself in the darkness. He turned carefully and reached his hands ahead of him for the door at the top of the steps, located the knob, and turned it. Locked. He leaned forward and pressed his full weight against it. The door felt substantial, unyielding. He wouldn't be able to attack it successfully in the dark.

Another pitiable moan issued from the room below.

Despite the cold, he felt sweat break out all along his brow. He felt his hands shaking. Afraid he might lose his balance, he turned and sat down on a step below him, trying to settle his nerves.

Who was in that room? The woman, Frau Escher? Maybe the SS had come through and injured her, or worse, then left her to die.

He used both hands and feet to slide down one step, then another, and work his way back down to the floor. On his hands and knees, he felt his way around the stairs, to the back of the risers, heading toward the spot in his mind's eye where he'd watched the lighter fall from sight. He spread his hands out ahead on the floor as he edged forward, trying to cover every inch of ground.

One of his hands came in contact with something smooth and fleshy and he scuttled back away from it, grunting in disgust. Another moan issued from the room behind the door at the end of the hall. Much louder and closer, and in the deep darkness the sound cut right through him.

What had he touched? He waited, but sensed nothing moving toward him. He reached out his hands again, angling in another direction, slowly at first, then more frantically as fear wormed deeper into his mind, until his thumb grazed something metallic on the floor. He chased after it with clawing fingers and finally got his hands around the lighter. Trying to stave off panic, he flicked it once, twice, but got no spark. He shook the lighter in his hand, breathed deeply, waited, then tried again. The small flame sprouted into the air and held, a pinpoint of light in a sea of black.

The geography of where he was faded back into view. His eyes

took in everything in snapshots, turning to look in each direction until he fixed his position.

The stairs. The short hallway. The door from which he'd entered from the storage room. The second door at the end of the hall.

Under the stairs near where he was crouched, a pile of gnawed and weathered bones.

Lying next to them, the object he'd grazed in the dark—a human hand.

Bernie scrambled backward across the floor, away from the thing, until his back collided with a wall. His heart thumped in his chest; adrenaline pumped through his gut. He stood up without realizing it. As his back bumped against the wall again, the door behind him swung open. Bernie turned when he heard the hinges yawn.

He stepped back from the open door and held the lighter out in front of him, waiting for the flame to penetrate the gloom inside. Two long shapes lay on the floor inside the small space. He took a step closer and saw that they wore olive green field uniforms. One rested motionless, and he knew on instinct the body had no life in it. The other moved slightly, seemed to sense his presence, then moaned again and feebly raised an arm in his direction. The arm ended in a bloody black stump.

Bernie heard the sharp bang of a door slamming shut upstairs, followed by heavy, shuffling footsteps crossing the room directly over his head, and the sound of something heavy dragging across the floor. Keys rattled in the lock of the door at the head of the stairs. Bernie killed the lighter, left the small room where the two bodies lay, and retreated back down the hall to the storage room. Hiding behind the closed door, he eased it open a crack and looked out.

The door at the top of the stairs swung open and a wedge of yellow light sliced down into the basement hallway. He saw her shadow first, then the woman's bulk appeared on the landing, almost obliterating the light. She clumped down two steps, then turned and reached back for something. She proceeded to back down the stairs, dragging a body behind her feet first, face up. Bernie saw black boots and the green field jacket of a GI. The head bounced heavily on each

step as she yanked the body after her like a sack of cement. She was wheezing with effort, and muttering under her breath in German.

"Sehen Sie, Amis, wie Sie es jetzt mögen."

When the body hit the basement floor, she turned and noticed the open door behind her to the room with the other soldiers. She dropped the feet of the body she'd just dragged down and entered the smaller room. She pulled a string to turn on a naked overhead bulb, setting it swinging. Bernie saw a concrete floor with a drain in the middle, dried blood on the walls. Hanging from a line, apparently to dry, he saw what looked like a stretched, mottled sheet of skin. The woman leaned down over the soldier who was still alive and viciously kicked him with her boot, prompting another moan.

"You open this door, *Ami*? You open this door? What I tell you? Maybe now I took your other hand, yes?"

She marched back into the hall. Bernie shut the door quietly and leaned back, feeling ill and weak. He thought about trying to identify himself, in the hope she'd remember him from the other day, but what he'd seen in that room made that unthinkable. Not in the dark hell of that basement, not in an American uniform. She'd crossed a border human beings never came back from. He heard the woman's weight burden the stairs as she made her way back up.

Bernie glanced around the room in the dim light from the broken window. The line of tools against the wall. A shovel. A pickax. A hatchet planted in a small stack of cut wood under the window. He moved over to pick up the hatchet and caught movement out of the corner of his eye.

Her bright, vacant blue eyes were staring down at him through the broken window. Then, in an instant, she was gone.

Bernie tried to pull out the hatchet, but it was wedged so deeply into the wood that he couldn't dislodge it. The woodpile collapsed around him, sending logs rolling across the room. He stepped over them, his hands found the shovel, and he threw open the storage room door. He heard her footsteps stomping across the floor above. He closed the door behind him, ran underneath the staircase, and planted his back against the wall.

He saw her shadow first, thrown down against the basement floor by the sharp yellow light as she stood at the top of the stairs. She held a meat cleaver in her hand.

"You come to steal my food again, *Ami*?" she called toward the closed storage room door. "Like those other boys?"

Bernie didn't move. He wasn't even sure he was breathing.

"Maybe I lock you in down here. See how you like that for a week, yes? No food? No water? You like that, *Ami*? With your friends here?"

She waited, then took a step down onto the first riser. Bernie heard the nails groan above him as they held her weight.

"They all lying in a meadow, *Ami*. All dead. All your friends. We take care of them good, huh? Like I take care of you. You come into our village. You kill my livestock. Take my food. We see how you like it."

She stepped down to the next riser. Now Bernie could see the back of her feet and thick, booted ankles through the open stairs.

"Come out, *Ami*. I have something for you," she said, her tone changing to a playful sing-song. "You must be hungry, yes? Come here, boy, I fix you something nice."

As she stepped down onto the third stair, Bernie reached both hands in from behind, grabbed her fat right ankle and yanked it toward him with all his strength. Her left foot lifted off the stair, and she struggled to maintain her balance. She planted her left leg and nearly pulled her right foot out of his hand. Leaning forward, she made a small hop to the left, then tried to skip down to the next stair onto her left foot. Bernie twisted the foot he still held in his grasp and felt it turn her body in midair. She toppled forward, arms extended, landing heavily on her left side down the rest of the stairs with a loud yelp. She slid the rest of the way, then rolled onto the floor on top of the dead soldier.

Bernie gripped the handle of the shovel, leaned out from under the stairs, and waited. The woman groaned, her breath rising and falling in a ragged rasp. He edged forward until he caught sight of her heaped form in the edge of the light. Bernie took a deep breath.

The woman jolted to life, scrabbling along the ground at him like

a rabid dog, the cleaver in her hand, gibbering incoherently. Bernie stumbled away from her until he slammed into another door. It crashed open behind him and he fell back into a narrow room lined with shelves on either side. The woman crawled after him. He kicked the door shut with his foot; it slammed into her face and bounced off, but she kept coming. Bernie crabbed backward, pulling down shelving between them. Glass jars exploded on and around her as she advanced. The room filled with noxious smells; he didn't want to know what was in those jars. He jumped to his feet, made his way around the shelving to the right, saw another door ahead, and threw himself at it. The door flew open. He slammed it shut and bolted it just as she drew herself up and threw her mass at the other side. The entire wall shuddered. She shrieked and hit it again, then went quiet.

Bernie looked around. He was back in the first room he'd entered. He peered through the door to the hallway. He could see the stairs. He glanced at the casement window he had broken, but didn't think he could climb through it in time.

Bernie made a break for the stairs, and she came running out of the darkness, cutting off his angle. He tried to leap up to the third stair, caught his toe on the edge, and landed hard, facedown on the stairs. She closed in behind him, the cleaver going up in her hand. Bernie turned, whipped the shovel around, and the cleaver scraped down along its shaft, sparks flying, metal ringing on metal. He swung the shovel back the other way and struck a glancing blow to the side of her head, but she shook it off and kept after him.

Bernie pulled himself up onto the next riser, parried another blow from the cleaver, then jabbed the blade at her fleshy mass to keep her at bay. She knocked the shovel aside and brought the cleaver down again, missing Bernie's hip by two inches, splintering the wood of the riser as he rolled out of its way.

Bernie swung the shovel again, but couldn't put much weight behind it. The blow struck her in the ribs and she hardly seemed to notice. She pinned the handle under one arm, turned her body, and wrenched the shovel out of his hands, letting it fall. Bernie turned and crawled frantically up the stairs.

Someone stood in the open doorway at the top, silhouetted. He

saw an arm point toward him, holding a pistol. Bernie threw himself flat on the stairs, turning his head away, and from the corner of his eye he saw her nightmare figure lurching up the stairs behind him, the cleaver high in the air. Then came the sharp report of the gun, twice, three, four shots, echoing harshly.

The bullets stopped the woman on the stairs, blossoms of blood spreading across her chest. She looked at Bernie in disbelief, wobbled in place, gave a soft, low groan, crumpled, and collapsed off the side of the staircase, hitting the concrete floor with a heavy crunch.

Bernie felt a hand on his shoulder. He raised his head up to look.

"Jesus Christ, Brooklyn," said Von Leinsdorf. "I leave you alone for a minute, look what you get yourself into."

"What the fuck. What the fuck."

Von Leinsdorf continued down the stairs. He walked into the room at the end of the hall where she'd stashed the bodies. Moments later, Bernie heard another shot.

16

rannit downshifted sharply, the gearbox of the Willys grinding in protest, fishtailing the rear tires around the hairpin turns. They'd taken ten minutes to drive up the hill. Going down, they reached the river road in five.

As they accelerated toward the bridgehead, they could see the other jeep parked alongside the checkpoint. All four passengers were still in their seats. An officer in the back was talking with the sergeant in charge of the bridge.

"Don't you want to slow down a little, Earl?" asked Carlson.

Grannit looked at him, annoyed. "Do you want to drive, Ole?"

"Just thought you'd want to come in slow so we don't tip 'em off."

"You want me to pull over so you can drive?"

"No."

"Why don't I just stop right here and you can take us in at the right speed?"

"Forget it. Sorry I asked."

"Jesus, you'd make coffee nervous."

Grannit hit the brakes before they made the final turn and reached the bridge emplacement ten seconds later. Grannit gave a casual wave to the sergeant as he pulled in front of the other jeep, cutting off their way forward. A captain in the passenger seat of the second jeep turned to look at them with a wave and a friendly smile.

"Everything okay, Sergeant?" asked Grannit.

"This is Captain Harlan," said the sergeant, turning to the new arrivals. "Did I get that right, sir?"

Harlan nodded. Grannit hopped out of the jeep and saluted.

"How are you doing today?" Harlan asked Grannit, returning the salute. "Where you fellas from?"

None of the four men appeared unduly nervous. Two wore their boots without leggings, like the dead German they'd found at the crossing, and one lacked a regulation belt. Only one man wore a unit patch on his shoulder. Keeping an eye on their movements, Grannit casually moved around their jeep. He noticed that the lettering on their hood looked freshly stenciled, showing no wear and tear. Four spare jerricans were tied to the back.

"We were near Liège this morning," said Grannit, taking out a pack of cigarettes. "Where you coming in from, sir?"

"We were in Holland yesterday, Eindhoven. Signal Corps, Third Armored. Orders to move came down in the middle of the night. It was hell just getting everybody on the road."

Grannit tried to light a cigarette, deliberately mistiming his roll of the flint. "See any Krauts on the way down?"

"We sure didn't. Guess the heavy stuff's still to the east, huh? Is it really as bad as they're saying?"

"Where you guys headed? Hey, you got a light?" asked Grannit.

Captain Harlan fished out his silver Zippo. "They said they wanted the whole outfit in Malmédy by tonight. Our CO told us to divert west and head down to Bastogne. We're looking for the turn to get us back on the highway, just stopped to ask directions—"

As the captain held out his lighter, ready to flick it on, Grannit grabbed his hand and took it from him. He pulled his .45 with the other and held it inches from the captain's head.

"Have your driver toss the keys to my partner," said Grannit.

On the other side of their jeep, Carlson pulled his handgun and covered the driver. The sergeant and his platoon stepped forward, training weapons on the other men in the jeep. None of them moved.

"What's this all about? What's the problem?" asked Harlan.

"Do it," said Grannit.

The driver looked at his captain, who nodded, then pulled the keys from the ignition and threw them to Carlson.

"You want to think about what you're doing, Lieutenant?" said Harlan. "Don't make yourself any trouble—"

"Climb down, all of you. Leave the weapons. Get on the road, hands and knees."

The men in the jeep obeyed.

"Don't do something you'll regret, Lieutenant," said Harlan. "There's obviously some kind of misunderstanding. I know tensions are running high—"

"Put your sidearm on the ground and slide it to me," said Grannit.

Captain Harlan did as he was told. "You want to check our ID again? Our pay books, what? We already showed our trip pass to these fellas; what more do you need?"

Grannit holstered his Colt and yanked the cover off the captain's Zippo. A small glass vial of clear liquid had been packed in next to the saturated wadding. Grannit pulled it out and took a sniff.

Bitter almonds.

Harlan saw the glass vial in Grannit's hand, and his eyes betrayed him.

"*Sprechen Sie deutsch*, *Captain?*" asked Grannit.

Von Leinsdorf helped Bernie up the stairs and set him on a sofa in the front parlor. He locked the door to the cellar and closed the blinds before turning on a light. He laid out an assortment of cold K rations and opened two bottles of ale he'd found in the kitchen. Bernie drank and ate greedily.

"How badly are you hurt?" asked Von Leinsdorf.

"I'm fine," said Bernie, his voice scratchy and hoarse. "Everything's working. She never got a piece of me."

He met Von Leinsdorf's eyes and didn't look away, to make sure he was believed. Leinsdorf appeared satisfied. He leaned back in his chair, threw a leg over its arm, and lit a cigarette.

"I lost you in that fog," he said.

"An American patrol pulled me out of there," said Bernie, biting into some crackers and cheese. "Tree knocked me on my ass."

"Never seen pea soup like that before, even in London. At least it let me get our jeep back." Leinsdorf tapped down a cigarette on the face of his wristwatch and watched Bernie wolf down the rations. "Where'd they take you?"

"Baugnez."

"You were in Baugnez?"

"Yeah. Just before the tanks got there."

"That was our main column. *Oberstürmbannführer* Peiper's command, the First SS Panzer Division. *Die Leibstandarte.* You know who they are, Brooklyn?"

"Hitler's bodyguard."

"Five thousand men. The most elite regiment in the army. Spearhead of the invasion."

"Is that why they don't take prisoners?"

Von Leinsdorf leaned forward. "You saw what happened?"

"Saw it, fuck, we were thrown in with 'em, I nearly got killed."

"For fuck's sake, Brooklyn, why didn't you tell them who you were?"

"I tried. Happened so fast I never got the chance. I saw you outside but couldn't get your attention. I made it into the woods when they started shooting."

"So you remembered this place."

"Regular four-star hotel. How'd you find me?"

"Not because I was looking. I met our *Abwehr* contact at that café. He said they left the package for us here this morning, so I came to find it. Lucky for you, old boy."

"So is it here?"

"I was about to take a look when I heard you romping around with your girlfriend. Christ, what a ghastly beast. What was she doing down there?"

Bernie shrugged, trying to deny the memory, but Von Leinsdorf read something on his face.

"You're not going to tell me she dragged those bodies here for . . . delicatessen purposes—"

"I don't want to think about it."

"Neither do I. But it makes you wonder about that meal she served us the other night—"

"I don't want to talk about that either."

"*La spécialité maison*: Frau Escher's secret recipe."

"Shut the fuck up."

"Her husband never joined the army," said Von Leinsdorf, trying to suppress a laugh. "That must have been him in the display case."

"It's not fucking funny," said Bernie, finishing his ale. "I could have ended up in a sausage."

"That's why we're always rushing through here on our way to France. No one comes to Belgium for the food." He tried to restrain himself and broke up even harder.

"Shut up!" As the alcohol hit his system, Bernie felt himself give in and slide over into laughter.

"Which explains her interest in poor old Preuss," said Von Leinsdorf. "That wasn't lust, it was hunger."

"There was a lot to love—"

"And she wanted to bring out the 'wurst' in him."

Bernie fell over on the sofa and banged his fists on the table until he rolled onto the floor. Both laughed until they had tears in their eyes.

"Oh shit," said Von Leinsdorf, drying his eyes.

"Fuck," said Bernie.

"Fuck, fuck, fuck. God damn it."

"So what do we do now?" asked Bernie when the laughter finally subsided.

"I'm going to find that package," said Von Leinsdorf, getting to his feet and searching the room.

"You make contact with corps command?"

"No. I talked to some of Peiper's men. They say Skorzeny and the rest of our brigade's stuck near the border."

"What's holding them up?"

"Logistical problems, across the entire front. We've broken through but can't get troops to the front. Half our divisions are still into Germany."

"What happened?"

Bernie followed him into the kitchen, where Von Leinsdorf rifled through the cabinets.

"Final shipments of fuel didn't arrive, so they're scavenging for gasoline. There's too much traffic for these country roads and the weather's turned them to skating rinks. The Americans blew some key bridges as they fell back; others can't bear the weight of the tanks. Now the roads are so congested the fuel can't get to the forward positions. Aside from that, everything's going splendidly."

"Snafu."

"Snafu is right. But Americans keep surrendering every time we make contact. Over ten thousand on the first day alone. Entire divisions."

"That's why they don't want prisoners. So they won't get slowed down. That's why those prisoners were shot."

"Maybe."

"You have any idea how the Americans are going to react when word gets out about that?"

"This is war. Happens all the time."

"Not to Americans it doesn't."

"It's the nature of the beast. On the Russian front neither side takes prisoners—"

"I got news for you, this isn't Russia, and your trigger-happy pals in the *Waffen*-SS can't go around killing American prisoners with impunity—"

"Take it easy, Brooklyn—"

"Take it easy? You know what this does to our chances if we're captured in these uniforms? If there was ever any doubt about a firing squad, forget it. We're in deep fucking water, both sides are shooting at us, we've lost half our squad—"

Von Leinsdorf moved into the workroom behind the kitchen and kept looking.

"The first thing they teach you in the military: Plans are only useful until the moment you meet the enemy."

"Here's a plan: Why don't we head back to Germany? I'm serious. If our brigade's not even across the border yet, what the fuck are we doing? Let's ditch these uniforms and get out of here."

"You're talking about desertion."

"That's just a word. It doesn't mean anything. Nothing means anything out here, it's just fucking chaos, and from what I've seen all it does is make people crazy. We're not going back to that bridge, are we?"

"No."

"Well, I don't see any point in getting killed for nothing, do you?"

"It wouldn't be for nothing, Brooklyn," said Von Leinsdorf. "You're forgetting. We have a second objective."

Bernie's heart thudded in his chest. Von Leinsdorf opened the cabinet where the woman hid her radio, reached to the back, fished around, and lifted out a large envelope. He opened it and looked inside.

"And now that we have these, we can get on with it."

"Why? What's in there?"

Von Leinsdorf showed Bernie four high-level U.S. Army security passes for Supreme Allied Headquarters.

"What did we need 'em for?" asked Bernie. "You already gave us one of these before we came over the line."

"There was a mistake in the printing," said Von Leinsdorf. "Our document team misspelled a word, but it wasn't discovered in time. These are the corrected versions. We can't use the old ones."

"Use them for what? Why are we even talking about this? Let's get the hell out of here."

Von Leinsdorf grabbed him by the collar and pulled him close. "I can be your friend, Brooklyn. In spite of our differences, after what we've been through I like to think that I am. But don't suggest that again."

Von Leinsdorf released him and put the passes back in the envelope.

Friend. That wasn't a word Bernie had ever used in relation to Erich Von Leinsdorf. There had been moments when he felt they could get along, even stumble toward some understanding of each other, and the man had just saved his life. But the question stuck: Did their mission demand this violence from him—seven killed now in two days—or give him an excuse to indulge it?

"This other objective," said Bernie. "You going to tell me what it is?"

"Why should I trust you, Brooklyn? Do you trust me? After Schieff and Preuss, I don't think so."

"Guy gets the sniffles around you, he ends up with a bullet in the head."

Von Leinsdorf pointed an emphatic finger at him. "They endangered our mission. Nothing else matters. We don't need them now anyway."

"What does that mean? You need me, so I get to live?"

"Put it any way you like," said Von Leinsdorf. "I can't complete the assignment without you. Go pack up the jeep, I'll use the radio."

Once Bernie left the room, Von Leinsdorf used the radio to contact his other squad leaders, Gerhard Bremer and William Sharper. Both squads had evaded capture through the first days of the invasion and picked up their corrected SHAEF security passes from the *Abwehr*. Von Leinsdorf told them that they were to move south into France, as scheduled, and pursue the Second Objective.

Karl Schmidt's squad failed to respond, but Von Leinsdorf considered that a plus; the man was a weak-kneed intellectual and chronic complainer. They were better off without him. He would have been no help at all where they were going.

17

The Bridge at Amay
DECEMBER 17, 7:00 P.M.

rannit and Carlson secured their four prisoners and sat them down behind the sandbag emplacement while the bridge detail stood watch. Carlson radioed headquarters about the arrests. Grannit searched their jeep. After assembling the evidence he found in an empty ammunition tin, he walked back to the prisoners.

"You're in charge, right?" he asked their captain.

The man nodded.

"Take a walk with me," said Grannit, gesturing toward the bridge.

The German stood up and started ahead of him. Ole Carlson hurried out of the radio tent as they neared the bridge.

"Command says bring 'em in to First Army Interrogation," said Carlson, falling into step with them. "They want Army Counterintelligence in on it, we should get 'em there ASAP—"

"I won't be long," said Grannit.

"They said they don't want to wait, Earl—"

"Give me a few minutes. And stand by for that other thing we talked about."

Carlson gave the German next to Grannit a long look. "Whatever you say."

Ole pulled his sidearm and walked back toward the other prisoners. Grannit waved the German on ahead of him. The man looked back at

Carlson, concerned. Grannit shoved him forward and told him not to turn around. By the time they reached the middle of the bridge, it was nearly pitch black.

"Stop here," said Grannit.

Grannit set the ammo box down on the ground between them, turned on a flashlight, and pointed it at the German. He had a long, intelligent face, and was trying at the moment to put up a hardened front.

"Let's get one thing straight. There's enough in that jeep to hang you five times. Unless you think you're going to pass these off as souvenirs." He held up a pair of red armbands with swastikas. "I ask questions and you answer them, got that? What's your name?"

"Karl Heinz Schmidt."

"What's your rank?"

"*Oberstürmführer.* Lieutenant."

Grannit held up the dog tags he'd taken earlier from the man's neck. "Who's Captain Ted Harlan?"

"I have no idea."

"Did you kill him?"

"No."

"Why are you wearing his tags?"

"They were given to me. I assume he must be an American prisoner of war."

"What unit are you with?"

"The 150th Panzer Brigade."

"Who's your commanding officer?"

Schmidt hesitated. "Colonel Otto Skorzeny."

Grannit recognized the name from military briefings, but showed no reaction.

"So what brings you to Belgium, Karl?" asked Grannit. "Sightseeing? Little vacation?"

"Could I have a cigarette, please?"

Grannit handed him a pack. Schmidt's hands were shaking as he tried to light a match.

"My understanding under the accords of the Geneva Convention, to which both of our countries are a party, is that I am required

to give you only the information you've already requested. Nothing more."

Schmidt tried to meet his eye with resolve. Grannit took a step closer to him.

"Here's the truth: I don't know shit about military procedure. I'm with a special investigative division and we do things differently, so let me put it on a plate for you: You got pinched behind our lines wearing an American uniform. The book says that makes you a spy and all bets are off. They teach you what that phrase means, Lieutenant Schmidt, all bets are off?"

Schmidt shook his head. Grannit took another step forward until they were nose to nose.

"It means I don't give a fuck. So you tell me what I want to know or I'm going to hurt you. I'll start with an easy question. How many other men are in your squad? How many were with you in that jeep?"

Schmidt appeared confused. "Three."

Grannit waved the flashlight back toward the edge of the bridge, switching it off and on. A moment later, a single shot rang out, followed by a scream, then another shot. Grannit turned back to Schmidt.

"I think it's two now," said Grannit.

Schmidt's knees buckled slightly. He backed up a step and went pale.

"You want a heads-up on your next few days? Military Intelligence questions you, you go before a court-martial and then a firing squad, and the court-martial's a formality."

Schmidt took another step and staggered when he felt the wall of the bridge behind him.

"Nobody on this side's going to defend you or care what happens to you, and nobody on your side's ever going to hear about it. The one chance you've got is to cooperate and tell us everything you know. If you don't come clean, I'll save everybody the trouble and drop your ass off this bridge right now."

Schmidt went down onto his haunches, head lowered, breathing in jagged bursts.

"You don't strike me as a stupid man," said Grannit. "I don't

want to lean on you if I don't have to. You're not a soldier, are you, Schmidt?"

Schmidt shook his head. Grannit knelt down next to him and lowered his voice, radiating sympathy.

"I didn't think so. You have a family?"

"Yes," said Schmidt. "A wife. Two boys. Twins. They're not even ten years old."

Grannit took out a notebook and pen and waited. "That's who you should be thinking about now. I can't make any promises but this: I'll do what I can for you."

Schmidt rubbed his eyes, struggling to compose himself. "We were part of a special brigade. Those of us who came over in American uniform. Our company was going to assemble here."

"To capture the bridge?"

"And two others, nearby, by tonight."

"So where's the rest of your brigade?"

"I don't know. We were sent ahead to scout. When the others came, we were to secure the bridges for the main offensive. We had tanks. Some captured American. Panzers and Panthers disguised to look like Shermans. We have also motorized artillery, antitank guns, three mortar platoons, an armored reconnaissance group, a full supply column—"

Grannit could hardly write fast enough to keep up. "How many men are we talking about?"

"I would estimate two thousand? There was supposed to be a paratroop drop also, regular Wehrmacht, to support us against the bridges. The main columns were supposed to reach this position within a day. By tonight."

"The main objective being Antwerp."

Schmidt looked at him, mildly surprised. "That's right. If all went according to plan, they said it would fall within a week." He continued as Grannit kept writing.

"I want you to know I had no choice in this. I am not in the Nazi Party; I didn't even enlist. I despise what has happened to my country. It's only that I spoke your language, you see? I worked as a translator before the war, at a Berlin publishing house; I studied English in

college. There were threats to my wife and children; they made me work as an intelligence officer, reading newspapers, interpreting reports; I've never been near the front line—"

"I'll be sure to note that," said Grannit. "So how many men in your company came over the line? How many were in the jeeps?"

"The commando unit? I don't know, maybe eighty men?"

"All in four-man teams."

"Yes, that was how they organized us."

"About twenty teams altogether?"

"That sounds right."

"Did you all have the same objective?"

"As far as the bridges were concerned? Yes, but different responsibilities. Some for reconnaissance, some trained for sabotage, others demolition."

"There's another team I'm looking for." Grannit described the two soldiers he'd tracked to the hospital and chased in the jeep. "I need to find the lieutenant in charge of that squad. You have any idea who I'm talking about?"

Schmidt's look hardened. "Yes, I do. I think I know exactly who that man is."

"What's his name?"

"I never knew his German name. He is using the American name Miller, Lieutenant George Miller."

"What else can you tell me about him?"

"He is SS. I think he came from Dachau."

"Where's that?"

"The SS training center. Near Munich."

Grannit wrote down the name, put his notebook in his pocket, and pulled the man to his feet.

"We can talk more while we're driving in," said Grannit. "You did all right, Schmidt. You did the right thing."

"What choice do I have? What choice have I had from the beginning?"

Grannit didn't answer. As they neared the bridgehead, he waved his flashlight. By the time they reached the emplacement, Carlson was waiting behind the wheel of a small transport with the engine

running. Guarded by two soldiers from the bridge, the other three Germans sat in the open payload. None of them had been wounded or harmed in any way. Schmidt looked at Grannit, who couldn't tell if he was angry or relieved.

"You think I'd shoot a prisoner of war?" asked Grannit. "Where the hell you think you are, Russia? Get in."

He pointed Schmidt into the back of the captured jeep. Grannit took the sergeant in charge of the bridge platoon aside and relayed what Schmidt had told him about the impending attack.

"Radio your unit, tell them to get you reinforced fast. Maybe they're coming in force, maybe they're not, but you've got to hold this bridge."

"Yes, sir."

Grannit climbed into the jeep beside Schmidt. One of the bridge platoon GIs jumped in to drive, and both vehicles headed north along the river road.

"They really thought you could pull this thing off," said Grannit, after a while.

"They hoped," said Schmidt.

"But you didn't."

Schmidt shrugged. "Hope is all they have left." He watched the river for a moment, a plaintive look on his face. "Is it up to you? Whether I live or die?"

"I'll have something to say about it," said Grannit.

"But is it your decision to make?"

"Why do you want to know?"

"Our brigade was to capture that bridge," he said, studying Grannit's reaction. "We were also given a second objective."

Grannit waited. "Why don't you tell me what it was."

Schmidt watched him closely. "I'll wait. To speak to your superiors."

"Why not tell me now?"

"You made the choice to spare my life, and I appreciate that. But I need to speak about this with someone who can offer me a more substantial guarantee."

18

efore they left, Erich Von Leinsdorf poured out the kerosene from every lamp in the house and set Frau Escher's butcher shop on fire. By the time they drove away, *Oberstürmbannführer* Peiper's main panzer column had advanced through to the west; the village was deserted. Fog curled in, and more snow began to fall as they picked their way south and west. Von Leinsdorf studied a road map with a flashlight.

"I made coffee," he said, holding up a thermos. "Drink a lot of it."

Von Leinsdorf poured him a cup, and Bernie choked downed the strong brew as he drove, blasting his senses awake. Von Leinsdorf handed him a new helmet.

"What's this for?" he asked.

"Some Americans have had a look at us. We're changing units."

"Fuck, I was just getting used to Jimmy Tenella."

"You don't have to change the name, just give me your helmet."

Bernie did, and Von Leinsdorf tossed it out of the jeep.

"We're with the 291st Combat Engineers now. Our CO sent us south with dispatches just before they pulled back from Malmédy." He held up a leather U.S. Army document tube.

"I'm supposed to remember all this?"

"You'd better, old boy, or we're fairly fucked."

"Where are we going?" asked Bernie.

"You drive, I'll get us there. The good news is we can take back roads the entire way. Left here."

Von Leinsdorf switched on the flashlight over the map again. Bernie glanced over and realized that at some point Von Leinsdorf had changed the color of his blond brush cut to a dirty brown.

"What'd you do to your hair?"

"Another of Frau Escher's secrets. Hair dye in the bathroom."

Von Leinsdorf put on a pair of square, black-framed glasses, which drastically altered his appearance, making him look years older.

"Where did you get all this stuff?"

"Downstairs."

Bernie fumbled off his helmet. "Jesus, this is from one of those stiffs in the basement?"

"The ones they gave us at Grafenwöhr were stamped with the wrong mark inside the shell, see here?" He showed him a factory insignia inside the rim of the new helmet. "It's a different stamp for officers and noncoms. Ours looked the same. I'd put that back on if I were you; there may be snipers out here."

Bernie uneasily set the helmet back on his head.

"I take it you lost your rifle, too," said Von Leinsdorf. "There's another M1 in the back. What do you think of this?"

He held a vicious-looking hunting knife into the light.

"The woman had it strapped to her thigh."

Bernie made a face. "You searched her thighs?"

"Be thankful she didn't use it on you," said Von Leinsdorf. "If anyone stops us or we hit a checkpoint, show them this." He handed Bernie another road pass. "If they ask you anything else, you defer to me."

"So what do you need me for?"

"In case they ask us some bullshit trick question about baseball or who's fucking Minnie Mouse. Then jump in with all deliberate speed. You are up to that, aren't you, Brooklyn?"

Bernie swallowed his frustration and kept driving; anxiety gnawed at him, his hands clutched the wheel. They reached the Ambleve River near midnight, crossing an ancient stone bridge pockmarked

with bullets. The highway south took them into a shadowy forest. Ancient hardwoods crowded the road, their branches intertwining overhead to create a fog-enshrouded canopy. The stripped trees took on an unearthly silver glow, like twisted knots of human limbs in the mist. Visibility narrowed to a few yards.

Bernie had to brake suddenly to avoid slamming into a burned-out troop transport. A shell had hit the gas tank flush and the wheels had melted right onto the road. The charred corpses inside were impossible to identify as either German or American. They slowly drove around it and edged forward. Bernie thought he saw a line of men sprint across the road in front of them and disappear into the woods, but he couldn't tell what uniforms they were wearing. Von Leinsdorf crouched in the passenger seat and raised his rifle. A volley of bullets whistled by them out of the fog from that direction and shattered the rearview mirror. Von Leinsdorf returned fire, emptying his clip. Bernie stepped on the gas, taking a chance that nothing else lay hidden ahead of them in the dense air.

At three in the morning they emerged onto a high rocky plain, and Von Leinsdorf directed Bernie to follow signs toward Bastogne. Artillery boomed in the distance and drew closer as they approached. They cleared a checkpoint outside the village and entered an entrenched stronghold in the middle of town. MPs directed them to central command for VIII Corps, and they parked around the corner. Rifle companies were digging in all around, fortifying positions for mortars and machine guns. Bernie changed field jackets, putting on one that bore the insignia of the 291st Engineers.

"Stay next to me," said Von Leinsdorf. "Don't talk to anybody."

Holding up the document tube, Von Leinsdorf showed their new, corrected SHAEF security passes at the door, and they were sent toward the signal office. The command center, hastily thrown together in the middle of an old cathedral, hummed with frantic energy, officers shouting over one another. Housed in one of the chapels off the main nave, a battery of radio, telex, and telegraph operators relayed updated messages. Von Leinsdorf stood near the back and observed for a minute, getting a grasp of the command structure.

"Keep your head down," said Von Leinsdorf. "Look busy."

Bernie took out a pad and began to write. His hands could barely hold the pen. A signal corps sergeant barked at them as he walked past, gesturing at the document tube.

"You got something for us, Lieutenant?" he said.

"Already handed 'em off," said Von Leinsdorf. "Waiting on dispatches for the Twelfth."

"Don't wait too long," said the sergeant. "You might not get back out."

Listening to the chatter, Bernie learned that German forces were advancing rapidly to the north and south of Bastogne. The mood in the room ran just short of panic that they were about to be overrun; Bernie felt it fire his overwrought nerves. Von Leinsdorf studied the radio operators. He picked out a small corporal who looked close to exhaustion, then moved toward him the next time he came off a call, holding up the document tube. He had to shout to be heard over the din in the room.

"God damn it, they told us General Bradley would be here," said Von Leinsdorf. "I've got to get these into his hands."

"Bradley? He was supposed to be here an hour ago, but we lost the main road between here and Luxembourg."

"Christ, you're telling me he's not coming?"

"They might try to fly him in later, or get him back down to France. Ike wants both him and Patton for a pow-wow—"

"Where the hell's that going to be?"

"Maybe Verdun, maybe in Paris, they haven't said yet."

"Well, when the fuck is it scheduled?"

Bernie moved closer, listening and watching Von Leinsdorf. His sudden interest in Bradley's movements alarmed him.

"I don't think before tomorrow, and you can forget about getting to Luxembourg before that, sir, the Krauts are swarming down there—"

"Then god damn it, Corporal, I've got to get into France today. I need to know which crossings are still open and if it's gonna be Verdun or Paris as soon as you get word."

"I'll stay on it, sir."

"Where's your signal officer? I need the fucking passwords."

"We were just about to put out today's list," he said.

"Well, don't let me stop you," said Von Leinsdorf.

As the radio operator went to work, Bernie saw Von Leinsdorf step back and assess whether he'd been overheard. Every man in the room was so caught up in his own corner of the war that no one paid any attention. Ten steps away, Bernie watched a group of officers knotted around a red-faced general, who was shouting angrily at them. A shell landed outside, close enough to shake dust from the ceiling and momentarily dim the lights. During the blackout, Von Leinsdorf brazenly snatched the password list from the operator's desk—Bernie saw it in his hand when the lights came back on. Von Leinsdorf put it in his pocket, looked over, caught Bernie watching, and winked at him.

He's crazy. He's enjoying this.

Until he found a way to stop Von Leinsdorf, Bernie had resigned himself to the consequences of sabotage, reconnaissance, even espionage. That at least gave him a chance to avoid killing Americans.

Until that moment, assassination hadn't even occurred to him.

The telex station behind where Bernie was standing jumped to life, startling him.

Bernie leaned forward to read the message as it came through. It was an urgent signal from First Army HQ in Liège. The headline identified it as an emergency override, the highest level of Allied security alert.

First Army Interrogation Center, Liège
DECEMBER 18, 4:00 A.M.

The contents of Karl Schmidt's satchel, jeep, and pockets lay on the table between Schmidt and Major Moran from the 301st Counter Intelligence Corps Detachment. Schmidt's wrists were in handcuffs, secured through the slats of the chair behind his back, and he still wore the undershirt and trousers of his American uniform. Major Moran asked questions, while Earl Grannit and a team of intelligence

officers watched through a one-way observation window in an adjoining room. From there, a stenographer transcribed the conversation, which was conducted in English, although a translator was also present if the need for one arose. A wire tape recorder ran throughout the interview, so that when they reviewed and transcribed, no detail would be overlooked.

In a money belt concealed around his waist, Schmidt had carried $2000 in American currency, a thousand in counterfeit British pounds, and smaller amounts in Belgian, Dutch, and French notes and coins. American soldiers in Europe rarely carried cash and were instead issued printed scrip they called "invasion money," a detail that had escaped the scrutiny of Skorzeny's quartermaster. A shortwave military radio of German origin was found hidden in the back of Schmidt's jeep. They also found ten Pervitin tablets—caffeine-based energy boosters—an assortment of concealed weapons, including brass knuckles, hand grenades, and a stiletto; an American officer's field manual; and an English pocket-sized edition of the New Testament. Hidden in an empty fuel canister they found fuses, detonators, and six pounds of Nipolite, a malleable plastic explosive.

Other cans held four regulation German uniforms and a number of more exotic weapons, including a piano wire garrote and a silencer. Grannit took particular interest in the silencer, a silver cylinder that slid neatly over the barrel of Schmidt's standard American issue M1911 automatic. It also fit onto the end of a compact machine pistol they found, which converted to an automatic rifle with the addition of an armatured stock and telescopic sight. Among the ammunition for it they found a clip of seven bullets containing a poisonous aconite compound encased in the head, which was scored to split upon contact, causing certain death.

Because of his forgery training, Ole Carlson worked with two officers to examine Schmidt's collection of maps and documents. They included credible versions of the highest security passes issued by the Allied forces.

Early in his interview, Lieutenant Schmidt repeated the information he had given Grannit about the commando unit known as

Einheit Stielau. In earlier interrogations the other three captured members of his squad corroborated the basics of Schmidt's story. However, none of those men admitted knowing anything about a so-called second objective, even after being subjected to severe physical abuse.

Major Moran hadn't yet resorted to coercion with the talkative Schmidt, when negotiations stalled over this second objective. Schmidt offered to reveal what he knew about it, but only if given written assurance that he would not be executed as a spy. Major Moran refused. An agitated and emotional Schmidt refused to say anything more.

Furious, Moran came out of the room and ordered his men to beat it out of him. Earl Grannit asked if he could be left alone with Schmidt for a few moments. The major agreed. Grannit entered and took Moran's seat across from Schmidt.

"It doesn't matter what you dangle in front of them, Karl. They can't make that promise to you."

"But it's not fair. From the moment they brought us to that camp, we had to obey orders or they would shoot us. I haven't conducted espionage, I haven't killed Americans, I haven't committed any crimes—"

"That's not for me to decide. For all I know it may be true, but right now you have to do better."

"How?"

"Tell them you'll go out on patrol, help them look for the other commando teams. You know who or what to look for, don't you?"

"Would they let me do that?"

"Of course. But first you have to tell them what they want to know. We already grilled your squad about this. Nobody's backing you up. They say they don't know anything about a second objective—"

"They don't know because I never told them. We were ordered not to tell them anything—"

"Where'd that order come from?"

"From the officer in charge, the one who called himself Lieutenant

Miller, the man you asked me about. Please, they must believe me, I'm telling you the truth, but I'm fighting for my life."

Grannit hesitated. "Let me see what I can do."

Grannit left the room, and walked right past Moran and his men. "I gotta take a piss."

He went across the hall into the room where Ole Carlson was examining Schmidt's documents.

"These forgeries are high-quality," said Carlson. "I can't find a single fault that gives 'em away—"

Grannit leaned in and whispered, "Come into the other room. Wait for my signal after I go back in with Schmidt, then buy me a minute alone with him."

Carlson's eyes went wide, and he followed Grannit back into the observation room where the CIC officers had congregated, keeping an eye on Schmidt through the window. Grannit lit a cigarette.

"So?" asked Moran, in a foul mood. "Is he bullshitting us?"

"I don't think so."

"We're through fucking around with this asshole. If he's got something, let him put it on the table."

"I've got a good sense of this man, Major. We need to work him carefully—"

"Yeah, well, he can go fuck himself. I think he's full of shit, I think he's bluffing—"

"I respectfully disagree—"

"Well, who made you the fucking expert?"

"Colonel Otto Skorzeny put their unit together," said Grannit. "That name means something to you college graduates, doesn't it? You think Hitler sent them over here to play patty-cake?"

"So take a billy club and beat it out of him. That's how the NYPD likes to work, isn't it? Or do you prefer a rubber hose?"

Grannit pulled his sidearm and chambered a round. "Why don't I just pump bullets into him until he comes clean. You want to give me your okeydokey on that, Major? I'll make him confess to the fucking Lincoln assassination if that does the trick for you. Is that how you want to utilize our only asset?"

"You've got five minutes," said Moran.

Grannit stubbed out his cigarette on the doorjamb and walked back into the interrogation room. He sat down, glanced back at the one-way window, and rubbed the bridge of his nose. Seeing that signal, Ole Carlson stepped into the room, stumbled over somebody's foot, and spilled his coffee all over Major Moran's trousers. During the confusion that followed, Grannit leaned forward and switched off the hidden microphone under the table.

"Okay, Karl, I got you your deal, let's hear it," said Grannit.

"They won't prosecute me as a spy, they'll treat me like any other prisoner of war?"

"You have my word on it."

Schmidt leaned forward and cradled his head in his hands on the table, shoulders heaving with emotion. Grannit guessed he had less than a minute before the CIC smart-asses rushed in to turn the microphone back on.

"Save it for your family reunion, Karl, we're short on time. Now, you're going to have to ride along on those patrols we talked about; I told them you agreed to that—"

"Yes, of course—"

"And this whole thing stays between me, you, and the officer in charge, because it's against regulations. You can't mention it, even to him when they all pile in here, okay?"

Schmidt lifted his head up from the table. "Yes."

"What was your second objective?"

Grannit reached down and turned the hidden microphone back on.

"After the first two days," said Schmidt, "we are supposed to move south. Into France."

"How many men?"

Schmidt didn't blink. He reasoned that if he exaggerated the scope of the threat, he had a better chance at clemency, and that the right lie might save his life.

"All of us," said Schmidt. "Eighty men. The entire company of Skorzeny's commandos. We're to meet in Reims on the nineteenth, at a cinema, then move south to Paris."

"What's in Paris?"

"We rendezvous at the Café de la Paix with our local support and then move on Versailles. That's our objective."

"What is?"

"To attack Allied headquarters command."

Grannit felt his throat tighten.

"And to kill General Eisenhower."

19

esus Christ, take a look at this."

The telex operator ripped off the printed cable and held it out to the radioman next to him before Bernie could read it. "Holy shit."

The corporal's reaction drew Von Leinsdorf's attention, and he stepped toward them, taking a look at it before Bernie did. He handed it back to the corporal, then smiled at Bernie.

"Read it, Corporal," said Von Leinsdorf.

"Let me have your attention!" The corporal stood up on his chair and read it out loud. "First Army HQ, emergency override alert for all units in Belgium, Luxembourg, and Holland. Be aware that squads of German commandos in American uniform, driving American vehicles, are operating in combat zone behind Allied lines—"

Bernie froze in place. The room quieted and soldiers gathered around them as the message continued.

"Be also warned brigade strength force disguised as same, equipped with Sherman tanks and mobile artillery, believed to be somewhere in the field, details to follow—"

Excitement radiated out around them. The corporal rushed the cable toward the CO's desk. News of the bulletin ripped through the room, generating an uproar.

Bernie backed up against the wall, out of traffic, trying to make himself invisible. He caught Von Leinsdorf's eye. Von Leinsdorf tilted his head toward the door and Bernie started toward the exit. A couple of HQ staff sergeants ahead of them looked like they were trying to stop people from leaving and to organize a stronger watch on the door. Von Leinsdorf grabbed one by the arm.

"Christ, can you fucking believe this?" asked Von Leinsdorf.

"I believe they'd do anything."

"But how are we gonna know the difference? How can we tell these fuckers apart? Nazis wearing our uniforms, what if they're standing right in front of us?"

"We'll know, sir. They can't pull something like this off."

"Jesus, I hope you're right. Station men here, check IDs coming in and out. We've got to secure our perimeter, get word to the MPs, let's jump on it."

"Yes, sir."

The sergeant hurried off. Von Leinsdorf grabbed Bernie behind the elbow, guiding him through the door. "Keep walking. Don't stop."

The MPs outside were just hearing the news. Von Leinsdorf barked at them, "CO needs you men inside, double time, move, move, move."

The news radiated out in front of them, jumping from man to man. Bernie kept waiting for someone to notice them, stop them, put an end to it, and some part of him half wished it would happen. As they reached the street, another artillery barrage began and lit up the morning sky, shells stepping progressively closer to the village.

"They caught one of us," said Von Leinsdorf. "Probably one of the scout teams."

"How much do you think they know?"

"Their alert didn't mention the Second Objective. So we keep going."

"To where?"

"Reims, France," said Von Leinsdorf.

"What are we doing there?"

"In Reims? We're going to the movies."

They turned the corner and saw an MP in the parking area examining the unit numbers on their jeep. Bernie saw Von Leinsdorf's hand move toward his belt as they approached.

"Corporal, what are you standing there for? Don't you know what's happening?" asked Von Leinsdorf.

"You from Twelfth Army, sir?" asked the MP.

"That's right," said Von Leinsdorf, climbing aboard and signaling Bernie to get in and drive, as he held up the document tube. "And we're heading back there now, got to get these to the Old Man."

The MP put a hand out and stopped Bernie from starting the jeep. "Where'd you come in from?"

"North," said Bernie. "Both roads to Luxembourg are cut off, case you haven't heard."

"I was just gonna say," said the MP. "Road north's cut off, too, if you planned on going back that way."

"How do we get out of here?" asked Bernie.

"You gotta head due west. I see your road pass, soldier?"

Bernie glanced at Von Leinsdorf and handed it to him. They waited while he shined his flashlight on it. Bernie saw Von Leinsdorf reach down into the seat for the hunting knife.

The MP took his time looking it over, then handed it back. "You better make tracks. Krauts just about got us buttoned up."

"Good luck to you," said Von Leinsdorf.

"You said something's going on inside?" asked the MP.

"Nothing to worry about," said Von Leinsdorf.

Bernie stepped on the gas and they drove due west out of Bastogne.

Liège
DECEMBER 18, NOON

They didn't turn off the tape recorders until Earl Grannit had squeezed every last detail out of Karl Heinz Schmidt. Less than three hours later, stripped of his uniform and dressed as a prisoner of war, Schmidt was handed over to a squad of Army Intelligence officers. They began roving patrols of the main highways south and

west of the front lines, using Schmidt as their watchdog, looking for elements of what Schmidt had called Operation *Greif*.

Ongoing Allied communications problems prevented First Army Interrogation from notifying Counter Intelligence in the city of Reims, France, about Schmidt's final revelation: that the German assassination teams were planning to rendezvous at a cinema there on the evening of December 19. Earl Grannit and Ole Carlson drove out of Liège at noon and headed south to deliver that news in person.

Carlson held Karl Schmidt's forged blue SHAEF pass in his hand, studying it as they drove, then suddenly slapped it against his leg. "Staring me right in the face. That's what's wrong with this thing."

"What?" asked Grannit.

"This is U.S. government issue watermarked paper, and everything else is so well crafted you'da thought the Krauts'd catch this, it's just so danged obvious once you notice—"

"Notice what, Ole?"

"They transposed the e and a in 'headquarters.' They misspelled the doggone word."

Carlson showed it to him.

"Get on the radio," said Grannit. "Make sure they know that at the border. With luck we'll get there before they cross over."

Carlson cranked up the radio, trying to find a signal. "They're gonna execute him, aren't they?" he asked. "Schmidt?"

"That's right, Ole." Grannit glanced over as he drove. "What's the problem?"

"You promised him he wouldn't die for it."

"We don't even know he's telling the truth. Maybe he made the whole thing up to save his ass."

"Sounded pretty straight to me. How many more teams you think they sent over?"

"He said eighty men."

"They're desperate enough to try something like this. He had too many details. I think it's real and he got caught up without knowing what it was about—"

"Every bad guy's got a sob story, Ole."

"I'm just saying that if he's shot for it after helping us and us telling him different so he'd talk, it's a raw deal—"

"Guy comes over the line, wartime, in our uniform, confesses he's got orders to kill our commanding general, and you feel sorry for him."

"We lied to him, Earl."

Grannit said nothing.

"Well, how do you feel about it?"

Grannit took a long look at him. "Do I look troubled to you?"

Lieutenant Karl Heinz Schmidt would not see the other three men from his own jeep squad again until two days before Christmas. That night a group of captured German nurses were brought outside their cells and sang Christmas carols to them in their native language.

The four men were marched out at dawn the next day, Christmas Eve, tied to posts, and executed by an American firing squad. Schmidt's protests about a secret arrangement with Counter Intelligence that was supposed to have spared his life fell on deaf ears.

By noon on December 18, First Army Headquarters at the Hotel Britannique in Spa had been abandoned, retreating northwest toward Liège. Supply dumps in the area were ordered to pull back fuel and ammunition stores and destroy whatever they couldn't move to prevent them from falling into enemy hands. The German offensive had caught First Army so off guard and undermanned that every available able body was pressed into front-line action. Around Malmédy that included clerks and cooks with no combat experience, who called themselves "canteen commandos." First Army's commanding officer, General Courtney Hodges, issued one last order just before retreating toward Liège. All Allied military personnel currently in the brig for court-martial offenses were offered a one-time amnesty if they volunteered to join units fighting the increasingly desperate defense.

On the afternoon of December 18, Corporal Eddie Bennings and

twenty-six other members of the 724th Railway Battalion accepted the offer. They were released from custody in Liège, re-armed, loaded onto a truck, and shipped toward Malmédy.

Fifteen minutes after being assigned to a front-line company, Eddie Bennings cut himself on the arm with his bayonet, spilling an impressive but inconsequential amount of blood. He feigned dizziness, and a medic walked him to a mobile field hospital. Bennings entered, slipped out the back of the tent as soon as he was alone, jogged half a mile down the road to the supply depot's fuel shed, came out carrying two cans of gas, hot-wired a parked jeep, and headed south toward France.

As the day wore on, the warning about Skorzeny's commandos paralyzed the American battle zone. Military police locked down every major intersection under Allied control. Effective immediately, no enlisted man or officer without the current password was allowed to pass through any checkpoint. Traffic piled up behind roadblocks, and movement of American troops, during critical hours of the offensive, came to a dead halt. Reinforcements were delayed, hundreds of soldiers ended up in custody, and important dispatches were held up for hours. Placards with information about the imposters appeared in every barracks. An army of men who had never felt any reason to distrust the American uniform now viewed one another through a lens of paranoia and suspicion. Like the rumors that had infected the Nazi camp at Grafenwöhr, wild speculation about the objectives of the 150th Panzer Brigade spread across the battlefield. Not even Otto Skorzeny would have dared to hope that the mere mention of his commando squads would create such chaos in the Allied ranks.

The bulletin that German spies were operating behind Allied lines was not the only news to hit hard on December 18. Late on the afternoon of December 17, three survivors of the massacre at Baugnez Crossroads were found by an American patrol and rushed to the field hospital in Malmédy. Two reporters from *Time* magazine encountered the survivors, heard their story, and rushed it to headquarters in

Liège. By nightfall, First Army senior staff released the story that invading SS forces had murdered a large group of unarmed American prisoners of war. Newspapers in the United States, which hadn't yet run a single story about the Ardennes offensive because of a blackout ordered by SHAEF, were encouraged to publish detailed accounts of the incident. Many compared the slaughter to the Japanese attack on Pearl Harbor. Anti-German sentiment spiked to a wartime high; war bond purchases and volunteer enlistments soared.

Americans all across the country were reading about the "massacre at Malmédy" before the bodies of the eighty-six victims had even been recovered, lying under a thick blanket of snow in the meadow at the Baugnez Crossroads.

20

eneral Eisenhower spent the morning with his staff in his Map Room, trying to piece together fifty disjointed dispatches into a coherent overview of the invasion. This much was clear: Twenty-four Wehrmacht and *Waffen*-SS divisions had already been identified in the attack, striking toward Allied positions in three broad columns. While the northern and southern thrusts had met with makeshift but effective American resistance, the center through the heart of the Ardennes had not held. As Allied forces there crumbled and fell backward before the bludgeoning thrust of *Kampfgruppe* Peiper, tens of thousands of Wehrmacht and SS troops poured into the elastic middle behind them. The German attack flowed out to the south and west from there like water collecting in a basin, creating a distinct bulge on the map centering around the town of Bastogne.

During those early, uncertain hours, Dwight Eisenhower maintained a remarkable evenness of spirit. He had never led a battlefield unit but knew the first obligation of command was to set an example for the men around him. Despite the unsettling possibilities the attack presented, he never showed a moment's panic, and his calm attitude flowed through SHAEF and down the chain of command. As a portrait of the battle began to emerge, Eisenhower's tactical mind made an intuitive leap toward his enemy's intent. He picked up a captured

German sword, pointed to the center of the map, then slashed it west, all the way to Antwerp.

"They're trying to split our army groups with this central thrust, and isolate the British to the north," said Eisenhower. "These flanking columns are only there to screen the main push."

General Strong asked him how he wanted to respond. Eisenhower stepped closer to the map, bringing the sword back to the middle of the Meuse River.

"If we keep them on this side of the river, pinch them in along both shoulders, and confine the central column along this corridor, there's a chance we can choke them off here."

The point of the sword came to rest on a nexus of interlocking roads south and east of the Meuse. Eisenhower immediately ordered his reserve divisions, the 82nd and 101st Airborne, to proceed with all haste toward Bastogne.

No longer able to reach Bastogne himself, General Omar Bradley summoned General George Patton to Twelfth Army headquarters in Luxembourg City. He told Patton that his Third Army's offensive across the Saar River to the south, set to launch within days, had been officially called off. Bradley ordered Patton to have three of his divisions on the march toward the Ardennes within twenty-four hours.

During their meeting, Eisenhower sent word that he wanted to meet both his senior field commanders the following day in the French fortress city of Verdun, halfway between their headquarters, to finalize their response to the Ardennes offensive. Before they parted that evening, Bradley sympathized with Patton that his scheduled attack would not be going ahead.

"What the hell, Brad," said Patton. "We'll still be killing Krauts."

To the east of the German border, at their battle headquarters in Ziegenberg, news of the invasion's successes during the first two days heartened the Wehrmacht general staff. Hundreds of miles of forfeited Belgian territory had been regained, and thousands of American soldiers had surrendered. *Oberstürmbannführer* Peiper's

panzer column appeared to be relentlessly carving its way toward the Meuse.

The truth was more complicated. On the first morning after a crucial paratroop drop fell ten miles off course, the northernmost of their three panzer columns encountered stiff resistance and stalled in its tracks. Their inability to keep pace with the swift western progress of Peiper's central column left his northern shoulder exposed and vulnerable to attack if the Allies were able to regroup. Peiper's advance to the Meuse had turned into a race against time.

Since the offensive began, the main battle group of Otto Skorzeny's 150th Panzer Brigade had been stuck behind the massive traffic jam that backed up to the Western Wall. Despite the work of its advance commando teams, Operation *Greif*'s success depended on the main force making a clean break into open territory within the first few hours. Skorzeny's American tanks would not even reach Belgian ground until the early hours of December 17. Shortly after they did, Skorzeny's commanding officer, Lieutenant Colonel Hardieck, attempted to avoid the traffic jam by driving around it on secondary roads. His Willys Jeep hit a land mine on a logging road that had not been cleared by scout teams. Hardieck, along with his driver and adjutant, was killed instantly.

Colonel Skorzeny decided to take personal command of the brigade, but the roads were so snarled with traffic that Skorzeny was forced to abandon his jeep and walk ten miles to reach their forward position. By which point, at dawn on December 17, realizing his tanks had no chance to reach the river that evening on schedule, Skorzeny nearly called off Operation *Greif*. Only the encouraging intelligence from his lead commando units that the bridges at the Meuse were still undefended kept Skorzeny from issuing that order.

After consulting with his staff, he decided to try to keep their first objective alive for one more day.

At midnight on December 17, after speaking with Von Leinsdorf by radio, the two other commando teams he had recruited for the Second Objective cut off contact with Skorzeny's corps command and made

their way south toward France. By late afternoon on December 18, disguised as a squad of MPs, SS *Unterstürmführer* Gerhard Bremer's team was less than forty miles north of the French border. After driving into the middle of a firefight, William Sharper's squad had been forced to spend the night in the basement of an abandoned tavern. The delay put them two hours behind Bremer when they headed south again that morning.

Neither of them knew that the squad headed by Lieutenant Karl Schmidt had been arrested, that Schmidt had confessed, and that the alert was spreading behind American lines.

21

Twenty miles west of Bastogne, Bernie slowed the jeep as they neared an American battalion's encampment. Forward security posts were unmanned, exterior gates had been left open and the camp abandoned, leaving behind the battalion's bivouac and heavy gun emplacements. The German vanguard had not moved through yet, but artillery fire from the southeast suggested they were closing fast. In an eerie silence, the two men searched the tents to scrounge for rations and supplies.

The Americans had left in a hurry. Scores of uneaten breakfasts still sat on mess hall tables. Canisters of hot coffee and oatmeal bubbled over on field stoves. Von Leinsdorf helped himself to coffee and a slice of toast off a plate, then filled a knapsack with K rations and medical supplies. Outside they squeezed the last few gallons of gas from the camp's depot and strapped four extra cans to the rear of the jeep, enough fuel to get them deep into France. By the time they finished, they could hear German tanks advancing behind them, less than a mile away.

A short drive beyond the camp, they neared a river and spotted a platoon of American engineers working on the far side of an old stone bridge. Bernie drove toward the eastern approach, then slammed on the brakes when four armed GIs jumped out of the bushes, blocked the road, and pointed their rifles at them.

"What's the password?" shouted the lead corporal.

"Jesus," said Bernie. "You almost gave me a fucking heart attack."

"The password is 'stamp,'" said Von Leinsdorf. "What's the countersign?"

"Powder," said the man.

"That's incorrect," said Von Leinsdorf.

That response seemed to confuse them, and they conferred noisily for a moment.

"Hurry up, for Christ's sake. We're carrying important dispatches," said Von Leinsdorf.

"The Krauts are right on our ass," said Bernie.

"Hold your horses." They finished talking among themselves. "Is it 'smoke'?"

"That's right," said Von Leinsdorf. "Now get the fuck out of the way."

Another one of the soldiers stepped forward to ask: "What's the capital of Illinois?"

"Springfield," said Bernie.

"That's the wrong answer, search 'em."

The other soldiers moved toward the jeep. Von Leinsdorf stood up and pulled his pistol.

"It's Springfield, for Christ's sake, what the fuck's the matter with you?" shouted Bernie.

"The capital of Illinois is Chicago."

"Who says it is?" asked Bernie.

The corporal pointed to one of his other men. "He does."

"Is he from Illinois?"

They asked the man. He shook his head.

"He's a fucking moron, it's not Chicago, it's Springfield."

The soldiers discussed it heatedly among themselves, and couldn't reach a decision, but didn't move out of the road.

"God damn it, we don't have time for this shit," said Von Leinsdorf, pulling his pistol. "You're grilling us? You didn't even know the countersign. What are you fuckups doing here? Is that your bivouac we just passed?"

"Yes, sir, we're the last company out. We got orders to blow this bridge. The Krauts are supposed to break through any minute."

"No shit, Einstein, I just told you they're on our ass," said Bernie.

"We can help," said Von Leinsdorf. "We're engineers."

"That wouldn't be up to us, sir. Ask over there," said the corporal, pointing to the far side of the bridge.

"Then get out of the fucking way," said Von Leinsdorf.

The soldiers finally stood aside.

"It's Springfield, I'm telling you, anybody else comes through and you're gonna ask 'em that," said Bernie, as they drove past them.

When Bernie reached the far side of the bridge, Von Leinsdorf pointed to three other Allied vehicles and ordered him to pull over.

"What the hell for?" asked Bernie.

"Because I told you to," said Von Leinsdorf. "Come with me and keep your mouth shut."

Bernie followed Von Leinsdorf down a steep path that ran along the base of the bridge to the edge of the river below. Half a dozen American engineers worked underneath, planting M85 satchel charges, stringing fuses to the western shore beneath the single span.

"How can we help?" Von Leinsdorf shouted.

"You guys techs?" asked the sergeant in charge.

"That's right."

"You can rig those last two charges," he said, pointing them toward a pile of demolition supplies stacked against the stone.

Von Leinsdorf opened one of the boxes and handed Bernie two twenty-pound satchels, packed tight with block charges. They hammered two spikes in between the stones in the base of the rampart and suspended the satchels on them. Looking across the river, Bernie could see six other satchels strung under the bridge, connected by fuses leading back toward the western approach.

"What are we doing here?" whispered Bernie.

"Give me the priming assembly," said Von Leinsdorf.

Bernie watched as he appeared to attach the detonating cord clip to the booster charge running from the satchel, but at the last moment folded the connector underneath the clip with a pair of pliers,

concealing it inside a fold of canvas. He then ran the fuse out to the main line running toward the shore.

"Here they come!" shouted one of the GIs on the far side of the bridge.

Moments later they heard the last patrol retreating over the bridge overhead. Bernie stepped out from under the span and looked east, but he was too far below the bank to see anything.

"Let's get the hell out of here," he said.

"Hold your horses," said Von Leinsdorf, working calmly.

He repeated the procedure on the second satchel. The other engineers had finished their work, running lines behind them as they backed toward the eastern shore. Von Leinsdorf tossed their fuse line to the sergeant who was making fast all the connections. Bernie turned to follow the engineers up to the road, looked back across the river, and saw a line of gray German scout cars advancing down the road, less than a mile away.

Instead of hooking their line to the main fuse, the sergeant stopped to check the connections on their satchels. Von Leinsdorf, who had started after Bernie, hesitated when he saw the man stop. He waved at Bernie to keep going. Bernie could see that the sergeant was about to come across their unconnected detonating cord. Von Leinsdorf pulled his knife, held it along his leg, and advanced toward the sergeant's back.

"Sarge, come on, they're closing in on the bridge," called Bernie.

The sergeant looked up and saw Von Leinsdorf ten feet away with the knife in his hand. Von Leinsdorf kept walking, trying not to appear threatening.

"I double-checked everything, Sarge," said Von Leinsdorf.

"Stop right where you are," said the sergeant.

The sergeant pulled a handgun on Von Leinsdorf. Von Leinsdorf turned to glance at Bernie, expecting him to react. Bernie slowly raised his rifle, unsure where to point it.

"Sarge, the Krauts are coming, what's the problem?" asked Bernie.

"Drop that knife, Lieutenant," said the sergeant. "Right now."

"Come on, Brooklyn," said Von Leinsdorf, glancing back at him. "What are you waiting for?"

"I'm counting to three, then I shoot," said the sergeant. "One, two—"

Von Leinsdorf dropped the knife and raised his hands. "Jesus, what are you so jumpy for, Sarge? Did I fuck up the connections? I didn't mean to—"

"Turn around and start walking."

"Brooklyn?"

"Drop the rifle, kid, or I'll fire. I'm not fucking around."

Bernie lowered the rifle, holding it to the side as he stepped toward them. "We lied, okay? So we're not engineers, we were driving past and saw the situation. He didn't mean to fuck up the fuse. We're just trying to give you a hand."

The sergeant hesitated, blinking his eyes, exhausted and anxious, trying to decide.

"For Christ's sake, what you gonna do, shoot one of your own?" asked Bernie. "With the fuckin' Krauts on top of us?"

"I'll fix it if you show me how," said Von Leinsdorf.

"I said stay where you are."

Bernie glanced back up toward the road and saw the engineers on the road hustling to attach the charge line to a detonator.

"We're running out of time—"

The whistle of an incoming tank shell split the air. It slammed into the surface of the bridge above them, clouding the air with dust. The blast staggered the sergeant, knocking him against the base of the bridge. Von Leinsdorf picked up his knife and was on him in two steps. He grabbed the sergeant's gun arm and bent it back against the rocks until the pistol fell. He brought up his knife with the other hand, planted it in the sergeant's chest, and rode him down into the dirt, covering his mouth, holding him there until he stopped moving.

Bernie kept the rifle trained on the tangle of their bodies. He was unable to draw a clear target as they wrestled, until the sergeant went still and he had a clean shot at Von Leinsdorf. His finger found the trigger, the second time he'd had Von Leinsdorf in his sights.

The way he cut that rifleman's throat in the cabin.

Bernie had made excuses for him after Von Leinsdorf saved his life. Telling himself Von Leinsdorf had only killed because war or their survival demanded it.

But not that one. Not that poor terrified kid in the cabin.

You need to know what the mission is first, thought Bernie. *Kill him now, there's still others out there trying to pull it off, with no way to stop them—*

Von Leinsdorf looked up from the dead man, saw the barrel pointing at him, and the uncertainty in Bernie's eyes. He raised his hands as he stood up, unafraid, inviting him to take the shot.

Another shell screamed toward them. Bernie turned and ran the rest of the way to the road as Von Leinsdorf dove to the ground. The shell landed to the left of the bridge. Showered with dirt but unharmed, Von Leinsdorf picked up his knife, sliced the main fuse line, and sprinted up the path.

The column of panzers rumbled down the road from the west. The rest of the GIs had fallen back a quarter mile, shouting at the engineers to hurry. Bernie started their jeep, pointed the wheels away from the bridge. The pop of small-arms fire erupted. Bullets kicked up around the engineers as they hooked up their detonator.

"Forget about that! Get out of here!" Bernie shouted to them.

He saw Von Leinsdorf running out from under the bridge, his uniform covered in dust.

"Where's the sarge?" one of the engineers shouted back.

Bernie stepped on the gas as Von Leinsdorf came alongside and jumped onto the running board. They skidded away as another shell exploded behind them on the road. The rest of the Americans scattered in every direction. In a quick look back, Bernie saw the last engineer push down the plunger on their detonator. When nothing happened to the bridge, and a second shell landed near them, the engineers followed the riflemen into the trees. Bernie skidded around the next turn and floored the jeep, desperate to leave the bridge behind them.

Von Leinsdorf fell into the passenger seat beside him. His whole body appeared to be shaking.

"What's wrong, are you hit?" asked Bernie.

Von Leinsdorf turned toward him and Bernie realized he was laughing.

"What's so fucking funny?" said Bernie.

"Why didn't you shoot him when you had the chance?"

"What are you talking about? He had a gun on you the whole time."

"I saved your life, the least you can do is return the favor—"

"I didn't have a shot. Jesus Christ, what am I supposed to do? We shouldn't have stopped in the first place."

"Keeping that bridge open could be the difference for the entire offensive. Did that ever occur to you?" Von Leinsdorf pulled out a cigarette.

"Well, don't mistake me for somebody who gives a shit."

Von Leinsdorf glared at him, then pulled his pistol and pointed it at Bernie's head. "Pull over. Pull off the road and stop right now."

Bernie did as he was ordered, steering onto the first dirt side road, concealed from the main highway by a thick stand of evergreens. Von Leinsdorf told him to stop near the ruins of an old country church. Bernie kept both hands on the wheel, his eyes on the road.

"I'm sorry," said Bernie. "I didn't mean that."

"Are you really that reluctant to shoot an American, Bernie? Before we go any further: You are a German soldier, aren't you?"

"I could've just as easily shot you, too," said Bernie, glancing sideways at the gun. "You think about that?"

"Oh yes. And what would you have done then? How long do you think you'd last after Counter Intelligence takes you for questioning? What sad story would you tell them, Brooklyn? This Nazi/GI took you hostage and forced you to drive all over Belgium? No credibility problem there. But tell us, Private, what about all these forged documents and German uniforms in the back of your jeep?"

"Okay, you made your point."

"The point is they'd break you in an hour. You'd give up your mother. You haven't the backbone for it." Von Leinsdorf looked disgusted. "Get out of the car."

"You said you needed my help, you couldn't do this without me—"

"Get out now."

"Look, put the gun down, all right?"

"Take your hands off the wheel."

Bernie kept his head down, clinging to the wheel, white-knuckled. "Just because I didn't kill that guy? Those other GIs would've heard the shot. What if they came after us? They had ten guys up there, there was no time, the panzers were on top of us. I did what I thought was best."

Von Leinsdorf hesitated. They heard heavy firing behind them. The German advance had crossed the bridge.

"I didn't ask to be here," said Bernie. "I didn't ask for any of this. I don't even know what we're doing."

Bernie glanced over and hardly recognized the man. The shell of civilized personality was gone. What he saw in its place was cold, hard, and sneering.

"I'm sick of your excuses. Get out."

"Why?"

"Because I don't want blood on my jeep."

Bernie climbed down and backed away. Von Leinsdorf followed, pistol raised, into the church's small graveyard. Shells had landed among the old headstones, cratering the field and scattering fragments of worm-eaten coffins and human remains.

"Try to appreciate the stunning degree of your own insignificance. You're here because a politician made a speech, another one rattled his saber, and in this way small men like you are marched out to fight their wars—"

"It has nothing to do with me—"

Von Leinsdorf shoved him forward. "It doesn't matter what you think about it, or what you think about anything. This is a business, and the business of war is killing. It's a job, like baking bread or carpentry—"

"That what they teach you at Dachau?"

"They didn't have to teach me. You learn on your own or you

can't go on. By now you should have figured it out for yourself. That's the lesson."

Bernie backpedaled as Von Leinsdorf advanced straight at him. "What lesson?"

"That it means nothing." Von Leinsdorf screwed the silencer onto the end of his pistol. "You value your sorry little life so highly. Tell me why, because of what? What have you ever done with it? What makes your life worth saving?"

"I don't know, I'm just me."

"How you could possibly know who that is? I grew up in two countries, too, but I never forgot. You've been too busy hiding all your life, making yourself invisible, a nobody so they wouldn't notice you. Because you're ashamed of what you are."

Bernie had no answer. He couldn't even mount an argument, his face burning at the painful truths the man had seen in him.

"None of it matters. That's what you don't know. You have no idea how cheap life really is. You have no idea. What you find when you get to the bottom of it. There's no honor, no dignity, no morality, no spirit. There's just blood and meat. Life is shit. It's *shit.*"

Von Leinsdorf leaned forward, inches from Bernie's face, looking haunted and skeletal under his handsome features. Bernie went down to his knees on the charnel house ground, beside a scattering of bones.

"This so-called gift you think is worth saving, that's just a reflex, a bug flinching at a boot. There's no majesty to it. You can take apart a human being as easily as a clock. I worked with a doctor in our camp at Dachau, Dr. Rasher, you know that name?"

Bernie shook his head.

"He organized our research. Identified what we could learn from these subjects. How they react to heat, cold, pressure and pain, wounds and bleeding. It's amazing how little fight they put up. They just hand it to you, that's what we learned: Killing's the easiest thing in the world."

He flicked Bernie's ear with the pistol, and he flinched.

"And the Jews were grateful for it. Because at some level they're aware of this disease they carry. The Jew is an infection. A genetic virus. Once it enters the bloodstream of a society, or an individual,

the only remedy is eradication. That's our lasting contribution to science. We found the cure."

Von Leinsdorf knelt down beside Bernie and grabbed his chin.

"You think your hands are clean? Your father works for IG Farben. They make the gas we use to kill them. All of them, Bernie. We're killing all of them."

Bernie felt paralyzed. He couldn't catch his breath.

"I'm no different. I've just had the benefit of a closer look at death. You think I value my own life?"

Von Leinsdorf pointed the gun to his own head.

"This endless series of humiliations and miseries? I'd end it right now if I didn't have this mission. And if I die in its service, at least I'll know it counted for something greater than myself. Can you say the same?"

"Believe whatever you want," said Bernie, shaking so hard he could barely speak. "It's none of my business."

"If you didn't learn the lesson in that basement back there, I don't know when you ever will. What you saw down there was child's play. Open your eyes, man. Declare yourself. This is as real as life is ever going to get. You won't last another day without deciding who you are or what is worth dying for."

"Why make it your problem?"

Von Leinsdorf touched the barrel to Bernie's chest. "Because I'm stuck with you. What am I going to do with you? If I kill you right now no one would mourn. No one would even know. Animals clean your bones, some peasant comes along one day and tosses them into these graves. All trace of you, all memory gone. Even your family will forget. As if you'd never existed."

Bernie saw a stark blackness in his eyes. He tried to steady his voice and ease him back to reality. "You said you needed me. To complete the mission."

"The next time you have a chance to shoot me, take it. If you can ever bring yourself to kill anybody."

Von Leinsdorf slumped, weary, as if he'd lost interest in what he'd intended to do. Then, a change. Businesslike again. He unscrewed the silencer and dropped it in his pocket. He picked Bernie

up off the ground, slung an arm around him, and walked him back toward the jeep. Now he took the affectionate tone of a confidant chiding a wayward friend.

"I don't think you're a physical coward, Brooklyn. Just a moral one. But if you do find it in your heart to kill me, you'll kill yourself as well. They'll catch you sooner or later, your American friends. To die in battle is one thing; execution is worse. I tell you from experience. It's not the dying, it's knowing when and where and how. That's the hell of it."

Bernie said nothing, the numbness in his body turning cold. Von Leinsdorf climbed back into the jeep. "Keep driving."

Bernie backed out and steered them onto the main road. They drove in silence for a while.

He's right about one thing, Bernie thought, glancing over at Von Leinsdorf. *I've gone too long thinking about myself, worried about my own life. Not anymore.*

Figure out what he's doing, a piece at a time. And then even if it kills me, I'll find some way to stop him.

22

Supreme Allied Headquarters, Versailles
DECEMBER 18, 1:00 P.M.

The news from Karl Schmidt's interrogation finally arrived by telex as General Eisenhower finished his strategy meeting in the Map Room. His chief of Counter Intelligence hurried in the dispatch after confirming the contents twice with First Army. Eisenhower scanned the report, that as many as eighty German commandos in American uniform targeting him for assassination might be in Paris, with characteristic calm.

"Just another crazy-ass rumor," he said, handing the pages back.

He was the only officer at Allied Headquarters who reacted that way. Over Eisenhower's protests, his chief of security ordered that the general's quarters be relocated immediately from a comfortable nearby villa into the Grand Trianon Palace in the Versailles compound. Ike relished what little privacy he had, and when he was off the clock, wanted to be left alone. His staff believed the reason for that was Ike's ongoing affair with his British aide-de-camp, a WAC lieutenant and former fashion model named Kay Summersby. When Eisenhower refused to make the move, his chief of staff told him that when his safety was involved, he had to follow orders like any other soldier. By the end of the day, America's only five-star general, commander of the entire Allied theater of war in Europe, had become, in effect, a prisoner of his own forces.

Within twenty-four hours, the Trianon Palace was transformed into a fortress. Two walls of thick barbed wire went up around the perimeter. Tanks and machine gun emplacements were installed at hundred-yard intervals around the compound. Roadblocks were set up for miles in every direction, and an elaborate new pass system was installed overnight. A platoon of MPs was added to the general's personal security detail, and he would be driven in an armored sedan with tinted windows, never using the same route twice. Accustomed to taking long, solitary walks through the gardens of Versailles, Eisenhower was confined to the building with the drapes closed, in case snipers had worked their way within range, while soldiers patrolled the grounds. Ike's protests that these men could better serve the war effort on the front lines were ignored.

"This must be what it feels like to be president," grumbled Eisenhower to a member of his staff.

By nightfall plainclothes Army Counter Intelligence officers in Paris had staked out the Café de le Paix, the restaurant Schmidt had identified as the assassins' rallying point. Machine guns were nested in nearby alleys. Otto Skorzeny's photograph was plastered to walls and lampposts throughout the city. Neighborhood watches organized patrols looking for disguised German agents. Any suspicious-looking GI who wandered into the area was detained and questioned.

Security officers tried using human bait to draw the killers into the open. One of Eisenhower's staff officers, Lieutenant Colonel Baldwin Smith, who bore a striking resemblance to his balding commander, volunteered to move into Eisenhower's vacated villa. For the next few days he dressed in one of the general's uniforms and was driven back and forth in the general's Cadillac along his normal travel routes. Eisenhower himself was neither asked nor told about the substitution.

The fallout from Lieutenant Schmidt's confession affected Allied soldiers all along the chain of command. Although he gave the correct password at a checkpoint, American General Bruce Clarke spent six hours in custody when an overeager MP decided that the general's placing of the Chicago Cubs in the American League constituted

proof he was a German spy. Driving back to his own headquarters, General Omar Bradley was stopped half a dozen times and grilled on Midwestern geography, the Notre Dame football team, and the infield of the St. Louis Cardinals.

British Field Marshal Bernard Montgomery, just arriving in Belgium from Holland, was waved down at an American roadblock near Malmédy. As a security precaution, all rank and insignia had been removed from his jeep, which aroused suspicion. Furious at having his authority questioned, particularly by an American, the imperious Montgomery ordered his chauffeur to drive on in the middle of the conversation. MPs responded by shooting out his tires, giving chase, and relieving Montgomery of his sidearm. They held the war's highest-ranking British officer in custody for three hours, until a Canadian colonel identified the apoplectic Montgomery. Exasperated by Monty's habitual grandstanding, Eisenhower reportedly relished hearing about his ordeal in detail.

Soldiers manning the checkpoints were no longer satisfied with passwords, and as the days wore on, their interrogations grew increasingly elaborate. Queries about sports, comic strips, and current Hollywood gossip supplied the most frequent stumpers. Some inventive MPs tried to trip up the putative assassins by demanding they recite poems filled with r's or w's, notoriously difficult for native Germans. "Round the rugged rock the ragged rascal ran" was a favorite.

For all the disruption they caused, these precautions were about to pay tangible dividends.

The French Border
DECEMBER 18, 9:00 P.M.

After driving all afternoon, Earl Grannit and Ole Carlson entered France at a heavily guarded crossing just north of the town of Givet. Grannit identified himself to MPs running the post and made sure they'd received the bulletin about Skorzeny's commandos. They showed him that it had been widely circulated and that more stringent

controls had been imposed. Traffic was backed up on the Belgian side of the border for a quarter of a mile.

Before pushing on for Reims, Grannit and Carlson were shown to the mess hall next door for a quick meal. Waiting for their food, they drank coffee by a window looking out on the post's supply depot on the French side of the line.

"You got a wife, Earl?"

"What do you want to know for?"

"I don't know, I just never asked you."

"I had one," said Grannit.

Carlson waited. "That's it?"

"Yup."

"What did your dad do?"

"He owned a gas station," said Grannit.

"Any brothers or sisters?"

"What is this, the third degree?"

"I'm just making conversation."

"I had a sister." Grannit spotted something out the window. "You got your binoculars with you?"

Carlson handed them over. Grannit focused them on an American jeep at a gas pump in the supply depot a quarter of a mile away. Two MPs stood near the jeep, one of them dispensing gas into the tank. From this distance and angle he couldn't make out any unit numbers on the jeep.

"Go ask at the post if a couple of MPs came across in the last hour."

"You got it."

Carlson immediately went next door to the border command office.

Grannit watched the MPs at the gas pump. He scanned the vehicle, looking for details that reminded him of Schmidt's jeep. Nothing jumped out. Carlson returned a few moments later.

"They came through about twenty minutes ago," said Carlson. "They had the password and SHAEF passes—"

"Did they check the spelling?"

"He said they had that detail from our bulletin, and that

'headquarters' was spelled correctly. They said they were from SHAEF, working security on the Skorzeny case."

"So they knew about it, mentioned it before they were asked."

"That's what he said."

Grannit saw a third MP returning to join the others at the jeep in the yard. "Anyway, there's three of them."

"You thought it might be our guys?"

"No, Ole, I thought it was Eleanor Roosevelt," said Grannit, lowering the glasses.

"You would've noticed her teeth," said Carlson. "Even at this distance."

Something caught Grannit's eye just as the binoculars came down, and he drew them back up. A fourth MP came out of a side building and climbed into the jeep.

"Hang on, shit, there's four of them."

"But their passes were good."

"Hold 'em up at the gate, we'll check ourselves. Go now."

Carlson hurried back to the post. Grannit hustled out the back of the mess hall into the yard and saw the jeep pull away from the gas pumps. It headed for the nearest exit, an open gate in a chain-link fence a hundred yards away. Heading after them, Grannit broke into a trot.

"Hurry up, Ole," he said.

As the jeep approached the gate, Grannit saw an MP in the guardhouse pick up a phone. He stepped outside and rolled the gate shut as the jeep got close. The MP leaned over to say something to the men inside.

The jeep slammed into reverse, spun around, and headed back across the yard toward another exit, quickly reaching top speed. The MP ran after it. Grannit pulled his pistol.

"Hey! Hey!"

The jeep careened straight at Grannit. He lowered the pistol, and emptied the clip. Shots cracked the windscreen and side mirror, but the jeep steered away from him. Ole and MPs from the border post ran out of the main building with guns drawn and angled toward the

gate across the yard. A machine gun on top of the post opened up, chasing the jeep with bullets across the yard but not connecting.

With no time to close the rolling gate at the far exit, two guards threw down a line of necklace mines across the opening. The jeep accelerated as it reached the open gate and hit the mines at fifty miles an hour. The mines detonated, blowing off the front tires. The full, oversized gas tank ignited in a fireball, flipping the jeep into the air. It landed upside down, enveloped in flames.

All four men aboard, including their squad leader SS *Unterstürm-führer* Gerhard Bremer, died instantly.

23

Bernie Oster and Erich Von Leinsdorf spent the night huddled in their jeep, side flaps and canvas roof raised, wrapped in blankets. Bernie was still too cold to sleep. They had driven west from Bastogne until after dark, sticking to back roads; eighteen hours to cover fifty miles, across empty fields, through abandoned or devastated villages. Twice they pulled into heavy woods to avoid American reinforcements entering from France. Using binoculars, Bernie spotted the screaming eagle insignia of the 101st Airborne on their sleeves.

Snow fell steadily through the night, wrapping the forest in silence. For the first time since the offensive began, they'd left the frenzy of battle behind. At first light they rolled down to a heavily wooded ridge overlooking a minor border post that Von Leinsdorf had selected on the map. Through binoculars he spotted two French soldiers manning a kiosk and guard gate spanning the dirt road. No traffic moved in either direction.

Von Leinsdorf fished around in his knapsack for traveling papers. "I'll do the talking," he said.

Bernie honked the horn and flashed headlights as they drove up to the gate, alerting a middle-aged French soldier, who stepped out to meet them. Von Leinsdorf waved the transit papers at the man as he emerged, and spoke in rapid-fire French. When the soldier asked

for a password, Von Leinsdorf lit into him. Bernie didn't understand a word, but it was clear that hearing fluent French from an angry American officer unnerved the man.

Von Leinsdorf held up his dispatch case. *"Je porte les expéditions importantes pour le chef du personnel Américain."*

Von Leinsdorf jumped out of the jeep, red in the face, using names that Bernie didn't need translation to understand. Cringing and apologetic, the Frenchman indicated he needed to show their papers to his superior inside.

"Wait here," Von Leinsdorf said to Bernie.

The sentry led him to their barracks, a squat concrete blockhouse twenty yards behind the kiosk. The Frenchman continued to apologize, backpedaling, tripping over his own feet. Von Leinsdorf waved at him to keep walking and followed, reaching for something on his belt.

Bernie lit a cigarette and waited until the two men entered the blockhouse, then climbed out of the jeep and hurried to the kiosk. He looked around for paper and pen, scribbled a note in English, until he saw the door of the blockhouse open.

Von Leinsdorf walked out, carrying a basket and a bottle of wine. He saw Bernie in the kiosk, studying a sheet of paper next to the window.

"What are you doing in there?"

"Take a look. They changed passwords overnight," said Bernie.

Von Leinsdorf scanned it, a telex from American command.

"Who's 'Dizzy Dean'?"

"He's a pitcher, for the St. Louis Cardinals."

"Well done, Brooklyn. You finally made a contribution."

Von Leinsdorf headed for the jeep. As he followed, Bernie noticed a body lying in the doorway of the blockhouse.

"At least the fucking Frogs know how to eat," said Von Leinsdorf, handing him the basket. "Let's get moving."

Bernie pointed to his cheek as Von Leinsdorf climbed back in beside him.

"What?" said Von Leinsdorf, then wiped his cheek. A spot of blood came off on his hand. "Did I get it?"

Bernie nodded, and started the jeep as Von Leinsdorf took the basket and rummaged through it.

"Not exactly Christmas dinner, but it'll do. Fruit and cheese, a baguette. Guess they already ate the foie gras," said Von Leinsdorf. "First time in France, Brooklyn?"

"Yeah."

"Beautiful country," said Von Leinsdorf, biting into an apple. "Dreadful people."

A phone began to ring inside the kiosk as they drove away.

The Border Crossing at Givet
DECEMBER 19, 6:00 A.M.

The burned hulk of the MPs' jeep didn't cool enough to be searched until halfway through the night. Searchlights were brought out illuminating the yard. Concern persisted that they'd killed four MPs until, near dawn, Earl Grannit turned up some burned German uniforms in a gas canister, and some of the same customized weapons they'd found in Karl Schmidt's jeep. Ole Carlson called Grannit over to look at a still-smoldering scrap of paper he had picked from the debris.

"One of their SHAEF passes," said Carlson.

The top had burned away, obliterating the word "headquarters."

"The guard who cleared them said it was spelled right," he said, troubled.

"Maybe he got it wrong," said Grannit. "You did for a while, and you were staring at it."

"I don't know. Something about it's bugging me."

Grannit asked the captain in charge to make sure every other border post had up-to-date intel about the two men they were looking for. The captain showed Grannit a large map of the French-Belgian border on his office wall.

"There's six crossings between here and the west edge of Luxembourg," said the captain. "Unless they cross on foot."

"They'll go through a checkpoint," said Grannit, studying the map. "They're not going to give up their jeep. We hauled ass getting here; they can't be that far ahead of us."

"Our reinforcements are moving into Belgium along these roads," said the captain. "They'll probably stay in this corridor. That leaves four crossings."

"You have MPs at all these posts?" asked Grannit.

"They were supposed to be there by this morning. We may not have reached all of 'em yet."

One of the MPs working the phones came back to confirm that three crossings had received the bulletin, and that MPs had arrived during the night. No other German teams had been stopped. The second MP was still on the phone.

"What's going on, son?" Grannit asked him.

"I can't get through to Pont-Colin," he said.

"Where's that?"

"Small post, twenty miles south," said the captain. "Used mostly by local traffic. Under French control."

"Get me a map. Ole, bring your breakfast."

The weather improved as Bernie drove out of the hills and made the last crossing over the Meuse as it twisted south through the high plains of northern France. Traffic on the highway from Reims was a solid flow of American military, all headed north, toward Belgium.

"What did you want to be when the war's over, Brooklyn?"

"Alive."

"Aside from that," said Von Leinsdorf.

Bernie glanced over. With a full belly and an open road ahead, the mercurial German had drifted into an unguarded mood, the ugly threats he'd made forgotten. He angled back in his seat, one foot on the dash, hands behind his head, looking up at the overcast sky. Bernie decided to keep him talking.

"I was supposed to go to college," said Bernie. "To figure that out."

"Where?"

"I was thinking NYU. New York University. Maybe study engineering, something like that."

"Yes, it would have suited you. Jolly good wheeze, campus life. I would have gone on to university in England, Cambridge, King's College. That was the plan anyway."

"Thought you'd always been in the army," said Bernie.

"Before the war? No. Politics, diplomacy, that's where I was headed. Peace between nations. Serving the greater good. That was my father's influence."

Bernie saw a shade of feeling flicker across his face.

"Where is he now?" asked Bernie.

"He died. Just after he retired."

"What was he like?"

"A decent man. His talent fell short of his ambition. He needed work to have a reason to live." Von Leinsdorf lit a cigarette, eager to shift the subject. "Is your father alive?"

"There's been heavy bombing in Frankfurt. I haven't heard from them."

"Terrible thing to lose your father."

Von Leinsdorf sounded genuine, as if he still possessed some trace of humanity.

"We were both taken from the life we were supposed to live, Brooklyn. Men our age should have more agreeable things on their minds. We should be out on the town, driving around with a couple of pretty girls."

Bernie looked at him. "Which town?"

"Paris isn't a bad place to start. Ever been?"

"No."

"Maybe once we finish there, we'll cruise down the Rivoli, pick up a couple of those fresh young things in their summer dresses. Champagne dinner at the Hotel Meurice, dancing, a midnight show in Pigalle. How does that sound?"

"Sounds pretty good."

So we're going to Paris. After Reims. That's our destination. Now all I need is the target.

Von Leinsdorf glanced up again. "Looks like it might rain."

"How many squads are working on this with us?" asked Bernie casually.

"Five altogether." He pointed at a road sign as they approached an intersection. "Take a right here."

The sign pointing to the right read "REIMS 60 KM."

Snow stopped falling as Grannit and Carlson parked a quarter mile shy of the post at Pont-Colin, on the French side of the border. Leaving the main highway three miles down, they hadn't passed a single vehicle as they drove up a series of mountainous switchbacks.

They advanced the rest of the way to the crossing on foot, weapons drawn. Grannit eased up to the window of the blockhouse barracks and saw the bodies of two French soldiers on the floor. He signaled Ole to check the kiosk, then went to work examining the scene.

The men's throats had been brutally and efficiently slashed; neither had put up a fight. They'd been cut with a heavy serrated blade, like a hunting knife. Grannit found a footprint in a pool of blood.

A GI combat boot.

"They were here less than an hour ago," he said as he came back out.

"Only one set of wheels came through that gate," said Carlson, pointing out tracks in the snow. "They parked here. Looks like a Willys."

"Two sets of footprints to the blockhouse, only one coming out. The other guy went in there."

Grannit followed a second set of footsteps to the kiosk. Grannit scanned the small room. Carlson stood back and watched.

"There's something going on with these two," said Grannit. "One does the killing. The other guy waited in the jeep outside the hospital. Same thing here. Same pattern."

Grannit's eye settled on a bulletin about Skorzeny's brigade tacked to the wall beside the guard window. He pulled out the thumbtack and saw two holes in the paper.

"They had the alert in plain sight," said Carlson. "Why didn't they stop 'em?"

"They probably couldn't read English," said Grannit. "Look at this."

He showed the back of the flyer to Carlson. The words "REIMS" and "MOVIE HOUSE" had been hastily scrawled.

"Schmidt said something about meeting at a theater in Reims," said Carlson.

"The second guy wrote this."

"Why?"

"I don't know. Get command on the radio. Somebody else has to clean this up."

They ran back to their jeep and Grannit took the wheel. Carlson cranked up the high-frequency shortwave, but all he got was static.

"God damned hills," said Carlson.

"Ole, I don't think I ever heard you swear before."

Carlson's cheeks flushed with color. "These guys really make me mad."

"Keep trying," said Grannit as they drove off. "We know where they're going and they weren't here that long ago. We need road-blocks every ten miles between Charleville and Reims."

24

In the middle of the night, General Eisenhower woke to the sound of gunfire just outside his window. His adjutant hurried out of their new quarters at the Trianon Palace in his pajamas and found Eisenhower's chief of staff, Walter Bedell Smith, running around with his carbine. Smith and four other soldiers emptied their rifles into a hedge where one of the MPs on duty said he had heard an intruder. No German assassins turned up, but at first light they found the bullet-riddled body of a stray cat. Eisenhower called the members of his enlarged bodyguard detail together and chewed them out, told them to calm their asses down and keep their fingers off the trigger. They weren't helping the war effort by denying him a good night's sleep. Six hours later, at their home in Fort Benning, Georgia, his wife, Mamie, received a telephone call from a reporter asking if she'd like to comment on the news that her husband had been shot. She spent the rest of the day on the phone frantically trying to track down the false report.

Eisenhower's motorcade left for Verdun early that morning, under heavily armed escort. General Patton was waiting when Eisenhower's motorcade arrived at eleven. Delayed on the road by checkpoints installed to catch the assassins, General Bradley drove in minutes later. They met in a spartan stone room, heated by an old potbelly stove, part of an ancient French barracks overlooking the

blood-drenched World War One battlefield. British Field Marshal Montgomery, held up by the MPs near Malmédy, sent a junior officer in his place. The overnight news that greeted them from the Ardennes painted an increasingly bleak picture of the battle. A dozen more towns had fallen under the pounding assault and thousands of American troops had surrendered. Eisenhower sensed the heavy spirits in the room.

"Gentlemen, there will be only cheerful faces at this table," he told them. "From this moment forward, our situation is to be viewed as an opportunity for us, not a disaster."

"Hell, let the sons of bitches drive all the way to Paris," said Patton. "Then we'll really chew 'em up and spit 'em out."

Laughter broke the tension. Over a large map set on the table, Eisenhower laid out the objectives of the German offensive. Under no circumstances could their tanks be allowed to threaten Antwerp. The Meuse was their last line of defense. He asked his generals for ideas, pointing out that because of bad weather they would have to succeed without offensive air support or reconnaissance. Only Patton offered a detailed response. He put three completely different approaches on the table, anticipating every contingency Eisenhower had to consider. The two men had known each other for thirty years, and had long recognized their complementary talents as strategic commander and battlefield tactician. Patton had always hoped they would have a war to fight together so he could play Stonewall Jackson to Eisenhower's Robert E. Lee, and this was that moment. His command of the battle's evolving dynamics and his vision of how to blunt the German advantage stunned everyone in the room.

"Talk us through it, George," said Eisenhower.

"First Army comes at their northern flank. My three divisions from Third Army hit from the south. Long as we hold 'em here they'll stop dead in their tracks."

He pointed with his cigar to the bulge on the map that was forming around Bastogne.

"How quickly can they get in there?" asked Eisenhower.

"Two days," said Patton. "The dumb bastard's stuck his head in a meat grinder. And this time I've got hold of the handle."

The Road to Reims
DECEMBER 19, NOON

"What other baseball players should I know?" asked Von Leinsdorf.

"What do you mean?"

"Who else might they ask about? Like Dizzy Dean."

"I thought that's what you needed me for."

"In case you're taking a piss."

"Well, everybody in America knows the Yankees," said Bernie. "Love 'em or hate 'em, they win the Series half the time."

"All right, good, who plays for them?"

"Bill Dickey, he's their catcher. Great talent. Red Ruffing's their best pitcher. Spud Chandler's a good arm. Joe Gordon at second, Phil Rizzuto's their shortstop. They call him Scooter. Not sure who's playing third this year—"

"Let's concentrate on who you do know. What's your favorite team?"

"Me? Hands down. You're from Brooklyn, it's the Brooklyn Dodgers, hands down."

"All right, so who plays for them?"

"Okay. One guy you gotta know. Biggest name in baseball. Center fielder, Brooklyn Dodgers. Best stick in the game."

"Who?"

"Joe DiMaggio." Bernie watched him closely.

"Yes. I've heard the name," said Von Leinsdorf. "DiMaggio. Center field. Brooklyn Dodgers."

"That's right."

Looking ahead on the highway, they noticed a line of American MP vehicles headed the other way, racing north, lights flashing.

"Pull over," said Von Leinsdorf.

Bernie steered onto the shoulder. Von Leinsdorf steadied his binoculars on the windscreen, looking at the road ahead. When he lowered them he pointed to a dirt road intersecting the highway a short distance ahead.

"Take that road," he said.

"What's going on?"

"They're putting up a roadblock."

Bernie drove onto the side road, while Von Leinsdorf studied the map.

"Take the first left," he said. "Runs parallel to the river. We'll cross farther downstream, come into Reims from the north."

"What if they've got that blocked too?"

"First things first."

"What happened? You think they found those guards at the border?"

"Just drive, Brooklyn."

Grannit and Carlson sped down the highway toward Reims. Roadblocks had gone up as ordered. They'd passed three already, but none had stopped any jeeps answering their detailed description.

"You divorced, Earl?"

"What is it with you and this?"

"You said you *had* a wife. I'm just curious."

"Is divorce such a fucking novelty?"

"It is in South Dakota."

"Marriage and police work go together like a match and a gas tank."

"Sorry to hear it."

"I'm doing just fine without your sympathy."

"I got a steady girl back home," said Carlson, after a while.

"So you said." Grannit glanced over. "You gonna marry her?"

"I was thinking about it."

"Tell me you're not going into police work after this."

"I been thinking about that, too," said Carlson. "I'm getting a pretty good feel for it, don't you think?"

"I got a pretty good feel for falling on hand grenades, but I'm not gonna make a career out of it."

"Well, what do you think I should do?"

"Marry the girl. Stick with insurance."

"It's not like we have that much crime. It's not like, you know, the murder capital of the high plains."

Grannit looked at him. "You gonna stay a volunteer fireman?"

"I guess so."

"So, you feel the need for a thrill coming on, set fire to a barn. You can rush in and put it out yourself. Sell the farmer his insurance beforehand, you win both ways."

"Why didn't I think of that?"

"Stick with me," said Grannit. "I specialize in the big questions."

Carlson laughed, slowing as they approached another roadblock, soldiers waving them down. Because they matched the description of the alert they'd sent out—two Americans in a Willys—it took fifteen minutes to convince the MPs they weren't the men every GI in France was now looking for.

Bernie and Von Leinsdorf skirted the town of Rethel until they reached an unguarded bridge that took them across the Aisne River and an adjoining shipping canal. A light rain started to fall as they passed a memorial for a World War One battle that took place on the strip of ground between the two bodies of water. The road continued to the southwest, parallel to the canal. When they came within sight of the highway south toward Reims, Von Leinsdorf took another look at the connecting road through the binoculars.

"There's another blockade," he said.

"We've got today's password, don't we?"

Von Leinsdorf glanced down the road. He spotted a French military ambulance outside a roadside café. It was early afternoon, lunch hour.

"Park off the road," he said, pointing to the right. "Next to those trees."

Bernie drove toward them. When they got close, Von Leinsdorf stepped on Bernie's foot, on top of the gas. The jeep lurched forward and crashed into the tree, crumpling the hood, sending up a column of steam.

"What the hell did you do that for?" asked Bernie.

"Leave everything. Follow me. Keep your mouth shut."

They walked in the rain to the café where the ambulance was

parked. Von Leinsdorf rushed inside and spotted the uniformed drivers eating at a table, the only customers.

"*Il y est eu un accident*," said Von Leinsdorf, in clumsy, American accented French. "*D'une juste la route. Veuillez nous aider.*"

The drivers followed them outside, asking questions in broken English which Von Leinsdorf, in his feigned urgency, did his best to avoid.

"Where is it?" asked the driver.

"*Nous vous montrerons,*" said Von Leinsdorf. "We'll take you."

The drivers gestured for them to climb in the back of the ambulance, and they drove back down the road until Von Leinsdorf directed them off to the left, where the jeep had hit the tree. The ambulance stopped a few yards away, and the drivers hurried toward the jeep.

Von Leinsdorf followed and shot one of the men in the back of the head with his silenced pistol. The other driver turned when he heard the pop, saw his comrade hit the ground. When he saw the gun in Von Leinsdorf's hand, he fell to his knees, pleading for his life, fumbling out his wallet, showing photographs of his wife and children.

"*Mon frère*, you're talking to the wrong Nazi," said Von Leinsdorf, turning to Bernie. "He actually thinks we're American—would you please just shut the fuck up? *Mettez ceux partis.* Silence!"

The man went quiet. Von Leinsdorf unscrewed the silencer and showed it to him before tucking it away.

"See? I'm not going to shoot you."

"What the hell are we doing?" asked Bernie.

"We need one of them alive," said Von Leinsdorf. Then, pointing to the dead man: "He's about your size, this one's a better match for me. Switch uniforms. Hurry up before there's too much blood on it. Don't ask questions."

Bernie knelt to the task. Von Leinsdorf turned to the survivor.

"*Enlevez votre uniforme,*" he said to him. "*Rapide!*"

The man unbuttoned his tunic. Von Leinsdorf did the same.

"Don't worry, *mon ami*," said Von Leinsdorf, with a reassuring smile. "*Je n'vais pas vous tuer*. Friends, yes?"

The driver smiled grimly as he dressed. Bernie put the driver's uniform on, then worked the dead man's loose limbs into his GI green.

"Don't put your jacket on him, just lay it over his face. Load everything into the ambulance," said Von Leinsdorf, slipping on the other driver's jacket. "Bring back a stretcher."

The second driver had finished changing into Von Leinsdorf's uniform when Bernie returned with the stretcher. Von Leinsdorf joked with the driver that the American uniform looked snug around the middle.

"Too many *pommes frites*, huh? Try them without mayonnaise next time, dummy. Put the dead one in back," said Von Leinsdorf to Bernie; then he waved at the driver, ordering him to lend a hand. "*Aidez-la.*"

Bernie and the Frenchman set the dead driver onto the stretcher and slid it in the back of the ambulance. Von Leinsdorf saw that Bernie had stacked the jerricans holding their equipment in the corner.

"Throw a blanket over those," he said. "Set up another stretcher next to that one."

When Bernie was finished, Von Leinsdorf pointed the driver at the second stretcher. "*Couchez-vous, monsieur, s'il vous plaît.*"

Eager to please, the driver lay down on the stretcher. Von Leinsdorf told Bernie to fasten the straps on the man, as he closed the rear doors.

"You know some first aid, don't you, Brooklyn?"

"A little."

Von Leinsdorf pulled a bottle from the stores of medicine in a footlocker. "Give him half a syringe, just enough to take the edge off."

Bernie took the bottle. Morphine. He prepared the syringe, then knelt beside the second driver, who stared anxiously at the needle.

"It's okay," said Bernie. "This won't hurt you."

"*Il ne blessera pas du tout,*" said Von Leinsdorf, translating.

The Frenchman tensed as the needle went in, then relaxed as the morphine hit his bloodstream. Von Leinsdorf patted his shoulder.

"But I'm afraid this will a bit," said Von Leinsdorf.

He touched the silencer to the man's cheek and pulled the trigger. The bullet tore through his mouth and burst out the other side. Blood spurted, the man screamed and strained against the straps, nearly flipping over the stretcher. Bernie struggled to hold him down.

"Why the fuck did you shoot him?"

"If he's not wounded, why would we be driving him to the hospital?" asked Von Leinsdorf.

"The other one isn't."

"The other one's dead. Why would we need the siren for a trip to the morgue?"

"Well, you didn't have to shoot him in the mouth, for Christ's sake," said Bernie.

"And have our wounded 'GI' spout French at the checkpoint? Think it through. That's why we gave him the morphine. Reduce his suffering, keep him from flopping off that stretcher. You don't speak French by any chance, do you, Brooklyn?"

"No."

"So keep quiet at the checkpoint or I'll shoot you, too."

Von Leinsdorf took the driver's seat, started the ambulance, and steered them back onto the road. He switched on the siren and flashers as they sped past the café. They rounded a curve, following the line of the canal as it turned south, then entered a roundabout, other vehicles yielding when they heard the siren.

South of the roundabout, they approached the American checkpoint. Two MPs stepped into the road, waving them down in front of the guard gate. Von Leinsdorf rolled to a stop. Soldiers were putting up a machine gun emplacement. Other MPs searched half a dozen American jeeps they'd pulled to the side of the road. One MP hurried to the driver's side of the ambulance, another moved toward the rear. As soon as the soldier reached his window, Von Leinsdorf unleashed an agitated torrent of fluent French, gesturing toward the back, shouting over the siren.

"Okay, take it easy, buddy. Where you headed?"

"Hospital," said Von Leinsdorf, in broken English. "Reims."

"What's on board?"

The other MP opened the rear doors. He saw Bernie in a driver's

uniform, sulfa packet in his hand, working on a badly wounded man, moaning and covered in blood.

"GIs," said Von Leinsdorf. "Automobile accident. *Un d'eux est mort et l'autre est critique. Nous devons nous dépêche!*"

The lead MP got the okay from his colleague, who closed the rear doors. Both men stepped back and waved the ambulance through. Von Leinsdorf stepped on the gas as the gate went up, and they sped off.

"How's he doing?" asked Von Leinsdorf.

"Great. He just asked for a daiquiri."

"He's not going to die; it's a superficial wound. We need him alive. There may be more checkpoints ahead."

"Ask him how superficial it is."

"Would you relax? It's just a Frenchman, for Christ's sake. Three aren't worth one German. I don't know that the going rate for Americans has been established. Do you?"

Bernie didn't answer. They passed another road sign: REIMS 20 KM.

25

Reims
DECEMBER 19, 7:00 P.M.

Carl Grannit parted the curtains of a second-story window and looked down and across the street at an old, ornate movie palace. Light rain continued to fall, thinning out foot traffic through the small square below. After arriving in Reims in the middle of the afternoon, Grannit and Carlson reported to the commander of the local military police. He placed a twenty-man detachment of MPs under Grannit's command. Half a dozen plainclothes agents from Army Counter Intelligence arrived an hour later, along with a platoon of regular army. Grannit pulled the entire detail together for a five o'clock briefing and broke down their assignments.

American forces used three movie houses in the downtown area to screen movies for Allied soldiers in Reims. Grannit's men had all three under surveillance by early that evening. This one, near the old shipping canal that split the city, was the largest and most popular, and seemed to Grannit the most likely for Skorzeny's men to use as a meeting place. He then commandeered as an observation post an apartment above and across a small square. Undercover men were assigned to circulate through the crowd at each of the theaters. The army detail deployed throughout the neighborhood with orders to stay off the streets until Skorzeny's men were identified. Once they were inside the theater, the soldiers would drop perimeter roadblocks into place and close the net.

The first show was scheduled for seven o'clock, a glossy Hollywood musical to help enlisted men forget their troubles. Lights on the theater's marquee remained dark, observing blackout restrictions, but Grannit had ordered that the foyer and lobby lights stay brightly lit so that anyone standing under the marquee could be seen from their post across the street.

Dozens of soldiers from different service branches milled around outside, smoking cigarettes, waiting for friends or dates to arrive. Behind-the-line types, thought Grannit, looking them over. He'd learned that the military was like an iceberg; only the small portion above the surface did the fighting. For every front-line dogface under fire in the Ardennes, there were six clerical types like these filling out requisitions in triplicate, calling it a day, and going to the movies. A police force ran the same way, a fraction doing the dirty work while everyone else cleaned up after them. Maybe it reflected basic human nature, this hunger for bureaucracy and order, and which side of that line you ended up on was a matter of luck. Everybody had a job to do. Some were just a whole lot worse than others.

Grannit scanned the soldiers' faces with binoculars, searching for the face of the "Lieutenant Miller" that he'd glimpsed for those few moments in Belgium. A sketch of the man, drawn from Grannit's recollection, had been distributed to everyone in the detail.

"I got a guy bringing over regulation SHAEF passes so I can compare 'em to our forgeries," said Ole Carlson, standing eating a meal they'd brought in from a local restaurant.

"Good."

"Think we'll get to Paris, Earl?"

"I don't know, Ole."

"Ever been?"

"No. You?"

"Heck no. I'd love to see it. See Paris and die, isn't that what they say?"

"I don't think they mean right away."

"Anyway, don't figure I'll ever get this close again." Carlson leaned

over Grannit's shoulder to look down at the theater. "I'm heading down there."

"The meet's supposed to happen between nine and twelve. That's not until the second show," said Grannit.

"I'm supposed to meet the guy with those passes. Don't want to miss him."

"While you're there," said Grannit, looking through the binoculars again, "go tell that MP swinging his nightstick around in the lobby like the house dick at Macy's to pull his head out of his ass. In fact, yank that half-wit out of there."

Grannit pointed the man out to him and Carlson headed for the door. "It would be my pleasure, Boss."

Grannit trained the glasses down each of the side streets and alleyways that fed into the old cobblestoned square. The neighborhood sported a flourishing nightlife, a number of hole-in-the-wall bars attracting heavy military traffic. Black-market profiteers flourished in an area with so many potential buyers and sellers. He spotted at least two brothels operating more or less in the open. He'd read in *Stars and Stripes* that in light of the attack in the Ardennes, dancing had been banned in Paris after dark, but young men in uniform still needed to get drunk or laid or both.

His walkie-talkie crackled to life, MPs reporting in from the other two theaters, each less than a mile away.

Nothing yet.

When they drove into Reims, Von Leinsdorf stashed the stolen French ambulance in an abandoned garage in a warehouse district near the canal. He ordered Bernie to exchange uniforms with the dead French driver again. While Bernie's back was turned, Von Leinsdorf killed the second driver with a single, silenced bullet, as if he were finishing some paperwork.

"We're GIs again," said Von Leinsdorf, unbuttoning the driver's tunic, searching both bodies for cash. "Not a moment too soon. I need to be fumigated. This bogtrotter was in desperate need of a

bath. Try to run their damn country properly for them and this is the thanks we get."

They dressed in silence. Bernie covered both dead drivers with blankets. Von Leinsdorf emptied the medicine and supplies from the ambulance footlocker into a knapsack.

"Leave the rest," he said. "We'll come back for it."

"What time are we supposed to meet?" asked Bernie.

"Nine o'clock."

"It's only five. What do we do till then?"

"So many questions, Bernie. I'm feeling a lack of confidence in my leadership. You don't hear any complaints from them, do you?" he asked, nodding toward the Frenchmen.

Von Leinsdorf put his black-framed glasses on, straightened his helmet, and opened the back of the ambulance. While his back was turned, Bernie slipped a syringe and a bottle of morphine into his pocket.

"Should I bring my rifle?" asked Bernie.

"We're going to the movies, Bernie."

"Who knows? It might be a western." Bernie jumped down and closed the ambulance doors. He caught a whiff of something foul and sniffed his uniform. "That's great, now I smell like a fuckin' dead guy."

"We could both use a bit of sprucing up," said Von Leinsdorf, handing him a forged seventy-two-hour pass. "Put on a happy face. We're supposed to be on leave."

They walked out into the empty street and a steady drizzle as the last daylight faded. Von Leinsdorf consulted a map with a flashlight as they walked until they reached a shopping district, studded with cafés and shops. Other off-duty GIs circulated in and out of store-fronts, so they didn't look or feel out of place. Von Leinsdorf directed Bernie to one of the cafés, where he ordered sandwiches and coffee, in French, paying with francs. They focused hungrily on the food, the first meal they'd eaten all day.

"It may help that they know about us, Brooklyn," said Von Leinsdorf. "He'll have gone to ground. Easier to find."

"Find who?"

"You're persistent," said Von Leinsdorf, admiring his sandwich. "I'll give you that."

Their table offered a view of an open produce market across the street. Von Leinsdorf kept staring in that direction. Bernie saw he was watching a plain young woman browsing through the market with a shopping bag.

"Follow me in a couple of minutes," said Von Leinsdorf. "And, Bernie, don't make me come back for you."

Bernie watched him cross the street and enter the market. He moved down an aisle, a preoccupied shopper checking out vegetables, and then bumped into the young woman. Her bag fell to the floor. All apologies, Von Leinsdorf bent to help her retrieve the items that tumbled out. Within moments he'd engaged her in conversation, taken the bag from her hand, and paid for her groceries at the counter. Bernie finished his sandwich, took what remained of Von Leinsdorf's with him, and followed them as they left the market.

Von Leinsdorf carried the woman's bag as they strolled down the street. When another burst of rain fell, he opened the umbrella she carried and held it over her head as she arranged a scarf around her hair. He maintained a respectful distance from her, holding the umbrella at arm's length, unthreatening and polite as a shy young suitor. Bernie shuffled along on the opposite side of the street, shoulders hunched, rain beating down on his helmet, about twenty yards behind them.

Two blocks later they stopped outside an apartment building. Bernie leaned back into the shadows of an alley across the street. He tried to formulate a plan, but he felt emptied out, cold, and miserable, and his mind refused to offer any clear ideas. From their body language and gestures, it was clear the woman was inviting Von Leinsdorf inside. He refused, she insisted, he agreed, as if it was the only gentlemanly thing to do, then waited while she fished out her keys and opened the door. Von Leinsdorf threw a glance back at Bernie—he knew exactly where he was standing—and followed her inside.

A minute later a light turned on in a window on the third floor.

Drapes were quickly pulled across the window, muting the glow. Bernie glanced at his watch: 5:35. Three minutes later, Von Leinsdorf appeared in the doorway again and waved Bernie over. Bernie trotted across the street to join him.

"Come on, hurry," said Von Leinsdorf, closing the door after him. "Keep quiet. Up the stairs. No one's seen us yet."

Bernie followed him up creaking stairs to the third floor and through the apartment door he'd propped open with a matchbook. Von Leinsdorf closed and locked the door as soon as they were inside. The furnishings looked more prosperous than the building's exterior suggested, tasteful and modern.

"This'll do for us," said Von Leinsdorf. "This'll do quite nicely. Would you like a cup of tea? She'd just put on the kettle."

"Where's the bathroom?"

"Through that door, off the bedroom."

Bernie opened the bedroom door. The woman lay on her back on the bed, legs sprawled, one shoe kicked off, lifeless eyes staring at the ceiling. She'd been strangled with the peach-colored scarf she'd worn on her head, still taut around her neck. Pooled blood had turned her face a bruised shade of scarlet; small capillaries had burst around her protruding eyes. Bernie covered her with a blanket, numb inside, then moved to the bathroom. He closed the door and turned on the faucet, the first running water he'd encountered in days.

The room's austere plainness seemed unreal. A sink, a toilet, hand towels, a bar of soap. The woman who'd used them lay dead, less than ten feet away. He caught a glimpse of his face in the mirror and for a moment didn't recognize what stared back at him, his face black with grime, eyes that belonged to an older, hollowed-out man. As he washed his hands, clots of dried blood dropped onto the porcelain, streaking red when they contacted the running water.

Von Leinsdorf was waiting with a hot cup of tea when he returned. "This'll bring you back from the dead, Brooklyn. Quite the scrounger, this one. She even had sugar and real cream in the icebox."

Bernie took the cup while Von Leinsdorf parted the curtains and looked down at the street. Bernie sat on the sofa, sinking into the

cushions, and took a sip of tea. The strong, bitter taste sent a shiver through him. He watched Von Leinsdorf, only a few feet out of reach. His free hand reached down to the syringe in his jacket pocket.

Stick him, and go find help. Make sure the Americans take him. They can make him talk, get the target out of him. They have to. Is it enough morphine to put him under? Will he kill me before it takes effect?

He realized Von Leinsdorf was talking to him.

"Our evening began with real promise, but I soon realized there was no future for us," said Von Leinsdorf, glancing at the bedroom.

"What's that?"

"She had another man in her life. His clothes are in the closet."

"Whose clothes?"

"You know, I never had a chance to ask. Anyway, treat yourself to a bath, then put on a fresh outfit; you're right, you do smell like the grave."

"And wear what? We're supposed to be soldiers."

"That's the beauty of it, Brooklyn. Her gentleman caller was a GI. His uniform's in the closet. Freshly laundered by his little French whore. A sergeant in the quartermaster corps."

He held up a khaki dress cap and twirled it on his index finger, looking at the sergeant's insignia.

"Not overly ambitious, was she?" said Von Leinsdorf. "For a camp follower. No doubt she shacked up with some of our boys before the Yanks showed up with better cigarettes."

"Maybe she saw you as a promotion."

"Frankly, it wasn't a face for an officer's pay grade. I'll fix us something else to eat. I paid for those groceries after all. Finish your tea."

Von Leinsdorf moved toward the kitchen. Bernie stared down at an issue of *Life* magazine on the table beside him. General de Gaulle was on the cover, posed heroically, staring into the distance at some idealized future for France, or at least for de Gaulle. Bernie heard a clock ticking somewhere, far louder than it should have sounded. An alarming sense of dislocation swept through his chest; his heart skipped a beat; his body flushed with heat. He banged the teacup

down on the table and staggered to his feet. De Gaulle's face began to wobble. The lines of every object in the room swam in front of his eyes; the air turned rubbery. Von Leinsdorf was beside him in a moment, taking his arm.

"Don't fight it, Brooklyn," he said, his voice distorting. "I put something in the tea. You'll sleep a few hours. Can't have you running off while I'm at the cinema. I'll come back with the others, if they're there. That's a good fellow. After all, you could use the rest."

Von Leinsdorf eased him back down onto the sofa. Bernie was out by the time his head hit the cushions.

The first show ended at eight-thirty, a wave of GIs spreading out from the theater into the surrounding bars and restaurants. The rain had passed through, and the night air warmed slightly under a lowering cover of clouds. Curls of fog spun in off the river, obscuring the square. Carlson and the rest of the men stationed on the ground scanned the faces of the exiting soldiers as they moved toward their evening's pleasures, while Grannit watched from his observation post. No one spotted his "Lieutenant Miller."

A brief lull in street traffic followed before uniforms began to trickle into the square again, lining up for the nine o'clock show. Grannit poured himself another cup of coffee. Ole and the five supervising MP sergeants returned to the apartment for a final briefing.

"Keep your men out of sight until the crowd builds in again," said Grannit. "Stay outside, watch the street. When they're about to start the show, button it up, put a hat on every exit, inside and out. Five minutes into the picture we kill the projector, bring up the houselights, announce we've got a security situation. Then we'll do it by the numbers. Bring 'em out row by row to the lobby, check IDs one at a time."

"What if anybody bolts?"

"Take 'em down," said Grannit. "If they draw a weapon, shoot 'em."

Grannit followed them downstairs. The fog had grown so thick he could no longer make out any faces from the window.

The American deserter William Sharper had spotted the MPs at a border post, abandoned the jeep, and led his squad into France the previous night on foot. After spending the night in a barn, they hitched a ride that morning with a middle-aged French farmer, who seemed thrilled to lend a hand to the American war effort. Before they reached the main highway, Sharper strangled the man and dumped his body in a field. Sharper put on the farmer's clothes, took his wallet and agricultural road pass, and drove his load of chickens into Reims. His other three men hid in the back with the birds. Sharper knew the city well enough to get them to the farmer's market, where they abandoned the truck and blended into the city.

By mid-day, Sharper had found the cinema that he'd suggested for their rallying point. Taking his men to a nearby brothel, he instructed them to play the part of randy soldiers on leave from the front, their easiest assignment yet. He paid for eight hours' time with the four girls in the house and the squad spent the rest of the day upstairs, getting laid, resting, and sleeping. Sharper put so much American cash on the table the madam agreed to wash their uniforms while they relaxed. She thought it odd that the Americans didn't ask for any wine or liquor, but dollars had a way of easing her curiosity.

At eight-thirty, Sharper and his men set out for the cinema, less than three blocks away, in their freshly laundered uniforms.

26

Von Leinsdorf walked slowly to the middle of the square outside the theater, on the edge of the gathering crowd. He took out a cigarette and scanned ahead for any unusual police presence. The fog thickened near the waterfront as soldiers lined up in front of the theater box office. Two MPs stood near the entrance to the lobby, but didn't look out of place. An American soldier materialized out of the fog, suddenly standing next to him, and offered a light for his smoke.

"Another Judy Garland picture," the man said, nodding toward the theater. "Louis B. Mayer's working her like a sled dog. You know she's not even five feet tall?"

"I might have read it somewhere."

"Just my size. A hot little number, if you like a babe with no waist and the ass of a ten-year-old boy. She do anything for you, Sarge?"

"She's no Marlene Dietrich," said Von Leinsdorf.

"Are you kidding me? Marlene Dietrich'd eat her like a chicken leg, spit out the bone."

Von Leinsdorf moved forward, trying to shake the man, but he fell into step alongside, holding out a hand. Short and fidgety, the man wore a corporal's stripes and pounded a wad of gum while he smoked.

"Eddie Bennings, Corporal Eddie Bennings, how you doing to-night?"

"Fine, thanks."

"A free night in France, fresh air, no bullets in the forecast, what could be so bad? I see you're with the quartermaster corps."

"That's right."

Looking ahead through the fog, Von Leinsdorf spotted William Sharper leading his three men into the theater lobby past the MP at the door.

"My line, too. Came in today from Belgium. Makes you appreci-ate the peace and quiet down here," said Bennings. Then, lowering his voice to a conspiratorial level: "My battalion does a lot of busi-ness with the quartermaster corps."

"Is that a fact?"

"And we're always looking for a good man to do business with—you going in to see the picture?"

"Yes."

"Let me spring for the tickets, my treat—you shouldn't have to stand on line, Sarge."

The persistent little man was starting to attract Von Leinsdorf's interest. "What sort of business?"

"I'll get the tickets, we'll have a chat. See if you're interested. Meet you in two shakes."

Von Leinsdorf moved on to the front lobby doors and waited as Bennings jumped the ticket line.

Bernie opened his eyes to a cat rubbing its face on his chin and purring. When he started awake, the animal vaulted off his chest into the kitchen. The room spun violently when he tried to stand. He lurched forward, tumbling over a table and vomiting as he hit the floor. Rolling onto his back, he took deep breaths, opening and clos-ing his eyes, waiting for the ceiling to stabilize. As his fractured thoughts reassembled and he remembered where he was, he raised his watch into view and waited for the hands to float into position. 8:40.

"Shit."

He pulled himself to his feet, made his way into the kitchen, stuck his head under the faucet in the sink, and ran cold water over his neck until his head began to clear. Taking a quick look around the apartment, he spotted Von Leinsdorf's GI field greens lying in a heap on the bedroom floor. The khaki dress uniform that had been hanging in the woman's closet was gone.

He remembered that Von Leinsdorf had mentioned the movie house was near the canal. A memory of the city map swam to the surface. He headed for the door.

Eddie Bennings handed Von Leinsdorf his ticket and they entered the lobby, blending into the crowd.

"Looking for somebody?" asked Bennings.

"Thought I saw someone I knew."

"You want a soda, popcorn or anything, Sarge?"

"No thanks."

"I never got your name."

"Dick Connelly."

"Okay, Dick. You want to talk about my proposition before the picture or after?"

"Now's fine," said Von Leinsdorf, scanning the lobby over the man's shoulder.

"As I was saying, we work with a lot of guys in the quartermaster corps. It's a first-class arrangement."

"Can you be slightly more specific?"

Bennings lowered his voice again and talked out of the side of his mouth, like a gangster.

He's seen too many Jimmy Cagney pictures, thought Von Leinsdorf.

"In the area of surplus supply and demand. Daily necessities. A drink, a smoke, a taste of home, whatever. We scratch their back, they scratch ours; everybody gets healthy, including the average GI who all he's looking for is a little relief."

Von Leinsdorf spotted Sharper standing near a door to the theater, his three men walking in just ahead of him.

"You want me to set it to music for you?" asked Bennings impatiently.

"I think I get the idea," he said. "Would you excuse me for a moment, Eddie? I want to say hi to my friend."

"Hope I haven't offended you, Sarge."

"You've got a little larceny in your heart, don't you, Eddie?" said Von Leinsdorf with an admiring smile.

"Troubled times. Is that such a terrible thing?"

"On the contrary. It's a character reference. I'll be right back."

Von Leinsdorf took one step toward Sharper, when Bennings grabbed him by the arm.

"Oh shit. Hang on a second. Don't move, Sarge."

Bennings turned away from the doors, then took another glance.

"It is him. Fuck. I had a run-in with that guy recently. He's a cop."

"Which one?"

Bennings nodded toward a man near the lobby doors, looking at his watch. A charge of adrenaline shot through Von Leinsdorf. It was the soldier he'd seen near Mallory's bed in the field hospital—the one who chased them.

Von Leinsdorf surveyed the lobby with new eyes, aware of half a dozen other men, in and out of uniform, with that same hard-eyed look. He turned his back to the doors fronting the street. Although he was sure the American wouldn't see through the alterations he'd made at a glance, that might change if their eyes happened to meet.

"If I had to guess, I'd say he's looking for me," said Bennings.

"Why is that?"

"Don't really have time for that story right now."

Music blared from the auditorium and the houselights started to dim. Von Leinsdorf saw Sharper head into the theater, unaware of either his or the Allied police's presence. On the side of the lobby nearest to them, he saw one of the uniformed MPs enter the men's room.

"Go to the bathroom," said Von Leinsdorf. "Wait in one of the stalls."

"What for?"

"I think I know him, too. Scratch my back, Eddie, I'll scratch yours."

Eddie headed toward the bathroom, turning his face away from the lobby doors.

Outside, out of breath, Bernie Oster ran up and joined the line at the box office window.

Ole Carlson came out of the auditorium to meet Grannit just after he entered the lobby.

"Think any of 'em showed?" he asked.

Grannit looked around. "We'll find out. You see your guy about the passes?"

"Yeah, got one here. Still doesn't add up, let me show you—"

Grannit looked at his watch. "Talk about it later. Everyone in place?"

Carlson picked up a walkie-talkie. "I'll double-check in back."

He moved into the auditorium just as the music started inside and the last GIs headed for their seats.

Von Leinsdorf entered the men's room, used the urinal, and then walked to a row of sinks to wash his hands. The MP was washing his hands in the next sink over. A muted swell of music reached into the room.

"Sounds like the show's starting," said Von Leinsdorf.

The only other soldier in the room finished drying his hands and exited. As the MP reached for a towel, Von Leinsdorf slid behind him and slipped a piano wire garrote around the man's throat. Yanking hard with both hands, he lifted the man off the ground, then walked him back into one of the stalls. The MP's heels kicked and dragged as he clawed at his throat. His helmet fell off and hit the ground. The stall door banged shut behind them. Von Leinsdorf

could anticipate the letting go down to the second. He counted in his head, and as he reached ten, the man went slack.

When the door swung slowly open, Eddie Bennings stood there staring wide-eyed at Von Leinsdorf. The MP's dead body slumped onto the toilet as Von Leinsdorf slipped off the garrote and dropped it into his pocket. He'd pulled so hard the wire had sliced the dead man's throat, a line of blood trickling down his neck.

"Holy shit," said Bennings.

Von Leinsdorf grabbed Bennings and pulled him into the stall. "If you want to get out of here alive, you need to do exactly as I tell you, Eddie. Do you have a problem following orders?"

"Not tonight."

Bernie Oster handed his ticket to the usher at the door and entered the lobby, one of the last men through the doors before they closed. The auditorium doors were still open; he could see the show had started and a newsreel was playing. As he hurried across the lobby, he noticed a number of MPs moving toward the doors behind him from outside, not quite in a line but organized, grouped around a tall officer in the middle of the lobby.

I know that guy, thought Bernie, trying to place him.

He moved to the concession stand and ordered a soda, keeping his back to the tall man. The line of MPs moved in to cover every door out of the lobby.

They found my note. They set a trap.

His eye caught two men walking out of the bathroom to his right toward the auditorium. A soldier followed by an MP in helmet and armbands, nudging the shorter man ahead of him with the butt of his nightstick.

"Let's go, pal, back to your seat," he said.

Von Leinsdorf.

The two men moved into the auditorium. Bernie followed. Entering the darkness, he was momentarily blinded by the illuminated screen, black-and-white wartime footage: destroyers at sea, fighters streaming overhead. Framed against the moving images, two men's

silhouettes stood out as they walked down the aisle toward the front of the theater. Bernie waited for his eyes to adjust to the light. His fingers found the syringe in his pocket.

Get close to him. Use the syringe. Slip out in the confusion. MPs are here, they'll take care of the rest.

William Sharper, sitting on the right aisle near the middle of the theater, noticed Erich Von Leinsdorf walk past him. A few moments later he whispered to one of his men to stay in their seats, and got up to follow him.

Grannit waited in the lobby for his MPs to reach their positions at the doors. He looked at his watch again. Three minutes until they stopped the film. His men should be in place by now. He picked up his walkie-talkie to check with Carlson when he overheard a nearby conversation.

"Where the hell's Whitey?" one of the MPs asked another.

"Still in the can," said another, glancing at his watch.

"What's taking him so long?"

Grannit looked toward the bathroom door. Sudden instinct propelled him through the door. The room was empty. He bent down and saw legs in one of the toilet stalls, a man's pants bunched around the ankles. He drew his gun and moved closer. The stall door swung open on a rusty hinge.

Ole Carlson reached the back of the theater stage, directly behind the screen, and put the beam of his gooseneck flashlight on the wall. A small rear door there had been left unlocked and unguarded, inside and out.

"Doggone it. What the heck are they thinking?"

He was about to call the lobby on his walkie-talkie and yell at them to get a body back here covering this door pronto. He turned and looked up at the huge moving images towering above him. He'd never realized you could see movies from the back side of the screen before, a reverse image, like you'd gone through the looking glass.

The newsreel was still running. There was Hitler, and that runt Himmler and the fat one, what was his name, he got Göring and Bormann mixed up sometimes. The crowd booed them. The jeers turned to cheers when the newsreel ended, the MGM lion gave a roar, and the movie began rolling lush Technicolor credits for the Judy Garland picture. He hadn't seen it before. He liked old-time pictures like this, a window back into the simple Midwestern world his parents had grown up in.

Two figures appeared from the left, black outlines against the screen, walking diagonally toward him. His hand went toward his sidearm; then he saw the MP's helmet on the second of the men and relaxed. The MP pushed a GI along in front of him, a shorter guy in a raincoat. He couldn't make out their faces and raised his flashlight.

"This joker was trying to sell hooch in the mezzanine," said the MP.

Carlson pointed the flashlight in the shorter man's face, and he raised a hand to shield his eyes.

"Well, if it ain't Corporal Eddie Bennings," said Carlson. "Seven-twenty-fourth Railway Battalion. Look what the cat dragged in."

Bennings shielded his eyes against the light and didn't answer. Another figure rose up behind the two men, ten paces away, framed against the movie screen.

"Lieutenant Miller, is that you?" asked William Sharper, moving closer. "Lieutenant Miller?"

Carlson's walkie-talkie crackled to life. Grannit's voice. "Ole, he's here. Miller's in the theater."

Carlson reached for his sidearm, but first had to transfer the flashlight to his left hand. In that moment the MP took a quick step toward him. Carlson saw something flash in the man's hand, moving toward him.

Grannit burst out of the restroom and through the doors into the auditorium, pulling his sidearm and shouting at the MPs in the lobby.

"Lock it down! Lock it down!"

Halfway down the aisle, Bernie felt more than saw a man rush past him, nearly knocking him over. He followed him until they'd

almost reached the front of the room and the houselights started to
fade up.

Behind the screen, Von Leinsdorf pulled the hunting knife out of
the man's chest; he'd gone up and under the ribs, into the heart, with
the practiced stroke of a surgeon. Looking at the soldier as he
dropped, he recognized the round face and close-cropped haircut.
This man had been at the hospital with the other one he'd just seen
in the lobby. He bent down, rifled through the man's coat, and
pulled out his badge and ID, sticking them in his pocket.

"Lieutenant Miller?"

Von Leinsdorf turned to see William Sharper standing above
him, anxious and agitated, trying to make him out in the dark. They
heard shouts from the auditorium; footsteps pounded toward them
down the aisles. Von Leinsdorf pressed the bloodied knife into
Sharper's hand, pulled Carlson's sidearm, and pointed it at him.

"Run," said Von Leinsdorf. "Run!"

"What the hell are you doing?" asked Sharper.

Sharper stepped back a few paces, confused, looking from Von
Leinsdorf and Bennings to the body on the floor.

"He's a Nazi!" shouted Von Leinsdorf. "Back here, he's a fucking
Nazi! I got the bastard! I got him!"

Sharper turned and ran toward the screen, where Judy Garland
was making her first appearance, singing and dancing in a hallway.
Sharper stopped short, startled by the image, then used the knife to
slice a gash in the screen, and as he burst through it, Von Leinsdorf
fired three times.

Earl Grannit was climbing the stairs to the stage when Sharper
came through the screen. When he heard the shots, Grannit turned
on instinct, knelt, and fired twice at close range, spinning the man
around. Sharper toppled forward and landed hard on the floor in
front of the stage. He wheeled around on the floor, crying out, in
death throes. MPs with guns drawn closed in around him from every
direction. One kicked the knife away from his hand.

The front of the theater emptied, soldiers crawling over seats,
scrambling toward the lobby exits, where MPs with riot guns stepped
in and held their ground. Grannit climbed the rest of the way onto

the front of the stage, fired a single shot at the ceiling, and shouted to the room.

"Nobody leaves! Get away from those exits! I want every man back in a seat!"

The projector shut down, the music died. A line of MPs and undercover men surged forward from the lobby and the exits to take control of the room. Grannit jumped down to take a close look at the face of the dead GI lying in front of the stage. There were five bullets in him, but he'd only fired twice.

Was it Miller? Maybe; he couldn't be sure. He was the right size, the right body type. But the face? He took a look at the serrated blade of the knife the man had carried, then jumped to the stage and pushed through the slash in the screen.

Ole was lying on his back ten paces away. A young kid, a private, was cradling his head in his hands.

"We need a medic back here!" Grannit shouted back to the auditorium. "Get me a medic!"

He knelt down next to them. Ole saw he was there, felt for him with a shaking hand. Grannit gripped it hard. He glanced down at the wound, saw how bad it was, and how fast he was losing blood. Ole's sidearm lay on the floor beside him, still smoking.

"We get him, Earl?"

"We got him. The same knife he used on the border guards."

"That's good. He was on me before I— He moved so fast— Hurts something awful."

"Take it easy, don't talk, help's coming."

"I can't figure what the hell Bennings was doing with him—"

"Bennings? What do you mean? Eddie Bennings?"

"Oh God, I don't feel good, Earl, I don't feel good."

The private was holding up a syringe so Grannit could see it, asking if he should use it on him. Grannit hesitated.

"Eddie Bennings was here, Ole? Is that what you're saying?"

"I think so. I just never figured an MP . . ." He started to fade, eyes blanking out.

"What MP? What MP?" He shook his head at the private. No morphine. Not yet. "Stay with me, Ole. Stay with me."

Ole's eyes focused again. "Those passes . . . meant to tell you . . . about those passes . . ." Blood bubbled out onto Carlson's lips. Grannit wiped it away with a handkerchief, holding the back of his head.

"Don't talk now."

"Don't think they knew about the mistake . . . Krauts for you, always think they got a better idea . . ."

Grannit nodded at the kid to give him the shot. He leaned in to do it. Ole's eyes met Grannit's in a moment of clarity, his grip grew stronger for a moment, then his hand went slack and he was gone.

27

The syringe shattered when it hit the floor. Bernie dropped his head, a hand covering his eyes, trying not to cry.

"You know him?" asked Grannit. "Do you know him?"

Bernie shook his head. Grannit looked up. There was an open door behind them, leading out into an alley.

"Did you see anything, Private?" asked Grannit. "What he was talking about?"

"I'm not sure what I saw," said Bernie.

"Somebody else was back here with him? An MP? Anybody else? Maybe two men?"

"Yeah, I think maybe."

"Where they'd go, out that way?"

"I heard the door close."

"You a medic?"

"No, sir."

Grannit took the dog tags off Carlson and slipped them into his pocket.

"Come with me," said Grannit, starting toward the door.

"What about him?" asked Bernie.

"Nothing we can do for him now. Come on."

They hurried out the back door into an alley. Grannit had his sidearm pulled, looking in both directions. He pointed to the left.

"Take that way, once around the block, meet back here. Give a shout if you see anything."

Grannit ran off to the right. Bernie headed down the alley like a sleepwalker, his thoughts thicker than the fog.

He knew this man. He remembered him now. The one who'd chased them at the hospital, who came after them on the motorcycle. He didn't think the man had placed him. Not yet, anyway.

Bernie reached the end of the alley and looked in both directions. Visibility was less than twenty yards. No sign of Von Leinsdorf.

Should he go back as the officer ordered him to do or keep walking? The darkness beckoned. He had a chance at least; now that he was free of the German, he could fade into the night. They were focused on Von Leinsdorf now but if he went back to that movie house, there'd be MPs all over him, questions he couldn't answer, then an American firing squad, just as Von Leinsdorf had predicted.

He could use the dead girl's apartment, at least overnight. Find a map, figure a way out of the city. But to do what? Go where? His life in Germany was finished, even if his parents were still alive. He could never set foot there again, not after what Von Leinsdorf had told him about the death camps. He'd heard the rumors, and he'd been around the Nazis long enough to know they were capable of it. Von Leinsdorf had only confirmed what he'd feared was true for years.

A sense of shame overwhelmed him. His impulsive little acts of rebellion in Berlin seemed so puny and inadequate. He could have done more, tried harder to fight them, but all he'd thought of when it really mattered was his own survival. When he faced his own death, whenever it might come, what damage had that done to his immortal soul? If he'd failed so miserably what difference did it make if he lived or died?

The bottom dropped out: Was Von Leinsdorf right? Did it all mean nothing? How could whatever he had left of his life make up for what he'd failed to do, if he didn't take a stand now?

He spotted something lying in a corner of the alley and picked it up. An MP's armband. Nearby a white helmet and billy club had been tossed in a trash can. They'd come this way, Von Leinsdorf and

the other man, after they'd left the theater. Bernie looked down the street. The girl's apartment was in that direction. That was where Von Leinsdorf would go first.

To take care of me. Another loose end. Unless I take care of him first.

He heard MPs' whistles blowing somewhere nearby, footsteps running down another street. A manhunt was under way and he remembered: *They're looking for me, too.*

He ran back toward the theater, until he saw the American officer rounding the corner. Bernie showed him the armband, then led him back to where he'd found it. Bernie watched as he examined the other articles.

"I think I know who did this," said Bernie.

"We killed that man in the theater."

"No, sir. I think it's someone else. Another GI. I followed him to the movie house."

"Why?"

"I saw him hurting this girl, earlier tonight."

"Where?"

"Through the window of an apartment, as I walked by. I'm not sure, but I think he might have killed her. I didn't know what to do so I waited. He came out a few minutes later."

"Where were you headed?"

"Me? I was going to the movies."

"Why didn't you say anything to an MP?"

"I saw him go inside, lost him in the lobby. Then I thought I saw him going behind the screen. That's why I followed him back there."

Grannit just looked at him. Bernie couldn't tell if he believed him or not.

"I think he might've gone back to that apartment," said Bernie.

"Take me there."

"Okay. It's this way."

Grannit called for a radioman to join them and they walked at a brisk clip, Bernie taking the lead. Grannit spoke into the radio most of the way, shouting orders to his men at the movie house.

"What's your name, Private?" the man snapped, as soon as he came off the radio.

"Bernie Oster, sir."

"What unit are you with?"

"Two hundred ninety-first Engineer Combat Battalion."

"Where you from?"

"Brooklyn, sir."

"Which neighborhood?"

"Park Slope."

"North or South?" asked Grannit.

Bernie looked over at him, but couldn't read the man's expression. "North."

"Where'd you live?"

"On Union Street, between Sixth and Seventh Avenue. You know Brooklyn, sir?"

"What'd your dad do?"

"He worked for Pfizer," said Bernie. "Research and development. He was a chemist."

"Was?"

"He's retired now. Turn right here."

Bernie led him to the front door of the woman's apartment building. Grannit ordered the radioman to call in support and wait for it on the street. He forced the lock and Bernie led him up to the third floor.

The door stood open a crack. Grannit drew his gun, gestured for silence, and listened. He silently eased the door forward.

All the lights were off. Bernie couldn't remember if he'd left them that way. Grannit pulled a flashlight from his belt. Bernie watched from the doorway as the beam edged around the apartment. Somehow, before even completing his sweep, the man knew the apartment was empty. He walked in and turned on the living room lamp.

"Stay by the door," said the man. "Don't touch anything."

Bernie stepped inside. Grannit walked straight into the bedroom. Bernie watched him lift the blanket covering the girl's body on the bed. He studied it for a moment, then replaced the blanket and examined the rest of the room. Bernie saw him pick up Von Leinsdorf's old discarded GI uniform from the floor. He glanced briefly at the jacket, ripped something off the shoulder, then dropped it again. Out

of nowhere, the dead woman's damn cat rubbed against Bernie's leg. He jumped half a foot and kicked at it.

"Get away. Get away."

Grannit came back into the living room, opened the window, and looked down at the street.

"Is she dead?" asked Bernie.

Grannit marched straight to Bernie, grabbed him by the throat, stuck the barrel of his gun under his chin, and cocked the hammer.

"Two hundred ninety-first Combat Engineers?" he said.

"That's right."

Grannit held up the patch he'd torn from the uniform in the other room so Bernie could see it. The same unit.

"You didn't tell me you were from the same unit," said Grannit.

"Guess I didn't realize—"

"You didn't see him do anything to that girl from the street, the curtains were pulled. You were up here with him—"

"No, only after he killed her," said Bernie, his voice shaking. "He made me come up with him."

"What are you doing in Reims?"

"We were delivering dispatches—"

"Don't fucking lie to me. Tell me what I want to know or I put your brains on the wall—"

"Okay, okay—"

"Your friend just killed my partner, you Nazi fuck!"

Grannit shoved Bernie down into a chair and pointed the gun at him. Convinced he was about to die, Bernie put his hands up and closed his eyes.

"You're with the 150th Panzer Brigade," said Grannit. "Your commanding officer's Otto Skorzeny."

Bernie opened his eyes.

Grannit took a step closer to him. "Your brigade was sent in to take three bridges over the Meuse. Your squad leader gave you a second objective in France. I've got three of your pals we just nailed in that theater ready to ID you. You want to deny any of that to me?"

Bernie shook his head.

"What's your friend's name?"

"His name's Von Leinsdorf. Erich Von Leinsdorf. He's a lieutenant in the SS," said Bernie.

"You came across the line with him into Belgium, with two other men, near Elsenborn. You killed three soldiers at the border crossing."

"He did. And one of ours. He was wounded, Von Leinsdorf shot him."

"Where'd you put the bodies?" asked Grannit.

"He ordered us to drag them into the woods. One of your men was still alive, a sergeant, so I tried to help him—"

"How?"

"I gave him morphine. Put sulfa and a pressure bandage on his wounds."

"You did that? Where'd you go from there?"

"We spent the night near Butgenbach. The next day we scouted that bridge—"

"Why were you at that hospital?"

"The fourth man with us got shot. An American convoy came along and took us there."

"Where Von Leinsdorf killed Sergeant Mallory and your own man."

"I guess he did—"

"You guess so? You were driving the fucking jeep!"

"He didn't tell me what he was going to do, and he didn't tell me after. He never told me anything."

"Why'd you come to Reims?"

"He said we were going to meet the other squads, at that movie theater. That's all I know."

"Where'd you cross the border?" asked Grannit.

"In the mountains this morning. A place called Pont-Colin. He killed the guards. I left a message in the booth to warn somebody, I was trying to stop him—"

Grannit held out a pen and a small notebook.

"Write down your name," he said.

"Which one?"

"Your real name."

Bernie did as he was told. Grannit took the notebook back from

him and compared it to a sheet of paper he took from his pocket. Then he held up the note he'd taken from Pont-Colin, the words "REIMS" and "MOVIE HOUSE" on it.

"You wrote this," said Grannit.

"Yes, sir."

"Why did you come to France, what's your target?"

"I don't know."

"Don't lie to me, god damn it—"

"I don't know, I swear to God he never told me. If you know anything, you know more than I do. There's a second objective, but he never told me what it was—"

"Why?"

"He didn't trust me."

Grannit moved closer to him and held up the note again. "Why didn't he trust you? Why the hell did you write this?"

"Because I'm an American."

Grannit stared hard at him. They heard multiple vehicles driving up fast outside. Grannit moved to the window, put two fingers in his mouth and gave a sharp whistle, then waved down to the radioman on the street.

Down to my last chance, thought Bernie.

"I am from Brooklyn, I swear to you it's true, I was born there, I grew up there. My parents are German; they immigrated to New York, then moved back here six years ago. We lived in Frankfurt till they drafted me into their fucking army. I've been fixing cars in Berlin, I've never been in combat, I never shot at anybody; I got pulled into this because I speak English. They didn't tell us what it was about and they killed anybody who didn't go along with it. We didn't even know where we were going until it happened."

Grannit walked back toward him. "What neighborhood in Brooklyn?"

"Park Slope North, like I told you. I was born in Brooklyn Hospital on DeKalb. I went to PS 109 on Snyder Avenue, just off Flatbush. Mrs. Quinn was my third grade teacher. I was supposed to start Erasmus Hall the year we moved away. My best friend was Jackie Waldstein from the south side; his dad worked for the Rheingold

brewery in Bushwick. We played ball every day in Prospect Park, on the diamonds by the boathouse."

"What was your address?"

"Three seventy-five Union Street. South side of the street, near Sixth. Big white house, two stories, a porch that ran all the way around the front. We'd sit out there summer nights listening to Jack Benny and Fibber McGee. My buddies and me went to the movies Saturday at Loews Palace near Grand Army Plaza. Matinees, all the serials, Red Ryder, Flash Gordon, kids' stuff. Three times a week I'd take the trolley down Flatbush to Ebbets Field; cost a quarter on Wednesdays for the right-field bleachers. I carved my fucking name in one of 'em with a penknife. If we didn't have the dough, we'd watch the game through this gap under the metal gate in right center. I caught a foul ball from Cookie Lavagetto, he signed it for me after the game, my parents still have the damn ball; I can tell you everybody who ever played for 'em."

Grannit hesitated. "They could've taught you all this."

"They could've but they didn't; I swear to God it's true; I lived it."

Bernie heard footsteps entering the building through the open front door down below.

"Where's the best cheesecake in Brooklyn?"

"Cheesecake? Junior's, on DeKalb and Flatbush; me and Jackie used to go there after school."

"Where'd your mother shop?"

"There was a greengrocer on the corner, corner of Polhemus and Garfield; she went over there almost every day—"

"What was it called?"

"Solly's, Solly's Produce. There was a Laundromat next door, a radio repair shop, then a coffee shop run by two brothers, they were Greek, a long name, lots of vowels in it. My dad used to get that sticky pastry they'd make on his way to work, what do they call it, baklava?"

"There was a candy store across the street."

"I know it, I know it, Foppiano's, this nice old Italian guy, had a big mustache, wore an old worn-out gray sweater every day, kept everything in glass jars behind the counter. Root beer sticks, Houten's chocolates, Black Crows, those little licorice deals? That's where I

bought comic books—and it wasn't right across from Solly's, it was diagonal."

"Tell me something that happened on that street. Something you'd only know if you were living there."

Bernie thought frantically. "When I was a little kid—I don't know, maybe six or seven?—there was a robbery at an Esso station. A girl got shot, I think she was a teenager. I remember it real clear; police were all over the place. I saw them put her in the ambulance, taking her away. Shook me up bad. There was blood on the sidewalk for a couple days."

Grannit looked as if he'd been slapped, and Bernie knew he remembered it, too. He could hear footsteps on the landing below. The other men would reach the apartment in less than a minute.

"You're from the neighborhood," said Bernie. "You are, aren't you? You're from Park Slope."

Grannit said nothing, but his look confirmed it.

"Jesus Christ, you know I'm telling the truth, what else do you need to hear?"

"I don't know what else."

"Please. I know you don't have to believe me, but I want to help you."

He waited. Grannit just stared at him.

"I'm sorry he killed your partner; I'm sorry he killed anybody, but he's not finished yet, and whatever's coming is going to be worse. Mister, I got reasons to want him dead every bit as bad as you. I've known this guy since he joined the brigade; I know a lot about him, I know how he thinks. If there's anybody in this whole fucking war who can help you stop him, it's me."

Grannit lowered the gun just as three MPs came through the door. He turned to them.

"Miller was here, before he went to the theater," he told them, then pointed to the bedroom. "He killed the woman who lived here, body's in there. Call the police."

"You really want to get the gendarmes involved?" an MP asked skeptically.

"You stay here and handle it. It was a Kraut killed her, make that

clear to 'em, the same guy we're looking for. He's an SS lieutenant, Erich Von Leinsdorf. He's dressed like a GI; he's one of Skorzeny's men—get that out on the radio. Make sure these cops know it wasn't an American did this. And get that old uniform out of there."

The MP looked at Bernie again. "We got those three guys downstairs. Like you asked. The ones from the theater."

"Any of 'em talk?"

"Only a little. Two of 'em hardly speakie the English. That sergeant you took out was their squad leader."

"His name was William Sharper," said Bernie. "He was an American deserter."

The lead MP looked at Bernie, even more puzzled, then back at Grannit. "You still want us to bring those Krauts upstairs?"

"No," said Grannit. "Hand 'em off to Counter Intelligence."

"So who's this then?" asked the MP, looking at Bernie again.

"He's a witness. He saw the hitter up close."

"Where you going, Lieutenant?"

"I'm going after him," said Grannit, grabbing Bernie's arm. "And this one's coming with me."

28

They left the apartment and climbed into an extra jeep Grannit's men had left downstairs. Grannit took the wheel. Bernie directed him to the warehouse where they'd stashed the French ambulance and told him how they'd made their way into the city. The bodies of the two drivers were still inside, but their weapons and the jerricans holding all their equipment were gone.

"He must've come back here," said Bernie. "After he knocked me out, before he went to the movie house."

Grannit wanted to know what was in the cans, and Bernie told him about what he'd seen in three of them: supplies, ammunition, German uniforms. There was one can that he'd never looked into that Von Leinsdorf had always protected. Grannit took a radio call from his detail, updates from the theater. Hearing one side of it, Bernie gathered that Von Leinsdorf had avoided capture. Grannit gave the address of the warehouse to his men, with orders to check it out, then ended the call.

Grannit lifted a box from the back of the jeep and handed it to Bernie. It held an MP's blouse, belt, and armband, puttees for his boots, a white-lettered helmet and nightstick.

"Put those on," he said. "As far as anybody's concerned, you're an MP, working with me on special assignment. Use your real name, don't talk to anybody, don't answer any questions unless you ask me first."

"Yes, sir."

"Don't leave my sight. If you run, if you touch a weapon, if you make one wrong move, I won't wait for a firing squad, I'll kill you where you stand."

"I understand."

Grannit waited while Bernie changed.

"What's your name, sir?" he asked.

"Lieutenant Grannit. That's all you fucking need to know."

"Yes, sir."

When Bernie had finished dressing, Grannit waved him toward the driver's seat. "They taught you how to handle a jeep. Drive back to the movie house."

When Erich Von Leinsdorf and Eddie Bennings walked out the back of the theater, the German turned left and led him down an alley. He had scouted the area earlier before going inside. After dumping his MP equipment in an alley that led deeper into the city, where he knew it would be found, they ran three blocks to the west, jumped a fence, and squeezed through a narrow gap between buildings.

"Where we going, Boss?" asked Bennings.

"Don't talk, Eddie. We're not out of this yet."

They emerged from the buildings onto the banks of the Aisne Canal, barely visible through the fog twenty feet below. They heard police whistles blowing, shouts, and men running through the fog behind them. Von Leinsdorf directed Bennings to a rope fixed to an iron ring hanging down a steep concrete wharf. Eddie glanced over the edge and saw that a small flatboat had been tied off on a narrow ledge at the bottom of the rope. Von Leinsdorf followed Bennings down, untied the boat, and they each took an oar. While Grannit's military detail dropped roadblocks into place on all the side streets feeding into the square, they were in the boat, rowing silently south on the still water.

They stayed close to the shoreline, working their oars without a splash. Unable to see the top of the bank through the fog, they twice

heard voices and car engines from above near the edge of the canal. Each time they shipped their oars and drifted until the voices and cars faded away.

They rowed downstream for half a mile, and Von Leinsdorf steered them to the left bank. Another small dock at the base of a quay appeared out of the mist, and he angled toward it, jumped out first, and tied off the boat. A small flight of stairs led up to the top of the bank.

They emerged onto a quiet street under a bridge that spanned the canal and the adjacent river. A single civilian car, a nondescript black Renault, was parked across the street. Von Leinsdorf took out keys and unlocked the trunk. Eddie Bennings had calmed down during the boat ride, impressed by the man's moves under pressure. He'd known a few guys with this kind of cool back home in Jersey—made men, guys he'd always looked up to—but never anybody in the army.

"I gotta say, Dick, whatever it is they want you for," said Bennings, "you got me beat by a mile."

"I didn't have a chance to tell you. Turns out we're in the same line."

"Black market? Can't say I'm surprised."

"I had to take out those MPs. They get their hands on me, it's like this . . ." He slashed his hand across his throat, then lifted a suitcase out of the trunk. "Don't know about you, I'm not that interested in firing squads."

"Brother, I'm picking up your frequency."

"Maybe they were looking for both of us back there. Doesn't matter now."

"Except you saw it coming, set up the boat, left this car here thinking about a way out."

"Helps to cover the bases, Eddie. We gotta lose the uniforms. Here, help yourself."

Von Leinsdorf opened a suitcase packed with everyday outfits. Both men picked some out and changed clothes by the side of the car. Eddie noticed a couple of jerricans sitting in the backseat.

"So, Dick, you a deserter?" asked Eddie.

"I am now." They both laughed. "You?"

"They had my whole battalion in the brig up in Belgium on a black-market beef. The Krauts come across a couple days ago, they tell us we're off the hook if we'll go catch a few bullets on the front line. I said hell yeah, why don't you just fit me for the pine overcoat while you're at it?"

They laughed again, Eddie in an aggressive, Woody Woodpecker staccato, his mouth contorted like the mask of tragedy.

"It was sayonara suckers before they even knew I was gone. This ain't my fight; I got no gripe with the Krauts. A freakin' Chinese fire drill getting down here; I can thank the Krauts for that."

"Why'd you stop in Reims?"

"That was a neighborhood we used to work; lotta freight moves on that canal. Thought I'd make a pass, see if I could pick up a few bucks." Eddie tried on a gray fedora, checking out his reflection in the car window. "That guy who came at us in the theater, he's one of these fellas you were supposed to meet?"

"I never saw him before."

"He called you Lieutenant Miller."

"Obviously he thought I was somebody else."

"Hey, it was him or us," said Eddie. "You won't hear me complaining."

"Who was the other cop, the one in the lobby?"

"That prick busted me the other night, Criminal Investigation Division, a real hard-on. Earl Grannit. New York homicide."

"He's a police detective?"

"That's right. He's on your tail, too?"

"He put some heat on us. I never knew his name."

"Well, fuck him, he can eat our dust," said Eddie. "I was gonna say we head down to Paris, what do you think?"

"You know your way around?"

"Been stationed there since August. Got that city wired. Our battalion was floating on a river of cash."

They heard sirens in the distance toward downtown Reims. When Eddie turned, Von Leinsdorf raised the silenced pistol, ready to shoot him in the back of the head.

"Our train yard's just west of the city, near Versailles," said Eddie.

Von Leinsdorf lowered the pistol. "Versailles?"

"Yeah. I'm telling you, you got to check out Paris. It's a fuckin' free-for-all. A guy with brass ones like you makes a killing in no time."

Von Leinsdorf put the pistol away before Eddie turned around.

"The Free French or de Gaulle or the U.S. Army may think they're running the joint, but nobody's got a handle on it. And the only God they bow down to in that town is the almighty American buck."

"You could introduce me to some people?"

"You got a stake we can use to prime the pump, get things rolling?"

"Sure," said Von Leinsdorf.

"Dick, I'm not pushing banana oil here. A couple weeks we could be running our own show. Just me and you, no brass skimming off the top."

"The army, the MPs, they're going to come looking for us."

"Forget it, I know places we could hole up for months. Local cops want nothing to do with the black market, and they're all on the pad anyway. You make your own law. There's parts of that city the army won't even come into."

"Will these get us there?" asked Von Leinsdorf, showing him some papers from his pocket.

"Road passes, regional business stamps, *laissez-passers*. Yeah, I'd say you got it covered."

"We're Danish businessmen looking into postwar oil contracts," said Von Leinsdorf.

"Let's get rich."

They shook hands, climbed into the Renault, and drove off. Von Leinsdorf had positioned the car less than a hundred yards from an entrance to the bridge that would carry them across the river, toward the highway to Paris. The army wouldn't throw roadblocks up on the bridge until half an hour after they crossed.

Von Leinsdorf glanced at Eddie as he drove. The man amused him, a common thief with a lust for money. So much more useful than Bernie Oster. That he'd left the young American alive remained

an irritant, but a minor one. Brooklyn didn't have the skills to survive alone for long on enemy ground. He'd get himself captured or killed. Even if he talked, he knew nothing about the Second Objective; Von Leinsdorf had seen to that. He smiled. Eddie grinned back.

Everybody needed a little luck now and then.

Bernie stayed behind Earl Grannit's right shoulder and kept his mouth shut, as ordered. A few of the other MPs shot questioning glances his way—where had *he* been all night?—but none said a word. Grannit was in charge and he was Grannit's man.

Grannit's temper flared once he'd gathered all his MPs and Army Counter Intelligence men in the theater lobby. The killer and a probable accomplice had walked out into the night and vanished. How was it possible that no one saw them or followed them or picked them up once they left the theater? Forty men looking for one man and "Lieutenant Miller" slipped the net like smoke.

Bernie could feel the other officers' frustration in the tense silence that followed. They had a bona fide deserter from Skorzeny's brigade dead and three men from his squad alive; didn't that qualify as a good night's work? Maybe other German agents had been there, and maybe they'd gotten away, but no one else had seen these two phantom killers in back of the stage or outside the movie house. Not even the three Krauts they'd captured knew anything about them.

It seemed obvious to everyone else in the room that William Sharper had murdered the MP and Ole Carlson. Sharper died with the knife that killed Carlson in his hand. He'd been shot with Carlson's gun. He even looked like the sketch Grannit had circulated.

An army intelligence officer summed up their reservations. "Even if this Lieutenant Miller was here and got away, what can one Kraut do alone in the middle of France?"

"First of all, Carlson didn't shoot Sharper," said Grannit. "He's got no powder residue on his hand. That knife Sharper had in his hand killed two French border guards earlier today. An SS officer named Erich Von Leinsdorf killed those two men. He came into Reims in an ambulance today, killed the drivers, a female civilian,

and our two men here tonight. He set up Sharper to take the fall, then killed him and walked away clean when we had him dropped, so don't fucking tell me what this man can't do."

Bernie wondered if anyone figured him as the source of all this, and if so, how he had come to know it.

"I want this sketch of Von Leinsdorf telexed to every checkpoint in France. Expand roadblocks to every road and highway leading out of town. Cover train and bus stations and canvass every street in this part of the city door to door. Do it now."

Grannit stormed out of the meeting; Bernie followed. They spent twenty minutes with a graves detail outside making sure Ole Carlson would be shipped home instead of being planted under a white cross in a French cemetery. Grannit wrote a letter to the man's father to accompany the casket. They were about to walk upstairs to the apartment Grannit used as his command post, when he heard the chug of a diesel motor cutting through the fog on the canal. Bernie followed him to the water's edge. Grannit lit a cigarette and walked along the bank, looking down through a break in the fog at a tug pushing a coal barge downstream.

"He used a boat," said Grannit, angry at himself for not seeing it earlier. "God damn it, he used a boat."

"He won't give up," said Bernie. "He won't stop until you kill him."

"Where's he going? Give me your best guess."

"Paris, I think. He said he spent time there before. He speaks the language like a native. I think he's supposed to kill somebody. Somebody important, I don't know who."

Grannit whistled sharply, and two MPs ran toward them from the movie theater. Grannit offered Bernie a cigarette while they waited. Bernie took it and accepted a light.

"Whoever he's after," said Bernie, "that's his next move."

Grannit didn't answer, but he turned to the MPs when they arrived. "Search the canal, both directions. Cut off the bridges. He took a boat."

They scrambled back toward the theater, blowing whistles to summon more men.

"He's halfway there by now," said Bernie.

"He's going after General Eisenhower," said Grannit. "That's the target."

Bernie felt what little strength he had left rush out of him. He stumbled slightly, and nearly went to his knees.

"Jesus Christ."

"You didn't know that."

"No, sir. He wouldn't tell me anything. I don't know what to say. It's my fault. They're all fucking crazy. I could've stopped him; I should've killed him when I had the chance."

Grannit just watched him. "How many men were assigned to this?"

"He said there were five squads, but I only saw four."

"Not the whole commando unit?"

"No, no, it was a small group. Four squads, four men apiece. How many are left?"

"Not counting you," said Grannit, "one."

"One squad?"

"Just him."

Grannit took out the keys to the jeep. Bernie could see he was thinking about tossing them to him, telling him to drive it around. He could also see that Grannit knew that he knew that Grannit was thinking about it. Grannit put the keys back in his pocket and tossed away the cigarette.

"Paris," he said.

29

General Eisenhower returned to Allied headquarters after his meeting at Verdun, and the jaws of the security detail protecting him from Skorzeny's assassins snapped shut. He would not be allowed to leave his heavily defended compound again.

For the first time that morning headlines about the "Battle of the Bulge" appeared in American newspapers, and it quickly became the catchphrase for the entire Ardennes offensive. As the American front continued to deteriorate, Eisenhower made a controversial decision to place Field Marshal Bernard Montgomery in charge of the northern half of the battlefield. In doing so, he transferred authority over two American army groups that had long served under General Bradley to the one British officer almost universally disliked by the American senior staff. Unable to communicate with his generals in that part of the field, Bradley had his hands full holding the southern half of the Ardennes until Patton arrived. Still, Bradley reacted furiously to the perceived slap at his performance and tried to tender his resignation. Eisenhower refused it, arguing that the Germans had surrounded the American divisions in Bastogne. The fight was entering its most critical hours, and Bradley was his man.

Bradley had until recently, and for years prior, been Eisenhower's superior officer, so this loss of command was a bitter pill to swallow, particularly since he knew Ike shared his antipathy for Montgomery.

When Bradley agreed to stay on, as a show of gratitude Eisenhower made arrangements for him to receive his fourth star. Although Montgomery conducted his new command effectively, conflicts that resulted between the senior staffs of the Allies nearly achieved Hitler's objective of tearing their delicate alliance apart. Throughout, Eisenhower maintained his unearthly composure, kept Montgomery in check, and held these two armies together by force of will and his own quiet decency.

Three hours before daylight on December 21, the 150th Panzer Brigade finally entered the Battle of the Bulge under the command of Otto Skorzeny. Realizing that Operation *Greif*'s plan to capture the bridges at the Meuse would never materialize, Skorzeny volunteered his brigade for a frontal assault to capture the key city of Malmédy, where the Allies had mounted a makeshift but tenacious defense. His ten tanks, German Panthers disguised as American Shermans, led the attack from the southwest. They did not enjoy the benefit of surprise; an attack in the Ardennes by a German force dressed as Americans had been anticipated for days. As the tanks approached, they set off trip wires that flooded the night sky with flares. Under the artificial light, American guns entrenched on the far side of a stream opened fire and destroyed four of the tanks. Two more were taken out as they forded the stream. By dawn and into the early afternoon, rallied by Skorzeny's leadership, the brigade fought its way into the outskirts of town, defended primarily by the 291st Combat Engineers. When two companies of American infantry arrived to reinforce them, Skorzeny assessed his precarious position from a hill overlooking the field and reluctantly ordered his brigade to retreat. None of his tanks and less than half of his infantry survived.

That night, while approaching German divisional headquarters near Ligneuville to make his report, Skorzeny's armored car was blown into a ditch by a barrage of American artillery shells. Skorzeny was thrown from the car. Shell fragments peppered him in the legs, and a splinter the size of a small pencil pierced his forehead

above the right eye. It caused heavy bleeding and carved off a flap of dangling flesh that impaired his vision. Taken to headquarters for treatment, he refused anesthetics and the doctor's recommendation that he be moved to a hospital for surgery, demanding that they stitch his forehead together so he could return to the field. He would command his remaining troops in a variety of actions for two more days before infection set in around the wound that nearly blinded him and forced his evacuation to a German hospital.

The Ardennes offensive, so far as Otto Skorzeny and what was left of his 150th Panzer Brigade were concerned, was effectively over.

30

Paris, France
DECEMBER 20

The City of Light had turned dark and cold. While the Allies' Liberation of Paris in August raised the spirits of those who had endured the German occupation, the early success of the Ardennes offensive leveled them in a single chilling blow. Amid wild rumors that circulated in the absence of hard news, the specter of Nazi columns marching back in along the Champs Élysées seemed all too easy to envision. Thousands of returning civilians who had just begun to reestablish their lives fled again in panic.

For those who remained, on the eve of what would be remembered as the coldest Parisian winter in modern memory, there was little fuel to heat their apartments and almost no food beyond the barest necessities to put on their table. Unstable gas lines resulted in random explosions that killed dozens every week. Curfews and blackouts, already in place but enforced more rigorously once fighting in the Ardennes began, emptied the streets. The power grid failed at least twice a night and the deep darkness provided cover for a campaign of terror, as the Free French who had resisted the Nazis during occupation took revenge against collaborators. Only two months in office, General Charles de Gaulle's provisional French government clashed repeatedly with the Allied high command, which retained de facto control of Paris as a war zone, and their conflicts strangled the

flow of essential goods and services. Anyone with means who sought to remedy their personal or household shortages had no alternative but to traffic in black-market goods.

Every block on every street in every *arrondissement* produced a broker, someone who knew someone who could connect him to the rising tide of illicit goods that flooded the city like an invisible sea. Enterprising citizens traveled back and forth by train to Normandy, returning with suitcases full of Spanish hams, wheels of English cheese, sacks of coffee from Morocco. Whether you were a GI looking to sell his daily ration of cigarettes to a man hawking Lucky Strikes outside the St. Denis Metro station, or a star chef trying to score a hundred pounds of veal for a three-star restaurant on the Rue Royale, the deal could be done if you greased the right wheels. In the Darwinian ecosystem that had sprouted up overnight to meet those demands, ruthlessness and amorality guaranteed success.

Montmartre, Paris
DECEMBER 20

As regular as banker's hours, the man known only as Ververt spent every night from eight P.M. to two A.M. at a table near the kitchen of a jazz club he owned on Rue Clichy at the foot of Montmartre. He chain-smoked cigarettes, nursed one milky glass of pastis each hour, and kept an eye trained to oversee the action on the floor. A squadron of underlings ran interference, screening every supplicant who asked for an audience with their boss. Most problems or requests they were able to handle, but occasionally something crossed the door that warranted Ververt's personal attention. Like the two thousand in American cash sitting on the table in front of him.

Ververt gestured to a couple of chairs. The two men looked and moved like Americans. Soldiers, out of uniform, probably deserters, like so many others who sought him out. Listening to *"le jazz Américain"* from the quartet on stage, the audience was filled with the usual assortment of Allied servicemen, more than 50 percent on any

given night. None had any idea they were paying for stolen U.S. Army liquor and cigarettes they should have been getting for pennies on the dollar at their officers' club or PX.

"Is it always this cold in Paris this time of year? I'm gonna complain to my travel agent," said the shorter one, rubbing his hands together. Then, to an appearing waiter: "How about a cup of coffee?"

Ververt could see that the taller man, who hadn't spoken, was in charge but wanted to let the little one do the talking. The second man shook his head to the waiter. His eyes met Ververt's for a moment, before respectfully looking away.

This one is interesting, thought Ververt.

"You speak English, right?" asked Eddie Bennings.

"I speak dollars," said Ververt.

"It's the universal language," said Eddie. "We're working from the same phrase book, my friend."

Ververt looked at the two thousand, without making a move to pick it up. "What are you trying to say?"

The man leaned toward him, in the overly familiar way that Americans mistook for charm. "I believe that you had some dealings with a few of my former associates. Captain John Stringer and other officers from the 724th Railway Battalion."

Ververt stared at him without responding until Eddie felt compelled to take a sudden interest in a book of matches.

"I don't know anyone by that name," said Ververt, pausing to light his next cigarette from the butt of his last. "Even if I did, and it happened that he had recently been arrested along with every other man in your battalion, why would I tell you about it?"

"Because you needed him," said Eddie. "It's left a hole in your supply chain. I worked closely with Captain Stringer, I kept his books, so I know how much business you did together. We never met, but that's how I know about you."

Ververt looked back and forth between the two men, as Eddie's coffee arrived.

"I misjudged you," he said.

"Sorry?"

"I thought you were military police. I am so relieved to learn

you're not working undercover," he said, then turned to Von Leinsdorf. "Such a disadvantage in my business. I take everyone at their word."

Eddie seemed bewildered by the man's deadpan cynicism, and looked to his companion.

"What is your name?" Ververt asked the other man.

Von Leinsdorf didn't seem to hear the question, looking toward the stage. "What's with the jungle music?"

"They've played this way in Montmartre for twenty years. *Le tumulte noir*; the tourists come for it. It's as much a part of Paris as our contempt for them."

"I thought the Germans put a stop to it."

"When the Nazis took over, they decided it is degenerate music. A Negro-Jewish conspiracy to undermine the morals of the French, as if they had any, but a more particular threat to the morals of the Germans. Theirs, as you know, are more established as a matter of public record."

"That's rich," said Eddie.

Ververt glanced at him again, then turned back to Von Leinsdorf. "My personal theory is that it reminds the *Boches* of the Jazz Age, Paris in the twenties, and the shame they suffered at Versailles. That's what it's about for them, this Nazi business. We're all paying for rubbing their noses in the shit. So American jazz was banned during the Occupation. The last four years we play only 'French jazz.'"

"The Liberation change that?"

"Now the locals can't get enough. And the soldiers, the Americans, they like it, too. And they like our women," said Ververt, looking out at the audience. "Especially the blacks."

"So why call it American jazz?" asked Eddie. "Sounds the same to me."

"These days if I called horseshit 'American' I could sell horseshit sandwiches. Paris will tire of you soon enough, you'll see. Liberators quickly turn into occupiers."

"You get any British in here?" asked Von Leinsdorf.

"Everyone comes to Montmartre. We create a fantasy here; that

sin can be packaged, contained, sold like chewing gum. It appeals to a fundamental part of human nature, whether it's Nazi, American, British, bourgeois, resistance, collaborator."

"I don't see any Brits."

"They're not allowed to wear their uniforms," said Ververt. "Some concern that they mustn't be seen in any *boîte de nuit* that traffics in this alleged black market."

"That's the English for you. Always erring on the side of propriety," said Von Leinsdorf. "They don't approve of premarital sex because it might lead to dancing."

Ververt snorted, his approximation of a laugh.

"Don't they have their own officers' club?" asked Von Leinsdorf casually.

"They've taken over Maxim's," said Ververt. "Do you know it? The Rue Royale?"

"Who's been to Paris and doesn't know Maxim's?" said Von Leinsdorf, with a Gallic shrug.

"It's not the same. The gendarmes arrested the maître d' recently, Albert, a very well-known, a very well-liked local personality."

"For what reason?"

"For extending the same courtesies to the Nazis that he has shown the *haute monde* for twenty-five years. This was not collaboration, it was hospitality. An essential part of his business."

"I'll bet those same gendarmes who arrested Albert," said Von Leinsdorf, "have been collaborating with the Nazis in Maxim's for the last three years. And the only reason was to prevent Albert from testifying against them in the reprisals."

"You see? *Exactement!* The perils of Liberation."

"That's what you can count on in times like these," said Von Leinsdorf. "*Égalité, liberté, hypocrisie.*"

Ververt picked up the two thousand from the table. "Money has no politics. It will outlast ideology."

"Ah yes, but will we, my friend?"

Ververt snorted in appreciation and pocketed the cash. "Come back tomorrow night. Seven o'clock, before we open."

Von Leinsdorf stood up to leave and Eddie followed suit. He

knew that Von Leinsdorf had forged a bond with the man, and that he'd gotten what they came for, but he wasn't clear about how or when it had happened.

"Where do the Brits keep their officers' mess?" asked Von Leinsdorf.

"The Hotel Meurice," said Ververt. "Rue de Rivoli."

"The Meurice. Ah yes. Walking distance from Maxim's."

"You get the idea."

Ververt gestured to his flunkies and they escorted Von Leinsdorf and Eddie away. Von Leinsdorf surveyed the cramped, low-ceilinged room as they moved through the mixed-race crowd that included a number of interracial couples. All eyes were on the tiny stage, where the quartet was heating up, sweat pouring off them under the lights, blacks playing saxophone and bass, white men on piano and bass.

"Hey, Dick, you want a drink?" asked Eddie, catching up with him near the door, flushed with success. "They say it's on the house."

"I don't drink with niggers," said Von Leinsdorf, and walked outside.

The neon sign outside, LE MORT RAT, threw garish red light onto the wet pavement. They turned up their collars against the cold and threaded through the tangled warren of steep, cobblestoned streets toward the small apartment a few blocks away that Eddie had rented with cash after they arrived that morning.

"Have to say, that couldn't have gone much better," said Eddie, breaking the silence. "You see that scar on his face? Bet that wasn't a cooking accident."

"He's a Corsican pimp and a drug dealer and he'll cut your throat the first chance he gets."

"Be that as it may, according to our books the son of a bitch always paid on time for goods received."

"It's one thing him doing business with the army, Eddie; the size of your outfit kept him in line. He knows we don't have that kind of weight behind us. You're sure your boys at the depot can deliver?"

"They're in like Flynn. It's the Christmas train, *le* jackpot of jackpots. Bringing in luxury rations for every dogface in Paris."

"And the branch line runs through Versailles."

"Yeah, I've worked it myself. Don't worry, this is a bull's-eye right down the stovepipe, baby. Pull off this one score, we retire to the land of tits and honey."

"Yes. The American Dream. Hedonism and sloth."

Eddie didn't catch the irony. "Man, it's a beautiful thing."

36 Quai des Orfevres, Paris
DECEMBER 20, 10:00 P.M.

Earl Grannit and Bernie Oster had been sitting on a bench in the cavernous lobby of the city's police headquarters for over two hours. A large electric clock ticked directly overhead, above a bulletin board plastered with sheets of official announcements. Grannit's badge hadn't made much impression on the harried civil servants manning the desks and scurrying through the halls. They watched as uniformed gendarmes hustled in a steady stream of suspects for processing through their overworked justice system. From a detective's bullpen beyond the foyer the clatter of multiple typewriters clashed with the sound of raised voices shouting at each other in French.

"Business is booming," said Bernie.

Grannit lit another cigarette, leaned forward, and ran a hand over his face. The man looked worn to the bone.

"You were a cop," said Bernie. "In New York."

"That's right."

Bernie looked around the room, turning the MP's helmet around in his hands. "Is it any different here?"

"The same shit flowing down a different sewer."

"Never been inside a police station before. Looks like a hell of a job."

"It's a hell of a world."

"Are people just born bad, is that what makes them do this shit?"

"It's a choice. Everybody's always got a choice."

Bernie hesitated. "Von Leinsdorf worked at a death camp."

Grannit looked at him. "What?"

"Dachau's a death camp. They're killing people. Jews mostly, others too. I don't know how many, maybe millions, all over Germany. Do they know about this back home?"

Grannit shook his head.

"Started with them taking people out of the cities. Deporting them to camps. We all knew about that. Nobody did anything. Then this started and nobody wanted to know."

"For how long?"

"I don't know. Maybe two years."

"Von Leinsdorf told you this?"

Bernie nodded. A wave of emotion hit him. "I want to be a good person. But I was in that army. I did what I could, but it wasn't enough. I don't see any way to make that right."

A clerk arrived to collect them. He led them into a warren of cubicles and offices and deposited them outside a door that read LE COMMISAIRE. The clerk knocked; someone inside bid them enter.

A weary, middle-aged man stood behind a desk lighting a pipe. He wore an ill-fitting hand-knit sweater against the cold, waved them forward, and pointed to chairs in front of the desk. A small sign on his cluttered desk read INSPECTOR GEORGES-VICTOR MASSOU.

"My apology," he said. "It took time to find someone of sufficient rank who could speak English. I have only just returned. How can I help?"

Grannit showed his credentials, referring to Bernie only as his associate. He unfolded the flyer with the sketch of Von Leinsdorf and handed it to Massou.

"We have reason to believe this man is in your city as of last night. He's a German soldier disguised as an American, part of Otto Skorzeny's commando brigade."

"Yes. The famous Café de la Paix assassins. We are well aware. There were rumors of paratroops landing outside the city last night. Unverified." From under the jumbled mass on his desk he located another flyer that featured Skorzeny's photograph. "The café is under constant surveillance. It was my understanding your army is handling this investigation."

"We spoke with senior security at SHAEF today as well as

provost marshal of the military police in Paris. They've moved Eisenhower into the Trianon Palace under heavy security. Because only one man is left they feel they have the situation under control. We don't think that's the case."

"How so?"

"We've been involved since this began six days ago. This individual we're looking for is a lot more dangerous than they know or want to admit. They're military men, not police officers."

"As you are."

"New York, homicide. That's your beat, isn't it?"

Massou nodded and puffed on his pipe, his gaze sharpening as he looked at them through the smoke. Bernie saw his polite formality fall away, leaving the same dispassionate, assessing eye that he'd seen in Grannit, a frank, collegial accord between the two men. Massou picked up the rough sketch of Von Leinsdorf again, taking a closer look.

"Tell me about this man," he said.

Grannit gave an account of Von Leinsdorf and his crimes, leaving out Bernie's role entirely. Massou listened without comment, occasionally taking a note. As Grannit finished, he handed Massou a mug shot and rap sheet on Eddie Bennings.

"Von Leinsdorf is probably in the company of this man, an American deserter and black marketer."

Massou looked at Eddie's picture. "Does *he* know who he is with?"

"We don't have a way of knowing that. We believe both men have spent time in your city."

"Then you must have some idea of the legion of places they could hide, yes? A city of ten million, in this kind of chaos? Montmartre, le Marais, Montparnasse. And everywhere scores are being settled. Over five hundred murders since the Liberation in August. Have you ever known such a period in New York?"

"Not while I've been there."

"The number sounds trifling compared to the battlefield, but in cities like yours or mine? Catastrophe, the end of civilization. Entire neighborhoods where our authority has regained no foothold! Paris

acquired some lamentable characteristics under the *Boches*. So, regrettably, did much of the police force."

The phone on his desk rang.

"I have spent these last years in retirement, returning only three months ago—excuse a moment." Massou answered the phone. "*Oui? Oui, oui, mon cher.*" He covered the mouthpiece with his hand and whispered: "Madame Massou." He went back to the call. "*Oui, cher, oui, un cassoulet serait beau. Oui, superbe. J'attends avec intérêt lui. Pas trop tard, j'espère. Est-ce que je puis apporter quelque chose? Oui, cher. Au revoir.*" He hung up. "Please *pardon*, she who must be obeyed, yes?"

"I'll take your word for it."

"If you could experience her cooking, you would understand completely." He looked suddenly to Bernie. "You are not a policeman."

"No, sir." He glanced at Grannit and corrected himself. "Military, yes, not civilian."

"It is somewhat different in the military. Doing this job on behalf of a nation, you may feel a sense of legitimacy." Massou fastidiously refilled his pipe and lit it again. "The lieutenant and I, you see, we are not a part of proper society. Nor can we be. I may have a wife, a pleasant home, an old cat who keeps me company, but the rest of the time we are immersed in these acts of violence. We study the end result to reconstruct the passions which created it. On occasion we find those responsible."

"You bring them to justice," said Bernie.

"We bring them here. What happens afterward is someone else's department. Murder has and always will have a place in the human heart, but no proper person cares to see this, or think about what we do; they simply want it done. Bodies keep appearing, in different form, day after day, so there are no lasting victories. We go on, too, but the work brings a sadness of spirit."

Grannit's head was down, nodding slightly in agreement. Massou looked at them both, not without sympathy. He seemed to know something was off center between them, but chose not to pursue it, out of professional courtesy. He focused his warm, liquid eyes again on Bernie.

"This is your first time seeing such things," he said.

"Yes, sir," said Bernie, wondering what else this man knew about him from a glance. He felt there wasn't much he'd be able to hide from him for long.

"The Romans had a phrase for it. If you need to catch a devil, set a devil on his trail." He turned back to Grannit, reached forward, and handed him a card. "I will do what I can. Reach me at this number at any time, provided the phones are working. Where are you staying?"

"We hadn't gotten around to that."

Massou hurriedly wrote down an address on a pad. "This hotel is just around the corner. Very small, very discreet, an estimable kitchen. If you don't mind my saying, Lieutenant, you both need a proper meal and some sleep." He ripped off the page and handed it to Grannit. "I'll call ahead."

"Thank you," he said.

"I'm certain you would do the same for me."

31

Walking from Montmartre toward the river, Von Leinsdorf turned a corner and found himself standing in
front of the Paris Opera. He stopped to stare at the
grand white wedding cake edifice, looked around the open square,
and smiled at the thought of what he was about to do. He crossed
the boulevard, sat down, and ordered a coffee at the Café de la Paix.
His eyes scanned across the square and intersecting streets, picking
out two undercover operatives in the crowded scene.

Looking for Lieutenant Miller, no doubt, he thought, amused.

When his coffee arrived, he offered a silent toast to Colonel Otto
Skorzeny and absent members of the 150th Panzer Brigade. None
of the men assigned to watch the square glanced his way. He knew
he could have sat there all day without attracting any attention.

Von Leinsdorf wore a conservative overcoat, a dark business suit
and hat, and he carried an ivory-headed cane. His hair had been
tinted steel gray, and to his three-day beard, similarly bleached, he'd
added a presentable white mustache. When he rose to leave, he
dropped a few francs on the table, along with the morning edition of
Le Monde, opened to a prearranged page. If anyone had thought to
look at it, they'd have seen a few words hastily scrawled in French in
one of the margins. It appeared to be a shopping list. He walked
away with a pronounced limp, leaning on his cane. The veteran's

service medal he wore on his lapel, a bauble he'd picked up in a Montmartre thrift shop, dated to the Great War. When he rounded the next corner, he looked up and caught a glimpse of two American soldiers on the roof of an adjacent building, manning a machine gun, its barrel aimed down toward the café. One of the soldiers was stifling a yawn. Von Leinsdorf quietly tipped his hat to them and limped away.

He was astonished to see no signs of the impending Christmas holiday enlivening the city's broadest avenues. None of those elegant, swan-necked women in the shopping arcades or haughty restaurants. He had spent Christmas here twice before, once as a London schoolboy with his family and two years ago with the SS, who used trips to Paris as morale-boosting rewards, a tourist attraction for overachievers. The city always wore its brightest colors at Christmas. Now it appeared drab gray and drained of life. Walking through the Place Vendôme, he glanced up at the statue of Napoleon atop its stark central column, fashioned from melted Prussian cannon captured at Austerlitz.

The French beat us that time, Von Leinsdorf remembered grudgingly. *Well, that was once.*

Turning right onto the Rue de Rivoli, he settled on a bench at the edge of the Tuileries, directly across from the entrance to the Hotel Meurice. A line of Allied flags rippled in formation, a harsh wind stirring up a dark, scudding sky. Dozens of military vehicles for ranking British and American officers were parked out front, flying pennants, jutting into the avenue. When Von Leinsdorf had last been here, the hotel served as the German Army's headquarters, until the surrender of the city. An artillery shell had since collapsed two of the arches—covered with scaffolding, under repair—that spanned its classical nineteenth-century facade.

He remembered climbing those same steps for the first time, proud and in awe, his father's sleek leather glove holding his hand. His father was still a high-ranking diplomat and they had been treated like royalty, shown all the sights, squired around the city in a chauffeured car. The happiest days his family had ever known, less than a year before they ended in a single day.

Twelve years later, after the Germans had taken France, he returned as an SS officer on leave, self-made, on his own merits. Everyone in that hotel, in Paris, showed him a respect that not so long before he'd had reason to believe would be denied to him forever. With that visit had come the assurance that his father's disgrace was at last behind him.

The sound of the chair hitting the floor in the next room.

The old man's obsequious, servile smile, the fluttering of his hands whenever a superior turned a corner. How pathetic and defeated he had looked when they found him out. The image still sickened Von Leinsdorf. The womanly tears as his father confessed the secret he'd kept from his wife and son all those years; everything they believed about him a lie. Packing his own bags for exile, unshaven, doubled over, sobbing as he folded every collar and crease like a ghetto tailor, the life already kicked out of him. The shameful legacy of the Jew visible in him from a mile away.

Von Leinsdorf had vowed to forget the man. He would cut the scar from his soul.

The creak of the rope when he walked in and found him swinging from that beam. The old man's pleading eyes meeting his, clawing at his own throat, his life ending with one last misgiving. Von Leinsdorf never moved. He watched him die and then he turned and left the room.

No one had ever worked harder to erase a memory; why would it come back now? Because Paris had fallen? Did that mean all his work had been for nothing? This hotel, the site of the only triumph he'd ever known, was back in the hands of the enemy, Americans and British crawling all over the city, smug and entitled, as if the war were already won.

They would soon be hearing from him about that.

The rattle of a passing bus broke his reverie. He studied the hotel, noting the security outside, the traffic patterns passing through its doors. After twenty minutes he crossed the street and climbed the stairs, leaning on his cane.

Stammering in excited French and broken English, he explained to the guards at the door that an unexploded German shell had been found in his neighborhood. They tried to explain that he needed to

report such a matter to his local police or SHAEF's offices near the Place Vendôme. With the wounded dignity of an outraged Great War veteran, his tirade resulted in a spell of breathlessness. The guards assisted him into the lobby to recover, promising he could speak to the next available officer. After bringing him a glass of water, they promptly forgot about him. Von Leinsdorf settled into a chair that offered him a view of the elevators and the front desk. He watched a steady stream of British officers who had taken up residence in the hotel as they came and went.

He waited for an officer of a specific age and size. Such a man hurried through the door at eleven-thirty-five, carrying two suitcases and an attaché case. Von Leinsdorf rose from his chair and hobbled past the front desk, patting his face with a handkerchief, in time to see this British lieutenant, just arrived from London, identify himself, receive his room key, 417, and carry his bags toward the lift.

Von Leinsdorf waited five minutes, then entered an enclosed lobby phone booth and placed a call through the switchboard to room 417.

"Hallo?"

"Is that Lieutenant Pearson?" asked Von Leinsdorf.

"Yes?"

"I've been ringing you for over an hour. This is Major Smyth-Cavender over at SHAEF. Where the blazes are you?"

"I literally just walked through the door, sir."

"Some problem with the flight, was there?"

"A bit delayed, actually, sir."

"Yes, well, RAF's got their own problems. We've had a cock-up down the hall here ourselves, pushed the clock right out of round. How are your quarters?"

"Fine, splendid."

"Beats a damp foxhole by a crushing margin. So listen, Pearson old boy, since there's no rush, why don't you pop round and meet me at Maxim's. Do you know where that is?"

"No, sir."

"Hard by the hotel there; ask at the desk. It's our officers' club for

the moment. I'll stand you to a glass and a spot of lunch, act the welcoming committee. Shall we say quarter past noon then?"

"That's only ten minutes, sir."

"Take you five to get there. You can unpack later."

"Yes, sir, right away, sir."

Von Leinsdorf hung up the phone and ducked through a nearby door into a service stairwell. He took the stairs to the basement and moved along a low corridor, following the smell of steam until he found the laundry. No one was there. Stepping into a storage area, he removed his overcoat and jacket and replaced it with a valet's coat, gloves, and hat. He walked into the bustling laundry area and searched through a hanging line of cleaned and pressed military uniforms ready for delivery. After finding what he was looking for, he walked out holding the suit up in front of his face. He waited for the service elevator, followed an Algerian housekeeper pushing a linen trolley on board, and rode it up to the fourth floor. The housekeeper stepped off first. He started down the hall in a different direction, looking at room numbers, then made a show of patting his pocket, groaned, and turned to the housekeeper.

"*Merde, j'ai oublié ma clef de passage. Cher, ouvriez-vous une salle pour moi pour satisfaire?*"

"*Quelle salle?*"

Von Leinsdorf pretended to look at the ticket attached to the suit. "*Quatre cents dix-sept.*"

"*Oui, oui,*" she said wearily.

She led him around the corridor to the room and knocked twice.

"Housekeeping," she said.

When there was no answer, she opened the door with her pass key. Von Leinsdorf slipped her an American five-dollar bill. She pocketed it and turned away, sensing that perhaps this was something she didn't wish to know any more about.

"*Merci beaucoup, chéri.*"

He entered, then closed and silently locked the door behind him. He hung the suit on a hook, closed the blinds, and turned on a lamp. He laid Pearson's two suitcases on the bed, opened and quickly searched through them, taking out the man's kit bag. He opened the

man's attaché and scanned a cache of letters and documents inside, pleased by what he found.

Walking into the bathroom, he removed his shirt and jacket and studied himself in the mirror. He eased off the false mustache, washed the gray from his hair, the makeup from his face, and used Pearson's razor and soap to give himself a close shave. He pulled a black eye patch from his pocket, covered his left eye with it, then turned to the uniform he'd just stolen from the basement.

"Pearson, old boy, dreadfully sorry, I had one foot out the door and our G2 rings me with the catastrophe du jour," said Von Leinsdorf.

"Isn't that always the way?" said Pearson, rising from the table to shake the major's hand.

Callow, late twenties, weak and sweaty grip. Perfect.

"They've not done you any favors with this table. We call this sector Outer Siberia."

"Really?" Pearson looked around as if he expected to be seized and carted away.

"Don't be afraid to buy yourself a better table. Nothing like the same service here since the gendarmes dragged Albert the maître d' off for crimes imagined. For all their bloody whining, you'd think they preferred feeding the Nazis. Maybe they tipped better. First time in Paris?"

"As a matter of fact it is, sir."

"Not what it was, of course, nor what it will be." Von Leinsdorf snapped his fingers, summoning a waiter. "Best let me order, old thing, or you'll end up with stewed boot on your plate. Garçon, bring us a decent claret, not that swill you decant at the bar, one of those '38 Lafittes you walled up in the basement before the Huns marched in. This is Lieutenant Pearson, just across the pond. Treat him exceptionally well, he's an important man, you'll be seeing a lot of him. We'll both have the tournedos, medium well. *Salade vert apres, c'est ca?*"

Pearson, as he'd expected, was cowed into respectful silence by the performance. Von Leinsdorf tore into a basket of bread. He

caught a glimpse of himself in the beveled mirrors on the walls, his image fractured and multiplied, and wondered for a split second whom he was looking at.

"It's all black-market fare, of course, but one can't afford to be a moralist; an army travels on its stomach. What do you know about the G2? Have you met him before?"

"General Strong? No, sir."

"Runs a first-rate shop. One of our finest men. Even gets along with the Americans. Do you know his deputy, Brigadier Betts?"

"Only through correspondence, sir."

"A capable second, Betts. So they're bringing you on board to calculate petrol use or something, have I got that right?"

"To analyze and increase the efficiency of petrol transport and distribution, yes, sir."

"In anticipation of the push to Hitler's front parlor."

"I believe that's the underlying incentive."

"Sounds riveting. Trained at the War College, were you? Sand-ringham?"

"Actually, no, sir. British Petroleum. I'm on loan."

"Their loss is our gain, we're lucky to have you. How's morale at home? With all this Ardennes business, it's been a week since I've laid my hand on *The Times*."

They chatted about London and the war effort and the exquisite challenges of domestic petrol distribution until their bottle arrived. Von Leinsdorf struggled to keep his uncovered eye open while attempting to appear engaged by this colorless bore. When he poured Pearson a second glass, along with it he emptied a small vial of the medicine that he palmed in his hand.

As they worked their way through the main course, Von Leinsdorf encouraged the man to drone on about the untapped yields of the Middle East while he shoveled in the food rapidly, in the English style, trying to finish his first decent meal in days before the drug took hold. When Pearson dropped his fork, complaining he felt dizzy and light-headed, Von Leinsdorf was instantly at his side and assisted him to his feet. Refusing offers of help from the staff, and berating them for serving his man some questionable beef, he

escorted Pearson out the door and four blocks down the street to a side entrance of the Hotel Meurice. By which time Pearson was laughing and mumbling incoherently; Von Leinsdorf got them past the guards with a brief, apologetic shake of the head.

"Too much *vin rouge*," he said.

He collected the key from the desk, moved them into an elevator, alone, and rode up to the fourth floor. Pearson was out on his feet by the time they reached the door to room 417. Von Leinsdorf carried him inside, dropped him on the bed, set out the DO NOT DISTURB sign, and closed and locked the door.

32

Grannit's eyes opened and automatically sought out Bernie Oster. He was sitting on the edge of a bed across the room, his right hand handcuffed to the bed frame, smoking a cigarette with his left. Bernie had suggested the cuffs himself before they bunked down, before Grannit had even considered it. For a moment, neither could summon the energy to speak. Grannit checked his watch; almost eleven o'clock. The fatigue that a full night's sleep had only begun to remedy weighed on them even more heavily. They dragged themselves downstairs, and the hotel kitchen laid out its version of an American breakfast: scrambled eggs and mounds of fried potatoes, buttered rolls with dark jam, and thick black coffee. They ate in silence and abundance, then walked out onto the Ile de la Cité and smoked cigarettes in the biting wind while they stood at the rail and looked down the river.

"What's that big church?" asked Bernie.

Grannit took a look. "I think that's Notre Dame."

"How's their football team doing? I don't see the stadium; is it around here?"

Grannit was about to respond until he saw the look on his face. "You always a wiseass?"

"Until Germany. Not a lot of laughs over here."

Grannit turned and looked out over the city.

"I know you have to turn me in, no matter what," said Bernie. "I want you to know I won't ask you not to do that. I don't expect any thanks. I just don't want to die knowing that son of a bitch is still out there."

"Why?"

"Once you told me about the general? A man like him's so much more important. I'm nobody. What happens to me doesn't matter at all."

Grannit didn't look at him.

"What did he say to you about Paris?"

"That he'd been here a lot. It's his favorite city, but he's not that nuts about the French."

"Gee, you think? Where'd he learn the language?"

"English boarding school."

Grannit flicked his cigarette into the river. "That could've prepared him for the SS."

"Got some wiseass in you, too, huh?"

"Must be a neighborhood thing," said Grannit, with as close as Bernie had seen to a smile.

"You never said. Which side of Park Slope you from?"

"South."

"Really? What'd your dad do?"

"Let's stay on Von Leinsdorf."

Bernie remembered something. "Could you get a question to the MPs, have them ask it at their checkpoints?"

"What question?"

"Who plays center field for the Dodgers."

"Most guys won't even know that; it's like a revolving door out there at Ebbets Field—"

"I know," said Bernie. "I talked about it with Von Leinsdorf. He thinks it's Joe DiMaggio."

Grannit stopped short, looked at him, then took out his notebook and jotted it down. "Not bad, kid. So what about Paris?"

"His style, he'd go for the fanciest joints," said Bernie. "Art, culture, he was up on all that stuff."

"I don't think he'll be taking in a museum today."

"Wait a second. He mentioned this hotel he liked once. I got the idea he must've stayed there. A good place to take a girl to dinner if you wanted to get laid."

"What's the name of it?"

"I don't remember."

"There's a thousand fucking hotels in this city," said Grannit.

"I know; it was like a guy's name, I think— Jesus, I'm so tired. Maybe if I saw a list."

Grannit headed back inside the hotel. The concierge handed them a dog-eared prewar Michelin guide from behind the counter. Bernie paged through it while Grannit placed a call to military police headquarters. He was on his way back when Bernie held up a finger, pointing with his other hand to a page of the book.

"Hotel Meurice."

When Von Leinsdorf left that morning for the Hotel Meurice, he told Eddie Bennings to stay inside their rented garret until he returned that afternoon. Eddie promised he would, content to start his day with the K rations they'd brought up from the car. Within ten minutes, prompted by an enticing view of Montmartre and the attention span of a hummingbird, Eddie had talked himself into needing a cup of coffee for an eye-opener—what the hell, it was Paris, he'd only go out for a few minutes—and then there was that bakery he remembered around the corner where they sold those buttery brioche. That led him to look for a newsagent, where he picked up *Stars and Stripes*, see if they had the latest college football scores. The *tabac* next door to the newsstand was open for business so he picked up a pack of cigarettes, and when he saw the attached bar, he thought, *What the fuck, after what I've been through the last few days, what's one beer?*

Three beers later, after exchanging pleasantries with the barkeep, a comely young woman sat down beside him at the counter and they struck up a lively conversation about her enthusiasm for all things American. Taken in by her adorable broken English, and forgetting that he was supposed to be a Danish businessman trying to

secure postwar oil leases, he owned up to being American, and twenty minutes later he was banging the living daylights out of the mademoiselle in her room at a fleabag pension.

The trouble didn't start for another twenty minutes, after they'd satisfied their physical needs and shared a few minutes of mutual, if not entirely sincere, postcoital appreciation. As Eddie was pulling on his pants, the young lady revealed that the joy they'd just shared was less the spontaneous expression of mutual affection he'd supposed it to be, so much as a routine, age-old business transaction for which she now expected to be paid accordingly. Eddie took exception, arguing, not without reason, that in order for such an arrangement between two parties to be considered binding it first required that he, the buyer, receive from her, the seller, adequate notification—prior to commencement of services and well before their conclusion—and then give answer to said proposal in the affirmative. The girl, who was seventeen, malnourished, and dumb as a ball-peen hammer, countered that as dazzled as she had been by his all-American personality, she had forgotten to mention it, and although she'd be happy to write off their brief encounter as a freebie, her pimp waiting in the *tabac* across the street would take a much dimmer view. Eddie responded that as far as he was concerned this fell under the category of "that's *your* problem, bitch." He slapped her around to reinforce his position, put on his overcoat, and left her place of business.

The pimp watched Eddie exit the pension, and waited a few minutes while finishing his first coffee of the day. On the short side, and swarthy, he bore a distinct tattoo of a knife between the thumb and fingers of his right hand. When his girl failed to appear, he sauntered up to her apartment. Appalled less by her physical condition and hysterical emotional state than by her failure to collect any cash, he gave her a more severe beating, emptied her purse, and went back to the street. Outraged that this American prick had flouted the conventions of their industry—the little whore claimed she'd been stiffed—the pimp asked the barkeep if he had seen which way the man went, then hurried off in that direction until he spotted his overcoat on a neighboring street. He followed the man until he entered a

transient apartment building a few blocks up the hill. A plan on how to collect his debt took shape immediately.

He walked four blocks south to the local police station, behind a nightclub on the Rue de la Rochefoucauld. The bicycle of a corrupt patrolman he bribed to protect his business sat in its usual parking space under the blue lantern outside. As much as it pained him to enter the station, for fear he might be perceived as a snitch, which in fact he was, the pimp did so just long enough to signal the patrolman that he needed a word. They met around the corner, where the pimp told the corrupt patrolman how his girl had just been taken advantage of by either an American GI or more likely a deserter. His behavior fit the profile of a dabbler in the black market, in which case he was probably sitting on a considerable pile of cash, from which the two of them might, without undue effort or risk, be able to separate the fucker. They agreed to pay the American a visit as soon as the patrolman came off duty later that day and then went their separate ways.

In this unwitting way, for want of a cup of coffee, would Corporal Eduardo DiBiaso, aka Eddie Bennings, make his only significant contribution to the Allied war effort.

The Hotel Meurice, Paris
DECEMBER 21, 2:25 P.M.

At 2:25, just before he left room 417, Von Leinsdorf called an office number at SHAEF headquarters that he found in Lieutenant Alan Pearson's address book. Speaking as a convincingly under-the-weather Pearson, he reported that he had taken desperately ill at lunch and would need to spend the rest of the day recuperating in bed. Hoping it wouldn't be too great an inconvenience, he would present himself for duty the following morning. The secretary asked him to hold the line.

"Right, sorry, just checking the schedule, sir," said the secretary. "The G2 will be out at our offices at Versailles all day tomorrow. I'm afraid you'd have to come out there."

Von Leinsdorf tried to sound neutral. "Whatever the general thinks is best."

"Will you be needing a driver then?"

"Yes. If you wouldn't mind sending a car around."

Before ringing off, she filled him in on how and where to present himself to clear SHAEF security upon arriving at Versailles.

An escort right into Versailles. Von Leinsdorf hung up the phone and laughed so hard he had to cover his mouth.

Earl Grannit and Bernie Oster entered the lobby of the Hotel Meurice at two-thirty P.M. After handing flyers with Von Leinsdorf's likeness to guards at the entrance, they were speaking with the front desk when Von Leinsdorf came off the elevator, carrying a small suitcase and attaché, with a British officer's greatcoat over his arm, dressed in the uniform of Lieutenant Alan Pearson. He saw Grannit and Bernie across the crowded lobby on his way to the desk. He turned away, patting his pockets as if he'd forgotten something, and headed back up the stairs. Badly shaken by the sight of them, he stopped in the stairwell to collect his thoughts, then ran back up to the fourth floor. He quickly rearranged how he had left things in room 417 in a way that he thought would solve this unwelcome development, then took a rear staircase to the back entrance, sorting through the problem as he walked away.

They had found the apartment and the dead girl in Reims, and Bernie Oster alive in the bargain. That had to be it. Had he convinced Grannit he was an American soldier? Unlikely, but why else would he still be a free man? Grannit and Bernie Oster together.

He walked back toward the Place Vendôme. Had he said anything to Bernie that could have put them on his trail? Why were they at the Meurice? Had he mentioned staying there during his last trip to Paris? Perhaps in passing. A block away he turned to look back at the hotel, saw no other police or military outside. They would have come in force if they were sure he was there, just as they had in Reims.

The two men had come alone then. He walked on, trying to

weigh how this affected his plan for the following day. The Lieutenant Pearson scenario had given him a straight-ahead path to the end, but the identity would be compromised by any thorough search of the hotel. He had to assume that would happen, and couldn't risk using it now.

His mind scrambled after solutions. Pearson had eliminated his need for Eddie Bennings—he'd planned to dispense with him on his return to Montmartre—but now he'd have to keep that scenario in play. And the Corsican, Ververt, as well.

He stepped off a curb without noticing and his foot hit the pavement, jarring him. He felt a violent, visceral shift disrupt his mind from his innermost self, and for a moment all thought of the mission was forgotten. His obsessive focus lifted, he was suddenly, keenly aware of the grid of the Paris streets and how much they reminded him of his own rigid mental discipline; straight lines and angles, geometric precision. He saw perfection and power in their clean, spare rigor. Civilization had reached an apex in this miracle of order, and he wanted nothing more than to inhabit them forever, walking down these broad avenues and regimented streets. He felt that if these buildings, all the people, even the streets themselves faded from view, the deep underlying meaning that their physical reality masked and could only hint at would be revealed. Patterns that unlocked all the uncertainties of existence. It was a moment of grace freed from time and circumstance, transcendent and full, but it was shadowed by a dawning awareness just beyond his comprehension that something dreadful had been done to him. A yawning darkness opened behind him, hideous forms of primal terror lurched at him out of it. He saw himself being held down in a malformed coffin, squirming to escape unseen hands. His head was missing, then it looked up at him from inside his attaché case, and horror like none he'd ever known lit up his mind—

A horn sounded, a screech of brakes. His attaché hit the pavement. He had walked blindly into the middle of a street and nearly been hit by a jeep full of MPs. He waved an apology, picked up his case, and walked on. They watched him go and he felt their eyes on

him until they drove away. As quickly as it had come, back in reality, his waking nightmare vanished. He saw the Café de la Paix straight ahead across the street.

The newspaper he'd left on the table was gone. In its place, a pair of gloves and a blue scarf.

The signal. Contact. His mind found navigable points again. Now he could make all the pieces fit together. He crossed the street, and stepped down the stairs to the Madeleine metro station.

Grannit and Bernie spent twenty minutes with the manager at the front desk, who promised them they could question the rest of their staff and the hotel residents. Over two hundred officers billeted at the Meurice, but most were out during the day. Grannit said they were prepared to wait until every last one had been cleared.

Bernie sat near the front desk while Grannit telephoned Inspector Massou. He was out of the office, so Grannit left word to call them at the hotel. He joined Bernie a short time later, waiting for the staff to assemble and keeping an eye on the door in case Von Leinsdorf showed.

As he walked up the stairs at the Abbesses metro station, Von Leinsdorf heard choral music, looked up, and caught sight of a modest Gothic church, St. Pierre de Montmartre, perched on the hill before him just below the Sacre Coeur. The voices drew him forward. He had never had religious feelings—following the Party line, he believed only in the Father, not the Son—but he craved a few minutes in the presence of that music. He slipped inside and stood near the back of the church. A choir stood in a stall below the altar, lit by candlelight, performing a medieval *chanson*. The ancient music fed a hunger in Von Leinsdorf he hadn't known he possessed. The mysterious feeling of peace that had overwhelmed him as he walked the streets crept back into his mind, shadowed by that same black foreboding. He went weak for a moment, breaking into a sweat, and had to brace himself against a pew.

What is this?

A priest appeared at his side. Was he all right?

Yes, yes, he just needed a rest.

Von Leinsdorf slid into a pew and let his eyes drift up and around the chapel. He vaguely remembered that this was the oldest church in Paris. A bank of windows on one side had been shattered by a bomb, and he could see a storm drawing into the late afternoon sky above. He closed his eyes for a moment.

When he opened them again, he saw through the broken windows that the sky had turned pitch black. He glanced at his watch. Over an hour had vanished. He looked around, startled. The music had stopped, the choir was gone. The same priest was talking with a gendarme at the back of the church. Von Leinsdorf got up quickly, gathered his things, and walked out.

ddie Bennings heard him on the stairs before he came through the door. Von Leinsdorf was wearing a long great-coat when he entered their garret and he immediately went into the second room to change. Bennings, who was pitching pennies against a bare wall in the front room, under the light of the room's only lamp, never saw the British uniform.

"Where you been, Dick? I was starting to worry," said Eddie.

"Nothing to worry about," said Von Leinsdorf from the other room. "Making arrangements. What was your day like?"

"Boring. Just sitting around on my ass."

Bennings had decided not to mention his own outing that morning. He picked up *Stars and Stripes* while he waited and made conversation.

"Did you hear they can't find Glenn Miller? They think his plane went down over the Channel."

"When did that happen?"

Von Leinsdorf came out dressed in civilian clothes. He carried a greatcoat and was using a needle and thread to sew a flap inside its left front panel. Bennings glanced at him without curiosity and went back to his paper.

"Don't know. Last few days. On his way to Paris to organize a Christmas concert."

"Was it the Krauts?" asked Von Leinsdorf.

"Had to be. Crying shame, isn't it? You know how many times that guy's music got me laid? I got no quarrel with the Krauts, but I'd like to get my hands on the punks who did this. Man, I'm starving. Haven't been out all day."

"Where did you get the newspaper?"

"Found it downstairs."

"So you did go out," said Von Leinsdorf.

"I went out once, briefly, for a pack of cigarettes."

Von Leinsdorf moved to the window and looked out the curtains. The clouds had lowered and the rain that had threatened was starting to fall.

"Did you speak to anyone?"

"No, Christ, no. You want to get something to eat? What time we meeting him?"

"Seven."

"What time is it now?"

"Half past six."

Von Leinsdorf saw two men standing across the street from the entrance to the building. Both were looking up at the attic window. He turned off the lamp inside the room, retrieved his binoculars, and took a closer look at them.

A gendarme and a smaller, swarthy-faced man, a civilian. Both unfamiliar. Not who he'd expected.

"Something wrong?" asked Eddie.

"I don't know yet."

"So what do you say we grab some grub?"

"We'll get something at the club."

When they walked outside and started down the hill through the winding streets toward Ververt's club, the two men across the street were gone. They arrived ten minutes ahead of schedule, tapped on the front window, and waited for someone to appear. Von Leinsdorf knew they were being followed, probably by the gendarme and his companion, but never caught a glimpse of them. One of Ververt's men opened the front door of the jazz club and they went inside.

Ververt sat at his table near the kitchen. He asked if they were hungry, more hospitable this time, as one of the men set down a bottle of red wine and a platter of bread, cheese, and green olives. Ververt asked to hear their proposal, and he listened carefully, saying nothing while Eddie laid out the details of the Christmas train job.

"How many trucks do we need?" asked Ververt when Eddie was done.

"That's up to you," said Eddie. "We can fill two or three."

"What time do they need to leave Paris?"

"We need a ride to the depot," said Von Leinsdorf. "We have to be there by midnight, so we should be on the road by nine. Have them meet us at the Invalides metro stop. They drop us at the yard, then drive back into Versailles."

"We'll hook up on the spur line at three when we bring the train in to load up," said Eddie.

"How long will that take?"

"Once the train's there, not more than an hour. The trucks should be back in the city by first light."

Ververt looked at his cigarette. "What about security on the train?"

"We've got that covered out of our end."

"And the money?"

"Fifty thousand," said Eddie. "Half now, half on delivery."

Ververt flicked his cigarette, a gesture of disdain. "I don't know what I'm buying."

"We've got to take care of the boys on the train before they'll open it up," said Eddie.

"Why should that be my concern?" asked Ververt.

"Because otherwise we don't have a deal," said Von Leinsdorf.

Ververt poured himself another glass of pastis. He nodded to one of his men, who stepped forward and set a gray strongbox down on the table. Ververt opened it and counted out ten thousand American dollars.

"The rest when we finish loading the trucks," he said.

The money sat on the table between them for a long beat. Ververt closed the strongbox to punctuate the finality of the offer. Finally, Von Leinsdorf reached over and picked up the money.

"Coffee?" asked Ververt.

The corrupt patrolman and the pimp had been taken aback by the appearance of the second man, who arrived at the rooming house soon after they took up their surveillance. They assumed he was another American deserter, and decided to alter their approach. Instead of charging up to the garret, they waited and followed the men, when they left their building, to a jazz club owned by a notorious local gangster. They observed them through a window, sitting down with Ververt. The connection to Ververt made the pimp question the wisdom of taking these two down, but the patrolman, who had collected payoffs from the Corsican for years, felt more certain than before that they were viable targets. These were unknown players with no local standing. Ververt was probably setting them up for a sting, so they might as well beat him to it.

Shortly after seven o'clock at the Hotel Meurice, a British major marched down to the front desk in his bathrobe and registered a noisy complaint about a missing dress uniform that he had sent for cleaning the previous day. Bernie and Grannit were on the house phones, calling each resident officer, working their way through the registration cards, when they overheard the major's tirade.

So did an Algerian chambermaid, who was standing in a nearby line of employees waiting to be questioned by the hotel's chief of security. She stepped forward to say she remembered seeing a valet returning a major's uniform earlier that day on the fourth floor. The major's anger went up a few decibels—he was staying on the *second* floor, so why the bloody hell was his uniform being delivered on the *fourth* floor? The major then answered his own question: because

theft was rampant in this bloody hotel, that was why, because of the overwhelming presence in this city of the bloody Wogs.

"Just another reminder that the Wogs begin at Calais," he was heard to say.

The chief of security called Grannit over to hear the maid's story, and inserted himself between them.

The maid, sensitive to the major's racism, mentioned that this valet was a man she had never seen in the hotel before, but not that he'd given her five dollars after she'd opened a room for him with her pass key. She failed to recall which room it was.

Grannit and Bernie pulled registration cards for every officer staying on the fourth floor. Five new arrivals had checked in that day, and Grannit called each room from the switchboard. Two of the men were in their rooms. Grannit identified himself and asked them to come down to the lobby for questioning. Three did not answer. Two of those room keys rested in their pigeonholes on the rack behind the desk, so those men were reasonably assumed to be out of the hotel.

One key was missing, room 417, registered to a Lieutenant Alan Pearson, who according to his card had checked in shortly after noon. One of the clerks behind the desk then remembered that Lieutenant Pearson had come back from lunch shortly thereafter looking the worse for wear from drink, in the company of another British officer who had asked for the key to 417 and then helped him upstairs.

"Who was this other man?"

A major, he thought. Pressed for details, the clerk recalled only that the major wore a black eye patch, although he couldn't say for certain which eye it covered, and that was all he could remember about him.

"That's exactly why he wore it," said Grannit.

Seconds later, Grannit and Bernie were in the elevator, accompanied by the manager and the hotel's chief of security.

Von Leinsdorf and Eddie Bennings walked back up the hill, heads down, collars raised against the cold as the freezing rain gave way to

snow. Large, fragile flakes danced down in isolation. Von Leinsdorf stopped for a moment to look up at them.

Like the discharge from the smokestack of the crematorium.

"You all right, chief?" asked Eddie, looking back at him.

Von Leinsdorf had always prided himself on his ability to shut off memories of the camp, all the unwanted pieces of his past, partition them from his waking mind. Now they were punching through those walls with alarming frequency. He didn't know what it signified, but it left him reeling.

"Yes, fine."

They continued, turning the corner into the narrow covered entrance to their rooming house. Von Leinsdorf pulled Eddie back into the shadows against the wall of the building. Moments later, the two men Von Leinsdorf had earlier seen standing outside their building stepped forward. One of them held a handgun and barked at them in French.

"Speak English," said Von Leinsdorf.

"Paris police. Put your hands against the building."

Von Leinsdorf took a step forward, shoving his hands down into the pockets of his raincoat. "I'd like to see a badge first."

The policeman took another step toward them. "Do as you are told."

Eddie started to turn around, but Von Leinsdorf stopped him with his voice. "We're not doing anything until we see a badge."

The policeman seemed thwarted by his lack of respect. The pimp stepped forward with a snarl, unfolding a straight razor from his pocket.

"*Faites ce qu'il dit, chien!*" He took a few threatening steps toward Eddie. "*Vous ne payez pas, ainsi nous vous faisons!*"

"What the fuck is your problem?"

"He said you didn't pay so he's going to *make* you pay," said Von Leinsdorf. "What's he talking about?"

Eddie swallowed hard and blinked, but didn't answer.

"Nobody move," said a distinctly American voice. "Any of you."

A man in a trench coat and hat stepped into view in the street just outside the passage behind Von Leinsdorf, holding with both hands

a Colt .45 and a flashlight lined up against its barrel. The gendarme turned toward the newcomer, irritated.

"This is a police matter," said the gendarme.

The man swung the flashlight onto the gendarme. "Put your gun down on the ground and we'll talk about it."

"Who the hell are you?"

"Military police."

"Good news," said Von Leinsdorf, pulling a badge from his pocket. "So are we. Criminal Investigation Division."

Eddie's head swiveled back and forth, trying to keep up.

The officer pointed his light on Von Leinsdorf and the badge he was holding. "Toss that over here. The rest of you put your weapons on the ground and kick them toward me. Right now."

Von Leinsdorf threw the badge toward the feet of the MP. The gendarme and the pimp laid the gun and razor on the ground and kicked them in his direction.

"Get down on your hands and knees," he said.

The Frenchmen obeyed. Before he picked up Von Leinsdorf's badge, the MP slid his light over onto Eddie Bennings.

"Who the hell are you?" he asked.

"I'm with him," said Bennings, pointing to Von Leinsdorf.

"A cooperative witness helping with our investigation," said Von Leinsdorf. "I've got his ID right here. These guys are cops, like they said, and they're dirty as hell."

"That is what *we* are doing," said the gendarme, pointing at Von Leinsdorf. "*They* are deserters, black marketers—"

Bennings glanced down and saw Von Leinsdorf pulling the pistol from his pocket, and a moment later the narrow corridor erupted in gunfire.

At five minutes to eight, the hotel's chief of security knocked on the door to room 417. He identified himself and announced to Lieutenant Alan Pearson that he had an urgent message for him from SHAEF headquarters. Grannit stood to the left side of the door

with his pistol drawn. Bernie Oster and the hotel manager waited just down the hall. The door Bernie stood directly in front of opened, and he came face-to-face with a woman on her way out. She looked at his MP gear in alarm, and he saw an officer getting dressed in the room behind her. Bernie held his finger to his lips and she quietly closed the door.

When Pearson failed to answer, the chief of security inserted his pass key with trembling hands and pushed open the door. Grannit pushed ahead of him into the room. Alan Pearson lay in bed, under a blanket pulled up to the chin, his face turned away from the door. Grannit felt for a carotid pulse and then yanked the covers away. Pearson's body had been stripped to his underwear. From the way blood had pooled in the body Grannit knew the man had been dead for at least five hours. He called the others inside, then examined Pearson's arms.

"He was here," said Grannit to Bernie, then turned to the manager. "Call Inspector Massou at the Prefecture of Police."

"I know him," said the manager, grateful for a reason to leave.

"He killed him with an injection," said Grannit, pointing out a wound on the inside of Pearson's arm.

Out of the corner of his eye Grannit saw the chief of security about to open an armoire at the foot of the bed. He spotted a piece of fabric sticking out of a gap at the bottom of the armoire door.

"Don't touch that!"

Grannit crossed to him and examined the door carefully. He opened it a crack and looked down its length, then turned to Bernie.

"Flashlight."

Bernie handed him the flashlight off his belt. Grannit used the beam to illuminate a line of monofilament stretched taut across the opening, then traced it down along the door to the bottom of the armoire, where it connected to the pin of a hand grenade, taped onto a small square pat of dark gray plastic explosive resting on the tunic of the uniform that had been inserted under the door.

"He left something for us," said Grannit. "Call the bomb squad."

When he saw the grenade, the hotel's chief of security turned

pale and backed out the door. A moment later they heard him running down the hall outside. Grannit gently closed the door to the armoire and held it there. He looked over at Bernie.

"You gonna have to hold that shut till they get here?" asked Bernie.

"Maybe," said Grannit. "Latch seems a little iffy."

"Want me to do it?"

"You could find some tape."

Bernie turned for the door, then stopped. "If I was gonna run, this would be a pretty good time to do it."

"I can't argue with that," he said.

"I'll get the tape," Bernie said.

Just after Bernie left the room, the phone on the bedside table rang. Grannit looked at it, looked at Pearson's body on the bed, looked at the closet door, and glanced at his watch: 8:25. Bernie returned not long after the phone stopped ringing, with a roll of black electrical tape. They applied the entire roll to the front of the armoire, then tested to make sure the door wouldn't swing open if they let go. When they were sure the tape would hold, they backed away toward the exit. The phone beside the bed rang again. They looked at each other.

"Want me to get that?" asked Bernie.

Grannit sighed, walked over, and picked up the phone, keeping an eye on the armoire.

"Four-seventeen," he said.

"I was asked to call," said the voice. "This is Inspector Massou."

"Inspector, this is Lieutenant Grannit. We're at the Hotel Meurice. Von Leinsdorf was here."

"When?"

"Earlier today, just after lunch."

In a Montmartre apartment, Inspector Massou turned with the phone in his hand and looked out the window, into the passageway of the boardinghouse.

"We've got him here now," he said. "Get downstairs. I'll send a car."

34

The police car deposited Grannit and Bernie outside the entrance to the boardinghouse. The area had been cordoned off by police, their black vans parked up and down the street, flares on cobblestones lighting up the night. Inspector Massou greeted them as they came out of the car and walked them toward the building. He gestured toward an ambulance that was pulling away.

"Two dead," said Massou. "This is one of the men you're seeking?"

He handed Grannit a pair of dog tags. Grannit checked them under his flashlight: Eddie Bennings.

"Yes," said Grannit.

"He died before they could get him in the ambulance."

"Where's Von Leinsdorf?"

"Army Counter Intelligence arrived ten minutes ago. They've got him in the car."

Massou nodded toward the first of two black sedans with U.S. plates. The back door of the first car was open, blocked by a man leaning down to talk to someone inside.

Grannit picked up his pace toward the car, just as the man leaning in closed the door and started toward him, followed by his partner. Both wore hats and belted trench coats, the CIC's unofficial uniform. Grannit showed his badge, ready to blow past them.

"Whoa, whoa, what's your hurry, soldier?" asked the CIC man.

"I need to see that man," said Grannit.

"CIC's taking this, Lieutenant," said the man, showing his credentials. "Major Whiting. Special detail to SHAEF Command."

Grannit trained his flashlight on the man's SHAEF pass. "Headquarters" was spelled correctly. He relaxed.

Bernie ran up alongside the sedan as it pulled away and saw Von Leinsdorf in the backseat. Von Leinsdorf met his eye for a moment, staring at him blankly, without emotion, then looked away before they drove out of sight.

Maybe he doesn't feel anything. Maybe he can't. Even when they line him up to shoot him in the heart. Somewhere in his sick soul he'll welcome the bullet.

Bernie signaled to Grannit that they had the right man.

"We've been tracking him for a week," said Grannit.

"I'm aware of that, Lieutenant," said Whiting, gesturing to his assistant to make a note. "You'll feature prominently in our report."

"Where you taking him?" asked Grannit.

"He'll be processed and questioned at SHAEF headquarters. After that it's up to the G2. We'd like your report, come in tomorrow morning, eight o'clock. Where do you think he was headed?"

"The Trianon Palace at Versailles. Where General Eisenhower's holed up."

"We'll let 'em know Ike can get back to business, thanks to you. Good work, Lieutenant."

Whiting shook Grannit's hand, saluted, and headed back to the second black sedan. His assistant got in to drive, alongside a third man, a uniformed MP.

Massou joined Grannit as they drove away, and walked him through the crime scene.

"An MP came on them here in the middle of a dispute," said Massou. "Between your two men and a Paris patrolman, from the local precinct. He's the other body. I'm told he has been under investigation for corruption. The MP says he drew a gun. They had officers here within fifteen minutes of the shootings."

"The MP that just left with them?"

"They wanted to get his statement," said Massou.

Grannit watched the sedan edge past the police vans and drive away. Bernie stood under the roofline, out of the way, looking out at the narrow, winding streets that reminded him of Greenwich Village set on the side of a hill. The rain that had fallen earlier had turned to snow.

"Did you question him first?" asked Grannit.

"I did, briefly."

Massou borrowed a flashlight and walked Grannit through the alley. "The patrolman had a gun on the two fugitives when the MP arrived. There was some confusion. He said the German, Von Leinsdorf, showed him a counterfeit American badge."

"How do you read it?"

Massou shrugged. "The patrolman waited for them here, under the stairs." With the end of his umbrella he pointed to a couple of cigarette butts near the back wall. "A robbery, or something more complex. The MP hears raised voices, walks into it. Our patrolman panics, shots are fired. Two men die. There's blood on the wall, on the ground. But the monster you're after is in hand, so does the rest really matter?"

"I guess not."

One of Massou's men brought him a glass of beer. "Would you care for something? Wine, or brandy? Coffee perhaps."

Grannit shook his head. Massou extended the invitation to Bernie, who declined.

"My officer's gun was never fired," said Massou. "It seems the MP was quicker on the draw. The only other anomaly is this."

He produced a straight razor from his pocket.

"It was lying on the street. Perhaps it belonged to the dead American, Bennings?"

"Hard to say," said Grannit.

"Just another night in Montmartre," said Massou, wearily. "Chasing a murderer, through the middle of a war."

Grannit pulled his flashlight, bent down, and took a look at a

bloodstain on the ground. Working back from there, he found a bullet hole in the wall and dug it out with a penknife.

"It's from a Colt," said Grannit, pocketing the slug. "The MP's gun."

Massou finished the beer and handed the glass back to one of his men. "You should have a look at the apartment upstairs."

Grannit and Bernie followed Inspector Massou upstairs to the apartment. He told them the concierge had confirmed that Von Leinsdorf and Bennings had lodged there for two days. Grannit took a look around, found an empty jerrican in the back room and an edition of *Stars and Stripes*, but little else of interest. They walked back downstairs a few minutes later.

"Is there anything else I can do for you, Lieutenant?" asked Massou.

"I don't know what it would be."

"The driver will take you where you wish to go," said Massou, putting on his hat. "The end of the hunt is never what it should be."

"No, it isn't."

Massou shook Grannit's hand and then turned to Bernie with penetrating but not unkind scrutiny. "It's none of my business, young man, but you're not a military policeman, are you?"

Bernie glanced at Grannit before answering. "No, sir, I'm not."

"I ask to satisfy my personal curiosity." Massou lit his pipe and studied Bernie as he spoke. "To the untrained eye it may seem that what we do, our methods, differ from those we pursue by only a matter of degree. Our authority may be sanctioned by law, but it can seem as harsh as these savages we hunt." He kept looking at Bernie, but the rest seemed directed at Grannit. "In certain instances, perhaps your own, which depend on the judgment of others, there are laws of nature that on occasion supersede those of men. I wish you well."

Massou tipped his hat. As he walked to a waiting car, a military police jeep drove up and the MP on board handed something off to a CID man, who walked it to Grannit.

"Addressed to you, sir," said the officer, handing over an envelope. "Came over in the pouch from London."

Grannit opened the envelope and found a manila folder insider. He opened it and turned on the flashlight. It contained a few clipped and weathered articles from London newspapers. Stories from the mid-thirties about the dismissal of a high-ranking diplomat named Carl Von Leinsdorf from the German embassy. There was a photograph of the man and his wife and teenaged son. Bernie could see Erich's face in the boy, smiling and untroubled. A briefer article, accompanied by a photograph of the father, mentioned the man's suicide in Stockholm a few months later.

"Is that him?" asked Grannit, nodding to the photograph.

"Yes."

"Doesn't mention why his father lost the job."

"From what I heard," said Bernie, putting it together, "I think they found out the father was Jewish."

"Don't know why they make such a big deal out of it." Grannit took the folder back. "So am I."

Bernie took a moment to register that.

"We stopped him, anyway. That's what matters."

"I gotta take you in, Bernie."

"I know."

"We could wait till morning."

"Let's get it over with."

SHAEF Headquarters, Paris
DECEMBER 21, 11:00 P.M.

They rode in the backseat as the same police driver steered them through the night streets toward SHAEF headquarters in the Place Vendôme.

"I'd like to try and write my parents," said Bernie. "Would you let me do that before . . . ?"

The rest of his question hung between them.

"Where are they?"

"I don't know. I don't even know if they're still alive. They live in

Frankfurt, at least they did a couple months ago. I'd like to let 'em know I tried to help. Help the Americans."

Grannit looked at him. "We can do that."

"Always thought I'd see the neighborhood again. I dream about Park Slope all the time, you know? That's where I always go. Think that means I'm really an American, deep down, if I dream that way?"

"Maybe so, kid."

"That's something, anyway," said Bernie, watching the city go by out the window. "Beautiful place, isn't it? Doesn't even look like anybody lives in it."

"It'll outlive all of us."

"You have to put cuffs on me when we go in, Earl?"

Grannit thought about it. "No."

"I'd appreciate that."

They pulled up outside of SHAEF headquarters, a ponderous bank building fronted by massive columns, commandeered after the Liberation. Grannit gestured for Bernie to get out first, then followed him, tipped his hat to the driver, and the police car sped off. Grannit took Bernie by the arm and they walked up the steps to the entrance. A heavily armed detail of MPs patrolled the front.

"Don't say anything," said Grannit. "I'll lay it out for 'em and do the best I can. When they weigh in your cooperation, we can get some—"

"Don't make any promises," said Bernie. "I appreciate it, but I know it's not up to you. I'll take whatever's coming."

When they reached the top of the stairs, Grannit showed his badge to the guards at the door. "I need to talk to the CO, whoever's got the watch."

"What's this regarding, sir?"

"The 150th Panzer Brigade."

"Follow me."

They entered the dimly lit lobby and waited while the MP went into the offices. Stripped of decoration, windows blacked out, the cold marble of the massive room extended to the edge of their vision. They stood under one of the columns and waited. Civilian aides and junior officers trafficked through the room, still bustling near

midnight. They all wore the familiar blue SHAEF pass on a chain around their neck.

Bernie felt a cold chill run down his neck. A shaking started in the pit of his stomach and spread outward. He blinked, having trouble seeing. His mind raced, involuntarily calculating how many days and hours he had left to live. Von Leinsdorf had been right about that, too: It was worse knowing when you were going to die.

He noticed Grannit's back suddenly straighten. Grannit pulled a charred piece of blue paper from his pocket and looked at it, then moved out to one of the junior officers crossing the room. Grannit stopped him, took the man's blue SHAEF pass in his hand, and examined it.

The letters e and a in "headquarters" were transposed.

Grannit stopped another person crossing, to look at his pass, then another and another. Bernie went to him as the last person moved off. He looked stunned.

"What's wrong?" asked Bernie.

"There is a mistake on the passes. But the army never corrected it."

"The blue one?"

"Did they give you one of these?"

"Yeah, and we got new ones in Belgium from the *Abwehr*—"

"After you came across?"

"Von Leinsdorf said their forgers didn't notice the mistake in time to fix it. He said these were the ones we were supposed to use."

"And they were spelled correctly."

"That's right."

"But Schmidt's wasn't corrected," said Grannit.

"Then you must have caught him before he could pick them up."

"God damn it, that's what Ole was trying to tell me. The fucking passes."

"What about them?"

"How many squads did Von Leinsdorf tell you were working on this?"

"Five."

"The men who took Von Leinsdorf had the corrected passes," said Grannit. "We only caught four teams."

"You're saying that MP, those guys from Counter Intelligence—"

"They're the fifth squad."

A young lieutenant came out to escort them into the CO's office. Grannit grabbed him by the arms.

"Has a suspect in the Skorzeny case been brought in during the last hour?" asked Grannit.

"I don't know—"

"Well, how fast can you fucking find out?"

The young lieutenant ran back toward his office. He returned at a trot leading his CO, a dyspeptic captain, who assured them that if any German operative in the Skorzeny case had been brought in, he would've been the first to hear about it.

"Is there anywhere else they would've taken him?"

"Maybe the SHAEF offices in Versailles."

"I need to use your phone," said Grannit.

Invalides Metro, Paris
DECEMBER 21, 11:00 P.M.

Ververt's two men had been parked outside the Invalides metro station in an empty bakery truck for an hour when a black sedan with U.S. military plates pulled up alongside. Two men climbed out, one in the uniform of an MP, the other in civilian clothes, who brought along a suitcase he lifted from the trunk of the car. One of Ververt's men opened the back panel door and they climbed inside. The black sedan sped off. Once the back panel of the truck rolled shut, the driver headed west toward the highway along the river, out of the city.

Paris City Morgue
DECEMBER 22, 12:30 A.M.

Inspector Massou was waiting for them at the front door. He led Grannit and Bernie downstairs to the examination room. An attendant

pulled the sheet off a body lying on a slab, next to one bearing the body of the dead French patrolman.

"This is the man who was wearing Bennings's dog tags," said Massou.

He had taken four gunshot wounds to the chest. One had gone clear through. He'd died quickly. About Bennings's age and with similar coloring, he had a tattoo of a knife on the back of his right hand.

The coroner showed Grannit the bullets he'd taken from the body. They matched the one Grannit had dug out of the alley wall. Each bore the same distinctive rifling as the silenced shots that had hit Sergeant Mallory.

"This isn't Bennings," said Grannit.

Versailles
DECEMBER 22, 3:00 A.M.

Eddie dozed off in the back of the truck during the ride out from Paris, which was slowed by the snowstorm blanketing the city. Von Leinsdorf pretended to sleep, listening to the two men up front speaking in French. They said little, but he gathered enough to know they'd been given orders from Ververt to kill them as soon as the goods from the train were on board their truck.

Von Leinsdorf woke Eddie as they neared the supply depot in Matelot. Bennings directed them to their rendezvous point near the back gate of the train yard. Moments after the truck came to a stop, Von Leinsdorf shot each of the Frenchmen in the back of the head with his silenced pistol.

"What the hell," said Bennings.

"They had orders to kill us, Eddie," said Von Leinsdorf. "I heard them on the drive."

"What the fuck we supposed to do with Ververt now?"

"Live in hope our paths cross again so we can make it up to him. I've arranged for the men who helped us out of Paris to meet us at the drop. They'll take the delivery off our hands and pay us on the spot. We're done."

Troubled that he still lacked a satisfactory explanation for exactly who those men were, Eddie followed Von Leinsdorf into the

train yard. Eddie's two contacts in the depot's railway battalion were waiting, as instructed, inside the gate. Eddie sounded anxious, but they were used to that, and in the dark of the train yard they couldn't see the sickly sheen of sweat on his face. The GIs led them to the Christmas train, waiting on a side track near the edge of the yards. Von Leinsdorf paid them out of Ververt's advance, and beyond that they showed no interest in the aftermath of their transaction.

Von Leinsdorf helped Eddie up into the last boxcar holding the luxury goods, and the train rolled out of the yard just after twelve-thirty. Eddie propped himself up against a stack of whiskey boxes in the corner. He watched Von Leinsdorf set down and open his suitcase, turn on a flashlight, and go to work.

"How long to the drop?" asked Von Leinsdorf.

"An hour, maybe more, depending on the switches," said Eddie. "Trouble you for a smoke?"

"A million cigarettes in this car and you're bumming one off me?"

"Old habits die hard."

Von Leinsdorf tossed a pack of Luckies over to him. Eddie fumbled through his pockets.

"Shit, sorry, you got a light?"

Von Leinsdorf moved over to him, taking out his lighter.

"This is a one-night career, Eddie. We collect our end, work our way down to Portugal, and buy passage home out of Lisbon."

"I can't wait to get back to New York. You can have fucking Europe, they're all out of their minds. There's some important guys I want you to meet in the city, Dick. Connected guys."

As Von Leinsdorf leaned down with the lighter, the car jolted sideways and he stumbled slightly and bumped into Eddie. When he straightened back up, Eddie was holding a pistol at his head.

"Now you tell me what the fuck is going on," said Eddie. "Or you're not leaving this car."

"Eddie, Eddie, I thought we understood each other."

"Fuck you. I bring you into this, now you try to hijack my job? Think I don't know a double-cross, bringing these new guys in—"

"Eddie, I told you, they're buddies from my old outfit, you can trust them—"

"Where'd they get the uniforms, the badges, the cars, all that shit, how'd you pull it off?"

"We have the resources of an entire army behind us."

"What unit are you with, and I want the truth."

"The 150th Panzer Brigade. Munich."

"Munich. That's a good one."

"No, seriously."

"I don't know what the fuck you're talking about, but I'm getting to the bottom of this before we stop this train."

"Do you mind if I change clothes with you?" asked Von Leinsdorf, back at his suitcase, unbuttoning his jacket and loosening his tie. "We don't have much time."

"What the fuck are you talking about? I'm gonna shoot you in a god damn minute. You're not changing anything."

Von Leinsdorf looked at his watch. "How's your hip, Eddie?"

"What about my hip?"

"Look at it."

Eddie looked down at his leg. A syringe was sticking straight out of the side of his right hip. He hadn't even felt the needle go in.

"Jesus, what did you do?" asked Eddie. "What the hell did you do?"

"Can you move your legs?"

Eddie tried. Each felt as if it weighed a hundred pounds; he could barely budge them. "What the fuck?"

"Drop the gun. Your hand won't work now anyway."

Eddie tried to squeeze the trigger, but his fingers wouldn't move. The gun fell to the floor. The progressive numbness branched in from his limbs toward the center of his body. Eddie gasped for air, his lungs aching for breath.

"What . . . what . . ."

"Don't fight it, Eddie. You'll only make it worse." Von Leinsdorf walked back across the car holding another syringe.

"What you doing?"

"That last one killed you. This one will keep you alive."

The Road to Versailles
DECEMBER 22, 4:40 A.M.

Massou left the siren on even after they left the city, even though the roads were empty. Another detective drove, riding next to him up front. Grannit and Bernie sat in back. Grannit gave him an uncorrected SHAEF pass to use when they arrived.

"Why correct the passes?" asked Grannit quietly. "Why would Skorzeny do that?"

"It's like your partner said," said Bernie. "The Nazis always think they got a better idea. That their way's the only way, and yours is wrong, no matter what."

"Our mistake and they had to fix it anyway. Couldn't stop themselves even when it gave 'em away. Arrogant fucks."

"And I can tell you," said Massou, turning around, "contrary to what you may have heard, they never made the trains run on time either."

Versailles
DECEMBER 22, 5:15 A.M.

Snow continued to fall as the American supply train rolled onto the side track forty-five minutes behind schedule. Once the train had stopped, the boxcars containing the luxury goods and the one trailing it were uncoupled. The rest of the train slowly chugged forward again, onto the main track, and out of sight.

The side door facing away from the compound slid open. Von Leinsdorf dropped to the ground and closed it behind him. The southern perimeter of the vast Versailles compound stood less than a hundred yards away, on the far side of a row of tall cypress trees and a service road that hugged the exterior fence line. Carrying a small knapsack, Von Leinsdorf stepped to the trees and walked south a quarter mile away from the train cars. He surveyed the double line of fence and barbed wire ahead of him and saw no movement up and down the service road.

He sprinted across the road, used bolt cutters to hack a small opening through the lines of barbed wire, and slipped through it into the compound. He ran forward into the shelter of a stand of evergreens. The heavily falling snow quickly erased his footsteps as he headed deeper into the trees.

Versailles
DECEMBER 22, 5:20 A.M.

After clearing security, Grannit and Bernie entered the provost marshal's office, a large, drafty room in the château at Versailles. Grannit presented his dossier on Von Leinsdorf to the provost's second in command and a junior officer from Army Intelligence, who looked like he'd been dragged out of bed. The men listened patiently while Grannit explained that they believed Von Leinsdorf had been taken from police custody in Paris by an undercover German squad posing as U.S. Counter Intelligence officers. They might try to gain access to Versailles with Von Leinsdorf as their prisoner, or perhaps posing as the British lieutenant he'd killed at the Hotel Meurice. Without telling them how, Grannit also mentioned that these men now knew that General Eisenhower had been moved from his regular quarters to the Trianon Palace.

Appearing to take their report seriously, the two officers reassured Grannit that security surrounding Versailles and the general had been elevated to extraordinary levels following the initial threat of Skorzeny's commandos. Eisenhower had spent every minute of the last few days inside the Trianon Palace, almost a mile across the gardens inside the compound. They appreciated this new information, but the idea that any alleged or actual assassin could endanger the general there was inconceivable, no matter what guise he arrived in or who was escorting him. They also mentioned that in just the last few hours, thanks to CID's efforts, the recent arrest of Skorzeny's last squad in Reims had resulted in a lowering of the threat

assessment. The general was chomping at the bit to get back to his usual hard-driving schedule. With that, the senior officer indicated their meeting was at an end.

"You men are welcome to bunk down here if you like," said the major. "Or grab a meal before you head back to town."

Grannit knew it was an order, not an invitation.

"Would you mind if we had a look around?" asked Grannit.

"Around the grounds?" asked the major. "It's five in the morning."

"The compound covers over fifteen hundred acres," said the intelligence officer. "There's an entire battalion stationed around the perimeter. A bedbug couldn't get into Ike's quarters without our knowing it. You think you're going to find something out there we've missed?"

"No. I'm really beat. Thinking it might help me sleep."

"Why don't you wait until after the war's over and come back as a tourist," said the intelligence officer, out of patience.

"No, that's all right, they're welcome to take the grand tour," said the major. "We'll arrange an escort as soon as someone's up and around. Save you the price of a ticket down the road."

Two MPs walked Grannit and Bernie through the palace's long corridors to the officer's mess. A long buffet table of breakfast food for early risers was being laid out by the kitchen staff. Grannit pulled cups of coffee from the silver urn and stood with Bernie next to a wall of windowed doors looking out onto the fabled gardens. The first light of dawn filtered into the eastern sky. Snow fell softly outside, accumulating in powdery drifts around the steps of a broad terrace outside, lending the marble of the columns an otherworldly glow. Bernie glanced through an old tourist brochure with a map of the grounds, then looked back at the two MPs, sitting at a table near the door.

"They're not going to leave us alone, are they?"

"No."

"I could try to distract 'em."

"Don't push it, kid. You got too much to lose."

"So we're just going to leave it up to them," said Bernie. "The army and the MPs—"

"We did our job."

"We didn't finish it."

Grannit looked at him, not disagreeing. He tried the door and to his surprise found it open. He held up a pack of cigarettes to show to their MP escorts at the rear table, then pointed to the terrace. The MPs nodded. Grannit stepped outside and Bernie followed him.

Standing under a portico on the terrace, they lit cigarettes and shivered against the cold. In the faint predawn light, they could just discern the enormous outline of the château spreading out around them. When they'd arrived earlier, it had been too dark to see the massive scale of the buildings.

"What a joint," said Bernie, looking at the map on the brochure. "Guess some big shot built this for himself way back when, was that the deal?"

"Labor was a little cheaper."

"No unions."

"In New York, they'd still be pouring concrete."

Bernie smiled. Their MP escorts stepped out to join them and borrow cigarettes.

Eddie Bennings's eyes opened with a jolt. He was lying in the dark and couldn't move, but he felt something cold and metallic in his hands. He identified it as his own automatic pistol. He heard the sound of a car engine approaching outside. His finger inched toward the trigger.

The GIs patrolling the compound perimeter heard a gunshot, then another. They pulled off the road and listened. Another shot. They appeared to be coming from a train car parked on the spur line to the south of the fence. They drove the jeep close and approached cautiously, with weapons drawn. Two boxcars sat on the tracks. The doors of the first car stood open, boxes of ammunition stored inside. They heard a muffled voice issuing from the second car, then noticed that the door was partially open.

. . .

A call came in on the MPs' walkie-talkies about an abandoned train car that had been found near the southern perimeter. The officer reported that shots had been fired and they were moving to investigate. One of the MPs listened on his walkie-talkie as the officers advanced on the train.

Grannit leaned in to listen.

With weapons drawn, the two soldiers slowly rolled open the rear boxcar door.

If they'd been alive long enough to register it, they would have caught a brief glimpse of Corporal Eddie Bennings lying on the floor of the car, bound hand and foot, a gag in his mouth, and a pistol taped into his hands. His body was surrounded by a chain of small gray bricks connected by fuses. Eddie looked up at them and screamed through the gag just as the opening door snapped a small cable, which set off a detonating cap and fired the fuses attached to the plastic explosives packed around his body.

In the next instant the explosion atomized Eddie Bennings, the two officers, and the boxcar. The explosion set off an even bigger secondary blast in the adjoining boxcar, which carried a full load of artillery shells. An arc of flame shot two hundred feet in the air, and the concussive blast knocked out windows in a row of suburban houses over a thousand yards to the south. Along the perimeter of the Versailles compound, American soldiers manning the guardhouses and entrenched defiles saw the flames, heard the explosions, and left their positions to investigate.

The MP escorts on the back terrace heard the explosion distort through their walkie-talkie. An unnaturally bright glow caught Grannit's eye on the southern horizon. A moment later a muffled thump echoed across the flat landscape in front of them like distant artillery. Bernie turned in time to see a lick of flame above the distant tree line and hear a second, larger concussion. Both

their MP escorts rushed down the stairs toward the explosion, pulling their weapons. "Go back inside!" shouted the MPs. "Back inside now!"

Grannit waited until the MPs were out of sight. Then he took a spare pistol from his pocket and handed it to Bernie.

"Fuck that," he said, and started down the steps. "Bring the map."

36

General Eisenhower woke at 4:30 A.M. after a restless night. He showered and dressed, then walked down from the small flat he was using as a bedroom in the Trianon to his office. His orderly served him coffee while he looked over the night's accumulated cables from the Ardennes. He looked at his watch; the Third Army's counterattack across the southern front of the Bulge was just getting under way, but it would be hours before any meaningful reports reached his desk. A full briefing was scheduled for ten. He looked out the window at the snow that had fallen throughout the night, worried about how much was coming down in Belgium and if it would hamper Patton's advance.

He picked up a pen and legal pad, prepared to compose the most important letter he'd written in weeks. Eisenhower had announced the night before that he wanted to issue an Order of the Day, a commander's prerogative he seldom exercised. Addressed to every Allied soldier in the European Theater, he wanted to send an inspirational message to rally their spirits as they faced this crucial hour. He had asked his staff to compose a draft for him by morning, but he'd tossed and turned all night because he knew he needed to write such a vital communication himself. With the pen in his hand, the words stalled; he could hear the tone he wanted, but nothing flowed.

On his desk he noticed that an order had come through

overnight to SHAEF high command, lowering the threat assessment from Skorzeny's commandos. Welcome news. He told his orderly to bring his hat, scarf, and overcoat. He was stepping outside. After three days cooped up in this eighteenth-century cuckoo clock, he knew a walk in the gardens at sunrise would clear his head.

By the time the explosion drew most of the security detail toward the southern perimeter, Von Leinsdorf was half a mile inside the compound. Under thick clouds, the blanket of fresh snow on the grounds amplified the first hints of dawn, giving the light the peculiar quality of emanating from the ground up. The storm had passed, but a lingering mist gave the air a granulated texture, as if viewed through cottony gauze. Von Leinsdorf walked just inside the tree line, following the linear shore of a large, frozen rectangular body of water to his left. The woods were empty, the air still as glass; all he could hear was his own breathing and the plush turning of the powdery snow underfoot. He had memorized the maps Skorzeny had given him before the mission, but the snow had erased all low-lying landmarks and made it difficult to orient himself. He knew he was skirting the Great Canal, but it wasn't until he reached this perpendicular intersection with another hard-edged line of water that he placed his location on the grid he'd built in his mind.

He stopped at the edge of the tree line, double rows of symmetrical beech and linden, and looked both ways. The arms of the canal, a grand cross, stretched out in all four directions nearly to the horizon. He could vaguely sense the outline of the main château looming up a slope a mile to the right. That meant he was headed north, toward the Trianon Palace. Not another soul in sight. He stepped out of the trees and crossed the canal. Halfway across the ice, he stopped, overcome with sudden awe. He had reached the geometrical center of the park, where the perfect balance and majesty of its architecture all flowed from this axis. In formal perfection, lines from every point of the compass converged where he was standing. Despite the urgency of his mission, he was stunned by this faultless ordering of space and angle, land and water and air.

After the brutality and chaos of the last week, his mind resonated in harmony. The secret meaning he had detected the day before hidden in the design of the Parisian boulevards broke through here in explicit expression. The landscape's spiritual precision meshed in his mind with the sure prospect of completing the mission he'd been given, and he knew in that moment that fate would guide him to the finish.

It would happen here, within sight of the palace where they'd signed the treaty that began Germany's long, slow humiliation at the hands of the Allies a quarter of a century before, setting in motion the chain of disasters that had brought him to this place and time. The insult would be answered at its source. Meaning and culmination merged in him as one, even in the same breath, an exaltation that caused his soul to soar.

The panzers would march on Antwerp. He would complete the Second Objective. The death of the American commander would fatally split the Allied alliance.

He continued on to the northern shore of the canal. Safely inside the cover of the tree line, he stopped and opened the attaché case. The ID cards he carried would get him close enough to the building to detonate the explosive device inside, but he was prepared if a better opportunity arose. He quickly screwed a wooden stock to the handle of the machine pistol and then attached the silencer and scope to the barrel. The assembled gun slid into the pocket he'd sewn inside the front left flap of his overcoat. He closed the coat, picked up the case, and continued walking.

Bernie tried to keep Grannit in sight before him as they sprinted through the snowbound gardens, past emptied round ponds and statuary and strange conical trees, down broad steps and around a frozen fountain. A long avenue opened up straight ahead of them leading to what looked like a frozen canal that extended beyond the end of the lane as far as the eye could see. They covered the ground between a dense narrowing of trees to another larger, empty circular pool. Startling sculpted figures, a godlike creature being drawn by

wild horses, burst out of the snow in its center. On the far side of the pool, they reached the edge of the canal and Grannit stopped for a moment.

"Where's the Trianon?" he asked as Bernie caught up to him.

Bernie quickly placed them on the map, found the Trianon Palace, then pointed toward the first of two diagonal lanes branching away from the canal to the right at a forty-five-degree angle.

"That way. About half a mile."

Grannit looked back in the direction where they'd seen the explosion, calculating distances and times. He looked straight down the canal, then pulled a small pair of field glasses from his pocket and pointed them in that direction.

A single set of footprints in the pristine snow, crossing the canal.

"Get there as fast as you can," he said. "Tell them he's coming. Go on!"

Grannit pulled his pistol and started toward the second diagonal path that ran closer to the canal. Bernie kept pace with him until the paths diverged, and he took the one bearing right. They ran at the same pace, Bernie glancing to his left, watching Grannit until the bare trees between them grew thick enough to obscure his view. Bernie slipped once on a patch of ice below the snow, and when he got back on his feet Grannit had disappeared.

Grannit sprinted down the symmetrical pathway, chuffing for breath, his lungs burning in the frigid air. He stopped briefly when it intersected with another diagonal that angled back toward the center of the water. He looked both ways, then pressed forward, the northern terminus of the crossbar of the Great Canal coming into sight at the end of the path.

Von Leinsdorf stopped in the woods just short of the water's northern shore. Fifty yards beyond the end of the canal a series of empty fountains cut into the slope of a gentle rise, framed on either side by curved staircases that led to a flat terrace and gardens on the upper level behind the Trianon. A solitary figure was walking through the snow in the formal gardens on that terrace, moving in and out of

sight behind an intermittent line of trees and high hedges. Von Leinsdorf dropped his attaché case and pulled the rifle from the slot in his coat. Keeping the man in view, he walked steadily forward into a small grove of conical evergreens, dropped to one knee, and focused down the barrel through the telescopic sight.

The figure came into focus, his face turned away. A middle-aged man wearing an American officer's cap, walking with a slight limp.

Grannit sprinted to the end of the diagonal pathway, where it reached the canal, saw the line of footprints continuing to the north, then spotted a leather case in the snow beside them twenty yards to his right. He hurried to it, opened the case, glanced inside, and knew who had brought it here. Movement against the white snowfield drew his eyes farther to the right.

A soldier in an overcoat kneeling in a nearby thicket held a rifle, pointed at the northern terrace.

The officer on the terrace turned, and Von Leinsdorf glimpsed Eisenhower's face. As he squeezed the trigger and heard the muffled snort of the silencer, he felt a sharp slap on the back of his left thigh and a jolt of searing pain rocked him forward. His bullet fired off-line, kicking snow off a branch above and to the right of the general. In that frozen moment, as a gunshot cracked the clear cold air, Von Leinsdorf realized he'd been shot from behind. He spun around onto his back, saw a man advancing toward him, pistol in hand, and fired the rifle at him. The shot caught the man between the neck and right shoulder and punched him off his feet.

Bernie had nearly reached the end of the path to the Trianon Palace, the barbed wire and defensive gun emplacements around the building in his sight, when he heard the single shot ring out through the trees in the distance to his left. He stopped and looked both ways, then turned to his left, the direction Grannit had gone, and kept running.

301

When Von Leinsdorf looked back up at the terrace, the general was out of sight behind the line of hedges. Von Leinsdorf limped out of the trees toward the staircases and fountains beyond the canal. By the time he reached the bottom of the stairs, he could hear shouts coming from the terrace above. Looking to his left, he noticed a gap in the back of the empty fountain complex and remembered something pleasing from his study of the maps.

Grannit pulled himself to his feet. His right arm hung uselessly at his side, the collarbone shattered, pain exploding along the arm, through the shoulder, and up into his neck. He bent down awkwardly to pick up his gun with his left hand and staggered after Von Leinsdorf, following a trail of blood and footprints in the snow. At the base of the stairs, the trail veered to the left into some empty fountains at the foot of the slope and toward a narrow three-foot gap at the bottom of the back wall, where it met the base of the hill. Grannit advanced to the opening, bent down to look inside, and saw smooth concrete walls below. He stuck the gun in his belt and lowered himself with one hand toward the edge, inched himself back over the lip, and then let go and dropped about four feet, stifling a cry of pain as he landed on a smooth concrete floor.

He had landed in an ancient reservoir below the fountains and terraces, emptied of water. A series of low keystoned arches branched up to form the ceiling from rows of square pillared foundations, stained by ageless watermarks. A distant light source illuminated the symmetrical edges of the pillars as they marched away in both directions. The air felt glacial and stagnant, as if it hadn't been disturbed in a hundred years. Grannit pulled his gun and stood up, nearly to his full height under the center point of the arches. He listened and heard nothing but a distant, steady drip of water. He saw no movement or shadows in either direction. He set down his gun, switched on the small flashlight and held it between his teeth, then picked up the gun again.

The trail of blood continued ahead of him on the smooth stone floor. The reservoir seemed to have no end, extending into infinite darkness. He advanced slowly, following the blood from pillar to

pillar with the light. His right arm felt dead, hanging as if by a string, its every involuntary movement shooting pain out through his upper body that took his breath away. He crept forward, half a step at a time, cautiously approaching the edge of each pillar before inching into the open again.

He heard footsteps moving ahead of him in the dark, then the sound of a scuffle, followed closely by two booming gunshots and a groan. He heard something heavy hit the ground.

"I got him!" he heard an American voice yell. "I got the son of a bitch!"

The fragile beam of the flashlight caught the edge of something moving two pillars ahead. Grannit leaned out, took the light into his good hand, focused it along the trail of blood, and followed it. His eyes blurred, refusing to focus, and he knew he was going into shock.

"Can I get some fucking help down here! He's still alive, I got him!"

Grannit saw the soles of a man's boots around the corner of the pillar. He took another step forward and saw the man in the overcoat moaning in pain, writhing on the ground in a spreading pool of blood. An MP stood over Von Leinsdorf, holding his gun pointed down at the body with both hands.

"Anybody there, god damn it! I need help!"

Grannit rubbed the back of his hand across his eyes, trying to will them to work. He took the gun back into his left hand, held it along with the light, and stepped forward with the barrel raised. It looked as if Von Leinsdorf had been shot in the face; he was covered in blood, his hands reaching up frantically to his head as he moaned in pain.

"Don't fucking move again!" said the MP, lowering the gun at him.

"Where'd you hit him?" asked Grannit.

"Head and neck, I think. I had patrol down here," said the MP. He pointed deeper into the darkness. "There's a door connects to the basement inside. I heard the shot outside so I came through. He jumped out at me; I was lucky I got some shots off."

"Is the general all right?" asked Grannit.

"I think he is, I think they got him back inside. Who the fuck is this guy? One of those Germans?"

"That's right," said Grannit, staggering as he leaned toward one of the columns.

"Jesus, you're hit, too. Cover him, I'll get help. Where the hell is everybody?"

Grannit rubbed his eyes again. He thought he saw a bloodstain on the back of the MP's left leg as he took a step toward the door in the darkness.

"Hold up," said Grannit.

"Come on, man, you're hurt—"

"Who plays center field for the Dodgers?" asked Grannit.

"What, are you fucking kidding me?"

"Just answer the question."

"Joe DiMaggio."

Grannit pulled the trigger. Von Leinsdorf spun around and dove to the ground, squeezing off three shots from his .45, deafening in the enclosed space. The first bullet caught Grannit just above the hip and drove him to the ground. His good arm braced to break the fall, his elbow cracked as it hit the concrete, and his gun and flashlight skittered a few feet away from his hand.

Von Leinsdorf stepped forward into the light, holding the Colt in both hands. Grannit's shot had grazed his ribs. He touched the blood, assessing his injury as he advanced slowly toward Grannit, staring at him with a mix of rage and curiosity. Grannit tried to inch his left hand toward his gun, but his legs wouldn't work properly and the area under his hip grew slick with blood, preventing any traction. Von Leinsdorf stopped three feet away.

"What do you want?" he asked. "What do you want?"

Grannit didn't answer, but didn't look away.

Von Leinsdorf raised the gun to fire point-blank at him when the reservoir exploded with a series of deafening shots that merged into one long, continuous blast.

Bernie advanced steadily toward Von Leinsdorf as he emptied the clip, and every shot caught him square in the back. The German jerked forward, spun to his left as he dropped the gun, tried to grab a pillar to hold himself up, then slid to the ground and onto his side. He looked up at Bernie in disbelief. Bernie stood over him, held his look

without flinching, pointed the gun at his forehead, and the trigger clicked again, the clip empty. And in that instant the dark light in Von Leinsdorf's eyes finally went out.

Bernie tossed the gun away and knelt down beside Grannit. He didn't like what he saw.

"They're coming," he said. "You're going to be all right. They'll be here soon."

"How's the other guy?"

Grannit nodded toward the man in the overcoat. Bernie went to check on him, a young military policeman.

"He's gone," said Bernie.

"Get out of here now," said Grannit. "Before they find you."

"I'm not leaving you here."

"Go on—"

"Forget that. Forget it. I'm not leaving you alone."

Grannit closed his eyes and struggled to breathe. They could hear shouts and footsteps entering a far end of the reservoir, voices echoing over the stone. Grannit pointed toward the left pocket of his coat.

"Here. In here."

Bernie helped him reach in, and they pulled out Ole Carlson's dog tags. Grannit pressed them into Bernie's hands, held his hand over them, and squeezed hard.

"You're with me, Bernie," said Grannit, fading away. "Tell 'em you're my partner. We came here together. We finished the job. You tell 'em that."

"All right."

"He dropped a case near the water. Make sure you get it first. There's papers in there you can use."

"Okay, Earl."

"Promise me you'll do that."

"I promise."

Grannit closed his eyes, but didn't loose his grip on Bernie's hand until the first soldiers arrived.

37

Late on the morning of December 22, General Eisenhower issued his Order of the Day to all the Allied troops in Europe, his first public acknowledgment of the seriousness and scale of the Battle of the Bulge.

The enemy is making his supreme effort to break out of the desperate plight into which you forced him by your brilliant victories of the summer and fall. He is fighting savagely to take back all that you have won and is using every treacherous trick to deceive and kill you. He is gambling everything, but already, in this battle, your unparalleled gallantry has done much to foil his plans. In the face of your proven bravery and fortitude, he will completely fail.

But we cannot be content with mere repulse.

By rushing out from his fixed defenses the enemy has given us the chance to turn his great gamble into his worst defeat. So I call upon every man, of all the Allies, to rise now to new heights of courage, of resolution, and of effort. Let everyone hold before him a single thought—to destroy the enemy on the ground, in the air, everywhere—destroy him. United in this determination and with unshakable faith in the cause for which we fight, we will, with God's help, go forward to our greatest victory.

Later that same day, for reasons that have never been adequately explained, the extraordinary security detail surrounding General Eisenhower at the Grand Trianon in Versailles was ordered to stand down. He soon returned to his former patterns of free movement behind the lines and among his forward troops.

On the morning of December 23, the weather over Belgium and the Ardennes Forest cleared. For the first time in the week since the battle had begun, combined Allied air forces took to the sky and entered the fight against the invading German armies with devastating effect. Within three days, elements of Patton's Third Amy reached the exhausted American defenders who had resisted the ferocious siege of Bastogne. Hitler's last gamble had reached its high-water mark. Within days, his bold offensive would devolve into a desperate retreat toward the German border to save what remained of his battered divisions from utter destruction. Although intense fighting would continue for weeks into the New Year, generating for both sides the highest casualty rate of the entire war, initiative and momentum had shifted back toward the Allies for the final time. Less than five months later, at SHAEF's field headquarters outside Reims, German field commanders signed the official articles of surrender.

After watching his staff struggle and fail to produce a satisfactory statement to commemorate the moment, with characteristic modesty General Eisenhower summed up the entire war effort in a single sentence:

"The mission of this Allied force was fulfilled at 0241 local time, May 7, 1945."

38

ach afternoon, outside the urgent-care wing of the Veterans Administration Hospital on Seventh Avenue, nurses wheeled their patients out onto a western-facing plaza overlooking a public golf course, to soak up the last heat of Indian summer. The play-by-play broadcast of the World Series could be heard from a dozen different radios, the voices of Red Barber and young Vin Scully setting the scene. After losing two of the last three championships to the despised Yankees, the Brooklyn Dodgers had once again carried the Series into a seventh and deciding game.

When Bernie arrived for his visit, he expected to find Earl on the plaza, but didn't see him there and went back to look for him in his room. A young, friendly nurse whom he didn't recognize was working the floor. They met just outside of the room, as Bernie glanced in at Earl.

"How's he doing today?"

"Feeling a little poorly this morning," she said.

"You're new, aren't you? What's your name?"

"Charlene. I've been here a few weeks."

"Charlene, I'm Bernie."

Bernie held out the small bouquet he always brought to brighten up the room and asked if she could help him find a vase. He walked with her to the nurses' station.

"Where you from, Bernie?"

"Here. Brooklyn."

"Yeah? Me, too," she said. "Mr. Grannit doesn't get many visitors."

"I come by every Sunday."

"See, that's why, I don't usually work weekends."

"Anyway, kind of a local holiday today, isn't it? For a Tuesday."

"For any day, you kidding? I'm living and dying with every pitch."

"You want to listen to the game with us? We'll put it on in his room."

"Thanks, I'll be in and out. Just about everybody in here's got it on the radio."

"They say you could walk from one end of Brooklyn to the other today and never miss a pitch," said Bernie.

"I believe that."

She held out the small vase she'd filled with water, and he nestled the flowers inside. She noticed the worked-in dirt and grime on his hands and under the nails. They walked back to the room.

"You a relative, Bernie?"

"No, just a friend."

"I don't believe Mr. Grannit has any immediate family, does he?"

"Not that I'm aware of."

They entered the room. Earl sat propped up in the bed, his face turned to the single window. He showed no sign that he'd noticed their arrival. Charlene set the flowers on the bedside counter. Bernie switched on the radio, and the sounds of the warm-up show came across, Red and Vinny running down the lineups as the crowd settled into Yankee Stadium. Bernie pulled up a chair beside the bed.

"What do you think?" asked Bernie. "You think today's the day, Earl? I really think we're going to do it. With Podres going for us, he had their number last game. I don't think they can touch him."

Earl's right arm sat folded up beside him, atrophied and useless. He had some movement in the left hand, to signal for things he wanted or needed. Bernie and the staff had learned how to read most of those requests. This time, as the game started, he gestured

in a way Bernie couldn't decipher. Finally, he realized Earl wanted to hold his hand for a while as they listened. Earl looked directly at him, which he didn't usually do. His features had been twisted by the series of strokes he'd suffered, and some days his eyes stayed dull, but today Bernie could see a spark. When Gil Hodges singled in the game's first run in the top of the fourth and Brooklyn took the lead, Earl slapped his hand on the bed a few times and nodded his head.

It looked like a sure thing. Podres was too strong. This time they were going to do it. After fifty-five years Brooklyn was finally going to win the Series.

Three weeks later, two days after Earl died, Bernie received a call at the station from an attorney named Jack Meyer, who worked out of a small storefront near Grand Army Plaza in downtown Brooklyn. He mentioned that he was handling the details of Earl's estate and had a couple of questions for him. Bernie arranged a time to see him during his lunch hour and took the trolley to his office.

Meyer worked alone in a cramped single room, piled halfway up the walls with accordion files and loose paperwork. A round, balding man in his mid-sixties with a welcoming smile, he welcomed Bernie in and gestured toward the chair in front of his desk, the only other place to sit.

"Apologies in advance for my filing system," said Meyer. "I'm a few weeks behind on my paperwork."

Bernie said he didn't mind, uncomfortable as always in an encounter with any form of authority.

"If you don't mind my asking, how did you know Earl Grannit?" asked Meyer.

"We met during the war."

"Did you serve together?"

"Not in the same unit. But that's where we met."

"Where are you from originally?"

"Brooklyn. That's what we realized. That we were from the same neighborhood."

Something of Bernie's reticence came across. "I don't mean to pry," said Meyer. "I'm just trying to understand the relationship. I knew Earl's father; I represented the family for many years. I never heard Earl mention you."

"He was never much of a talker," said Bernie.

"No," said Meyer, with a warm smile. "But he made the most of the words he let go of."

"Yes, sir. After the war, we stayed in touch. When he had the stroke, I started helping out at the gas station. I'm a mechanic."

"I see."

"Earl had a rough time of it."

"I know he was badly wounded over there. Took him years to recover."

"See, I don't think he ever really did."

"It's a blessing his suffering is over," said Meyer. "So our business here today is short and simple. If you knew him as well as you say, you won't be surprised to hear that Earl took very precise care of his affairs."

Bernie smiled slightly.

"I have his will here. He's left everything to you."

Bernie couldn't speak for a moment. "Excuse me?"

"You're his sole heir. Don't run right out and move to Westchester; there's not a lot, aside from the gas station and a few savings bonds."

"I thought . . . He had no other family at all?"

"He had a sister growing up."

"Where is she?"

"She was killed. There was a robbery at the station. Some punk emptied the till, she walked in on him. A long time ago now, over twenty-five years. She couldn't have been more than twelve or thirteen."

Bernie's own vivid impressions of that day came flooding back and his eyes filled with involuntary tears. He could even pick a young policeman out of the crowd in his memory who might have been . . .

"As I understand it, Earl had just joined the police force. Had to

work a double shift that day when he would normally have been at the station. Terrible, terrible business. They never found the killer. Family never got over it. Two years later Earl's father dies of a heart attack. His wife went the next year. There's one theory that she killed herself. Didn't he ever tell you any of this?"

"No, sir. He never did."

"Well," said Meyer, sympathetic to Bernie's show of emotion. "He was a hard man to know."

Bernie composed himself before he spoke again. "You have no idea what he did. Over there. Nobody knows what he did. More than any man I know. Did he ever tell you what happened?"

"No. And I never asked. Nor, in putting this document together, and this is a little awkward, could I find any mention of your service record. No entry or discharge. Nothing with the Veterans Administration." He let that sink in for a moment, then turned to a legal pad. "I did verify that your family lived in Park Slope, as you say. Then it appears you moved away for some time in '38? Eight years later you're back in the area. Alone. Living in a one-room apartment. Unmarried. No trace of your family."

Meyer appeared to be waiting for an explanation, but when none was forthcoming he showed no disappointment.

"The fact is Earl Grannit vouched for you," said Meyer. "And that is as far as my curiosity extends. I require your signature here, and here."

Meyer set two copies of the will down in front of him and handed Bernie a pen.

"I owe him my life," said Bernie, about to elaborate.

"Please, feel no obligation to say anything more. Earl obviously had his reasons as well."

Bernie signed the documents. Meyer efficiently gathered them from him and showed him to the door.

"Anyway, one hopes that's what we've learned about what happened over there, isn't it?" he said. "In those black hours."

As Meyer looked at him over his glasses, behind the easy congeniality, Bernie wondered exactly how much he did know.

"What's that, sir?"

"What we were fighting for. And against."

"Yes, sir."

"Not every hero came home with a medal."

They shook hands, and Bernie stepped out onto the quiet tree-lined street, a chill in the wind, the leaves just starting to turn, and walked all the way back to Park Slope.

n May 19, 1945, near Salzburg, Austria, where he had led his commandos into the Alps to mount a final defense, *Oberstürmbannführer* Otto Skorzeny turned himself in to American forces. News of the surrender of "the most dangerous man in Europe" created a sensation throughout the Continent, America, and the rest of the world. When General Eisenhower learned of Skorzeny's capture, he sent his personal chief of security to interview him and ordered a film crew from Army Counter Intelligence to record the interrogation. Eisenhower reviewed the resulting footage personally, but his reaction was never made public. Skorzeny would spend the next two years in prisoner-of-war camps at Nuremberg and later at Dachau, awaiting trial in the Allies' war crimes court. Although he was universally described in newspaper accounts as "the man who tried to kill Eisenhower," Skorzeny skillfully defused the accusation through the English-speaking press. Charming and formidable, easily the most charismatic of the surviving Nazi hierarchy, in dozens of interviews he claimed that he had never seriously intended to assassinate the Allied commander, adding, with a sly smile, that if he had, "no one would have been left in doubt about what I was trying to do."

Despite working steadily for the next two years, Allied officials were unable to produce any written orders or compelling eyewitnesses

who would testify to Skorzeny's direct involvement in the plot to kill Eisenhower. Skorzeny had received his orders directly from Hitler, and had made certain that no paper trail survived. The only other men with direct knowledge of the Second Objective had all been killed in combat or shot by American firing squads. Only the interrogation of the unfortunate Karl Heinz Schmidt and a few others testified to its existence, and those files would remain classified by Army Counter Intelligence for the next fifty years. The reason for that had something to do with the fact that, while in custody, after weeks of fruitless interrogations about Operation *Greif* by Allied interrogators, Skorzeny was visited by the legendary Bill Donovan, head of the Office of Strategic Services, forerunner of the CIA, and Skorzeny's opposite number on the American side. Donovan recognized a kindred spirit in Skorzeny, and although no record of their discussions remain, they were apparently amiable and far-reaching. What they shared in earnest, besides an appetite for spy craft, was a serious dread of the Soviet Union and its emerging designs on Eastern Europe. Shortly after their encounter, all pursuit of charges against Skorzeny in the Eisenhower assassination attempt was dropped. For a while, frustrated prosecutors considered including Skorzeny with the dozens of soldiers and officers responsible for the massacre of American troops near Malmédy, but the idea was dismissed for an obvious lack of evidence.

Skorzeny was finally brought to trial before a military tribunal in 1947 on a lesser charge that his deployment of German commandos disguised as Allied soldiers during the Ardennes offensive constituted a war crime. Press from around the world gathered to cover the proceedings. With the help of a tenacious American defense attorney, Lieutenant Colonel Robert Durst, Skorzeny argued that every side in the war had at one time or another employed the exact same tactic. If his actions were considered a war crime, any similar Allied effort would have to be held to the same criminal standard. At the eleventh hour, Skorzeny's attorney called a surprise defense witness to the stand, a decorated British RAF war hero who testified that he and his commando unit had worn German uniforms on a

number of missions during the war. The tribunal acquitted Otto Skorzeny of all charges. Afterward, the thwarted and furious chief prosecutor told the press: "I still think Skorzeny is the most dangerous man in Europe."

Although technically free, Skorzeny remained in American custody while they debated what to do with him. Attempts by the Soviets and the Czechs to extradite him for war crimes in their own tribunals, where he faced certain execution, clouded the issue. While those efforts were tied up in the courts, he was finally transferred to a German detention camp in early 1948. A few months later, with help from agents of the recently formed Central Intelligence Agency, three former SS officers arrived at the camp disguised as American military policemen and presented forged documents that authorized them to transport Skorzeny to a hearing at Nuremberg the following day. The American soldiers on duty signed the release, and Skorzeny walked out of the prison in the custody of the disguised MPs. He promptly disappeared. When his absence was discovered and his cell searched later that day, officials found a letter Skorzeny had left behind, addressed to the German court, explaining his actions:

After the capitulation of the German Army, Mr. Chairman, I, as a soldier, which is all that I was, freely gave myself up with a trust in the justice of the victors without making any effort to avoid my responsibility. For over two years I tried to clear myself and restore the honor of my name to the world. The American military tribunal in Dachau cleared me of all charges and therewith declared to the public that I had acted and fought purely as a decent soldier and had only done my duty to my Fatherland. In spite of this official release I was kept under arrest. The American authorities offered me the choice to go to either a DP camp or a German internment camp. I chose the latter in the hope of finding only justice before a German court and have prepared myself for months for these proceedings. However, I will not allow myself to fall under a one-sided, outside influenced decision and thus lose the honor which was restored to me by the American court. For these reasons I have withdrawn myself

*from further German court proceedings. If I'm given an opportu-
nity to come before a German court which stands only under the
law and is strong enough to resist the hatred exerted from outside
sources as is worthy of German justice traditions, I will immediately place myself at your service. As a German who fought for his
country, as did every German man, I have only one wish: to live in
honor in my Fatherland.*

Yours sincerely, Otto Skorzeny

Hindsight makes it clear that in the utilitarian opinion of Bill
Donovan and the CIA, Skorzeny possessed more value as a living
intelligence asset than a dead war criminal. Although rumors reported his whereabouts all over the globe, one of the world's most
sought after fugitives spent the next two years living in Paris, where
he regularly dined at the Café de la Paix. Recently declassified documents confirm that he was now working on behalf of the Western
Allies, gathering intelligence against the French Communist Party.
After his identity was revealed in France, he published his memoirs
and moved back to Germany, where he lived under an assumed
name for a few years, before finally settling in General Franco's fascist Madrid. He would spend the next twenty-five years straddling
an unsettling line between Western intelligence informant and
godfather to the surviving remnants of the *Waffen*-SS, known initially as "The Brotherhood" and later more notoriously as Odessa.
During that time, drawing on his early training as an engineer,
Skorzeny founded a technical consulting company and amassed a
considerable personal fortune. He amplified that fortune with a
number of less savory business ventures, among them industrial espionage, assassination for hire, and international arms dealing.
Throughout these years Skorzeny lived the social life of a dissolute
playboy, romancing dozens of glamorous socialites and minor royalty, including, for a time in Argentina where he worked as a consultant with that fascist regime, Eva Perón. Operationally conceived
on the back of Skorzeny's World War Two commando force, to this
day Odessa remains the original prototype for the modern terrorist
organization.

When he finally succumbed to cancer in 1975, Otto Skorzeny was laid to rest in a Madrid cemetery. In surviving footage of the funeral, a band plays *"Deutschland Über Alles"* while the aging members of his organization offer their dead leader a sustained Nazi salute as his casket lowers into the grave.

A Note on Sources

The 150th Panzer Squad, Operation *Greif*, and all the details about training at the Grafenwöhr camp are based on fact, most of which remained classified by American Military Intelligence for fifty years after the end of World War Two. Much of what the Allies learned about the objectives of the operation during the Battle of the Bulge, including the plot to kill General Eisenhower, came from a captured German commando named Karl Schmidt. Two American-born soldiers took part in the attack; one was a deserter by the name of William Sharper. Another of the German commandos, the son of a diplomat, had learned English while growing up in England.

Less than half of the men who trained at Grafenwöhr and served in Skorzeny's Brigade 150 survived the war. The casualty rate among the commando group, Company Stielau, approached 75 percent. Of the twenty members of the commando group who took part in the Second Objective, eighteen were either killed in action or captured and executed by American forces during the Battle of the Bulge.

The remaining two men have never been accounted for.

Los Angeles, California
November 2006

ACKNOWLEDGMENTS

Many thanks to my agent, Ed Victor; editor in chief Will Schwalbe; my editor, Gretchen Young; and my expert researcher, Jennifer Bidwell.

THE SECOND OBJECTIVE

Belgium
Dec. 14 — Dec. 22, 1944

River Thames

London

ENGLAND

Dover

Strait of Dover

Brugge

Dunkirk

Calais

Boulogne

Lille

Lys

Canche

Authie

N

Somme

FRANCE

Bresle

Dieppe

2000 ft.

St. Quentin

Bethune

Trianon

Bassin Neptune

GRAND CANAL

Oise

Seine

Rouen

Petit Parc

Château

Risle

Aisne

Versailles

Piece d'Eau des Suisses

Eure

Seine

Oise

St. Denis

Paris

Avre

Versailles

Illustrated map by Laura Hartman Maestro ©2007

IT ALL STARTED WITH COLUMBUS

FERDINAND AND ISABELLA REFUSED TO BELIEVE THE WORLD WAS ROUND, EVEN WHEN COLUMBUS SHOWED THEM AN EGG.

It all started with Columbus

BEING AN UNEXPURGATED, UNABRIDGED, AND UN-
LIKELY HISTORY OF THE UNITED STATES FROM
CHRISTOPHER COLUMBUS TO THE PRESENT FOR THOSE
WHO, HAVING PERUSED A VOLUME OF HISTORY IN
SCHOOL, SWORE THEY WOULD NEVER READ ANOTHER.

BY RICHARD ARMOUR, A.B., C.D., E.F.

Lavishly illustrated by CAMPBELL GRANT

MC GRAW-HILL BOOK COMPANY, INC.

NEW YORK   TORONTO   LONDON

IT ALL STARTED WITH COLUMBUS. Copyright, 1953, by Richard Armour. All rights in this book are reserved. It may not be used for dramatic, motion-, or talking-picture purposes without written authorization from the holder of these rights. Nor may the book or parts thereof be reproduced in any manner whatsoever without permission in writing, except in the case of brief quotations embodied in critical articles and reviews. For information, address McGraw-Hill Book Company, Inc., 330 W. 42 St., New York 36, N. Y.

Library of Congress Catalog Card Number: 53–5181

Published by McGraw-Hill Book Company, Inc.

First printing, March, 1953
Second printing, June, 1953
Third printing, October, 1953
Fourth printing, November, 1953
Fifth printing, December, 1953
Sixth printing, January, 1954
Seventh printing, February, 1954
Eighth printing, July, 1954
Ninth printing, December, 1954
Tenth printing, March, 1955
Eleventh printing, November, 1955
Twelfth printing, March, 1956
Thirteenth printing, October, 1956

PRINTED IN THE UNITED STATES OF AMERICA

HUMBLY

DEDICATED

IN AN ATTITUDE OF GRATITUDE

TO WALTER CARRUTHERS SELLAR

AND ROBERT JULIAN YEATMAN

WHO WROTE THE WONDERFUL

1066 AND ALL THAT

ACKNOWLEDGMENT.

The author
wishes to thank
Christopher Columbus,
Captain John Smith, George
Washington, and the many others
who made this book possible. He is also
grateful to the Red Skins, the Red Coats, the
Red Badge of Courage, and the inventor of gun powder,
without whom the history of our country would
have been sadly lacking in bloodshed and
would have made dull reading.

Nota bene: The author will appreciate
assistance in eliminating, in future
editions, any accurate dates or
undistorted facts that may
have insinuated them-
selves despite the
most painstaking
research and
proofread-
ing.
R.A.

APOLOGIA.

THE AUTHOR APOLOGIZES FOR BEING UNABLE
TO AFFORD A GHOST WRITER, WHICH EXPLAINS
THE LACK OF A DISTINCTIVE PROSE STYLE.

CHAPTER I

THE DISCOVERY OF AMERICA.

AMERICA was founded by Columbus in 1492. This is an easy date to remember because it rhymes with "ocean blue," which was the color of the Atlantic in those days. If he had sailed a year later the date would still be easy to remember because it would rhyme with "boundless sea."

Columbus fled to this country because of persecution by Ferdinand and Isabella, who refused to believe the world was round, even when Columbus showed them an egg. Ferdinand later became famous because he objected to bullfights and said he preferred to smell flowers if he had to smell anything. He was stung in the end by a bee.

Before Columbus reached America, which he named after a man called American Vesuvius, he cried "Ceylon! Ceylon!" because he wanted to see India, which was engraved on his heart, before he died. When he arrived, he cried again. This time he cried "Excelsior!" meaning "I have founded it." Excelsior has been widely used ever since by persons returning with chinaware from China, with indiaware from India, and with underware from Down Under.

Columbus was mistaken in thinking he had reached India when actually he had not got even as far as Indiana. There is still a great deal of confusion about the East and the West. As Columbus discovered, if you go west long enough you find yourself in the east, and vice versa. The East and the West are kept apart by the Date Line, just as the North and

South are kept apart by the Masons' Dixon Line. In the New World most of the eastern half of the country is called the Middle West, although it is known as the East by those who live in the Far West.

Columbus, who was as confused as anybody who has been at sea for a long time, called the first people he saw "Indians." It is not known what they called Columbus. His unfortunate error has been perpetuated through the centuries. The original Americans are still known as "Indians," while all manner of immigrants from England, Ireland, Angora, and Lichtenstein are referred to as "Americans." [1]

Accompanied by his devoted followers, the Knights of Columbus, Columbus made several other voyages in search of India. Try as he might, however, he kept discovering America, and finally returned to Spain to die. He lived for a time in Madrid, but spent his last days in Disgrace.

Some say it was not Columbus who discovered America but a man named Leaf Ericson. Leaf came from one of the Scandi-

Leaf Ericson.

navian countries with a shipload of people, all of whom were called Yon Yonson or Ole Olson or Big Swede, and went straight to Wisconsin, where he unloaded his passengers and went back for more.

[1] Or, by their mathematically inclined friends, "100 percent Americans."

2

On his next trip he went to Minnesota. We know all this from some undecipherable remarks he made on a piece of stone. This stone has since become an utter rune.

After Columbus proved the world was round, a great many people went around it. Marco Polo, who was one of the earlier explorers, had the misfortune to live several centuries before Columbus. Therefore, although he got around a good deal, he did not get completely around. He went far to the north, however, and is remembered for his discovery of the Polo regions.

Sir Francis Drake.

The chief rivals in exploration were England and Spain. England had men like Cabot, who spoke only to a man named Lowell, and Sir Francis Drake, who had a singed beard and a ship called the *Golden Behind.*

Nor should we forget Sir Martin Fourflusher.[1]

The struggle between England and Spain came to a climax in an epic sea battle off the Azores known as the Last Fight of the Revenge. In this decisive conflict, Sir Richard Grenville and Alfred Lord Tennyson proved conclusively that the lighter English warships could get more miles to the galleon.

England has ruled the waves ever since and has kept the sun

[1] A direct descendant of the early Saxons, who knew all the Angles.

3

from setting anywhere on her empire, thus providing a longer working day than in other countries.

STILL FURTHER EXPLORATIONS.

Other explorers included Bilbo, Cabbage de Vaca, Cortez (known as The Stout, who traveled much in realms looking for gold), and Pantsy de Lion, a thirsty old man who was looking for a drinking fountain.[1] He never found it, but he founded Florida, to which a great many thirsty old men have gone ever since.

Pantsy de Lion.

CHAPTER II.

THE VIRGINIA COLONY.

ALL this time there was not much happening in the New World, except that it was steadily growing older.

This period, known as the Doldrums, came to an end in fifteen-something-or-other when Sir Walter Raleigh, a man with a pointed beard and a pointless way of muddying his cloak, established a colony in America in the hope of pleasing the Queen, whose favor he had been in but was temporarily out of.

[1] Some historians say that in his wanderings through the South he invented the Dixie cup, just in case.

Although he claimed the new land in the name of Elizabeth, he called it Virginia, which aroused suspicions in Elizabeth's mind and caused her to confine Sir Walter in a tower. While imprisoned, Sir Walter made good use of his time by writing a history of the world on such scraps of paper as he could find, and filling other scraps of paper with a weed brought back from Virginia.

Sir Walter lost his head.

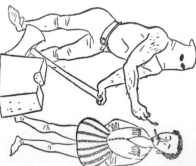

He had barely completed his history when he lost his head. Had he been permitted to keep it a few years longer he might have become the first man to roll a cigarette with one hand.

The Virginia Colony was lost for a time, and its name was changed to The Lost Colony, but it was subsequently found at about the place where it was last seen. Its original name of Virginia was restored because Elizabeth no longer cared, being dead.[1]

THE INDIANS.

The people who were already in the New World when the white men arrived were the first Americans, or America Firsters. They were also referred to as the First Families of Virginia.

The early colonists found the Indians living in toupees, or wigwams, and sending up smoke signals, or wigwags, with piece

[1] The end of Elizabeth is known as the Elizabethan Period.

5

pipes. Apparently because of a shortage of pipes, they sat in a circle and passed one pipe around, each biting off a piece as it passed. The chief Indian was named Hiawatha, and his squaw, whose name was Evangeline, did all the work. This was later to become an Old American Custom.

The Chiefs, it must be said in all fairness, were too busy to work. They were engaged in making wampum, or whoopee, when they were not mixing war paint or scattering arrowheads about, to be found centuries later.

In order to have their hands free to work, the squaws carried their babies, or cabooses, on their back, very much as kangaroos carry their babies on their front, only different.

The Indians were stern, silent people who never showed their feelings, even while being scalped. They crept up on their enemies without breaking a twig and were familiar with all the warpaths. Despite their savage ways, they sincerely loved peace, and were called Nobel Savages.

Nobel savages.

Their favorite word was "How," which the colonists soon learned was not a question.

The whites feared the redskins and considered them the forest's prime evil. Some went so far as to say that "The only good Indian is a wooden Indian." The redskins resented the whiteskins because they thought they had come to take their lands away from them, and their fears were well grounded.

Captain John Smith was the first of a long line of Smiths who came to this country to keep up with the Joneses.

He was captured by the great Indian Chief, Powhatan, and was about to be killed when Popocatepetl, the fiery young daughter of the Chief, stepped in. We are not told what she stepped in, but she saved Captain John Smith's life, for which he thanked her. Later she married an Englishman, which improved relations.

CHAPTER III.

THE PILGRIMS.

THE PILGRIMS were a branch of the Puritans, and were proud of their family tree.[1] They wore tall hats, which they had to

The Low and High Church.

take off when they went inside because they attended a low church. This displeased King James, who raised the roof. He demanded that they attend the same church as he did. At least

---

[1] These, it should be noted, were the first Puritans. The last Puritan was a Spanish nun named Santa Anna.

this is his side of the story, which became known as the King James Version.

Although the King insisted, the Puritans, who were very stiff-necked from years of wearing truffles on their collars, stubbornly declined. They would probably still be declining if they had not left England and gone to Leyden, a city in Holland noted for the discovery of electricity in a jar. (Electricity was subsequently lost for a while, but was rediscovered, by accident, when Benjamin Franklin was told to go fly a kite, and did. See below.)

While in Holland, the Pilgrims suffered from pangs of sin,[1] and sent their children to Dutch Reform Schools when they misbehaved. These children, naturally enough, became Protestants, but their protests were ignored.

THE PLYMOUTH COLONY.

After several years in Holland, the Pilgrims decided to set out for the New World. This decision to move is known as Pilgrims' Progress.

The ship on which they sailed was the *Mayflower*. In stormy weather the women and children descended below the heaving decks, thus becoming the *Mayflower* descendants. There they huddled with the Colonial Dames and other early settlers and passed the weary hours comparing genealogies.

It was a long and perilous voyage across the Atlantic. Several times they were blown off their course. But finally, in 1620, which was a doubly Memorable Year because it was also the year in which they set sail, they sighted the rocky coast. The rock on which they landed they called Plymouth Rock because it reminded them of another rock of the same name in England. They built a small picket fence around it and made it a national shrine.

The first four men ashore became our fourfathers.

THE FIRST WINTER.

After a short stay on Plymouth Rock, which was windy and damp, the Pilgrims sought a more sheltered place to build a

[1] Some years later a man named Sigmund Fraud claimed they enjoyed it.

town. One party went in one direction and one went in another. This was the beginning of the two-party system. When the two parties met, they held the first town meeting.

The first winter was cold,[1] which was a distinct surprise to the Pilgrims. Indeed, they might not have survived but for the corn that was given them by friendly Indians. By a curious quirk of history, it has since become illegal for white men to give Indians either corn or rye.

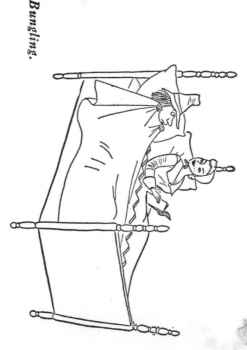

Bungling.

One thing that helped the Pilgrims get through the winter was the economical practice of putting young men and women into bed together, fully clothed. This odd practice, known as bungling, was endured by the young people of the colony until the weather became milder and a sufficient supply of bed-warmers could be imported from England.

The next spring the crops were good, and in the fall the Pilgrims celebrated their first Thanksgiving, which fell, that fall, on a Thursday. The friendly Indians were invited, and the unfriendly Indians stayed in the background, muttering.

[1] Probably responsible for the blue noses which became one of the Pilgrims' outstanding features.

9

CAPTAIN MILES STANDISH.

One of the leaders of the little band [1] at Plymouth was Captain Miles Standish. He was known throughout the township for his courtship.

He was an exceptional man. Except for him, almost all the Pilgrims were named William or John. One of the latter was Miles Standish's friend, quiet John Alden, a man who did not speak for himself until spoken to. He was spoken to, and sharply, by the fair Priscilla, whom he married, much to the annoyance of Miles Standish, who thought he was stood up by his stand-in.

CHAPTER IV.

THE COLONIES GROW.

Let us leave the Pilgrims in Plymouth and see what was happening elsewhere in New England.

Education took a forward step with the founding of Harvard in a yard near the Charles River. Among the early benefactors of Harvard was a plantation owner from the South known as "Cotton" Mather. The first library was only a five-foot shelf, given to the college by T. S. Eliot, a graduate who no longer had need of it. [2] The books on this shelf are known as the Great Books and have grown to one hundred.

With the founding of two other old colleges, Old Eli and Old Nassau, the educational system was complete. Because of the ivory towers which were a distinctive feature of many of the early buildings, the three colleges became known as the Ivory League.

To provide recreational facilities for students at Harvard, the city of Boston was established. Boston became famous for its two famous hills, Beacon and Bunker, its two famous

[1] A precursor of such bandleaders as Paul Whiteman and Benny Goodman.
[2] Having made a fortune in real estate by the sale of wasteland.

churches, North and South, and its two famous bays, Back and Front.

The people of Boston became wealthy by exporting baked beans and codfish, which they were smart enough not to eat themselves. Many, who were pillars of the church and pillars of society, came to be known as Propper Bostonians.

WILLIAMS AND PENN.

One who was unhappy with life in Plymouth was Roger Williams, who thought the Pilgrims were intolerable. The Pilgrims, in turn, thought Williams was impossible. He proposed that they pay the Indians for their land instead of simply taking it from them. This utopian suggestion was dismissed by the Pilgrims as economically unsound.

*Roger Williams'
reluctant departure.*

Because of his unorthodox views, the Pilgrims branded him. They branded him a heretic, and drove him from town to town, although he preferred to walk. This was why Roger Williams reluctantly left Plymouth and founded Rhode Island, which is really not an island and is so small that it is usually indicated on maps by the letters "R.I." out in the Atlantic Ocean. It was once densely wooded. It is now densely populated.[1]

William Penn, on the other hand, came to America to collect some land the King owed his father. He belonged to a frightened religious sect known as the Quakers. So that he would not be

[1] Many, with leftist political leanings, became Rhode Island Reds.

11

forgotten, he gave his name to the Pennsylvania Railroad, the Pennsylvania Station, and the state prison, which is known as the Penn.

MASSACHUSETTS BAY.

The English had always been a seafaring race, ever since they were Danes. Therefore one of their first acts in the New World was to make Massachusetts Bay a colony. From Massachusetts Bay and the nearby bayous they went out in their high-masted vessels looking for whale oil, which they found mostly in whales. The men who went away on voyages to capture whales were called whalers. So, by coincidence, were their sturdy ships. This is more confusing to us now than it was then.

The most famous whale, in those days, was an ill-tempered, unpredictable old whale called Moody Dick. Everyone was on the lookout for him, especially whalers whose legs he had bitten off in one of his nastier moods. The one-legged whaler who was most resentful was Captain A. Hab, who persisted until he finally managed to harpoon Moody Dick where it hurt the most. The whale had the last word, however, for he overturned Captain A. Hab's ship, the *Peapod*, which went down with all hands, including both of Captain A. Hab's.

Thomas Hooker.

12

Fortunately for those who liked to visit New York (see below) but preferred not to live there, Connecticut was founded within commuting distance.

It was founded by Thomas Hooker, a clergyman who, in a dim church, interpreted the Gospel according to his own lights. He would also accept no money for his preaching, which set a low wage standard for others; he was therefore scorned as a free thinker. So he left under a cloud. Many of his parishioners believed his stern words about hell and followed him to Hartford, where he guaranteed them protection in the hereafter and sold them the first fire-insurance policies.

Connecticut is usually spelled Conn, which is easier.

CHAPTER V

LIFE IN OLD NEW ENGLAND.

Most of the Puritans were ministers. Each week they could hardly wait until Sunday, when they preached for several hours on such subjects as "Hellfire" and "Damnation." In those days, church attendance was as good every Sunday as it is today on Easter.

Adulthood in old New England.

13

All of the Puritans, except a few who should never have left England, were opposed to sin. When a woman sinned, they pinned a scarlet letter "A" on her breast, where it would be conspicuous. Women who won their letter year after year were disdainfully called Scarlet, like Scarlet O'Hara and Scarlet Pimpernel. Children were kept in innocence of the meaning of the "A" and thought it stood for "Adulthood," when such things usually happened.

The homes of the Puritans were simple and austere, but their furniture was antique and therefore frightfully expensive. The chairs were as straight and stiff as the Puritans themselves, and had hard bottoms. They became known as period pieces because they went to pieces after a short period of sitting on them. The women had large chests, or collector's items, of which they were extremely proud. Some of these have been handed down from generation to generation and are displayed proudly by their owners today.

Stores were known as Shoppes, or Ye Olde Shoppes. Prices were somewhat higher at the latter.

The Puritans believed in justice. A woman who was a witch, or a man who was a son of a witch, was punished by being stuck in the stocks. These were wooden devices that had holes to put the arms and legs through, and were considered disgraceful. They were also considered uncomfortable.

Every day the men went out into the fields in their blunderbusses and sowed corn. The women, meanwhile, were busy at

Puritan justice.

14

home embroidering the alphabet and the date on a piece of cloth. One of the women, Hester Primmer, one of the New England Primmers, never got beyond the first letter of the alphabet. She also had only one date. That was with a young minister and was enough.

Other amusements were pillories, whipping posts, and Indian massacres.

THE LAND.

The land was stony and hilly, except in places where it was hilly and stony. The stones were useful for making millstones and milestones. The Indians sharpened them and used them for scalping and other social purposes.

The hills were useful to watch for Indians from, unless the Indians were already on them. They were hard to plow up, but they were relatively easy to plow down.

THE CLIMATE.

The winters in New England were long. Largely for this reason, the summers were short. In keeping with the seasons, long underwear was worn in the winter and short underwear in the summer.

CHAPTER VI

THE DUTCH AND THE FRENCH COME TO AMERICA.

Many believed there was a shorter way to get to Asia than around America. Not yet having discovered the Panama Canal, they were looking for the next best thing, which was the Northwest Passage. Since it did not exist, it was, of course, hard to find. Nevertheless many Intrepid Explorers made their reputation hunting for it.

One of those who sought the Northwest Passage was Henry

15

Hudson. In a ship of which he was part owner, called the *Half Mine*, he led a crew of Dutchmen to the mouth of the Hudson River, which he was pleased to find named after himself.

Stopping only to make friends with the Indians and to buy the island of Manhattan from an Indian named Minnehaha (or "Laughing Minnie") for a handful of beads,[1] he pushed on up the river. When he stopped pushing he was in Albany, and he was disappointed. The water was getting shallower and shallower and it was clear. It was clear that this was not the Northwest Passage, and that instead of founding an important route to the Orient, he was about to founder at the state capital. The choice was also clear. He must remain in Albany or make the hard and perilous voyage back across the Atlantic. Without hesitation he chose the latter.

Henry Hudson.

On a second trip to the New World in search of the elusive Passage, Henry Hudson sailed into Hudson Bay. This, again, was not the Northwest Passage, but its name had a familiar ring.

It is not known what became of this Able Navigator who had not been able to find what he was looking for. One theory is that

[1] Beads were then selling at $24 a handful.

16

Hudson met Cadillac and De Soto, and that together they discovered Detroit.

NEW AMSTERDAM.

Because of Henry Hudson's explorations, the Dutch laid claim to the mouth of the Hudson River, which in their systematic way they divided into the North River and the East River. A stubborn race, they named Manhattan New Amsterdam, although it was obviously New York.

Poltroons.

New Amsterdam was soon swarming with wealthy Dutch traitors known as poltroons. These were bluff, hearty men who smoked long pipes and loved to eat burghers. They frequently had their pictures painted, and one of the most picturesque was their Governor, Rip Van Wrinkle, a one-legged gentleman who fell into a deep sleep while watching a bowling game.

The English also claimed Manhattan, in view of the fact that the beads with which it was purchased were plainly stamped "Made in England." The Dutch could not see the merits of their claim, but they could see that the English had more guns on their warships, so they left.

This was a turning point.

The clever English changed the name Amsterdam to **York**, but they retained the New.[1]

[1] The city was later called New York, New York, for the sake of those who did not catch it the first time.

LA SALLE.

The French, although exhausted by the Hundred Years' War, were not too tired to try to establish themselves in the New World. There were still mountains which had not been planted with flags, and there were still rivers that had not been sailed up. So they sailed up them. Many of these still rivers ran deep and led into fastnesses where no white man had ever trod and very few had walked.

At last the only river remaining to be sailed up was the Mississippi. In this instance the French explorer La Salle defied convention. A headstrong young man, he began at the headwaters of the mighty river and sailed down it. He thus not only opened up a vast new territory but discovered an easier means of navigating the rivers of America. La Salle's interesting account of his trip down the river, called *Life on the Mississippi*, is available in an English translation by Mark Twain.

Thanks to La Salle, the Mississippi basin remained in French hands until they grew tired of holding it and sold it for $15,000,000, which many thought was a high price for a second-hand basin.

It is to the French also that we owe the establishment of the beautiful city of Quebec, which was named, according to custom, after the King of France, whose name, according to custom, was Louis (pronounced kwė-bĕk'). The English later

The English dominated the French.

18

seized Quebec and its outskirts, called Canada, from the French, but not without a struggle.

Henceforth the French were dominated by the English, who became our Good Neighbors to the north. We have had amicable relations ever since by agreeing that there are two sides to everything, for example Niagara Falls, which has an American side and a Canadian side.

FIRST TEST.

1. Why do you think Columbus was so interested in traveling to distant places? What else do you know about his home life?

2. Are you really convinced that the world is round? Do you worry much about it?

3. To what extent would the course of American history have been altered if America had never been discovered?

4. What would you say about the Puritans? Would you say the same if they were listening?

5. Can the passengers on the *Mayflower* be considered immigrants? With their strong sense of duty, do you suppose they tried to conceal anything from the customs officials?

6. Have you ever thought how much of a Pilgrim was wasted when an Indian kept only his scalp?

7. Trace on a map the voyages of Henry Hudson. Use a solid line to show where he went and a dotted line to show where he thought he was going. Sign on the dotted line.

8. What would you have done if you had been in La Salle's shoes? How do you know he wore any?

CHAPTER VII

BEGINNINGS OF THE AMERICAN REVOLUTION.

Mosr of the people in the American colonies at this time were English, as were the people in England, who were older because England was the mother country.

As a result of costly wars with the French and Indians, England found herself in need of money. The King, who was George III for a long time, thought of taxing postage stamps used by the colonists. This tax was to be only on outgoing letters, however, and is not to be confused with the income tax, which was a later development.

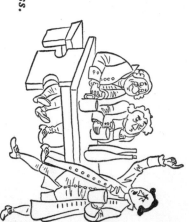

A spirited address.

Nevertheless the colonists objected. They met clandestinely in taverns and made many spirited addresses. Watchwords such as "Death and Taxes" were on every lip, both upper and lower. The colonists were further enraged because, even if they paid taxes on their stamps, they would have no representatives in Parliament, which had only M.P.s.[1] Tempers were at the breaking point. The situation was grave, even serious.

THE BOSTON TEA PARTY.

The colonists, who were now called Americans, which was only fair in view of what the British were being called, tried to

[1] Military Police.

avoid the stamp tax by writing fewer and fewer letters. They became Bad Correspondents. This made the King mad,[1] so mad that he thought up a diabolical scheme of forcing the Americans to drink tea instead of coffee. This led to the first act of violence.

A storm of protest swept Boston. Many Bostonians actually preferred tea, but they objected to being told what to drink, especially by a King three thousand miles away who had never gone to Harvard.

The Boston Tea Party.

A shipload of tea was then in Boston Harbor. This was too much for the good people of Boston. Half a shipload, in fact, would have been sufficient. Disguising themselves as Indians, they crept across Boston Harbor and clambered up the side of the anchored ship. There, armed with knives and war hoops, they quickly subdued the crew and threw tea bag after tea bag into the water. Then they crept back across the harbor and returned to their homes, where they rebelliously drank coffee.

[1] Ironically enough, George III died insane. It is an interesting commentary on American history, not hitherto noted by any historian, that every British sovereign since George III has also died,[2] except the present one.

[2] The sole exception to the historical principle formulated above is King Edward VIII, who not only married an American but, when last seen in New York, was still alive.

The British suspected that the Indians were really Americans, but they could not be sure without seeing the whites of their eyes. The Americans, employing a method of disguise later popular in Hollywood, wore dark glasses.[1]

As coming events were to disclose, this was no mere prank but a Blow for Freedom. Although humorously called the Boston Tea Party, it is more correctly referred to as the Boston Massacre, or, in its abbreviated form, Boston Mass.

The King (who was still George III) stubbornly persisted in his plan to tax the American colonists, whom he considered upstarts, pipsqueaks, and rabble rousers. Since the Americans did not like to be thought of in these terms, they held secret meetings in such unexpected places as Faneuil Hall and the belfry of Old South Church, and thought up one or two terms for the King. A conservative faction was opposed to more than two terms.

One of the most memorable meetings was that known as the First Continental Congress. Among the leaders at this meeting were Samuel and John Adams, who were cousins, and Patrick and Henry, whose last name has been forgotten but who were probably brothers, since everyone was closely related in those days. Sam Adams was born with a silver spoon in his mouth, but once it was removed he became a fine orator. A generous man, he made an Important Contribution.

Patrick and Henry were even more influential. Despite the fact that they had been in business in a country store and had failed, they were highly successful in public affairs. Such success stories came to be a commonplace in the 19th and 20th centuries, owing largely to writings by Ralph Waldorf Emerson and Horatio Algae on behalf of ragged individualism.

Patrick and Henry often arose in meetings, such as the Continental Congress, and spoke as with a single voice. Their speeches were invariably rousing. Once they called the King a

[1] Had the British used similar cunning at Bunker Hill, the course of history might have been altered.

23

Tyrant and a Despot, and were wildly applauded. This was Dangerous Talk. Another time they rose to oratorical heights and delivered a speech that was long remembered, even after the meeting was over. It was the famous Battle Cry of the Republic, reaching its climax in a forthright demand for better clothing for the colonists, "Give us livery, or give us death!" The audience was deeply moved, although some remained in their seats until it was time for the Second Continental Congress, which followed immediately.

The die was cast. The American Revolution would have begun then, but it was not yet 1776.

CHAPTER VIII

THE AMERICAN REVOLUTION.

ONE last effort to avoid the American Revolution was made by a friendly Englishman. He was Edmund Burke, the author of

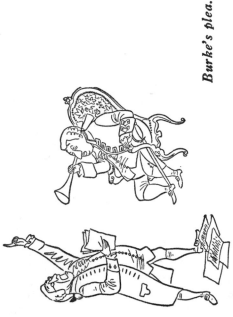

Burke's plea.

Burke's Works. Although he did not believe in giving the colonies their independence, he was in favor of reconciliation.[1]

---

[1] Later called appeasement.

His speeches on behalf of the colonies were so long and loud that they were called oratorios. In one of these, he pleaded with the King to lift the tax burden from the colonists and put it back on the English, who were accustomed to it. But by the time Burke had finished speaking the King was an old man and had become hard of hearing. Thus Burke's plea fell on deaf ears.

CONCORD AND LEXINGTON.

By various means, such as the grapevine, the underground, and the subway, the British learned that the Americans were collecting powder in a room in Concord. A detachment of British soldiers was therefore detached, although not without difficulty, from Boston, and sent with orders to break into the powder room. The whole country was scandalized.

Paul Revere.

Fortunately for the Americans, they had been forewarned. Although hardly a man is now alive who remembers the entire poem that was written about his exploits, Paul Revere got up at midnight and awakened everyone with his cries. He had seen a light in the steeple of Old North Church, and knew at once that the British were coming by land or sea. Accompanied by William Dawes,[1] he carried the news from Boston to Concord

[1] Who, unfortunately, had an inferior press agent and thus did not go down in history.

and from Ghent to Aix. When dawn broke, the countryside swarmed with countrymen.

At Lexington, the British found a little band of Americans playing in the town square and shouted to them to disband. This was the "shout that was heard round the world." Loud as it was, the Americans pretended not to hear, and the British marched on to Concord, still shouting. There they met a larger band of Americans and the same thing happened except that shouts were exchanged, and the rate of exchange was unfavorable to the British, who thought it advisable to return to Boston. As they marched down the road, rolling their drums in front of them, the Americans hid behind trees, bushes, and billboards and derisively shouted "Redcoats" and "Reds" at the British, who were humiliated.

BUNKER HILL.

Smarting under their defeat, the British began a series of intolerable acts. One of these was to quarter [1] colonists who failed to cooperate. Another was to raid military stores, where the thrifty merchants were selling Army surplus.

A Minute Man.

The colonists fought back with muskets (which they kept hanging on the nearest wall), pitchforks (with which they fought pitched battles), and teeth and nails of various sizes. They were always ready to fight within an hour, which is why they were called Minute Men.

[1] The British never did anything by halves.

26

One of the first battles took place at Bunker Hill, where a tall monument afforded an excellent view of Boston and the surrounding countryside. Although the Americans were finally driven from this strategic point, they proved their courage and marksmanship by firing only at the whites of eyes, disdaining any larger target. The British, despite having a superior force of major generals, knew they had met a Worthy Foe.

GEORGE WASHINGTON.

It was time for the colonists to have a leader, and who better than George Washington? He had all the desired qualifications, to wit:

(1) He was widely known, since everyone had seen his picture on stamps and dollar bills.

(2) He was a person of social standing, being a country gentleman with a large estate which was open to the public on Sundays.

(3) He was a man of great physical strength, having chopped down a cherry tree when he was a small boy.

(4) He cared nothing for money, on one occasion having thrown a silver dollar across a river.

(5) His birthday, which would be a holiday if he became famous, came in February, which at that time was badly in need of holidays.[1]

George Washington was therefore chosen to lead the brave but outnumbered colonists. He took command of his forces under a spreading chestnut tree in Cambridge, after which he returned home only long enough to marry Martha Washington and make preparations to become the father of his country.

[1] It was not known then that Lincoln would also be born in February.

FAMILY TREE* OF GEORGE WASHINGTON.

King George (Royal George, or Gorge) = Lady Windermere (Fan)   →A long and distinguished line

Henry George = Single (until married) Tax   S.S. Washington = Takoma (Indian maiden, illegiti-mate daughter of Seattle)

Gilbert = Sullivan   John L. Sullivan

By George **   Lloyd George = Miss Washington Irving   Gilbert Stuart   Parson Weems
(one of the Lloyds of London)   (later Miss America)

George Washington = Martha Custis

D.A.R.   His Country   Republicans, Democrats, etc.

28

* Cherry, of course.
** Said to be founder of Society for Prevention of Calling Pullman Porters George.

CHAPTER IX

THE AMERICAN REVOLUTION (CONTINUED).

THE war that followed divides itself easily into three periods. These are called, for convenience, the First Period, the Second Period, and the Third Period. They should be kept carefully in mind for a clearer understanding of the following events, each of which is bound to fall in one period or another.

SIEGE OF BOSTON.

General Gage and the British were inside the city and wanted to get out. Washington and his men were outside the city and wanted to get in. Both leaders knew this sort of thing could not go on for long. It was a question of nerve. Fortunately for America, General Gage had less than Washington. He soon lost heart, as well as nerve, and sailed for England, which he preferred to Boston anyhow.

CROSSING OF THE DELAWARE.

In order to save British lives, Lord Charles Cornwallis hired several regiments of German Hushians from Germantown. These were quiet, soft-spoken soldiers except when they were roaring drunk, as they were inclined to be at places like Brandywine. With the help of the mercenary Germans, who received pay rather than medals, Cornwallis threw Washington across

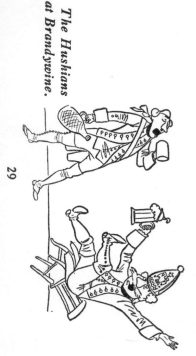

The Hushians at Brandywine.

29

the Delaware River. Washington, however, was not injured, and decided upon a Bold Stroke. Leaving his campfires burning, because he expected to be back shortly, he swiftly recrossed the storm-tossed Delaware in a small boat. Hazardous as it was, Washington stood up during the rough crossing in order that his portrait might be painted by a famous artist in an accompanying boat. Cornwallis could not match Washington; the best English portrait painters were in England, busy painting Lord Nelson, Lady Hamilton, and their Blue Boy.

VALLEY FORGE.

Along with his successes, Washington suffered reverses. Many of the places at which he failed are now commemorated with signs that read, "Washington Slipped Here." His darkest hour, and also his coldest, came at Valley Forge. As he told his friend Tom Paine, who had brought him a new pair of boots, these were the times to try men's soles. For days he trudged about in the snow looking downcast and discouraging his men. Little did he know, because he was several miles inland, that the tide was turning.

A TRAITOR AND A HERO.

Benedict Arnold, though at first thought a well-born American, was ultimately found to be a dastard. He tried to turn West Point, which was then a fort, over to the British. Had he succeeded, he would doubtless have done the same with Annapolis. The plot was discovered, however, when Major John André, the British messenger, stuffed Arnold's message in his boot and developed a limp. André was hanged, and Benedict Arnold took to the high seas and changed his name to Edward Everett Hale, The Man Without a Country.

To vindicate the family name, Nathan Hale, who was on the American side and thus a good spy, went to his death bravely when he was caught by the British. He cheerfully remarked that he wished he could be hanged more often for his country. Benedict Arnold, as we have seen, refused to be hanged even once, which was niggardly and disloyal.

Most of the war was fought on land, but there were a few important battles at sea, owing to demands from the Navy. Chief among our naval heroes was John Paul Jones, who is well remembered. At least he is better remembered than if his name had been merely John Jones. He commanded a stout vessel named the *Bonjour Richard*. It was he who, after his ship was sunk, declared, "I have just begun to fight." He was a brave man, but slow to anger.

*John Paul Jones,
slow to anger.*

FOREIGN AID.

For a time the colonists fought without allies, which was at least better than fighting with them. Foreign shipowners being afraid of England's sea power, almost nothing could be imported in foreign bottoms, and domestic bottoms were all rust and barnacles. The outlook was dim. The issue hung in the balance.

After a while, however, the valiant colonies began to look like a Good Risk, and several first-class powers came to their aid. Had they delayed much longer, America might have won without their help, which would have been embarrassing. Germany sent Baron Steuben and France sent Lafayette. When Lafayette arrived, he declared, "I am here." He did not want to

be overlooked. Poland, having no barons or officers handy, sent Ostroski and Wojukowitz, whose progeny have been distinguishing themselves at left guard [1] and right halfback ever since.

YORKTOWN: THE LAST BATTLE.

Feeling between Cornwallis and Washington had grown tense, and the stage was now set for the final act. This came at Yorktown with the unexpected suddenness which one learns to expect at the end of wars. Cornwallis was hemmed in and was unable to extricate himself. After an agonizing struggle, he gave up like a soldier and gentleman.[2] On hearing the news of the surrender of the British, King George (still the III), who had been half mad for some time, went wholly mad and shouted "Let them eat cake!" Henceforth the British were required to send diplomats to America, when they needed funds, instead of tax collectors.

◆

CHAPTER X.

THE FOUNDING FATHERS.

OUR COUNTRY owes a great deal to its founding fathers. These were a group of parents who were determined that their children should have the advantages which they themselves had been denied. One of these advantages, coveted by children ever since, was the opportunity of going to school, which is why schools all over America are named after one or another of the founding fathers, *viz.*, Thomas Jefferson High School, Alexander Hamilton Grammar School, and P.S. 127.

THOMAS JEFFERSON.

Thomas Jefferson is best known as the author of the Declaration of Independence, which is responsible for two holidays,

[1] Not to be confused with the Old Guard.
[2] Lord Cornwallis, handing his sword to General Washington, is reported to have said, "Good show, old boy." This expression is untranslatable.

July Fourth and Declaration Day. Although he was the author of this important document, he failed to secure a copyright, and it was therefore signed by a great many persons, including Charles Carroll of Carrollton, a high-stepper named Francis Lightfoot Lee, and a slovenly fellow called Unbuttoned Gwinnett, all of whom became known as signers, co-signers, or tangents. These men signed in such space as was left them by John Hancock, who had taken a course in penmanship and was still practicing.

Unbuttoned Gwinnett.

It was also Jefferson, an exceedingly handy man with tools, who framed the Declaration of Independence and hung it on the wall of the Library of Congress, where it may be observed today by those interested in seeing John Hancock's John Hancock.

Jefferson was not only a statesman but an inventor. His many inventions include the dumb-waiter, the decimal system of coinage (enabling us to make change, which is still impossible in England), the swivel chair, the University of Virginia, and the Democratic Party.[1] An extremely versatile person, he was also an architect, thus saving a fee when he built his home.

[1] The Democrats first called themselves Republicans, to distinguish themselves from the Federalists. When the Federalists discovered how successful the Democrats were as Republicans, they decided to become Republicans too. To preserve the two-party system, the original Republicans generously became Democrats, and let the new Republicans have Lincoln, which was a serious error.

More equal than others.

Deeply religious, Jefferson was for a time a minister to France. In his spare time, he was a farmer and an aristocrat.

Jefferson made a great contribution to American political philosophy. He believed that all men are created equal, but that some are created more equal than others.

ALEXANDER HAMILTON.

It is a little-known fact that Alexander Hamilton was born in the West Indies. It is also of little importance. Hamilton became known as the best Secretary of the Treasury until Andrew Mellon. Both he and Mellon, it should be noted, were helped by the fact that the country enjoyed good times during their terms of office. This is always a good thing for a Secretary of the Treasury.

Hamilton, a reactionary, was opposed to debt. In order to pay the costs of the war against the British, he established a mint. It was the sale of mint, for mint juleps, to army officers from the South, that put the new government on its feet and removed a good many Southern colonels from theirs. Hamilton also instituted a system of taxes, which the people of America accepted willingly as soon as Hamilton assured them he was not British.

Because he was a Federalist and Jefferson was a Republican (Democrat), Hamilton and Jefferson never saw eye to eye, which caused considerable strain. Hamilton supported the

34

businessman and Jefferson supported the farmer. This was generous of them, but they were both well able to afford it.

Just before the end of his life, Hamilton engaged in a duel with Aaron Burr, a disappointed presidential candidate who never got beyond the vice-presidency. It is not known whether Burr shot (1) straighter or (2) sooner, but (3) he was declared the winner, and Hamilton, his time being up, (4) expired. One of the unanswered questions of history is why the ambitious Burr shot Hamilton instead of Jefferson, which would have given him the presidency. It would, however, have established a bad precedent for vice-presidents.

BENJAMIN FRANKLIN.

As a boy, Benjamin Franklin helped his father make candles, which were thought to look more romantic than electric lights. Later his father apprenticed him to a printer, and Benjamin became a printer's devil, much to the printer's dismay.

He was self-educated, which means that he was too poor to go to school and therefore got a good education.

When he was twelve, Benjamin became so interested in reading that he gave up eating in order to buy books. A few months later, his appetite getting the better of him, he ran away to Philadelphia, where he sold his books and thereafter walked around with an enormous loaf of bread under each arm.

In between trips to the bakery, young Franklin was hard at work flying kites, putting up lightning rods, discovering electricity, and thinking up wise sayings like "A penny saved is the best policy" and "Early to bed and early to rise keeps the dark circles from under your eyes." These sayings he contributed to *Poor Richard's Almanack*, which published them because he was the owner. He printed this periodical by hand, since he could never learn to do it with his feet.

Franklin was a plump, well-rounded man who invented almost as many things as Jefferson, including silkworms, whisk brooms, the Franklin stove, and bifocals. As Postmaster General, he instituted general delivery, and also established the dead-letter office, a place for keeping letters from people who

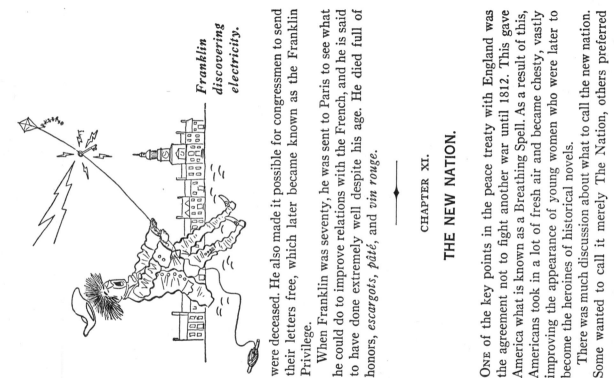

Franklin discovering electricity.

were deceased. He also made it possible for congressmen to send their letters free, which later became known as the Franklin Privilege.

When Franklin was seventy, he was sent to Paris to see what he could do to improve relations with the French, and he is said to have done extremely well despite his age. He died full of honors, *escargots*, *pâté*, and *vin rouge*.

CHAPTER XI.

THE NEW NATION.

ONE of the key points in the peace treaty with England was the agreement not to fight another war until 1812. This gave America what is known as a Breathing Spell. As a result of this, Americans took in a lot of fresh air and became chesty, vastly improving the appearance of young women who were later to become the heroines of historical novels.

There was much discussion about what to call the new nation. Some wanted to call it merely The Nation, others preferred

the New Republic. Those who believed in States' Rights insisted on the United States. Those who supported Labor wanted it called the Union. It was finally decided, as the result of what is known as the XYZ Affair, to call it the U.S.A., the U.S., or, when one is abroad, The States. The U.S.A. was the first of a long series of alphabetical agencies which reached an impasse in the time of F.D.R., when the alphabet was exhausted.

THE FLAG.

The first flag of the United States was made by Betsy Ross, assisted by Molly Pitcher (a little woman who had big ears), Barbara Frietchie, and other members of the Philadelphia Sewing Circle. In the original flag there were thirteen stars, but since many persons were superstitious, more stars were quickly added.

THE CONSTITUTION.

The thrifty English had an unwritten constitution, which saved them a large printing bill. But the Americans decided to write theirs out in order to have something for the Supreme Court to interpret.

The Constitution provided for the following:

1. Two houses, a lower and an upper, with a stairway, or escalator clause, between. Bills, which were afterwards to be sent to taxpayers for collection, would first be thrown into a large hopper and allowed to age. Members of the lower house were to be elected according to population—that is, according to whether enough of the population voted for them. Members of the upper house were to represent the states instead of the people. To get into the upper house, it was necessary to have:

   (*a*) A broad-brimmed hat
   (*b*) A flowing bow tie
   (*c*) A good name
   (*d*) A key or a ladder

2. Congressional immunity: a special health program under which senators were inoculated against lawsuits.

3. A system of checks and balances, which led to the national debt.

4. Committees: smaller groups which killed bills, tabled proposals, played poker, and generally ran things.

THE FIRST AND SECOND PRESIDENTS.

George Washington was the first president. He might have stayed in office for life, but he wanted to get out for some fresh air.[1] Furthermore, he had prepared an eloquent farewell address, which he was impatient to deliver.

He was followed, at a respectful distance, by John Adams. Although Adams was the second president, he was the first vice-president, and this was some consolation.

THE NEW CAPITAL.

The capital (which is spelled capitol when it is the building and not the city or vice versa) was first New York City, but since all of the presidents came from Virginia, commuting was a problem. It was therefore moved to Washington, which

[1] He also wanted to go back to the farm. In this, Washington set a precedent. Almost every figure in American public life has expressed a desire to go back to the farm, even when he didn't come from one.

Adams followed Washington.

was called Washington, D.C., to differentiate it from Washington, George.

CHAPTER XII.

DIFFICULTIES OF THE NEW GOVERNMENT.

In its first years, the United States was visited by trials and tribulations. United in war, the new nation was now torn by dissension and tormented by doubt. The Minute Men had grown old, and were taking longer. The Navy consisted chiefly of the Ship of State, which many considered unseaworthy. As if all this were not bad enough, our presidents failed to measure up to Washington, who was a very tall man.

ALIEN AND SEDUCTION ACTS.

Among the ill-advised laws passed by the new government were the Alien and Seduction Acts, which gave foreigners the choice of either ceasing their acts of seduction or becoming citizens. These laws were soon repealed, however, when it was found that seduction was also practiced by native-born citizens.

39

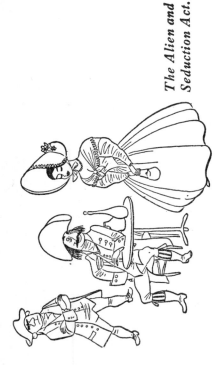

The Alien and Seduction Act.

WHISKY REBELLION.

Another unwise act was perpetrated when the government sent its officials to collect a tax from farmers who were allowing their grain to stand in the fields until it spoiled and turned into whisky. Since it was hard to reach the outlying farms, owing to unpaved roads, this was called the Exercise Tax. The farmers objected to paying such a tax and said they would drink their own whisky first, which some of them courageously did. The entire country was in a ferment. A force of militiamen [1] was sent against the rebellious farmers, who sobered up when they saw they were outnumbered. The whisky was seized by the Federalists. This practice of taking over spoiled grain, known as the Spoils System, lost the Federalists the farm vote at the next election, as well as the support of the WCTU, which believed that confiscated whisky should be poured down the drain instead of down the hatch.

INDECISION.

Unable to wait for the next war with the United States, England was at this time at war with France, which was closer anyhow. The United States considered entering the war also, but could not decide which country would win. Throughout the

[1] Soldiers who had taken the Pledge.

40

war it remained undecided, or neutral, and looked around for a smaller country to fight.

WAR WITH TRIPOLI.

This opportunity came unexpectedly when a band of Barbarian Pirates, or Coarse Hairs, seized one of our ships and took it into the port of Tripoli, one of the Barbarian States in North Africa. The Bad Shaw of Tripoli, insulted by the smallness of the bribe he was offered, declared war on the United States. The United States was in turn insulted, thinking that it should have been permitted to declare war first.

In the war that followed, none of the admirals received as much publicity as Lieutenant Stephen Decatur, who daringly rowed into the harbor of Tripoli and afterwards rowed out again, despite the fact that the Coarse Hairs had batteries all along the shore and turned the current against him. This heroic exploit did not end the war, however, which dragged on until we finally made a Bold Move. We caught the enemy by surprise, on the shores of Tripoli, by making a landing with our Marines, who came on the run from the halls of Montezuma.

The Bad Shaw declared war.

SECOND TEST.

1. Which of these was most unbearable to the colonists:

   (*a*) Taxes?

   (*b*) Tea?

   (*c*) Letter writing?

2. Was King George resentful because he was always third?

3. Why was the year 1776 chosen for the Revolution? Were there any other good years along about then?

4. Look into the mirror. Examine the whites of *your* eyes. What if the Redcoats at Bunker Hill had been suffering from pinkeye?

5. Write a brief essay of twenty-five words or less on "I like George Washington because. . ." Your answer should be accompanied by twenty-five cents and a box top.

6. How would you have dealt with Aaron Burr if you were no better a shot than Alexander Hamilton?

7. Name three inventions which Jefferson and Franklin overlooked. Explain why.

8. Come to some sort of a conclusion.

EXPANSION.

ALL this time the population was growing. People were getting larger and larger. Crowded conditions in the Eastern part of the United States, or the East Side, were becoming intolerable. At first people in the East refused to go West, but as the population continued to grow, they finally came to their census. Before long many farmers, who had heard about the fertile lands to the west (or to the left, if a map is being used), shouldered their hoes and set forth, shouting their stirring cry, "Westward Hoes!" A few people from Massachusetts joined the westward movement, but because of their Boston accent they had difficulty making themselves understood west of the Hudson River.[1]

LOUISIANA PURCHASE.

West of the Atlantic seaboard and from Canada to the Gulf of Mexico stretched a vast territory that was owned by a wealthy Frenchman named Napoleon. Even without stretching, it was a large area. It was heavily wooded, having been seeded by the King of Spain some years before.

An inexpensive way of exporting American products from the interior was to send them down the Mississippi River on rafts, riffrafts, log jams, and showboats, piloted by such experienced rivermen as Mark Twain, Mark Time, Mark Hopkins (on one end of a log), Huckleberry Finn, Mickey Finn, and Old Man River. The French controlled New Orleans, however, and thus were able to bottle up the Mississippi, which they did and sold to American tourists.

This situation could not continue. The United States therefore asked Napoleon if he would sell New Orleans, bottling works and all. To everyone's surprise, Napoleon, who was in financial straits because of the lavish tomb he was building

[1] Their broad "A" is not to be confused with the Scarlet Letter.

himself in Paris, accepted the offer and threw in the environs (see Mississippi Basin, above), which stretched northward to Canada and included East St. Louis.

LEWIS N. CLARK.

The region west of the Mississippi was a trackless wilderness, and without tracks railroads were useless. Transportation was therefore extremely slow. To open up this new country and to find such states as Oregon and Washington, which were thought to be out there somewhere, a brave young explorer named Lewis N. Clark was told to go west, which he did.[1]

Lewis N. Clark.

Lewis N. Clark was a trail blazer and a path breaker and a very good man in the bush because he never got poison ivy. He carried beads to give to the Indians, who sewed them on bookmarks, handbags, and watch fobs to sell to tourists at Albuquerque.[2]

Starting from St. Louis, Lewis N. Clark went northwestward until he found the headwaters of the Missouri, and thence to the

[1] The person who told him was probably Horace Greeley, who sent many young men West to die with their boots on. Mr. Greeley died in the East, in bed.

[2] A city in New Mexico, whose name the Indians avoided spelling by refusing to learn to write.

44

mouth of the Columbia River, where he spent a trying winter. Mostly he was trying to keep warm. The next spring, secure in the knowledge that he was the first white man to reach the Pacific Ocean by the land route, he turned his face homeward. On the way east he saw many huge herds of bison, which he mistakenly called buffalo. But for this error, one of our noted plainsmen (see below) would be known as Bison Bill.

CHAPTER XIV.

THE WAR OF 1812.

A SENSIBLY NAMED war was the War of 1812, the date of which can easily be remembered by anyone who can remember its name. The chief causes of the war were the following:

1. The British were then fighting against Napoleon (who had not as yet met his Waterloo at Waterloo) and would not allow our ships to enter French ports. They established blockheads, or port authorities, to see that this edict was enforced.

2. The British claimed the right to search American ships

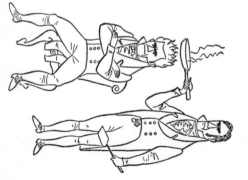

Hotheads.

45

and take from them any British sailors born on board. Sometimes they took American sailors also, and occasionally the British Americans were flattered, or impressed, into helping the British sail their ships.

3. Hotheads like John C. Calhoun and Henry Clay held a war party, at which they entertained all the congressmen and played war games. By the time a considerable amount of firewater had been consumed, there was hardly a cool head left in the government.

NAVAL BATTLES.

The War of 1812 was fought mostly at sea. One of our greatest victories was when the warship *Constitution*, captained by the immortal Barnacle Bill, thundered volley after volley at the British fleet. One of the British ships, a frigid named the *Derrière*,[1] was quickly sent to the bottom. Another victory occurred when Commodore Perry, on his way back from discovering the North Pole, swept the British from Lake Erie. The place has been kept tidy ever since.

BURNING OF WASHINGTON.

A dastardly act of the British was their landing soldiers on the shores of Chesapeake Bay without warning, and then proceeding to burn Washington. Fortunately Dolly Madison, the mistress of the White House, was a woman of great strength and presence of mind. She carried off everything of value, including the Declaration of Independence, the Mint, and the Washington Monument. After the British had gone, she returned everything to its place,[2] thus establishing herself as the most honest public servant until Lincoln.

THE BOMBARDMENT OF FORT MC HENRY.

In an attempt to take Baltimore, the British attacked Fort McHenry, which protected the harbor. Bombs were soon burst-

[1] Which shot only grapes.
[2] See Webster's definition of *dolly*: "a small wheeled truck for moving heavy beams, columns, etc."

46

ing in air, rockets were glaring, and all in all it was a moment of great historical interest. During the bombardment, a young lawyer named Francis Off Key wrote "The Star-Spangled Banner," and when, by the dawn's early light, the British heard it sung, they fled in terror.

Dolly Madison.

THE BATTLE OF NEW ORLEANS.

General Andrew Jackson, who was on his way to Florida for the winter, heard that the British were going to New Orleans to force their way into the Mardi Gras, to which they had not been invited. After days of hard riding, he reached the city, where he immediately threw up redoubts. Feeling somewhat better, he awaited the British attack. According to custom, the British advanced in a solid line, which our marksmen soon perforated, turned back, and folded under.

Jackson won a great victory and thereby became presidential timber, or Old Hickory. Little did he know that the war had already been over for two weeks and that it was no longer 1812, but 1815.

CHAPTER XV.

PRESIDENT MONROE.

JAMES MONROE came from Virginia, the mother of presidents. Little is known of his father, except that he was devoted to Virginia.

Monroe's presidency was a period of much political strife, when everyone enjoyed being angry at everyone else. It was therefore known as the Era of Good Feeling. The Federalists, however, took a dim view of things. In fact they felt so low about losing the election to Monroe that they went underground. Despite a thorough search, no trace has ever been found of them.

The only war at this time was a halfhearted one called the Semi-No War. It came about when General Andrew Jackson chased some Florida Indians into the Everglades, which was their last resort. He also proved to the King of Spain that Florida was not only indefensible but worthless. The King sold it to the United States for a good price and celebrated his shrewd sale by firing a great number of cannons. The noise was deafening and gave rise to the expression, "boom prices."

It was during Monroe's presidency that the Cumberland Road

Jackson chased the Florida Indians.

48

was built to make it easier to get to Ohio and Illinois. When completed, it was found equally useful in getting *from* Ohio and Illinois, with the result that some weird types began to show up on Broadway and along 42d Street.

MISSOURI COMPROMISE.

Missouri felt left out of things and wanted to join the Union. But it was a slave state (where slaves had to be bought), and was opposed by the free states (where slaves were given away to anyone who wanted them). About the same time, Maine also wanted to join the Union, in order to get Union wages, and of course the slave states objected. This knotty problem was resolved by letting both Missouri and Maine into the Union, thereby making an equal number of persons angry on both sides. This was called the Missouri Compromise and was considered extremely clever by those who thought it up.

MONROE DOCTRINE.

Monroe is best remembered for the Monroe Doctrine. This was fair warning to European nations not to establish any more colonies in America. The United States in turn promised that its colonies in Europe, such as the American colony on the Left Bank, would not make any more trouble.

The chief purpose of the Monroe Doctrine was to protect the new republics in South America from Spain. Shortly afterwards these republics decided they wanted to be protected from the United States.

CHAPTER XVI.

THE SECOND ADAMS.

JOHN QUINCY ADAMS was the second Adams to become president. He is not to be confused with his father, John Adams, who was the first Adams but the second president, or with his Uncle

Sam Adams (who was not the real Uncle Sam, except to his nieces and nephews).[1] It was fortunate for us, if not for the second John Adams, that he had the Quincy, which the first John did not.

THE EERIE CANAL.

It was at this time that the Governor of New York, a man of action known as "Do It" Clinton, made a momentous decision. He decided to build a canal from Lake Eerie to the Hudson River in order to bring together the waters of the Great Lakes and the Atlantic Ocean, which he thought should never have

A large floating population.

been separated. People laughed at him and called the canal "Clinton's Big Ditch" and "Do It's Folly," but he lived to laugh at those who laughed at him, and the canal was built. Before long, people from Detroit and Cleveland came barging into New York City, which has had a large floating population ever since.

STEAMSHIPS AND RAILROAD TRAINS.

Steam had already been invented by James What, an inquisitive and observant young fellow who noticed it coming out of a teakettle. By putting two and two and a number of teakettles together, he found he could not only make more tea but press clothes and unseal envelopes.

[1] It becomes all the more confusing when we consider the various Madams Adams.

Transportation was revolutionized by Robert Fulton, who built the first steamboat, and Casey Jones, who invented the steam locomotive. The latter invention led to a number of significant developments that profoundly affected life in America. Chief among these were:

1. Cinders.
2. Windows that could be opened only by someone else.
3. Timetables, with asterisks, daggers, and "Sundays only" in very small type.
4. Railroad tracks, which people lived on the right or wrong side of.

CHAPTER XVII.

ANDREW JACKSON SPOILS THE SYSTEM.

ANDREW JACKSON was a popular president. He swore he would shake hands with everyone in town and kept his promise. This delayed the business of his administration for several weeks, until they could take off the bandages. One of the first things President Jackson did, after flexing his fingers, was to reward those who had cast more than one ballot for him by appointing

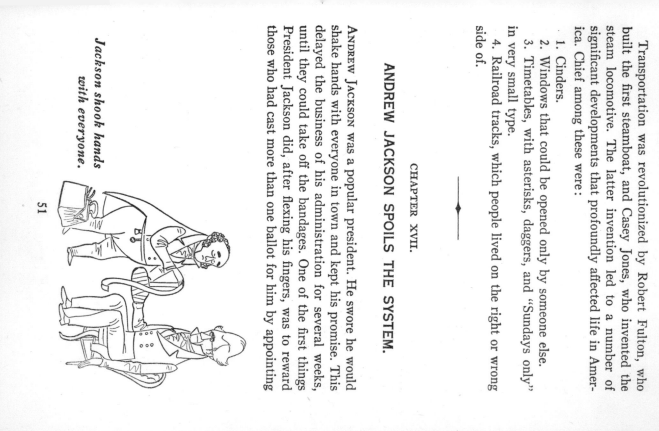

Jackson shook hands with everyone.

them postmasters, judges, generals, and garbage collectors. It was in this last connection that one of his friends made the famous remark, "To the victors belong the spoils."

Trouble was caused by South Carolina, an agricultural state, that raised cane over some of Jackson's laws that favored manufacturing states. When South Carolina demanded nullification of these laws, on the grounds that there were enough states already without manufacturing any more, Jackson threatened nullification of South Carolina.

Although nullification was finally nullified, Jackson handled this and other cases so highhandedly that his enemies nicknamed him King Andrew the First, and many wanted to crown him. His friends, however, hailed him as the Great Democrat. This was called an Honest Difference of Opinion.

FURTHER ACCOMPLISHMENTS OF JACKSON.

Jackson is best remembered for having founded the Democratic Party and the Jackson Day Dinner. The latter is a meal where plates are sold for as much as a hundred dollars apiece and are still not supposed to be taken home. The Jackson Day Dinner has grown to be so expensive that only Republicans can afford it.

CHAPTER XVIII.

THE BEGINNINGS OF INDUSTRY.

THUS FAR, although people were industrious, there was little industry in America. Smokestacks rarely belched. In cities like Pittsburgh and St. Louis the air was so free of smoke that many persons grew impatient at the lack of progress and disgustedly said they might as well move back to the country. This dearth of industry was largely caused by:

1. A shortage of captains of industry, it being the age of private enterprise.

2. A feeling on the part of some that it was morally wrong to invent things. These persons were mindful of the Biblical saying, "Hell is paved with good inventions."

3. Opposition to change by those who wanted to stop where they were and preferred the *status whoa.*

COTTON GIN.

Industry was furthered at this time by a graduate of Yale, "Old Eli" Whitney. Cotton was causing trouble because it was full of little seeds that had to be picked out by hand, one at a time. Whitney invented a long stick for knocking the seeds out of cotton two or more at a time. This practice came to be known as cotton batting. The far-reaching consequences of progress were immediately apparent: many cottonseed pickers gained additional leisure by being thrown out of work. Whitney also invented a stimulating drink called cotton gin, which enabled one man to do the work of fifty.

THE REAPER.

In the early days, grain was cut with a scythe or sickle by a sickley old man who carried around an hourglass so that he would know when it was quitting time. He was called the Grim Reaper. This slow procedure was speeded up by Cyrus McCormick, familiarly known as Jack the Reaper, who developed a machine with a belt conveyer, which conveyed belts throughout the Middle West and was responsible for establishing the Corn Belt and the Bible Belt.

THE SEWING MACHINE.

Howe, like What, the inventor of the teakettle (see above), was exceedingly curious. He was destined to succeed, because as a young man he lived in a garret. It came to him, in a flash of inspiration, that if McCormick could make a machine that would reap, he should be able to make one that would sew. The only question was Howe, and he answered that for himself.

53

THE TELEGRAPH.

Communication was improved by S. O. S. Morse, who invented the telegraph and organized the first union of telegraph operators in the West, known as the Western Union. He also developed the secret code that bears his name. Morse's first message on the telegraph was the reverent question, "What hath God wrought?" which is Morse code for "Don't write, telegraph."

CHAPTER XIX

HARD TIMES.

WHEN Martin Van Buren became president, he found government positions for all his supporters. This led to a Great Depression on the part of those who had not supported him. Van Buren was not reelected, but his campaign was so hilarious that he was popularly acclaimed the Panic of 1837.

HARRISON AND TYLER.

Many thought Henry Clay should be the next president, especially the Wigs, a group of bald-headed men who admired his fine head of air. But others felt that Clay, who had said in a speech, "I know no North, no South, no East, no West," was too ignorant to hold such a high office. When he further said, "I would rather be right than be President," the country took him at his word.

William Henry Harrison, who was more careful about stating his preferences, was elected president to succeed Van Buren. John Tyler was elected vice-president on the same ticket. (The ticket read, "Admit W. H. Harrison and Friend.") Their opponents tried desperately to defeat them by circulating a cartoon showing two men in a boat. Underneath the cartoon was the caption, "Tip the canoe and Tyler too."

Harrison was the first president to die in office. He had been

Clay's fine head of hair.

in his office for thirty days, working on new tariff laws, and probably overtaxed himself.

DANIEL WEBSTER.

A famous statesman and orator at this time was Daniel Webster. When he was on the Dartmouth College debating team, he spoke against the best-known debaters of the country, including the Devil, who represented Harvard. The trophies he won for debating are kept in the Dartmouth College Case. Although he was admitted to the bar when he was only nineteen, he never overindulged.

Webster was famous for using long words that other people could not spell, and therefore is said to have held his audiences spellbound. As he talked, his cousin Noah took these words down and eventually published them in a large volume called *Webster's Dictionary*.

CHAPTER XX

THE WINNING OF TEXAS.

THE FRONTIER continued to move westward. Many adventurous persons, not wishing to be left behind, moved along with it. Some went by the Sante Fe, which at that time was only a trail, and had no diner. Some, who followed the inland waterways, used prairie schooners. There were many dangerous characters abroad, and not a few in our own country. Cardsharps and outcasts from places like Poker Flat were always ready to get up a game in a Canasta wagon.

KIT CARSON.

Kit Carson was one of the famous frontiersmen of his day. He was also a backwoodsman. For this reason he is said to have known the West backwoods and forewoods. As a young man, he was a scout; as a boy, he was a boy scout. The daring deeds of Kit Carson are in no way minimized in a book about them which was written by Kit Carson.

DAVY CROCKETT.

Another of the famed frontiersmen was Davy Crockett. He early proved his prowess with a rifle by shooting matches, which

Davy Crockett.

were too small a target for most of the sharpshooters of the day. His favorite costume was a coonskin cap and a buckskin jacket. It is assumed that he wore trousers of some sort, although they are never mentioned. After many exploits in Tennessee, he went on to Texas, which welcomed men of his caliber (.45). He wound up in the Alamo.

THE ALAMO.

Texas was then a part of Mexico because of Spain. Mexico had thrown off the Spanish yoke a few years earlier, but Texas was still wearing the Mexican yoke. Because this was before Theodore Roosevelt (see below), America was not yet an Imperialist Nation.

Americans living in Texas disagreed with the Mexicans who lived there; and Mexicans, and especially Mexican food,[1] disagreed with the Americans.

Finally the Americans declared that Texas was no longer a part of Mexico, and a small body of Americans moved into a landmark called the Alamo and waited to be outnumbered.[2] They were soon accommodated by a huge army of Mexican generals, who killed the defenders of the Alamo to the last man, whom they also killed.

The triumph of the Mexicans was short-lived, as also were many of the Mexican generals. If they expected the Americans to forget all about the Alamo, they were wrong. By saying "Remember the Alamo" over and over, especially just before going to sleep, the Americans were able to remember the name of the place for weeks and weeks. Later they remembered the Maine and after that Pearl Harbor.

SAM HOUSTON.

The leader of Texas's fight for independence was Sam Houston. He was in a class by himself, having gone to a small country school. When Texas became a republic, he was its first president.

[1] Notably Mexican jumping beans, which refused to stay down.
[2] Being outnumbered is a requirement for going down in history, or even for going down.

dent, and when Texas joined the Union [1] he became a senator. In Washington, he was feared and respected by his fellow senators, possibly because he always carried a knife. They addressed him as "the distinguished Senator from Texas." He referred to them as "You-all."

WAR WITH MEXICO.

A dispute arose over the boundary between Texas and Mexico. The Americans thought that South of the Border was too far north, and the Mexicans did not like the way the Americans took the final "e" off the Rio Grande. There was a clash

General Infield Scott driving to Mexico City.

of arms. And then legs. War was on. Three of our finest leaders were the great generals Zachary Taylor, Old Rough, and Ready, who joined forces to defeat the Mexicans at Buenas Noches. General Infield Scott, who liked to fight up close, then drove all the way to Mexico City. This, considering the condition of Mexican roads, was such an impressive feat that the Mexicans were glad to sue for peace. The United States won the suit and was awarded California, Nevada, Utah, and a number of other states that were badly needed to fill up the map.

[1] Or, from the point of view of Texans, when the Union joined Texas.

CHAPTER XXI

THE WINNING OF CALIFORNIA.

CALIFORNIA was discovered by John C. Frémont. This was thought unnecessary by the Mexicans and the Indians who were living there at the time, but they could not speak English and so did not count. On his way to California, Frémont followed the north fork of the Platte, which was just above the south fork. He endured terrible hardships, including the failure of many persons to put the accent in his name, even though he reminded them repeatedly. On one occasion his food supply ran so low that he was forced to eat his own horse, from which he first dismounted. Altogether he traveled six thousand miles, partly on horseback and partly on a full stomach.

Frémont discovering California.

THE GOLD RUSH.

More important than the discovery of California was the discovery of gold, a soft metal which nevertheless comes in for some hard use. Gold was discovered in a sawmill belonging to a Mr. Sutter. Since it interfered with the operation of the saw, it was removed as quickly as possible.

Thanks to clear atmospheric conditions, the cry, "Gold!

Gold!" was heard across the country. The Forty Niners, a group of forty-nine unkempt old men who chewed tobacco and never shaved, were among the first to arrive. Others were not far behind, including O. Henry, O. Susanna, and Mother Lode. They came by the thousands, and also by the Horn, which was several months slower. With them they brought picks, shovels, and a generous supply of stakes with which to stake claims. Because their wagons were so full of household goods, they carried their banjos on their knees.

Gold was mostly found in creek beds and was removed in bedpans. Since it was necessary to squat while at work, many of the miners were called squatters.

LIFE IN OLD CALIFORNIA.

Californians who were unsuccessful in finding gold went into other enterprises. Some went into business. Some went into professions. Almost everyone went into saloons. There were no lawyers, since people took the law into their own hands.

Because of lust for gold, morals reached a low point, known as the gold standard. No respectable woman would be seen in a music hall, and very few respectable women were seen anywhere, except young schoolteachers who had recently come from the East and still had a lot to learn. Card players, who

The Quick and the Dead.

60

played for high stakes and sometimes for money, had a nervous habit of shooting each other over trivial matters, such as almost invisible marks on cards or one or two extra aces in a deck. Persons who pulled their pistols out of their holsters first were known as the Quick; the others were the Dead.

CHAPTER XXII

THE WINNING OF OREGON.

OREGON was discovered when someone followed the Oregon Trail right out to the end.

Early settlers in Oregon were mostly fur traders looking for beaver hats. These they obtained by swapping sticks, or trading posts. One of the leading traders was John Jacob Astor, a wealthy New York hotel man who wished to take furs back to Lady Astor so that she could keep up with the Vanderbilts.

The journey over the Oregon Trail took several months. The plains were crossed in wagon trains or caravans, and the streams were crossed in Fords. At night the wagons were lined up around a hollow square. The women and children were put in the square, and the men, who were known as "square shooters," shot off Indians as they rode around and on their horses. The Indians who had not been shot off, rode off. Crossing the desert was especially hazardous because of mirages, which were

Trading posts.

61

pools of water caused by thirst. The early travelers were slow to realize that the water in these pools was not good for drinking.

TROUBLE WITH THE BRITISH.

The British were in possession of most of Oregon and scornfully referred to the American fur traders as "furriners." The Americans offered to buy Oregon for $54.40, but the British considered this a disgracefully low figure, and wanted more latitude. This, however, was the Americans' last offer, and they said, "Fifty-four forty or fight." Rather than risk another war, the British let Oregon go for this price and withdrew across the Canadian border, taking their customs with them. Owing to American enterprise, the population doubled in a short time, which was the reason for cities like Walla Walla.

CHAPTER XXIII

THE MORMONS.

THE MORMONS are a group of people who became saints later than others and are thus known as Later-day Saints. Because their customs were different, they were forced to move from place to place. For settlers, this was an unsettling experience.

Bigamy Young.

But cheerfully, they pushed their handcarts over the mountains, thus becoming known as Good-humor Men.

They finally took over Utah and the Great Salt Lake, which no one else wanted. This was called the Mormon Conquest.

Their leader in the early days in Utah was Bigamy Young. When he arrived in Salt Lake City he said to his followers, "This is the place," although he had never been there before. It was uncanny.

Under Young's leadership, the Mormons prospered. They were industrious, thrifty folk, and good at arithmetic and keeping accounts, as for instance the number of their cattle, sheep, and wives. They multiplied rapidly. The women who objected to plural marriages were considered singular.

The Mormons are credited with having made the desert bloom, which it continues to do each spring.

CHAPTER XXIV

FOUR PRESIDENTS.

ALL this while there were several presidents, one at a time. Being small men, they stood on platforms to make themselves look bigger. These were built by party hacks, who made use of such devices as old saws and the rank and file. In order to be elected it was necessary to make campaign promises, which had to be kept for the duration of the campaign. Upon election, it was the custom to swear oaths. These were listened to without flinching by the Chief Justice of the Supreme Court, who was considered a good judge of such things.

JOHN TYLER.

As we have seen, John Tyler was in the tippy canoe with Harrison, and paddled to office up the Potomac. He was the first vice-president to become president through the death of a president, which was a good thing for him but a bad thing for Harrison.

63

Although he was elected to office as a Wig, the Wigs later disowned him because he insisted on wearing his own hair. For a time he was a man without a party, which annoyed his wife, who loved to entertain.

It was during Tyler's presidency that China opened its doors to American traders, with the proviso that they take off their shoes before coming inside. This led to friendly relations with the Chinese, who came to the United States in large numbers to open laundries and restaurants and to teach young Americans to play "Chopsticks" on the piano.

JAMES K. POLK.

Polk was the first president to enter the race as a dark horse. Only after he had won the race and was installed in the White House was it discovered that he was actually a horse of another color. He was forgiven for this deception, but never became popular.[1]

Much trouble was caused during Polk's term by the Free Soilers, a group of unreasonable men who wanted to get everything dirty and refused to pay their laundry bills. On the other hand, progress was made by the invention of the Rotary printing press. This went around and around and preceded by several years the next development in this field, the Kiwanis.

ZACHARY TAYLOR.

Owing to his defeat of the Mexicans at Buenas Noches, General Taylor became a national hero. It turned out to be only a step from Buenas Noches to the presidency, and the General took this in his stride.

General Taylor is remembered as the only president who ever rode a horse up the steps of the Capitol. Eminent historians agree that he was probably the only president who ever wanted to. At any rate, it is fortunate for the custodians of the building that this bad precedent has not been followed.

[1] He redeemed himself slightly by introducing the folk dance that bears his name, the Polka.

One of the most important pieces of legislation during Taylor's term was the Omnibus Bill, introduced by Henry Clay. This would have provided omnibuses in California, Utah, New Mexico, and Texas, which were large territories and badly in need of transportation. Taylor opposed the Omnibus Bill, however, because he thought it would mean the end of the horse. He was not sure which end, but he had always been a horse lover.[1]

It was also while Taylor was president that the Department of the Inferior was created to improve conditions among the underprivileged third of the nation.

After a brief period in office, Zachary Taylor died with his boots on, but in bed.

MILLARD FILLMORE.

Millard Fillmore inherited the presidency from Zachary Taylor. This was discovered when Taylor's will was read.

*Commodore Perry
opens up Japan.*

Fillmore achieved a certain amount of distinction by the Compromise of 1850, in which he gave away a little to the North and a little to the South. The possessor of a keen his-

[1] Cf. Taylor's classical expression, "Equus vincit omnibus."

torical sense, Fillmore was saving the Civil War for Lincoln, who could handle it.

A significant development at this time was Commodore Perry's expedition to open up Japan so that Americans could see what was inside.[1] They were startled to discover that it was teeming with Japanese, who enjoyed a high birth rate.

Perry's opening of Japan caused many Japanese to come out where they could see the rising sun. As a result of this, Japan soon developed modern methods. (See Pearl Harbor, below.)

[1] This was later viewed with alarm by a funereal-looking newspaperman named William Randolph Hearse. He wrote so much about the Yellow Peril that his journalism took its distinctive coloration from the subject.

THIRD TEST.

Some of these statements are either true or false. Indicate which ones are neither.

1. Napoleon sold Louisiana because he knew he could not compete with Huey Long.

2. If the British owned Oregon today, and it were worth $54.40, what would they receive for it, net? (Hint: Convert the price into sterling at $2.80 to the pound, then deduct British income tax at the rate of 9 shillings 6 pence to the pound, and you'll find it a lot easier to move on to the next question.)

3. You can reach the high notes in "The Star-Spangled Banner" by standing on tiptoe.

4. Dolly Madison was stronger than Dolly Varden.

5. The Morse code is so profane that it is necessary to resort to dashes.

6. Housewives in early California were constantly annoyed by the gold dust.

7. No one ever traveled east on the Oregon Trail because it was longer that way.

8. The Alamo is easier to remember than Polk, Tyler, or Fillmore.

CHAPTER XXV

THE SLAVERY QUESTION.

THE QUESTION that was most often asked at this time was the slavery question. It was hardly ever answered. John C. Calhoun, a champion of the Southern cause, asked the question more often than anyone else in the South. William Lloyd Garrison, a champion of the Northern cause, out-asked everyone in the North. Calhoun thought slavery was a good thing. Garrison, on the other hand, was an Abolitionist. He wanted to do away with slaves—a bloodthirsty proposal that made the kindly Southern plantation owners shudder.

H. B. STOWE.

The slavery question would probably have remained a question had it not been for Harriet Beechnut Stowe, a self-reliant, determined woman who lived with her Uncle Tom in a humble cabin. At first she was only mildly against slavery, and called it a Little Evil, but later she changed her mind because of an unpleasant experience with a planter named Slimy Legree, who pursued her across the ice while she was carrying Topsy. Despite her condition, she managed to get away by jumping from one piece of ice to another faster than her pursuer.[1] This left her terribly cold toward Legree and all he stood for. As a result, she wrote a famous book praising the Negro, called *Black Beauty*, that incited people in the North to acts of violence, including setting fire to slave-owners' barns.

The slavery question then became a Burning Issue.

THE UNDERGROUND RAILROAD.

Slaves were sold in the South by being auctioned off. Entire city squares, called auction blocks, were devoted to these sales. Buyers often felt slaves' muscles to see whether they would be good workers. They also looked at their teeth, in case they were to be used for plowing.

[1] While she was slowed down by Topsy, Legree was slightly tipsy.

As if they were their own children.

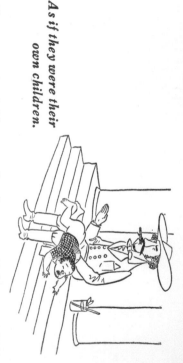

Slaves were treated by many Southerners as if they were their own children, and yet some of them ungratefully ran away. For this purpose the slaves cleverly built an underground railway all the way to Canada. Trains (including the extra-fare *Dixie Fl'yer*) left almost daily from tracks on the lower level called the Deep South. Slaves usually bought a one-way ticket.

THE DREAD SCOTT DECISION.

The Dread Scott Decision was one that frightened everybody. It decided that a slave who lived in a free state was free to be a slave, but would be happier if he lived in a slave state where slavery was appreciated. This was not only frightening but confusing. Even the Supreme Court was forced to admit it had no jurisdiction, which meant that it was unable to figure it out. As might be imagined, everyone was in a state.

JOHN BROWN.

John Brown was a brave but foolhardy man (*i.e.*, a Fanatic) who tried to seize arms from Northerners and give them to slaves. The Northerners were willing to give him a hand, but thought this was going too far. So they hanged poor John Brown and left his body on Harper's Ferry, where it lay moldering until the passengers complained. War was in the air.

69

PRESIDENTS PIERCE AND BUCHANAN.

MANY PERSONS have difficulty remembering what President Franklin Pierce is best remembered for, and he is therefore probably best forgotten.

President James Buchanan is known as The Only President Who Never Married, and thus has become extremely useful in quizzes and crossword puzzles. An important event of his administration was the establishment of the pony express, which made it possible to ship ponies anywhere in the United States as long as they were securely wrapped.

The Pony Express.

The Civil War was ready to begin during Buchanan's term, but everyone thought it better to wait until Lincoln so that it could begin and end under the same president.

ABRAHAM LINCOLN.

ABRAHAM LINCOLN was the Man of the Hour. In those days this was almost as important as being Man of the Year or Book of the Month.

During his youth he lived in several different log cabins, a style of architecture favored by his father. He was born in only two of them, the Original and the Reconstructed.

Young Abe loved to read. Since he had no library card, he had difficulty borrowing books and obtaining advice about what to read. On one occasion he walked many miles to get Blackstone's commentaries. Blackstone apparently suggested the Bible, from which Lincoln copied out favorite passages with a piece of charcoal on a shingle and thus evolved a simple, if rather wooden, style. Lincoln always read lying on his stomach in front of an open fireplace. Thus he developed an insatiable curiosity and a sacroiliac condition.

Lincoln became known as Honest Abe when he was working as a clerk in a store. Once he walked three miles to return six cents to a woman. When he told the woman he had overcharged her, she was surprised and said, "Honest, Abe?" The name followed him through life, and often caught up with him.

Renowned for his feats of strength, Lincoln was of great use to the early railroads. A champion rail-splitter, he was able to split a rail with one blow of his ax, thus making two tracks out of it.[1]

Lincoln had one term in Congress and then ran for the Senate because, as he said in a famous speech, "The House is divided against itself and cannot stand." He wanted to get out before the roof caved in.

As president, Lincoln was always traveling about the country to meet people and to sign commissions which were kept in attics until the value of Lincoln's signature went up. It was difficult to get his mail to him because of his many addresses, such as the First Inaugural, the Second Inaugural, and the Gettysburg. This latter he jotted down on the back of an envelope instead of the front, but it came through all right.[2]

Lincoln is now popularly known for being "heads" when one is matching pennies.

---

[1] Lincoln's ability as a rail-splitter later proved useful in politics. Most of his opponents, considerably weaker men, were hair-splitters.

[2] The Post Office Department was then at the peak of its efficiency.

CHAPTER XXVIII.

THE CIVIL WAR.

War finally broke out when some of the Southern states decided to secede. It was their firm belief that nothing succeeds like secession. They named Jeff Davis their president and raised their own flag, it being possible to raise almost anything in the fertile soil of the South.

Lincoln, who was a kindly man, insisted that if there had to be a war it should at least be fought as decently as possible. It was therefore spoken of as the Civil War. It was fought between the boys in blue (who wore Union suits) and the boys in gray, although most of the boys were old enough to have whiskers and did.

The battle cries of the two forces were "On to Washington" and "On to Richmond." Each was after the other's capital, and the North, being industrial, had more capital than the South. If the North had permitted the South to take Washington and the South had permitted the North to take Richmond, the war might have been won by both sides and everyone would have been happy. Apparently the opposing generals did not take this under serious consideration.

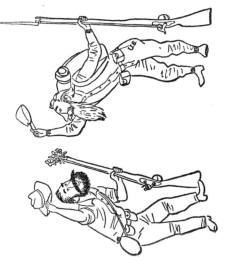

The Civil War.

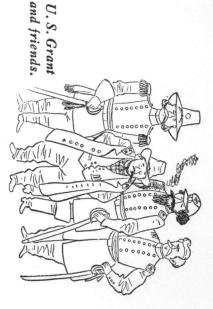

U. S. Grant and friends.

GRANT AND LEE.

The greatest general of the North was U. S. Grant, who is not to be confused with U. S. Mail or U. S. Steel. In a picture of the Northern generals, all of whom have identical untidy black whiskers, he is usually the one in the center with his coat unbuttoned. Grant was the victim of repeated attacks. After one of these he took Vicksburg, which had a tonic effect.

The Southern leader was Robert E. Lee, who had better manners but fewer soldiers than Grant. Promotion was slow in his army, and most of his high-ranking officers never became more than Lee's lieutenants. To distinguish him when he is in a picture with Grant, Lee is the one with the white whiskers sitting on Traveller, who was a horse. After the war, Lee bought a half interest in Washington and Lee University in nearby Virginia.

OTHER GENERALS.

Two of the leading generals of the North were Sheridan and Sherman. Sheridan is known for his famous Ride and Sherman for his famous March, which is noteworthy because it lasted well into December. Some of Sherman's exploits are almost unbelievable. We are told that he cut a path sixty miles wide through the South, although this was surely wider than neces-

sary. He also sacked Atlanta, after which he carried it all the way to the sea.

Lee's most able general (or lieutenant) was Stonewall Jackson. When Jackson died, it is said that Lee lost his right arm, which made it difficult for him to hold the reins.

Most of the other generals were named Johnston.

FAMOUS BATTLES.

The first great battle of the Civil War was fought in a cow pasture and was known as Bull Run. The battle was such a success that it was repeated by popular request.

The other important battles were all fought at some burg or other, such as Petersburg, Fredericksburg, Gettysburg, and Williamsburg. Williamsburg was so badly damaged that it had to be restored.[1] The most decisive of these battles was Gettysburg, where the Confederates, who by this time were low on ammunition, swept up the hill with sharpened stakes in what was called Pickets Charge.

At sea, meanwhile, there was a famous engagement between two "ironclads," the *Christian Science Monitor* and the *Merrimac*. Since neither could sink the other, and they could not wait to see which one would rust first, they agreed to call it a draw.

SURRENDER.

The end came in a memorable action at Appomattox Court House, where Grant, who was more experienced at the bar, won a clear-cut decision. This brought tears to the eyes of Lee's soldiers, and they were overcome. Lee then gave his sword to Grant, but Grant gave it back to him, since he already had one. Jefferson Davis joined the ranks of the unemployed.

[1] The Rockefellers paid for this, even though they had not been responsible for the damage.

MID-TERM PROJECTS (OPTIONAL).

1. Read one other book about the Civil War. This will make you a specialist.

2. Split a rail in remembrance of Abe Lincoln. If this is too difficult, lie on the floor in front of an open fireplace. If you have no fireplace and happen to work behind a cash register, shortchange your next customer and then follow him for six miles through a raging blizzard to see that he gets what's coming to him.

3. Draw detailed maps of the following:
  (*a*) Sheridan's Ride
  (*b*) Lee's Surrender
  (*c*) Grant's Tomb

4. Prepare a thirty-minute talk on the Siege of Richmond. Then find someone who will listen to it.

5. Visit the chapel at Washington and Lee University and look at the mounted skeleton of Traveller. If you were a college, couldn't you think of a more appropriate way to dispose of a dead horse?

CHAPTER XXIX

RECONSTRUCTION.

AFTER the Civil War, the South was swept by a wave of carpet-beggars who went from door to door begging carpets from the poor Southerners, many of whom did not even have floors. They were told to come back after the Reconstruction.

Carpetbeggars and Ku Klux Klan.

The carpetbeggars were especially disliked by the Ku Klux Klan, a group of Southerners who had nothing to wear but sheets with holes in them [1] and always looked as if they had just come from a Halloween party. It was these Klux who introduced phonetic spelling and gave us such words as Kleenex, Krispies, and Krazy Kat.

PRESIDENTS JOHNSON AND GRANT.

Reconstruction was begun by President Johnson and completed by President Grant, who financed it by selling copies of his two-volume *Memoirs* to everyone in America.

MONEY TROUBLES.

During Grant's administration a good deal of trouble was caused by money, which people had previously considered

[1] Thus they became known as "poor whites."

man's best friend. Outstanding troubles were the following:

1. *Black Friday.* This was due to Jay Gould, who wanted to buy up every bit of money and make the United States go on the Gould standard. He was assisted in this nefarious plan by an ex-slave called Black Friday, who was always leaving foot-prints in unexpected places. It was because of Friday that Gould was finally tracked down.

2. *Specie Payments.* The origin of the Specie is attributed to Darwin. It is often called Hard Money, as opposed to Easy Money. In order to make hard money easier, bits of specie were buried in government vaults until they mildewed and became greenbacks.

3. *Silver Act.* This was one of Grant's unwisest acts. It was put over by the hard-money people, who considered gold too soft and thought it should be made harder by adding bits of silver.[1]

WHISKY RING.

One of the things that caused Grant's cabinet a great deal of trouble was the way a whisky glass, when set down on it, would leave a ring. Although Grant tried his best to cover it with whitewash, the Whisky Ring still showed through. This finally forced Grant to leave the White House in disgrace.

CHAPTER XXX.

THE WILD WEST.

WHILE the rest of the country was being reconstructed, the West was still being constructed for the first time, and there was a great deal of wild life everywhere, especially in the towns. Men were men and women were women, and this simple ar-

[1] The only good that came of this was the popular song, "Silver Threads Among the Gold."

rangement proved quite satisfactory. Men who were in business together called each other "podner."

Life was hard in the Great Plains region. On the one hand there were the badmen, or Desperate Characters, like the James brothers, William and Henry. They held up stagecoaches, thus making them late, and withdrew other people's money from banks. On the other hand there were the Indians, like Geronimo and Sitting Bull, stubborn chieftains who claimed the Indians were there first and refused to budge.

BUFFALO BILL AND OTHERS.

Fortunately there were half a dozen crack shots,[1] known as the Six Shooters, on the side of law and order. One of these

General Custer (right) vs. Crazy Quilt.

was Wild Bill Hiccup, a man of few words, such as "Reach" and "Now git." He is said never to have killed a man except in self-defense, but he was defending himself almost constantly. Another was Buffalo Bill, a sharpshooter who had poison ivy on his hands and thus was bothered by an itching

[1] Able to shoot through narrow cracks and knotholes. To be distinguished from crackpots.

trigger finger. In his later years Buffalo Bill went into the circus business and shot it out with Annie Oakley.

CUSTER'S LAST STAND.

The badmen were usually defeated by the goodmen and the redmen by the whitemen, but occasionally there was a temporary setback. This was permanent in the case of Custer, who bravely stood up in plain sight and fought against all sorts of odds, including an Indian named Crazy Quilt. His last stand was at a place of uncertain size called Little Big Horn.

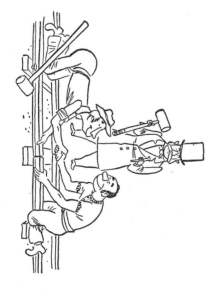

Without overlapping.

THE HOMESTEAD LAW.

To induce people to leave the East and face the hazards of life in states like Oklahoma, the government passed the Homestead Law. This gave everyone free land, provided he would guarantee to stay alive on it a certain length of time.[1] The Homesteaders lined up in their covered wagons and buggies at the state boundary and at a given signal were off on a race for choice lands. The best land seemed to be on top of a high mountain called Pikes Peak (or Bust), which rapidly became overpopulated. Those who could find no room there settled in

[1] See Edgar Guest's "It takes a heap o' livin' on to make a house a homestead."

79

Oklahoma and worked diligently to turn its rich land into the Dust Bowl.[1]

TRANSCONTINENTAL RAILROAD.

A great stride was taken in the development of the West when a railroad was finally built all the way across the country. This railroad was begun at both ends and came together, without overlapping, somewhere in Utah. To celebrate this instance of making ends meet, the two parts were fastened together with a gold spike, and the wilderness was no longer trackless.

[1] Oklahoma's answer to California's Rose Bowl.

CHAPTER XXXI

FROM HAYES TO HARRISON.

THE PRESIDENTS in this period are difficult to tell apart, even though their parents gave them first names like Rutherford, Chester, and Grover to make it easier. To add to the confusion, Grover Cleveland was elected twice, with one president in between, which was constitutional but highly irregular.

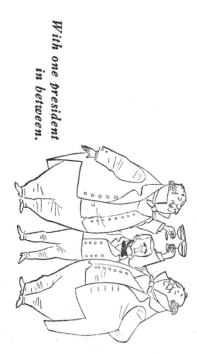

With one president in between.

Another thing that makes the presidents at this time hard to distinguish is that they were not very distinguished; so if some of them get mislaid here, it is a safe assumption that they will never be missed.

GROVER CLEVELAND.

As a politician, Cleveland made his name in Buffalo. Unlike Chester A. Arthur, who became honest after becoming president, Cleveland started earlier. When he ran for governor of New York, he said he was an "unowned candidate." This proved quite upsetting to the members of Tammany Hall, who thought he said he was an "unknown candidate," which would have been all right.

Cleveland was elected president as a Democrat with the help of the Mugwumps, a group of uncertain Republicans who, as

we have often been told, sat with their mugs on one side of the fence and their wumps on the other. In some cases it was hard to tell which was which.

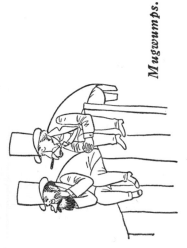

Mugwumps.

As soon as he became president, Cleveland instituted a number of reforms, the first of which was to remove Republicans from office. This was a distinct surprise to them, because for years they had thought, as they put it, that "public office is a Republican trust."

The Republicans still caused trouble, however, because they had won most of the seats in Congress and the Democrats were forced to stand.

BENJAMIN HARRISON.

Harrison is best remembered because he is the president who was sandwiched in between Cleveland's first term and second term. With Cleveland both over and under him in the list of presidents, his place in history is secure and he is not likely to move an inch.[1]

[1] The reader may be interested to know that President Benjamin Harrison was the grandson of President William Henry Harrison. And then again he may not.

CHAPTER XXXII

THE AGE OF INDUSTRY.

New factories began springing up everywhere. Articles that had formerly been made by hand were now made by machines, although a few continued to be handmade, with irregularities and imperfections, for the lucky persons who could afford them. In addition to factories, there were numerous sweatshops. These were rooms in overheated homes, where women and small children worked long hours so that the man of the house could maintain his credit at the corner saloon. Sometimes the golden-haired daughter would go to the saloon and beg her dear father to come home with her, which he often would do in order to beat up his family. This was called Intemperance and was frowned on.

Intemperance.

IMMIGRATION.

People came from all over the world to work in American factories, standing in long assembly lines to seek employment. When they left their home country, they were called "emigrants," but this was Anglicized to "immigrants" when they reached the Land of Opportunity, as the United States was called on maps printed in Europe.

Before being permitted to work in American factories, immigrants had their foreign customs removed by customs officials

and were thoroughly cleaned in what was called a melting pot. Those who could stand the intense heat were considered ready for the sweatshops.

LABOR UNREST.

In the early days [1] a laborer sometimes worked twelve or fourteen hours. He had little time for sleep, and this unfortunate situation became known as Labor Unrest. Workingmen decided to strike (a blow for freedom) and thus, unwittingly, started the Industrial Revolution.

In order to help the laborers strike better, or at least to strike the right people, Samuel Gompers organized the American Federation of Labor. Members of the AFL carried cards and thus were always able to get up a game when not working. [2]

The greatest contribution made by labor was the ingenious reform of the calendar, resulting in the eight-hour day and the five-day week.

CHAPTER XXXIII.

CAPTAINS OF INDUSTRY.

THIS was a period of great opportunities for enterprising young men. Most of the factories were one-story buildings, so it was easy to get in on the ground floor. As soon as additional stories were built, those who had started at the bottom worked their way up.

CORNELIUS VANDERBILT.

Vanderbilt made his money in ships. Thus, while others became captains of industry, he became a commodore. He also

[1] The early days were so called because the workingman had to get up at five o'clock.
[2] They also carried signs, reading "Unfair," to keep from getting struck themselves.

bought up railroads so that he could always be sure of getting a lower berth. His control of carts and cartels gave him a virtual monopoly of transportation. One of his favorite expressions, which endeared him to everyone, was "The public be damned."

ANDREW CARNEGIE.

Carnegie made his money in steel. Although he was a mild, soft-spoken man, his steel had quite a temper. Most of it was made in open hearths, then fashionable in the better homes of Pittsburgh. Thanks largely to Carnegie's efforts, steel rapidly came to replace wood in almost everything but trees.

In a short while Carnegie, who had come to this country as a poor boy from Scotland, amassed such wealth that he was loved by everyone. He was especially popular because of his determination to give away all his money before he died.[1] In order to succeed in this, he was forced to retire early, since he was making money faster than he could give it away. He is best remembered for having given away libraries, with his name on them, in which everyone was asked to be quiet out of respect for the donor. Carnegie was so well known for his philanthropy that he became an Institution.

JOHN D. ROCKEFELLER.

Rockefeller made his money in oil, which he discovered at the bottom of wells. Oil was crude in those days, but so was Rockefeller. Now both are considered quite refined.

Almost everyone called Rockefeller "John D." A few called him something else, but not to his face. He was admired for his skill in a game called Monopoly, which was an effective way of eliminating competitors and establishing a single standard, such as Standard Oil.

Rockefeller's huge fortune seemed even larger than it was because he kept it in dimes.

[1] See his book on giving away money, *How to Win Friends and Influence People.*

J. P. MORGAN.

Morgan, who was a direct sort of person, made his money in money. He lived in an airy mansion, full of bank drafts, called the House of Morgan. One of the gayest persons in the house was Helen Morgan, who sat on top of the piano when she sang.

An ingenious invention of Morgan's was a means of floating government loans which made it possible to send large sums of money across the Atlantic without using ships. He became immensely wealthy because of his financial interests, most of which were around eight or ten per cent. This Morgan is usually spoken of as "J.P." to distinguish him from Henry Morgan, the pirate.

HENRY FORD.

Henry Ford manufactured one of the early automobiles, known as the Model T. This led to such modern conveniences as traffic signals, parking meters, back-seat drivers, and carbon monoxide. In time it came to replace the horse for almost all purposes except horse racing and horsemeat. An idealist and a dreamer, this great inventor dreamed of two cars in every garage—both of them Fords. Henry Ford was fond of saying, "History is bunk." Historians, in turn, called Henry Ford "a damned old crankshaft."

CHAPTER XXXIV.

NEW INVENTIONS.

Inventions were necessary at this time so that factories would have something to manufacture. Before an invention could be invented, however, four things were required:

1. Necessity, the mother of inventions.
2. An inventor, the father of inventions.
3. A basement, back room, or small shed, where the birth of the invention could take place.
4. A patent, or birth certificate.[1]

THE ELECTRIC LIGHT.

The man who was first with almost all the new inventions was Thomas ("Alpha") Edison. He is best remembered for having been thrown off a train for inventing things in the baggage car when he should have been selling newspapers. He lit on his head and became so deaf that he was unable to hear discouraging remarks and soon became successful.

Since Edison suffered from insomnia, he invented the electric light, so that he could read at night. He had to sweat it out, and this led him to make his famous remark: "Genius is about 2 per cent inspiration and 98 per cent perspiration."

THE TELEPHONE.

The telephone was invented by Alexander Graham Bell, after whom the telephone bell is named. He was also responsible for the telephone exchange, where old phones could be traded in for French models. Other outgrowths of the telephone include the telephone booth, in which one has the choice of light or air, and the telephone book, a large volume that permits almost everyone to see his name in print.

The telephone revolutionized American life and introduced such improvements as the party line, the wrong number, the busy signal, and the long distance.

[1] Important patents included patent leather and patent medicine.

THE RADIO.

We are indebted for the radio to an Italian by the name of Macaroni. An inconspicuous person, he was not recognized in his native land and was forced to make his career in England and the United States.

The radio is also called the wireless, especially in England. This is because, although there are a great many wires in it, there are less than there might be. The great improvement of the radio over the telephone is that it may be turned off without offending the speaker.

THE AIRPLANE.

The airplane was invented by the Wright brothers and a girl friend named Kitty Hawk. They were at first thought crazy, which assured them of ultimate success. The airplane revolutionized transportation, making it possible to cross the United States in a few hours and crash almost anywhere.

At first they were thought crazy.

CHAPTER XXXV.

PRESIDENT MCKINLEY.

THE ELECTION of 1896 was one of the most stirring in American history. Sediment ran high. McKinley ran on the Republican

The Vested Interests.

ticket and Bryan, who had the wind but not the legs, ran on the Democratic ticket. One of the important issues in the election was gold versus silver. Bryan was for silver, and talked about it so much that he was said to have a silver tongue.

On the other hand, McKinley was for gold, which gained him the backing of a group of well-dressed financiers known as the Vested Interests. He conducted a front-porch campaign (Bryan meanwhile skulking around in the back), and was assisted by a bossy woman always referred to simply as Hannah. The election was finally won by McKinley, but Bryan was not discouraged. He ran in several more presidential races until Clarence Darrow finally made a monkey out of him in Tennessee.

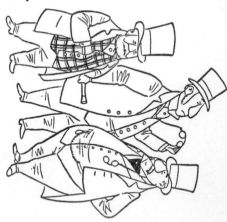

THE BOXER REBELLION.

One of the disturbing events of McKinley's administration was the Boxer Rebellion. This occurred when Chinese prize fighters thought they were being treated unfairly by foreign referees, such as an Irishman by the name of Hoyle, whom everything was always according to, and that notorious rake, the Marquis of Queensberry. After a good deal of unpleasantness, the matter was settled amicably by giving the boxers

scholarships to study the rules of the ring at American universities.

CHAPTER XXXVI

THE SPANISH-AMERICAN WAR.

THE SPANISH-AMERICAN WAR, which occurred at the turn of the century,[1] was caused by Cuba. The United States wanted Cuba free [2] but Spain would not even sell it. It was thought that if Cuba could throw off the Spanish yoke, which increased the overhead, Havana tobacco would be less expensive. And it was widely believed that what this country needed was a good five-cent cigar.

So much to remember.

Conditions became tense when the battleship *Maine*, which was in Havana Harbor, exploded and sank to the bottom. Americans resented this, because they recalled the old saying. "As the *Maine* goes, so goes the nation." All over the country, citizens, so goes the nation." All over the country, citi-

[1] The turn of the century encompasses the period from 1875 to 1925. The nineteenth century turned very slowly.

[2] Whence the name of the popular drink of that day, the *Cuba Libre*.

zens who had been busy remembering the Alamo were now asked to remember the *Maine*. With so much to remember, nerves were on edge and war was inevitable.

The first blow was struck in Manila Bay, where the American fleet was stationed to protect our interest in Manila envelopes and other indispensable commodities. The fleet was under the command of Commodore Dewey, who cleverly sailed up behind the Spanish ships and for this exploit was made a rear admiral. A considerate commander, his immortal words on this occasion were, "You may fire when ready, Gridley." Unfortunately for the Spanish fleet, Gridley was ready.

On land, meanwhile, the Americans won a great victory when Colonel Roosevelt's Rough Riders, a band of cavalrymen who were hard on their clothes and easy on their horses, crawled up San Wan Hill on their stomachs. Their mounts were therefore fresh when they reached the top, and they were able to dash down again in fine style.

The United States did not get Cuba out of the Spanish-American War, but it got Puerto Rico, the Philippines, Guam, Typhoid, and Malaria. These were considered sufficient to make her a world power and only one or two possessions short of imperialistic.

FOURTH TEST.

1. How would you confuse

   (*a*) Black Friday and Blue Monday?

   (*b*) The James brothers?

2. Discuss the following terms :

   (*a*) Greenbacks

   (*b*) Whitewash

   (*c*) Blackmail

3. How many pear-shaped vowels do you find in the word "Mugwump"? Do you still like pears?

4. Complete the quotation, "Where men were men and women were ———."

5. Do you think any of the present-day wonder drugs would have helped Buffalo Bill's itching trigger finger?

6. Estimate the relative temperature of

   (*a*) Sweatshops

   (*b*) Turkish baths

7. Why on earth did Rockefeller want so much money?

8. List five situations in which it would have heen better if the electric light had not been invented.

CHAPTER XXXVII

THEODORE ROOSEVELT.

THEODORE ROOSEVELT was one of our best-known presidents, being known as T. R., Teddy, and Not Franklin. He was an Oyster Bay Roosevelt, which is one of the two principal varieties.

As a boy, Roosevelt was weak and sickly, but he built himself up by boxing and taking exercises with dumbbells in a gymnasium. Gradually he became more and more robust, despite several years at Harvard. He liked the out-of-doors, and bought a large amount of it on a ranch in North Dakota, the acquisition of which he modestly described as "The Winning of the West."

Roosevelt grew so muscular that the politicians deemed it wise to put him on a shelf in the vice-presidency, where they thought he would be safe, not knowing that McKinley was so close to being shot.

When Roosevelt got down from the shelf and moved into the White House, the United States was at peace. The former Rough Rider found this intolerably dull and decided to make war on someone. The British, Japanese, Germans, Canadians, Russians, and Venezuelans were all considered. In a final act of desperation, Roosevelt sent the American fleet around the world

T. R. looks for a war.

93

looking for a suitable enemy. Unable to find one, he was forced to accept the Nobel Peace Prize as a consolation.

Roosevelt was known as a man of unquenchable energy. He paid little attention to rank, money, and social position, perhaps because he had so much of all three. He was deeply interested in nature, which he tried to conserve. He did this by collecting such natural resources as butterflies and birds, which he thought were being wasted. At the same time he was violently opposed to Big Business, then busily engaged in collecting money, Trusts, and other unnatural things. As might be expected, Roosevelt was greatly annoyed when the Trusts sneeringly referred to him as "Buster."

At the conclusion of his term, Roosevelt went West to find his successor and picked a hearty, pioneer type named William Howard Taft. This done, he went off to Darkest Africa where, despite the poor light, he bagged many magnificent specimens and brought them home for zoos and museums. One specimen of which he was especially proud was the bull moose, which he captured by speaking softly and then hitting it on the head with a big stick.

THE MUCKRAKERS.

The Muckrakers were exceedingly fond of muck, which they raked up into large piles and gazed at admiringly.

One of the leading muckrakers was Upton Sinclair, who raked up a huge pile in South Chicago. While raking, Sinclair could not help noticing the terrible conditions in the nearby stockyards, where innocent cattle were being driven to slaughter instead of being coaxed. He wrote a book about this called *The Jungle*, which was read by President Roosevelt, who thought it was about Africa. Roosevelt was indignant when he read about the treatment being given these poor animals, and introduced a law providing that they should be killed only by sportsmen wearing pith helmets.

A lady muckraker named Carrie Nation was responsible for legislation that required printing the alcoholic content on the label so that sick people would know whether they were getting

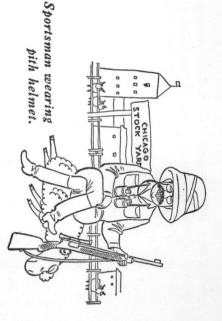

Sportsman wearing pith helmet.

enough alcohol to do them any good. Soon afterwards came the Poor Food and Drug Act. This made it mandatory for manufacturers to tell whether their product was a poor food or a drug so that the consumer would know whether to keep it in the kitchen or in the bathroom.

THE PANAMA CANAL.

The Panama Canal was built to make it possible for the Atlantic and Pacific Oceans to come together without having to go clear around South America. Digging was begun under Roosevelt (but, luckily, not directly under him), and was finished several presidents later. For a time work was delayed by mosquitoes, which the workmen were kept busy slapping with their shovels. Science came to the rescue when the bothersome insects were injected with yellow fever and died like flies.

CHAPTER XXXVIII.

TAFT.

The next president is chiefly remembered for his size. He was about as big around as two ordinary men, and was fortunately

named both William and Howard. His great hunger (and wealth) led him to demand steaks for breakfast.[1] Since he was too large for most chairs, he spent most of his life on the bench. Roosevelt leaned heavily on him when he was in his cabinet, but Taft was very good-natured about it.

Fortunately named both William and Howard.

DOLLAR DIPLOMACY.

Because of his long years on the bench, Taft was no longer a young man when he finally got into the game. Once in, however, he made his weight felt. His policy of dollar diplomacy, *i.e.,* hiring dollar-a-year men, was considered a master stroke of economy.

THE PROGRESSIVES.

When Taft ran for reelection, the Republican Party was unable to get anywhere. It had been bolted by the Progressives,[2] under a pugnacious chap with a fine head of hair named "Fighting Bob" La Follicle.

Taft tried to keep in the middle of the road and succeeded. He was run over by the Democratic machine.

[1] Thus becoming widely known as the Autocrat of the Breakfast Table.
[2] Laborers very handy with a wrench.

96

CHAPTER XXXIX

WILSON.

WOODROW WILSON is the president who is usually pictured sitting in the back of an open car with a top hat and an overcoat on. The man sitting next to him is the head of some European government who also wears a top hat and would wear an overcoat if he had one. A Princeton man, Wilson was known as The Scholar President, and even after he got to the White House he was always in a brown study.

FINANCIAL REFORM.

Money continued to be badly distributed, and the demand was greater than even the counterfeiters could satisfy. Conditions were somewhat improved by establishment of the following:

1. *Federal Reserve System.* This involved the printing of Federal notes, which the government generously sent to banks all over the country to save them the expense of printing their own.

2. *Income Tax.* The income tax came into being with passage of the Underwood Act (sometimes referred to as the Underhand Act). People were put into tax brackets where they were held securely until they gave up. Most of them gave up plenty.[1]

MEXICAN BORDER WAR.

An obscure little war took place at this time with Mexico. As a matter of fact it only bordered on war, whence it derived its name. It was caused when a fat fellow named Pauncho Villa and his followers, known as the Four Horsemen of Acapulco, made daring raids into United States territory and breathed garlic into the faces of the terrified citizenry. President Wilson sent General Pershing (familiarly known as Blackjack because of his fondness for licorice chewing gum) down to capture

[1] Other taxes included sails taxes, aimed principally at yachtsmen, and hidden taxes, which were ashamed to come out in the open.

Villa. But Villa eluded his pursuers by hiding behind mesquite, mesquitoes, mustachios, and other features of the rugged Mexican terrain. All the Americans got out of the war was calluses, which the infantry and cavalry got in different places.

Pauncho Villa breathing garlic.

CHAPTER XL

WORLD WAR I.

WORLD WAR I was fought to make the world safe for the Democrats. There are different theories regarding its cause.[1] It is variously attributed to:

1. The fact that Germany wanted a place in the sun and was determined to take the French Riviera.

2. The Balkan powder keg, which was set off by a guy named Guy Fawkes who mistook the lower part of Europe for the lower house of Parliament.

3. The mistaken belief of Kaiser Wilhelm that the English would not fight against him because he was related to Queen Victoria.

4. A serious shortage of paper, which made a mere scrap of it worth fighting for.

[1] Any three of these constitute the Triple Intent.

The United States at first kept out of the war. President Wilson wrote numerous notes to the Kaiser, asking him to stop fighting. The Kaiser either ignored them or boorishly replied in German, which he thought Wilson could not read. Moreover he played Havoc (a German game) with American shipping, even though he soon ran through his first-string submarines and was down to his U-boats.

Finally Wilson, who had turned a deaf ear to those who wanted war, turned his good ear. He was shocked at what he heard.

THE WESTERN FRONT.

The AEF, later referred to as the American Legion, was sent to a part of France known as the Western Front or Over There. The first soldiers were enthusiastically greeted by Lafayette, the Mademoiselle from Armentières, and other French dignitaries, who kissed them on both cheeks. After a terrifying taxicab ride from Paris, they reached the trenches, where they soon acquired trench mouth, trench foot, and other soldierly habits that qualified them for membership in the Veterans of Foreign Wars.

The Americans fought bravely, frequently going over the top and over the hill and running into Germans who said

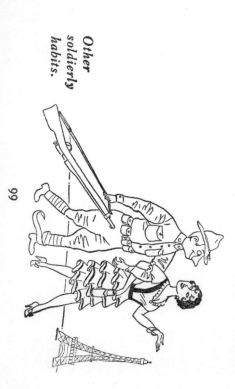

Other soldierly habits.

99

"Kamerad" or "Don't you remember me? We met in a beer garden in St. Louis." The hero of the Western Front was Sergeant York, who captured several regiments of Germans by popping up in unexpected places and making noises like an armored division. When the Germans discovered York was only one man, and a noncom at that, they threw up their hands in disgust. Once their hands were up, it was an easy matter to take them prisoner.

Our boys were under the splendid leadership of Pershing, while the British were stimulated by Haig and Haig. The Germans put their faith in generals named von Hindenburg, von Moltke, and von Zeppelin, and boasted that the war was "as good as von." The German soldiers were often called Huns by the Americans, and the ones with bad dispositions were known as Sour Krauts.

CHAPTER XLI.

PEACE.

WORLD WAR I was ended by declaring an Armistice Day. Troops were urgently needed at home for parades.

President Wilson at once sailed for France to help redraw the map of Europe, which badly needed it because the colors had run. He traveled all over Europe and was triumphantly hailed at a number of points.[1] Streets, railroad stations, and children were named after him as quickly as they could be built or born.

Wilson brought home with him an engraved invitation to join the League of Nations, a fashionable club in Geneva, and thought everyone would be pleased. But Senator Lodge, who was not a joiner, thought there were enough good clubs right here in this country. Some say he turned his back on the future, which was discourteous, to say the least. At any rate America

[1] Fourteen, to be exact.

100

never joined, and the League couldn't get along without American support, which had been included in the budget.

The war left Europeans with huge debts, and they were at first discouraged about their ability to pay them. When they discovered that they only owed the money to the United States, their relief was considerable. This was called War Relief.

Redrawing the map of Europe.

CHAPTER XLII.

PROHIBITION.

About this time a group called the Drys, who wore tall hats and carried umbrellas, got into a terrific wrangle with a group of thirsty people called the Wets.

At first the Wets did not take the Drys seriously, and were mildly amused at their dry humor. They became alarmed, however, when the Drys commenced trying out on them what was called a Noble Experiment. This lasted for about thirteen years and led to the development of the following:

1. *Home brew*—a drink made in bathtubs that left a dark brown ring.[1]

---

[1] See Whisky Ring, above.

2. *Moonshine*—a brew made in caldrons under the light of a new moon while chanting incantations like:

Toil and worry,
Tongue feels furry;
Trouble, trouble,
Seeing double.
Newts and lizzards,
Burns through gizzards;
Awful, awful,
Quite unlawful.

3. *Bootleggers*—men who delivered liquor to Wild Parties in boots, after which it was divided up and drunk out of ladies' slippers.

4. *Speakeasies*—places where people spoke more easily after their tongues had been loosened.

Wild parties.

CHAPTER XLIII.

HARDING: A WEAK PRESIDENT.

HARDING became president as the result of mistaken identity. The Republican presidential convention was held in a smoke-

filled room, and visibility was so poor that Harding was mistaken for Hoover.[1] Once he was nominated, the Republicans had no choice but to go through with it and elect him. They apologized to Hoover, however, and assured him that his turn would come soon.

Harding came from a small town in Ohio called Normalcy, which he was always wanting to return to.

DISARMAMENT CONFERENCE.

About the only good thing for which Harding is remembered is the Disarmament Conference. This was a meeting held in Washington at which each nation sought to disarm all the others. There was great enthusiasm, and the delegates all went home with souvenirs which they melted down and made into cannons.

TEAPOT DOME.

The government had a large, dome-shaped mountain full of oil that it was quietly saving for the Navy. Unfortunately, Harding shared this secret information with one of the boys in

Fall sneaked out the
oil in teapots.

the back room, a poker player by the name of Fall. Then the trouble started. Fall sneaked out the oil in teapots and sold them to Big Businessmen, who got a few cents back for returning.

[1] Both of them wore high stiff collars. In difficult times, these helped them keep their chins up.

ing the empties. As might be imagined, tea drinkers all over the country were indignant and demanded that Fall be sent to prison for causing a shortage of teapots. They also said that President Harding's hands were not clean, though he had always been considered a neat dresser back in Normalcy. All of this upset Harding and made it hard for him to digest crab meat, which led to Coolidge.[1]

CHAPTER XLIV.

COOLIDGE: A QUIET PRESIDENT.

COOLIDGE was sworn in by his father, who was a justice of the peace, at two o'clock in the morning. He wanted to lose no time drawing his pay as president. He swore to uphold the Constitution, which Harding had let sag a bit, and then went back to bed and slept soundly until time for his inauguration.

The most memorable thing about Coolidge was his dour silence. He is widely known for what he did not say. His favorite expressions were "Yes" and "No," and even these he used sparingly and often delegated to a subordinate.

A thrifty New Englander, Cal (as he was called to save a syllable) also saved string, paper clips, and picture calendars from the general store in Plymouth, Vermont.

Coolidge was reelected on the slogan, "Keep Cool With Coolidge." Since it had been an unusually hot summer, this campaign promise won widespread support, and Coolidge lived up to it through the fall and winter. Just before the next election he made one of his longest and most eloquent speeches. This speech is of such importance that its full text is printed here.

"I do not choose to run."

[1] Many believe that Harding was innocent and put the whole blame on Fall. This is the source of the expression "Fall guy."

CHAPTER XLV

THE ROARING TWENTIES.

This was a very noisy time. Business was booming, the stock market was crashing, and racketeers were making a racket. There was a great deal of roaring, especially by young persons in their twenties who, being members of the Lost Generation, were always bumping into things. Because of all this noise, people could not hear themselves think. It was therefore not an especially thoughtful period.

Among the popular pastimes of this era were such strenuous activities as channel swimming, flagpole sitting, goldfish swallowing, and trial marriage. A dance called the Charleston was engaged in by people known as "hot" dancers because they never took off their raccoon coats.

Gangsters, or Big Shots, who had scars on their faces to identify them, were driven around in long black limousines by Little Shots. Among the most famous gangsters were Al Capone, Little Caesar, and a sinister Oriental woman by the name of Ma Jong. Big Shots loved funerals, and were always shooting other Big Shots so they could send them horseshoe-shaped floral pieces inscribed "Good Luck."

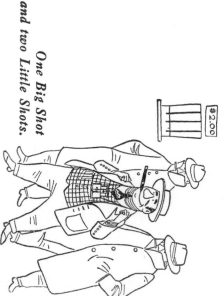

One Big Shot
and two Little Shots.

It was the heyday of sports. Famous sports included Babe Ruth, Jack Dempsey, and Bobby Jones. In a spectacular boxing upset, Dempsey was knocked out by a college man named Tunney, who had a volume of Shakespeare's plays tucked in his glove and was thus able to give his opponent the works.

Important writers at this time included such persons as H. L. Mencken, who was known as "The American Mercury," and Theodore Dreiser, who was known as "The American Tragedy." Many of the leading writers, like F. Scott Fitzgerald and Ernest Hemingway, lived in Paris to be near Gertrude Stein and Alice Talkless, whom they could understand better in French.

THE CRASH.

About this time stocks became exceedingly common. Everyone had a few thousand shares and turned at once to the financial section of the newspaper to see how much richer he was than yesterday. Stocks were usually bought on the margin, especially by those who wanted to be closer to the gilt edge.

Financial experts, called Paper Prophets, were forecasting that stocks would go higher. But suddenly, on a dark day known as Black Tuesday, the stock market, which was a big building on Wall Street,[1] collapsed. The accident is attributed to panic among stock-exchange employees when someone shouted that bears were loose in the place.

After this unfortunate occurrence everything was quieter and the Roaring Twenties died to a whimper.

CHAPTER XLVI.

THE GREAT DEPRESSION.

THE FALL of the stock market caused a great depression right in the middle of Wall Street. For most of his term, President

[1] Near the corner of Dun and Bradstreet.

Visibility was limited.

Hoover tried manfully to fill it up. He used ticker tape, raccoon coats, pocket flasks, unsold copies of books on Technocracy, and notes from foreign governments thanking him for declaring a moratorium, which permitted them to delay paying debts they did not intend to pay at all. The hole remained about as large as ever, though, and was a menace to traffic.

Hoover insisted that "prosperity was just around the corner," along with rainbows and cups of coffee and pieces of pie in the sky. But people distrusted him because they didn't believe he could see around the corner with so many apple sellers in the way. Visibility was also limited by the grass that was growing in the streets.

THE BONUS ARMY.

The only war during Hoover's administration was with the Bonus Army. This was an ill-housed and ill-clothed band of veterans, so ill-fed that they were down to skin and bonus. They mistakenly marched on Washington in order to get some money from the government, not knowing that all the money was at Fort Knox. They camped for a while in the lobby of one of the large hotels, but finally left in tears, partly from disappointment and partly from tear gas.

CHAPTER XLVII

F.D.R.

F.D.R., or That Man, as he was known by Republicans, was born with a silver cigarette holder in his mouth. He was elected president despite the opposition of those who were in his class at Groton and Harvard, and thus became known as a Traitor to his Class. Except for his persistence in wearing an old school tie, he dressed very well.

As president, he surrounded himself with a group of intimates known as Fireside Chaps. These included men with such picturesque names as Harry the Hop, Tommy the Cork, The Old Curmudgeon, Moley,[1] and Ironpants Johnson, a chap who must have had trouble sitting down. Most of F.D.R.'s aides had been college professors all their lives, and insisted on wearing mortarboards instead of top hats. They formed a society known as the Brain Trust—so called because they trusted each other's brains —and let themselves into the White House by a back door that could be opened only with a Phi Beta Kappa key.

F.D.R.'s alphabetical agencies.

F.D.R. was elected president four times, largely because he was on a horse in the middle of the stream every November. A vote for F.D.R. was a vote for progress, and everyone wanted to see him get ahead, at least until he reached dry land.

Outstanding accomplishments of F.D.R. were the following:

[1] A character out of *The Wind in the Willows.*

1. Priming the pump. This led to a flow of milk, honey, 3.2 beer, and ultimately to the Repeal of Prohibition.

2. Packing the court. F.D.R. packed the Supreme Court in a large box and was about to ship it off when cries were heard inside. He had forgotten to leave air holes.

3. Establishing alphabetical agencies, chief of which were AAA (obviously the first), NRA (which set up game laws to protect the vanishing blue eagle), CCC (Spanish for "Yes, yes, yes"), and FDR.

4. Inventing such things as bonedogging (a means of feeding a dog the same bone over and over), the New Deal (with the help of Ely Culbertson), the Roosevelt Dollar (which had the gold content taken out of it to keep it from turning yellow), etc.

5. Giving away overage destroyers, such as the Nine Old Men.

6. Recognizing Russia. Since Russia was a bear that walked like a man, this wasn't easy.

CHAPTER XLVIII.

WORLD WAR II.

———◆———

WORLD WAR II began because the Germans felt they needed a *Lebensraum*, or living room. They already had a kitchen, bedroom, and bath, but they wanted a place where they could entertain guests. The Germans at that time were under the leadership of a Furor named Heil Hitler, who looked like Charlie Chaplin but was only in the newsreels.

Hitler, who never tired of walking, marched into Poland with his panthers. He also marched into the Low Countries. This was easier because it was downhill all the way. When people resisted, despite their having signed a treaty of friendship, Hitler blew them to blitz and destroyed their favorite dives with his dive bombers.

A furor.

THE AXES.

The Germans thought themselves supermen, that is to say *Deutschlandersuberalles*, and drove all who were not 100 percent into grottoes. Everyone had to be full of Nordic blood, grade A and pasteurized, and had to have a blond grandmother. The only exceptions were the Italians and Japanese, who made the team because of what they did to the Ethiopians and the Chinese. The leader of the Italians was an unwell person called Ill Duce, who made the trains run on time because he had a horror of being late to meet Hitler.

Russia was one of the Axes for a while, and helped chop up Poland and Finland,[1] but there was a change of plans.

AMERICA ENTERS THE WAR.

At first England did most of the fighting, despite the fact that it was overrun by exiled kings related to the Royal Family and seeking refuge in the House of Windsor.

The United States did not enter the war until the Japanese

[1] The Russians were afraid of Finland, a large and powerful nation that constantly threatened their security with warlike acts such as playing the music of Sibelius.

110

attacked Pearl Harbor, whereupon our forces landed in North Africa to confuse the Japs. Among the important contributions made by the United States to the war effort were:

1. Lend-Lease, which was a delicate way of giving things to our proud Allies.

2. American No, How? We were always asking our Allies if they knew how to do something or other. When they said, "No, How?" we told them.

3. Ingenious instruments of war. These included hedge-clippers used to trim the hedgerows in France; pogo sticks for island hopping in the Pacific; atom bombs, used to tidy up Japan; and floating harbors, which turned the tide.

CHAPTER XLIX.

TRUMAN: A NOT-YET-CLASSIFIED PRESIDENT.

NEAR the end of World War II, Harry S. Truman stepped into F.D.R.'s shoes. Since he had once owned a haberdashery, he knew that the shoes didn't fit, and said so.

His election to a second term was an upset. It particularly upset the Republicans and the poll takers.

Truman was an accomplished pianist, but there is a difference of opinion as to what else he accomplished.

THE COMMUNISTS.

A great deal of trouble was caused during this period by the Communists. During what was called the Century of the Common Man,[1] they claimed to be the commonest of all. They lived in underground cells, but came out once a year, on May 1st, to see whether they cast a shadow. They always did.

The Communists owe their origin to Karl, the oldest of the Marx Brothers, who described the rest of the world in a book

[1] A phrase coined by Henry Wallace, the Great Commoner, while experimenting with hybrid corn.

Hard to shake hands with.

called *Das Kaput-all.* Although no one has ever read it, it is widely discussed. Communists go around with clenched fists and thus are terribly hard to shake hands with.

UN.

UN stands for the United Nations. It also stands for a great many other things, since it is remarkably patient. It is made up of slightly deaf delegates who wear earphones and always have the name of their country on a sign in front of them so they can remember where they are from.

The UN is dominated by the Great Powers, which are the United States, England, France, Russia, and China. The Great Powers are in turn dominated by the Veto Powers, which are mostly Russia. At times there is more power than light.

The chief purpose of the UN is to keep the peace, which is kept in the top drawer of the Security Council, along with olive branches, laurel wreaths, arsenic, and old lace.

112

CHAPTER L.

CONCLUSION.

WE HAVE now traced the development of the United States from a struggling colony to a struggling great power. With Jefferson's immortal words (which we cannot recall at the moment) ringing in our ears, and until more history is made, this is

THE END.

FINAL EXAMINATION.

1. Contemplate the consequences if World War II had been waged before World War I.

2. Write a short factual or imaginative composition on one of the following subjects:

 (a) Why I Was Not Old Enough to Vote for McKinley.

 (b) A Descent into the Depths of the Depression.

 (c) Should Prohibition Have Been Prohibited? Or, Denatured vs. Good-natured Alcohol.

 (d) Incidents in the life of Roosevelt. (Before you conclude, explain in detail which Roosevelt you have been writing about.)

3. Quote at length.

4. Aren't you glad it's the government that owes the national debt and not you?

5. Make a list of the modern conveniences in your home that you would not have had to repair in 1865.

6. Lock all the doors and try to corner a market.

7. Discuss in detail whatever you still do not know about American history.

8. How can you become a better citizen? What's stopping you?

GLOSSARY OF TERMS.

America: Same as United States of America, much to the annoyance of persons living in Canada and the Latin American countries.

Ambassador: Person with enough influence to be appointed and enough wealth to be able to serve.

Boom: Opposite of Bust.

Bust: Opposite of Boom, except when applied to women.

Communist: 1. A Communist. 2. (*Americanism, unfortunately not yet obsolete*) Anyone who disagrees with you.

Conservative: A man who saves his money (even before women and children).

Damnyankee: Southernism for Vermonter.

Democrat: Opposite of Republican.

Frontier: Area occupied by persons always in the van, along with their furniture.

Inauguration: Ceremony during which the President stands in the rain with his hat off.

Liberal: Something everyone claims to be.

Peace: Short period of preparation for the next war.

Platform: Structure intended to give a lift to party morale.

Puritan: Person opposed to sin, especially in others.

Republican: Opposite of Democrat.

Radical: Opposite of almost anything.

Red: See Russia.

Russia: See red.

Satellite: Neighboring country attracted into Russian orbit by removal of trade barriers, food supplies, and leading citizens.

Suffrage: Pain caused women by unaccustomed exercise of their franchise.

Two-party System: Political system composed of two parties, the Ins and the Outs.